ECONOMIC REFORM AND THE POOR IN AFRICA

Economic Reform and the Poor in Africa

Edited by

DAVID E. SAHN

CLARENDON PRESS · OXFORD
1996

Oxford University Press, Walton Street, Oxford OX2 6DP

Oxford New York
Athens Auckland Bangkok Bogota Bombay
Buenos Aires Calcutta Cape Town Dar es Salaam
Delhi Florence Hong Kong Istanbul Karachi
Kuala Lumpur Madras Madrid Melbourne
Mexico City Nairobi Paris Singapore
Taipei Tokyo Toronto

and associated companies in
Berlin Ibadan

Oxford is a trade mark of Oxford University Press

Published in the United States
by Oxford University Press Inc., New York

British Library Cataloguing in Publication Data
Data Available

Library of Congress Cataloging-in-Publication Data
Data available

ISBN 0-19-829035-7

1 3 5 7 9 10 8 6 4 2

Typeset by BookMan Services, Oxford
Printed in Great Britain
on acid-free paper by
Biddles Ltd., Guildford and King's Lynn

ACKNOWLEDGEMENTS

The work contained in this volume was prepared with funding under a Cooperative Agreement between the Africa Bureau of the U.S. Agency for International Development (AID) and the Cornell Food and Nutrition Policy Program (CFNPP). The support of AID is greatly appreciated, especially Jerome Wolgin, Yoon Lee, and Jay Smith.

CONTENTS

PART IV   AGRICULTURE, FOOD POLICY REFORMS, AND WELFARE OUTCOMES

CONTRIBUTORS

Harold Alderman, Senior Economist, World Bank, Washington, DC, and formerly Senior Research Associate, Cornell Food and Nutrition Policy Program, Cornell University.

Jehan Arulpragasam, Economist, World Bank, Washington, DC, and formerly Research Support Specialist, Cornell Food and Nutrition Policy Program, Cornell University.

Carlo del Ninno, Economist, World Bank, Washington, DC, and formerly Senior Research Associate, Cornell Food and Nutrition Policy Program, Cornell University.

Paul Dorosh, Associate Professor of Economics, Cornell Food and Nutrition Policy Program, Cornell University.

Steven Haggblade, Senior Research Associate, Cornell Food and Nutrition Policy Program, Cornell University.

Solomane Koné, Research Associate, Cornell Food and Nutrition Policy Program, Cornell University, and Professor of Economics, University of Abidjan.

Mattias Lundberg, Michigan State University, and formerly Research Support Specialist, Cornell Food and Nutrition Policy Program, Cornell University.

Bradford Mills, Research Fellow, International Service for National Agricultural Research, Namibia, and formerly Research Associate, Cornell Food and Nutrition Policy Program, Cornell University.

B. Essama-Nssah, Economist, World Bank, Washington, DC, and formerly Senior Research Associate, Cornell Food and Nutrition Policy Program, Cornell University.

David E. Sahn, Associate Professor of Economics, and Director, Cornell Food and Nutrition Policy Program, Cornell University.

Ousmane Samba-Mamadou, Professor of Economics, University of Niamey.

Alexander Sarris, Senior Research Fellow, Cornell Food and Nutrition Policy Program, Cornell University, and Professor of Economics, University of Athens.

Gerald Shively, University of Wisconsin and formerly Research Support Specialist, Cornell Food and Nutrition Policy Program, Cornell University.

Shankar Subramanian, Assistant Professor of Economics, Cornell University.

Erik Thorbecke, Professor of Economics, Cornell University.

Yves Van Frausum, formerly Senior Research Associate, Cornell Food and Nutrition Policy Program, Cornell University.

Stephen Younger, Senior Research Associate, Cornell Food and Nutrition Policy Program, Cornell University.

TABLES

FIGURES

PART I

Introduction

1

Economic Reform and Poverty: An Overview

David E. Sahn

1.1. *Introduction*

Has economic reform hurt the poor in Africa? Little disagreement exists that most African countries faced an economic crisis in the early 1980s, characterized by worsening budget and balance-of-payments deficits, stagnant growth, and slow improvement in social indicators. Far less consensus exists, however, on the appropriateness and effectiveness of macroeconomic and sectoral economic reforms that such conditions motivated. More contentious still is the subject of this book: the impact of economic reforms on poverty and income distribution in Africa.[1]

Economic recovery programs in Africa have emphasized state disengagement from roles such as rationing foreign exchange, administering prices, marketing productive inputs and economic output, controlling and managing enterprises, allocating credit, and guaranteeing employment for university graduates. Understanding the growth and distributional effects of such a transition is difficult. While economic theory provides a framework for analyzing the outcomes of economic liberalization, an assessment of the actual effects on poverty and income distribution must consider who it was that received rents associated with rationing of goods, received subsidized inputs and food, had access to government provided services, benefited from public employment, and produced products facing high implicit taxation associated with overvalued exchange rates and state interference in output markets. Detailed empirical analysis is therefore required to understand how macroeconomic and sectoral reforms affect households. This volume compiles the findings of a body of quantitative research that addresses the question of whether the poor are hurt, in absolute and relative terms, by the

[1] An earlier, companion volume describes this economic malaise and the reform programs instituted to confront them, focusing on the same ten countries studied here (Sahn 1994). Building on that early, largely descriptive, ground work, this volume extends that research effort through analytical assessments of the impact these reform programs have had on Africa's poor.

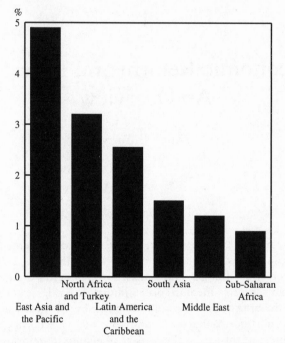

Fig. 1.1. Average annual GDP per capita growth, 1965–1985
Source: World Bank (1994: 18).

adoption of economic policies designed to restore macroeconomic stability, reinvigorate markets, and rationalize resource allocation in Africa.

For many African countries, the policy changes of the 1980s associated with economic liberalization represent an important paradigm shift. Post-independence governments in most of Africa often assumed the commanding heights of the economy, attempting to control much of the country's productive resources and to market much of the output. This approach was based on an idea in good currency at the time of independence: that markets and other existing civil institutions were not adequate to build a strong economy and achieve expressed objectives of growth and poverty alleviation.[2] Such thinking fostered an adherence to the principles of state socialism and centralized planning.[3]

Policies adopted in post-independence Africa contributed to dismal economic performance where growth lagged far behind other regions of the

[2] For further discussion, see Sahn and Sarris (1994).
[3] See e.g. von Freyhold (1979), Yasané (1990), Azarya and Chazan (1987), and Abernathy (1988). It is also noteworthy that failed institutional models were not only the domain of governments, but were also promoted by international organizations, including the World Bank, which, for example, was instrumental in the development of parastatal grain marketing agencies in much of Africa (SIDA 1994).

developing world (Figure 1.1). Likewise, structural features of African economies that made them vulnerable to negative external shocks were in part to blame. Even so, other developing country regions faced similar shocks and still performed impressively. Recent attempts to unravel the role of policy from external shocks conclude that ill-conceived policy was primarily responsible for Africa's poor economic performance, with deterioration in the terms of trade playing only a small part in explaining the stagnation of growth and the worsening internal and external account imbalances (World Bank 1994; Elbadawi et al. 1992; Easterly et al. 1993; Thorbecke 1994).

Regardless of the relative contribution of shocks and policy to declining output per capita and an untenable balance-of-payments position, most African governments had little choice but to alter their policy stance. In general, this transition involved increasing their reliance on markets, and reducing the interference of the state in administering prices and allocating productive resources. The underlying assumptions of this paradigm shift was that the state had contributed to the economic inefficiencies and stagnation that gripped much of Africa in the late 1970s and early 1980s; and that even the inevitable market failures that would occur in a liberalized economy would be less damaging than the bureaucratic failures observed prior to reform (Bauer 1984; World Bank 1981).

Prominent among the economic recovery programs instituted in Africa during the 1980s were trade and exchange rate liberalization, designed to alter the relative prices of tradables to non-tradables,[4] and attempts to restore fiscal discipline and to rationalize spending.[5] Also of major importance were reforms in the food and agricultural sector, particularly in light of agriculture's critical role in generating employment, providing wage goods, and earning foreign exchange. Most of the policy changes in the food and agricultural sector revolved around liberalizing markets and reducing the role of parastatals that were involved in procurement, transformation, and marketing of food and export crops.[6]

Opinion is far from uniform about the effectiveness and equity of these trade and exchange rate, fiscal, and agricultural reforms, which are frequently associated with structural adjustment and stabilization programs and often undertaken with the urgings of the World Bank, International

---

[4] Helleiner (1994) and others make a distinction between trade policy and exchange rate policy, limiting the former to policies that affect the relative prices of tradables. However, such measures will alter supply and demand and, thus, the relative prices of tradables to non-tradables (Dornbusch 1975). Therefore, as in Thomas and Nash (1991), the chapters in this book concentrate on how both trade and exchange rate liberalization affect prices of tradables to non-tradables.

[5] Sahn, Dorosh, and Younger (forthcoming) and Ferroni and Kanbur (1991) dispel the myth that economic reforms were contractionary in Africa, and that social sector spending, in real terms or as a share of total expenditures, declined as a consequence.

[6] For a further discussion of the evolution of thinking that contributed to agricultural sector reforms, see Paarlberg and Grindle (1991), Bates (1981), and Lele (1989).

Monetary Fund (IMF), and bilateral donor agencies.[7] In fact, there is perhaps no issue that has generated a more lively debate among those concerned
with Africa's social and economic development than the appropriateness of
reform measures associated with adjustment programs.[8] Proponents contend
that sustained economic reform leads to improved performance.[9] Critics
maintain, however, that the macro and sectoral reform measures begun
during the 1980s failed, mistakenly concentrating on promoting macroeconomic stability and getting prices right, rather than addressing, more
importantly, underlying structural and institutional weaknesses (Taylor
1993; Cornia, van der Hoeven, and Lall 1992; Jespersen 1992).

In addition to the arguments over the ability of adjustment policies to
restore internal and external balance at a macro level, an active debate over
the equity of such policies has been a central part of the overall discussion
of policy in Africa. In particular, important critics (e.g. UNICEF; United
Nations Economic Commission for Africa (UNECA)) have argued that even
if orthodox policies make sense at a macro level their social costs are too
high. While macroeconomic policies are best evaluated in terms of macro
outcomes, questions of whether the process of adjustment imperils the poor
should not be ignored. On the contrary, an important measure of the success
of economic reforms is their eventual impact on poverty. Moreover, efforts
to mitigate any social costs of reforms require an understanding of their
adverse consequences.

Criticisms that adjustment policies hurt the poor[10] have focused on how
economic reforms in Africa, particularly exchange rate devaluation, fiscal
policy reform, retrenchment of state workers, market and trade liberalization,
higher taxes, and so forth, further imperil the already tenuous living conditions of the poor. More specifically, the concern is that, as a result of such
reform initiatives, real wages fall, unemployment rises, prices of staple goods
increase, and the availability of vital social services declines. The prospect of
economic reform further imperilling the poor, or at least the historical fact
that adjustment programs have failed to offer an immediate solution to
poverty, is viewed as a fatal flaw, regardless of their macroeconomic impacts.

---

[7] The terms *structural adjustment* and *stabilization* are closely associated with the policy-based
lending of the World Bank and International Monetary Fund, respectively. Structural adjustment generally focuses on improving resource allocation and economic efficiency to raise output
and productivity, while stabilization focuses on demand restraint. In practice, however,
structural adjustment and stabilization are inextricably intertwined, with key policy changes (e.g.
devaluation) being common to both. In the remainder of this book, the term *adjustment*
encompasses the broad range of policy reform initiatives associated with structural adjustment
and stabilization.

[8] See e.g. the discourse between the World Bank and United Nations Development Programme (1989) and the United Nations Economic Commission on Africa (1989), which is
analyzed in detail by Mosley and Weeks (1993).

[9] See e.g. World Bank (1994).

[10] See e.g. Jolly and Cornia (1984); Singh and Tabatabai (1993); Jamal and Weeks (1993);
and UNECA (1989).

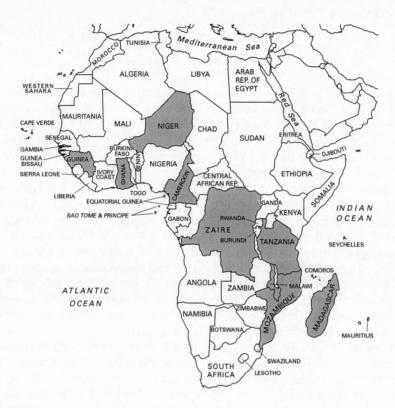

Fig. 1.2. Map depicting countries studied
Source: Sahn (1994).

The broad indictment of adjustment policies has in turn generated a number of responses, which revolve around two principal tenets. The first holds that living standards have not, in fact, declined, in contrast with what the critics of adjustment policies would suggest. The second maintains that any deterioration that did occur was not attributable to the process of economic reform.[11] Resolving the different viewpoints on the impact of economic adjustment is beyond the scope of this book, as we make no pretense of providing a complete assessment of all the economic reforms instituted throughout sub-Saharan Africa during the past decade. Rather, the chapters in this volume use appropriate empirical methods and models to examine particular reform policies and their implications for the welfare of the poor in the sample of ten countries where we have worked—Cameroon, The

---

[11] See e.g. Preston (1986), Behrman (1988), Thorbecke (1994), and Berg et al. (1994).

Gambia, Ghana, Guinea, Madagascar, Malawi, Mozambique, Niger, Tanzania, and Zaire (see Figure 1.2).

1.2. *Methodological Approach*

It is important to clarify at the outset the general research approach used in this book and how the analysis fits within the context of the contentious debate over the impact of economic reform in Africa. Unlike much of the analysis of economic reform conducted to date, this book employs empirical methods to separate the effects of the economic crisis that induced countries to begin to adjust from the impact of the economic reforms themselves. This approach contrasts with the more typical practice of comparing economic performance and household welfare before and after reform, and attributing observed changes to the process of economic reform.[12] The disadvantage of such before-and-after analysis is, first, a tendency to blame the unconscionably low living standards of Africa's poor on the process of adjusting to policy failure, instead of on the recessions and interventionist excesses that generally preceded reform; second, such analysis fails to distinguish the effect of policy change from the array of exogenous influences that affect growth and income distribution. To avoid these shortcomings, we rely on counterfactual simulations from empirically based models.

With these models, the chapters in this book examine the impact of specific policy reforms (e.g. currency devaluation, eliminating taxes on export crops, retrenching civil servants) in specific country contexts. We adopt this approach for two closely related reasons, rather than purporting to examine the impact of broadly defined and generally misunderstood efforts, such as structural adjustment programs. First, in many countries the economic reforms modeled have been only partially implemented, or else rapidly reversed.[13] Thus, exploring the impact of adjustment programs is not synonymous with examining the impact of policy reform. Second, the complexity of adjustment programs cautions against broad statements about their impact and commends being context- and policy-specific in order to sort out the net effect of adjustment policies on poverty. Toward this end, we go beyond anecdotal accounts when measuring the impact of adjustment on poverty. Instead, we employ solid analytical techniques based on a com-

---

12 Much of the discourse of the effects of adjustment has simply been based on such before-and-after comparisons, often attempting to group countries according to their degree of reform (e.g. Cornia, Jolly, and Stewart 1987; Elbadawi et al. 1992; Corbo and Rojas 1991; World Bank 1992).

13 This failure to reform or to stay the course reflects the fact that governments often do not embrace fully the reform agenda and that the process of negotiating adjustment loans with the international financial institutions fails to encourage ownership over, and enthusiasm for, the loan conditions (Mosley, Harrigan, and Toye 1991; Husain and Faruqee 1993; World Bank 1993).

prehensive understanding, largely from household-level, producer, and market surveys, of the structure of African economies. In the absence of this type of careful analysis based on appropriate data and economic models, both critics and supporters of reform programs have based their arguments on perceptions and accounts that are not representative, not put into proper context, or not based on appropriate data sources.[14]

This book thus presents a series of studies that brings both analytical rigor and a wealth of empirical information to the question of how economic reform programs impact poverty in Africa. Although this volume takes an eclectic approach to examining different aspects of the complex question of the impact of economic reform on poverty and income distribution, the chapters share a common focus on understanding the linkages between macro and sectoral policy and the welfare of the poor. Our purpose is to understand where adjustment has had deleterious consequences for the poor (if at all) and to better understand the linkages between macro and sectoral policies and household-level outcomes. The challenge therefore is to go beyond simple characterizations such as "adjustment is harmful, or beneficial, to the poor" and instead to use appropriate economic models to understand the mechanisms and channels through which different macro and sectoral policies filter through the economy, eventually affecting household welfare. Only by gaining such insight will it be possible to ensure that adjustment policies are "pro-poor," or that reform at least will not address macro imbalances and economic inefficiencies at the expense of those least able to assume the cost.

1.3. *Organization of the Book*

The case study material in this book is organized by substantive policy areas: trade and exchange rate policy; fiscal policy; and agricultural sector policy. Each chapter is placed in the section of the book where the policy reforms examined are most important, and impacts the greatest on the poor.

1.3.1. *Trade and exchange rate policy*

We begin in Part II with an analysis of the implications of trade and exchange rate reforms. These reforms were intended primarily to increase the openness of the economy by facilitating competitiveness and promoting export growth.

During the 1970s and 1980s, most African states rationed foreign

---

[14] For example, analysis based on official prices neglects the reality that the relevant price for the poor is often that in parallel markets (Lindauer 1989). The important distinction between official and parallel markets must also be made when analyzing foreign exchange and credit markets, and farmgate, input, and food prices. Likewise, official wage and employment statistics gathered in the formal sector are generally irrelevant for the poor.

exchange and engaged in trade policy, ostensibly for the purpose of conserving foreign exchange for imports that were "essential" to an inward-looking development strategy intended to protect certain key economic activities and sectors. Such policies meant that the demand for foreign exchange at the official price far exceeded foreign exchange reserves and revenues. As a result, tradable goods were taxed implicitly. At the same time, overvalued exchange rates yielded substantial benefits for those privileged with access to foreign exchange at the official price. Official imports with rationed foreign exchange were being valued domestically at a much lower price than their scarcity value. Furthermore, an array of tariffs and non-tariff barriers contributed not only to distortions in the relative price of tradables to non-tradables but also to the existence of large rents for traders who had access to officially priced foreign exchange and import licenses. Likewise, domestic producers that successfully lobbied for protection of their products captured the rents from such distortions. In the highly distorted pre-reform environment, these rents reached enormous heights. They averaged $500 million per year in the ten countries studied, reaching a maximum of $1 billion annually in Zaire.

We explore the implications of moving away from the grossly overvalued official exchange rates characterized by large premiums for foreign exchange on parallel markets, and trade policy that involved arbitrary and highly variable tariff structures and quantitative restrictions. The effects of correcting such policy distortions are addressed, focusing on the growth and distributional impact of eliminating foreign exchange rationing and liberalizing trade regimes.

The magnitude and direction of the changes in income distribution that result from devaluation and trade reforms are not known *a priori*, nor are they easily determined. For one thing, the extent to which policy changes, such as a devaluation of the nominal exchange rate, contribute to an increase in the price of tradables relative to non-tradables is determined by an array of factors, including commercial trade policy and monetary and fiscal policy. Of particular significance is the degree to which inflation erodes the effectiveness of nominal devaluation. Another complicating factor is the pervasiveness of parallel markets, where a large share of the poor's foreign exchange transactions occurred prior to reform. The importance of the dual market structure must therefore be taken into account in any analysis. But most critical, the implications of changes in relative prices for functional income distribution in general, and the poor in particular, are determined by an array of factors that require empirical investigation. The models presented in Part II quantify the share of a household's income that is derived from the production and consumption of tradable versus non-tradable goods, as well as the extent to which households benefited from rents that were generated by policy distortions.

Five country studies—for Cameroon, The Gambia (included in Part III of the book), Madagascar, Niger, and Tanzania—inform the question of the impact of trade and exchange rate reform on poverty and income distribution. All five case studies employ a common methodology, that of using computable general equilibrium models (CGEs), to capture the underlying socioeconomic structure and the behavior of major actors. These models, each described in their respective chapters, permit an analysis of the impact of alternative policy options and external circumstances. In all cases, the CGEs are built around social accounting matrices (SAMs),[15] constructed as part of the Cornell multi-country study, which describe economic flows between production activities, factors of production, and institutions in the economy.[16] The advantage of this modeling approach is that it allows one to analyze the direct and indirect effect of a given policy change in the entire economy in a comprehensive, consistent, and disaggregated fashion.

Chapter 2, by Paul Dorosh, discusses the impact of trade liberalization on Madagascar's poor. Dorosh evaluates the impact of Madagascar's structural adjustment program, in which trade liberalization was a key element, as well as the country's prior stabilization effort, which slashed government spending. The chapter highlights a number of important aspects of trade and exchange rate policy reform in an archetypical case of a country forced to respond to excessive and unsustainable borrowing that was used to finance imports and unproductive investment. Madagascar's unrestrained borrowing ended rather abruptly in the early 1980s when the availability of foreign exchange declined sharply. Consequently, the government had little choice but to stabilize the economy through aggregate demand management. A few years later, the country embarked on an economic liberalization program. This sequence of events, where a massive but ineffective, externally financed public investment program brought about the need for a stabilization program, which was subsequently followed by trade liberalization, provides some important lessons. First, the findings indicate that pre-reform policies that encourage large inflows of foreign savings primarily benefited the urban households, while the adverse effects of stabilization measures, including declines in foreign savings and reduced rice imports, were concentrated among the same groups of households. This, in large part, reflects a typical situation in Africa, where the urban and, more specifically, high income

[15] For a complete discussion of SAMs, see Alarcon et al. (1986); Pyatt and Thorbecke (1976); and Pyatt and Round (1985). Likewise, the CGEs in this book share many of the characteristics discussed by Dervis, de Melo, and Robinson (1982) and Sarris (1990).

[16] Since the SAMs present only a snapshot of an economy, they are limited in terms of their ability to describe the behavioral and technical relations that govern how the flows are generated. That is, a SAM does not provide any information about how the economy responds to changes in policy or external shocks. To create a model that shows new flows in the economy in response to changing policies, or external conditions, it is necessary to add a series of behavioral equations or to specify technical relationships that allow the flows captured by the SAM to be updated and evolve. In the CGE models presented in this book, prices, quantities, and the value of transactions involved in production, consumption, generation of income, and trade in the economy are all determined through sets of simultaneous equations.

households control most of the capital and skilled labor in the economy. Second, trade and exchange rate reform resulted in a redistribution of income in favor of the poor by raising the relative prices of tradable goods they produce and eliminating quota rents. Third, there are lessons in terms of sequencing and timing of reforms insofar as trade liberalization was delayed for a number of years after the commencement of stabilization measures. This delay had costs in terms of both efficiency and equity since, when finally adopted, liberalization contributed to higher economic growth and rural incomes, particularly for the poor.

In Chapter 3, Shankar Subramanian evaluates the impacts of external shocks and government policies in Cameroon, using a CGE model. Cameroon differs from the other study countries discussed in the volume on account of its higher income per capita and its status as an oil exporting country. Two major periods of the country's economic history are analyzed. In the first period, rapid growth of oil exports fueled a phenomenal GDP growth rate that averaged 14 percent per year during the last half of the 1970s, before slowing to just over half that during the first part of the 1980s. Later, the response of policy-makers to the subsequent terms of trade shock (falling by 47 percent between 1985 and 1987), when world oil prices plummeted, is examined.

The model results show that the losses from lower oil earnings adversely affected primarily nonfarm households—rural nonfarm (both poor and rich) and urban rich households. In fact, the lower consumer prices that resulted from the decline in oil prices led to higher real incomes for the urban poor and rural farm households. In contrast, the deleterious price shock for agricultural exports that occurred synchronously with the oil shock had substantial adverse effects on the rural farm households, rich and poor alike. Thus, it was the adverse movements of agricultural export prices, and not the oil shock, that contributed to the rural poor's stagnant and falling incomes in the mid-1980s. Furthermore, the strong linkage between agricultural exports and the remainder of the economy, coupled with the price responsiveness of, and forward and backward linkages with, agriculture, meant that the effects on GDP growth of the decline in agricultural export prices were greater than the effects of the oil shock. Moreover, even the urban non-poor lost from the fall in agricultural export prices.

Other simulations for Cameroon show that there were high costs of maintaining a fixed nominal exchange rate, a fact that stemmed from being a member of the CFA (Communauté Francophone Africaine) zone. If, in fact, the government could have undertaken a devaluation of the exchange rate, instead of adjusting to the oil price shock solely through expenditure-reducing policies, real household incomes for farming households would have risen, despite small losses for some other groups. Likewise, Cameroon's external imbalances would have effectively been addressed. The chapter also shows that the high implicit tax on agriculture during the years of the oil boom had significant negative consequences for income distribution and rates of return on agricultural investment. Similarly, a more prudent investment policy would have reduced the cost of stabilizing the economy after the oil price shock, without appreciably affecting output during or after the oil boom.

In Chapter 4, Alexander Sarris presents the results of policy experiments in Tanzania, where a series of adjustment measures have been underway since 1984. The model simulations of the dynamic CGE model that Sarris employs suggest that the structural adjustment policies, as envisioned in the economic recovery program, will impose the major burden of adjustment on the non-poor. Specifically, simulations of major policy reforms, including a 20 percent devaluation, an increase in public nominal investment expenditures financed by a corresponding reduction in public current expenditures, a reduction in public sector employment, a reduction in indirect taxation of agricultural exports, and an increase in foreign loans, all result in short-term declines in real income for all household groups. Declines for the poor, both rural and urban, are minimal; losses for the non-poor, however, are much higher, on the order of 4–5 percent of their incomes. The large magnitude of the non-poor's losses largely reflect the fact that they benefit most from rent seeking in the pre-reform economy. In the medium-term, however, GDP growth accelerates and the public and foreign deficits shrink as inflation is moderated and real domestic investment recovers. Relative to not undertaking adjustment, in the medium term, the welfare of the poor and middle income households is markedly higher.

When adverse terms-of-trade shocks are superimposed on economic reforms, the consequences for the poor and non-poor alike are not so favorable. Although no great surprise, this result is likely to be one reason why adjustment programs assume the blame for external factors beyond the control of the state. Furthermore, when each of the policies included in the adjustment scenario described above are considered separately, they work in different directions, through different linkages in the economy. The results in this regard are informative insofar as they point to the fact that the choice of, or emphasis on, alternative reform options in the context of an adjustment program will influence household welfare, as well as macroeconomic outcomes.

The final chapter in Part II, by Paul Dorosh, B. Essama-Nssah, and Ousmane Samba-Mamadou, discusses the options for responding to a large terms-of-trade shock in Niger and the implications of devaluation of the CFA franc, a policy reform option that was widely debated throughout the region, and is particularly relevant in light of the devaluation that occurred in 1994. Chapter 5 reports how Niger, like many of its neighbors, was confronted in the early 1980s with the need to adjust to declines in the historically high prices in the 1970s of primary product exports. Niger's need to adjust to declines in uranium earnings was exacerbated by drought as well as by economic reforms undertaken in neighboring Nigeria. The rapid appreciation of the CFA franc relative to the Nigerian naira (on the parallel market), coupled with the declining incomes in Nigeria which depressed demand, dramatically reduced Niger's exports.

Like other CFA countries (including its wealthier neighbor Cameroon, discussed in the previous chapter), exchange rate devaluation was not a policy alternative during the 1980s (although, owing to the low level of inflation, Niger's real exchange rate did depreciate relative to its major trading partners). The results of this chapter show that the fall in uranium prices led to declining investment and savings, reducing the demand for labor and the real incomes of all households. The ability to devalue would have accelerated the adjustment process and raised real incomes. Nevertheless, exchange rate devaluation would not resolve Niger's fiscal crisis, a pressing need in light of excessive spending relative to falling revenues from taxes on uranium exports. Reducing government spending, however, has adverse consequences primarily for urban households employed by the public administration. In total, while Niger would have been better off, in terms of both growth and income distribution, if it had been able to devalue earlier on, there have been considerable positive benefits of CFA membership, enabling Niger (and other CFA countries) to avoid the foreign exchange rationing and import licensing restrictions so prevalent and harmful in non-CFA countries. Furthermore, at the heart of Niger's long-standing economic woes is excessive government spending, which can be reduced only through politically perilous initiatives such as public sector retrenchment programs, discussed in Part III of the book.

1.3.2. *Fiscal policy and investment priority*

Part III discusses fiscal policy reforms and their effects on Africa's poor. To begin with, two studies on Ghana and Guinea examine the impact of retrenchment programs designed to reduce public sector employment in order to contain the wage bill that contributes to fiscal deficits. Most countries in Africa greatly expanded the size of the public sector during the 1970s, resulting in bloated and notoriously inefficient state bureaucracies. Later, as budgetary pressures limited wage increases, a decline and compression of salaries ensued, contributing to the deterioration in the morale and effectiveness of civil service employees. Moonlighting and absenteeism became widespread problems (Lindauer and Nunberg forthcoming). The spillover effects of this overstaffing are manifested in a variety of ways, ranging from the distortions that result in the private wage labor market to the heightened demand for higher education often perceived as a means of obtaining a public sector job.[17] Overstaffing and painfully low civil service salaries also

---

[17] For an informative case study of how education was perceived as the modality to gain access to the bureaucracy, see Abernathy (1969).

encourage patronage, corruption, and rent-seeking.[18] Moreover, harm to the economy often results from poorly trained and over-zealous state workers imposing ineffectual and counterproductive rules and regulations that interfere with the activities of productive enterprises.

Civil service reform, however, has proven difficult. One important reason is that such reforms may have large costs for those who lose their jobs, which in turn may prove politically perilous for the government instituting such policies. The concern thus expressed over the actual social consequences of retrenchment is the focus of the chapters included in this part of the book.

In the first of the two case studies (Chapter 6), Stephen Younger examines the effort in Ghana to reduce the size of the public sector, focusing on the plight of former public sector employees and, in particular, on whether they were able to find remunerative employment after losing their jobs. The experience of retrenched workers indicates that the transition to finding private sector employment was rapid in Ghana. In fact, the rates of unemployment and non-participation among redeployees were remarkably similar to those of the population at large. In large measure this was attributable to the fact that nearly half of the redeployees had held second jobs while on the public sector payroll.

However, even though many retrenched workers had second jobs and were rapidly absorbed into the non-wage sector, the earnings losses of retrenched workers were significant. On average, wages fell by around one-half, as compared with earnings while in the civil service. This loss reflects a decrease in the earnings premium to civil servants after redeployment rather than lower returns to human capital compared with the remainder of the population. Comparisons of welfare status of redeployees' households indicates that poverty has thus increased among laid-off workers. Nonetheless, the prevalence of poverty among redeployees is no worse than that of the population at large.

Chapter 7, by Bradford Mills and David E. Sahn, is a case study on retrenchment in Guinea. The results contrast with the findings of the Ghana case. Overall, the transitions between public and private sector jobs were more costly than in Ghana. As in Ghana, however, the cost of these transitions was mitigated by a relatively effective severance and retirement scheme for those who left their jobs. Savings out of these schemes were also lower in Guinea than in Ghana. This may have reflected that in Guinea severance was paid out over a longer period of time, instead of as a large lump-sum payment. Findings also indicate that the labor market in Guinea was segmented into the wage and non-wage (self-employment) sectors, with the former being preferred and therefore leading to queuing, especially for men. Among those who did finds jobs after retrenchment, however, a large

---

[18] See e.g. Price (1975) and Gould (1980).

share became self-employed workers. The level of education was of prime importance in determining who got the more valued wage sector jobs as well as the level of earnings for wage and self-employed workers. In addition, the results suggest that females faced longer durations of unemployment in the wage sector but shorter durations in the non-wage sector. The durations of the former group were also lengthened as a result of receiving severance pay. Once a new job was found, around half the workers were earning less and half were earning more than at the time of their public sector departure.

Controlling the wage bill in order to reduce fiscal account imbalances is an important element of adjustment programs. There remains, however, a complementary requirement of most reforming economies: increasing revenues to reduce structural budget deficits. More specifically, the literature on the social impact of adjustment programs, while raising the prospects of deleterious consequences as a result of reduced government spending, has rarely raised the issue, "Who pays the taxes?"

Problems of thin financial markets, a narrow tax base, and weak administrative structures have often contributed to countries' resorting to means of financing that are intrinsically distortionary. Of particular concern is the high level of taxes on international trade. For example, export taxes on primary products are widespread, despite the fact that the taxed commodities are often an important source of income for the poor. Raising revenues thus has important distributional implications and is an issue of great concern, since in most countries a change in the source and level of taxes has been a component of the reform program.

Measuring the incidence of taxation is a complicated and understudied topic in Africa. In Chapter 8, Stephen Younger uses data from the Ghana Living Standards Survey to examine the evolution of tax incidence prior and subsequent to the economic recovery program. The study finds that most direct taxes are progressive, while the distributional incidence of indirect taxes is more variable. The sales tax, for example, is essentially proportional, while taxes on fuel in general, and gasoline in particular, are progressive. The most regressive of the major revenue sources in Ghana is taxes on cocoa. In fact, a sharp decline in the share of taxes from cocoa has contributed to a substantial increase in the progressivity of taxes in general since the onset of the Economic Recovery Program in Ghana. Nevertheless, the cocoa duty remains high. While taxing cocoa is easy, it is both distortionary, discouraging production of one of Ghana's most competitive exports, and highly regressive. In its place, enhancement of the progressivity through, for example, increasing direct taxes and the petroleum duty is commended.

Another critical issue is that of the allocation of investment resources. The importance of this allocation is highlighted during the course of adjustment programs that are, in part, a response to the severe balance-of-payments problem. Contributing to this problem were the low-quality investments, which were financed by unsustainable foreign borrowing. Furthermore, private investment has not been very responsive to adjustment programs and public investment is generally the first item to be cut during fiscal stabilization programs. Thus, it is critical to ensure that available investment resources are well used. Of particular concern is both the efficiency of investment and its equity implications.

One country study that typifies low quality and excessive investment contributing to a severe balance-of-payments problem is Madagascar. This problem, which eventually precipitated the adoption of a stabilization program, was a direct consequence of the development strategy, *investir a outrance* (to invest to the hilt), particularly targeting industry, as well as large-scale irrigated rice perimeters. In the wake of having restored macroeconomic discipline, however, Madagascar is faced with the question of formulating appropriate priorities for the public investment program, an exercise that is proving central to its economic recovery program.

In Chapter 9, Paul Dorosh and Steven Haggblade employ a semi-input–output model to examine investment alternatives. Although reducing the balance-of-payments deficit is a key component of whatever investment priorities are adopted, this objective can be achieved through increasing either exports or import substitutes. Thus, three basic options are highlighted: investing in coffee production (the major export crop), in paddy (the major food crop, for which imports are still large), or in formal manufacturing. The results show clearly that investing in agriculture, particularly in small irrigated paddy perimeters, is a superior strategy. This investment strategy generates the most rapid growth in income, the most jobs, and the most equitable income distribution. In addition to benefiting rural households, urban households profit from the increased demand for private services and informal sector industrial products as rural incomes expand. Government revenues also rise in accordance with increased economic output. This chapter also clearly contrasts the detrimental actions of the state prior to reform (e.g. taxing farmers and engaging directly in purchasing and marketing key crops) with more appropriate roles (e.g. investing in rural infrastructure to foster growth and equity).

The final study included in this section of the book, Chapter 10 by Solomane Koné and Erik Thorbecke, documents the high costs of failing to sustain economic reforms, both for growth and for poverty alleviation in Zaire. The case of Zaire is perhaps the most egregious example in sub-Saharan Africa where, despite a wealth of natural resources, the economy lies in ruins owing to fiscal policy run amok. This alarming situation is reflected in an inflation rate of in excess of 7000 percent per year. Using a SAM as the basis for a multiplier model, the authors find that traditional agriculture, followed by commerce, private services, and construction, are the activities in the economy that will best improve household incomes. The sectors that the government has most heavily invested in, however, are manufacturing, mining, and transport, which will have the least beneficial effect for incomes, particularly of the poor. More significantly, policy experiments show that the poor would have greatly benefited if the government had followed the broad prescriptions suggested in the failed structural adjustment program, in conjunction with access to foreign financing through a structural adjustment loan. The results also indicate that fiscal discipline, as manifested through reducing government recurrent spending, will not have harmful consequences for most of the poor, even in the short term. This in large measure reflects the anti-poor bias in expenditures of the state.

1.3.3. *Agriculture and food markets*

Part IV explores the performance of agriculture and food markets in reforming economies, and the impact of such changes on the poor. Agriculture remains the most important sector in Africa, both in terms of providing jobs and incomes for the poor and as a share of GDP and exports. Agriculture was also generally the sector most adversely affected by the distortions that were so pervasive prior to the policy changes of the past decade. Consequently, policies that affect agriculture and food markets have been central to concerted efforts at sectoral reform.

Prior to adjustment, agricultural marketing parastatals that engaged in forced procurement and restrictions on inter-regional trade, and oligopsonist millers and processors sanctioned by the state, contributed to a situation where farmgate prices were heavily taxed and/or food markets were inefficient, and inequitable in terms of who got access to goods at low official prices. Liberalization of agricultural marketing arrangements has thus been at the center of many adjustment programs in Africa, with the underlying objective of raising exports and food production through turning the terms of trade in favor of agriculture. While reducing taxation of agriculture and raising incentives for and incomes of producers are objectives that receive broad support, a number of concerns still arise in terms of the welfare implications of such measures. First there is a concern that large numbers of the poor are net consumers of staple foods and, as such, stand to witness a fall in incomes if real food prices rise as a consequence of market liberalization and the disengagement of marketing parastatals. Likewise, the prospect of only large farmers, not poor smallholders, benefiting from export crop liberalization has also dampened enthusiasm for market reforms.

These concerns raise the issue of how the changes in marketing arrangements and the performance of agriculture will affect the poor, in both urban and rural areas. Or put in other terms, the question is whether on balance, given the poor's characteristics as consumers and producers, do changes in producer incentives and market prices raise or diminish their incomes?

This part of the book begins with the three chapters that report the results of economic models of Malawi, Mozambique, and Guinea. In the case of Malawi, an econometric model is used to explore the growth and distributional implications of a variety of macro and sectoral policies. In Chapter 11,

Yves Van Frausum and David E. Sahn point out that Malawi was regarded as one of Africa's best performing economies during the 1970s and was lauded for its agriculture-based, export-promotion development strategy. Adverse external shocks in the 1980s, particularly the war in Mozambique, which cut Malawi's main supply routes for export and imports, exposed underlying structural weaknesses and policy failures. The resulting increase in the transport margin adversely affected smallholders who comprise the vast majority of Malawi's poor. The inadequate response of the government during the 1980s to changing external conditions, including a failure to eliminate excessive taxation of smallholder export crops, exacerbated the adverse effects of the shock for small farmers. Government instead chose to pass the increase in the transport margin onto the poor farmers engaged in producing exports, both through maintaining low procurement prices and by not allowing the currency to depreciate sufficiently in response to such adverse external conditions. Model results indicate that failure to reduce taxation of smallholder export crops reduced GDP growth and the share of value added that accrue to the poor. The study also points out that foreign borrowing, while providing some short-term relief from negative external shocks, was on balance a net drain on the economy over the long run owing to the accumulation of debt.

Chapter 12 presents the multi-market modeling results from Mozambique. Here, Paul Dorosh, Carlo del Ninno, and David E. Sahn explore how the enormous foreign aid flows contributed to an overvaluation of the exchange rate. Results indicate that any policy to reduce foreign capital inflows would on balance result in a contraction in demand and incomes in the short term, even though the depreciation of the exchange rate, *ceterus paribus*, would improve incomes and raise producer incentives. In addition, the chapter focuses on the implications for the urban poor of liberalizing domestic food markets and eliminating the system of food rationing for staple commodities (e.g. rice, maize, sugar) that was in effect in the capital city, Maputo. The authors find that the existing system of state interference in urban food markets has created enormous rents, with little of the benefit accruing to the poor. They also present model results indicating that yellow maize is an inferior good, self-targeting to the poor. Thus, maintaining high levels of yellow maize food imports into Maputo will substantially ameliorate poverty and eliminate the justification, or need, for the existing food rationing scheme. Furthermore, the analysis indicates that yellow maize imports will not have significant adverse effects on incentives for rural producers who grow and market white maize and other domestically produced food crops. A number of factors contribute to this result: yellow and white maize products are weak substitutes among consumers, most of the white maize in Maputo is imported, and the region around the capital city is not a major maize-producing area. Thus, allowing markets, instead of administrative controls, to allocate yellow maize imports is found to be an effective approach to alleviating poverty in Maputo, in contrast with the expensive and ineffectual system of rationing a range of staple goods.

A similar multi-market model to that for Mozambique was developed for Guinea to explore the implications of trade and agricultural policy reforms on urban consumers and rural producers. Since the liberalization of trade and exchange rate policy in 1986, Guinea has witnessed a dramatic increase in rice imports and, to a lesser extent, wheat imports. Driven by twin concerns for protecting rural producer welfare and increasing fiscal revenues, the government has increased tariff and non-tariff barriers. In Chapter 13, Jehan Arulpragasam and Carlo del Ninno focus on the appropriateness of this response while exploring alternative policies. Model simulations suggest that protectionist policies will lead to only small increases in production of local rice. The consumption of imported rice, a product of lower quality and desirability, declines sharply among both the urban and rural poor as a result of falling trade barriers; thus, real incomes of all poor, rural and urban, fall despite increased agricultural production and higher nominal incomes of farmers. Government revenues also increase from the imposition of higher tariffs, although the negligible improvement could be easily achieved through taxing other commodities that are not of such great importance in the budget shares of poor consumers. While the results of the policy simulation on tariffs suggest that using such an instrument to increase domestic agricultural production has a high welfare cost, at least in the short term, it is also shown that investments that lower the high marketing and transportation costs of agricultural output will help both urban and rural consumers. Likewise, policies that promote the growth of local private enterprise from non-agricultural sources will generate significant demand for agricultural products, a much more favorable approach to raising demand than that of increased protectionism.

In Chapter 14, Paul Dorosh and Mattias Lundberg employ a general equilibrium model to examine the distributional and growth effects of economic reforms in the groundnut sector, as well as the role of foreign aid in the economic recovery in The Gambia. Results indicate that groundnuts play a crucial role in determining foreign exchange earnings and rural incomes and that groundnut prices have large effects on income distribution. Pre-reform policies of implicitly taxing producers to generate revenues used for investments were detrimental to the welfare of the poor given the concentration of government investment in urban areas. In addition, government spending and foreign aid inflows contribute to an appreciation of the exchange rate and to lower real incomes of the rural poor. This negative effect, however, is outweighed by targeting development expenditures to agriculture and rural infrastructure. But regardless of government policy, The Gambia, to a considerably greater extent than other countries discussed in this book, is vulnerable to external shocks owing to a combination of its high reliance on foreign aid and its general characteristics as a small open economy. As a consequence, domestic agricultural pricing policy has a much lesser impact than in other countries elsewhere in Africa, while in fact policies abroad, particularly in Senegal, are of greater importance.

While CGE, econometric, and multi-market models effectively explore the links between agricultural policy and household-level outcomes, they do not focus on the specific topic of the impact of economic reform on market performance. This issue is taken up by Harold Alderman and Gerald Shively in Chapter 15, which presents a Ghana case study using a dynamic model of price integration, cointegration techniques, and an autoregressive conditionally heteroskedastic model to examine the relationship between commodity prices over time, price variability, and seasonal price movements. These issues, of interest in their own right, are also critical in terms of the food security implications of reform programs. Simply, the evolution of commodity prices under adjustment, both their level and the degree of instability, are key factors in determining the living standards of the poor. Furthermore, this chapter provides an unusual and detailed analysis of the performance of commodity markets and their ability, in a liberalized economy, to successfully transmit incentives to producers and price signals to consumers.

Interestingly, the results from Ghana show that, contrary to widespread perceptions of the effect of adjustment policies, food prices have fallen in Ghana since the beginning of economic reform and price volatility has declined slightly. These observations, along with declining marketing margins, are taken as evidence that the efficiency of markets has improved since adjustment. The findings suggest that there is no compelling argument for the government to increase its involvement in commodity markets in order to mitigate the social cost of liberalizing markets.

1.4. *Overall Findings*

The results of the research in this volume reject the proposition that economic reforms are inherently harmful to the poor or that the poor bear the disproportionate cost of adjustment. In fact, they provide evidence quite to the contrary. Removing distortions in markets and altering relative prices in the directions typically associated with economic reform policies generally improve income distribution and raise the income of the poor, albeit marginally, even in the absence of large supply responses. More specifically, policies such as exchange rate devaluation and agricultural market liberalization, which are often portrayed as harmful to the well-being of those at the lower end of the income distribution, have just the opposite effect in the countries studied. This is not to say that there are no losers from adjustment policies; they are, however, predominantly the non-poor, such as public sector workers and traders who had access to rationed foreign exchange. Furthermore, most of the decline in living standards that follows from efforts at reform is a result of eliminating rents and privileges—not of demand contraction, as is often assumed.

The fundamental lesson of the case studies in this volume is that changes in relative prices, liberalization of markets, and reduction of state intervention in the allocation of resources and directly productive activities will generally have positive effects on growth and income distribution. The case studies show that, ironically, government interference in markets, often undertaken in the guise of promoting welfare, has a propensity to generate distortions that are in fact anti-poor. When the merits of state intervention in markets were initially put forth, whether it be administering food subsidies, providing public employment for university graduates, or reserving limited foreign exchange for essential imports, they were often compelling. In practice, such actions are rarely considered in the broader context of macroeconomic sustainability and administrative feasibility. As a consequence, original objectives were unmet and the most needy target groups unserved. Instead, inefficiencies and rent-seeking became debilitating to the broader context of development, further imperiling the objective of poverty alleviation.

An important policy implication that follows from our conclusion that the process of economic reform is not inherently anti-poor, or undertaken at the expense of the poor, is that concern for the welfare of the poor is a weak excuse for inaction and the perpetuation of failed policies. The evidence presented here instead suggests that most of the poor continue to lose when the pace of reform is retarded, since they are not the main beneficiaries of subsidized food, protection from global competition, public sector employment, grossly underpriced foreign exchange, and so forth. In addition, continued economic stagnation that accompanies egregious economic distortions offers little prospect for poverty alleviation, regardless of the equality of income distribution. In many cases, the greater the longevity of the old rules and regulations that governed the economy and perpetuated the distortions, the slower the rate of economic recovery. The failure to reform inappropriate economic structures thus lengthens the duration of the economic crisis and worsens poverty.

While the general conclusion, then, is that the macro and sectoral economic reforms discussed in this book have had little to do with causing poverty in sub-Saharan Africa, they should not be expected to be a panacea either. Eliminating predatory actions of the state and restoring good macroeconomic management, the goals most commonly associated with adjustment programs, are just initial steps in what needs to be defined as a broad development agenda for Africa. The remainder of this agenda, however, is in many ways more challenging than broad-stroke-of-a-pen reforms such as devaluation and market liberalization. More emphasis needs to be placed on addressing structural and institutional weaknesses, including measures to enhance the quality of human resources, developing infrastructure, revising legal and regulatory frameworks, divesting state enterprises, and restoring investors' confidence through reinvigorating markets and other indigenous institutions. These institutional and structural considerations need to be addressed as integral components of a broad development strategy. However, as that strategy is developed and implemented, maintaining macroeconomic stability is paramount. This message is reinforced by the finding in this book that macro and sectoral policy reforms are generally consistent with the objective of equity and poverty alleviation.

References

Abernathy, David B. 1969. *The Political Dilemma of Popular Education: An African Case Standard.* Stanford: Stanford University Press.

—— 1988. "Bureaucratic Growth and Economic Stagnation in Sub-Saharan Africa." In *Africa's Development Challenges and the World Bank*, Stephen K. Commins, ed. Boulder, CO: Lynne Rienner.

Alarcon, Jorge, Jan van Heenst, Steven V-Zunig, Willem de Ruijter, and Rob Vos. 1986. *The Social Accounting Framework for Development: Concepts, Construction and Applications.* The Hague: Institute of Social Sciences.

Azarya, Victor and Naomi Chazan. 1987. "Disengagement from the State in Africa: Reflections on the Experience of Ghana and Guinea." *Comparative Studies in Society and History*, 29(1): 106–131.

Bates, Robert H. 1981. *Markets and States in Tropical Africa.* Berkeley: University of California Press.

Bauer, P.T. 1984. *Reality and Rhetoric: Studies in the Economics of Development.* London: Weidenfeld and Nicolson.

Behrman, Jere. 1988. "The Impact of Economic Adjustment Programs on Health and Nutrition in Developing Countries." In *Health, Nutrition and Economic Crises: Approaches to Policy in the Third World*, D.E. Bell and M.R. Reich, eds. Dover, MA: Auburn House.

Berg, Elliot, Graeme Hunter, Tom Lenaghan, and Malaiku Ray. 1994. Trends and Living Standards in Latin American and Africa in the 1980s: UNICEF Myths and Statistical Realities. Bethesda, MD: Development Alternatives. Mimeo.

Corbo, Vittorio, and Patricio Rojas. 1991. *World Bank-Supported Adjustment Programs: Country Performance and Effectiveness.* PRE Working Paper Series No. 623. Washington, DC: World Bank.

Cornia, Giovanni Andrea, Richard Jolly, and Frances Stewart, eds. 1987. *Adjustment with a Human Face: Protecting the Vulnerable and Promoting Growth.* Oxford: Oxford University Press.

—— Rolph van der Hoeven, and Sanjaya Lall. 1992. "The Supply Side: Changing Production Structures and Accelerating Growth." In *Africa's Recovery in the 1990s: From Stagnation and Adjustment to Human Development*, Giovanni Andrea Cornia, Rolph van der Hoeven, and Thandika Mkandawire, eds. New York: St Martin's Press.

Dervis, Kemal, Jaime de Melo and Sherman Robinson. 1982. *General Equilibrium Models for Development Policy.* Washington, DC: World Bank.

Dornbusch, Rudiger. 1975. "Exchange Rates and Fiscal Policy in a Popular Model of International Trade." *American Economic Review*, 65(5): 859–871.

Easterly, William, Michael Kremer, Lant Pritchett, and Lawrence H. Summers. 1993. "Good Policy or Good Luck? Country Growth Performance and Temporary Shocks." *Journal of Monetary Economics*, 32(3): 459–483.

Elbadawi, Ibrahim, Dhaneshwar Ghura, and Gilbert Uwujaren. 1992. *Why Structural Adjustment Has Not Succeeded in sub-Saharan Africa.* WPS 1000. Washington, DC: World Bank, Country Economics Department.

Ferroni, Maro A., and Ravi Kanbur. 1991. *Poverty-Conscious Restructuring of Public Expenditures, Structural Dimensions of Adjustment-Lending*. Working Paper No. 9. Washington, DC: World Bank.

Gould, David J. 1980. *Bureaucratic Corruption and Underdevelopment in the Third World: The Case of Zaire*. New York: Pergamon.

Helleiner, Gerald K., ed. 1994. *Trade Policy and Industrialization in Turbulent Times*. New York: Routledge.

Husain, Ishrat and Rashid Faruqee. 1993. *Adjustment in Africa: Lessons from Country Case Studies*. Washington, DC: Work Bank.

Jamal, Vali, and John Weeks. 1993. *Africa Misunderstood, or, Whatever Happened to the Rural–Urban Gap?* London: International Labour Organization.

Jespersen, Eva. 1992. "External Shocks, Adjustment Policies and Social Performance." In *Africa's Recovery in the 1990s: From Stagnation to Adjustment to Human Development*, G.A. Cornia, R. van der Hoeven, and T. Mkandawire, eds. New York: St Martin's Press.

Jolly, Richard, and Giovanni Andrea Cornia. 1984. *The Impact of World Recession on Children: A Study Prepared for UNICEF*. 1st edn. New York: Pergamon Press.

Lele, Uma. 1989. "Aid to African Agriculture: Lessons from Two Decades of Donor Experience in Managing Agricultural Development in Africa." Washington, DC: World Bank, Special Studies Division, Country Economics Department.

Lindauer, David L. 1989. "Parallel, Fragmented, or Black? Defining Market Structure in Developing Economies." *World Development*, 17(12): 1871–1880.

—— and Barbara Nunberg, eds. Forthcoming. *Rehabilitating Government: Pay and Employment Reform in Developing Countries*. Washington, DC: World Bank.

Mosley, Paul, Jane Harrigan, and John Toye. 1991. *Aid and Power*. London: Routledge.

—— and John Weeks. 1993. "Has Recovery Begun? African Adjustment in the 1980s Revisited." *World Development*, 21(10): 1583–1606.

Paarlberg, Robert L., and Merilee S. Grindle. 1991. "Policy Reform and Reform Myopia: Agriculture in Developing Countries." *Food Policy*. 16(5): 383–394.

Preston, Samuel H. 1986. Review of Richard Jolly and Giovanni Andrea Cornia, eds., *The Impact of World Recession on Children*. *Journal of Development Economics*, 21(2): 373–375.

Price, Robert M. 1975. *Society and Bureaucracy in Contemporary Ghana*. Berkeley: University of California Press.

Pyatt, Graham, and Jeffrey Round, eds. 1985. *Social Accounting Matrices: A Basis for Planning*. Washington, DC: World Bank.

—— and Erik Thorbecke. 1976. *Planning Techniques for a Better Future: A Summary of a Research Project on Planning for Growth, Redistribution, and Employment*. Geneva: International Labour Organization.

Sahn, David, ed. 1994. *Adjusting to Policy Failure in African Economies*. Ithaca, NY: Cornell University Press.

—— Paul Dorosh, and Stephen Younger. Forthcoming. "Exchange Rate, Fiscal and Agricultural Policies in Africa: Does Adjustment Hurt the Poor? *World Development*.

—— and Alexander Sarris. 1994. "The Evolution of States, Markets, and Civil Institutions in Rural Africa." *Journal of Modern African Studies*, 32 (2): 279–303.

Sarris, Alexander. 1990. *A Macro–Micro Framework for Analysis of the Impact of*

Structural Adjustment on the Poor in sub-Saharan Africa. Monograph No. 5. Ithaca, NY: Cornell Food and Nutrition Policy Program.

SIDA. 1994. *State, Market and Aid.* Stockholm: International Development Authority.

Singh, Ajit, and Hamid Tabatabai. 1993. *Economic Crisis and Third World Agriculture.* Cambridge: Cambridge University Press.

Taylor, Lance. 1993. *The Rocky Road to Reform: Adjustment, Income Distribution, and Growth in the Developing World.* Cambridge, MA: MIT Press.

Thomas, Vinod, and John Nash. 1991. "Reform of Trade Policy: Recent Evidence from Theory and Practice." *World Bank Research Observer*, 6(2): 219–240.

Thorbecke, Erik. 1994. Performances in Sub-Saharan Africa under Adjustment and Components of a Long-Term Development Strategy. Paris: OECD. Unpublished paper.

United Nations Economic Commission for Africa (UNECA). 1989. "Statistics and Policies: ECA Preliminary Observations on the World Bank Report: Africa's Adjustment and Growth in the 1980s." Addis Ababa: ECA.

von Freyhold, Michael. 1979. *Ujamaa Villages in Tanzania: Analysis of a Social Experiment.* New York: Monthly Review Press.

World Bank. 1981. *Accelerated Development in Sub-Saharan Africa: An Agenda for Action.* Washington, DC: World Bank.

—— 1992. *Adjustment Lending and Mobilization of Private and Public Resources for Growth.* Washington, DC: World Bank.

—— 1993. *Adjustment in Sub-Saharan Africa: Selected Findings from OED Evaluations.* Report No. 12155. Washington, DC: The World Bank.

—— 1994. *Adjustment in Africa: Reforms, Results, and the Road Ahead.* Oxford: Oxford University Press for World Bank.

—— and United Nations Development Programme. 1989. *Africa's Adjustment and Growth in the 1980s.* Washington and New York: World Bank and UNDP.

Yasané, Aguibou Y. 1990. "Guinea: The Significance of the Coup of April 1984 and Economic Issues." *World Development*, 18(9): 1231–1246.

PART II

Trade and Exchange Rate Policy:
*A General Equilibrium Approach to
Examining Welfare Outcomes*

2

Rents and Exchange Rates: Redistribution through Trade Liberalization in Madagascar

Paul Dorosh

2.1. *Introduction*

In Madagascar, as in a number of countries, IMF stand-by agreements in the early 1980s were followed by a succession of World Bank and bilateral structural adjustment and sectoral loans designed to restore macroeconomic balances and liberalize markets. No representative household survey data exists with which to trace the actual evolution of household incomes and expenditures in Madagascar during the 1980s. Using available information on prices, household income and expenditure patterns, Dorosh, Bernier, and Sarris (1990) provided evidence suggesting that in Madagascar, the adverse effects of adjustment policies, per se, were more limited. This study, based on computable general equilibrium (CGE) model simulations of external shocks and policy changes, attempts to shed more light on the important linkages between macroeconomic adjustment and welfare of lower-income households in Madagascar.

The case of Madagascar is important for several reasons. The immediate cause of the balance of payments crisis of the early 1980s is similar to that in a number of other countries of sub-Saharan Africa: a sharp decline in foreign exchange availability. And, as in other countries, stabilization efforts included cutbacks in imports of food and a reduction in food subsidies. Unlike in many other developing countries, however, there is evidence that a large share of these subsidies actually reached lower-income urban groups. Finally, Malagasy agriculture is sufficiently diverse to enable an analysis of effects on both smallholder export crop producers and food crop producers.

This chapter first presents a brief overview of the economy of Madagascar and a summary of key economic policies in Madagascar in the 1980s. A

I am grateful to Nancy Benjamin, Shanta Devarajan, and Erik Thorbecke for their many useful suggestions on CGE modeling; to David Sahn for his comments on this paper; and to René Bernier for his work as a research assistant.

brief description of the CGE model and of the data base follows. In Section 2.3, results of model simulations of major elements of the investment boom, stabilization and structural adjustment policies adopted by Madagascar are presented. Conclusions are found in the final section.

2.2. *The Malagasy Economy and Economic Policy in the 1980s*[1]

Madagascar is typical of many low income countries of sub-Saharan Africa with large agricultural and service sectors and a small industrial sector. Less than 20 percent of the population lives in urban areas. Although some large farms managed by parastatals exist, the bulk of agricultural production is carried out by traditional smallholders whose average farm size is only 1.15 hectares.[2] Madagascar's agriculture differs from that of most of sub-Saharan Africa because of the dominance of irrigated land, especially on the densely populated high plateau which ranges from the north to the south in the center of the island. Irrigated area, planted primarily with rice or cotton, accounts for 44 percent of traditional cultivated area nationwide (MPARA 1988). Rice consumption alone represents 54 percent of total calorie consumption (FAO 1984).

The relative importance of agricultural exports (mainly coffee, cloves and vanilla) declined during the 1980s because of a decline in world prices of coffee and cloves, yet agricultural exports still accounted for 51.5 percent of Madagascar's total exports in the 1987–1989 period[3] (down from a share of 65.7 percent in 1980) (World Bank 1986, 1991).

Production of the formal industrial sector is concentrated in import-substitution sectors such as food processing, textiles and beverages, and in nontraded sectors such as water and electricity. Imports of raw materials, energy, and capital goods make up about 70 percent of the import bill (World Bank 1991). High transport and marketing costs contribute to the large size of the service sector; marketing alone accounted for 21 percent of value added in 1984.

Based on poverty lines for rural and urban households calculated using food requirements and typical expenditure patterns, approximately 37 percent of rural households, 26 percent of households in small urban areas, and 18 percent of households in the seven large urban areas can be classified as poor (Dorosh, Bernier, and Sarris 1990). Nationally, 34 percent of all households are poor, 90 percent of which are in rural areas.

[1] This discussion draws heavily from Dorosh, Bernier, and Sarris (1990) and Dorosh and Bernier (1994).

[2] Traditional farmers, as defined in the 1984 Agricultural Census, are farmers owning 10 or fewer hectares, hiring fewer than five full-time, paid workers, and not using any specialized modern equipment or machinery.

[3] Including agro-industrial exports such as cloth, preserved meats, and essences of cloves and ylang ylang, the share rises to 62 percent (IMF 1991).

2.2.1. *Economic policies in the 1980s*

At the start of the 1980s, severe macroeconomic imbalances plagued the Malagasy economy. The "investment to the limit" development strategy of the late 1970s had led to a huge surge of imports, an unsustainable balance of payments deficits, large government budget deficits and accelerating growth in the money supply (Table 2.1). The current account deficit reached 16.9 percent of GDP in 1981, and inflation jumped from 9.1 percent per year in 1977 to 23.8 percent per year in 1981.

Between 1981 and 1984, macroeconomic adjustment in Madagascar focused largely on stabilization efforts endorsed by the IMF. Aggregate demand was quickly reduced through cuts in public investment and other

Table 2.1. Madagascar: macroeconomic summary, 1973–1989

	1973–77	1978–80	1981–82	1983–87	1988–89
Real GDP					
(bn 1984 FMG)	1712.90	1797.60	1667.00	1719.00	1880.00
Real GDP per capita					
(bn 1984 FMG)	224.30	212.10	183.60	170.30	164.60
Average GDP growth					
rate (%)	−0.01	2.70	−5.80	1.40	4.40
Annual percentage change					
in GDP deflator					
Average	11.60	11.00	27.60	16.10	16.30
End of period	8.60	15.00	28.60	22.80	10.20
Trade deficit/GDP (%)					
Average	−4.10	−13.00	−10.40	−5.90	−5.90
End of period	−3.60	−16.40	−9.40	−4.60	−5.20
Budget deficit/GDP (%)[a]					
Average	−3.28	10.05	−9.60	−3.70	−5.60
End of period	−6.28	14.51	−7.10	−3.30	−7.90
Rice imports (1000 tons)					
Average	86.00	161.00	272.00	130.00	101.00
End of period	95.00	176.00	351.00	94.00	112.00
Exchange rate (FMG/$)					
Average	233.00	217.00	311.00	683.00	1505.00
End of period	226.00	211.00	350.00	1069.00	1465.00
Industrial value added					
(bn 1984 FMG)					
Average	252.70	267.60	204.00	203.00	241.00
End of period	262.40	265.50	197.00	22.00	250.00

[a] Budget deficit on a commitment basis.

Sources: World Bank (1991); IMF (1988, 1991).

government expenditures. Initial efforts at liberalization of rice marketing were begun, including a large reduction in the subsidy on rice for consumers. These stabilization efforts proved successful in terms of their major goals: by 1984 inflation had dropped to 10.3 percent per year and the trade deficit was cut to only 5.0 percent of GDP. However, real GDP also fell sharply, by 5.4 percent between 1979–1981 and 1982–1984.

Structural adjustment reforms aimed at restoring growth enjoyed relatively little success until 1988, the year a major trade liberalization was completed. Thereafter, in 1989 and 1990, Madagascar enjoyed positive growth in per capita GDP for the first time since the unsustainable surge of the investment boom at the start of the decade.

Unfortunately, many of the gains from adjustment unraveled in the early 1990s. A decline in world export prices together with domestic credit expansion contributed to balance-of-payments difficulties in 1991. More important, political protests led to a temporary closing of the major port, Toamasina, in mid-1991 and marked the beginning of a two-year transition to a new constitution and a new democratically elected president. The political uncertainty during this period hindered government development efforts, discouraged private investment, and stalled foreign aid inflows.

The major channels by which adjustment policies and external shocks affected the poor are relatively clear. Rice subsidies and large quantities of imports heavily favored urban consumers, especially in the capital city, Antananarivo, to the detriment of producers of rice. The investment boom of the late 1970s and the early 1980s was concentrated in large industrial projects, spurring economic activity and (especially urban) incomes. And, despite changes in the real exchange rate brought about by nominal devaluations and fiscal discipline, real producer prices of export crops changed little during the decade, initially because of increases in the rate of taxation on exports, and then later because of a decline in world prices that coincided with, but was independent of, a liberalization in export crop marketing. The magnitudes of the above effects and their interactions are not straightforward, however, and require a more formal analysis, which is the main purpose of this chapter.

2.3. Model Description[4]

The CGE model used for these simulations is a variant of the "neoclassical structuralist" model originating with Dervis, de Melo, and Robinson (1982) and later applied to Cameroon (Benjamin and Devarajan 1985; Condon, Dahl, and Devarajan 1987) and other developing countries.[5]

---

[4] A complete model description is found in Dorosh (1994).
[5] The model also draws some of its features from Sarris (1990).

A social accounting matrix (SAM) for Madagascar's economy in 1984 is the data base for the model. The SAM is constructed from the 1984 national accounts and input–output table, supplemented by data from national household surveys in 1978 and 1980, an agricultural census in 1984, and smaller surveys of rice producers and consumers in the early 1980s (see Dorosh et al. 1991).

Twenty-seven production activities are specified, producing 15 commodities (Table 2.2). Given the importance of rice in Madagascar's economy, three separate technologies (activities) are specified for paddy (small farm irrigated, large farm irrigated, and upland), and both paddy and milled rice are included as a separate commodities. Separate technologies are modeled for most agricultural activities (large and small farm) and non-agricultural activities (formal and informal sector).

Three types of labor (highly skilled, skilled and unskilled) are modeled, each with a non-zero elasticity of supply with respect to the real wage. Capital is fixed in the short run and is updated with additions of new investment net of depreciation. Only aggregate capital enters the production functions. Returns to capital are allocated among six types of capital: non-farm capital in the formal and informal sectors, farm capital/land belonging to small farmers in three regions of the country (the Plateau, East Coast, and West and South zones), and farm capital/land owned by large farmers.

The model specifies 11 institutions: eight household groups, formal enterprises, government, and the rest of the world.[6] The three urban household groups are classified according to the skill level of the head of household (which corresponds with income levels, as well) (Table 2.3). Per capita incomes of the urban high-income households are nearly seven times those of urban low-income households. Per capita incomes of the rural poor, comprised of rural small farmers and a small non-farm rural poor population (5.0 percent of total population), are approximately 40 percent of the national average. Rural small farmers are disaggregated by agro-ecological zone: Plateau (where irrigated rice is the major crop), East Coast (a region with export crops), and West and South (the rest of the country, where livestock are a dominant source of rural income). Large farmers throughout the country and rural non-farm households with a skilled head of household are classified as rural high-income households. In the model, all transfers between institutions (including households) have been netted out.

Value added generated by production activity j is specified as a constant elasticity of substitution (CES) production function; quantities of intermediate inputs are modeled as fixed shares of the quantity of output

---

[6] The published Madagascar SAM (Dorosh et al. 1991) has 13 institutions. In addition to the 11 institutions listed above, private nonprofit institutions (included with high-income urban households in the model) and financial enterprises (included with formal sector enterprises in the model) have separate accounts in the full SAM.

Table 2.2. Madagascar: subsectors in SAM

	Gross value added	Sectoral gross value added as a % of total GVA
Primary sector	568,709	35.8
Paddy	119,036	7.5
Small farm irrigated	44,227	
Large farm irrigated	58,947	
Upland	15,682	
Other food crops	197,855	12.5
Export crops	37,573	2.4
Small farms	27,283	
Large farms	10,290	
Industrial crops	11,680	0.7
Small farms	8,030	
Large farms	3,650	
Livestock and forestry	202,565	12.8
Informal sector	189,548	
Formal sector	13,017	
Mining, energy, and water	31,969	2.0
Rice milling	3,807	0.2
Informal sector	0	
Formal sector	3,807	
Other food processing	59,944	3.8
Informal sector	12,118	
Formal sector	47,826	
Textiles	24,545	1.5
Informal sector	4,391	
Formal sector	20,154	
Other industry	44,447	2.8
Informal sector	10,664	
Formal sector	33,783	
Construction	42,752	2.7
Informal sector	5,339	
Formal sector	37,413	
Transportation and communication	160,758	10.1
Informal sector	130,818	
Formal sector	29,940	
Commerce	331,933	20.9
Informal sector	219,161	
Formal sector	112,772	
Services, private	188,787	11.9
Public administration	130,301	8.2
Total	1,587,954	100.0

Source: Dorosh et al. (1991).

Table 2.3. Madagascar: household groups

Household Group	Population		Revenue per capita
	('000s)	(%)	(1000 FMG)
Urban high-income	210.7	1.9	877.0
Urban middle-income	1120.8	10.9	181.2
Urban low-income	291.4	3.5	126.2
Urban subtotal	1622.9	16.3	172.7
Small farmers/Plateau	1910.7	20.0	102.7
Small farmers/East Coast	1996.1	20.9	104.9
Small farmers/West and South	1345.5	14.1	118.3
Rural rich (all regions)	2258.2	23.7	271.3
Rural poor (non-farm)	474.3	5.0	103.3
Rural subtotal	7984.9	83.7	150.1
All Madagascar	9607.8	100.0	171.8

Source: Dorosh et al. (1991).

produced. Elasticities of substitution between capital and labor are chosen so as to give conservative magnitudes for elasticities of supply, equal to 0.1 for mining and energy, 0.3 for most formal sector industrial activities (including formal sector construction) and all agriculture except for upland paddy and "other crops," and 0.5 for all other activities (mainly services and informal sector industry).

Internationally traded goods are treated as imperfect substitutes for goods domestically produced and consumed. A constant elasticity of substitution (CES) aggregation function defines the composite of imports and home goods (Armington 1969). Similarly, a constant elasticity of transformation (CET) aggregation is used to define a composite production good of export goods and goods produced for domestic consumption. Elasticities of substitution and levels of trade and domestic production are given in Appendix Table 2A.1. Madagascar is assumed to be a price taker both for imports and exports.

Incomes of households derive from their ownership of factors of production and access to rents (Table 2.4). Earnings from highly skilled labor accrue only to the urban non-poor households. Incomes of the poor derive from unskilled labor, informal sector capital, and land. Household consumption is specified as a function of prices and incomes, using a linear expenditure system (LES) formulation. Savings is a linear function of income. Household budget shares and demand parameters are given in Tables 2A.2 and 2A.3.

Table 2.4. Madagascar: estimated household income shares, 1984

	Urban non-poor	Urban middle	Urban poor	Small farmer Plateau	Small farmer East Coast	Small farmer West/South	Rural non-poor	Rural nonfarm poor	All households
Highly skilled labor	0.404	0.000	0.000	0.000	0.000	0.000	0.000	0.000	0.071
Skilled labor	0.014	0.584	0.000	0.000	0.000	0.000	0.068	0.000	0.082
Unskilled labor	0.006	0.248	0.681	0.711	0.708	0.621	0.308	0.575	0.401
Informal capital	0.000	0.168	0.319	0.077	0.076	0.067	0.406	0.425	0.190
Land—Plateau	0.000	0.000	0.000	0.213	0.000	0.000	0.000	0.000	0.027
Land—East Coast	0.000	0.000	0.000	0.000	0.215	0.000	0.000	0.000	0.029
Land—West/South	0.000	0.000	0.000	0.000	0.000	0.312	0.000	0.000	0.032
Land—Large farm	0.000	0.000	0.000	0.000	0.000	0.000	0.218	0.000	0.068
Dividends	0.292	0.000	0.000	0.000	0.000	0.000	0.000	0.000	0.051
Rents	0.284	0.000	0.000	0.000	0.000	0.000	0.000	0.000	0.050
Total	1.000	1.000	1.000	1.000	1.000	1.000	1.000	1.000	1.000

Source: Madagascar CGE model.

Government recurrent and investment expenditures are fixed in real terms. Savings determine the level of private investment. This specification reflects the situation in Madagascar during most of the 1980s, when the commercial banks were controlled by the state and allocation of credit for investment was determined largely through rationing. The value of investment by sector of destination j is assumed to be a fixed share of total fixed investment, and the composition of capital by activity is likewise fixed.

Quantitative restrictions on the imports of manufactured goods and rice are modeled by fixing imports of these commodities exogenously at the quota levels. The rents generated from these quotas are modeled as accruing to the urban high-income households. In the base run of the model, implicit tariffs on manufactured goods and rice are set at 100 and 47 percent, respectively.

Apart from quantitative restrictions on imports of rice and manufactured goods in some model runs, prices adjust to equate supply and demand. Labor markets also clear through adjustment in real wages, though the substantial underemployment in the Malagasy economy in the 1980s is reflected in high elasticities of the supply of labor. Savings determines private investment given fixed values of real government investment and government expenditure. The nominal exchange rate and foreign savings are also fixed exogenously, leaving changes in the aggregate price index to bring about movements in the real exchange rate and equilibrium in the Rest of World accounts.

In the dynamic simulations, capital stock is updated each year according to the previous period's net investment by sector. The base-level labor supply is also increased exogenously by a constant population growth rate.

2.4. Simulation Results

How did the stabilization and structural adjustment policies of the Malagasy government during the 1980s affect income distribution and the welfare of the poor? To address this question, the CGE model previously outlined is used to simulate key aspects of stabilization and structural adjustment policies. Four model simulations which illustrate the effects of major changes in external conditions and government policy in Madagascar are presented.

The first two simulations focus on the effects of the major stabilization policies adopted in the early 1980s. Simulation 1 models the impact of a large increase in foreign borrowing and investment and subsequent stabilization where foreign debt is repaid. This simulation also illustrates the effects of the investment boom of 1978–1981 and the stabilization of 1982–1984. Simulation 2 models the impact of the large increase in rice imports in the early 1980s. From these results we can also deduce the effects of the subsequent reduction in rice imports as part of the stabilization effort of 1982–1984.

Simulations 3 and 4 model trade policy reform, the centerpiece of the structural adjustment effort in the late 1980s. Simulation 3 shows the effects of a removal of import quotas with no change in foreign capital inflows. Simulation 4, which includes a reduction in foreign capital inflows along with the elimination of quotas, more closely simulates the historical trade liberalization in 1988.

The model emphasizes three major channels through which changes in government policy or external shocks affect income levels and distribution in Madagascar. First, the level of foreign capital inflows and other factors, which in turn influence the level of aggregate demand, helps determine the overall level of economic activity and incomes earned by all household groups. Second, the level of investment spending, heavily concentrated in urban goods and services, has a major influence on the distribution of economic benefits between rural and urban groups. Third, and most important, changes in the real exchange rate, which affect producer and consumer incentives throughout the economy, are shown to be an important determinant of the sectoral distribution of production and the distribution of real incomes of households.

In all the simulations, real government investment and expenditures are exogenous. The base run of the dynamic model fixes foreign savings, real government current expenditures, and real government investment at their 1984 per capita values in each of the six years of the simulation. The base run also keeps quotas on imports of rice and manufactured goods constant on a per capita basis. In the dynamic policy simulations, the model maintains the changes in exogenous variables in real per capita terms over six years, except in simulation 1. The model results presented in the following tables compare the outcomes of simulated policies with the base solution of the model.

2.4.1. *Investment boom and stabilization: simulation 1*

In the late 1970s and continuing in the early 1980s, the *investir à outrance* ("invest to the limit") development strategy spurred a large increase in foreign borrowing and imports of capital goods. A balance of payments crisis ensued as interest and principal on the foreign debts came due before the new investments generated sufficient additional foreign exchange. Madagascar rapidly cut imports by tightening import quotas (rather than by a real devaluation or by increasing tariffs).

Simulation 1 illustrates the effects of an investment boom like that of the late 1970s by specifying gross capital inflows of US$50 million (1984) in the first and second years of the simulation, and a gross capital inflow of US$30 million (1984) in year 3 of the simulation (Table 2.5). Principal and interest (at 5 percent per year) repayments begin in year 2 and increase steadily until

Table 2.5. Madagascar: foreign capital inflows for simulation of investment boom and stabilization

Simulation year	Gross capital inflow	Interest	Principal repayment	Net Flow	Debt
1	50.0	0.0	0.0	50.0	50.0
2	50.0	2.6	10.0	37.6	92.6
3	30.0	4.6	20.0	5.4	107.2
4	0.0	5.4	30.0	−35.4	82.4
5	0.0	4.2	40.0	−44.2	46.6
6	0.0	2.4	49.0	−51.4	0.0

Source: Madagascar model simulations.

the full debt is repaid in year 6. This simulation adjusts the quota on manu-factured goods imports each year by an amount equal to 50 percent of the value of the net capital inflow.

In an economy with no quantitative restrictions on trade, a large increase in foreign capital inflows normally leads to a large appreciation of the real exchange rate (i.e. a decrease in the price of traded goods relative to nontraded goods).[7] As aid inflows are spent in the country (either directly or through the counterpart funds), prices of domestic goods, particularly nontraded goods, tend to rise. Prices of traded goods, which are tied to world prices, rise less, thus reducing the real domestic prices of traded goods. In Madagascar, as in most developing countries, the agricultural sector is the largest producer of traded goods (e.g. rice, export crops, and cotton). Thus, agricultural production and agricultural real incomes tend to decline when the real exchange rate appreciates.

For the Malagasy economy in the late 1970s and early 1980s, however, import quotas for most goods were binding. A higher level of capital inflows enables an increase in the import quota, and much of the increase in demand is channeled into imports instead of nontraded goods. With less change in demand, the rise in the price of nontraded goods is small and the real exchange rate appreciation is limited.

Apart from the loss of quota rents, the major beneficiaries of the invest-ment boom (years 1–3 of the simulation) were the urban rich, although all groups gained (Table 2.6). The effects of the stabilization (years 4–6) are the reverse, with the urban rich seeing a larger decline in their real non-rent incomes than the poor. Three major mechanisms determine these results:

[7] This appreciation, and the negative effects on tradable goods production resulting from the change in producer incentives, is often referred to as the "Dutch disease" after the decline in the industrial sector of the Netherlands following an increase in natural gas export revenues in the 1970s.

Table 2.6. Madagascar: investment boom and stabilization: simulation result 1

| | Investment Boom | | Stabilization |
	Year 1	Year 3	Year 6
Real GDP	2.62	0.69	−3.27
Private consumption	3.16	0.82	−3.10
Total real investment	18.79	3.10	−26.56
Private investment	28.89	4.80	−41.67
Government investment	0.00	0.00	0.00
Government consumption	0.00	0.00	0.00
Government revenue	1.99	0.36	−2.19
Real exchange rate	−4.33	−1.17	3.03
Exports ($m)	−1.71	−0.46	0.83
Imports ($m)	9.67	1.41	−8.94
Foreign savings/GDP	1.49	0.24	−1.32
Sectoral production			
Agriculture	1.15	0.21	−1.38
Industry	3.06	1.20	−5.06
Formal	3.81	1.99	−6.63
Informal	2.21	0.26	−2.96
Services	1.80	0.81	−2.15
Formal	6.15	1.62	−6.17
Informal	0.16	0.65	−0.66
Public administration	0.01	0.02	−0.01
Total	2.02	0.77	−2.87
Household incomes			
Urban I (high-income)			
Total income	1.08	2.70	−2.23
Non-rent income	19.88	1.40	−14.09
Urban II (middle-income)	4.83	0.97	−5.83
Urban III (low-income)	2.55	0.55	−3.25
Small farm Plateau	2.60	0.56	−2.69
Small farm East	2.65	0.49	−3.15
Small farm West/South	2.55	0.47	−2.59
Large farm rural high-income	4.34	0.37	−4.28
Nonfarm rural low-income	3.05	0.35	−2.98
Total	3.12	0.91	−3.48

Source: Madagascar model simulations.

direct income effects of changes in capital inflows, investment spending linkages, and variations in the real exchange rate.

Increased foreign savings (the inflow of foreign capital) increase the pool of funds available for government expenditures and investment, thus raising aggregate demand. Given the high level of underemployment of labor, particularly unskilled labor, the supply of many goods and services, especially nontraded goods and services, is relatively elastic. Thus, an increased demand for these goods will elicit an increase in supply with a relatively small increase in price. This effect of increased aggregate demand on output is partly responsible for the 2.6 percent increase in real GDP per capita in year 1.[8]

Increased foreign savings also add to the pool of total savings in the economy, enabling an 18.8 percent rise in total investment in year 1, which translates into increased demand for investment goods and services. Historically, investment spending (apart from certain large irrigation projects) has been heavily concentrated in urban areas, both in terms of the location of investments and in terms of the composition of investment goods (largely urban construction services and to a lesser extent domestic industrial goods).[9] In response to increased investment demand, industrial output (which here includes construction), grows by 3.1 percent, and demand for highly skilled and moderately skilled labor increases so that real wage rates rise by 2.6 and 0.8 percent, respectively. Returns to formal sector capital also increase, along with increased dividends paid to urban high-income households. Because of this investment spending bias, urban households with skilled and highly skilled labor tend to gain more in real non-rent incomes than other households. Real incomes of the urban II households (those with skilled heads of households) rise by 4.8 percent, compared with the national average gain of 3.1 percent. Apart from the change in quota rents, real incomes of urban I (highly skilled) households rise by 19.9 percent.

The increase in the quota on imports of manufactured goods helps to limit the appreciation of the real exchange rate resulting from the increased capital inflow. Thus, the real exchange rate appreciates by only 4.3 percent in the first year. In general, the real exchange rate appreciation has the expected effects on traded and nontraded sectors: output of the nontraded services sector rises by 1.8 percent, while agriculture (a mix of traded rice and export crops with nontraded crops and livestock) increases by only 1.2 percent.

Table 2.7 shows the contribution of the various income components to

---

[8] See Dorosh (1994) for sensitivity analysis regarding the elasticity of labor supply. Even with labor supply fixed, real GDP and personal incomes rise by 1.3 and 1.7 percent, respectively, as labor resources are reallocated toward higher productivity industrial sectors.

[9] Purchases of imported intermediate and capital goods also account for much of the investment spending.

Table 2.7. Madagascar: breakdown of household income changes: simulation 1—investment boom

	Urban non-poor	Urban middle	Urban poor	Small farmer Plateau	Small farmer East Coast	Small farmer West/South	Rural non-poor	Rural nonfarm poor	All households
Highly skilled labor	4.512	0.000	0.000	0.000	0.000	0.000	0.000	0.000	0.789
Skilled labor	0.143	5.941	0.000	0.000	0.000	0.000	0.691	0.000	0.833
Unskilled labor	0.043	1.905	5.234	5.464	5.444	4.774	2.370	4.422	3.083
Informal capital	0.000	1.579	3.001	0.721	0.719	0.632	3.815	3.993	1.784
Land—Plateau	0.000	0.000	0.000	1.782	0.000	0.000	0.000	0.000	0.226
Land—East Coast	0.000	0.000	0.000	0.000	1.644	0.000	0.000	0.000	0.219
Land—West/South	0.000	0.000	0.000	0.000	0.000	2.532	0.000	0.000	0.259
Land—Large farm	0.000	0.000	0.000	0.000	0.000	0.000	3.002	0.000	0.940
Dividends	10.327	0.000	0.000	0.000	0.000	0.000	0.000	0.000	1.807
Rents	−13.020	0.000	0.000	0.000	0.000	0.000	0.000	0.000	−2.278
Total	2.004	9.425	8.235	7.967	7.807	7.938	9.878	8.416	7.662
Change in national CPI	4.520	4.520	4.520	4.520	4.520	4.520	4.520	4.520	4.520
Real income change I	−2.407	4.692	3.554	3.298	3.145	3.270	5.126	3.727	3.006
Change in household CPI	0.914	4.386	5.545	5.232	5.027	5.259	5.307	5.212	4.408
Real income change II	1.081	4.827	2.549	2.599	2.647	2.545	4.341	3.045	3.117

Source: Madagascar model simulations.

changes in real household incomes in simulation 1. Increased wages from highly skilled labor increase nominal incomes of the urban non-poor by 4.5 percent, and larger dividends raise nominal incomes by 10.3 percent. The decline in rents, given a partial relaxation of the foreign exchange constraint with increased capital inflows, reduces nominal incomes of the urban non-poor by 13.0 percent. Thus, total nominal incomes of these households increase by only 2.0 percent and real incomes rise by just 1.1 percent.

Nominal income gains are roughly similar for small farmers in all agro-ecological zones, although slightly smaller for those on the east coast, since returns to land and capital on export crop production are dampened by the real exchange rate appreciation. Real incomes of small farmers on the east coast actually increase slightly more than those of other small farmers because the price of their consumption bundle rises less. As the direction of new net capital inflows reverses after year 3 (modeling the effects of stabilization measures), the economy contracts and real incomes decline. By year 6 of the simulation, real GDP is down by 3.3 percent *vis à vis* year 6 of the base run, and investment has fallen by 26.6 percent. (Relative to year 1 of the investment boom, investment in year 6 is lower by 31.5 percent.) The real exchange rate in year 6 depreciates by 3.0 percent relative to the base run, helping to limit the reduction in agricultural output to −1.4 percent but worsening incentives for services, which fall by 2.2 percent.

With the exception of urban I households, all household incomes (per capita) decline continuously after year 1 of the simulation.[10] And, for all households except the urban non-poor, real per capita income in year 6 of the simulation is lower than in year 1 of the base SAM. The present value of the per capita income streams (using a 10 percent discount rate) in simulation 1 is about 0.1 percent lower to 0.2 percent higher than in the base run for all household groups except the urban non-poor. For these households, the discounted per capita income stream is 0.9 percent higher in simulation 1 than in the base run.

This simulation of increased foreign capital inflows, increased investment expenditures, and subsequent stabilization suggests that the urban high- and middle-income households benefited the most from the investment boom in the late 1970s. The skilled labor of these groups was in demand by the construction and manufacturing industry to produce investment goods. Apart from the loss of quota rents, the percentage gain for urban high-income households was more than six times the national average. Lower-income households (especially rural households) benefited less from the investment boom, as the negative effects of the real exchange rate appreciation somewhat offset the benefits of the increase in aggregate demand on employment.

---

[10] Real per capita income for urban I households declines continuously after year 2 of the simulation.

The simulation results also suggest that, just as the investment boom benefited urban households the most, the stabilization policies that cut back foreign capital inflows and government investment likewise hurt these same households the most. The investment boom itself, however, was unsustainable. The large increase in foreign capital inflow in the form of loans could not continue indefinitely: the stabilization effort was inevitable.

Finally, although the calculations of the present value of the income streams for many household groups in simulation 1 are nearly identical to those in the base run, the present value measure may not adequately reflect people's perception of their own welfare. From a political economy standpoint, if expectations of higher incomes are raised during the investment boom period, the subsequent decline may lead to more dissatisfaction with government policies than the base scenario where a long-term trend is maintained.

2.4.2. *Increased rice imports: simulation 2*

Not all of the increase in foreign savings in the late 1970s was spent on imported capital goods. Rice imports also increased substantially in this period: imports in 1980 were nearly double those in 1984. Simulation 2 models a 90 percent increase in rice imports funded by an increase in foreign savings of equal value (Table 2.8).

As in simulation 1, the increase in foreign savings permits an increase in investment. The value of the additional rice imports is added implicitly to government total revenues, as parastatals sold the imports, reducing government borrowing and increasing availability of loans to parastatals for investments. Total investment rises by 7.1 percent in year 1 of this scenario, although real GDP declines by 0.1 percent, owing in part to disincentive effects on rice production. Real incomes rise by 0.2 percent on average.

Although investment demand increases, the continued quotas on manufactured goods inhibit production of the formal manufacturing sector, which requires imports of intermediate goods. Thus, industrial output falls by 0.4 percent (compared to a gain of 3.1 percent in simulation 1 with an increase in total investment of roughly twice the magnitude). The gains in real incomes for urban households arising from the investment spending bias thus are limited.

Changes in relative prices play a major role in the effects of an increase in rice imports. As domestic rice prices fall, domestic paddy production declines by 5.4 (6.0) percent in year 1 (year 6). Net supply (production plus imports) increases, however, and rice consumption increases by 1.7 percent in year 1 and 1.1 percent in year 6. In this simulation, the value of additional rice imports exactly matches the increase in foreign savings, so that no large gain is seen in foreign exchange available for other imports. The real exchange rate depreciates slightly as the decline in rice prices depresses prices of competing nontraded food commodities as well.

Table 2.8. Madagascar: increased rice imports: simulation result 2

	Year 1	Year 3
Real GDP	−0.08	0.06
Private consumption	0.26	0.37
Total real investment	7.10	8.03
Private investment	10.92	12.60
Government investment	0.00	0.00
Government consumption	0.00	0.00
Government revenue	2.62	2.00
Real exchange rate	0.99	0.46
Exports ($m)	0.11	0.12
Imports ($m)	6.32	6.26
Foreign savings/GDP	0.83	0.85
Sectoral production		
Agriculture	−1.28	−1.55
Industry	−0.38	−0.04
Formal	0.28	1.18
Informal	−1.22	−1.65
Services	0.12	0.50
Formal	−0.42	0.10
Informal	0.44	0.88
Public administration	0.02	0.02
Total	−0.41	−0.20
Household incomes		
Urban I (high-income)		
Total income	1.65	2.58
Non-rent income	−0.76	−1.06
Urban II (middle-income)	0.66	0.43
Urban III (low-income)	1.51	0.77
Small farm Plateau	−0.11	−0.22
Small farm East	−0.03	0.03
Small farm West/South	−0.48	−0.47
Large farm rural high-income	−0.59	−0.67
Nonfarm rural low-income	2.09	0.80
Total	0.20	0.31

Source: Madagascar model simulations.

Not surprisingly, the household groups that do not produce rice benefited most from the large increase in rice imports in the late 1970s. Urban households and the non-farm rural poor enjoy the largest increase in real incomes, since the decline in rice prices brings about a more significant reduction in the cost of their consumption basket (1.7 and 1.9 percent, respectively), while their incomes are not directly tied to rice farming. Given that the rice imports in this simulation are funded through additional foreign borrowing, the net effect of the rice import policy on rural farmers is minimal, since the effects of greater aggregate demand offset the adverse effects of lower rice prices (and thus lower returns to land) for producers. Of course, without a change in foreign capital inflows, a policy of increased rice imports would have no positive aggregate demand effects and rural producers would bear the brunt of lower producer prices.

While increasing the imports of rice does increase real incomes, this policy leads to lower overall growth. Comparing year 1 of simulations 1 and 2, using foreign capital inflows to finance rice imports instead of manufactured goods and other diverse imports results in lower overall investment and real GDP growth.[11] Real income gains for the rural non-farm poor and the urban poor, both large net consumers of rice, enjoy similar gains in real incomes in the two scenarios. Other household groups also see larger gains in real incomes with the investment boom scenario. These results are derived mainly from the larger production disincentives arising from imports of a highly tradable commodity (rice) compared with imports of goods that are less perfect substitutes for domestic production (imported manufactured goods).[12]

2.4.3. Trade liberalization: simulations 3 and 4

Though a key to Madagascar's economic reforms, trade was not liberalized until 1988, six years after stabilization efforts were begun in earnest. Until that time, import licenses and import quotas were used to control the outflow of foreign exchange. In simulation 3, the quota on manufactured imports is removed and the import tariff is kept at its 1984 value of 19.3 percent. Since foreign savings are held constant in this simulation, changes in the real exchange rate and the level of investment dominate the results (Table 2.9).

With the quota (and implicit import tariff) removed, imports of manufactured goods rise by 15.4 percent in year 1 and domestic production of

---

11 Real GDP increases under the investment boom scenario (simulation 1, year 1), while it falls slightly in year 1 of the rice import scenario and is only slightly higher by year 6.

12 Sensitivity analysis on the impact of using a higher degree of substitutability of imported and domestic rice in the model simulations results in a slightly greater decline in paddy production (−5.7 percent in year 1 compared with −5.4 percent in year 1 of simulation 2 above) and a smaller rise in rice consumption and real incomes for most households (See Dorosh 1994).

Table 2.9. Madagascar: trade liberalization: simulation results 3 and 4

	Simulation 3: liberalization		Simulation 4: liberalization with 20% reduction in foreign savings	
	Year 1	Year 6	Year 1	Year 6
Real GDP	2.76	6.56	2.39	5.92
Private consumption	1.56	4.40	0.83	3.48
Total real investment	18.99	38.01	16.55	34.01
Private investment	29.20	59.63	25.45	53.36
Government investment	0.00	0.00	0.00	0.00
Government consumption	0.00	0.00	0.00	0.00
Government revenue	9.25	16.56	10.06	16.92
Real exchange rate	11.81	18.01	15.32	21.02
Exports ($m)	6.99	12.94	8.36	13.97
Imports ($m)	5.89	10.92	3.87	8.66
Foreign savings/GDP	0.00	0.00	−0.42	−0.43
Sectoral production				
Agriculture	1.61	3.12	1.53	2.94
Industry	2.88	8.80	2.48	7.91
Formal	3.86	12.71	3.41	11.48
Informal	1.78	3.57	1.44	3.13
Services	1.66	4.90	1.40	4.39
Formal	5.81	12.32	4.93	11.05
Informal	0.09	2.51	0.07	2.24
Public administration	−0.06	−0.04	−0.07	−0.05
Total	2.03	5.67	1.78	5.12
Household incomes				
Urban I (high-income)				
Total income	−11.49	−8.29	−13.62	−10.66
Non-rent income	23.89	35.83	21.25	32.61
Urban II (middle-income)	4.51	9.83	3.83	8.82
Urban III (low-income)	2.04	4.77	1.63	4.20
Small farm Plateau	2.76	5.30	2.42	4.82
Small farm East	4.28	8.29	4.23	7.99
Small farm West/South	2.80	5.05	2.50	4.63
Large farm rural high-income	4.15	6.58	3.52	5.91
Nonfarm rural low-income	2.61	4.22	2.11	3.71
Total	1.07	3.87	0.32	2.94

Source: Madagascar model simulations.

manufactured goods falls by 2.5 percent. Quota rents are of course eliminated, sharply reducing the real incomes of urban I households by 11.5 percent. Demand is shifted toward imported manufactured goods, from other goods in the economy, so that the price of non-tradable goods falls relative to the price of tradable goods. The real exchange rate depreciates by 11.8 percent in year 1 (18.0 percent relative to the base run in year 6).

When relative prices are higher, more tradable goods are produced. Exports increase by 7.0 percent in dollar terms, permitting an increase in imports of 5.9 percent. Revenues from import tariffs and export taxes increase as well, so government revenues rise by 9.3 percent in real terms. Since government real expenditures are held fixed in the simulation, the increased government revenues add to total savings. These additional funds enable investment to increase by 19.0 percent in year 1. Real GDP increases by 2.8 percent in year 1, and since investment is 19–38 percent higher each year, the capital stock grows faster than in the base run and real GDP in year 6 is 6.6 percent higher than in year 6 of the base run.

Apart from those households that suffer a loss of rents, all households enjoy significant gains in real incomes as a result of trade liberalization. Urban households with skilled labor again gain most from the surge in investment spending. Non-rent incomes of urban I households rise by 23.9 percent; urban II household incomes rise by 4.5 percent. Rural per capita incomes rise between 2.6 and 4.3 percent, and small farmers on the east coast who produce export crops gain the most. Land on the east coast and formal sector capital are the only two factors of production for which nominal returns rise in this simulation (Table 2.10). Thus, liberalizing trade, even without a change in foreign capital inflows, increases total output (a gain in efficiency) and improves income distribution (a gain in equity).

Historically, a reduced trade deficit accompanied the trade liberalization in 1987 and 1988. In simulation 4, foreign savings are reduced by 20 percent. In this scenario, the depreciation of the real exchange rate in year 1 increases to 15.3 percent. Smaller capital inflows reduce the funds available for investment compared with those in simulation 3, but because of the increase in government tax revenues, investment still increases by 16.6 percent. With less of a boost in earnings from the construction sector, urban incomes increase less dramatically than in simulation 3. Real incomes of urban II households increase by 3.8 percent in year 1 compared with 4.5 percent in simulation 3. With reduced capital inflows, small farmers on the east coast see only a small decline in real incomes *vis à vis* simulation 3, because the greater real exchange rate depreciation raises the real price of export crops and thus the returns to land (in real terms) on the east coast. Rural households still gain from 2.1 to 4.2 percent in year 1 of simulation 4 relative to the base run.

The above simulations of trade liberalization (with and without reduced foreign capital inflows), a cornerstone of the structural adjustment measures

Table 2.10. Madagascar: breakdown of household income changes: simulation 3—trade liberalization, no change FSAV

	Urban non-poor	Urban middle	Urban poor	Small farmer Plateau	Small farmer East Coast	Small farmer West/South	Rural non-poor	Rural nonfarm poor	All households
Highly skilled labor	-2.084	0.000	0.000	0.000	0.000	0.000	0.000	0.000	-0.365
Skilled labor	-0.084	-3.489	0.000	0.000	0.000	0.000	-0.406	0.000	-0.489
Unskilled labor	-0.041	-1.849	-5.080	-5.304	-5.284	-4.634	-2.301	-4.293	-2.992
Informal capital	0.000	-1.263	-2.401	-0.577	-0.575	-0.505	-3.053	-3.195	-1.427
Land—Plateau	0.000	0.000	0.000	-1.456	0.000	0.000	0.000	0.000	-0.185
Land—East Coast	0.000	0.000	0.000	0.000	0.131	0.000	0.000	0.000	0.017
Land—West/South	0.000	0.000	0.000	0.000	0.000	-2.066	0.000	0.000	-0.211
Land—Large farm	0.000	0.000	0.000	0.000	0.000	0.000	-0.113	0.000	-0.036
Dividends	5.946	0.000	0.000	0.000	0.000	0.000	0.000	0.000	1.040
Rents	-28.563	0.000	0.000	0.000	0.000	0.000	0.000	0.000	-4.997
Total	-24.827	-6.601	-7.481	-7.337	-5.729	-7.206	-5.872	-7.488	-9.644
Change in national CPI	-10.561	-10.561	-10.561	-10.561	-10.561	-10.561	-10.561	-10.561	-10.561
Real income change I	-15.950	4.428	3.443	3.605	5.403	3.751	5.242	3.436	1.025
Change in household CPI	-15.072	-10.632	-9.335	-9.822	-9.601	-9.733	-9.622	-9.843	-10.597
Real income change II	-11.486	4.511	2.044	2.756	4.283	2.799	4.149	2.612	1.065

Source: Madagascar model simulations.

undertaken in Madagascar, show that these policies tended to benefit rural households, especially export crop producers. Government revenues increase in these simulations, so that, with government recurrent expenditures held in check, the trade liberalization increases total savings and investment in the economy. The size of the decline in foreign capital inflows largely determines total investment and the extent of the real exchange rate depreciation.

2.5. *Conclusions*

Together, the four simulations of macroeconomic policy changes in the 1980s suggest that stabilization and structural adjustment policies in Madagascar did not adversely affect the bulk of the poor, that is the rural poor. An inflow of foreign savings benefited all household groups to some extent, but the investment boom benefited the urban households the most, largely because of patterns of investment spending. Stabilization measures such as a decline in foreign savings and reduced rice imports had their largest negative impact on urban households, and, in the case of a decline in rice imports, on rice deficit rural households as well. Trade liberalization improved both efficiency and equity, redistributing income away from those who had captured quota rents and boosting incentives to produce tradable goods, an important income source in rural areas.

Three key factors largely determine the impact of macroeconomic policies on household incomes in these simulations: the real exchange rate, the level of investment, and aggregate demand effects. Real exchange rate changes, whether caused by changes in trade policy, foreign capital inflows, or other factors, to a large extent determine production and consumption incentives in the economy. Policies leading to depreciations of the real exchange rate tend to benefit the agricultural sector and small farmers, who constitute the bulk of the poor in Madagascar. Increased government savings and total investment, on the other hand, tend to benefit higher-income urban households, who gain most from gains in the industrial and construction sectors. These latter effects result from an urban bias in the destination of investment as well as in the composition of investment goods, factors held fixed in the model simulations.[13] Investment concentrated more heavily in rural activities, using more unskilled labor and local materials, is likely to have a more positive effect on alleviating poverty. Finally, given the assumption of relatively elastic supplies of non-traded goods in the Malagasy economy arising from considerable underemployment of unskilled labor, there are positive multiplier effects resulting from an increase in aggregate demand, from whatever the source.

[13] See Pryor (1990) for a discussion of urban bias in Madagascar's long-term economic development.

In most of the simulations, urban high-income households, not the poor, are more affected by policy changes and external shocks than are other household groups. Urban high-income households, because they own significant amounts of two of the most scarce resources in the Malagasy economy (capital and skilled labor) see major changes in their incomes from policy-induced changes in the formal sector and the levels of investment. That these households were among the biggest beneficiaries of the investment boom and the biggest losers from the contraction in the economy during the stabilization period suggests one major reason why adjustment policies were initially so strongly resisted in Madagascar, as in other countries of sub-Saharan Africa.

Sectoral and household level interventions can of course offset the negative effects of macroeconomic and other policies on income distribution. But interventions such as food subsidies and income transfers can be expensive and difficult to target and administer. Although tax policies can be used to adjust relative prices of key goods in favor of the poor, targeting and enforcement can be problematic.

The urban bias in development policy is not unchangeable, however. Investment can be more concentrated in rural areas where the bulk of the poor live and in labor-intensive urban activities. More unskilled labor-intensive means of capital construction can be used to increase demand for labor supplied by poor households. An appropriate blend of fiscal, monetary and exchange rate policies can prevent real exchange rate appreciations that hurt the rural poor. The investment boom of the late 1970s did not greatly benefit the poor, and rice policies, while benefiting the urban poor, had little positive impact on small farmers who constitute the bulk of Madagascar's poor.

Appendix 2.1.
Equations of the Madagascar
Model

Definitions of the variables are given at the end of the appendix. Exogenous parameters are demonstrated by lowercase italics.

Prices

(1) $PM_i = \overline{PWM_i} \bullet (1 + \overline{TM_i}) \bullet \overline{ER}$

(2) $PE_i \bullet (1 + \overline{TE_i}) = \overline{PWE_i} \bullet \overline{ER}$

(3) $PPT_i \bullet XPT_i = PPD_i \bullet XPD_i + \dfrac{PE_i}{(1 + margx_i)} \bullet E_i$

(4) $PVA_j = PPT_j(1 - tprod_j) - \displaystyle\sum_i PC_i a_{ij}$

(5) $PC_i \bullet XT_i = PPD_i(1 + margd_i + dtax_i) \bullet XPD_i + PM_i(1 + margm_i + itax_i) \bullet M_i$

(6) $PK_j = \displaystyle\sum_i PC_i \bullet imat_{ij}$

(7) $PPTACT_j = \displaystyle\sum_i PPT_i \bullet outmat_{ji}$

(8) $PINDEX = \displaystyle\sum_i \theta_i \bullet PC_i$

Production

(9) $XPTACT_j = CES(L_{1j}, L_{2j}, L_{3j}, K_j)$

(10) $XPT_i = \displaystyle\sum_j XPTACT_j \bullet outmat_{ji}$

Trade

(11) $XPT_i = AT_i(\gamma_i E_i^{\psi_i} + (1 - \gamma_i)XPD_i^{\psi_i})^{1/\psi_i}$, for i = exported goods

(12) $\dfrac{E_i}{XPD_i} = \left[\dfrac{PE_i^*}{PPD_i} \bullet \dfrac{(1 - \gamma_i)}{\gamma_i} \right]^{\phi_i}$, $PE_i^* = \dfrac{PE_i}{1 + marg_i}$,

$\phi_i = \dfrac{1}{\varphi_i - 1}$, for i = exported goods

(13) $\quad XT_i = AC_i \left[\delta_i M_i^{-\rho_i} + (1-\delta_i) XPD_i^{-\rho_i} \right]^{-(1/\rho_i)}, \qquad$ for $i =$ imported goods

(14) $\quad \dfrac{M_i}{XPD_i} = \left(\dfrac{PPD_i^*}{PM_i^*} \cdot \dfrac{\delta_i}{1-\delta_i} \right)^{\sigma_i}, \qquad \sigma_i = \dfrac{1}{1+\rho_i}, \qquad$ for $i =$ imported goods

$\qquad PPD_i^* = PPD_i(1+ margd_i + dtax_i), \qquad$ and $PM_i^* = PM_i(1+ margm_i + itax_i)$

(15) $\quad XT_i = XPD_i, \qquad$ for $i =$ non-imported goods

(16) $\quad XPT_i = XPD_i, \qquad$ for $i =$ non-exported goods

Factor markets

(17) $\quad W_{lc} \bullet wdist_{j,lc}/r_j = \dfrac{\alpha_{lc,j}}{1 - \displaystyle\sum_{lc} \alpha_{lc,j}} \cdot \dfrac{K_j^{1+\rho_j}}{L_{lc,j}^{1+\rho_j}}$

(17a) $\quad LS_{lc}/\overline{LS0}_{lc} = \left(W_{lc}/\overline{W0}_{lc} \right)^{BLE_L}$

(18) $\quad \displaystyle\sum_j L_{lc,j} = \overline{LS}_{lc}$

(19) $\quad r_j = (1 - \displaystyle\sum_{lc} \alpha_{lc,j}) \bullet AD_j^{-\rho} \bullet K_j^{-\rho-1} \bullet PVA_j \bullet Q_j^{1+\rho}$

Household incomes, saving

(20) $\quad LCSAL_{lc} = \displaystyle\sum_j wdist_{j,lc} \bullet W_j \bullet L_{lc,j}$

(21) $\quad RETK_{kc} = \displaystyle\sum_j \left(PVA_j \bullet XPTACT_j - ACTSAL_j \right) \bullet shrkc_{kc,j}$

(22) $\quad ACTSAL_j = \displaystyle\sum_{lc} WA_{lc} \bullet wdist_{j,lc} \bullet L_{j,lc}$

(23) $\quad RENT_i = \overline{PWM}_i \bullet (TM_i - tmr_i) \bullet \overline{M}_i, \qquad$ for $i = imq$

(24) $\quad Y_h = \displaystyle\sum_{lc} \left(shr_{lc,h} \bullet LCSAL_{lc} \right) + \displaystyle\sum_{kc} \left(shr_{kc,h} \bullet RETK_{kc} \right)$

$\qquad + \displaystyle\sum_{imq} \left(rentshr_{imq,h} \bullet RENT_{imq} \right)$

(25) $\quad SAVHH_h = sO_h \bullet \left(\dfrac{PINDEX}{PINDEX0} \right) + mps_h \bullet Y_h$

(26) $\quad YD_h = Y_h - SAVHH_h - \overline{TDIR}_h \bullet Y_h$

Intermediate demand

(27) $INT_i = \sum_j a_{ij} XPTACT_j$

(28) $INT_{11} = \sum_j a_{ij} XPTACT_j$
$$+(MARGXTOT + MARGMTOT + MARGDTOT)/PC_{11}$$

(29) $MARGXTOT = \sum_i PE_i \bullet margx_i/(1 + margx_i) \bullet E_i$

(30) $MARGMTOT = \sum_i PM_i \bullet margm_i \bullet M_i$

(31) $MARGDTOT = \sum_i PPD_i \bullet margd_i \bullet XPD_i$

Household consumption

(32) $PC_i \bullet CD_{ih} = LES(PC, tcx, YD_h)$

(33) $CD_i = \sum_h CDHH_{i,h}$

Government

(34) $GD_i = \beta_i^G \bullet \overline{GDTOT}$

(35) $GR = TARIFF + DUTY + PRODTX + DSALETX + ISALETX$
$$+ DIRTX$$

(36) $TARIFF = \sum_i \overline{TM_i} \bullet \overline{PWM_i} \bullet M_i \bullet \overline{ER}$

(37) $DUTY = \sum_i \overline{TE_i} \bullet PE_i \bullet E_i$

(38) $PRODTX = \sum_j tprod_j \bullet PPTACT_j \bullet XPTACT_j$

(39) $DSALETX = \sum_i dtax_i \bullet PPD_i \bullet XPD_i$

(40) $ISALETX = \sum_i itax_i \bullet PM_i \bullet M_i$

(41) $DIRTX = \sum_h tdir_h \bullet Y_h$

(42) $SUBSIDY = \sum_h \sum_i PC_i \bullet \overline{TCX_i} \bullet CDHH_{i,h}$

(43) $\quad GOVSAV = GR - \sum_i PC_i \bullet GD_i - SUBSIDY$

Investment

(44) $\quad ID_i = \sum_j imat_{ij} \bullet DK_j$

(45) $\quad GID_i = gio_i \bullet \overline{GOVIVT}$

(46) $\quad VGOVIVT = \sum_i PC_i \bullet GID_i$

(47) $\quad PK_j \bullet DK_j = KIO_j \bullet (SAVINGS - TOTDSTK - VGOVIVT)$

(48) $\quad TOTDSTK = \sum_i PC_i \bullet DST_i$

(49) $\quad SAVINGS = TOTHHSAV + GOVSAV + ENTFSAV + \overline{FSAV} \bullet \overline{ER}$

(50) $\quad TOTHHSAV = \sum_h SAVHH_h$

(51) $\quad YENTF = RETK_{kform}$

(52) $\quad ENTFSAV = YENTF - \sum_{inst} \overline{TRANSFER}_{inst,entf}$

(53) $\quad DEPRECIA = \sum_j DEPR_j \bullet PK_j \bullet K_j$

(54) $\quad DKTOT = \sum_j DK_j$

National income

(55) $\quad YGDP = \sum_j PVA_j \bullet XPTACT_j + PRODTX + TARIFF + DUTY$

$\qquad\qquad + DSALETX + ISALETAX - DEPRECIA - SUBSIDY$

Model closure

(56) $\quad \sum_i \overline{PWE}_i \bullet M_i = \sum_i \overline{PWE}_i \bullet E_i + \overline{FSAV}$

(57) $\quad XT_i = INT_i + CD_i + GD_i + ID_i + GID_i + \overline{DST}_i$

Dynamic equations

(58) $\quad LS0_{1c,t+1} = \overline{LSO}_{lc,t} \bullet (1 + lsgr_{lc})$

(59) $\quad \overline{K}_{i,t+1} = \overline{K}_{i,t} \bullet (1 - depr_i) + DK_i + gkio_i \bullet \overline{GOVIVT}$

Endogenous variables

ACTSAL	Wage bill by activity j
CD	Total consumer demand of good i
CDHH	Consumer demand for good i by household h
DEPRECIA	Total value of depreciation
DIRTX	Direct tax
DK	Real investment by activity j
DXTOT	Total real investment
DSALETX	Sales tax on domestic goods
DST	Change in stocks of good i
DUTY	Export duties
E	Exports
GD	Government consumption of good i
GID	Government investment demand for good i
GOVSAV	Government savings
GR	Government revenue
ID	Private investment demand for good i
INT	Intermediate use of good i
ISALETX	Sales tax on imported goods
L	Labor use (demand) in activity j
LCSAL	Total wage bill for labor of type lc
M	Imports
MARGDTOT	Total marketing margin on domestic goods
MARGMTOT	Total marketing margin on imports
MARGXTOT	Total marketing margin on exports
PC	User price of good i
PE	Domestic price of exported goods
PINDEX	National consumer price index
PK	Price of capital goods in activity j
PM	Domestic price of imported goods
PPD	Price of domestically produced goods
PPT	Price of output of good i
PPTACT	Price output of activity j
PRODTX	Revenue from producer taxes
PVA	Price of value added of activity j
RETK	Total returns to capital of type kc
SAVHH	Savings by household h
SAVINGS	Total value of savings
TARIFF	Tariff revenue
TOTDSTK	Total change in stocks
TOTHHSAV	Total household savings
WA	Average wage rate
XPD	Domestic sales of production of commodity i
XPT	Domestic output of commodity i
XPTACT	Output of activity j
XT	Supply of commodity i
Y	Household income

YGDP   Definition of GDP

Exogenous variables

ER   Exchange rate (FMG/$)
FSAV   Foreign savings
GDTOT   Total government consumption
GOVIVT   Total government investment
K   Capital stock in activity *j*
LS   Labor supply
PWE   World export price in dollars
PWM   World import price in dollars
TM   Import tariff rate

Activities (20)

Grains, export crops, other crops, livestock, forestry, mining, meat processing, food processing (F, I), manufacturing (F, I), construction (F, I), transport (F, I), private services (F, I), public services.

Labor types

Skilled, unskilled

Household types

Urban I (skilled head of household)
Urban II (unskilled head of household)
Semi-urban
Rural north—high-income
Rural north—low-income
Rural south—high-income
Rural south—low-income

Capital

Formal sector
Informal sector
Agricultural—corresponding to each rural household group

Table 2A.3. Madagascar: household demand parameters

	Urban I	Urban II	Urban III	Small farm Plateau	Small farm East Coast	Small farm South and West	Rural rich	Rural nonfarm poor
Income elasticity of demand								
Paddy	0.00	0.00	0.00	0.00	0.00	0.00	0.00	0.00
Other food crops	0.39	0.64	0.63	0.77	0.61	0.46	0.55	0.79
Export crops	0.00	0.00	0.00	0.00	0.50	0.50	0.50	0.50
Industrial crops	0.00	0.00	0.00	0.00	0.50	0.50	0.50	0.50
Livestock/fishing	0.80	1.00	1.00	1.00	1.00	1.00	1.00	1.00
Mines/energy/water	0.80	1.00	0.80	0.80	0.80	0.80	0.80	0.80
Rice	0.20	0.50	0.60	0.35	0.35	0.35	0.35	0.35
Processed food	1.00	1.20	1.50	1.50	1.50	1.50	1.40	1.50
Textiles	1.00	1.20	1.50	1.50	1.50	1.50	1.40	1.50
Manufactures	1.30	1.30	1.50	1.50	1.50	1.50	1.80	1.50
Construction	1.00	1.00	1.00	1.00	1.00	1.00	1.00	1.00
Transport/communications	1.00	1.20	1.20	1.20	1.20	1.20	1.20	1.20
Commerce	0.00	0.00	0.00	0.00	0.00	0.00	0.00	0.00
Private services	1.00	1.20	1.20	1.20	1.20	1.20	1.00	1.20
Public services	1.00	1.00	1.00	1.00	1.00	1.00	1.00	1.00
Frisch parameter (marginal propensity to save)	-1.6	-2.5	-3.5	-3.5	-3.5	-3.5	-2.0	-3.5

Source: Madagascar CGE model.

References

Armington, Paul. 1969. "A Theory of Demand for Products Distinguished by Place of Production." *IMF Staff Papers*, 16: 159–176. Washington, DC: International Monetary Fund.

Benjamin, Nancy, and Shantayanan Devarajan. 1985. *Oil Revenues and Economic Policy in Cameroon: Results from a Computable General Equilibrium Model*. World Bank Staff Working Paper No. 745. Washington, DC: World Bank.

Condon, Timothy, Henrik Dahl, and Shantayanan Devarajan. 1987. *Implementing a Computable General Equilibrium Model*. Report No. 290. Washington, DC: Research Department, World Bank.

Dervis, Kemal, Jaime de Melo, and Sherman Robinson. 1982. *General Equilibrium Models for Development Policy*. Washington, DC: World Bank.

Doosh, Paul. 1992. *A Computable General Equilibrium Model for Madagascar: Equations and Parameters*. Washington, DC: CFNPP.

——1994. *Structural Adjustment, Growth, and Poverty in Madagascar: A CGE Analysis*. Monograph No. 17. Ithaca, NY: CFNPP.

—— and René Bernier. 1994. "Staggered Reforms and Limited Success: Structural Adjustment in Madagascar in the Eighties." In *Adjusting to Policy Failure in African Economies*, David E. Sahn (ed.). Ithaca, NY: Cornell University Press.

—— Armand Roger Randrianarivony, and Christian Rasolomanana. 1991. *A Social Accounting Matrix for Madagascar: Methodology and Results*. Working Paper No. 6. Ithaca, NY: CFNPP.

—— and Alexander H. Sarris, 1990. *Macroeconomic Adjustment and the Poor: The Case of Madagascar*. Monograph No. 9. Ithaca, NY: CFNPP.

Food and Agricultural Organization (FAO). 1984. *Food Balance Sheets, 1979–81 Average*. Rome: FAO.

International Monetary Fund. 1988. "Madagascar—Statistical Annex." Unpublished paper.

——1991. "Madagascar—Statistical Appendix." Unpublished paper.

Ministère de la Production Agricole et de la Reforme Agraire (MPARA). 1988. *Généralités et Méthodologie, Campagne Agricole 1984/85*. Projet Recensement National de l'Agriculture et Système Permanent des Statistiques Agricoles, 4 vols. Antananarivo: MPARA.

Pryor, Frederick L. 1990. *The Political Economy of Poverty, Equity, and Growth: Malawi and Madagascar*. Oxford: Oxford University Press.

Sarris, Alexander H. 1990. *A Micro–Macro Framework for the Analysis of the Impact of Structural Adjustment on the Poor in Sub-Saharan Africa*. Monograph No. 5. Ithaca, NY: CFNPP.

World Bank. 1986. *The Democratic Republic of Madagascar: Country Economic Memorandum*. Report No. 5996-MAG. Washington, DC: World Bank.

——1991. *Madagascar: Beyond Stabilization to Sustainable Growth*. Washington, DC: World Bank.

3

Vulnerability to Price Shocks under Alternative Policies in Cameroon

Shankar Subramanian

3.1. *Introduction*

After almost a decade of rapid growth fueled by the discovery of petroleum in the 1970s, Cameroon's economy was hit hard in the mid-1980s by the steep fall in world prices for oil and for coffee and cocoa, its other principal exports. Cameroon had to scale back spending in 1987/88 and finally in 1989/90 to take recourse in a structural adjustment program. After growing at an annual rate of 11.5 percent from 1976 to 1981 and 5.9 percent from 1982 to 1985, GDP decreased at 2.6 percent annually between 1986 and 1990 (see Table 3.1).[1] By 1990, Cameroon's external debt was more than double that of a decade before. Despite the massive contraction between these years, per capita GNP in 1989/90 was $1010, one of the highest in sub-Saharan Africa. As Blandford et al. (1994) note, given its high per capita income, its relatively steady growth, and the apparent prudence of the government in husbanding its oil revenues, the magnitude of Cameroon's economic crisis was unexpected.

This study uses a computable general equilibrium model of Cameroon to examine several key issues. First, what was the impact on income distribution of the different components of the price shocks and of the adjustment program? Second, what alternative adjustment policies could the government have followed and how would they have affected growth and distribution? Third, would the economy have been less vulnerable to the

I would like to thank Paul Dorosh, Elisabeth Sadoulet, and David Sahn for their comments and suggestions. Of course, any errors remain my own. My thanks also to Madeleine Gauthier for supplying me with the Cameroon input–output table and to Nancy Benjamin for providing her CGE model for Cameroon.

[1] The Cameroon fiscal year runs from June 1 to July 31. Thus, 1984 refers to the year 1984–1985. It should be noted that data on GDP for the period after 1985 are not reliable. The data used here are from the 1992 *World Tables* (World Bank 1992), but they differ substantially from more recent data obtained from the World Bank. However, the latter are clearly in error because they show a 50 percent decrease in real value added in the petroleum sector in 1986 even though there was no significant change in oil production.

Table 3.1. Cameroon: macroeconomic summary, 1975–1990

	1975	1976–81	1982–85	1986–90
Real GDP (bn 1987 CFA francs, market prices)				
End of period	1624.9	3118.9	3930.5	3451.4
Real GDP/capita ('000 1987 CFA francs/person)				
End of period	218.4	347.2	386.6	294.0
Annual change in GDP (%)	−0.75	11.48	5.95	−2.57
Annual change in GDP deflator (%)				
Average	18.93	9.08	11.37	−0.16
End of period	18.93	11.80	9.04	−1.92
Budget surplus/GDP (%)				
Average	−2.12	−0.46	0.51	−1.20
End of period	−2.12	−2.95	0.79	−3.15
Trade deficit (G+NFS)/GDP (%)				
Average	7.81	5.87	−7.09	0.60
End of period	7.82	2.31	11.00	−2.06
Exchange rate (CFA francs/$)				
Average	222.4	228.8	383.0	322.6
End of period	222.4	235.3	471.1	300.7
Total external debt ($m)				
Average	420.1	1717.2	2779.3	4557.1
End of period	420.1	2548.3	2939.9	6023.4

Source: *World Tables* (World Bank 1992).

adverse shock in the terms of trade had the government adopted a different set of trade and investment policies during the oil boom?

Section 3.2 summarizes the major features of the process of growth in Cameroon over the past two decades. Section 3.3 is in two parts. The first part describes the structure of the Cameroon economy using the Gauthier–Kyle (1991) social accounting matrix, and the second part presents the CGE model. Section 3.4 describes the simulation experiments and the results, and Section 3.5 concludes the study.

3.2. *Cameroon's Economic Growth*[2]

3.2.1. *The oil boom*

Until the discovery of petroleum in the mid-1970s, Cameroon was a predominantly agricultural economy. Agriculture accounted for 36 percent

---

[2] This section is based on Blandford et al. (1994).

of GDP, 84 percent of employment, and 87 percent of exports during the early 1970s. The share of industry in GDP was about 16 percent during this period.

Petroleum production grew swiftly after the mid-1970s, its share of GDP rising to 20 percent by 1984/85. Under the stimulus of the oil boom the economy grew rapidly. Gross domestic product growth was 14 percent per annum from 1977/78–1980/81, falling off to about 7.5 percent per annum for the period 1982/83 to 1985/86. Though population also increased rapidly at 3.2 percent annually, per capita GDP growth was high, about 6 percent annually from 1978/79 to 1984/85. This period was marked by massive expansion in investment funded by oil revenues. The share of gross domestic investment in GDP increased from 21 percent in 1979/80 to 33 percent in 1985/86.

Not unexpectedly, there was substantial variation in growth rates across sectors. Manufacturing, in particular, was aided by protectionist policies. Export agriculture, however, remained stagnant because the increase in world market prices was not passed on to producers and because the oil boom led to some real exchange rate appreciation. As petroleum exports surged, total exports expanded rapidly at an average rate of 17 percent annually from 1978/79 to 1984/85. Imports also increased, but at a slower rate, so that Cameroon ran a sizable current account surplus in 1984/85.

Government revenue increased substantially, both in absolute terms and as a share of GDP, rising from 16 percent of GDP during the late 1970s to 25 percent in 1982/83. From 1981/82 to 1985/86, oil revenues accounted for over 40 percent of total revenues. Government expenditures also increased rapidly, but rarely exceeded revenues (Table 3.1). However, towards the end of the oil boom, in 1985/86 and 1986/87, government expenditure surged by 13 and 30 percent, respectively, in real terms, the result of substantial increases in public investment. And, as government revenues fell sharply in 1986/87, the deficit mounted to 71 percent of revenue and 13 percent of GDP. A key aspect of the evolution of government expenditure during these years was the rapid increase of current transfers and subsidies to a level of 25 percent of current expenditure by 1985/86, much of it accounted for by subsidies to loss-making public enterprises.

Public investment was a major factor behind the economic boom, accounting for over 45 percent of gross fixed capital formation by 1984/85. In addition, capital expenditures accounted for between 38 and 51 percent of total expenditure from 1980/81 to 1986/87. However, public investment was not as fruitful as it might have been, for two reasons. First, actual investment in agriculture, rural development, and social infrastructure was far lower than planned investment in these areas. Second, much of the oil revenue was held abroad in an attempt to prevent the building up of popular pressure for greater government expenditures and was transferred at the discretion of the president, largely to finance capital expenditures. These expenditures were poorly coordinated with capital expenditures funded through the budget and from foreign sources, resulting in wasteful investment.

Cameroon is a member of the Communauté Francophone Africaine (CFA), and its currency, the CFA franc, is tied to the French franc. In addition, membership carries with it the ceding of autonomy in setting monetary policy to the CFA central bank. Despite the CFA franc's progressive overvaluation, French policy was to maintain the exchange rate at 50 CFA francs to the French franc. Indeed, it was not until early 1994, after much speculation about devaluation and in the face of opposition from many governments in Francophone Africa, that the CFA franc (CFAF) was devalued to 100 CFA francs to the French franc.

Two other features of this period are worth noting: the performance of the financial sector and of agriculture. The boom years saw a large expansion in credit from the formal sector. A high proportion of bad loans, however, brought the banking system close to bankruptcy, which was to have grave consequences when the oil boom came to an end.

Agricultural growth during this period was uneven across commodities. While food crop output increased, production of export crops stagnated after 1982. One reason for the slow growth of agriculture was the low priority this sector received in the allocation of public investment and formal-sector credit. Another is that the smallholder sector, which produces 90 percent of output and 80 percent of marketed surplus, was neglected and much of the investment went to the estate sector. Moreover, in the case of export crops, price policies in effect insulated domestic producers from world market prices. The gains from the commodity price boom accrued largely to the parastatal marketing agencies, and producers had no incentive to invest and increase capacity.

3.2.2. The boom ends

Cameroon's export boom came to an end in 1985/86, when the dollar-denominated prices of its major exports—oil, coffee, and cocoa—began to fall steeply. The fall in prices was exacerbated by the 40 percent fall of the US dollar against the French (and CFA) franc between 1985 and 1988. Cameroon's terms of trade declined by 47 percent between 1985 and 1987, much of it the result of a 65 percent decrease in the oil export price index. Total exports fell by 30 percent for two years in a row. The balance of payments went from a surplus of 4.4 percent of GDP in 1984/85 to a deficit of 8.8 percent in 1986/87.

Though government revenues fell by 19 percent in real terms in 1986/87, the government was unable to halt the growth of expenditure, which increased by 30 percent in real terms that year. Government spending fell precipitously thereafter, in real terms by 34 percent in 1987/88 and 12 percent in 1988/89. Capital expenditures were scaled back even more sharply.

As the economy contracted sharply, private investment also declined. Total investment fell by 44 percent in 1987/88, 25 percent in 1988/89, and 12 percent in 1989/90.

Already in precarious shape, the banking sector was a major casualty of the economic crisis. A liquidity crisis developed as major depositors, such as the government and parastatal agencies, began to make large withdrawals to cover current expenditures. Real GDP fell rapidly as the contraction continued, by 6.5, 7.7, 3.4, and 2.5 percent in 1986/87, 1987/88, 1988/89, and 1989/90, respectively.[3] Confronted by a crisis of this magnitude, Cameroon was forced to undertake a structural adjustment program under the auspices of the World Bank and the International Monetary Fund. Key aspects of the program are fiscal, public enterprise, and agricultural reforms. The fiscal reforms have had little success in increasing non-oil tax revenues, primarily because the economic contraction has reduced the number of tax-paying enterprises and employees and because of increased tax evasion and smuggling. Public enterprise and banking sector reform has been slow and has yet to yield results. Agricultural sector reform has gone the furthest. The monopsonist marketing boards have been replaced by quality control boards, which do not control trade, and producer prices are to be aligned with world market prices.

Several factors have impaired the adjustment process. The government's reluctance to curb current expenditures and reform public enterprises is indicative of the political strength of those who stand to lose from these measures. The inability or unwillingness to reduce current expenditure has meant that capital expenditure has borne the brunt of adjustment, thus compromising future growth. Finally, because of Cameroon's inability to devalue its currency, the economic contraction resulting from the adjustment program has been harsher than would otherwise have been the case.

3.3. The Cameroon Economy

3.3.1. The structure of the economy

The base year data for the model come from a social accounting matrix (SAM) for 1984/85 by Gauthier and Kyle (1991), which was based on the 1984/85 input–output table for Cameroon and on data from a household survey. The SAM has four labor categories: agricultural and informal sector labor, formal sector unskilled labor, skilled labor, and highly skilled labor. Agricultural and non-agricultural capital are also separated. The households are disaggregated into five rural and two urban groups: poor farm households in (1) the northern and (2) the southern regions, (3) rich farm households, (4) poor non-farm households, (5) rich non-farm households,

---

[3] These are based on the 1992 *World Tables* data (World Bank 1992).

(6) poor urban households, and (7) rich urban households. Poor households are those in the lower 60 percent of the income distribution.

This SAM was modified in several ways for the purposes of this study. First, the oil sector was separated from the manufacturing sector and the public administration sector was separated from the public services sector. Second, oil exports were under-reported and private consumption over-reported in the input–output (I–O) table; these were corrected using unpublished World Bank estimates for exports and using the budget share for petroleum products from a household survey in Côte d'Ivoire.[4] Third, the original I–O table ignored the state marketing agencies' levy on agricultural exports. In the new SAM, this levy on exports is treated as a tax on the producer which is transferred to the public services and public administration sectors.[5] Fourth, the household consumption matrix, the matrix of payments by sectors to the different factors and the matrix of payments by factors to households in the original SAM had to be corrected for various computation mistakes. Finally, the structure of taxes in the Cameroon national accounts was incorrect in that indirect taxes were too high and direct taxes and petroleum-related taxes were too low compared with the figures in the World Bank's *World Tables* (1992) and the IMF's *International Financial Statistics Yearbook* (1992). This was corrected to some extent by decreasing trade margins for the petroleum sector and increasing indirect taxes on this sector.[6] It should be noted, however, that the original I–O table is not consistent with the Cameroon national accounts (Cameroon 1989) or with the 1992 *World Tables*. Thus, GDP in the original I–O table is 4.421 billion CFA francs while GDP in the national accounts and the *World Tables* is 3.839 billion CFA francs. After correcting for the understatement of oil production, GDP in the modified SAM increases to 4.706 billion CFA francs.[7]

As Table 3.2 shows, the service sectors accounted for over 50 percent of value added in 1984/85. The petroleum sector's share in GDP was 17 percent, while that of agriculture was 21.3 percent and that of manufacturing, 8.7 percent. Major exporting sectors were oil (62.7 percent) and export agriculture (15.8 percent).[8] The manufacturing sector's (excluding food

[4] The budget share in the original I–O table was 14 percent. This was lowered to 3.8 percent, the budget share observed in Côte d'Ivoire.

[5] This treatment is based on the understanding that the incomes of the marketing agencies were expended on their own operations and not transferred to the government. The implicit export taxes were computed using unpublished World Bank data on the marketing agencies' margins.

[6] A more complete revision of the I–O table to make the direct and indirect taxes consistent with World Bank and IMF data was not performed because it would have required extensive changes in the I–O table and because no other data on sectoral indirect tax rates were available.

[7] In the case of imports and exports, the figures in the national accounts do not agree with those in the *World Tables* or in the original I–O table. In addition, the sectoral shares in value added in the national accounts, the I–O table, and the *World Tables* are also inconsistent.

[8] Export agriculture includes the estate sector.

Table 3.2. Cameroon: sectoral shares in value added, imports and exports, 1984/85 (%)

Sector	Share of value added	Export tariff	Share of exports	Share of imports	Import tariff
Food agriculture	11.90	—	0.53	2.05	0.152
Export agriculture	7.34	0.614	14.71	2.00	0.295
Forestry	1.66	—	2.74	0.00	0.000
Estate sector	0.57	0.614	1.14	0.15	0.295
Food proc. (private)	1.30	—	1.55	3.39	0.256
Food proc. (public)	0.15	—	0.19	0.42	0.258
Manufacture (private)	7.04	—	8.31	82.20	0.253
Manufacture (public)	1.68	—	0.78	4.37	0.213
Construction	7.85	—	—	—	—
Services (private)	31.23	—	6.21	3.01	0.000
Services (public)	4.67	—	1.12	0.55	0.000
Public administration	7.46	—	—	—	—
Oil	17.13	—	62.72	1.87	0.152

Source: computed from 1984/85 Social Accounting Matrix; export tariff computed from data on trading margins of marketing boards.

processing) share in exports was 9.1 percent. As is to be expected in an import-substituting economy, the manufacturing sector was the largest importer, with a share of 86.6 percent. Import tariffs on the manufacturing sectors were moderate, between 21 and 25 percent. Export taxes (representing the marketing boards' margins) applied only to the agricultural export sectors. These were high in 1984/85 at 61.4 percent.[9]

Turning to factor incomes, all labor income in the non-estate agricultural sectors accrues to agricultural and informal sector labor. Informal sector labor is also employed in the private service sector, which accounts for over a third of labor income in this category. Formal unskilled labor is employed mostly in manufacturing, construction, public services, and public administration. Skilled labor income is concentrated in private services, manufacturing, and public administration. Highly skilled labor is also concentrated in public and private services and public administration. Agricultural capital income is evenly divided between traditional food crops and agricultural export crops. The private services and oil sectors are the major sources of non-agricultural capital income, with the oil sector accounting for over half of the total.

Table 3.3 shows per capita incomes and sources of income for the

[9] That is to say, producer price (including transport and trade margins) was 1/1.614 or 0.62 times world price.

Table 3.3. Cameroon: sources of household income and savings rates (%)

	North farm poor	South farm poor	Farm rich	Nonfarm rural poor	Nonfarm rural rich	Urban poor	Urban rich
Labor							
Agricultural and informal sector	77.07	84.53	48.22	42.05	6.51	20.08	2.17
Formal unskilled	19.88	5.19	16.76	32.14	11.40	34.98	6.77
Skilled	0.00	5.43	19.89	16.37	33.58	28.35	25.11
Highly skilled	0.00	1.81	3.22	9.44	25.10	16.59	14.39
Agricultural capital	3.05	3.04	11.15	0.00	0.00	0.00	0.00
Non-agricultural capital	0.00	0.00	0.00	0.00	23.42	0.00	47.04
Transfers from government	0.00	0.00	0.75	0.00	0.00	0.00	4.51
Savings rate[a]	4.00	4.00	14.20	4.00	21.80	4.00	21.80
Per capita income ('000 CFAF)	164.8	148.0	480.2	160.3	749.3	310.2	852.8
Number of households	159,273	322,327	523,077	127,503	241,394	11,053	155,647

[a] The factor income distribution was obtained using data on sector of employment and skill classification for household members in the survey. These data were not of good quality and it proved necessary to work out household income from household consumption using an assumed savings rate under the constraint that total household savings were consistent with the figure in the aggregate social accounting matrix.

Source: Computed from household survey data and Cameroon input–output table.

different household groups.[10] The rural farm and non-farm poor have the lowest annual incomes per capita, between 148,000 and 165,000 CFAF (US$314–$350 at 1984/85 exchange rates). Rich farm households are significantly less well off than rich non-farm rural households. The urban poor appear to have higher incomes than the rural poor. The highest incomes are those of the rural non-farm rich and urban rich households. Agricultural and informal sector labor is the major source of income for poor farm and non-farm households and also for the rich farm households. It is also an important source of income for the urban poor. While poor farm households are almost entirely dependent on agricultural labor income, however, the other household groups receive substantial parts of their incomes from skilled and highly skilled labor, and from capital income.[11] Non-agricultural capital incomes accrue by assumption only to the rural non-farm rich and the urban rich. These groups also receive a large part of their income from skilled and highly skilled labor. Transfers from government are assumed to flow only to rich farm and rich urban households and are only a small part of these groups' incomes.

3.3.2. *The model*

The model, found in Appendix 3.1, is a standard neoclassical computable general equilibrium (CGE) model in the tradition of Dervis, de Melo, and Robinson (1982).[12] Each sector employs capital and a labor aggregate of the four kinds of labor. Output is given by a CES function of the factor inputs. Demand for intermediates is obtained using the input–output coefficients. Labor demand is determined by the usual marginal conditions. Sectoral capital stocks are fixed in the short run and sectoral rates of return will, in general, not be equal. The petroleum sector is treated differently in that output is specified exogenously and capacity utilization adjusts. The reason for this is that petroleum production does not respond in the short run to prices (which are well above marginal cost) and is determined largely by past investment and production capacity. Payments to capital and the

10 The savings rates shown in table 3.3. need some explanation. The factor income distribution was obtained using data on sector of employment and skill classification for household members in the survey. These data were not of good quality and it proved necessary to work out household income from household consumption using an assumed savings rate under the constraint that total household savings were consistent with the figure in the aggregate social accounting matrix.

11 Agricultural capital income from food agriculture and export agriculture was allocated to the different farm household groups in a two-step process using data from Cameroon's agricultural census. In the first step, profits from food agriculture and export agriculture were divided between northern and southern regions in proportion to cultivated areas. In the second step, profits in the northern and southern regions were allocated to poor and rich farm households again in proportion to areas cultivated by them by assuming that small farms (as identified by the census) were operated by poor households.

12 The model presented in this paper extensively draws upon a CGE model for Cameroon developed by Benjamin (1991).

different kinds of labor are aggregated across sectors. Labor income accrues only to households, while capital income flows to both firms and households. Firms are only accounting entities; they receive capital income and transfers from government, and they pay taxes and save, transferring the residual to households.[13] Their marginal propensity to save is assumed to respond to the average rate of return to capital with a constant elasticity. Similarly, households' propensity to save is also sensitive to the average rate of return to capital. This specification attempts to capture the large increase in domestic savings experienced during the oil boom.

Households receive transfers from firms and government and labor and capital income. Household consumption is determined by subtracting personal taxes and savings from household incomes. Consumer demand is found by using a linear expenditure system of demand (LES) for each household group.[14]

Trade flows are determined by making the assumption that domestic sales and exports are imperfect substitutes, as are domestic production and imports. We also assume that firms and consumers operate as price-takers and respond to the prices of imports and exports relative to domestic prices. Import and export prices are determined by applying the exchange rate and the relevant tariff rates to world prices. Thus, firms operate on a transformation frontier between domestic sales and exports and allocate their production between the two markets in such a way as to maximize revenue. Similarly, what consumers buy is an aggregate of imports and domestic production.[15] The ratio of imports to the domestic product is determined by cost minimization on the part of consumers. The only exception to this is in the petroleum sector, in which imports and domestic production are assumed to be perfect substitutes. This was necessary to prevent unrealistically large swings in the domestic price of oil in response to the large increase in oil production and exports that occurred in the mid-1970s.

Government revenue is endogenous, consisting of domestic indirect taxes, tariff revenues, and corporate tax. However, the export tax on agriculture, which is really part of the marketing boards' margins, does not accrue to government but is treated as a subsidy to the public administration and public services sectors. Government expenditure is essentially exogenous, but in some of the simulations simple rules are used to endogenize some of its components. Government savings is a residual.

Total investment can be treated either as exogenous or endogenous. Total investment less changes in stocks is allocated across sectors according to an investment allocation rule. The vector of sectoral investment is

---

[13] Not all capital income is taxed at the same rate. Profits from the oil sector are taxed at a higher rate than profits in other sectors.

[14] Each group's LES was estimated using estimates of the flexibility of money or the Frisch parameter; see Bieri and de Janvry (1972).

[15] CET and CES aggregation functions are used for exports and imports, respectively.

translated into a vector of investment demand by sector, using a capital composition matrix. Total savings is the sum of domestic and foreign savings. Foreign savings or the current account deficit is the trade deficit plus net remittances abroad.[16]

In general, commodity and factor prices are determined by market clearing, except that rates of return to capital are determined residually and need not be equal across sectors because sectoral capital stocks are fixed in the short run.

Two kinds of simulation can be distinguished. In one, the model is used to track the historical performance of the economy. In this case, gross investment, changes in stocks, government consumption and transfers, and net remittances to the rest of the world are exogenous.[17] In addition, since Cameroon has been on a fixed exchange rate regime with respect to the French franc, the exchange rate is fixed at unity and the price index is allowed to adjust. The current account balance is then endogenous. The attempt in these simulations is to calibrate the model so as to track the behavior over time of the current account balance, the price index, and real GDP.[18]

In the second kind of simulation, one wishes to examine counterfactual scenarios. In these, many of the exogenous variables follow their actual time paths, but alternative trajectories will be specified for other exogenous variables, e.g. for oil export prices or total investment. In a different kind of counterfactual scenario one may endogenize investment by assuming that investment and savings are equal *ex ante* (what is known as the neo-classical closure) and by postulating simple rules for endogenizing other variables, such as government expenditure, remittances, and foreign savings. One such rule is to assume that these quantities grow at the same rate as GDP.

In both kinds of simulations, investment is allocated to the different sectors according to some rule. Typically, one would expect sectoral investment allocation to respond to changes in sectoral rates of return. The different rules used in the simulations are described in the section on results below.

3.3.3. *Limitations of the model*

In analyzing and interpreting the results from model simulations, it is necessary to bear in mind the limitations of the model and the data. On the

16 As noted above, the Cameroon government made extensive use of overseas accounts to conceal oil revenues. This form of financial investment is not examined here because the accumulation of debt and financial assets and interest payments on debt are not modeled here.

17 Information on other quantities, such as transfers by firms, is not available over time. These variables are kept endogenous in these simulations by making the assumption that they are proportional to some other flow, such as firms' income in this example.

18 Since GDP in the base year does not agree with that in the World Bank data, for purposes of calibration the World Bank series is multiplied by a constant to bring it into agreement with the GDP in the base year SAM.

data side, as noted above, there are conflicting estimates for the major macroeconomic aggregates, taxes, and data relating to the petroleum sector. As a result, the model's ability to track macroeconomic aggregates will be limited. Second, the commodity classification was imposed by the published results from the Cameroon budget survey and is highly aggregated. As a result, substitutability between imports and domestic production is likely to be overstated. In addition, the consumer demand system is not based on econometric estimates. Third, the income distribution sub-model is based on employment-related data from the budget survey, which are not of high quality. Several adjustments had to be made, as described in the section on the SAM above, to arrive at an internally consistent income distribution.

On the modeling side, there are two major limitations. First, because the base year for the model is 1984/85 and the key issues to be examined in the simulations pertain to the period after 1984/85 (which was also a period of economic crisis), the model could not be calibrated in the usual fashion using a dynamic simulation forward in time. Instead, a "calibration" using simulations backward in time was employed to validate the model. This must be viewed with some caution, however, because investment allocation decisions in dynamic models are typically made forward in time and cannot be run in reverse. A second limitation is that the neoclassical, Walrasian CGE model is ill-suited for examining situations of macroeconomic disequilibrium, as when the economy is not at full employment. Even large price shocks produce little change in real GDP in full-employment CGE models. A greater degree of realism can be injected by incorporating non-Walrasian features, such as mark-up pricing or unemployment. The Cameroon model implements this through the device of a highly elastic labor supply when the economy is not at full employment. Clearly, a more realistic model of the labor market, embodying institutional details such as wage formation mechanisms and indexation, would be desirable.

3.4. Results

3.4.1. The oil boom, 1976–1984

This experiment seeks to simulate the growth of the Cameroon economy from 1976/77 (when oil production commenced) to 1984/85 (the height of the oil and commodity price boom). As noted previously, in this simulation oil production, gross investment, changes in stocks, government consumption and transfers, remittances to the rest of the world, and world prices (in CFA francs) for Cameroon's imports and exports take on their historical values and are exogenous. The exchange rate is fixed and the price index and balance of payments are endogenous.

Since the sectoral allocation of investment, labor supply growth by skill category, and sectoral productivity growth are not known over this period, some assumptions have to be made about these variables. Aggregate labor supply is assumed to grow at 4 percent annually, slightly in excess of the annual 3 percent rate of population growth. Labor supply in all categories, except that of agricultural and informal sector labor, is assumed to grow at 5 percent annually, a rate higher than the rate of growth of aggregate labor supply, reflecting both increased urbanization and skill upgrading. However, agricultural and informal sector labor supply grows at a rate of 3.8 percent, only slightly slower than aggregate labor supply growth. This is not unreasonable, because this labor category includes both rural and urban informal sector workers and need not decrease with urbanization. Total factor productivity growth is assumed to be 4 percent annually in manufacturing and public sector food processing and 2 percent per year in private sector food processing.[19]

No attempt is made to incorporate in the model the phenomenon of urbanization and the movement of households across household groups associated with urbanization and economic growth because no data are available that would permit modeling these changes. As a result, the simulations do not directly address the issue of how the gains from growth were distributed, though some conclusions may be drawn from sectoral growth rates and growth rates of wage payments for the different labor categories.

Starting from the base year of 1984/85, the model is solved backward in time. Since sectoral investment shares are only known in the base year (1984/85), some assumptions are required to find previous years' sectoral investment shares. The equations describing these are shown below:

$$K_i(1-d_i) + DK_i = K_i^0$$

$$P_i^K DK_i = \rho_i I$$

$$\rho_i = \mu \rho_i + (1-\mu)\rho_i^0$$

$$\dot{\rho}_i = \mu_i^1 P_i^K K_i (1-d_i) / \sum_j \mu_j^1 P_j^K K_j (1-d_j)$$

Here d_i is the depreciation rate in sector i and P_i^K is the price of capital in sector i. The first equation above states that next year's sectoral capital stock, K_i^0, is this year's capital stock, K_i, less depreciation plus this year's sectoral investment DK_i. The value of investment in sector i, $P_i^K DK_i$, is the sectoral investment share ρ_i times total investment I. The sectoral investment share ρ_i is a weighted average of the current sectoral share, ρ_i^0, and a desired sectoral share, $\hat{\rho}_i$. The desired sectoral share is proportional to the

---

[19] These total factor productivity (TFP) growth rates were chosen by trial and error. That for the private food processing sector is smaller than that for the public sector, the reason being that, unlike the public sector, the private sector includes household and small-scale enterprises, which are likely to be less dynamic and exhibit lower TFP growth than the large-scale public sector.

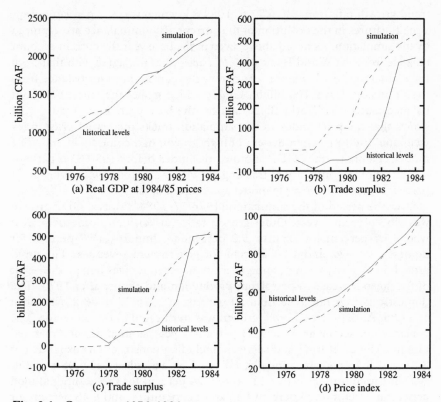

Fig. 3.1. Cameroon, 1976–1984

value of the sectoral capital stock, so that the desired sectoral investment is one that would lead to an equal rate of growth of capital across sectors. This specification makes it possible to solve the model recursively backward in time by endogenizing the current year's sectoral capital stocks and sectoral investment, given the next year's sectoral capital stocks. Thus, after solving for the base year equilibrium, all exogenous quantities (including labor supply and total factor productivity) are "updated" to their values in 1983/84, the model re-solved for, among other things, sectoral capital stocks and investment in 1983/84, and so on, until the year 1976/77.

The model was calibrated by attempting to match trends (see Figure 3.1) in GDP, the current account balance, and the price index over the period 1976/77–1984/85. Among the parameters that were varied for this purpose were the sectoral capital stocks in the base year and the total factor productivity growth rate. Real GDP increased at almost 14 percent annually from 1976/77 to 1980/81 before slowing down considerably. The simulation does not capture this break in the growth rate and merely matches the trend growth rate from 1976/77 to 1984/85, which was 9.7 percent a year. Broad features in the evolution of the current account balance are captured by the simulation. As noted above, even in the base year the current account balance from the World Bank's *World Tables* does not agree with that from the Cameroon SAM. Figure 3.1c shows the current account balance from the simulation less a 100 billion CFAF, which makes the current account balance match the World Bank data for the base year. Last, Figure 3.1d shows that the price index in the simulation tracks the actual price index well after 1980/81, when the era of high growth had come to an end. The model's failure to track GDP and the price index before 1980/81 is perhaps indicative of the difficulty of tracking growth in an economy growing at 14 percent a year with a simple model and limited data.

Over the period of the simulation (1976/77–1984/85), real GDP growth was 9.63 percent a year. Other growth rates (at constant domestic prices) were 15.3 percent for exports, 5.2 percent for imports, 15.7 percent for domestic savings, and 13.4 percent for government revenues. The rapid growth in exports, savings, and government revenues was largely the result of the steep increase in petroleum production and export after 1976. The domestic savings rate rose from 20 percent in 1976/77 to 28.2 percent in 1984/85. At the sectoral level, growth was most rapid in the oil sector. The construction sector grew at 9.93 percent a year as investment expanded rapidly. Manufacturing and services (including construction) expanded at 8.85 and 8.25 percent annually, followed by agriculture at 6.05 percent. Within agriculture, growth rates were 5.24 percent for the traditional food agriculture sector, 6.25 percent for export agriculture, and 8.48 percent for the forestry sector. The sectoral growth rates based on data from the 1992 *World Tables* are agriculture 5.1 percent, manufacturing 14.9 percent, and services 7.0 percent. It is clear that the simulation underestimates the growth rate in manufacturing.

Real wage rates grew at 8.6 percent for agricultural and informal sector workers, 4 percent for unskilled formal sector workers, 6.3 percent for skilled workers, and 5.4 percent for highly skilled workers, reflecting differences in growth rates of labor demand and differences in labor supply growth rates. The rapid wage growth for agricultural and informal sector workers is thus partly the result of the comparatively low rate of labor supply growth for this labor category. Wage payments to agricultural and informal sector workers increased in real terms at 12.7 percent annually, to unskilled formal sector workers (9.4 percent), skilled workers (11.9 percent), and highly skilled workers (11 percent). Non-agricultural capital incomes to households increased at 21.4 percent in real terms while agricultural capital incomes to households decreased at 17.1 percent annually. Non-agricultural profits accruing to households grew rapidly because of increasing revenues from the petroleum sector and because of the oil boom's stimulus to the rest of the economy. The decline in agricultural profits may be associated with the increasing level of the implicit tax on export agriculture and the protection granted the non-agricultural sector during the boom years.

How were the gains from growth distributed? The rapid growth of manufacturing, services and petroleum production, the slow growth of agriculture, and the growth of non-agricultural profit income and decline in agricultural profits would suggest that farm households gained less than did non-farm households. But, to the extent that poor farm households migrated to cities and entered the informal sector workforce, these households would have gained from the increasing wage payments to informal sector labor. Since Cameroon experienced a significant increase in urbanization from 27.9 percent in 1976 to 35.4 percent in 1984, this shift in population would have had a significant effect on the distribution of gains from growth.

3.4.2. *The price shock and its aftermath*

As noted above, Cameroon's export earnings were hit hard by the sharp decrease in world prices for its major exports after 1985/86. Coupled with a steep fall in government revenues and expenditures, the price shock resulted in a substantial contraction in economic activity after 1987/88. As is well known, a full employment model will fail to replicate such a contraction. One way to obtain a contraction when aggregate demand declines is to have inflexible real wages. Real wage inflexibility is introduced by making labor supply highly responsive to the real wage after 1987/88.[20]

A second change is in the treatment of sectoral investment allocation. As before, the actual sectoral investment share is a weighted average of the previous year's sectoral investment share and a desired sectoral investment share. However, the desired sectoral investment share, $\hat{\rho}_i$, is now the previous year's sectoral investment share, ρ_i^0, multiplied by a factor which depends on the change in the sectoral profit rate, r_i, from its previous value, r_i^0. Thus, sectors with increasing profit rates will have larger desired and actual investment shares. The parameter v_i determines how responsive the investment share in sector i will be to a change in that sector's profit rate.

$$P_i^K DK_i = \rho_i I$$

$$\rho_i = \mu \rho_i + (1 - \mu)\rho_i^0$$

$$\hat{\rho}_i = (r_i / r_i^0)^{v_i} \rho_i^0 \bigg/ \sum_j (r_j / r_j^0)^{v_j} \rho_j^0$$

This model is used to examine how these shocks affected output and distribution in Cameroon. Several simulations or runs are presented (see

---

[20] A constant elasticity of labor supply with respect to the real wage was assumed. This elasticity was taken to be 1.4 except for the agricultural and informal sector labor, for which it was specified as 0.6. The market for the latter labor category therefore exhibits greater wage flexibility than those for the other, more skilled, labor categories. It should be noted that the modeling here of labor market outcomes is rudimentary. There is no unemployment as such in the model, and those who "leave" the labor market share incomes with those who continue to be employed.

Tables 3.4–3.9). In these runs, total investment, government expenditure, oil production, and remittances are exogenous and take on their observed values (except for investment, when alternative investment scenarios are considered).[21] Run 1 simulates the actual trajectory of the economy from 1984/85 to 1989/90. The simulations were not extended beyond 1989/90 primarily because data for many exogenous variables were not available beyond this date. The other runs are counterfactual. Runs 2 and 3 simulate the separate impacts of the oil and agricultural export price shocks. Since a major factor behind the crisis in 1986/87 was the large increase in investment in 1985/86 and 1986/87, run 4 simulates the outcome of a more restrained build-up of public investment, in which total investment is maintained at its level in 1983/84, instead of rising 44 percent in 1984/85 and 34 percent in 1985/86 before falling steeply in 1987/88 and 1988/89.[22] As was seen above, Cameroon's adjustment program had to depend entirely on expenditure-reducing policies because its membership in the CFA zone precluded the use of devaluation to encourage expenditure switching from non-traded to traded goods. Run 5 examines the outcome of instituting an expenditure-switching policy through a 25 percent devaluation in 1986/87. The last simulation (run 6) reduces the implicit tax on agricultural exports in 1985/86. This reduction is expected in the short run to increase farm incomes and raise incentives for investment and in the long run to increase sectoral productivity.

3.4.3. *Run 1: the base run*

This run seeks to replicate the growth of the economy from 1984/85 to 1989/90. All exogenous variables are at their observed values. In 1985/86 gross investment rose by 34 percent and the world price for Cameroon's petroleum exports fell by 36 percent. Gross domestic product (at 1984/85 prices) in the simulation rises by 6.7 percent, exports fall by 169 billion CFAF (13 percent), imports rise by 84 billion CFAF (15 percent), and the trade balance falls from 534 to 282 billion CFAF (Table 3.4). Gross domestic product continues to increase in 1986/87, but by only 1.6 percent. Gross investment falls thereafter, by 1989/90 reaching a level (in nominal terms) almost two-thirds below its peak in 1986/87. In the simulation GDP falls by 1989/90 to a level close to its value in 1984/85 and 8.5 percent below its peak in 1986/87. Figure 3.2 compares the simulation with data from the 1992 *World Tables* and more recent unpublished World Bank

21 The (nominal) exchange rate is fixed. In addition, since remittances are exogenous, an increase in the current account deficit will imply an increase in absorption and in real incomes.

22 In addition to these simulations, other simulations are discussed in Subramanian (1994). Among these are one in which there is no increase in nominal investment in 1985/86 and 1986/87 and investment in these years is kept at its level in 1984/85, and two that combine the price shocks (one at a time) with the restrained investment build-up scenario of run 4. For lack of space, only the more important results from these runs will be discussed in this chapter.

Table 3.4. Cameroon: the base run, 1984/85–1989/90

	1984/85	1985/86	1986/87	1987/88	1988/89	1989/90
(bn CFAF)						
Real GDP	4706	5022	5104	4971	4944	4678
Price index	100	110.1	109.3	91.5	83.3	80.4
Government revenue	821	803	713	573	529	486
Government expenditure	501.8	556.2	556.0	530.0	559.4	567.0
Exports	1262	1094	839	899	847	795
Imports	728	811	834	693	614	587
Balance of trade	534	283	5.2	206	233	208
Gross domestic saving	1328	1327	1134	759	643	521
Savings rate[a]	0.282	0.249	0.223	0.197	0.178	0.169
Real per capita incomes ('000 CFAF)						
North farm poor	164.8	184.3	183.2	159.5	161.4	126.9
South farm poor	148.0	162.9	161.4	147.6	147.5	114.9
North and South farm rich	480.2	522.8	503.2	428.5	428.5	337.3
Rural nonfarm poor	160.3	176.7	179.4	155.8	158.4	135.3
Rural nonfarm rich	749.3	781.2	754.8	631.3	656.9	574.7
Urban poor	310.2	329.8	325.7	268.3	268.1	231.0
Urban rich	852.8	794.5	692.4	577.5	579.6	511.9

[a] Savings rate is gross domestic savings divided by nominal GDP at market price.

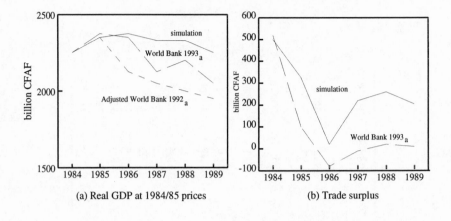

(a) Real GDP at 1984/85 prices   (b) Trade surplus

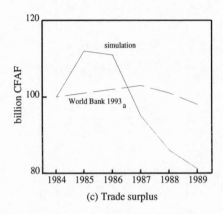

(c) Trade surplus

Fig. 3.2. Base run, 1984/85–1989/90

data.[23] Unfortunately, the World Bank data appear to be incorrect: they show that value added at constant prices in mining and quarrying fell by almost half between 1985/86 and 1986/87 despite the fact that oil output fell by only about 4 percent.[24] The impact at the sectoral level is mixed. In 1989/90 output in sectors other than manufacturing and public administration is 6–8 percent below the base year level. Output in the agricultural export crop sector and in construction falls even more steeply, by 13 and 34

[23] The 1993 World Bank data are from the Cameroon country desk and the constant price series is at 1979/80 prices. To facilitate comparison with the simulation, the 1993 and 1992 World Bank data are converted to 1984/85 prices and the GDP series is scaled to match with the GDP in the 1984/85 SAM.

[24] The understatement in oil value added is approximately 270 billion CFAF at 1984/85 prices. If this is the only error in the World Bank data, the fall in real GDP in Figure 3.2 is seriously exaggerated.

percent, respectively. Output in manufacturing grows by 37 percent as exports double and imports fall by 43 percent.

Turning to the trade surplus, as Figure 3.2 shows, the simulation captures, reasonably well, broad changes in trade surplus over this period, especially the decrease in trade surplus between 1984/85 and 1986/87. In the simulation, however, the trade surplus recovers far too rapidly after 1986/87. The reason for this appears to be that the economy deflates quickly after this date, stimulating net exports. The behavior of the price index in the simulation is clearly unrealistic.[25] The increase in the simulation of 10 percent in the price level between 1984/85 and 1985/86, when gross investment increased by 34 percent, does not appear unrealistic, however, when compared with the increase of 9 percent in the price level between 1983/84 and 1984/85, when gross investment went up 44 percent. Gross domestic savings also declines rapidly, from 1327 billion CFAF in 1984/85 to 521 billion CFAF in 1989/90. The savings-to-GDP ratio falls from 0.282 to 0.169 over this period.[26]

Real per capita incomes show much larger changes than does real GDP because of the large terms-of-trade effects. In 1985/86 real incomes are higher by 6–11 percent for all except the urban rich, whose incomes fall by 6.8 percent, largely because of the decline in profit income from oil revenues. The decrease in real incomes is especially pronounced starting in 1987/88, when gross investment begins to shrink rapidly, inducing a recession. Real incomes fall the most in 1989/90, when the decline in real GDP is largest. The decrease in real income between 1984/85 and 1989/90 ranges from 15 percent for the rural non-farm poor to 40 percent for the urban rich. The income of the urban rich decreases more than those of the other groups because oil revenues—which fall steeply—represent a significant part of this group's income. Incomes for farm households and for rural non-farm rich and urban poor households fall by 22–29 percent. Both urban and rural groups face similar declines in incomes because the decline in agricultural export prices and the reduction in aggregate demand affect almost all sectors equally.

3.4.4. *Run 2: no oil price shock*

In this run, Cameroon's oil export price remains at its 1983/84 level while all other exogenous variables are as in the base run. Real GDP is not much higher than in the base run because petroleum production is exogenous and does not increase in response to the higher oil price (Table 3.5). Exports

---

[25] The steep fall in the price index is not the result of introducing an elastic supply of labor. If labor supply is kept fixed in the base run, the fall in the price index is even steeper.

[26] Historically, domestic savings fell much faster than is captured by the simulation. Note that gross domestic savings in the base year SAM does not equal that in the simulated base year because the trade surplus in the simulation differs from that in the base SAM (see Subramanian 1994, Table 14).

Table 3.5. Cameroon: run 2 (no oil price shock)

| | Changes from base run (%) | | | | | | |
	1984/85	1985/86	1986/87	1987/88	1988/89	1989/90
Real GDP	0	0.54	0.69	0.28	0.13	−0.14
Price index	0	2.26	3.48	4.26	4.84	4.92
Government revenue	0	22.11	38.99	45.47	51.41	50.97
Exports	0	32.70	65.74	55.34	60.90	58.10
Imports	0	2.43	3.61	3.95	4.34	4.22
Balance of trade	0	119.59	100.38	228.38	210.27	209.89
Balance of trade (bn CFAF)	534	620	527	676	722	645
Real per capita incomes						
North farm poor	0	−1.83	−3.60	−5.52	−6.51	−7.55
South farm poor	0	−1.16	−2.50	−4.23	−5.04	−6.10
North and South farm rich	0	−2.05	−3.98	−6.21	−7.29	−8.30
Rural nonfarm poor	0	−1.75	−3.13	−4.80	−5.62	−6.53
Rural nonfarm rich	0	3.98	5.80	6.60	6.46	6.29
Urban poor	0	−1.97	−3.35	−5.05	−5.89	−6.73
Urban rich	0	11.68	19.96	24.41	25.97	25.77

increase in value substantially and in 1986/87 are 65 percent higher than in the base run, and the steep reduction in the trade surplus seen in the base run is averted. Total exports do not grow over time because oil production is stagnant and agricultural exports fall because of falling world prices. However, the trade surplus remains high throughout the period.

The gains from higher oil earnings accrue only to the rural non-farm rich and urban rich households. The other household groups' real incomes are lower than in the base run, in large part because consumer prices rise faster than these groups' nominal incomes. Compared with the base run, in 1989/90 real incomes are 25 and 6 percent higher for the urban and rural non-farm rich, respectively, and 6–8 percent lower for other groups, and real wages for all categories of labor are 6 percent lower.

Government revenues are tied closely to oil earnings and are 40–50 percent higher than in the base run. Had oil prices not fallen so drastically, both internal and external imbalances may have remained manageable for a period of time.[27] The economy may well have weathered the steep fall in agricultural export prices without massive reductions in public investment and a recession.

3.4.5. *Run 3: no price shock for agricultural exports*

The price index for Cameroon's agricultural exports peaked in 1984/85. By 1986/87 it was 10 percent below its 1983/84 level. In this simulation, prices for agricultural exports remain at their 1983/84 level in every year after 1984/85, the base year (Table 3.6). It is assumed that export prices facing producers increase proportionately, i.e. that the marketing boards' margins (as a fraction of export price) remain at their observed levels. Real GDP in 1985/86 and 1986/87 is close to that in the base run because the agricultural export price index in these years is not far from its value in 1983/84. In later years, this price index is 60–120 percent higher than in the base run and real GDP is 4–9 percent higher than in the base run. Unlike the oil sector, output in the agricultural export sector is price-responsive, so higher prices lead to increased output and are expansionary. Agricultural export prices in 1989/90 are 125 percent higher than in the base run, stimulating an increase of 64 percent in output in the agricultural export sector and increases of 13 percent in the CPI and 19 percent in real wages for agricultural workers. The expansionary impact of higher agricultural production varies from sector to sector. Output in sectors with small trade shares is about 10 percent higher. Output in sectors with large trade shares, such as manufacturing, is only 1 or 2 percent higher. Compared with the base run, in 1989/90 real value added is higher in agriculture by 35 percent, in services by 6 percent, and in manufacturing by 3 percent. Real GDP increases until 1988/89, reversing the decline seen in the base run. The expansionary effect of higher

---

[27] Adjustment could not have been put off indefinitely because Cameroon's oil reserves are limited in extent and are close to exhaustion.

Table 3.6. Cameroon: run 3 (no agricultural export price shock)

	Changes from base run (%)						
	1984/85	1985/86	1986/87	1987/88	1988/89	1989/90
Real GDP	0	−0.09	0.21	3.78	5.19	9.05
Price index	0	−0.92	1.84	9.06	10.16	13.04
Government revenue	0	−0.75	1.74	13.10	16.15	22.77
Exports	0	−2.29	5.83	31.05	36.54	48.98
Imports	0	−0.81	1.59	11.80	15.09	21.28
Balance of trade	0	−6.54	685.74	95.88	93.17	127.00
Balance of trade (bn CFAF)	534	264	40.8	404	449	473
Real per capita incomes						
North farm poor	0	−0.80	1.70	12.86	15.80	28.07
South farm poor	0	−1.00	2.21	15.20	18.75	33.84
North and South farm rich	0	−0.95	1.93	22.41	22.93	31.11
Rural nonfarm poor	0	−0.33	0.56	3.92	6.70	14.74
Rural nonfarm rich	0	−0.06	0.00	0.15	2.23	7.48
Urban poor	0	−0.12	−0.03	0.34	2.48	7.82
Urban rich	0	0.20	−0.39	−0.53	1.22	4.75

agricultural production is thus larger than the contractionary effect of falling investment for much of the period. Government revenues also increase more or less in step with nominal GDP, but the increase is less than half of that seen in the no oil-price-shock scenario of run 2.

Since the agricultural export price is higher than in the base run after 1986/87, exports are 30–49 percent higher in these years. However, the increase in total exports is not as large as in run 2, when there is no oil price shock, so that agricultural export prices would have had to rise above their 1983/84 level in order to compensate for the loss of export earnings resulting from the oil price shock. Even if prices of agricultural exports had held firm, Cameroon would have faced a balance-of-payments crisis because of the oil price shock.

Since the difference in export prices between this run and the base run is small in 1985/86 and 1986/87, there is little difference in real per capita incomes between these runs in these years. The differences are pronounced in later years, when the difference in export prices is large. In 1987/88, all rural groups are better off, especially the rich farmers, while there is little difference in the real incomes of the urban groups. The reason for this is that the increase in urban groups' nominal incomes is of course much smaller than that for the rural groups and is more or less counterbalanced by the increase in their consumer price indices because of higher agricultural prices. In later years, the increase in real GDP is larger and real incomes are higher for all groups. The difference is especially pronounced in 1989/90, when GDP is 9 percent higher and real incomes are between 4 and 31 percent higher than in the base run. What is notable is that real income gains for poor farm household groups are comparable to the gains made by rich farm households. One reason for this is that real wages for agricultural workers increase, in part because the consumer price index does not rise as fast as agricultural export prices.[28]

Several important conclusions emerge from a comparison of the run with no oil price shock (run 2) and this run (run 3). First, higher prices for agricultural exports are more effective in maintaining real GDP than are higher prices for petroleum exports. This is because higher oil prices do not result in increased petroleum output, while output in the agricultural export sector is highly price-responsive. However, it should also be noted that government revenues are tied much more to oil prices than to agricultural export prices. Thus, had oil prices remained stable, the government would have been able to make far smaller cuts in investment spending, which would also have been less contractionary.

---

[28] In addition, income gains are comparable for poor farm households in the north and in the south despite the fact that the share of the northern region in agricultural export crops is small. The reason for this is that the agricultural labor market is not disaggregated by region so that gains in agricultural wage incomes will accrue proportionately to poor households in both regions.

3.4.6. *Run 4: investment kept constant at 1983/84 level after 1984/85*

Since average investment from 1985/86 to 1989/90 was more than 25 percent above investment in 1983/84, it would have been feasible to keep investment in these years at the 1983/84 value even after making allowances for inflation. In this scenario, investment after 1985/86 is kept at its 1983/84 level. Since investment in 1985/86 and 1986/87 is now almost 50 percent lower than in the base run and investment in 1987/88 is 7 percent lower than in the base run, GDP is between 1.3 and 2.9 percent lower than in the base run (Table 3.7). But in the last two years of the simulation, 1988/89 and 1989/90, investment is 25 and 40 percent higher than in the base run, respectively. Gross domestic product is marginally lower in 1988/89 and is 2 percent higher in 1989/90. The changed time profile of investment initially results in lower capital stocks and GDP, but in higher GDP in later years.

As expected, government revenue is below its base run trajectory until 1987/88. Household incomes exhibit similar behavior. Real incomes are lower for all groups until 1987/88, as much as 8 percent lower than in the base run. Real incomes fall more steeply than does GDP because with the decrease in investment the price level falls, stimulating net exports and decreasing absorption. Only in 1989/90 do all households have higher real incomes than in the base run. The lesson here is that the pay-off in terms of higher future growth appears only in the medium term. This strategy of restrained but steady investment would clearly be superior if the simulation were extended beyond 1989/90. Not modeled here are other factors favoring such a strategy. First, a slower build-up of investment after 1983/84 would have been more efficient in increasing productive capacity because investment projects would have been better coordinated and implemented. Second, had investment not risen so sharply, the financial system and public finances would have been more resilient and the economic crisis brought on by falling export revenues would have been less severe.

The sharp fall in the balance-of-trade surplus seen in the base run is absent because investment in 1985/86 and 1986/87 is much lower than in the base run. The trade surplus in later years is lower because real GDP is higher and the domestic price level is higher, resulting in higher imports and lower exports. Thus, the economy would still face the need to adjust to the growing external imbalance brought about by falling export prices, an imbalance that is now *larger* in later years than in the base run because of higher growth. But the total imbalance, as measured by the increase over the period in stock of foreign debt (or decrease in reserves), is smaller in this run.[29]

[29] This result also appears in a simpler scenario (see discussion of run 4 in Subramanian 1994 for details) in which only the investment build-up in 1985/86 and 1986/87 is avoided by keeping investment in these years at the same nominal level as in 1984/85, a level that is 42 percent above the level in 1983/84, which is the level used in this run.

Table 3.7. Cameroon: run 4 (investment kept constant at 1983/84 level after 1984/85)

	Changes from base run (%)						
	1984/85	1985/86	1986/87	1987/88	1988/89	1989/90
Real GDP	0	-1.27	-2.43	-2.93	-0.12	1.98
Price index	0	-15.97	-16.53	-0.23	4.34	6.61
Government revenue	0	-15.29	-19.19	-3.46	4.79	9.63
Exports	0	9.85	12.59	-2.00	-4.19	-3.60
Imports	0	-17.45	-19.28	-3.47	5.34	10.67
Balance of trade	0	88.22	5126.69	2.94	-29.36	-43.82
Balance of trade (bn CFAF)	534	531	272	212	164	117
Real per capita incomes						
North farm poor	0	-4.63	-6.41	-4.17	-0.81	2.83
South farm poor	0	-1.78	-3.54	-4.21	-1.54	2.01
North and South farm rich	0	-3.97	-5.01	-2.92	0.42	3.45
Rural nonfarm poor	0	-6.55	-7.96	-3.88	-0.10	2.84
Rural nonfarm rich	0	-6.11	-8.10	-3.22	0.68	2.91
Urban poor	0	-7.35	-8.51	-3.53	0.47	2.89
Urban rich	0	-3.08	-6.28	-2.74	0.93	2.74

This simulation demonstrates the trade-off between more sustainable investment and growth. The investment trajectory considered here produces what may initially be unacceptably large real income losses. A higher level of investment would then be called for. In a second simulation, investment was kept constant at its average between 1985/86 and 1989/90, a level 28.8 percent above that in the simulation discussed above. At this level of investment, GDP and household incomes are above their base run values after 1987/88. In addition, the present value of real incomes is higher than in the base run for interest rates up to 5 percent. In hindsight, it is clear that a sustainable investment policy would have been superior.

A related question is how the economy would have fared in the absence of a price shock for agricultural exports if investment had not risen so substantially as to cause enormous macroeconomic strains, which is to ask how the economy would have fared if the only difficulty facing Cameroon had been the oil price shock. The results from a simulation combining the specifications of runs 3 and 4 show that: (1) real GDP grows throughout except for a slight dip in 1989/90, and (2) the current account (trade balance less remittances) is in surplus throughout, suggesting that the oil price shock by itself need not have brought the economy to its knees.[30]

3.4.7. *Run 5: 25 percent devaluation in 1986/87*

This scenario is identical to the base run except for a 25 percent devaluation of the CFA franc in 1986/87, the year when the balance of payments was under greatest pressure. With a 25 percent devaluation, exports increase 11 percent and imports fall by 10 percent (both in dollars terms) in 1986/87 (Table 3.8). The trade surplus increases to 230 billion CFAF in 1986/87 and to 445 billion CFAF in 1987/88 compared with 5.1 billion and 206 billion CFAF for these years in the base run. Devaluation is clearly expansionary. However, the increase in real GDP is not uniform over time. Real GDP in 1986/87 is only 0.6 percent above its value in the base run because in the simulation the economy is maintained at full employment until this year. Starting from 1987/88, the economy is not at full employment, and so the expansionary effect of devaluation is larger and real GDP is 2.4–3.1 percent higher than in the base run. The price index after 1986/87 follows a trajectory about 10 percent higher than that in the base run. Government revenues are 12–18 percent higher than in the base run.

However, even though devaluation is expansionary, the impact on real incomes is ambiguous because real GDP does not increase uniformly over the period of the simulation. Compared with the base run, real wages are lower after 1986/87 by 1.7–3.4 percent for agricultural and informal sector workers and by 5.7–9.1 percent for other categories of labor. Initially, real incomes are lower for all groups because real GDP increases only 0.6

---

[30] For details see the discussion of run 7 in Subramanian (1994).

Table 3.8. Cameroon: run 5 (25% devaluation in 1986/87)

| | Changes from base run (%) | | | | | |
	1984/85	1985/86	1986/87	1987/88	1988/89	1989/90
Real GDP	0	0	0.60	2.36	3.06	2.50
Price index	0	0	9.63	10.63	10.87	10.09
Government revenue	0	0	11.75	16.69	18.49	17.91
Exports	0	0	11.22	11.00	12.19	10.44
Imports	0	0	−10.17	−7.43	−6.43	−7.26
Balance of trade	0	0	4330.1	116.35	101.70	100.39
Balance of trade (bn CFAF)	534	283	230	446	469	417
Real per capita incomes						
North farm poor	0	0	−2.22	−0.48	0.69	−2.05
South farm poor	0	0	−0.10	1.82	3.02	0.28
North and South farm rich	0	0	−1.72	2.12	2.25	−1.92
Rural nonfarm poor	0	0	−3.31	−2.54	−0.97	−2.04
Rural nonfarm rich	0	0	−3.89	−2.99	−1.19	−1.15
Urban poor	0	0	−3.99	−3.56	−1.93	−2.46
Urban rich	0	0	−2.35	−0.21	1.49	1.98

percent in the year of the devaluation. Later on, generally speaking, the farm and urban rich household groups stand to gain. Farm households gain because the devaluation increases export demand for agriculture. The urban rich gain because devaluation increases oil sector revenues. Other groups' real incomes tend to be somewhat below their levels in the base run. Poor farm households in the north stand to gain less than the other farm household groups because they produce predominantly for the domestic market and gain little from better export crop prices.

These results suggest that a devaluation would have been an effective means of addressing the external imbalance facing the Cameroon economy following the export price shock. In addition, any adverse effect on real incomes from such a devaluation would likely have been small.[31] The devaluation would have also resulted in improved government revenue, making a less drastic reduction in expenditure possible and mitigating the harshness of the adjustment process.

3.4.8. *Run 6: reduction of tax on agricultural exports*

The implicit tariff on Cameroon's agricultural exports resulting from the marketing boards' price-setting policies was 32 percent in 1985/86; i.e., producer prices were 32 percent below world prices that year. This tax fell during the economic crisis, becoming negative in 1987/88 and 1988/89 before rising to 14 percent in 1989/90. In this scenario, this tax is reduced so that the producer price is 20 percent above its level in the base run (Table 3.9). The implicit tax collected by the marketing boards is transferred to the public administration and services sectors as a subsidy. A reduction in this tax will therefore affect income distribution. In addition, it will also increase incentives for investment in agriculture, resulting in greater productivity in the medium to long run.

The reduction in tax results in a 7–12 percent increase in agricultural export crop production. However, the impact on sectoral capital stock of this reduction in tax is not large. Capital stock in 1989/90 in the agricultural export sector is only 1 percent higher than in the base run. One reason why the increase in capital stock is small is that investment is lower in real terms

---

[31] The recent devaluation of the CFA franc from 50 to 100 per French franc has provoked major protests throughout the CFA countries, triggered by the sharp increase in prices of imported consumer goods, such as drugs and other necessities. How can this be reconciled with the small changes in real income observed in the simulation discussed here? First, the devaluation discussed in the simulation is not as large—from 50 to 62.5 CFA francs per French franc. Second, the sectoral disaggregation in the model is broad, so that even if large price increases were to occur for certain "politically sensitive" commodities, these would be less noticeable at the level of aggregation employed here. Third, the simulation does not examine the process by which the economy makes the transition from one equilibrium to another. The predicted increases in exports, production, employment, and wage incomes occur with a lag, while the prices of imports go up immediately after the devaluation. During the initial stage of the transition, the costs for many groups may well exceed the benefits, and future benefits would still be uncertain, providing cause for dissatisfaction and protests.

Table 3.9. Cameroon: run 6 (reduction of implicit tax on agricultural exports)

	Changes from base run (%)						
	1984/85	1985/86	1986/87	1987/88	1988/89	1989/90
Real GDP	0	0.12	0.14	0.38	0.75	0.66
Price index	0	2.22	2.37	2.99	2.69	1.15
Government revenue	0	1.43	1.70	2.20	2.61	1.50
Exports	0	4.15	5.31	4.96	5.52	2.96
Imports	0	1.49	1.49	1.90	2.35	1.35
Balance of trade	0	11.77	37.3	15.28	13.91	7.50
Balance of trade (bn CFAF)	534	316	618	237	265	224
Real per capita incomes						
North farm poor	0	1.86	2.09	3.26	3.77	2.61
South farm poor	0	2.65	3.12	4.40	5.05	3.58
North and South farm rich	0	2.52	2.48	5.27	4.53	2.14
Rural nonfarm poor	0	−0.25	−0.30	−0.63	0.36	0.94
Rural nonfarm rich	0	−1.33	−1.53	−2.69	−1.65	−0.13
Urban poor	0	−1.30	−1.61	−2.70	−1.68	−0.24
Urban rich	0	−1.66	−1.83	−2.82	−1.83	−0.33

in this scenario because nominal aggregate investment is exogenous and the price level is 2–3 percent higher than in the base run.

The short-run impact of the tax reduction is therefore of greater significance here. Undoubtedly, a tax reduction undertaken five to ten years before the boom in commodity prices would have had a larger impact on agricultural investment and productivity because world prices for Cameroon's agricultural exports were higher and the implicit tax was large and positive during much of the economic boom after 1975.

As one might expect, real GDP, exports, and the trade surplus are all higher than in the base run. The increase in GDP is higher after 1986/87— between 0.4 and 0.7 percent—when the economy is not at full employment. Changes in real incomes are larger, with farm households gaining between 2 and 5 percent and non-farm households usually losing between 0.2 and 2.7 percent. The gains are smaller for the north farm poor household group because their share in export crop production is small, and so, they gain mostly as a result of increased employment.

While the impact of a 20 percent increase in producer prices is not very large, it should be kept in mind that a similar decrease in taxation during the commodity boom would have resulted in a substantially larger increase in producer prices. In addition, the volume of agricultural investment, and therefore total investment, is likely, in reality, to be sensitive to the producer price so that higher producer prices would have led to increased investment by farm households, which is not taken into account in this simulation. Thus, the high implicit taxation of export agriculture during the boom years would have had a major impact on income distribution, agricultural investment, and productivity.

3.5. Conclusion

After nearly a decade of rapid growth, the Cameroon economy plunged into an economic crisis triggered by the steep fall in the prices of its major exports. Unable to devalue its currency because of its membership in the CFA zone, the government had to depend exclusively on expenditure-reducing policies to reduce aggregate demand and bring about a new equilibrium. In addition to these macroeconomic policy changes, the government also undertook other systemic and sectoral reforms. These included attempts to reform public sector enterprises and the financial system, and pricing reforms in agriculture aimed at aligning producer prices closer to world prices and eliminating the large implicit tax on agriculture.

What was the impact on growth and income distribution of the terms-of-trade shock and of the reductions in public expenditure and investment that followed? The base run simulation presented here suggests that by 1989/90 real GDP had fallen 8.5 percent from its peak in 1986/87. By 1989/90, real income for most household groups was at least 25 percent lower than in 1984/85, the simulation's base year, suggesting that the external shocks and the attempt to adjust to these shocks have had a drastic impact on the economy.

In addition to the base run, other simulations examined the impact of different components of the price shocks and the role of investment policy and agricultural price policy in the adjustment process. The implications for policy from these simulations are examined below.

3.5.1. *The terms-of-trade shock*

As the simulations demonstrate, the oil and agricultural export price shocks are transmitted to the economy by very different mechanisms. The sectoral and multisectoral impact of the oil price shock was small because of the unresponsiveness of output to price and the weak linkages between the petroleum sector and the rest of the economy. However, government revenues are tied closely to petroleum earnings and so the major impact of the oil price shock was macroeconomic, operating through the government budget and the balance of payments. Faced with falling oil revenues and no external source of finances, the government had no recourse but to reduce expenditures. In addition, the price shock affected income distribution because profits flowing to households from the petroleum sector accrue mostly to the urban rich.

On the other hand, the fall in world prices for Cameroon's agricultural exports led directly to a substantial reduction in production in this sector and a decline in real incomes for farm households. Reduced output also occurred in other sectors, as a result of production and consumption linkages with agriculture. While the price shock undoubtedly reduced the implicit transfers paid by farmers to the marketing boards, the shock had little direct impact on government revenues narrowly defined because these transfers were used to subsidize the operations of the boards and did not accrue to the state treasury.

Had the government been able to adjust gradually, the impact of the oil price shock would have been moderated. By all accounts, the government had built up considerable financial assets abroad during the oil boom. Presumably, these assets were depleted in financing the investment boom prior to the price shock. Had a more prudent investment policy been followed, these assets could have been used to finance a gradual reduction in government expenditure and in the current account deficit after the price shock.

In the case of the agricultural export sector, a similar argument can be made about the marketing boards. If the marketing boards and other parastatal agencies had not dissipated the large revenues accruing to them during the years of high commodity prices, they would have been better placed to moderate falling producer prices and revenues when export prices fell. The agricultural export sector would have contracted as adjustment proceeded, but at a slower pace and with less drastic an impact on the rest of the economy.

Another factor impeding adjustment to the price shock was Cameroon's inability to devalue its currency. As the simulation shows, devaluation is expansionary and results in increased government revenues and an improvement in the current account balance. Since government revenues are higher and the trade deficit is lower after devaluation, the government could have relied less on expenditure reduction, which would have moderated the severity of the adjustment process.

3.5.2. Investment policy

The simulations of alternative investment policies demonstrate that the investment build-up after 1983/84 was of little benefit because the increased production capacity added little to output in a situation of economic contraction and excess capacity. In addition, the simulations demonstrate that a more prudent investment policy, which avoided this rapid increase in investment, would have made it possible (as pointed out above) to sustain a substantially higher level of investment after the price shock, resulting in a smaller reduction in GDP and a less severe contraction of the economy. Moreover, with a more prudent investment policy, far smaller macroeconomic imbalances would have appeared in the wake of the price shocks, making it easier to restore macroeconomic balance and stabilize the economy.

3.5.3. Agricultural price policy

The high degree of implicit taxation of the agricultural export sector during the commodity boom has been criticized extensively, both because it transfers income from agricultural households to mostly better-off urban government employees and other non-farm groups and because it reduces incentives for agricultural investment. However, there is little scope for increasing the producer price in the period after the boom because the wedge has become small, and sometimes negative, and the government and parastatal agencies do not have the wherewithal to finance a producer subsidy. The lesson here is that the years of the commodity boom were the time for reducing the wedge between producer price and world price. At that time, the wedge was large, world prices were high, and its reduction would have had a large impact on rural incomes and, over time, on sectoral investment.

3.5.4. Structural adjustment and poverty

It is clear from an examination of macroeconomic data that the Cameroon economy experienced a marked contraction after the mid-1980s. For insight into the consequences for poverty and income distribution of the continuing economic crisis and the structural adjustment policies, one has to turn to the model simulations discussed earlier.

Largely dependent on agriculture, the rural poor constitute the bulk of the poor in Cameroon. Their incomes are not directly tied to government expenditures through large-scale public employment or anti-poverty transfers. Consequently, structural adjustment—chiefly expenditure reduction—has affected these households indirectly: through the multiplier, through reductions in the quality and supply of infrastructural and agricultural services and in public investment in agriculture, and through its impact on investment and growth in the non-agricultural sector.[32] With the collapse of oil revenues, the Cameroonian state has been unable to maintain the already low pre-existing level of support for agriculture. The long-term consequences of reduced public spending on agriculture, though unknown and hard to quantify, provide cause for worry.

On the other hand, the steep fall in world prices for Cameroon's major export crops had a direct and substantial effect on rural poverty, especially in the more export-oriented southern region. While this price shock was one of the factors precipitating the economic crisis, its effect must be distinguished from the effects of the structural adjustment policies *per se*. Indeed, as the simulation demonstrates, had export crop prices not fallen, the impact of structural adjustment and the associated expenditure reduction policies on rural incomes would have been comparatively small.

That the direct impact of the structural adjustment policies on poverty has been small (when compared with the reduction in GDP caused by the price shocks), and has been concentrated in the relatively better-off non-agricultural and urban sectors, is cold comfort indeed. The inability of the state to restore public and private investment and revive economic growth, coupled with Cameroon's rapid population growth, can only lead to rapidly increasing poverty in the long run.

---

[32] Of these, the reduction in the quality of infrastructural and agricultural services is not modeled here.

Appendix 3.1.
Equations of the Cameroon Model

Definitions of variables are given at the end of the appendix.

Prices

(1) $\quad PM_i = ER \bullet PWM_i(1 + tm_i + mr_i^m)$, $\quad$ for $i \in I_M$

(2) $\quad PE_i(1 + te_i) = ER \bullet PWE_i$, $\quad$ for $i \in I_E$

(3) $\quad P_i X_i = PD_i XXD_i$, $\quad$ for $i \in \bar{I}_M$

$\quad\quad P_i X_i = PD_i XXD_i + PM_i M_i$, $\quad$ for $i \in I_M$

(4) $\quad PD_i = PM_i$, $\quad$ for $i \in \bar{I}_{M2}$

(5) $\quad s_b \sum_{i \in I_b} PX_i XD_i = \sum_i te_i PE_i E_i$, $\quad I_b =$ set of public administration sectors

(6) $\quad PX_i XD_i = PD_i XXD_i$, $\quad$ for $i \in \bar{I}_E$

$\quad\quad PX_i XD_i = PD_i XXD_i + PE_i E_i$, $\quad$ for $i \in I_E$

(7) $\quad PT = \sum_i tt_i^0 P_i$

(8) $\quad PVA_i + \sum_{\mathcal{J}} A_{ji} P_j = PX_i(1 - it_i + s_b \delta_{ib}) - mr_i^x PT$, $\quad \delta_{ib} = \begin{cases} 1 \text{ if } i \in I_b \\ 0 \text{ otherwise} \end{cases}$

(9) $\quad PK_i = \sum_j B_{ji} P_j$

(10) $\quad \bar{P} = \sum_i w_i P_i$

Production

(11) $\quad XD_i = \kappa_i AD_i \left[\lambda_i LA_i^{\rho_i^P} + (1 - \lambda_i) K_i^{\rho_i^P} \right]^{1/\rho_i^P}$

(12) $\quad W_{lc} wd_{i,lc} = XD_i PVA_i \alpha_{i,lc} \lambda_i LA_i^{\rho_i^P} / \left[\lambda_i LA_i^{\rho_i^P} + (1 - \lambda_i) K_i^{\rho_i^P} \right]$

(13) $\quad (PVA_i XD_i - \bar{r} rd_i K_i)(1 - \lambda_i) K_i^{\rho_i^P} = \bar{r} rd_i K_i \lambda_i LA_i^{\rho_i^P}$

Factor markets

(14) $\quad LA_i = \prod_{lc} L_{i,lc}^{\alpha_{i,lc}}$

(15) $\displaystyle\sum_i L_{i,lc} = LS_{lc}$

(16) $LS_{lc} = LS_{lc}^0 (W_{lc} / W_{lc}^0)^{\delta_{lk}}$

(17) $\displaystyle\sum_i K_i = \overline{K}$

Trade

(18) $XD_i = AT_i \Big[\gamma_i E_i^{\rho_i^T} + (1-\gamma_i) XXD_i^{\rho_i^T} \Big]^{1/\rho_i^T}, \qquad i \in I_E$

(19) $\dfrac{E_i}{XXD_i} = \left(\dfrac{PE_i}{PD_i} (1/\gamma_i - 1) \right)^{1/(\rho_i^T - 1)}, \qquad i \in I_E$

(20) $XXD_i = XD_i, \qquad$ for $i \in \bar{I}_E$

(21) $X_i = AC_i \Big[\delta_i M_i^{\rho_i^C} + (1-\delta_i) XXD_i^{\rho_i^C} \Big]^{-1/\rho_i^C}, \qquad$ for $i \in I_M$

(22) $\dfrac{M_i}{XXD_i} = \left(\dfrac{PD_i}{PM_i} \dfrac{\delta_i}{1-\delta_i} \right)^{1/(1+\rho_i^C)}, \qquad$ for $i \in I_M$

(23) $X_i = M_i + XXD_i, \qquad$ for $i \in I_{M2}$

(24) $XXD_i = XD_i, \qquad$ for $i \in \bar{I}_E$

(25) $X_i = XXD_i, \qquad$ for $i \in \bar{I}_M$

Marketing margins

(26) $MM_i = mr_i^x XD_i + mr_i^m ER \bullet PWM_i M_i / PT$

(27) $TT_i = tt_i^0 \displaystyle\sum_j MM_j$

Income distribution

(28) $TW_{lc}^{ag} = W_{lc} \displaystyle\sum_{i \in I_{ag}} wd_{i,lc} L_{i,lc}$

$TW_{lc}^{nag} = W_{lc} \displaystyle\sum_{i \in \bar{I}_{ag}} wd_{i,lc} L_{i,lc}$

(29) $TW_{lc} = TW_{lc}^{ag} + TW_{lc}^{nag}$

$YH_{h,lc} = \sigma_{h,lc} TW_{lc}$

(30) $\quad DEP_{ag} = \sum_{i \in I_{ag}} dr_i PK_i K_i$

$\quad DEP_{nag} = \sum_{i \in \bar{I}_{ag}} dr_i PK_i K_i$

(31) $\quad YK_{agf} = PVA_{agf} XD_{agf} - \sum_{lc} W_{lc} wd_{agf, lc} L_{agf, lc} - PK_{agf} dr_{agf} K_{agf}$

(32) $\quad YK_h^{ag} = \theta_h^{ag} \left(\sum_{i \in I_{ag}} PVA_i XD_i - \sum_{lc} TW_{lc}^{ag} - DEP_{ag} \right) + \theta_h^{agf} YK_{agf}$

(33) $\quad YK_h^{nag} = \theta_h^{nag}(1 - \theta_f) \left(\sum_{i \in I_{nag}} PVA_i XD_i - \sum_{lc} TW_{lc}^{nag} - DEP_{nag} \right)$

(34) $\quad YF = \theta_f \left(\sum_{i \in I_{nag}} PVA_i XD_i - \sum_{lc} TW_{lc}^{nag} - DEP_{nag} \right) + GFT - ER \bullet YFW$

(35) $\quad FTAX = dt_f YF$

$\qquad\qquad +(dt_{oil} - dt_f)\theta_f \left(PVA_{oil} XD_{oil} - \sum_{lc} W_{lc} wd_{oil, lc} L_{oil, lc} - dr_{oil} PK_{oil} K_{oil} \right)$

(36) $\quad Y_h = \sum_{lc} YH_{h,lc} + YK_h^{ag} + YK_h^{nag} + g_h GT + f_h FT$

(37) $\quad GFT = (1 - a_h)GTT$

$\quad GT = a_h GTT$

$\quad FGT = a_{fg}(YF - FTAX)$

$\quad FT = a_{fh}(YF - FTAX)$

Savings

(38) $\quad mps_h = mps_h^0 (\bar{r} / \bar{r}_0)^{v_3}$

(39) $\quad S_h = \sum_h mps_h(1 - dt_h)Y_h$

$\quad S_f = YF - FTAX - FT - FGT$

$\quad S_g = GR - GTT - \sum_i P_i GD_i$

$\quad S_T = S_f + S_h + S_g + DEP_{ag} + DEP_{nag} + ER \bullet FSAV$

Demand

(40) $D_j^{int} = \sum_i A_{ji} XD_i$

$\Delta S_i = ds_i XD_i$

$P_i CD_{ih} = P_i CD_{ih}^0 + \beta_{ih} \left[(1 - mps_h)(1 - dt_h)Y_h - \sum_j P_j CD_{jh}^0 \right]$

$P_i GD_i = \alpha_i^g GDTOT$

Government

(41) $GR = ER \sum_i tm_i PWM_i M_i + \sum_i it_i PX_i XD_i + \sum_h dt_h Y_h + FTAX + FGT$

Investment

(42) $\bar{r} \bullet \overline{K} = \sum_i PVA_i XD_i - \sum_{lc} TW_{lc}$

(43) $r_i = rd_i \Big/ \sum_j rd_j$

(44) $DST = \sum_i P_i \Delta S_i$

(45) $INVT = DST + DKTOT$

(46) $\tau_i = \left(r_i / r_i^0 \right)^{v_i} \tau_i^0 \Big/ \sum_j \left(r_j / r_j^0 \right)^{v_j}$

$\tau_i^1 = (1 - \mu)\tau_i + \mu \tau_i^0$

$PK_i DK_i = \tau_i^1 DKTOT$

$ID_i = \sum_j B_{ij} DK_j$

Current account

(47) $\sum_i PWM_i M_i = \sum_i PWE_i E_i + FSAV - YFW$

Commodity market equilibrium

(48) $X_i = D_i^{int} + \sum_h CD_{ih} + GD_i + ID_i + \Delta S_i + TT_i$

Exogenous variables

GTT	Transfers from government to firms and households
LS_{lc}^0	Labor force in base year in labor category lc
mps_h^0	Marginal propensity to save in base year for household group h
PWM_i	World market price of imports in sector i
PWE_i	World market price of exports in sector i
r_i^0	Base year sectoral rate of return in sector i
$\bar{r}_0$	Base year average rate of return
τ_i^0	Previous year's investment shares
W_{lc}^0	Base year wage rate for labor category lc
YFW	Net factor payments to rest of the world

Endogenous variables

CD_{ih}	Private consumption demand by household group h for sector i
DEP_{ag}	Depreciation of agricultural sectors
DEP_{nag}	Depreciation of non-agricultural sectors
D_i^{int}	Intermediate demand for sector i
DK_i	Investment in sector i
$DKTOT$	Total investment
ΔS_i	Inventory investment demand for sector i
DST	Total inventory investment
E_i	Exports by sector i
ER	Exchange rate
$FSAV$	Foreign savings
$FTAX$	Direct tax on firms
FGT	Firms to government transfer
FT	Firms' transfers to households
GFT	Government to firms transfer
GT	Government transfers to households
GD_i	Government consumption demand for sector i
$GDTOT$	Total government consumption
GR	Government revenue
ID_i	Final demand for productive investment from sector i
$INVT$	Total investment
$\bar{K}$	Aggregate capital stock
K_i	Capital stock in sector i
κ_i	Capacity utilization factor (for oil sector only)
$L_{i,lc}$	Employment by sector and labor category
LA_i	Labor aggregate in sector i
LS_{lc}	Labor supply by labor category lc

M_i	Imports in sector i
MM_i	Marketing margins in sector i
mps_h	Marginal propensity to save by household group h
P_i	Price of composite good in sector i
PD_i	Domestic consumption good price in sector i
PE_i	Domestic price of exports in sector i
$\bar{P}$	Aggregate price index
PK_i	Price of capital in sector i
PM_i	Domestic price of imports in sector i
PT	Price of trade margins
PVA_i	Value added price in sector i
PX_i	Domestic supply price in sector i
r_i	Rate of return on capital in sector i
$\bar{r}$	Average rate of return to capital
S_h	Household savings
S_f	Firms' savings
S_g	Government savings
S_T	Total savings
s_b	Subsidy to public sector financed by export tax
τ_i	Desired share of investment in sector i
τ_t^1	Share of investment in sector i
TW	Total wage bill
TW_{lc}^{ag}	Total wages in agriculture by labor category
TW_{lc}^{nag}	Total wage in nonagriculture by labor category
W_{lc}	Average wage rate by labor category
X_i	Composite goods supply in sector i
XD_i	Production in sector i
XXD_i	Domestic sales by sector i
Y_h	Household income for household group h
YF	Firms' income
$YH_{h,lc}$	Labor income by household and labor category
YK_{ag}	Non-food agricultural sector profits
YK_{agf}	Food agricultural food sector profits

Sets

I_M	Sectors with imports (all except public administration)
I_{M2}	Oil sector (imports and domestic sales are perfect substitutes)
$\bar{I}_M$	Sectors with no imports (public administration)
I_E	Sectors with exports (all except public administration)
$\bar{I}_E$	Sectors with no exports
I_b	Sectors subsidized by tax on agriculture (public administration, public services)

Sectors

Traditional food crops   Traditional export crops
Forestry   Agriculture, modern sector
Food industries, private sector   Food industries, public sector
Manufacturing, private sector   Manufacturing, public sector
Construction   Services, private sector
Services public sector   Public administration
Petroleum

Labor categories

Agriculture and informal, unskilled Formal sector, unskilled
Skilled   Highly skilled

Household groups

Farm north poor   Farm south poor
Farm north and south rich   Non-farm poor
Non-farm rich   Urban poor
Urban rich

References

Benjamin, Nancy. 1991. Income Distribution in an Agricultural Economy: A General Equilibrium Analysis of Cameroon. Ithaca, NY: Cornell Food and Nutrition Policy Program, Cornell University. Mimeo.

Bieri, J., and A. de Janvry. 1972. *Empirical Analysis of Demand under Consumer Budgeting*. Giannini Foundation Monograph No. 30. Berkeley: Department of Agricultural & Resource Economics, University of California.

Blandford, David, Deborah Friedman, Sarah Lynch, Natasha Mukherjee, and David E. Sahn. 1994. "Oil Boom and Bust: The Harsh Realities of Adjustment in Cameroon." In *Adjusting to Policy Failure in African Economies*, David E. Sahn, ed. Ithaca, NY: Cornell University Press.

Cameroon. 1989. "Comptes Nationaux du Cameroon (Version SCN), Resultats 1985/86, Projections 1986/87 et 1987/88." Direction de la Statistique et de la Comptabilite Nationale, Ministere du Plan et de l'Amenagement du Territoire, Yaounde.

Dervis, K., J. de Melo, and S. Robinson. 1982. *General Equilibrium Models for Development Policy*. Cambridge University Press.

Gauthier, M., and S. Kyle. 1991. *A Social Accounting Matrix for Cameroon*. Working Paper No. 4. Ithaca, NY: Cornell Food and Nutrition Policy Program.

International Monetary Fund. 1992. *International Financial Statistics Yearbook*. Washington, DC: IMF.

Subramanian, Shankar. 1994. *The Oil Boom and After: Structural Adjustment in Cameroon*. Working Paper No. 67. Ithaca, NY: Cornell Food and Nutrition Policy Program.

World Bank. 1992. *World Tables*. Oxford University Press.

4

Macroeconomic Policies and Household Welfare in Tanzania

Alexander H. Sarris

4.1. *Introduction*

Efforts to reform economic policies have a long history of heated debate in Tanzania. (For a recent review, see Sarris and Van den Brink 1993.) One of the main arguments used by those against economic policy reform has been the alleged adverse impacts on the poor. In this paper we present results based on a dynamic macro–micro general equilibrium model for Tanzania which is explicitly designed to trace the links from macro policies to household activities.

Tanzania is one of the poorest countries in the world, with a per capita GDP of only about $130. Since its independence in 1961, the country has undergone a series of major shocks and upheavals. After a period of continuation of pre-colonial policies, it embarked on a path of socialization in 1967 as embodied in the Arusha declaration. This was accompanied by wide-ranging nationalizations and price controls, and in the early 1970s culminated with the unique Ujamaa campaign of villagization, during which the bulk of rural residents was forcefully relocated in planned villages. The coffee boom of 1967–1977 eased the external financial constraints that had appeared since 1973. However, the war with Uganda in 1978–1979, and the subsequent reluctance of the government to adjust to adverse external conditions and domestic policy failure, plunged the economy into a long economic crisis in the early 1980s.

Since 1984 the Government of Tanzania (GOT) has adopted a series of stabilization and structural adjustment measures, such as devaluation, an own-funded import scheme, price liberalization, and relaxation of marketing controls. The economy appears to have stopped its downward trend, and official statistics show an increase in total and per capita GDP since 1984.

There are two major channels through which macroeconomic policies affect households (Bourguignon, Branson, and de Melo 1989). The first involves the effects of changes in public spending and production incentives, brought about by changes in relative prices. The second involves changes operating through the financial sector, such as the inflation tax, and wealth effects. The model outlined here is designed to incorporate all these effects and to allow an empirical investigation of the effects of economic reform on the poor.

Section 4.2 describes the social accounting matrix (SAM). Section 4.3 outlines the model. Section 4.4 describes the calibration and the reference simulation. Section 4.5 presents the results of simulations, while the final section summarizes the conclusions.

4.2. *The Social Accounting Matrix (SAM)*

The SAM constructed for this analysis, which is thoroughly described in Sarris (1994b), incorporates substantial household-specific detail. Its main drawback is that it is based on 1976, just like the SAM by Rutayisire and Vos (1991). However, as the main objective of the analysis is to investigate impacts of changes in policies from a given reference, the date of the initial year does not matter. Rather, what matters is the specification of the economy links between the macro and micro variables, as well as how equilibrium is achieved (the so-called closure rules of the model). In any case, it must be realized that 1976 and 1977 were probably the last "normal" years in the recent Tanzanian economic history.

The main accounting categories of the Tanzanian SAM appear in Table 4.1. The matrix is too large for presentation here, but its main flows can be described.

The SAM has 54 rows and columns. The accounting period is one calendar year. Rows and columns 1–41 represent the current accounts, while rows and columns 42–54 represent capital accounts. All figures in the SAM are in millions of Tanzanian shillings (mTsh). As exhibited in Table 4.1 there are 15 sectors of production which have been aggregated from the 73-sector 1976 input–output table of Tanzania. There are five factors of production distinguished in the model, two of which are labor (skilled, un-skilled) and three of which refer to capital (household capital and two types of formal enterprise capital (for parastatal and private firms)).

The major feature of the SAM is its rich institutional structure. There are six types of household distinguished by place of residence (rural, urban) and income (poor, middle, rich). The classification has been based on the 1976 National Household Budget Survey. The SAM also includes formal private enterprises and parastatals as separate institutions. This distinction is important in the Tanzanian context. Other institutions include the government, which is standard, and the financial sector institutions, namely the Bank of Tanzania (BOT) and all the commercial and state banks together. The rest of the world is separated into official and unofficial transactions. The unofficial transactions simulate the parallel market for foreign exchange.

A major departure from standard SAMs (and consequently CGEs) is the

Table 4.1. Accounting categories of the Tanzanian SAM

Sectors of production	Factors of production	Institutions (market participants)
Cereals	Unskilled labor	Households
Other food staples	Skilled labor	Rural poor
Other food crops	Household capital	Rural middle income
Export crops	Parastatal capital	Rural rich
Livestock, forestry, fishing	Formal private firm	Urban poor
Food and beverage manufacturing	capital	Urban middle income
Consumer good manufacturing		Urban rich
Intermediate and capital good		Private enterprises
manufacturing plus mining and		Parastatals
utilities		Government
Home-based small-scale industries		Bank of Tanzania
Construction		Commercial banks
Commerce		Rest of the world
Transport, communications		official
Health, education		Rest of the world
Other services		unofficial
Public administration		

explicit inclusion of assets and liabilities of all institutions. Households can own physical capital, cash, domestic and foreign deposits, and the equity of private formal enterprises. Their only liability is their wealth. In other words, they are assumed not to borrow directly from banks or from abroad. This is not the case with firms and parastatals (and of course the government), who can borrow from both domestic and foreign banks.

Inter-industry current transactions, income flows, and generation of final demand expenditures are in the northwest section of the SAM (rows and columns 1–41), and are fairly standard (Taylor 1983; Dervis, De Melo, and Robinson 1982; Pyatt and Round 1979). Households receive income from wage payments, returns to unincorporated capital, inter-household transfers, distributed profits from private firms, interest from bank deposits, and transfers from the government and rest of the world (ROW). Their expenditures are basically consumption expenditures, taxes, transfers to other households, and current savings. Enterprises receive income from payments to formal capital (operating surplus), interest on bank deposits, and transfers (from the government and abroad). They in turn distribute profits to households (private firms) and the government (parastatals), pay taxes, pay interest on domestic and foreign loans, and retain the remainder as savings (which can be negative). The current transactions of the banks (interest receipts and payments, as well as profits) are included in the account of parastatals.

Payment flows	Assets and liabilities
Wages Operating surpluses Distributed profits Interest payments Taxes, tariffs, subsidies Transfers	Physical capital Currency Deposits with commercial banks Equity of firms and parastatals Foreign deposits Loans from commercial banks Loans from Bank of Tanzania Loans from abroad Commercial bank balances with Bank of Tanzania (reserves) Loans from Bank of Tanzania to commercial banks Net worth (wealth)

The government account is standard. The income of government comes from indirect and direct taxes as well as parastatal distributed profits. Expenditures include spending on health and education, as well as public administration (the purchases of goods from various sectors are included in the input columns for the health and education and public administration industries), current transfers to households and enterprises, and transfers to the ROW (basically, payments on foreign debt). The official ROW current income includes official good imports, interest payments on foreign loans of the formal institutions (firms, parastatals, and government), and official transfers abroad. Its expenditure consists of official exports and foreign transfers to formal institutions. The current transactions of the unofficial rest of the world are derived as follows. First, from the original SAM (see Sarris 1994b) the household changes in foreign assets can be observed (see below). The sum of all these changes amounts to "foreign savings" of the unofficial external sector. It is also assumed that household interest income from foreign deposits, and household transfers to and from the rest of the world, are also part of the unofficial foreign exchange market. Finally, it is assumed that a fixed share (20 percent) of all base year exports occur through the parallel market. The above assumptions imply a corresponding volume of parallel imports which are taken out of all good imports recorded in the base year, and allocated to the various sectors and households in proportion to their base year imports. The official exports and imports are obviously the difference between the total SAM exports and imports, and the estimated unofficial amounts. These manipulations do not change the base year structure of the SAM, as the parallel exchange rate is assumed equal to one.

Turning to the capital accounts, the households' sources of finance are only own savings (rows 42–47). Very little direct bank lending to households occurs in Tanzania. Households do borrow and lend from each other in the informal financial market, but very little is known about the size of this market. The assumption made in the Tanzanian SAM is that each group of households is self-financed, i.e. does not borrow from other types of household or from banks. This essentially assumes away the informal financial market.

Households can invest their savings in purchasing physical capital. As will be seen, household capital is basically the capital in the unincorporated "informal" sector. Physical capital purchases can be from domestic and foreign sources, and any purchases incur taxes, which, of course, accrue to the government. Besides real capital, households can invest in various financial assets. They can invest in formal private firms by "buying firm equity," namely "shares" in old or new private firms, they can hold domestic currency, and they can hold domestic bank deposits, as well as foreign deposits. This last item in the household portfolio simulates capital flight.

Enterprises obtain investment funds from own savings, by issuing "new shares," which in the case of private firms are purchased by households while in the case of parastatals are purchased by the government, and by borrowing from domestic and foreign banks. Their assets include physical capital, stocks of goods, domestic currency, and deposits with domestic banks.

Government of Tanzania (GOT) investment funds derive from current savings, loans from domestic banks (commercial as well as the Bank of Tanzania (BOT)), and from foreign loans. GOT assets include physical capital (through public investment), equity of parastatals, and deposits with the BOT and commercial banks.

The banks are portrayed separately in the capital accounts only with respect to their balance sheet. In other words, the productive activities of banks are summarized with those of parastatals. The BOT derives funds (liabilities) through its own savings, which are separated out in the parastatal current expenditure column, from currency held by the private and public sectors, from deposits of commercial banks (required reserves), and from foreign liabilities. Its assets include loans to the government and commercial banks, and foreign assets. Commercial banks' sources of funds (liabilities), besides own savings, include deposits of the private and public sectors, loans from the BOT (rediscount), and foreign liabilities. Their assets are reserves with the BOT, loans to private and public sectors, and foreign assets.

The official foreign sector derives funds from the official current account deficit, namely current foreign savings, and foreign assets of banks, and accumulates assets through loans to enterprises, the government, and banks. The unofficial sector balances its current savings by household capital flight (foreign deposits). The SAM is structured so that initially (namely at the beginning of a period) all institutions (except the foreign sectors) have a balanced asset liabilities table. Changes in assets and liabilities from current transactions in the model result in a new balanced asset liability table for each institution. Hence dynamic time consistency is maintained.

Estimation of the SAM (Sarris 1994b) implies that the base year GDP is 13.3 percent above official GDP (Tsh 24,533.9 million vs Tsh 21,652 million). This is lower than other estimates of the second-economy GDP (Sarris and Van den Brink 1993; Maliyamkono and Bagachwa 1990) which raise the unobserved GDP in 1976 to 40–60 percent of official GDP, but there was no empirical information by sector on which to base another estimate.

The flows in the SAM were obtained from various sources. Fortunately, the yearbooks of the BOT provided enough information on financial flows to describe most of the cells in the flow of funds accounts (the southeast portion of the SAM, composed of rows and columns 42–54). However, one of the items that was residualized was changes in foreign deposits of households (namely capital flight).

Considerable effort went to estimating the stocks of initial assets of the various institutions. While for financial institutions this is no problem, since the stocks can be estimated from BOT yearbooks, initial financial assets of households and enterprises did not exist. These were derived by allocating some aggregate totals found in BOT yearbooks to institutions (e.g. households) according to shares obtained from the 1976 household budget survey, concerning financial investments of households. Initial stocks of household foreign deposits were estimated by applying simple money demand rules, such as that the ratio of total money held (domestic and foreign) to income be fixed, and subtracting estimates of domestic money held from estimates of total money held. Stocks of formal institution and GOT foreign loans were obtained from the World Bank World Debt Tables. Stocks of physical capital were obtained from the base year calibration of the model.

4.3. *Specification of the Model*

The model explicitly incorporates real as well as financial flows and gives nominal as well as real magnitudes. There are very few models of this sort for developing countries, both because it is quite difficult to incorporate nominal financial (namely portfolio) behavior in a real general equilibrium setting, and also because financial data at a disaggregated level is difficult to obtain. The only other available studies known to the author are those of Rosensweig and Taylor (1990), Bourguignon, Branson, and de Melo (1989), and Thorbecke et al. (1992). A more complete description with the full equation specification is given in Sarris (1994a).

The logic of the model is as follows. Given end of last period stocks of real capital (assumed fixed for the current period), domestic prices dictate production of commodities by the various sectors and institutions. Since capital stocks are fixed, the supply curves are positively sloped on the real side. The demands for the product of the various sectors are determined by current incomes and exogenous nominal elements such as government current and investment spending. Real investments of all institutions are determined endogenously—for households and firms by available savings, while for parastatals and government by deflating exogenous nominal investment expenditures by current capital good prices. Labor demands are determined from the production of commodities, while labor supplies are determined endogenously by household labor–leisure choices. Within each period, nominal savings flows add to current valuation of previous period asset and liability stocks, and financial equilibrium for each institution (namely, balance of the end of current period total assets and liabilities) is achieved by credit rationing or real investment adjustments.

While equilibrium in the goods and factors markets is achieved through price variations, by equating supply and demand in a neoclassical fashion, equilibrium in the financial markets is achieved by quantity adjustments. In Tanzania, like in many developing countries with undeveloped financial systems, interest rates are fixed, and the central bank rations credit. This has the implication that private investment expenditures are constrained.

In the official foreign exchange market, the exchange rate is fixed and balance is achieved by variation of a premium on official imports. In the parallel foreign exchange market the exchange rate varies to balance demand and supply of unofficial foreign exchange.

There are several distinctive features of the model. First, it is solved in nominal terms. This is necessary since changes in current year prices imply changes in the wealth of households and net worth of firms, and these in turn have real effects. Second, asset redistribution between households is allowed. Portfolio choices of households determine their desire to hold real and financial assets. The aggregate national demand for real assets, e.g. unincorporated capital, while it can be larger than current stocks (in which case there is new household investment), cannot fall below the existing total stock. Hence, in such cases market prices of the real assets decline until the demand for the real assets equals the existing supplies.

Third, while each household at the beginning of a period owns given amounts of real productive capital in crop agriculture, animal production, and unincorporated capital, it can allocate these given amounts to various products within the period depending on current relative prices. Hence there is substitution in the short run among sectors by the households. Finally, household expenditure (and savings) are affected by wealth. The flow equations of the model (namely those that make the model balance within a year) are grouped in 12 blocks, which are briefly described below.

The first block of equations describes price formation. Official import prices are determined by world prices (at official exchange rates) and tariffs. Unofficial import prices are determined by world prices and the parallel exchange rate. The imports sold domestically are a composite of official and parallel imports, which has a CES (Armington) specification with a corresponding price index. Domestic actors purchase a composite good made up of domestically produced goods and composite imports in a standard Armington constant elasticity of substitution (CES) fashion (see Dervis, De Melo, and Robinson 1982), whose composite price is given by a standard CES aggregator function. Each institution can face different net prices as indirect tax and subsidy rates can differ. A composite good "leisure" made up in an Armington fashion by inputs of leisure of skilled and unskilled household labor is consumed by households, and its composite price depends on the market wages of the two types of labor. Consumer purchase prices are the composite good prices, modified by excise taxes. Producing sectors demand a composite labor input, whose composite wage is given by a CES function. Purchase prices of investment goods are equal to domestic composite good prices modified by investment taxes. Finally, purchase prices for new capital stocks of institutions depend on capital coefficients.

The second block determines production. Commodity supplies are determined by profit maximization given Cobb–Douglas (CD) production functions. For government the supply of public services is determined by exogenous public labor input. Value added and demands for labor are derived in a standard way from profit maximization. Unit returns to capital and total returns to capital are also derived from profit maximization.

The third block determines household production and incomes. Households enter the year with three types of stock of productive capital. One is capital in crop agriculture (trees, tools, land, etc.), the second is animal stock, and the third is stock of "informal" or unincorporated capital. Households can allocate crop capital in the four types of crop activity, and unincorporated capital in ten non-agricultural activities (households do not produce public services), according to the current unit returns to these products. Since there is only one livestock activity, no allocation is necessary for animal capital. Allocation of household capital determines the total capital that is devoted by the household sector for production of commodities. Each household type receives a different average return to its three types of capital depending on current allocations.

Households enter the current period with stocks of various types of financial asset (currency, domestic and foreign deposits, and a share in private firm equity), and real assets. These stocks are valued at current period prices and they constitute the entering wealth of the households. Notice that implicit in this definition is appreciation or depreciation of assets. Full income of the households includes, except from current income from agriculture or informal enterprises, the value of available labor of different skills, a share of firm distributed profits, according to the previous period equity ownership of the household, interest income on domestic and foreign deposits, transfers from the government, abroad, and other households, and shares in official import rents and unofficial export implicit income.

The amount of composite leisure is determined by a linear expenditure type of function. In essence, households are assumed to choose between leisure and expenditure. The value of leisure for each labor type and the value of labor withdrawn from the market for education are subtracted from full income to determine monetary income of the household. Disposable income is monetary income less direct taxes and transfers to other households. Household expenditure is a function of current disposable income and wealth, while savings are determined residually. Note that savings can be negative. The final equation determines rents from official imports.

The fourth block concerns the current accounts of enterprises. Enterprises, namely private formal firms (herein firms) and parastatals, have income (operating surplus) from the returns to firm and parastatal capital. They distribute profits out of this, and pay direct taxes. Their other current transactions include interest received on domestic deposits, and interest (including amortization) paid on domestic and foreign loans. Parastatals also pay the interest on bank deposits of firms since the parastatal sector includes the banks, and they collect the interest from bank loans. Retained profits of enterprises (savings) are the result of all these current transactions.

The fifth block determines the investment and portfolio of non-household institutions. Real investments of parastatals are determined by deflating observed parastatal investment expenditures by destination, with the price of new capital. The same holds for government. For private firms, investment is given by investment functions, which depend on current profit rates, the average depreciation rate of firms, and the cost of capital. The latter is a weighted average of domestic and foreign real loan rates which are in turn determined by nominal rates and current inflation and exchange rates. Private firm investment is adjusted by an endogenous shift parameter to account for domestic credit rationing.

Working capital requirements for firms and parastatals are a multiple of current revenue, which is endogenously adjusted to reflect credit rationing. Working capital is apportioned between currency and domestic deposits, according to a share that depends on real domestic deposit rates. The total financing requirements of enterprises include the value of total outstanding assets of the enterprises plus the value of new investments minus the value of current equity minus current savings. Enterprises obtain financing via endogenous domestic and exogenous foreign loans, on the basis of a share that depends on real domestic and foreign loan rates. The mechanism is similar to the one outlined in Rosensweig and Taylor (1990).

For enterprises, the current price of their equity is determined by the current valuation of their previous period balance sheet. In essence, given a lagged value of the stock of outstanding shares, the current price of these shares is determined by the current value of the assets of enterprises. Given current share prices, private firms determine the stock of new equity so as to equate their new current net worth with the nominal supply of equity from households plus current firm savings. Parastatals do the same except they accept exogenous new equity from the government.

The household portfolio is determined in block 6 in a nested way. The mechanism adopted is a combination of the formulations found in Bourguignon, Branson and de Melo (1989), and in Rosensweig and Taylor (1990). First the unit returns to the various types of household capital are determined. Then the real return to foreign deposits, and firm equity are determined. Then the average real returns to real and financial assets are determined by weighted averages. Given the new total wealth of households, it is first allocated between financial and real assets, according to a share that depends on the relative returns to financial and real assets. Once the total amount of financial and real household wealth is determined, allocation to the various types of financial and real assets occurs by the use of a set of shares that depend on the rates of return.

The value of the desired amount of wealth held in real capital of some type by households at current prices might be smaller than the current valuation of total existing capital of that type at current new capital acquisition prices. In such a case there are no new investments in this type of capital by households, and its market price falls below the current acquisition price so as to equilibrate household demand for this type of capital with the existing supply. By this mechanism, household current investments in real capital can be negative for some type of household, implying sales of existing real capital and hence a reallocation of household wealth. To my knowledge, this mechanism, crucial as it is for household welfare, has not been empirically simulated before.

The demand block (block 7) is quite standard. Private consumer demand is determined by a linear expenditure system. Demand for investment goods by origin is determined by capital coefficients. Total demand for the composite good includes demands for intermediate use, the real value of exogenous nominal public expenditures and of exogenous changes in stocks. Demand for the domestic and imported goods is given by the standard Armington equations, while demand for exports is composed of separate demands for official and parallel ones. This specification implies that Tanzanian exports are differentiated in the world market. Once demand for the composite import is determined, it is allocated in standard Armington fashion among official and parallel imports.

Government current revenue and expenditure (block 8) is given in a standard form, and includes the implicit export taxes that arise from differences between domestic and world prices. Government saving is just the difference of current revenue and expenditure. (It is the negative of current public deficit.) The government capital account includes exogenous public nominal investment expenditures, exogenous equity investments in parastatals, and exogenous changes in deposits with the BOT and commercial banks. The government finances its deficit by exogenous foreign borrowing, and endogenous domestic borrowing from the Bank of Tanzania and commercial banks.

Commercial banks (block 9) keep as required reserves with the BOT a fixed share of their total deposits. Furthermore, they loan another given share to the government. This simulates the practice, widespread in many developing countries, through which the government pre-empts a share of the total bank deposits. The commercial banks' excess demand for funds is accommodated by the BOT. This excess demand is conditioned by the current valuation of commercial bank assets at the end of the previous period. In essence, the central bank supplies to the commercial banks whatever funds they need.

Turning finally to the central bank (block 10), its function is to balance the market. Given the current valuation of its previous period assets, namely the current valuation of lagged net worth, the BOT assets are set equal to BOT liabilities, and this implies the aggregate savings investment identity and the balance of the domestic money market. Notice that interest rates are fixed and that what balances the domestic money market is adjustments in investments and in the foreign assets held by the BOT. The adjustments in the latter act like additional foreign capital inflows, and can be interpreted as official foreign arrears.

Official and unofficial foreign current savings are determined in block 11 in a standard way. The final set of equations (block 12) is the balance of the various excess demands. There are two equations that balance the labor markets, 15 equations that balance the commodity markets and two equations that balance the foreign exchange market (one for the official and another for the parallel market).

Given the asset liabilities balance for all households, enterprises, and the banks, and the equilibria in real, foreign exchange, and domestic money markets, the savings investment identities for these actors obtain automatically. For the government and the foreign sector, there is explicit balance in the flow accounts. However, no asset liability balance is explicitly included for these actors. Basically, their asset liabilities tables balance by the equilibrium of the rest of the system.

The dynamic part of the model that does not involve simple updating of end of period stock variables (such as financial stocks) is described below. The capital stock of non-household institutions is updated in the standard way. The equity shares of households are recomputed in every period. Basically, because of portfolio effects households can trade between them the equity of firms (this does not necessitate the existence of a stock market), and this alters dynamically their equity ownership.

The updating of population for each household class is done on the basis of the same overall observed growth rate in the Tanzanian population (2.8 percent annually). This implies that the rural and urban populations grow at the same rate. While this does not appear correct, the incorporation of rural–urban migration in a model of this type presents serious conceptual and empirical problems, because of the reallocation of assets it entails.

A migrating person in traditional CGE models basically disappears from one group (rural) and appears with transformed consumer tastes in another (the urban group). In the model outlined here, however, we keep track of the assets and hence the wealth of the households. A migrating person or household must decide what to do with his/her assets. If he/she leaves them behind (e.g. physical capital) they must either augment the per capita assets of the remaining households of the same type as the one migrating or they must disappear. If not, then these assets must be added to those of some urban group. In either case there are a lot of arbitrary assumptions involved.

The decision in this model to leave groups as they are initially and have them grow uniformly does not mean that people cannot or do not migrate. It rather implies that those migrating do not change consumer or other habits. They keep the habits of the group they came from. Furthermore, they keep their assets as part of the household group they originally came from, and these assets produce and give them income. In other words, the migrants are assumed implicitly to take all their assets with them and to make them work in the same fashion as before. This simple implicit assumption seems less objectionable and more straightforward than what is assumed in standard non-asset-including CGEs.

The overall population growth rate and education rates imply growth rates for the unskilled and skilled labor force. The current year skilled labor force is given by the previous year skilled labor force adjusted by the death rate (which can be estimated for Tanzania at 3.2 percent annually), plus a fraction of the labor that in the previous period was educated. The current unskilled labor force is the previous one adjusted for the death rate and the growth in unskilled labor force, minus those that join the skilled labor force. The growth rate of the unskilled labor force is derived so that the growth in total labor force is the same as the growth of the general population.

Finally, the constants in the production functions are updated by public sector investments. This formulation amounts to assuming that real public investments influence the infrastructure, which in turn affects production. The model as outlined is a full employment neoclassical type of model, with flexible factor and goods prices and a quantity-adjusting money market. The assumptions of flexible goods and factor markets, which are the basic "closure rules" of the model, can be debated in the context of any economy. Recent evidence, however, suggests that unemployment in developing countries is mostly of the "luxury variety," namely among the educated groups. It also appears that people who lose formal jobs often become employed in the informal sector although they declare themselves unemployed (Horton, Kanbur, and Mazumdar 1991, Beaudry and Sowa 1990).

The assumption of flexible commodity markets must be discussed in the case of Tanzania. It is well known that throughout the late 1970s and early 1980s the GOT imposed price controls on almost all domestic sectors. This involved official prices for the products of the formal sector (private formal enterprises and parastatals). In the household "informal" sector the controls, albeit strict, were not very effective, with the result that widespread parallel markets with flexible prices evolved on all products. In essence, then, the goods markets were fixed price in one part (the formal sector) and flexible price in another (the household sector). However, the household sector constitutes the largest segment of the Tanzanian economy. In 1976, as estimated in the SAM, the gross value of output (GVO) of the formal private firm sector was Tsh 8177 million, the GVO of the parastatal sector was Tsh 7476 million, while the GVO of the household sector was Tsh 21,918 million, and this must be an underestimate, given that the SAM predicts an unofficial economy of only 13 percent. Hence, a minimum of 58 percent of the GVO in the economy was produced in the "flex-price" sector.

The above observation, plus the observed fact that a large share of the products of the official sectors were diverted to the parallel markets (Bevan et al. 1989), leads one to lean toward a flexible market representation of the Tanzanian economy, even throughout the crisis period. The equilibrium prices then represent a mixture of official and parallel market prices. Of course, it would have been more correct to model the simultaneous operation of both official and parallel markets. Besides the formidable analytical problems posed, as well as the unavailability of any data on which to base empirical analysis, the well known widespread evasion of controls implies significant rents generated and appropriated, probably by those with access to goods at official prices (civil servants, formal sector employees, etc.). This would result in an income and wealth distribution favoring the middle and upper income groups that constitute the bulk of formal sector employees. Hence the results of the model would tend to overestimate the real welfare of the poor during the period of the crisis (mainly 1980–1983). This must be kept in mind in interpreting the results.

4.4. *Calibration and the Reference Scenario*

Following standard practice, the 1976 SAM is used to derive a base year solution of the model. Key parameters are chosen and the remaining ones

Table 4.2. Tanzania: base year per capita income and wealth endowments of households[a]

| Sector[b] | POP ('000) | Incomes and wealth (Tsh) | | | | | | | | |
		HHINC	CURRH	DDH	FDH	EQH	Crop capital	Animal capital	UC capital	Total wealth
RURP	11,008	799	11	20	46	878	20	148	829	2,142
RURM	3,139	1,490	36	81	145	1,287	77	318	1,322	3,578
RURR	750	2,711	63	356	257	3,959	97	362	4,354	10,437
URBP	669	871	4	24	62	407	2	225	619	1,481
URBM	992	2,253	96	103	392	615	0	145	1,336	2,986
URBR	556	7,418	525	924	2,079	11,651	0	5	10,060	27,481

[a] All variables are in per capita terms. Symbols are as follows: HHINC, household current income; CURRH, household currency holding; DDH, domestic demand deposits; FDH, foreign deposits; EQH, private equity in formal enterprise; UC, unincorporated sector (informal)

[b] Sectors are: Rural poor, Rural middle-income, Rural rich; Urban poor, Urban middle-income, Urban rich.

are estimated, so that the equations are solved to replicate the base year SAM (Sarris 1994a). The base year sectoral capital stocks are estimated from the base year SAM returns to capital. The household endowments are for the most part estimated from non-SAM based information (see Table 4.2). For instance, estimates of total household endowments of financial assets from data of the BOT are allocated to households according to shares obtained from a household survey; similarly for total stocks of real capital. Rich households turn out to have a much larger ratio of wealth to current income (3.85 and 3.70 respectively for rural rich and urban rich), compared with poor households (2.68 for rural poor, 1.7 for urban poor). The full calibration results are presented in Sarris (1994a).

The model described in the previous section was simulated for Tanzania for the period 1976–1984. Historical (observed and hypothesized) values of various exogenous and policy variables were utilized to simulate a reference run, and the impact of various policies was then examined. Since exact values for several exogenous and policy variables were not available, it is not possible to replicate Tanzanian history exactly. Also, since the model is simulated in nominal terms, it tends to not converge in some of the later years (1985 and later), as the nominal variables increased substantially. However, the objective is not to replicate Tanzanian history exactly, but to outline the broad dynamic features of the economy during the crisis period, and to examine in a comparative dynamic sense the impact of various policies on household welfare.

Exogenous variables in the model include the world prices for Tanzanian exports and imports, foreign transfers to institutions, the external interest rates, and various items in the balance sheets of the Bank of Tanzania and commercial banks. World prices were all assumed to stay at their 1976 (dollar) levels (equal to 1 in the model), while time series on the other variables were obtained from Tanzanian statistical sources and from the World Bank Debt Tables.

Policy variables in the model include the level of nominal public current and investment expenditures, indirect tax and subsidy rates, direct tax rates, tariff rates, domestic interest rates, parastatal investment expenditures, and public employment. For the reference run all tax, tariff, and subsidy rates were left at their 1976 values for lack of reliable time series. For the rest, again a range of Tanzanian sources were used to compute relevant time series.

Given the several assumptions, and particularly the one whereby world prices and domestic tax and tariff rates stay unchanged, it is to be expected—and indeed it turns out to be the case—that, the longer the period for which one simulates the model, the further away from observed values of endogenous nominal variables one goes. In fact, it is for this reason that the results are exhibited only for the period 1976–1984. After 1984, the changes in the nominal magnitudes are substantial, and this led in some cases to the non-convergence of the model equilibria. Nevertheless, the simulation of a period as long as this (nine years), depends on the simulated dynamic equations of the model, which are rather simple. In fact, notice that the expectations behavior embedded in the model is of the "naive" type, whereby agents act, save, and invest on the basis only of current and one-period-lagged information. In any event, considerable amount of experimentation was done with model parameters in order to arrive at a "reasonable" base run. (See Sarris 1994a for further details.)

4.5. *Policy Simulation Results*

In this section we discuss the results of various policy simulations. Since the model tends to diverge from the (imperfectly) observed behavior of the Tanzanian economy in the latter part of the reference simulation run, all simulations were run for the five-year period 1977–1981. Since it is deviations from reference that are analyzed, it does not really matter which year one starts with. It is the behavior of the economy that counts. In fact, simulations starting with a later year produced similar percentage deviations from reference.

Basically, what changes when one starts with a later year are the initial conditions of the economy, and the relevant exogenous variables. In other words, there is a different reference scenario with which to compare the counterfactual simulation. However, the basic structure of the economy modeled, namely the basic behavioral and other closure rules, and equations describing the economy do not change. This is reasonable, as the stabilization and structural adjustment programs affect only specific policies, at least in the short run. In the medium run there might be some changes in economic structure—if for instance some parastatals are privatized, and hence not financed by the government, or if parallel markets are eliminated. However, even if there are structural changes of this sort, the overall nature of the counterfactuals does not depend much on the initial year. Another issue is whether the counterfactuals depend on the particular reference scenario. If this were the case, then starting at a different year would get one a different counterfactual. The exact magnitudes of the counterfactuals do indeed depend on the dynamic path, as the model is a dynamic one. But it still turns out that the general direction and nature of the results do not.

Table 4.3 gives the results from several policy simulations. Simulation 1 (SIM1) examines a 20 percent devaluation of the official exchange rate in all five years of the simulation (year 1 is 1977 while year 5 is 1981), with all other variables and policy instruments held fixed at their reference values. The second simulation explores a 10 percent reduction in nominal public current expenditures from their reference values in all five years. The third

Table 4.3. Tanzania: results of adjustment type of policy runs

		% deviation from reference[a]					
	Year	Reference	SIM1	SIM2	SIM3	SIM4	SIM5
Real per capita GDP	1	1,412	0.1	0.0	0.0	-0.1	0.0
(Tsh in 1976 prices)	5	1,412	-0.7	1.8	-2.4	-0.2	-1.1
End-of-period money supply	1	10,186	19.0	-2.9	-0.4	0.2	1.6
(m current Tsh)	5	21,887	14.7	-5.0	-0.4	0.1	4.3
Consumer price index	1	1.203	6.3	-5.6	-0.4	1.0	2.7
(1976=1)	5	1.530	3.1	-9.9	1.8	0.6	7.6
Household welfare (1976=1)[b]							
RURP	1	0.979	-0.6	0.8	-0.2	0.2	-1.0
	5	0.982	-0.9	2.4	-2.6	0.1	-3.3
RURM	1	0.996	-0.5	1.1	-0.2	0.4	-1.6
	5	1.083	-1.1	2.4	-2.7	0.3	-4.6
RURR	1	1.145	-6.5	-3.2	0.0	-0.3	3.1
	5	1.246	-7.2	-2.5	-1.9	-0.6	4.8
URBP	1	0.978	-0.5	0.9	-0.2	0.3	-1.7
	5	1.014	-1.2	2.5	-2.8	0.3	-4.6
URBM	1	1.182	-6.3	-3.6	0.1	-0.3	2.8
	5	1.359	-7.1	-2.4	-2.1	-0.6	3.5
URBR	1	1.232	-7.4	-4.4	0.1	-0.4	3.7
	5	1.366	-7.8	-2.9	-2.0	-0.7	5.4

Real wage ('000 Tsh, 1976 prices)							
Unskilled	1	5.08	1.0	1.4	-0.2	1.0	-2.2
	5	5.33	-1.3	2.4	-2.8	0.8	-4.7
Skilled	1	27.95	-0.9	0.2	-0.1	0.1	-4.4
	5	32.07	-2.8	1.9	-3.1	0.1	-8.3
Parallel exchange rate (1976=1)	1	1.198	4.8	-6.5	-0.3	-0.7	4.9
	5	1.343	3.6	-9.8	1.3	-1.4	13.0
Rents/GDP (%)	1	6.3	3.4	4.1	6.4	5.9	8.7
	5	3.8	1.6	2.0	4.0	3.4	7.5
Real public current expenditures ('000 Tsh, 1976 prices)	1	4,979	-5.9	-4.7	0.4	-0.9	-2.6
	5	7,230	-2.9	-0.2	-1.7	-0.6	-6.9
Total real domestic investment expenditures ('000 Tsh, 1976 prices)	1	5,349	-4.7	2.1	1.1	-0.7	-0.4
	5	6,680	-5.0	4.9	-3.2	-0.4	-2.2
Total real investment of private formal enterprises ('000 Tsh, 1976 prices)	1	1,440	1.7	3.3	0.6	0.6	-1.9
	5	1,710	-7.1	-0.2	-3.9	-0.2	0.8
Total real household investment expenditures ('000 Tsh, 1976 prices)	1	1,315	-9.3	-6.5	3.0	-1.7	5.6
	5	1,864	-6.7	-0.4	-5.0	-0.4	-7.6
Household end-of-period foreign assets (m FCUs)	1	3,123	-1.9	1.2	-0.4	0.7	21.8
	5	4,844	-3.8	0.1	-1.1	1.5	-3.6
Government real deficit (m Tsh, 1976 prices)	1	538	-104.3	-67.1	5.2	1.7	-10.1
	5	1,476	-11.2	-12.5	5.0	0.8	-21.3
Foreign official deficit (m FCUs)	1	1,461	-58.5	-10.0	-3.5	-0.3	-15.1
	5	5,005	-17.6	-5.3	-1.9	0.7	-11.4

[a] The figures indicated under the simulations are the *actual* percent rations, and not deviations from reference.

[b] See Table 4.2 for definitions.

simulation is of a 10 percent cut in nominal public investment expenditures in all years; simulation 4 involves a 20 percent reduction in the indirect tax rate on export crops in all years; and simulation 5 simulates a 10 percent reduction in public sector employment in all years falling equally on both sectors on which the governments spends.

Official devaluation, which contributes to a substantial fall in foreign capital inflows as the foreign deficit declines, still leads to a marginal increase in real per capita GDP in year 1, albeit to a small decline by year 5. If foreign capital inflows remained constant, GDP would have been higher even in year 5. Since the model is a full employment one, and the capital stocks in year 1 are predetermined, not much change in real GDP in year 1 is expected, and this can be verified for the other simulations as well. A great impact on GDP is felt in the medium run when dynamic adjustments have had time to take place.

The basic initial domestic influence of an official devaluation in the short run is to increase the prices of official imports, and hence the prices of all domestic composite goods. The CPI is seen to increase by 6.3 percent in year 1. The ensuing domestic inflation in the face of fixed nominal public expenditures (current and investment) implies declines in real public expenditures (current and investment), and real investments of parastatals. This implies a decline in domestic demand from the public sector, but an increase from the private sector via the expenditure switching to domestically produced goods. Given the different composition of public and private expenditures, domestic demands for labor turn in favor of unskilled and against skilled labor, and this is reflected in the decline in real wages of the skilled simultaneously with an increase in real wages of the unskilled.

Household real incomes (not shown) decline only slightly for the poor groups, once again despite substantial declines in foreign capital inflows, which if maintained would have resulted in an increase in the poor's welfare. Without maintaining foreign capital inflows, incomes fall substantially for the middle and upper groups. The reasons are the opposing changes in the real wages of different labor skills, coupled with the declines in rents that accrue mostly to the middle and rich groups. Inflation makes real wealth smaller, and this, along with the decline in real current incomes, leads to reduced real consumption and savings. The former implies lower levels of welfare for all; the latter implies lower levels of household real investments.

The large decrease in the foreign deficit, which permits the decline in foreign capital inflows, is due mainly to the large increase in official foreign exports, which are assumed to be quite price elastic, while official imports decline by a small amount. The parallel exchange rate increases by amounts much smaller than the 20 percent official devaluation, implying a narrowing of the parallel premium as expected. This relative price shift in the foreign exchange market makes households rearrange their portfolios favoring domestic assets, and this can be seen by the increase in money supply and the decline in the end-of-period aggregate foreign assets held by households. The public sector current nominal and real deficit declines substantially and this is expected, since nominal expenditures stay unchanged while tax income increases because of increases in both nominal incomes and domestic prices owing to inflation.

In the medium run, the declines in real public, as well as in real private, investment expenditures lead to a decline in GDP per capita, and a worsening of household welfare, but they still imply substantial reductions in domestic public and foreign official deficits. Therefore, the impact of an official devaluation *ceteris paribus* in a repressed economy of the type analyzed, while improving the external accounts, has a stagflationary domestic impact. The major reason for this is the decline in real public expenditures implied by the fixed nominal magnitudes in the face of inflation. Notice, however, that, despite the decline in GDP per capita, the welfare of the poor is reduced much less than the welfare of the middle and upper income groups.

A 10 percent cut in nominal current public expenditure in all periods (simulation 2) leads to decreased demand for domestic goods and hence to declines in prices which, however, are not enough to prevent short run declines in real current public expenditures. Given that public nominal investment expenditures are fixed, the price declines imply increases in real investment expenditures. The change in real demands for the different sectors has favorable implications for real wages (especially for unskilled wages). The welfare of poor households is affected positively by this, while the welfare of richer households is affected negatively, mainly by a decline in rents. The decline in public deficit releases funds for domestic private investment by enterprises, but household investments decline, as current incomes, especially by richer groups decline. Overall, however, total domestic real investments increase. Public sector real deficits decline considerably and so does the external deficit. In the medium run the increases in real investments lead to significant gains in per capita GDP, further welfare gains for poor groups, and smaller losses for richer ones.

A 10 percent reduction in public nominal investment expenditures over the whole simulation period (simulation 3) has meager impact on GDP and household welfare in the short run as it only affects demand. However, in the medium run it affects the volume of real infrastructure investment, which was modeled so as to affect production of all sectors. The implication in period 5 is a substantial 2.4 percent reduction in per capita real GDP. In Tanzania, real public investment took a precipitous dive in the late 1970s and early 1980s, and this, as the model makes explicit, must have had adverse implications for real incomes and household welfare.

Simulation 4 in Table 4.3 is a reduction by 20 percent of the indirect taxes on agricultural export crops, which in Tanzania constitute the most important source of foreign exchange. This leads to an increase in public current deficit through the loss of revenue, but a short run decline in the foreign deficit as export production is enhanced. The financing of the increased public deficit in the face of fixed nominal public expenditure is through crowding out of private investments, and consequently real GDP slightly falls in the medium run, and the foreign deficit is increased again. Nevertheless, the welfare of the poor is improved, as agricultural incomes are boosted, while that of the wealthier groups declines, mainly because of the decline in rents.

Simulation 5 has rather drastic effects. Release of public sector labor, keeping all other nominal magnitudes fixed in this full employment model, implies reductions in the real wages of both types of labor. This implies reductions in real incomes and welfare of households, but for rural rich and urban middle and rich households this is counterbalanced by increased rents. These are due in turn to the depreciation in the parallel rate, as the official rate stays fixed. Both official imports and exports decrease, with imports decreasing by more, owing to declining demand, and this accounts for the reduction in the external official deficit. However, given the fixity of the official exchange rate, the parallel market is enhanced, and this is evidenced by both the substantial increase in the parallel exchange rate and the increase in the foreign assets held by households.

Another single policy simulation run but not shown for space economy involves increases in the availability of foreign loans to the government. The latter, if not combined with any other measures, such as increases in nominal public spending, has negligible real implications, as it basically affects the foreign assets held by the central bank, except that it increases the external deficit in the medium run (via interest payments).

Given the impact of individual policy measures the next task is to simulate the impact of a policy package, as well as of external shocks. Starting in 1984, the Tanzanian economy has been implementing a structural adjustment program (SAP), which originally met severe resistance by the government. At the same time, the external environment facing Tanzania has deteriorated with the world price of its major export, coffee, declining and the world prices of imported intermediates rising. In the next simulations we try to assess the implications of the adoption of structural adjustment policies in the face of external shocks.

Table 4.4 illustrates the results from the following types of policy experiments. Simulation 6 is of an adjustment program which consists of the following measures:

1. A devaluation of 20 percent in all years (re SIM1);
2. An increase in public nominal investment expenditures by 20 percent in all years, financed by a corresponding reduction of all public current expenditures. The total reduction is equal in magnitude to the 20 percent increase in public investments, and apportioned proportionally to the sectors which are "purchased" by the government. (It turns out that the nominal

public expenditure cut is about 5 percent in the five-year period 1977–1981.) Hence, this part of the package combines attributes of SIM2 with those of SIM3 (with the reverse signs, however, as public investment is increased while in SIM3 it is decreased);

3. A reduction by 10 percent in all years of public sector employment (re SIM5);

4. A reduction by 20 percent in the indirect tax rate of agricultural exports (re SIM4);

5. An increase in foreign loans to government by 10 percent in all years.

The above package seems typical of the type of recommendations made by the Bretton Woods institutions (IMF and the World Bank).

Simulation 7 simulates a permanent (i.e. in all years) 20 percent decline in the world price of agricultural exports. Simulation 8 simulates a permanent 20 percent increase in the world price of imported manufactured intermediate products. The above two simulations, independently or combined, are intended to simulate an adverse external terms-of-trade shock, as agricultural exports constitute the bulk of Tanzanian exports, and manufactured intermediate imports constitute the bulk of imports. Simulation 9 combines the assumptions of SIM6, SIM7 and SIM8. It is intended to capture the combined impact of an adjustment program in the context of an adverse terms-of-trade shock.

The impact of the adjustment policies in simulation 6 can be visualized in terms of its component parts. Albeit the model is nonlinear, one can approximate the impact of the policies to the first order by adding up the separate impacts indicated in Table 4.3 (with double the magnitudes and with the opposite signs for SIM3, and multiplying the changes in SIM2 by 0.5). For instance, the impact on year 5 per capita GDP according to this rough approximation is 3.7 percent ($= -0.7 + 0.9 + 4.8 - 0.2 - 1.1$), compared with 3.2 percent indicated in SIM6. The SAM package has very drastic short and medium term effects. In the short run (year 1), real per capita GDP increases marginally (by 0.1 percent), but domestic money supply jumps by 21 percent, pulling the CPI up by 9.5 percent. The parallel premium is significantly reduced, as the parallel exchange rate increases by 8.1 percent, which is much lower than the 20 percent increase in the official exchange rate. This pulls down the rents on official imports, which fell from 6.3 percent of GDP in the reference run to 4.8 percent in SIM6, and also leads to a reduction in foreign assets held by households.

Total public real current expenditure declines significantly, both because of the nominal reduction necessitated by the financing requirements for public investment, and also because of the substantial domestic price increases. While public real investments increase, private real investments decline in the short run (mainly by the household sector, as formal private firm investments marginally increase by 0.2 percent).

Table 4.4. Tanzania: simulation of structural adjustment package and external shocks

	Year	Reference	SIM6	SIM7	SIM8	SIM9
		% devaluation from reference[a]				
Real per capita GDP (Tsh in 1976 prices)	1	1,412	0.1	0.2	0.0	0.2
	5	1,412	3.2	0.5	-0.3	3.6
End-of-period money supply (m current Tsh)	1	10,186	21.0	-0.4	0.1	20.2
	5	21,887	18.0	0.2	0.0	18.1
Consumer price index (1976=1)	1	1.203	9.5	-2.4	0.3	6.0
	5	1.530	4.2	-1.1	0.3	2.5
Household welfare (1976=1)[b]						
RURP	1	0.979	-0.8	0.1	-1.0	-2.2
	5	0.982	1.8	0.2	-1.1	0.5
RURM	1	0.996	-0.9	-0.6	-1.2	-3.5
	5	1.083	0.4	-0.4	-1.4	-2.0
RURR	1	1.145	-4.0	1.8	0.0	-1.8
	5	1.246	0.2	2.0	-0.2	3.0
URBP	1	0.978	-1.2	-0.5	-1.1	-3.3
	5	1.014	0.4	-0.4	-1.3	1.8
URBM	1	1.182	-4.6	1.7	0.2	-2.4
	5	1.359	-0.9	1.8	-0.1	1.7
URBR	1	1.232	-4.9	2.1	0.2	-2.3
	5	1.366	0.0	2.2	-0.1	3.1

Real wage ('000 Tsh, 1976 prices)					
Unskilled	1	5.08	0.8	-3.1	-1.6	-5.1
	5	5.33	1.1	-1.5	-1.5	-3.4
Skilled	1	27.95	-5.0	0.4	-1.4	-6.1
	5	32.07	-4.7	0.4	-1.3	-5.8
Parallel exchange rate (1976=1)	1	1.198	8.1	3.8	0.5	12.4
	5	1.343	8.3	5.4	0.5	15.5
Rents/GDP (%)	1	6.3	4.8	7.5	7.0	7.2
	5	3.8	4.0	4.7	4.3	6.0
Real public current expenditures ('000 Tsh, 1976 prices)	1	4,979	-8.5	2.3	-0.4	-5.7
	5	7,230	-3.9	1.2	-0.3	-2.3
Total real domestic investment expenditures ('000 Tsh, 1976 prices)	1	5,349	-7.3	2.7	-0.9	-4.6
	5	6,680	-0.4	1.3	-1.0	0.4
Total real investment of private formal enterprises ('000 Tsh, 1976 prices)	1	1,440	0.2	1.3	-9.6	-8.8
	5	1,710	0.2	1.5	-2.0	-0.5
Total real household investment expenditures ('000 Tsh, 1976 prices)	1	1,315	-13.1	5.2	7.6	2.2
	5	1,864	5.0	1.5	-1.3	5.7
Household end-of-period foreign assets (m FCUs)	1	3,123	-1.4	-2.3	-0.1	-4.1
	5	4,844	-3.2	-4.4	-0.3	-8.5
Government real deficit (m Tsh, 1976 prices)	1	538	-140.8	29.2	6.7	-93.0
	5	1,476	-47.5	3.8	2.6	-36.6
Foreign official deficit (m FCUs)	1	1,461	-71.0	14.3	2.6	-47.0
	5	5,005	-25.6	0.7	1.1	-22.2

[a] The figures indicated under the simulations are the *actual* percent rations, and not deviations from reference.

[b] See Table 4.2 for definitions.

The release of 10 percent of public labor in the domestic labor market, combined with other measures, has a differential impact in the real wages of the two skill types. The real wages of unskilled labor increase, while those of skilled labor decline.

The intention of any adjustment program is to reduce both domestic and external deficits, and the simulated adjustment program performs superbly on both fronts, turning the public sector from a real deficit (in the reference run in 1977) of Tsh 538 million to a real surplus of Tsh 219 million. Similarly, the official foreign deficit of 1461 million foreign currency units (FCU) is reduced to only FCU 424 million in the first year of the simulation. As can be seen from the individual policy experiments of Table 4.3, these effects are due primarily to the official devaluation, and to the reduction in public current expenditures (SIM1 and SIM2).

The impact on welfare of all households is negative, but very differentiated according to household type. The poor rural and urban households, as well as the rural middle income ones, who do not partake in the rents, lose about 1 percent of real welfare. The wealthier ones, however, lose from 4 to 5 percent of their real welfare in the short run. It thus appears that there is a significant short run cost of the adjustment package, although this is very limited for the poor households. Once again, however, if foreign capital inflows had been maintained at a level commensurate with that prior to the decline in the deficit, the welfare outcomes would have been quite positive.

Turning to the medium run, however, things are substantially different. Inflation is moderated, and real domestic investment, especially that of households, recovers. GDP per capita increases in year 5 by a substantial 3.2 percent compared with the reference run. This is helped by the improved public infrastructure, which on the assumptions of the model has an impact on domestic production of almost 4 percent. (The value of the constant coefficient in the production functions grows from 0.96 in the reference run for 1981 to 0.99 in SIM6.) The public and foreign deficits appear to be kept substantially below their reference values.

Household welfare improves considerably in the medium run, especially for the rural poor and middle income households, and by lesser but still positive amounts for the urban poor and rural rich. The urban rich also recover in their welfare, and by year 5 they are at the reference level. The only major losers in the medium run appear to be the urban middle income households, who even after the period of growth end up being worse off by 0.9 percent. It thus appears that the major burden of adjustment is by the better off households, while the poor ones, despite small early losses, emerge as overall gainers. These results are of similar nature to the ones reported by Sarris and Van den Brink (1993), using a different partial equilibrium model.

The consequence of the decline in the world price of agricultural exports (SIM7) is to decrease the world demand for agricultural exports. The official exchange rate does not respond, but the free parallel rate responds, and devalues by 3.8 percent in year 1 and 5.4 percent in year 5. This helps maintain domestic demand, in the face of a substantial decline in official exports (manifested in the increase in the official foreign deficit). Real wages of unskilled labor decline, but those of skilled labor marginally increase. Domestic prices fall in both the short and the medium run, and this, in the face of fixed nominal public expenditures, leads to increases in real domestic public demand (current and investment) which has a positive impact on GDP and real welfare of most groups. The major groups hurt are the rural middle income ones (that derive significant incomes from agricultural exports) and the urban poor (mainly through the unskilled labor market). Public sector deficit increases as expected.

An increase in the world price of imports increases the domestic price of imports, and this helps to increase domestic prices, and hence to reduce the real values of constant nominal public expenditures. Real wages are affected negatively for both skill types, and the parallel exchange rate is devalued by smaller amounts compared with SIM7. The impact on real welfares of households is negative in the short run for the poor groups. The richer ones benefit from small increases in rents, and are not affected in the short run. In the medium run, real GDP per capita declines by 0.3 percent, and welfare of all households is negatively affected.

SIM9 combines all influences simulated in SIM6, SIM7, and SIM8. It is thus intended to give an idea of the type of expected impact of a SAP combined with adverse terms-of-trade effects. If the model were linear, the sum of all percentage deviations under the three individual simulations would be exactly equal to the percentage deviation under the column for SIM9. The differences reflect the degree of non-linearity in the model. For instance, in year 5 the sum of the changes in real GDP per capita in SIM6, SIM7, and SIM8 is 3.4 percent, while that shown in the last column is 3.6 percent. Generally the differences are larger for household welfare, but the overall directions of change do not appear to be different from what can be inferred by summing the individual impacts in the first three columns.

The implications of the combined simulation are quite favorable from a macro perspective. Real GDP per capita increases considerably in the medium run, while the public domestic deficits and official foreign deficits are reduced substantially. Real wages for both skill types decline in both the short and medium run, and this favors the buyers of labor, namely private firms and household informal activities.

Households in fact are seen to increase their real domestic investments, while decreasing their foreign assets. The parallel rate increases by amounts less than the official devaluation, but the rents generated are still larger than those in the reference run. This, however, is mostly a consequence of the external shocks.

Household welfare declines for all households in the short run by roughly equal amounts. It is important to realize, however, by reference to the simulations in the previous three columns, that for the poor households this is mostly the consequence of the adverse external shocks, and less so the consequence of the adjustment policies, as already discussed. In the medium run, the rural poor household welfare recovers, and so does that of the rural rich, urban middle, and urban rich. The rural middle and urban poor households are seen to be still negatively affected.

It thus appears that, when adjustment policies are combined with adverse external shocks, the beneficial effects tend to be blurred, and this might be one of the reasons why adjustment programs have been blamed for consequences that in fact might have been due to adverse external causes.

The experiments up to now have involved policy or exogenous changes without a real structural change. However, most adjustment programs try to create such structural changes, especially in the foreign exchange market, by attempting to unify the official and parallel markets. Table 4.5 presents two simulations designed to explore such complete exchange rate liberalization. Simulation 10 involves the same exogenous and policy variables as in the reference run, except that now there is no parallel market for foreign exchange, and all foreign transactions occur in the official market, which however has a flexible exchange rate. Hence simulation 10 must be compared with either the reference run or simulation 1, which involves a 20 percent devaluation in the official market only. Simulation 11 simulates the adjustment package of simulation 6, but under completely unified exchange rate.

Comparing SIM10 with SIM1, it can be seen that the signs of all the deviations from the reference run are the same. Hence, all the discussion concerning the impact of a devaluation that was given while discussing SIM1 carries over here as well. However, the magnitudes are all less favorable. The reason is that a completely unified exchange rate regime implies a much larger exchange rate devaluation and inflation under the same nominal exogenous and policy influences. It can be seen for instance that the unified exchange rate under SIM10 in year 1 is 15.5 percent above the parallel market rate in the reference run; in year 5 it is 12.6 percent above the reference parallel rate. These numbers compare with the 4.8 and 3.6 percent devaluations of the parallel rate under SIM1. The larger domestic price increases imply larger contraction on the demand side compared with SIM1 as the nominal magnitudes in SIM10 are the same as in SIM1, and hence larger declines in per capita GDP. Household welfare declines for all households, but substantially so for wealthier ones, as they lose all the rents. Note, however, that both the government and the foreign deficits improve considerably more under this scenario.

Comparing SIM11 with SIM6, it can again be seen that, while the signs of the deviations from reference are the same, the magnitudes are less favorable compared with SIM6, and the welfare of households is worse.

Table 4.5. Tanzania: simulation of flexible exchange rate regime, without and with adjustment program

		% devaluation from reference[a]		
	Year	Reference	SIM10	SIM11
Real per capita GDP	1	1,412	0.1	0.1
(Tsh, 1976 prices)	5	1,412	−1.3	1.9
End-of-period money supply	1	10,186	40.1	55.7
(m current Tsh)	5	21,887	45.7	49.8
Consumer price index	1	1.203	13.3	21.9
(1976=1)	5	1.530	4.8	9.9
Household welfare (1976=1)[a]				
RURP	1	0.979	−0.8	−1.2
	5	0.982	−2.6	0.6
RURM	1	0.996	−0.4	−1.0
	5	1.083	−2.4	−0.3
RURR	1	1.145	−13.4	−14.0
	5	1.246	−12.4	−10.7
URBP	1	0.978	−0.4	−1.2
	5	1.014	−2.9	−0.6
URBM	1	1.182	−12.9	−1.9
	5	1.359	−12.4	−11.8
URBR	1	1.232	−15.0	−15.8
	5	1.366	−14.0	−12.2
Real wage ('000 Tsh, 1976 prices)				
Unskilled	1	5.08	3.0	3.7
	5	5.33	−2.8	0.8
Skilled	1	27.95	−1.0	−5.4
	5	32.07	−6.4	−7.8
Parallel exchange rate (1976=1)	1	1.198	15.5	25.4
	5	1.343	12.6	14.7
Rents/GDP[b](%)	1	6.3	0.0	0.0
	5	3.8	0.0	0.0
Real public current expenditures	1	4,979	−11.8	−20.0
('000 Tsh, 1976 prices)	5	7,230	−4.9	−0.8
Total real domestic investment	1	5,349	−7.9	−14.4
expenditures ('000 Tsh, 1976 prices)	5	6,680	−7.7	0.1
Total real investment of private	1	1,440	5.7	4.1
formal enterprises ('000 Tsh, 1976 prices)	5	1,710	7.7	4.7
Total real household investment	1	1,315	−14.8	−23.5
expenditures ('000 Tsh, 1976 prices)	5	1,864	−26.4	−2.8
Household end-of-period foreign	1	3,123	−6.7	−8.1
assets (m FCUs)	5	4,844	−6.0	−6.7

Table 4.5. (*cont.*)

		% devaluation from reference[a]		
	Year	Reference	SIM10	SIM11
Government real deficit	1	538	−194.4	−252.3
(m Tsh, 1976 prices)	5	1,476	−65.8	−89.8
Foreign official deficit	1	1,461	−119.9	−157.7
(m FCUs)	5	5,005	−41.6	−54.6

[a] See Table 4.2 for definitions.
[b] The open market exchange rate in the reference run is the parallel exchange rate.

However, this is explained by the fact that the public and foreign deficits are much smaller under this scenario.

The gist of this and the previous story is that devaluations or exchange rate unifications involve increased inflation. If net capital inflows decline (if official capital inflows do not offset any reduction in commercial borrowing) and nominal public expenditures remain constant, then there is a danger of stagnating the economy from the expenditure side. A possible remedy, which is explicit in SIM3, is that increased public investment expenditures seem to offer the best option for counteracting any stagflationary impacts. However, in most cases the adjustment lending that has accompanied exchange rate reforms in Africa has prevented sharp increases in real government spending, and in particular public investment.

4.6. *Concluding Remarks*

The chapter has made both methodological and policy related points. On the methodological front, the results of the analysis illustrate both the flexibility and power of the type of model constructed for Tanzania, and the significant interaction of nominal and real variables, mediated through the money market. The empirical incorporation of a parallel foreign exchange market, and the detailed specification of production, investment, labor-leisure, and portfolio behavior of households, including asset redistribution, are methodological innovations, which could help in more detailed subsequent analyses in other economies. Since the objective of the exercise was to analyze the impact of largely macro policies on households, it was necessary to be quite detailed on the description of the relevant links.

The simulations illustrated that the short and medium run impacts of policies can be opposite, as short run measures can affect investments. The model has a consistent dynamic structure, as it keeps detailed track of both real and financial accounts. However, it must be acknowledged that the parameters that influence dynamic behavior, such as household savings rates, the various depreciation rates, and the structure of investment functions, are not well known. Hence more research is needed in these areas.

The policy simulations considered both individual and combined policies, and external shocks. The major conclusion is that the impacts of individual policies on given variables are often in opposite directions. Hence the impact of a combination of policies, as normally included in an adjustment program, is often a matter of relative emphasis.

This point was made even more forcefully when the impacts of external shocks were considered. These were seen to reverse in some cases the beneficial impacts of the adjustment policies, reinforcing the need to distinguish between the influence of policy and exogenous factors.

The impacts on poor household welfare, a major concern of many African governments and donors alike, were seen to be positive in the medium run from most types of adjustment policies, despite small early losses in some cases. The impacts on non-poor household welfare were seen to be influenced by the evolution of rents in the economy. In this chapter rents were apportioned to the non-poor, and this meant that the reduction of the large pre-reform rents implied by adjustment policies tend to hurt the non-poor. The question of rent generation and appropriation in an economy is an important and not very well studied topic at the empirical level. However, it is mostly with models of the type illustrated here that one can analyze them, and it is hoped that the analysis here will stimulate further research in this area.

In the Tanzanian context, the empirical results of the model seem to support the general conclusion that the recent positive post-1986 developments are certainly related to adjustment policies, especially the devaluation of the official exchange rate; and in fact they could have been even better, had it not been for the adverse external developments.

Appendix 4.1.
Equations of the Tanzania Model

Variables are defined at the end of the appendix.

1. Price formation

(1)　$PM_i = EXR\,PMW_i(1 + tar_i)$

(2)　$PRC_i = \left(ad_i P_i^{1-\sigma_{mi}} + am_i PM_i^{1-\sigma_{mi}}\right)^{1/(1-\sigma_{mi})}$

(3)　$PEF_{i,I} = P_i(1 - tind_{i,I} + subs_{i,I}) - \sum_j a_{ji} PRC_j$

(4)　$PLEIS_h = \left(\sum_l al_{h,l} W_l^{1-\sigma_{lh}}\right)^{1/(1-\sigma_{lh})}$

(5)　$PRCH_i = PRC_i(1 + taxc_i)$

(6)　$WC_{i,I} = \left(\sum_l \delta_{l,i,I} W_l^{1-\sigma_{4i,I}}\right)^{1/(1-\sigma_{4i,I})}$

(7)　$PIN_{i,I} = PRC_i(1 + txinv_I)$

(8)　$PK_{i,I} = \sum_j b_{j,I} \bullet PIN_{j,I}$

(9)　$PKH_{hk} = \sum_i bh_{i,hk} \bullet PIN_{i,H}$

2. Production and factor demand

(10)　$Q_{i,I} = A^{1/\gamma_{2i,I}} \left(\dfrac{\gamma_{1i,I} PEF_{i,I}}{WC_{i,I}}\right)^{\gamma_{1i,I}/\gamma_{2i,I}} \bullet CAPL_{i,I}$

(11)　$Q_{i,G} = cg_i LABC_{i,g}^{ag_i}$

(12)　$VAD_{i,I} = PEF_{i,I} \bullet Q_i$

(13)　$LABC_{i,I} = \left(\dfrac{A\gamma_{1i,I} \bullet PEF_{i,I}}{WC_{i,I}}\right)^{1/\gamma_{2i,I}} \bullet CAPL_{i,I}$

(14)　$LABC_{i,G} = \overline{LABCG}_{i,G} \bullet INDX\,GL_i$

(15)　$LAB_{l,i,I} = LABC_{i,I} \bullet \delta_{l,i,I} \bullet \left(\dfrac{W_l}{WC_{i,I}}\right)^{-\sigma_{4i,I}}$

$$(16) \quad PIK_{i,I} = \gamma_{2i,F}(APEF_{i,I})^{1/\gamma_{2i,I}} \bullet \left(\frac{\gamma_{1i,I}}{WC_{i,I}}\right)^{\gamma_{1i,I}/\gamma_{2i,I}}$$

$$(17) \quad PCAP_{i,I} = PIK_{i,I} \bullet CAPL_{i,I}$$

3. Household production and income

$$(18) \quad CRCAP_{h,i} = HHKL_{h,CRCAP} \frac{acr_{h,i}PIK_{i,H}^{\sigma_{h,L}-1}}{\sum_{i \in CR} acr_{h,i}PIK_{i,H}^{\sigma_{h,L}-1}}$$

$$(19) \quad UCAP_{h,i} = HHKL_{h,UC} \frac{auc_{hi}c_{h,i}PIK_{i,H}^{\sigma_{h,u}-1}}{\sum_{i \in UC} auc_{h,i}PIK_{i,H}^{\sigma_{h,u}-1}}$$

$$(20) \quad CAPL_{i,H} = \sum_h CRCAP_{h,i}, \qquad i \in CR$$

$$(21) \quad CAPL_{LIVF,H} = \sum_h HHKL_{h,ANM}$$

$$(22) \quad CAPL_{i,H} = \sum_h UCAPL_h, \qquad i \in UC$$

$$(23) \quad PIKH_{h,CRCAP} = \frac{\sum_{i \in CR} PIK_{i,H}CRCAP_{h,i}}{HHKL_{h,CRCAP}}$$

$$(24) \quad PIKH_{h,ANM} = PIK_{LIVF,H}$$

$$(25) \quad PIKH_{h,UC} = \frac{\sum_{i \in UC} PIK_{i,H}UCAP_{h,i}}{HHKL_{h,UC}}$$

$$(26) \quad WEALTH_h = CURRHL_h + DDHL_h + EXR \bullet FDHL_h$$
$$+ \sum_{hk} PRCAPH_{hk} \bullet HHKL_{h,hk} + SHEQL_h \bullet PEQTY_f \bullet EQTYL_f$$

$$(27) \quad LED_{h,l} = LAV_{h,l} \bullet edr_{h,l}$$

$$(28) \quad FINC_h = \sum_l W_l \bullet LAV_{h,l} + \sum_{hk} PIKH_{h,hk} \bullet HHKL_{h,hk} + SHEQL_h \bullet DPROF_f$$
$$+ id_h \bullet DDHL_h + irt_f \bullet EXR \bullet FDHL_h + TRGH_h$$
$$+ EXR \bullet TRFH_h + TRHHR_h$$

$$(29) \quad QLEIS_h = QL0_h + \frac{mleis_h}{PLEIS_h}(FINC_h - PLEIS_h \bullet QL0_h)$$

(30) $LLEIS_{h,l} = QLEIS_h \cdot \alpha l_{h,l} \cdot \left(\dfrac{W_l}{PLEIS_h} \right)^{-\sigma_{lh}}$

(31) $HHINC_h = FINC_h - \sum\limits_l W_l \cdot (LED_{h,l} + LLEIS_{h,l})$

(32) $YDISP_h = HHINC_h - TRHHS_h - DIRTX_h$

(33) $EXP_h = (1 - ms_h)YDISP_h + \gamma_h WEALTH_h$

(34) $SAV_h = YDISP_h - EXP_h$

4. Enterprise current accounts

(35) $OS_e = \sum\limits_i PCAP_{i,e}$

(36) $DPROF_e = dpr_e \cdot OS_e$

(37) $DIRTX_e = dtx_e \cdot OS_e$

(38) $SAV_e = OS_e + INTR_e - INTP_e - DPROF_e - DIRTX_e + TRGE_e + TRFE_e$

(39) $INTR_f = id_f \cdot DDL_f$

(40) $INTP_f = \ln rtd_f CBLNL_f + EXR \cdot \ln rtf_f \cdot FLNL_f$

(41) $INTR_p = lurtdf_f \cdot CBLNL_f$

(42) $INTP_p = id_f DDL_f + EXR \cdot \ln rtf_p \cdot FLNL_p$

5. Investment and portfolio of non-household institutions

(43) $ID_{i,p} = \dfrac{PARINV_i}{PK_{i,p}}$

(44) $ID_{i,G} = \dfrac{GOVINV}{PK_G}, \qquad i = PUBA$

(45) $ID_{i,f} = CAPL_{i,f} \cdot GF_i \left(\dfrac{1 + \dfrac{PIK_{i,f}}{PK_{i,f}}}{1 + deprt_f + CSTKF} \right)^{\varepsilon_i}$

(46) $CSTKF = \dfrac{\ln rtd_f \cdot CBLNL_f + EXR \cdot \ln rtf_f \cdot FLNL_f}{CBLNL_f + FLNL_f}$

(47) $WCAP_e = awc_e \cdot \sum\limits_i P_i Q_{i,e}$

(48) $CURR_e = SHCUR_e \cdot WCAP_e$

(49) $DD_e = (1 - SHCUR_e)WCAP_e$

(50) $\quad SHCUR_e = \dfrac{acur_e}{acur_e + (1 - acur_e)\left(\dfrac{1 + id_e}{1 + \overline{id}_e}\right)^{\sigma_{wc,e} - 1}}$

(51) $\quad QL_e = \sum_i PK_{i,e}(CAPL_{i,e} + ID_{i,e}) + CURR_e + DD_e - SAV_e$

$\qquad\qquad - PEQTY_e \bullet EQTYN_e$

(52) $\quad CBLNN_e = PHICB_e \bullet QL_e$

(53) $\quad EXR \bullet FLNN_e = (1 - PHICB_e)QL_e$

(54) $\quad PHICB_e = \dfrac{acb_e\left(\dfrac{1 + \ln rtd_e}{1 + \ln \overline{rtd}_e}\right)^{1 - \sigma_{port,e}}}{acb_e\left(\dfrac{1 + \ln rtd_e}{1 + \ln \overline{rtd}_e}\right)^{1 - \sigma_{port,e}} + afb\left(\dfrac{1 + \ln rtf_e}{1 + \ln \overline{rtf}_e}\right)^{1 - \sigma_{port,e}}}$

(55) $\quad PEQTY_f \bullet EQTYN_f = \sum_h EQ_h$

(56) $\quad PEQTY_p \bullet EQTYN_p = PEQTY_p \bullet EQTYL_p + \Delta EQPARG$

(57) $\quad id_I = (1 + idn_I)\left(\dfrac{CPIL}{CPI}\right) - 1$

(58) $\quad \ln rtd_e = (1 + \ln rtdn_e)\left(\dfrac{CPIL}{CPI}\right) - 1$

(59) $\quad \ln rtf_e = (1 + \ln rtfn_e)\left(\dfrac{EXR}{EXRL}\right)\left(\dfrac{CPIL}{CPI}\right) - 1$

(60) $\quad PEQTY_e \bullet EQTYL_e = \sum_i PK_{i,e}CAPL_{i,e} + CURRL_e + DDL_e$

$\qquad\qquad + \sum_i P_i STKL_{i,e} - CBLNL_e - EXR \bullet FLNL_e$

(61) $\quad deprt_f = \dfrac{\sum_i PK_{i,f} \bullet CAPL_{i,f} \bullet deprt_i}{\sum_i PK_{i,f} \bullet CAPL_{i,f}}$

6. Household portfolio

(62) $\quad r_{h,hk} = \dfrac{PIKH_{h,hk}}{PKH_{hk}} - deprt_{hk}$

(63) $\quad rdf = (1 + irtf)\left(\dfrac{EXR}{EXRL}\right)\left(\dfrac{CPIL}{CPI}\right) - 1$

(64) $\quad req = \dfrac{OS_f}{PEQTY_f \bullet EQTYL_f} - deprt_f$

(65) $\quad rK_h = \dfrac{\sum\limits_{hk} r_{h,hk} PKH_{hk} \bullet HHKL_{h,hk}}{\sum\limits_{hk} PKH_{hk} \bullet HHKL_{h,hk}}$

(66) $\quad rF_h = \dfrac{id_h DDHL_h + rdf\, EXR \bullet FDHL_h + req\, SHEQL_h \bullet PEQTY_f \bullet EQTYL_f}{CURRHL_h + DDHL_h + EXR \bullet FDHL_h + SHEQL_h \bullet PEQTY_f \bullet EQTYL_f}$

(67) $\quad WEALTHN_h = WEALTH_h + SAV_h$

(68) $\quad WF_h = G_{lh} \bullet WEALTHN_h$

(69) $\quad WK_h = (1 - G_{lh})WEALTHN_h$

(70) $\quad G_{lh} = \dfrac{G_{2,h}}{1 + G_{2,h}}$

(71) $\quad G_{2,h} = \psi_h \left(\dfrac{1 + rK_h}{1 + \overline{rK}_h} \right)^{\varepsilon_h}$

(72) $\quad QK_h = \sum\limits_{hk} \bullet ahk_{h,hk} \left(\dfrac{1 + r_{h,hk}}{1 + \bar{r}_{h,hk}} \right)^{(\sigma_{K,h} - 1)}$

(73) $\quad QF_h = afcur + afdd \left(\dfrac{1 + id_H}{1 + \overline{id}_H} \right)^{\sigma_{F,h} - 1} + afdf \left(\dfrac{1 + rdf}{1 + \overline{rdf}} \right)^{\sigma_{F,h} - 1} + afeq \left(\dfrac{1 + req}{1 + \overline{req}} \right)^{\sigma_{F,h} - 1}$

(74) $\quad CURRH_h = \dfrac{afcur}{QF_h} WF_h$

(75) $\quad DDH_h = \dfrac{afdd \left(\dfrac{1 + id_H}{1 + \overline{id}_H} \right)^{\sigma_{F,h} - 1}}{QF_h} WF_h$

(76) $\quad EXR \bullet FDH_h = \dfrac{afdf \left(\dfrac{1 + rdf}{1 + \overline{rdf}} \right)^{\sigma_{F,h} - 1}}{QF_h} WF_h$

(77) $\quad EQH_h = \dfrac{afeq \left(\dfrac{1 + req}{1 + \overline{req}} \right)^{\sigma_{F,h} - 1}}{QF_h} WF_h$

(78) $\quad DESK_{h,hk} = \dfrac{ahk_{h,hk} \left(\dfrac{1 + r_{h,hk}}{1 + \bar{r}_{h,hk}} \right)^{\sigma_{K,h} - 1}}{QK_h} WK_h$

$$(79) \quad PHHK_{hk} = \frac{\sum_{h} DESK_{h,hk}}{\sum_{h} HHKL_{h,hk}}$$

$$(80) \quad PRCAPH_{hk} = \min(PK_{hk}, PHHK_{hk})$$

$$(81) \quad IDH_{h,hk} = \left(\frac{DESK_{h,hk}}{PRCAPH_{hk}}\right) - HHKL_{h,hk}$$

7. Demand for commodities

$$(82) \quad QDC_{i,h} = \overline{Q}F_{i,h} + \frac{MQ_{i,h}}{PRCH_i}\left(EXP_h - \sum_i PRCH_i \cdot \overline{Q}F_{i,h}\right)$$

$$(83) \quad INVOR_{i,I} = b_{i,I}\sum_j ID_{j,F}$$

$$(84) \quad INVOR_{i,H} = b_{i,H}\sum_{hk}\sum_h IDH_{h,hk}$$

$$(85) \quad DEMC_i = \sum_j a_{ij}\sum_I Q_{j,I} + \sum_h QDC_{i,h} \cdot POP_h + \sum_I INVOR_{i,I}$$
$$+ \frac{GEX_i}{PRC_i} + DSTK_i$$

$$(86) \quad DEMD_i = DEMC_i \cdot ad_i\left(\frac{P_i}{PRC_i}\right)^{-\sigma_{mi}}$$

$$(87) \quad DEMM_i = DEMC_i \cdot am_i\left(\frac{PM_i}{PRC_i}\right)^{-\sigma_{mi}}$$

$$(88) \quad EXP_i = \overline{EXP}_i\left(\frac{P_i}{EXR \cdot PEXW_i}\right)^{-\eta_i}$$

8. Government portfolio

$$(89) \quad GREV = \sum_I\sum_i P_i \cdot tind_{i,I}Q_{i,I} + EXR \cdot \sum_i PMW_i \cdot tar_i \cdot DEMM_i$$
$$+ \sum_i PRC_i \cdot taxc_i \cdot \sum_h POP_hQDC_h$$
$$+ \sum_i\sum_I PRC_i \cdot txinv_I \cdot INVOR_{i,I} + \sum_i (EXR \cdot PEXW_i - P_i)EXP_i$$
$$+ \sum_h DIRTX_h + \sum_e DIRTX_e + DPROF_p + EXR \cdot TRFG$$

(90) $\quad GEXP = \sum_i GEX_i + \sum_I \sum_i P_i subs_{i,I} Q_{i,I} + \sum_h TRGH_h$

$\qquad\qquad + \ln rtf_G \bullet EXR \bullet FLNL_G + \sum_e TRGE_e$

(91) $\quad SAV_G = GREV - GEXP$

(92) $\quad EXR \bullet \Delta FLN_G = GOVINV + \Delta EQPARG + \Delta CURR_G + \Delta DD_G - SAV_G$

$\qquad\qquad\qquad - \Delta BTLNG - \Delta CBLN_G$

9. Commercial bank portfolio

(93) $\quad CBABTN = cbrr\left(\sum_h DDH_h + \sum_I DD_I \right)$

(94) $\quad CBLNN_G = acb \ln g\left(\sum_h DDH_h + \sum_I DD_I \right)$

(95) $\quad CBNWL = \sum_I CBLNL_I + CBABTL + EXR(CBFAL - CBFLBL)$

$\qquad\qquad - \sum_I DDL_I - \sum_h DDHL_h - BTLNBL$

(96) $\quad BTLNBN = \sum_I CBLNN_I + EXR(CBFA - CBFLB) - \sum_h DDH_h$

$\qquad\qquad - \sum_I DD_I - SAV_{GB} - CBNWL$

10. Bank of Tanzania portfolio

(97) $\quad BTNWL = BTLNGL + BTLNBL + EXR(BTFAL - BTFLBL)$

$\qquad\qquad - \sum_h CURRHL_h - \sum_I CURRL_I - CBABTL$

(98) $\quad BTLNGN = BTNWL + SAV_{BOT} + \sum_h CURRH_h + \sum_i CURR_I$

$\qquad\qquad + GBABT + EXR(BTFLB - BTFA) - BTLNB$

11. Foreign sector

(99) $\quad SAV_{FOR} = EXR\left(\sum_i PMW_i \bullet DEMM_i + \sum_I \ln rtf_I \bullet FLNL_I - \sum_i PEXW_i \bullet EXP_i \right.$

$\qquad\qquad \left. - \sum_h TRFH_h - TRFG - \sum_h irt_f \bullet FDHL_h - \sum_e TRFE_e \right)$

12. Excess demands

$$(100) \quad \sum_h \left(LAV_{h,l} - LED_{h,l} - LLEIS_{h,l} \right) = \sum_I \sum_i LAB_{l,i,I}$$

$$(101) \quad DEMD_i = \sum_I Q_{i,I}$$

$$(102) \quad SAV_{FOR} + EXR \left(\sum_h \Delta FDH_h + \Delta BTFA + \Delta CBFA \right)$$

$$= EXR \left(\sum_I \Delta FLN_I + \Delta BTFLB + \Delta CBFLB \right)$$

1. Price variables

P_i	Domestic production price of commodity i
EXR	Exchange rate
PMW_i	World price of import i
PM_i	Domestic price of import i
PRC_i	Domestic purchase prices for composite product i
$PEF_{i,I}$	Effective producer price for commodity i produced by institution I
$PLEIS_h$	Price of composite leisure for household h
$PRCH_i$	Domestic purchase price for private consumption of commodity i
W_{lc}	Wage of skill class lc
$WC_{i,I}$	Composite wage index in sector i, institution I
$PIN_{i,I}$	Purchase price for investment good i by institution I
$PEQTY_e$	Current period price of equity of enterprise e (e = firms, parastatals)
$PK_{i,I}$	Current period purchase price for new capital of sector i, when purchased by institution I
PKH_{hk}	Current period purchase price for new household capital type hk

2. Production variables

$Q_{i,I}$	Production of commodity by sector i and institution I
$VAD_{i,I}$	Value added in sector i, institution I
$LABC_{i,I}$	Composite labor demanded in sector i, institution I
$LAB_{lc,i,I}$	Demand for labor type lc, in sector i, institution I
$PIK_{i,I}$	Return to a unit of employed capital in sector i, institution I
$PCAP_{i,I}$	Total payments to employed capital in sector i, institution I
$INDXGL_i$	Index of the exogenous growth of public labor in sector i
$CAPL_{i,I}$	Initial (end of last period) amount of capital employed in sector i, institution I

3. Household production and income variables

$HHKL_{h,hk}$	Initial ownership of household capital type hk ($hk = LAND$, ANM, UC) by household h
$CRCAP_{h,i}$	Amount of crop capital devoted to crop i, by household h
$UCAP_{h,i}$	Amount of unincorporated capital devoted to product of sector i by household h
$PIKH_{h,hk}$	Average return per unit of household capital type hk, for household h
$WEALTH_h$	Current period value of assets held by household h at the end of the previous period
$LED_{h,lc}$	Amount of household labor type lc devoted to education by household h
$LAV_{h,lc}$	Total available labor of type lc in household h
$FINC_h$	Full household income of household h
$SHEQL_h$	Share of privated firm equity owned by household h at the end of previous period
$EQTYL_e$	Outstanding amount of equity of enterprise e at end of previous period
$PRCAPH_{hk}$	Actual market price of household capital of type hk
$DPROF_e$	Distributed profits of enterprise e
$DDHL_h$	Lagged household domestic bank deposits
$CURRHL_h$	Lagged household domestic currency holdings
$FDHL_h$	Lagged household foreign deposits
$TRGH_h$	Transfers from government to household h
$TRFH_h$	Transfers from abroad to household h
$TRHHR$, $TRHHS$	Inter-household transfers received ($TRHHR_h$) or sent ($TRHHS_h$)
$QLEIS_h$	Quantity of composite leisure for household h
$LLEIS_{h,lc}$	Quantity of labor type lc, devoted to leisure by household type h
$HHINC_h$	Monetary household income of household h
$YDISP_h$	Disposable household income of household h
EXP_h	Household current expenditures by household h
SAV_h	Household savings of household type h

4. Enterprise current accounts variables

OS_e	Operating surplus of enterprise e
$DPRPOF_e$	Distributed profit of enterprise e
$DIRTXe$	Direct taxes of enterprise e
SAV_e	Current savings of enterprise e
$INTR_e$	Interest received by enterprise e
$INTP_e$	Interest paid by enterprise e
$TRGE_e$	Transfers from government to enterprise e
$TRFE_e$	Transfers from abroad to enterprise e

5. Investment and portfolio of non-household institutions variables

$ID_{i,I}$	Investment by destination of institution I in sector i
$CSTKF$	Private firm cost of capital
$CBLNL_I$	Outstanding (lagged) domestic commercial bank loans to institution I
$FLNL_I$	Outstanding foreign loans to institution I
$PARINV_i$	Parastatal investment expenditures in sector i
$GOVINV$	Public investment expenditure
$WCAP_e$	Working capital requirements of enterprise e
id_I	Domestic real deposit rate for institution I
$CURR_e$	Stock of currency held at the end of current period by enterprise e
DD_I	Domestic commercial bank deposits held by institution I at the end of the current period
$SHCUR_e$	Share of working capital held as cash at end of current period by enterprise e
QL_e	Requirements for current total bank (domestic and foreign) financing of enterprise e
$CBLNN_e$	Total domestic commercial bank loans to enterprise e at end of current period
$FLNN_e$	Total foreign loans to enterprise e at end of current period
$EQTYN_e$	Total stock of enterprise e equity at end of current period
$PHICB_e$	Share of loan needs of enterprise e provided by domestic banks
$lnrtd_e$	Effective real domestic loan rate to enterprise e
$lnrtf_e$	Effective real foreign loan rate to enterprise e
$EQTYL_e$	Lagged stock of enterprise e equity
$CURRL_I$	Lagged stock of institution I currency holdings
DDL_I	Lagged stock of institution I domestic deposits with commercial bank
$CBLNL_I$	Lagged stock of institution I loans from domestic commercial banks
$FLNL_I$	Lagged stock of institution I foreign loans
$STKL_{i,e}$	End of previous period stock of commodity i in enterprise e
$CPI(L)$	Aggregate consumer price index (lagged)

6. Household portfolio variables

$r_{h,hk}$	Real return to household capital type hk for household h
rdf	Real return to foreign deposits
req	Return to firm equity
rK_h	Average return to household physical capital for household h
rF_h	Average return to household financial capital for household h
$WEALTHN_h$	Value of new wealth of household h
WF_h	Amount of new wealth of household h held in financial assets
WK_h	Amount of new wealth of household h held in physical capital
G_{2h}	Allocation parameter between financial and non-financial wealth of household h

G_{1h}	Share of wealth of household h held in financial assets
QK_h	Index of aggregation for physical capital of household h
QF_h	Index of aggregation for financial capital of household h
$CURRH_h$	New stock of currency held by household h
DDH_h	New stock of domestic bank deposits held by household h
FDH_h	New stock of foreign deposits held by household h
EQH_h	Desired value of private firm equity held by household h
$DESK_{h,hk}$	Desired value of household h wealth invested in physical capital type hk
$PHHK_{hk}$	Ratio of desired wealth of household h invested in physical capital type hk to the outstanding total stock of household capital type hk
$PRCAPH_{hk}$	Actual market price of household capital of type hk
$IDH_{h,hk}$	Actual investment of household h in physical capital of type hk

7. Demand for commodities variables

$QDC_{i,h}$	Per capita private consumption of composite commodity i by household h
$INVOR_{i,I}$	Demand of commodity i for investments of institution I
$INVOR_{i,H}$	Investment demanded by origin for sector i for household new capital
$DEMC_i$	Total domestic demand for composite commodity i
POP_h	Current population of household type h
$DEMD_i$	Demand for the domestic good i
$DEMM_i$	Demand for competitive differentiated imports of good i
EXP_i	Demand for exports of good i

8. Government portfolio variables

$GREV$	Government current revenue
$TRFG$	Foreign current transfers to government
$GEXP$	Government current expenditures
SAV_G	Government savings
$\Delta FLNG$	Change in outstanding foreign loans of government
$\Delta EQPARG$	Change in government financing of parastatal equity
$\Delta CURR_G$	Change in currency holdings of government (deposits with BOT)
ΔDD_G	Change in commercial bank deposits of government
$\Delta BTLNG$	Change in BOT loans to government
$CBLN_G$	Change in commercial bank loans to government

9. Commercial bank portfolio variables

$CBABTN$	New total commercial bank assets with BOT (required reserves)
$CBLNN_I$	New total commercial bank loans to institutions

BTLNBN	New total BOT loans to commercial banks
SAV_{CB}	Net savings of commercial banks
CBNWL	Current period value of previous period assets of commercial banks (current value of lagged net worth)
CBFA(L)	End of current period commercial bank foreign assets (lagged)
CBFLB(L)	End of current period commercial bank foreign liabilities (lagged)

10. Bank of Tanzania portfolio variables

BTNWL	Current period value of previous period assets of BOT (current value of lagged net worth)
BTLNGN	New total outstanding BOT loans to government
BTFA(L)	End of current period BOT foreign assets (lagged)
BTFLB(L)	End of current period BOT foreign liabilities (lagged)

11. Foreign sector variables

SAV_{FOR}	Foreign savings

References

Beaudry, P. and N.K. Sowa. 1990. "Labor Markets in an Era of Adjustment: A Case Study of Ghana," Boston University, mimeographed, May.

Bevan, D., P. Collier, and J.W. Gunning, with A. Bigsten and P. Horsnell. 1989. *Peasants and Governments: An Economic Analysis*. Oxford: Clarendon Press.

Bourguignon, F., W.H. Branson, and J. de Melo. 1989. *Macroeconomic Adjustment and Income Distribution: A Macro-Micro Simulation Model*, OECD Development Centre, Technical Papers, No. 1, Paris, March.

Dervis, K., J. de Melo, and S. Robinson. 1982. *General Equilibrium Models for Development Policy*. Cambridge: Cambridge University Press.

Horton, S., R. Kanbur, and D. Mazumdar. 1991. *Labor Markets in an Era of Adjustment: An Overview*. Policy Research and External Affairs Working Papers No. 694. Washington DC: World Bank.

Maliyamkono, T.L., and M.S.D. Bagachwa. 1990. *The Second Economy in Tanzania*. London: James Currey.

Pyatt, G., and J. Round. 1979. "Social Accounting Matrices for Development Planning". *Review of Income and Wealth*, Series 23, No. 4.

Rosensweig, J.A., and L. Taylor. 1990. "Devaluation, Capital Flows, and Crowding-out: A CGE Model with Portfolio Choice for Thailand," in L. Taylor (ed.), *Socially Relevant Policy Analysis*. Cambridge, Mass.: MIT Press.

Rutayisire, L., and R. Vos. 1991. *A SAM for Tanzania*, Institute of Social Studies, Finance and Development Research Programme, Working Paper, Sub-Series on Money, Finance and Development, No. 39, September.

Sarris, A.H. 1994a. *Macroeconomic Policies and Household Welfare: A Dynamic Computable General Equilibrium Analysis for Tanzania*, Cornell University Food and Nutrition Policy Program, Working Paper No. 68. Forthcoming.

—— 1994b. *A Social Accounting Matrix for Tanzania*, Cornell University Food and Nutrition Policy Program, Working Paper No. 62.

—— and R. Van den Brink. 1993. *Economic Policy and Household Welfare during Crisis and Adjustment in Tanzania*. New York: New York University Press.

Taylor, L. 1983. *Structuralist Macroeconomies: Applicable Models for the Third World*. New York, Basic Books.

Thorbecke, E., with R. Downey, S. Kennig, B. Kim, D. Roland-Holst, D. Berrian, and the Center for World Food Studies. 1992. "Adjustment and Equity in Indonesia." OECD Development Centre. Paris.

5

Terms of Trade and the Real Exchange Rate in the CFA Zone: Implications for Income Distribution in Niger

Paul Dorosh, B. Essama-Nssah, and Ousmane Samba-Mamadou

5.1. *Introduction*

Dependence on primary commodity exports characterizes the economies of a number of countries in sub-Saharan Africa. During most of the 1970s, when commodity prices reached historic highs, real incomes rose along with exports in Cote d'Ivoire (cocoa and coffee), Cameroon (petroleum) and Guinea (bauxite). Subsequent reversals in the terms of trade contributed to balance of payments crises and led to the adoption of stabilization and structural adjustment measures. For Niger, a sharp increase in both the volume and price of uranium exports in the 1970s spurred an economic boom. Subsequent declines in uranium earnings in the early 1980s, combined with drought and macroeconomic reforms in Niger's large neighbor to the south, Nigeria, reduced foreign exchange earnings, real incomes, and the stock of wealth.

Structural adjustment measures in Niger in the 1980s involved a combination of efforts to reduce government budget deficits, limit bank credits to the domestic economy, decontrol prices, and liberalize agricultural markets. Exchange rate devaluation, a central aspect of the adjustment process in most countries of sub-Saharan Africa, was not an option in Niger, a member of the CFA (Communauté Financière Africaine) zone.[1] Nevertheless, movements in the real exchange rate, both *vis à vis* Niger's trading partners in officially recorded trade and *vis à vis* Nigeria, played an important part in determining economic incentives throughout the economy and the distribution of income.

In this chapter, we analyze the impacts of changes in external conditions

---

[1] The value of the CFA franc was fixed at 50 CFAF per French franc until the devaluation of January 1994.

and government policies on real incomes of various household groups in Niger using a computable general equilibrium (CGE) model. After a brief overview of major developments in Niger's economy in the 1970s and 1980s, we describe the CGE model and the data base. A set of six simulations follow, focusing on the effects of the decline in uranium revenues that occurred between 1987 and 1990, the impacts of government policy, and the role of real exchange rate movements in influencing income distribution in Niger. The concluding section discusses implications of real exchange rate movements in light of the debate surrounding a possible devaluation of the CFA franc.

5.2. *Structural Adjustment in Niger*

Niger is one of the poorest members of the CFA zone, having a per capita income of only US$300 (1991) per person (World Bank 1993). More than two-thirds of the country is located in the Sahara desert of West Africa. Ninety percent of its population of 7.25 million live in a narrow band along the Niger river in the southwest corner of the country or within 150 kilometers of the country's southern border with Nigeria.

Although the country has important mineral resources, in particular uranium, the economy remains dominated by agricultural and livestock activities, which produced 35 percent of GDP in 1987. Millet and sorghum are the major food staples, accounting for 80 percent of area cultivated in 1989. Livestock, cowpeas, and onions are exported (mainly to Nigeria). The share of the mining and industrial sector is small—only 15 percent (Table 5.1).[2]

Formal sector enterprises (those registered for tax purposes by completing a *declaration statistique et fiscale* (DSF)), dominate the mining, energy, industry, modern construction, and transport and communications sectors. Informal sector activities (mainly agriculture, livestock, trade) account for more than two-thirds of GDP.

During the 1980s, Niger experienced an economic crisis largely as a result of four external shocks: a fall in uranium export revenues, reduced foreign capital inflows, drought, and adverse effects of economic fluctuations in neighboring Nigeria.

The expansion of world demand for uranium in the 1970s, linked to the steep rise in petroleum prices in these years, boosted uranium prices and exports for Niger. The value of Niger's uranium exports increased from 2.0 billion CFAF in 1971 to 100.8 billion CFAF in 1980, when they accounted for 74 percent of Niger's export revenues. With additional uranium

---

[2] For more detailed discussion of the Nigerien economy, see Dorosh (1990), Jabara (1991), SEDES (1987, 1988), and Horowitz et al. (1983).

Table 5.1. Niger: production activities in the Niger SAM

SAM subsector	National accounts subsector	Production (bn FCFA)	Value added (bn FCAF)	Value added (%)
Grains	11	70,932	64,211	9.8
Export crops	11	23,821	18,314	2.8
Other crops	11	56,835	53,157	8.1
Livestock	12	84,772	83,441	12.7
Forestry, fish	13	23,384	22,319	3.4
Mining[a]	21	91,194	43,948	6.7
Meat processing	31	63,935	9,487	1.4
Food processing	31	17,189	7,048	1.1
Formal		10,279	3,573	0.5
Informal		6,910	3,475	0.5
Manufacturing	32–39, 41–42	84,553	41,413	6.3
Formal		56,880	22,262	3.4
Informal		27,673	19,151	2.9
Construction	51, 52	55,835	20,674	3.2
Formal		37,303	14,583	2.2
Informal		18,532	6,091	0.9
Trade	61	165,827	123,781	18.9
Formal		31,179	18,926	2.9
Informal		134,648	104,855	16.0
Transportation/ communication	63, 71, 72	56,602	34,169	5.2
Formal		25,099	16,392	2.5
Informal		31,503	17,777	2.7
Private services	81, 83, 94,	76,920	58,928	9.0
Formal	95	16,576	10.745	1.6
Informal	91, 96	60,344	48,183	7.4
Public services		106,291	73,962	11.3
Total		**968,089**	**654,852**	**100.0**
Primary sectors		259,744	241,443	36.9
Formal industry[b]		158,353	69,783	10.7
Informal industry[c]		88,518	32,113	4.9
Formal services		110,157	60,646	9.3
Informal services		245,026	176,905	27.0
Public services		106,291	73,962	11.3
Total		**968,089**	**654,854**	**100.0**

[a] Mining and meat processing subsectors include both formal and informal activities.
[b] Formal industry figures include informal mining activities.
[c] Informal industry includes formal meat processing activities.

Source: Dorosh and Essama-Nssah (1991).

revenues as collateral, the government of Niger (and parastatals) were able to borrow heavily on world markets, greatly increasing foreign capital inflows into Niger and spurring domestic investment. From 1978 to 1980, the modern sector's share of GDP rose rapidly from 15 to 25 percent.

During the 1980s, however, world supply of uranium grew faster than a stagnating demand. Niger's export receipts fell as quantities exported declined between 1981 and 1985. And beginning in 1987, Niger's contract price, negotiated with French importers, also dropped from 38,800 CFAF per kilogram in 1987 to 25,000 in 1989 and 20,400 in 1990 (Hugon 1990). Niger's uranium export earnings fell from a peak of 110.0 billion CFAF in 1983 to only 50.3 billion CFAF in 1992, a decline equivalent to 9.0 percent of GDP in 1992.

A stabilization program beginning in 1984 succeeded in sharply reducing imports, so that, with the exception of the drought year of 1984/85, Niger's merchandise trade deficit averaged only 1.4 percent of GDP from 1984 to 1987. Between 1987 and 1992, however, export earnings fell more rapidly than imports and the merchandise trade deficit reached 5.0 percent of GDP (Table 5.2).

The poor performance of the uranium sector also contributed to Niger's fiscal problems through reductions in royalties, income taxes, and export duty. Fiscal revenues from the uranium sector declined from 9.8 billion CFAF in 1987 to 6.2 billion CFAF in 1990. The major explanation for the 23.6 billion CFAF increase in the government deficit between 1987 and 1990, however, was a 27.6 percent (17.2 billion CFAF) increase in government expenditures (Figure 5.1). More recently, political turmoil limited tax collection in 1991, and with central bank credit to the government near the statutory limits on borrowing, the government resorted to arrears on both domestic payments to government workers and suppliers, and external obligations.

Related to the drop in uranium revenues and the drop in world uranium prices was a decline in foreign capital inflows in the 1980s. Until 1975 Niger's foreign debt was fairly small, although from 1970 to 1975 public and publicly guaranteed debt increased from 5 to 12 percent of GNP. Beginning in 1976, Niger used rising export revenues as collateral to greatly increase foreign borrowing, much of it from commercial banks. After 1981, Niger's ability to obtain credit on world markets declined together with the large fall in world uranium prices, and net transfers fell. Counting foreign grants, net transfers declined from 10.6 percent of GDP in 1981 to 0.3 percent in 1982. The grant component of these transfers fell as well, from 50.2 to 20.9 percent of budgetary receipts.

Climatic conditions were also disastrous. During the decade of the 1980s, rainfall was satisfactory only in 1986 and 1990; 1984 and 1987 were both drought years. The drought in 1984 was especially severe, causing large declines in the livestock herd and crop production. Food production per

Table 5.2. Niger: macroeconomic trends, 1985–1991

	1985	1986	1987	1988	1989	1990	1991
Uranium exports							
Unit value (m CFA/MT)	30.0	30.0	29.3	27.6	25.0	20.4	19.0
Quantity (metric tons)	3042	3026	2948	2966	2967	2964	2960
Value (bn CFA francs)	91.3	90.8	86.4	81.9	74.2	60.5	56.2
Uranium fiscal revenues (bn FCFA)	10.8	9.3	9.8	9.4	8.3	6.2	7.2
Total exports G&NFS (bn CFA)	135.7	130.9	139.1	140.5	129.1	114.5	114.5
Total imports G&NFS (bn CFA)	195	166.5	156.4	148.6	151.1	142.4	119.2
Trade deficit (bn CFA)	59.3	25.6	17.3	8.1	22	27.9	4.7
Trade deficit/GDP (%)	9.2	5.4	2.6	1.2	3.2	4.1	0.7
Real GDP (bn 1987 CFA francs)	665.5	695.9	671.1	708.7	709.7	696.9	710.2
Consumer price index (1985=100)	100	96.8	90.3	89	86.5	85.8	79.1
Nominal exchange rate (FCFA/$)	449.26	346.3	300.54	297.85	319.01	272.26	282.11
Real exchange rate index (1980=100)	83.9	79	71.8	67.7	62.8	62.1	54.2
Naira index (1980=100)	135.9	184.8	187.1	205.2	183.8	213.9	251.8

Sources: IMF (1992a, 1992b) and Dorosh (1994).

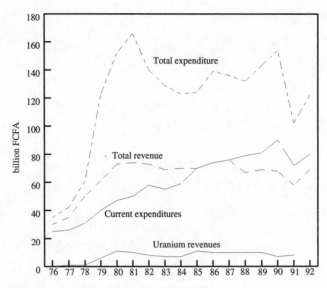

Fig. 5.1. Niger, government budget, 1976–1992
Source: International Monetary Fund (1992a, 1992b).

capita fell 22 percent in 1984, but recovered in subsequent years of higher rainfall. The effects on livestock were more long-lasting: the cattle population fell 40 percent in 1984 and continued to decline until 1986, when it was 59 percent below 1983 levels.

Finally, economic policies and economic conditions in Nigeria, Niger's neighbor to the south, with an economy nearly ten times as large, had large negative impacts on Niger. Niger's overall real exchange *vis à vis* its major trading partners, as calculated by the IMF, actually *depreciated* by 41.5 percent between 1980 and 1990, in part because of Niger's very low rate of price inflation over the period. Yet, the CFA franc *appreciated* by 113.9 percent relative to the Nigerian naira on the parallel market during the 1980s as Nigeria undertook macroeconomic reforms and devalued its currency. This movement in the bilateral real exchange rate with Nigeria diminished the profitability of Niger's exports to Nigeria and encouraged imports from Nigeria, to the detriment of Niger's domestic industries and rural producers of livestock, cowpeas, and onions. Declining real incomes in Nigeria during the 1980s also reduced demand for Niger's export products. Niger's parallel market exports of textiles to Nigeria fell by an estimated 60 percent between the early 1980s and 1989 (Ministère du Plan 1991).

5.3. *Model Specifications*

The CGE model for Niger (Dorosh and Essama-Nssah 1993) is a standard neo-classical CGE model following Dervis, de Melo, and Robinson (1982). The basic structure of the CGE model is reflected in the underlying data base, a social accounting matrix (SAM), derived from the 1987 national accounts and household survey data.[3]

Twenty activities producing 14 commodities are modeled (see Table 5.1). This level of disaggregation reflects important differences in technologies between the formal and informal sectors and the importance of certain traded goods in the economy (e.g. uranium and cowpeas). For a number of industrial goods and various services, two separate production technologies (for formal and informal sectors) are modeled, each producing the same commodity output. Thus, for these commodities the output of the corresponding formal sector activity is treated as a perfect substitute for the production of that same commodity by the informal sector.

The model includes eight primary factors of production: skilled and unskilled labor, formal and informal capital, and four types of agricultural capital (corresponding to the total value of the land, livestock, and implements of each of four rural household groups (rural north poor and non-poor, and rural south poor and non-poor). Ownership of cattle is used to distinguish poor and non-poor households in rural areas and the 400 mm rainfall isohyet demarcates north and south. Three urban household types (urban non-poor, urban poor, and semi-urban[4]) and three other institutions (formal enterprises, informal enterprises, and the government) are also included in the model. Per capita income of urban non-poor households is 2.6 times that of the urban poor (Table 5.3). In all, the rural poor account for 51.4 percent of total population; the urban poor comprise only 6.4 percent.

Domestic production (value added) of each good is modeled as a constant elasticity of substitution (CES) function of land, labor, and capital; quantities of intermediate inputs are assumed to be fixed shares of the quantity of output produced. Profit maximization determines demand for skilled and unskilled labor[5] by each activity, and real wages adjust to clear the labor market. In the comparative static simulations presented, labor supply is fixed.[6] Elasticities of substitution between capital and labor are

---

[3] Details of the construction of the SAM are found in Dorosh and Essama-Nssah (1991).

[4] Semi-urban households are defined as those residing in cities with a 1988 population less than 50,000.

[5] Skilled labor is defined as urban workers employed as military personnel, administrative staff, specialists, scientific personnel, and office employees, using data from the population census of 1987 (see Dorosh and Nssah 1991).

[6] This differs from Dorosh and Nssah (1993), where labor supply is a positive function of the real wage.

Table 5.3. Niger: revenue shares by household, 1987

	Urban non-poor	Urban poor	Semi-urban	Rural North non-poor	Rural North poor	Rural South non-poor	Rural South poor
Factor income shares							
Skilled labor	0.769	0.000	0.000	0.000	0.000	0.000	0.000
Unskilled labor	0.057	0.499	0.746	0.375	0.884	0.639	0.881
Informal capital	0.174	0.481	0.218	0.458	0.057	0.229	0.031
Land: North non-poor	0.000	0.007	0.012	0.167	0.000	0.000	0.000
Land: North poor	0.000	0.003	0.006	0.000	0.059	0.131	0.000
Land: South non-poor	0.000	0.007	0.013	0.000	0.000	0.000	0.000
Land: South poor	0.000	0.003	0.005	0.000	0.000	0.000	0.088
Total	1.000	1.000	1.000	1.000	1.000	1.000	1.000
Population							
('000)	228.0	451.5	344.3	729.6	2188.8	1660.1	1414.2
(% of total)	3.2	6.4	4.9	10.4	31.2	23.7	20.2
Total income							
(m FCFA)	94.5	72.2	20.6	84.3	107.3	112.6	69.6
(% of total)	16.8	12.9	3.7	15.0	19.1	20.1	12.4
Per capita income (FCFA/person)	414.5	159.9	59.8	115.5	49	67.8	49.2

Source: Dorosh and Nssah (1991).

chosen to correspond with guesstimates of magnitudes for elasticities of supply, equal to 1.0 for agricultural activities, 0.1 for mining, and 0.5 for most other sectors of the economy.[7]

Both imports and exports are assumed to be less than perfect substitutes for domestic goods. For each imported commodity, we use a constant elasticity of substitution (CES) aggregation function to define the composite of imports and domestically produced goods (Armington 1969). For export commodities, a constant elasticity of transformation (CET) aggregation is used to define a composite commodity of export goods and goods produced for domestic consumption. Appendix Table 5A.1 gives elasticities of substitution and levels of trade and domestic production for the commodities in the model. Niger is assumed to be a price taker for imports. For exports, the price elasticity of world demand (in large part from Nigeria) is 4.0.

Household incomes are determined as the sum of earnings from factors of production owned by the household (Table 5.3). In simulation 2, where foreign exchange is rationed, rents accrue to urban non-poor households and consumers pay an implicit tariff on imported goods. By definition, earnings of skilled labor accrue solely to urban non-poor households. Formal enterprises receive returns to formal sector capital. Incomes of the poor derive from unskilled labor, informal sector capital, and land; by definition, the rural poor own no livestock. Consumption of each commodity is a fixed share of total expenditures for each household group (Table 5A.2). Savings is a linear function of income.

Government recurrent and investment expenditures are fixed in real terms. Savings determines the level of private investment. The value of private (public) investment by sector of destination j is assumed to be a fixed share of total fixed private (public) investment, and the composition of capital by activity is likewise fixed.

In all commodity markets, prices adjust to equate supply and demand. Labor markets also clear through adjustment in real wages. Savings determines private investment given fixed values of real government investment and government expenditure. With the nominal exchange rate and foreign savings fixed exogenously, changes in the aggregate price index bring about movements in the real exchange rate and equilibrium in the Rest of World accounts.

The model solves for a sequence of solutions to the static model by updating capital stock according to the previous period's net investment by sector. Labor supply is also increased exogenously by a constant population growth rate.

---

[7] The livestock sector is modeled with an elasticity of substitution of 1.0 to allow greater flexibility in simulating reduction of capital stock resulting from drought (see Dorosh and Essama-Nssah 1993).

5.4. *Simulation Results*

Six simulations, analyzing various aspects of real exchange rate adjustment and fiscal policy, are presented. In each simulation, revenues from uranium exports are lowered by 25.9 billion CFAF (equal to 3.9 percent of GDP in 1987), reflecting the fall in uranium export revenues from 1987 to 1990. Given that the quantity of uranium exports remained essentially unchanged over this period, we model the loss in revenues as an exogenous decline in capital inflows. Real government expenditures are held fixed, unless otherwise noted. Total investment in the economy (private and government) is determined by the level of total savings (private, public, and foreign). With no changes in trade or fiscal policy, adjustment in the real exchange rate restores the external balance to its initial level.[8]

The first three simulations focus on the size and consequences of a real exchange rate depreciation to restore external equilibrium. Simulation 1 models the effects of the real exchange rate depreciation required with no changes in fiscal or trade policies. The major policy alternative to real exchange rate depreciation, rationing of foreign exchange, is modeled in simulation 2.[9] Simulation 3 highlights the role of Nigeria's economic policies for real exchange rate adjustment in Niger. Here it is assumed that exchange rate policy in Nigeria keeps the real exchange rate between the CFA franc and the Naira unchanged from its base level; changes in the real exchange rate between Niger and its other trading partners equilibrate the external accounts.

Simulations 4–6 show the impact of alternative fiscal policies. In simulation 4, government recurrent expenditures are reduced to offset the negative impact of the fall in uranium revenues on the government budget deficit. Simulation 5 models the effects of increased income taxes on urban households, again designed to restore the budget deficit to its original level. Finally, simulation 6 shows the effects of an increase in government recurrent expenditures, a scenario not unlike actual government policy in the late 1980s.

5.4.1. *Real exchange adjustment to a terms-of-trade shock*

In the absence of any fiscal or trade policy interventions (simulation 1),

---

[8] Note that in this non-monetary model only relative prices are determined. In the Niger model, we do not distinguish between a real exchange depreciation resulting from a devaluation with a fixed domestic price level and one resulting from a deflation of domestic prices with a fixed exchange rate. Fixing another price (such as the real wage rate) in addition to either the nominal exchange rate or the domestic price level would permit a distinction between nominal exchange rate devaluation and real depreciation with a fixed exchange rate (see Devarajan and de Melo 1987b).

[9] In the CFA zone, effective rationing of foreign exchange can take place through import licensing restrictions (Nash 1993) or through cutbacks in bank credit that fall largely on public enterprises with heavy propensities to import.

lower uranium export earnings lead to lower incomes and reduced spending on domestic goods so that the price of non-tradable goods falls relative to tradable goods (whose prices are linked to world market prices). The real exchange rate depreciates by 9.7 percent in year 1 of the simulation (the relative price of tradables *vis à vis* non-tradables rises), helping to reduce import demand and spur non-uranium exports (Table 5.4).[10] Imports decline by 9.9 percent and exports of cowpeas and livestock rise by 10.8 and 17.3 percent, respectively.

In addition to forcing a depreciation of the real exchange rate, the decline in uranium revenues also affects the macroeconomy by directly lowering incomes and total savings. Total investment falls by 23.2 percent because of the reduced pool of savings, lowering demand for construction services and investment goods. With government investment assumed fixed in real terms, private investment falls by 58.8 percent.

Urban households suffer most in this scenario. Wages for skilled labor fall by 5.4 percent as the construction sector, a large employer of skilled labor, declines by 8.9 percent. Since skilled labor accounts for 77 percent of non-transfer income for urban non-poor households, the decline in wage payments reduces their incomes by 4.1 percent (Table 5.5). The impact of higher relative prices for tradable goods (which comprise a larger budget share for urban households than for rural households) raises the consumer price index (CPI) for the urban non-poor by 1.6 percent more than the national CPI, so that their total decline in real incomes is 6.5 percent. Similarly, a rise in consumer prices contributes to the 4.8 percent reduction in real incomes of the urban poor.

The depreciation of the real exchange rate helps mitigate the adverse effects of the decline in uranium revenues by raising real prices of agricultural tradables such as cowpeas, whose production increases by 6.6 percent. The rural poor experience the smallest percentage declines in real income (2.0–2.3 percent) since returns to agricultural land rise with the real exchange rate depreciation. Returns to livestock fall, however, as lower private investment demand for livestock partially offsets the benefits of higher real prices for livestock exports. As a result, returns to agricultural capital (including both land and livestock) decline or increase only slightly for owners of cattle (the rural non-poor households).

Thus, although the effects of the decline in uranium prices are felt throughout the economy, urban households are most severely affected. Rural households suffer less because the real exchange rate depreciation helps boost earnings from agricultural production.

---

[10] Results from year 5 of each of the simulations are given in Table 5A.3 and do not vary qualitatively from those discussed in the text. For simulation 1, the real exchange rate depreciation in year 5, relative to the reference run with no decline in uranium revenues, is 10.1 percent.

Table 5.4. Effects of a terms-of-trade shock: Niger simulation results

	(1) Full RER adjustment	(2) Import quotas	(3) Naira depreciation	(4) Reduced public spending	(5) Increased taxes	(6) Increased public spending
Real GDP	-1.82	-1.70	-1.97	-1.85	-1.81	-1.81
Consumption	-2.80	-1.56	-3.65	-3.08	-3.27	-2.30
Total investment	-23.19	-31.69	-18.10	-19.77	-20.42	-30.60
Private investment	-58.81	-80.37	-45.92	-50.15	-51.80	-64.56
Public investment	0.00	0.00	0.00	0.00	0.00	-8.50
Government consumption	0.00	0.00	0.00	-2.16	0.00	5.00
Government revenues	-8.48	-6.43	-7.81	-8.49	-4.38	-8.53
Real exchange rate	9.73	0.00	14.90	9.93	9.77	9.27
Exports (dollars)	-13.25	-16.07	-17.41	-13.14	-13.31	-13.56
Imports (dollars)	-9.91	-12.02	-13.02	-9.83	-9.96	-10.14
Foreign savings/GDP	-3.94	-3.94	-3.94	-3.94	-3.94	-3.94
Real output growth						
Cereals	1.10	2.50	1.50	0.99	0.90	1.23
Export crops	6.59	3.36	2.36	6.65	6.54	6.42
Other food crops	0.51	1.21	0.87	0.40	0.34	0.66
Livestock	-1.28	-3.33	-1.92	-0.70	-0.90	-1.67
Fish, forestry	-1.66	-0.70	-0.67	-1.62	-1.61	-2.84
Mining	1.61	0.10	2.27	1.81	1.62	1.23
Meat processing	0.99	3.89	0.78	0.60	0.51	1.44

Other food processing	0.10	0.15	0.28	0.20	-0.12	-0.17
Manufacturing	-0.36	-0.65	0.63	0.04	-0.43	-1.27
Construction	-8.85	-12.00	-6.86	-7.54	-7.82	-16.16
Commerce	0.16	0.54	0.17	0.36	0.15	-0.18
Transport	-0.56	-0.76	-0.70	-0.60	-0.63	-0.46
Private services	-0.93	0.18	-1.01	-0.92	-1.11	-1.12
Public administration	-0.03	0.07	-0.04	-2.15	-0.05	4.87
Factor incomes						
Unskilled labor	-3.00	-5.97	-4.19	-3.10	-2.91	-2.72
Formal capital	2.73	-12.32	9.10	4.19	3.05	-1.11
Informal capital	-3.98	-5.28	-4.25	-4.28	-4.06	-3.81
Land: North non-poor	-3.01	-7.97	-5.46	-2.29	-2.59	-3.61
Land: North poor	6.31	4.53	2.01	6.27	5.70	5.33
Land: South non-poor	1.07	-1.92	-1.67	1.32	0.90	0.68
Land: South poor	7.11	6.81	3.74	6.72	6.12	6.89
Real household income						
Urban non-poor	-6.52	15.76	-6.77	-7.95	-8.65	-3.86
Urban poor	-4.76	-7.68	-5.83	-4.94	-5.92	-4.49
Semi-urban	-2.51	-4.79	-3.44	-2.64	-2.47	-2.31
Rural North non-poor	-2.25	-4.16	-3.17	-2.37	-2.25	-2.16
Rural North poor	-2.43	-5.16	-3.66	-2.51	-2.37	-2.27
Rural South non-poor	-1.98	-4.14	-3.01	-2.08	-1.97	-1.84
Rural South poor	-1.83	-4.27	-3.00	-1.93	-1.81	-1.65
Total household income	-3.14	-1.36	-4.07	-3.47	-3.09	-2.56

Source: Niger model simulations.

Table 5.5. Niger: real income effects on households, simulation 1: full RER adjustment

	Urban non-poor	Urban poor	Semi-urban	Rural North non-poor	Rural North poor	Rural South non-poor	Rural South poor
% change in nominal income arising from:							
Skilled labor	-4.124	0.000	0.000	0.000	0.000	0.000	0.000
Unskilled labor	-0.170	-1.498	-2.237	-1.126	-2.653	-1.918	-2.643
Informal capital	-0.694	-1.914	-0.869	-1.823	-0.227	-0.913	-0.125
Land: North non-poor	0.000	-0.020	-0.037	-0.501	0.000	0.000	0.000
Land: North poor	0.000	0.019	0.035	0.000	0.371	0.000	0.000
Land: South non-poor	0.000	0.008	0.014	0.000	0.000	0.140	0.000
Land: South poor	0.000	0.021	0.038	0.000	0.000	0.000	0.625
Total change	-4.988	-3.384	-3.056	-3.450	-2.508	-2.691	-2.142
Household consumer price index	101.6	101.4	99.4	98.8	99.9	99.3	99.7
Real income (% change)	-6.517	-4.758	-2.508	-2.253	-2.432	-1.980	-1.828

Source: Niger model simulations.

5.4.2. *Real exchange rate adjustment with foreign exchange rationing*

Niger and the other countries of the CFA zone have thus far to a large extent avoided a real exchange rate depreciation like the one modeled in simulation 1. Instead, they have largely postponed adjustment through a combination of a resort to the operations account with the French Treasury (akin to a drawdown of reserves), accumulation of arrears to creditors, and additional borrowing.[11] To the extent that the decline in Niger's uranium export revenues are offset by additional net capital inflows, total foreign exchange earnings are unchanged and the short run impact on the domestic economy is minimal.[12] Of course, postponement of the consequences is not a substitute for solution of the problem.

The main alternative to allowing a real exchange rate depreciation used in non-CFA countries has been a rationing of foreign exchange either explicitly or through import controls. Niger removed most of its quantitative restrictions on trade as part of its structural adjustment effort in the mid- to late 1980s. Simulation 2 models the re-imposition of trade restrictions so as to keep both the nominal exchange rate and the general price level unchanged. Equilibrium in the external accounts is achieved through implicit import tariffs on all imports, simulating rationing of foreign exchange for imports. The resulting rents are modeled as accruing solely to the urban non-poor households.

By design, the depreciation of the real exchange rate, measured as the nominal exchange rate deflated by the consumer price index, is zero (Table 5.4). The implicit tariff on imports is 15.0 percent, however, implying a depreciation of the real exchange rate for imports of the same magnitude. With no change in the real exchange rate for exports, exports rise by only 1.8 percent, compared with 4.6 percent in simulation 1.

Although the urban non-poor enjoy a large gain in real incomes (15.8 percent) because of the rents received, total savings and investment decline as returns to capital in the formal sector drop sharply (Table 5.6). All other households suffer sharply lower real incomes in comparison with a policy of real exchange rate adjustment. Rural households suffer an income decline of 3.0–3.3 percent, compared with the 1.9–2.5 percent declines when the real exchange rate adjusts freely (simulation 1).

---

[11] Given a decline in uranium export revenues of 25.9 billion CFAF, Niger financed a trade deficit of 27.9 billion CFAF in 1990, 10.6 billion CFAF greater than its trade deficit of 1987 (Table 5.2). Without this additional foreign capital inflow, it is argued here that real exchange rate depreciation by 1990 would have been even greater than historically observed (15.6 percent between 1987 and 1990). Further adjustment did take place in 1991, however, as indicated by the real exchange rate depreciation of 14.6 percent that accompanied the decline in the trade deficit of 4.7 billion CFAF.

[12] Recall that production of the uranium export sector has not been affected. Possible long-term effects of increased debt on investment incentives and future debt repayments are ignored here.

Table 5.6. Niger: real income effects on households, simulation 2: import quotas

	Urban non-poor	Urban poor	Semi-urban	Rural North non-poor	Rural North poor	Rural South non-poor	Rural South poor
% change in nominal income arising from:							
Skilled labor	-8.202	0.000	0.000	0.000	0.000	0.000	0.000
Unskilled labor	-0.339	-2.978	-4.448	-2.238	-5.275	-3.814	-5.255
Informal capital	-0.922	-2.541	-1.154	-2.420	-0.301	-1.212	-0.166
Land: North non-poor	0.000	-0.054	-0.098	-1.329	0.000	0.000	0.000
Land: North poor	0.000	0.014	0.025	0.000	0.267	0.000	0.000
Land: South non-poor	0.000	-0.014	-0.025	0.000	0.000	-0.252	0.000
Land: South poor	0.000	0.020	0.036	0.000	0.000	0.000	0.599
Rents	28.370						
Total change	18.908	-5.553	-5.663	-5.988	-5.310	-5.278	-4.822
Household consumer price index	102.72	102.31	99.08	98.10	99.84	98.82	99.42
Real income (% change)	15.76	-7.68	-4.79	-4.16	-5.16	-4.14	-4.27

Source: Niger model simulations.

5.4.3. *Impact of Nigeria's macroeconomic policy*

Given the extent of cross-border trade, changes in Nigeria's macroeconomic policy can have a significant impact on the extent of real exchange rate depreciation required to restore external balance in Niger. Here, we model an exchange rate policy in Nigeria that prevents any real depreciation of the CFA franc versus the Nigerian naira. The required real exchange rate adjustment *vis à vis* Niger's other trading partners is thus heightened.

In simulation 3, we adjust the world price (expressed in dollars) of goods traded with Nigeria so that there is no change in the border price expressed in CFA francs.[13] Instead of a 9.7 percent depreciation of the real exchange rate as in simulation 1, the overall depreciation of the real exchange rate is now 14.9 percent. With no gain in price incentives for exports to Nigeria, total exports (measured in dollars) increase by only 0.5 percent, compared with 4.6 percent in simulation 1. Export crop production increases by only 2.4 percent (compared with 6.6 percent in simulation 1) and livestock production falls by 1.9 percent (compared with 1.3 percent in simulation 1). Real incomes of all groups decline further than in simulation 1, with rural households for whom cattle and cowpeas are important income sources suffering declines of 3.0–3.7 percent (Table 5.7).

5.4.4. *Fiscal policy considerations*

Because the uranium sector is a major source of government revenues, the decline in uranium exports has implications for the budget deficit. Taxes on uranium exports and production equalled 9.8 billion CFAF in 1987, 13 percent of government revenues. With the decline in uranium exports, uranium revenues fell to only 6.2 billion CFAF by 1990, a 37 percent decline.

Since much of this decline was in the form of reduced royalties, corporate profits and export tax revenues, we model this as a transfer from the uranium sector to the government. Tax revenues also decline because of general equilibrium effects, in particular the loss of import tax revenues as imports decline. In simulation 4, government recurrent expenditures are reduced by an amount equal to the total decline in government revenues, so as to maintain the budget deficit at its pre-shock level.

The total reduction in government recurrent expenditure is only 3.7 billion CFAF, equivalent to just 4.4 percent of total government recurrent expenditures on goods and services. The impact of this cut falls mainly on urban households who are employed by the public administration. Real incomes of the urban non-poor fall by 8.0 percent (Table 5.8), compared

---

[13] The world prices of cowpeas and cattle are adjusted downward by the full amount of the CFAF/dollar depreciation. The world price of imports of grains and manufactured goods are adjusted downward by 23 percent of the CFAF/dollar depreciation, reflecting the estimated share of total imports of these products coming from Nigeria.

Table 5.7. Niger: real income effects on households, simulation 3: naira depreciation

	Urban non-poor	Urban poor	Semi-urban	Rural North non-poor	Rural North poor	Rural South non-poor	Rural South poor
% change in nominal income arising from:							
Skilled labor	-3.868	0.000	0.000	0.000	0.000	0.000	0.000
Unskilled labor	-0.238	-2.092	-3.125	-1.572	-3.706	-2.680	-3.692
Informal capital	-0.742	-2.044	-0.928	-1.947	-0.242	-0.975	-0.133
Land: North non-poor	0.000	-0.037	-0.067	-0.910	0.000	0.000	0.000
Land: North poor	0.000	0.006	0.011	0.000	0.118	0.000	0.000
Land: South non-poor	0.000	-0.012	-0.022	0.000	0.000	-0.219	0.000
Land: South poor	0.000	0.011	0.020	0.000	0.000	0.000	0.328
Total change	-4.848	-4.168	-4.111	-4.430	-3.830	-3.874	-3.497
Household consumer price index	102.06	101.76	99.30	98.70	99.82	99.11	99.48
Real income (% change)	-0.048	-0.042	-0.044	-0.044	-0.038	-0.039	-0.035

Source: Niger model simulations.

Table 5.8. Niger: real income effects on households, simulation 4: reduced public spending

	Urban non-poor	Urban poor	Semi-urban	Rural North non-poor	Rural North poor	Rural South non-poor	Rural South poor
% change in nominal income arising from:							
Skilled labor	−5.504	0.000	0.000	0.000	0.000	0.000	0.000
Unskilled labor	−0.176	−1.548	−2.312	−1.163	−2.742	−1.982	−2.731
Informal capital	−0.747	−2.059	−0.935	−1.961	−0.244	−0.982	−0.134
Land: North non-poor	0.000	−0.015	−0.028	−0.382	0.000	0.000	0.000
Land: North poor	0.000	0.019	0.035	0.000	0.370	0.000	0.000
Land: South non-poor	0.000	0.009	0.017	0.000	0.000	0.173	0.000
Land: South poor	0.000	0.020	0.036	0.000	0.000	0.000	0.591
Total change	−6.427	−3.575	−3.188	−3.506	−2.616	−2.791	−2.275
Household consumer price index	101.65	101.44	99.44	98.84	99.89	99.28	99.64
Real income (% change)	−7.95	−4.94	−2.64	−2.37	−2.51	−2.08	−1.93

Source: Niger model simulations.

with 6.5 percent in simulation 1. Rural households are only marginally worse off than in simulation 1.

The alternative to a cut in government expenditures, a tax increase, is modeled in simulation 5. Here, direct taxes on urban households are increased by an amount sufficient to restore the government budget deficit to its pre-shock level. We assume that the increased tax rate for the urban poor is only one-half of that for the non-poor, given the greater share of incomes of the urban poor from the informal sector.

The resulting 2.4 percent increase in the marginal tax rate on the urban non-poor (1.2 percent for the urban poor) reduces real incomes of the urban non-poor by 8.6 percent, 0.7 percent more than with the government expenditure cut modeled in simulation 4 (Table 5.9). Rural households are marginally worse off in this scenario, compared with simulation 4, because lower urban incomes lead to reduced total savings and investment spending and to a 0.2 percent smaller real exchange rate depreciation.

The decline in uranium revenues has not been the major cause of the fiscal crisis, however. The widening gap between expenditures and revenues is due mainly to continuing increases in government expenditures (Figure 5.1). Unable to fund these commitments, the government's domestic arrears increased substantially in 1990.

Simulation 6 shows the effects of the increased government spending in spite of the decline in uranium revenues. Real government recurrent expenditures are increased by 5 percent, reflecting the 12 billion CFAF increase in expenditures on goods and services between 1987 and 1990, expressed in per capita terms. Government investment is reduced by 8.5 percent.[14] The net result is a small (0.3 percent) drop in total government spending.

The major beneficiaries of this policy are the urban non-poor, who receive the largest share of government salaries. Their income decline is only 3.9 percent, compared with 6.5 percent with full real exchange rate adjustment but no change in government spending modeled in simulation 1 (Table 5.10). By contrast, the urban poor are only 0.3 percent better off than in simulation 1 because lower government investment spending reduces incomes from the construction sector. Output of construction services falls 16.2 percent relative to the base 1987 level, and 8.0 percent relative to simulation 1. Rural households are affected only marginally by this shift in government spending.

---

[14] Historically, real government investment increased by only 1 percent between 1986/87 and 1990. With population growth estimated at 3.1 percent per year, real government investment per capita fell by 8.5 percent (IMF 1992a).

Table 5.9. Niger: real income effects on households, simulation 5: increased taxes

	Urban non-poor	Urban poor	Semi-urban	Rural North non-poor	Rural North poor	Rural South non-poor	Rural South poor
% change in nominal income arising from:							
Skilled labor	−3.951	0.000	0.000	0.000	0.000	0.000	0.000
Unskilled labor	−0.165	−1.455	−2.173	−1.093	−2.577	−1.863	−2.567
Informal capital	−0.709	−1.954	−0.887	−1.861	−0.231	−0.932	−0.127
Land: North non-poor	0.000	−0.017	−0.032	−0.432	0.000	0.000	0.000
Land: North poor	0.000	0.017	0.032	0.000	0.336	0.000	0.000
Land: South non-poor	0.000	0.006	0.012	0.000	0.000	0.118	0.000
Land: South poor	0.000	0.018	0.033	0.000	0.000	0.000	0.538
Total change	−4.825	−3.384	−3.016	−3.386	−2.472	−2.677	−2.156
Household consumer price index	101.64	101.44	99.44	98.84	99.90	99.27	99.64
Real income (% change)	−6.36	−4.75	−2.47	−2.25	−2.37	−1.97	−1.80

Source: Niger model simulations.

Table 5.10. Niger: real income effects on households, simulation 6: increased public spending

	Urban non-poor	Urban poor	Semi-urban	Rural North non-poor	Rural North poor	Rural South non-poor	Rural South poor
% change in nominal income arising from:							
Skilled labor	-1.554	0.000	0.000	0.000	0.000	0.000	0.000
Unskilled labor	-0.154	-1.358	-2.029	-1.021	-2.406	-1.740	-2.397
Informal capital	-0.665	-1.833	-0.832	-1.746	-0.217	-0.874	-0.119
Land: North non-poor	0.000	-0.024	-0.044	-0.603	0.000	0.000	0.000
Land: North poor	0.000	0.016	0.030	0.000	0.314	0.000	0.000
Land: South non-poor	0.000	0.005	0.009	0.000	0.000	0.089	0.000
Land: South poor	0.000	0.020	0.037	0.000	0.000	0.000	0.606
Total change	-2.373	-3.175	-2.831	-3.369	-2.309	-2.525	-1.911
Household consumer price index	101.55	101.38	99.47	98.76	99.96	99.30	99.73
Real income (% change)	-3.86	-4.49	-2.31	-2.16	-2.27	-1.84	-1.65

Source: Niger model simulations.

5.5. *Concluding Observations*

Niger faces severe economic difficulties: declining uranium revenues, fiscal shortfalls, and mounting debt. Model simulations indicate that restoring external equilibrium in the aftermath of a sharp decline in uranium export revenues from 1987 to 1990 would have required a real exchange rate depreciation of 9–15 percent greater than actually observed in that period. Historically, Niger temporarily postponed the consequences of the terms of reduced export earnings through increased foreign capital inflows.

Reductions in uranium revenues lead unambiguously to lower household incomes. In the model simulations, with no change in foreign capital inflows, all household groups suffer as a result of the terms-of-trade shock, as economy-wide savings and investment decline, leading to reduced labor demand and real incomes. Without a depreciation of the real exchange rate (achieved through rationing of foreign exchange or import licensing restrictions in many non-CFA countries), however, simulation results indicate that real incomes of most household groups in Niger would decline by an additional 2–3 percent. The exceptions are the recipients of economic rents that result if foreign exchange and/or import licenses are rationed. Thus, adjustment of the real exchange rate is superior to non-adjustment, particularly for the poor.

With the nominal exchange rate of the CFA franc fixed relative to the French franc, adjustment in the real exchange rate in Niger has been slow. Real depreciation takes place through either a decline in domestic prices or slower price increases in Niger than in its trading partners. A nominal exchange rate devaluation could speed the adjustment process and raise real incomes.

In recent years, several options for changes in exchange rate policies have been put forth for the CFA member countries, including moving to a flexible nominal exchange rate, a one-time devaluation of the nominal exchange rate, and a one-time devaluation of the nominal exchange rate of varying magnitudes for the different countries of the CFA zone (Devarajan 1992). This latter option would in effect mean the end of the monetary union.

Niger's membership in the monetary union entails both benefits and costs. The stable fixed nominal exchange rate and currency convertibility encourages foreign investment and growth, while restrictions on government borrowing in the CFA zone tend to produce low inflation and encourage fiscal discipline.[15]

---

[15] By the rules of the monetary union, the amount of a central government budget deficit that can be financed through domestic credit from the central bank is limited to 20 percent of the government's fiscal receipts in the previous year. This rule has not prevented financing of government spending from abroad through commercial bank loans to governments and parastatals (see Guillaumont and Guillaumont 1984, and Bhatia 1985).

Up until the adjustment period of the early 1980s, the evidence suggested that overall impact of membership was positive. Cross-country regression analysis by Devarajan and de Melo (1987a) showed that the CFA countries had significantly higher growth than other countries in sub-Saharan Africa over the 1960–1982 period. Guillaumont, Guillaumont, and Plane (1988) attributed the better economic performance of the franc zone countries "in part to their strong investment efforts and relatively greater degree of commercial openness," factors linked to convertibility, monetary discipline, and stability of real exchange rates. For Niger, the sharp increase in uranium exports was the major factor explaining the country's rapid GDP growth during this period (see Jabara 1991).

Difficulties in adjusting the real exchange rate in response to adverse external shocks, however, led to a deterioration in the economic performance of franc zone countries in the 1980s (Devarajan and de Melo 1990). Sharp falls in world prices of major exports played a major role in economic decline in a number of CFA countries. Focusing only on "the costs of maintaining a fixed exchange rate regime in the context of a highly variable external terms of trade," Devarajan and Rodrik (1991) suggest that membership in the CFA zone has resulted in a tradeoff between output and inflation that has been "a bad bargain for CFA member countries."

Adjustment of the real exchange rate, however achieved, would not solve the fiscal problems that also burden Niger, as indicated by the model simulations.[16] A devaluation may make it easier politically to slow real government spending, by enabling a reduction in real wages in the public sector through limiting nominal wage increases to a level less than the rise in domestic prices. Yet devaluation could discourage private investment, at least in the short to medium term, owing to increased uncertainty regarding exchange rate policy. And a policy of worker retrenchment may be a more effective solution to the government wage bill problems in the long run.

Thus, more rapid adjustment in the real exchange rate, achieved through a nominal exchange rate devaluation, is not a panacea for solving the country's economic woes, in particular the fiscal crisis. Moreover, membership in the CFA zone has worked to avoid the economic inefficiencies and lost incomes for the bulk of the population (including the rural poor) that would result from foreign exchange rationing and import licensing restrictions prevalent in non-CFA countries of sub-Saharan Africa.

---

16 In periods of high export receipts the inflow of foreign exchange in itself leads to increases in money supply. See Lane (1989) for a discussion of the monetary expansion in Côte d'Ivoire in the 1970s.

Appendix 5.1.
Equations of the Niger Model

Definitions of the variables are given at the end of the appendix. Exogenous parameters are demonstrated by lowercase italics.

Prices

(1) $\quad PM_i = \overline{PWM}_i \bullet (1 + \overline{TM}_i) \bullet \overline{ER}$

(2) $\quad PE_i \bullet (1 + \overline{TE}_i) = \overline{PWE}_i \bullet \overline{ER}$

(3) $\quad PPT_i \bullet XPT_i = PPD_i \bullet XPD_i + \dfrac{PE_i}{1 + margx_i} \bullet E_i$

(4) $\quad PVA_j = PPT_j(1 - tprod_j) - \sum_i PC_i a_{ij}$

(5) $\quad PC_i \bullet XT_i = PPD_i(1 + margd_i + dtax_i) \bullet XPD_i + PM_i(1 + margm_i + itax_i) \bullet M_i$

(6) $\quad PK_j = \sum_i PC_i \bullet imat_{ij}$

(7) $\quad PPTACT_j = \sum_i PPT_i \bullet outmat_{ji}$

(8) $\quad PINDEX = \sum_i \theta_i \bullet PC_i$

Production

(9) $\quad XPTACT_j = CES(L_{1j}, L_{2j}, L_{3j}, K_j)$

(10) $\quad XPT_i = \sum_j XPTACT_j \bullet outmat_{ji}$

Trade

(11) $\quad E_i / \overline{E0}_i = \left(\dfrac{\overline{PWE0}_i}{PWE_i} \right)^{\eta_i}$

(12) $\quad XPT_i = AT_i[\gamma_i E_i^{\psi_i} + (1 - \gamma_i)XPD_i^{\psi_i}]^{1/\psi_i}, \qquad$ for i = exported goods

(13) $\quad \dfrac{E_i}{XPD_i} = \left(\dfrac{PE_i^*}{PPD_i} \bullet \dfrac{1 - \gamma_i}{\gamma_i} \right)^{\phi_i}, \qquad PE_i^* = \dfrac{PE_i}{1 + margx_i}$

$\quad \phi_i = \dfrac{1}{\rho_i - 1}, \qquad$ for i = exported goods

(14) $XT_i = AC_i [\delta_i M_i^{-\rho_i} + (1 - \delta_i) XPD_i^{-\rho_i}]^{-1/\rho_i}$,   for i = imported goods

(15) $\dfrac{M_i}{XPD_i} = \left(\dfrac{PPD_i^*}{PM_i^*} \bullet \dfrac{\delta_i}{1 - \delta_i} \right)^{\sigma_i}$, $\sigma_i = \dfrac{1}{1 + \rho_i}$,   for i = imported goods

$PPD_i^* = PPD_i (1 + margd_i + dtax_i)$,   and $PM_i^* = PM_i (1 + margm_i + itax_i)$

(16) $XT_i = XPD_i$,   for i = non-imported goods

(17) $XPT_i = XPD_i$,   for i = non-exported goods

Factor markets

(18) $\dfrac{W_{lc,j}}{r_j} = \dfrac{\alpha_{lc,j}}{1 - \displaystyle\sum_{lc} \alpha_{lc,j}} \bullet \dfrac{K_j^{1+\rho_j}}{L_{lc,j}^{1+\rho_j}}$

(19) $\displaystyle\sum_j L_{lc,j} = \overline{LS}_{lc}$

(20) $r_j = \left(1 - \displaystyle\sum_{lc} \alpha_{lc,j} \right) \bullet AD_j^{-\rho} \bullet K_j^{-\rho-1} \bullet PVA_j \bullet Q_j^{1+\rho}$

Household incomes, savings

(21) $LCSAL_{lc} = \displaystyle\sum_j wdist_{j,lc} \bullet W_j \bullet L_{lc,j}$

(22) $RETK_{kc} = \displaystyle\sum_j (PVA_j \bullet XPTACT_j - ACTSAL_j) \bullet shrkc_{kc,j}$

(23) $ACTSAL_j = \displaystyle\sum_{lc} WA_{lc} \bullet wdist_{j,lc} \bullet L_{j,lc}$

(24) $RENT_i = \overline{PWM}_i \bullet (TM_i - tmr_i) \bullet \overline{M}_i$,   for $i = imq$

(25) $Y_h = \displaystyle\sum_{lc} (shr_{lc,h} \bullet LCSAL_{lc}) + \displaystyle\sum_{kc} (shr_{kc,h} \bullet RETK_{kc})$

$+ \displaystyle\sum_{imq} (rentshr_{imq,h} \bullet RENT_{imq})$

(26) $SAVHH_h = sO_h \bullet \left(\dfrac{PINDEX}{PINDEX0} \right) + mps_h \bullet Y_h$

(27) $YD_h = Y_h - SAVHH_h - tdir_h \bullet Y_h$

Intermediate demand

(28) $INT_i = \displaystyle\sum_j a_{ij} XPTACT_j$

(29) $\quad INT_{11} = \sum_j a_{ij} XPTACT_j$

$\qquad\qquad +(MARGXTOT + MARGMTOT + MARGDTOT)\,/\,PC_{11}$

(30) $\quad MARGXTOT = \sum_i PE_i \bullet margx_i \,/\,(1 + margx_i) \bullet E_i$

(31) $\quad MARGMTOT = \sum_i PM_i \bullet margm_i \bullet M_i$

(32) $\quad MARGDTOT = \sum_i PPD_i \bullet margd_i \bullet XPD_i$

Household consumption

(33) $\quad PC_i \bullet CD_{ih} = cles_{ih} \bullet YD_h$

(34) $\quad CD_i = \sum_h CDHH_{i,h}$

Government

(35) $\quad GD_i = \beta_i^G \bullet \overline{GDTOT}$

(36) $\quad GR = TARIFF + DUTY + PRODTX + DSALETX + ISALETX$

$\qquad\qquad + DIRTX + (PVA_{11} \bullet XPTACT_{11} - ACTSAL_{11})$

(37) $\quad TARIFF = \sum_i \overline{TM}_i \bullet \overline{PWM}_i \bullet M_i \bullet ER$

(38) $\quad DUTY = \sum_i \overline{TE}_i \bullet PE_i \bullet E_i$

(39) $\quad PRODTX = \sum_j tprod_j \bullet PPTACT_j \bullet XPTACT_j$

(40) $\quad DSALETX = \sum_i dtax_i \bullet PPD_i \bullet XPD_i$

(41) $\quad ISALETX = \sum_i itax_i \bullet PM_i \bullet M_i$

(42) $\quad DIRTX = \sum_h tdir_h \bullet Y_h$

(43) $\quad GOVSAV = GR - \sum_i PC_i \bullet GD_i - SUBSIDY$

Investment

(44) $\quad ID_i = \sum_j imat_{ij} \bullet DK_j$

(45) $GID_i = gio_i \bullet \overline{GOVIVT}$

(46) $VGOVIVT = \sum_i PC_i \bullet GID_i$

(47) $PK_j \bullet DK_j = KIO_j \bullet (SAVINGS - TOTDSTK - VGOVIVT)$

(48) $TOTDSTK = \sum_i PC_i \bullet DST_i$

(49) $DST_i = dstr_i \bullet XPT_i$

(50) $SAVINGS = TOTHHSAV + GOVSAV + ENTFSAV + \overline{FSAV} \bullet ER$

(51) $TOTHHSAV = \sum_h SAVHH_h$

(52) $DEPRECIA = \sum_j DEPR_j \bullet PK_j \bullet K_j$

(53) $DKTOT = \sum_j DK_j$

National income

(54) $YGDP = \sum_j PVA_j \bullet XPTACT_j + PRODTX + TARIFF + DUTY$

$\qquad\qquad + DUTY + DSALETX + ISALETX - DEPRECIA$

Model closure

(55) $\sum_i PWM_i \bullet M_i = \sum_i PWE_i \bullet E_i + \overline{FSAV}$

(56) $XT_i = INT_i + CD_i + GD_i + ID_i + GID_i + DST_i$

Dynamic equations

(57) $\overline{LS}_{1c,t+1} = \overline{LS}_{1c,t} \bullet (1 + lsgr_{lc})$

(58) $\overline{K}_{i,t+1} = \overline{K}_{i,t} \bullet (1 - depr_i) + DK_i + gkio_i \bullet \overline{GOVIVT}$

Endogenous Variables

ACTSAL	Wage bill by activity j
CD	Total consumer demand of good i
CDHH	Consumer demand for good i by household h
DEPRECIA	Total value of depreciation
DIRTX	Direct tax
DK	Real investment by activity j
DXTOT	Total real investment
DSALETX	Sales tax on domestic goods
DST	Change in stocks of good i
DUTY	Export duties
E	Exports
GD	Government consumption of good i
GID	Government investment demand for good i
GOVSAV	Government savings
GR	Government revenue
ID	Private investment demand for good i
INT	Intermediate use of good i
ISALETX	Sales tax on imported goods
L	Labor use (demand) in activity j
LCSAL	Total wage bill for labor of type lc
M	Imports
MARGDTOT	Total marketing margin on domestic goods
MARGMTOT	Total marketing margin on imports
MARGXTOT	Total marketing margin on exports
PC	User price of good i
PE	Domestic price of exported goods
PINDEX	National consumer price index
PK	Price of capital goods in activity j
PM	Domestic price of imported goods
PPD	Price of domestically produced goods
PPT	Price of output of good i
PPTACT	Price output of activity j
PRODTX	Revenue from producer taxes
PVA	Price of value added of activity j
PWE	World export price in dollars
RENT	Rent from import quotas on good i
RETK	Total returns to capital of type kc
SAVHH	Savings by household h
SAVINGS	Total value of savings
TARIFF	Tariff revenue
TOTDSTK	Total change in stocks
TOTHHSAV	Total household savings
VGOVIVT	Nominal value of government investment
WA	Average wage rate
XPD	Domestic sales of production of commodity i
XPT	Domestic output of commodity i

XPTACT	Output of activity *j*
XT	Supply of commodity *i*
Y	Household income
YGDP	Definition of GDP

Exogenous Variables

ER	Exchange rate (FCFA/dollar)
FSAV	Foreign savings
GDTOT	Total government consumption
GOVIVT	Total government investment
K	Capital stock in activity *j*
LS	Labor supply
PWM	World import price in dollars
TM	Import tariff rate

Activities (20)

Grains, export crops, other crops, livestock, forestry, mining, meat processing, food processing (F, I), manufacturing (F, I), construction (F, I), transport (F, I), private services (F, I), public services

Labor types

Skilled, unskilled

Household types

Urban I (skilled head of household)
Urban II (unskilled head of household)
Semi-urban
Rural north—high-income
Rural north—low-income
Rural south—high-income
Rural south—low-income

Capital

Formal sector
Informal sector
Agricultural—corresponding to each rural household group

Appendix 5.2.
Base Data and Model Parameters

Tables 5A.1 and 5A.2 present trade levels and parameters, and household budget shares, respectively. Table 5A.3 shows the levels of model variables in year 5 of the policy simulations.

Table 5A.1. Niger: trade levels and parameters, 1987 (m FCFA)

	Domestic production	Exports	Imports	Elasticity of substitution
Cereals	70.93	1.62	11.61	2.0
Export crops	23.82	14.12	0.21	2.0
Other food crops	56.84	2.71	6.44	0.9
Livestock	84.77	11.57	1.50	2.0
Forestry products	23.38	0.09	0.41	0.9
Mining	91.19	85.51	6.17	2.0
Meat	53.93	0.11	0.12	0.9
Processed food	17.19	1.35	20.02	0.9
Manufactures	84.55	13.91	141.14	0.7
Construction	55.83	0.00	0.00	0.4
Commerce	165.83	0.00	0.00	0.4
Transportation/ communication	56.60	0.00	4.85	0.4
Private services	76.92	0.00	5.75	0.4
Public services	82.12	0.00	0.00	0.4
Total	943.92	131.00	198.21	n.a.

Source: Dorosh and Essama-Nssah (1993).

Table 5A.2. Niger: household budget shares, 1987 (%)

	Urban non-poor	Urban poor	Semi-urban	Rural North non-poor	Rural North poor	Rural South non-poor	Rural South poor
Cereals	11.07	16.22	17.74	10.41	24.57	15.03	19.58
Export crops	0.66	0.98	1.43	0.84	1.98	1.21	1.58
Other food crops	7.59	11.17	15.77	4.01	9.48	22.02	28.69
Livestock	0.56	0.83	11.45	29.59	3.68	12.55	1.62
Forestry products	2.53	3.72	2.48	2.55	2.79	2.28	2.25
Mining	2.70	1.66	0.00	0.00	0.00	0.00	0.00
Meat	10.69	6.14	11.06	11.38	12.44	10.15	10.01
Processed food	5.13	7.03	7.31	7.53	8.23	6.71	6.62
Manufactures	40.62	34.52	12.21	12.56	13.73	11.20	11.05
Construction	0.61	0.65	0.25	0.26	0.28	0.23	0.23
Commerce	3.04	4.48	5.19	5.34	5.84	4.76	4.70
Transportation/communication	2.04	2.99	5.57	5.73	6.27	5.11	5.04
Private services	12.34	8.83	9.45	9.73	10.63	8.67	8.56
Public services	0.43	0.79	0.08	0.08	0.08	0.08	0.08
Total	100.00	100.00	100.00	100.00	100.00	100.00	100.00
Total expenditures (m FCFA)	178.54	169.07	34.27	198.67	210.60	161.83	479.86

Source: Dorosh and Essama-Nssah (1991).

Table 5A.3. Niger: effects of a terms-of-trade shock: simulation results, year 5

	(1) Full RER adjustment	(2) Import quotas	(3) Naira depreciation	(4) Reduced public spending	(5) Increased taxes	(6) Increased public spending
Real GDP	−3.99	−4.53	−3.88	−3.75	−3.75	−4.36
Consumption	−4.29	−3.60	−4.96	−4.34	−4.57	−4.05
Total investment	−26.68	−35.58	−21.47	−23.18	−23.85	−34.44
Private investment	−58.88	−78.52	−47.39	−51.16	−52.63	−65.75
Public investment	0.00	0.00	0.00	0.00	0.00	−8.50
Government consumption	0.00	0.00	0.00	−2.16	0.00	5.00
Government revenues	−5.30	−4.33	−4.09	−4.88	−1.04	−5.97
Real exchange rate	10.05	0.37	15.84	10.25	10.08	9.40
Exports (dollars)	1.58	−2.35	−2.34	2.14	1.90	0.64
Imports (dollars)	−12.69	−15.59	−15.58	−12.27	−12.45	−13.38
Foreign savings/GDP	−13.33	−13.33	−13.33	−13.33	−13.33	−13.33
Real output growth						
Cereals	1.20	3.04	1.86	1.05	0.92	0.77
Export crops	8.01	4.62	3.59	7.99	7.91	5.90
Other food crops	0.14	0.64	0.47	0.07	0.02	0.08
Livestock	−6.72	−10.94	−6.10	−5.34	−5.68	−7.80
Fish, forestry	−0.18	2.37	1.12	−0.39	−0.35	−0.33
Mining	−4.33	−7.44	−2.77	−3.41	−3.71	−5.34
Meat processing	−1.75	−0.24	−1.34	−1.69	−1.84	−1.63
Other food processing	−1.58	−2.06	−1.08	−1.20	−1.59	−2.08
Manufacturing	−3.28	−4.43	−1.81	−2.51	−3.05	−4.70
Construction	−11.44	−15.14	−9.20	−9.95	−10.26	−19.00
Commerce	−1.57	−1.89	−1.22	−1.14	−1.39	−2.08

Table 5A.3. (cont.)

	(1) Full RER adjustment	(2) Import quotas	(3) Naira depreciation	(4) Reduced public spending	(5) Increased taxes	(6) Increased public spending
Transport	-3.73	-5.03	-3.36	-3.36	-3.46	-4.07
Private services	-2.24	-1.72	-2.08	-2.06	-2.25	-2.50
Public administration	-0.05	0.03	-0.06	-2.17	-0.07	4.85
Factor incomes						
Unskilled labor	-1.74	-5.24	-2.80	-1.61	-1.49	-2.10
Formal capital	4.14	-10.86	11.07	5.71	4.62	0.88
Informal capital	-2.09	-3.47	-2.48	-2.30	-2.12	-1.78
Land: North non-poor	-2.34	-8.89	-4.88	-1.29	-1.63	-2.77
Land: North poor	11.50	5.38	4.42	11.67	11.05	16.48
Land: South non-poor	2.10	-3.14	-1.12	2.66	2.21	3.86
Land: South poor	9.62	6.01	4.87	9.44	8.84	14.86
Real household income						
Urban non-poor	-10.37	10.54	-10.24	-11.26	-9.83	-8.27
Urban poor	-5.43	-8.52	-6.63	-5.49	-5.36	-5.33
Semi-urban	-3.63	-6.35	-4.42	-3.55	-3.44	-3.82
Rural North non-poor	-4.16	-6.83	-4.80	-3.96	-3.92	-4.23
Rural North poor	-3.31	-6.55	-4.5	-3.21	-3.12	-3.45
Rural South non-poor	-3.15	-5.91	-4.08	-3.04	-2.97	-3.13
Rural South poor	-2.55	-5.51	-3.73	-2.49	-2.41	-2.52
Total household income	-4.70	-3.64	-5.51	-4.77	-4.47	-4.38

Source: Niger model simulations.

References

Armington, P. 1969. "A Theory of Demand for Products Distinguished by Place of Production." *IMF Staff Papers*, 16. Washington, DC: International Monetary Fund.

Bhatia, Rattan J. 1985. *The West African Monetary Union*. Occasional Paper No. 35. Washington, DC: International Monetary Fund.

Dervis, Kemal, Jaime de Melo, and Sherman Robinson. 1982. *General Equilibrium Models and Development Policy*. Washington, DC: World Bank.

Devarajan, S. 1992. "Preserving the Union: Lessons of History, Theory and Thirty Years of Experience." Paper presented at the Symposium on the 30th Anniversary of the UMOA, Dakar, Senegal, November 30–December 1, 1992.

—— and J. de Melo. 1987a. "Evaluating Participation in African Monetary Unions: A Statistical Analysis of the CFA Zones." *World Development*, 15(4): 483–496.

—— —— 1987b. "Adjustment with a Fixed Exchange Rate: Cameroon, Cote d'Ivoire, and Senegal." *World Bank Economic Review*, 1(3): 447–487.

—— —— 1990. *Membership in the CFA Zone: Odyssean Journey or Trojan Horse?* PPR Working Paper No. 482. Washington, DC: World Bank.

—— and D. Rodrik. 1991. *Do the Benefits of Fixed Exchange Rates Outweigh Their Costs? The Franc Zone in Africa*. National Bureau of Economic Research Working Paper No. 3727. Cambridge, MA: NBER.

Dorosh, Paul A. 1994. "Economic Fallout from a Uranium Boom: Structural Adjustment in Niger." In *Adjusting to Policy Failure in African Economies*, David E. Sahn, ed. Ithaca, NY: Cornell University Press.

—— and B. Essama-Nssah. 1991. *A Social Accounting Matrix for Niger: Methodology and Results*. Working Paper No. 18. Ithaca, NY: CFNPP.

—— 1993. *External Shocks, Policy Reform, and Income Distribution in Niger."* Working Paper No. 40. Ithaca, NY: CFNPP.

Guillaumont, P., and S. Guillaumont. 1984. *Zone Franc et developpement Africain*. Paris: Economica.

—— —— and P. Plane. 1988. "Participating in African Monetary Unions: An Alternative Evaluation." *World Development*, 166(5): 569–576.

Horowitz, Michael et al. 1983. *Niger: A Social and Institutional Profile*. Binghamton, NY: Institute for Development Anthropology.

Hugon, Philippe. 1990. *Aspects Methodologiques et Comparatifs des Programmes d'Ajustement Structurel: Le Cas du Niger*. Niamey, Niger: Ministère du Plan et PNUD, Projet NER/88/014.

International Monetary Fund. 1992a. *Niger—Statistical Annex*. Washington, DC: IMF.

—— 1992b. *International Financial Statistics Yearbook*. Washington, DC: IMF.

Jabara, Cathy L. 1991. *Structural Adjustment and Stabilization in Niger: Macroeconomic Consequences and Social Adjustment*. Monograph No. 11. Ithaca, NY: CFNPP.

Lane, C. E. 1989. *The Effectiveness of Monetary Policy in Cote d'Ivoire*. Working Paper 30. London: Overseas Development Institute.

Ministère du Plan, Direction de l'Analyse Economique et de la Planification. 1991. *Etudes et Conjoncture*. Niamey: Ministère du Plan.

Nash, John. 1993. *Implementation of Trade Reform in Sub-Saharan Africa: How Much Heat and How Much Light?* Policy Research Working Paper 1218. Washington, DC: World Bank, Policy Research Department, Trade Policy Division.

SEDES. 1987. *Etude du secteur agricole du Niger: Bilan-Diagnostic-Phase 1*. Paris: SEDES.

——1988. *Etude du Secteur Agricole du Niger: Bilan-Diagnostic-Phase 2*. Paris: SEDES.

World Bank. 1993. *World Development Report 1993*. New York: Oxford University Press.

PART III

Fiscal Policy and Welfare Outcomes:
*Retrenchment, Tax Reform, and
Investment Priorities*

6

Labor Market Consequences of Retrenchment for Civil Servants in Ghana

Stephen Younger

6.1. *Introduction*

During the past decade, inefficiencies in the public sector have drawn the attention of development economists working to understand the causes of Africa's worsening economic performance. Governments and state-owned enterprises have not been able to provide the services and goods they were created to provide in an efficient, cost-effective manner. One important cause of these inefficiencies is the public sector's employment practices. Driven in part by the widely held notion that the public sectors should lead their countries' development efforts, and in part by political patronage, African governments and their agencies increased staffing levels at a rapid pace after independence; most continue to do so. At first, these practices cause fiscal problems as the wage bill increases and fiscal deficits grow. But that is only the first manifestation of excessive employment. The problems run much deeper in Africa. Once governments reach the limit of what they can finance through tax revenue, aid, and the inflation tax, they are forced to cut back other expenditures to make wage payments. Typically, capital spending goes first.

It is not uncommon for African governments to have virtually all of their capital expenditures financed by donors (who do not place such a high priority as local officials on maximizing the payroll). If eliminating locally financed capital expenditures is insufficient, expenditures for operations and maintenance come next. These reductions tend to make public sector employees less productive as they do not have the appropriate equipment or materials to work with.

In the most extreme cases of this retrogression, governments are forced to cut public sector real wage rates in order to support the ever-growing number of employees. As an alternative, however, very few governments have been willing to address the root cause of the excessive wage bill by reducing public sector staffing levels. While some governments have instituted voluntary departure programs, actually laying off employees is seen as a politically risky and inhumane policy option that even the most authoritarian regimes shy away from. Behind these reservations lies a strong belief that retrenched public sector employees cannot find other gainful employment if they were laid off, so that retrenchment would either leave them destitute or create a politically volatile population concentrated in the capital city.

Despite the almost universal reluctance to retrench, a few African governments have risked public sector layoffs as part of the structural adjustment programs of the 1980s. Ghana is one such case, and the Cornell Food and Nutrition Policy Program (CFNPP) has collected survey data on retrenched civil servants which allow us to analyze the economic and social impact of the redeployment program on the affected civil servants. This paper summarizes that research, with a particular emphasis on the issue of primary concern to policy-makers: can and do former public sector employees find remunerative employment after they are dismissed from their public sector jobs? Section 6.2 gives a brief overview of Ghana's retrenchment program. Section 6.3 reviews the CFNPP work on unemployment spells and earnings potential after retrenchment, and section 6.4 concludes with a discussion of our results' policy implications.

6.2. *The Redeployment Program in Ghana*

The circumstances that brought Ghana to its redeployment program are similar to those in many other African countries. Ghana suffered years of declining real incomes under governments that followed highly interventionist economic policies. It also experienced rapid growth in public sector employment, to the extent that public employees represented 4.5 percent of the entire population, one of the highest levels in Africa (de Merode 1992). Civil service salaries collapsed under the weight of such extensive employment combined with a poorly performing economy, reaching a minimum of $8.50 per month in 1983 for the lowest echelons and $22.60 for the highest.

Ghana began a long-term Economic Recovery Program in 1983 that encompassed major fiscal reforms and market liberalizations, including the civil service redeployment program.[1] In addition to dismissing civil servants over the mandatory retirement age (60), the government first redeployed workers who were hired in excess of the approved levels for an office, agency, etc., as well as those whose qualifications for employment were falsified. Volunteers came next in the queue, followed by redeployments on

---

1 The redeployment program pertained only to civil servants because established collective bargaining agreements with employees at the state-owned enterprises required levels of severance pay that were impossible to meet, so those institutions were not included in the program.

a "last in, first out" basis. Teachers and employees at the Ministry of Health were exempt because the government viewed these posts as critical to its development plans. In addition, the government reserved the right to refuse redeployment to volunteers whose service was indispensable.

From 1987 to June 1992, the government retrenched 59,810 civil servants, about 20 percent of the 1986 total civil service staff. While there has been some further hiring within the civil service since 1987, especially in the education service, the redeployment program has succeeded in reducing overall civil service staffing levels by about 47,000 employees net of new hires.[2]

All civil servants past retirement age received only their regular pension as compensation for their retrenchment. Other redeployees, whether volunteers or not, received severance pay equal to four months' base pay plus two months' base pay for each year of service. In addition, redeployees were technically eligible to receive tools and one year's subsistence food allowance if they chose to go into farming, or to have their fees paid for an apprenticeship in another field. In practice, the apprenticeship program did not take off until 1991 (four years after the redeployment program began), too late for our survey to find any such redeployees.

The average amount of severance rises steadily from 1987, when the average was $383 per worker, to 1992, when it reached $1102 per worker. This marked increase is due in part to increases in real civil service salaries, and in part to the fact that employees in the lower salary scales were more likely to be redeployed early in the program. This may explain why the earliest redeployees seem to be the most dissatisfied with the program. In addition, civil service salaries were "unified" in 1991; i.e. a variety of allowances for transport, clothing, lunches, etc., that were previously paid separately from the base salary were enveloped into it. While this did not increase overall compensation, it did increase the "base" salary, and thus severance benefits. Nevertheless, even the amounts received in 1992 are at the lower end of severance payments for civil service employees compared with those in other countries for which we have data.[3] Total severance payments have exceeded 2 percent of government expenditures during the entire period.

The fiscal impact of the redeployment program has been positive, but not as significant as some had hoped for. Particularly in the early years, the costs of severance pay outweighed any savings on salaries. What's more, over 80 percent of redeployees came from the lower echelons of the civil service and

---

[2] See Mills et al. (1993) for a discussion of appropriate administrative methods for insuring that gross staff reductions are translated into net reductions.

[3] In Mali, for example, volunteers for retrenchment received about $4000 on average (Kingsbury 1992b). In Senegal, the government made loans to volunteers who wished to start a business; these loans averaged about $7500 per volunteer, and should probably be viewed as transfers rather than loans because the repayment rate is only 10 percent (Karp-Toledo 1991). In Guinea, severance payments ranged between $1130 and $2257, although they were paid over a 30-month period.

Table 6.1. Ghana: cash flow of severance pay and salary savings for redeployment program (m 1987 cedis)[a]

Item	1987	1988	1989	1990	1991	1992
Severance pay	851	2,141	3,686	2,968	3,624	3,983
Compensation savings	281	1,321	3,301	5,845	8,868	11,431
Net savings	−570	820	−385	2,877	5,244	7,448
Discounted savings	−1,621	−1,756	−651	3,464	5,269	6,703
Sum of discounted savings	−1,621	−3,377	−4,027	−564	4,705	11,408
Net savings/government expenditures	−0.006	−0.006	−0.002	0.012	0.015	0.019

[a] For 1992, the CPI is for June; for all other years, it is the monthly average. 1992 government expenditures are based on the budget; all other years are actual expenditures. Discounting is at a real rate of 10% per year.

Sources: de Merode (1992).

had correspondingly low salaries, limiting the fiscal benefits of the program in any particular year. Nevertheless, the government continues to save on its wage bill in each year after a redeployment (assuming that the post is not refilled later), so that over the long run the rate of return on the program for the government has been quite high. Table 6.1 shows that the discounted flow of salary savings less severance paid out turned positive in 1991, and the net savings amounted to about 2 percent of government expenditures by 1992. If we assume that the redeployment program ended in 1992, we can calculate a rate of return for all redeployments from 1987 to 1992, which is 60 percent.[4] In sum, the redeployment program has been fiscally advantageous for the government and will continue to be so in the future, but the gains to date are modest when compared with current expenditures or GDP.[5]

6.3. *Consequences of Redeployment for Public Sector Employees*

While the government of Ghana has reaped fiscal benefits from the redeployment program, many policy-makers in Ghana and abroad still harbor a fear that laid-off workers will not find other work and thus may become either destitute or a politically dangerous force. The results from the CFNPP surveys in Ghana help shed light on these concerns.[6] In this section, we discuss the unemployment spells that redeployees experienced and the impact of redeployment on redeployees' earnings. We also review the evidence on the socioeconomic characteristics of redeployees compared with public employees and the general population.

6.3.1. *Employment patterns for redeployees*

Table 6.2 shows the labor force participation status of redeployees in Ghana along with comparable information for the adult population in general.[7]

---

[4] In a similar study, Svejnar and Terrell (1991) found rates of return from 22 percent to more than 300 percent for retrenchments of public employees in the transit sectors of six countries.

[5] We should note in passing that these calculations assume that the government (and the Ghanaian public in general) did not receive any benefit from the retrenched civil servants' efforts when they were publicly employed. If those employees had in fact been productive, we would have to value their output and subtract it from the stream of benefits to get a (reduced) rate of return to the redeployment program. Nevertheless, given the nature of public employment in Ghana and the large number of redeployees who held lower echelon jobs, the argument that these employees had zero productivity is valid.

[6] For the record, Ghana has not experienced significant political problems in the wake of its redeployment programs, although it has made concessions to former and current public service employees since the program began.

[7] Information on the general population for Ghana comes from the 1987/88 round of the Ghana Living Standards Survey (GLSS). See Glewwe and Twum-Baah (1990) for a description of that survey. To maintain comparability with our sample, we have used information from the GLSS for only the three regions in which we sampled redeployees. See Alderman, Canagarajah, and Younger (1993) for details.

Table 6.2. Ghana: labor force participation status of redeployees and the general population in three regions

	Working	Under-employed agriculture	Unemployed	Out of labor force	Student	Total
GLSS						
Number	2301	12	89	244	150	2796
Proportion	0.823	0.004	0.032	0.087	0.054	
Redeployees						
Number	392	43	17	45	9	506
Proportion	0.775	0.085	0.034	0.089	0.018	

Source: Alderman, Canagarajah, and Younger (forthcoming).

The participation rate of redeployees is remarkably close to that for the entire population, with only 3 percent of redeployees unemployed and 9 percent out of the labor force not working and not actively seeking work. As we will discuss later, another 8 percent of redeployees appear to be under-employed; including this group with those openly unemployed yields a significantly higher unemployment rate and suggests that some former civil servants in Ghana have had difficulty finding gainful employment. Nevertheless, these data clearly refute the general notion that former civil servants either could not find jobs after redeployment or would not work at the jobs available. The majority of redeployees are in fact working.

For those redeployees currently working, the transitions from public sector employment to their new jobs have been generally brief. In the first place, 235 redeployees, 46 percent of the total, held second jobs while they were in the civil service. All but 3 of these redeployees had no spell of unemployment after they were laid off, but simply continued to work at that second job, often increasing the hours they dedicated to it; redeployees who carried over a second job which they held while in the civil service and spent an average of 16 hours per week at that job (or jobs) before being redeployed, were now spending 39 hours per week on it. Increased hours are especially notable among farmers and other self-employed workers who have a considerable amount of discretion in choosing how much time to dedicate to these activities.[8] Even the redeployees who had to seek another

---

8 The high hours for wage workers reflect the fact that some are security officers who can, in theory, work up to 24 hours a day because their job usually allows them to sleep and eat while working. Several people in our sample reported working regular eight-hour days in the civil service followed by a 12-hour shift as a watchman, for example.

job usually had little difficulty: 73 percent of this group (39 percent of all redeployees) had found new work within a year of redeployment.[9]

More careful analysis of redeployees' earnings, however, suggests that finding a job is not the end of the story: the type of work a redeployee does is important. In particular, our data on redeployees' earnings and time allocation suggest that a significant number of redeployees who claim to be farming are not working very intensively at that activity. As discussed in Alderman, Canagarajah, and Younger (1993), this group's earnings are very low, both because their yields are far below normal yields for Ghanaian farmers, and because they are farming small plots of land. Social custom in Ghana generally requires that a village allocate land to every villager who wants it, even if they have been away for some time. Thus, farming is always available as a fallback employment option for the desperate. Nevertheless, some redeployees appear to view farming as a temporary, part-time activity to carry them over until they find other employment. For that reason, we have classified any redeployee who is only farming and who is working less than one acre as "underemployed." While almost no one in the GLSS sample falls into this category, 8 percent of redeployees do.

To emphasize the importance of these distinctions, I have grouped redeployees into five states: not working, farming less than one acre ("underemployed"), working one job only (but not underemployed), working one job plus farming less than one acre, and working two "full" jobs. Being redeployed shifts a worker down two states (because the civil service job is full time), after which we can ask, how long does it take a redeployee to recover his or her pre-redeployment state? Note that this is somewhat more demanding than simply exiting unemployment: the redeployee must maintain any second job held at the time of redeployment and find another full-time job.

Figure 6.1 shows the proportion of redeployees who recovered their initial state, by months after redeployment.[10] As one can see, even though a large number of redeployees were working within one year of redeployment, less than half had actually recovered their initial state.

Table 6.3 shows the average monthly transition probabilities from state to state.[11] It is evident that holding post-redeployment jobs is not difficult: the probability of moving down a state (or more) from any job is always less than 0.01. It is also true that the probability of leaving the not-working state

[9] Note that these figures include even the redeployees who are out of the labor force, i.e. not working and not looking for work. If we limit the sample to only those who were actively working or searching at the time of the survey, the numbers are even more favorable.

[10] The results are biased by the fact that some redeployees are censored: we interviewed them only x months after redeployment and thus cannot say what state they would be in at $x + 1$ and more months after redeployment. This bias is more severe as the lag grows. In the sample, 16 percent are censored at 12 months and 43 percent at 24.

[11] Censored observations are omitted from the calculations.

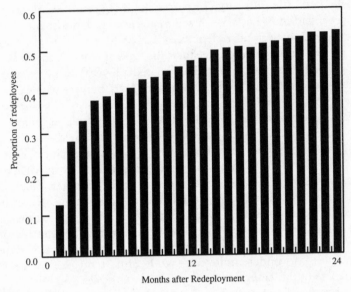

Fig. 6.1. Proportion of Ghanaian redeployees recovering their employment status, by months after redeployment

is reasonably high, considering that most redeployees in this state after the first two or three months of redeployment are probably out of the labor force. The odds of exiting underemployed agriculture are much less favorable, however, exemplifying this state as a particularly difficult one.

Are there any identifiable characteristics of former public sector employees which make them more or less likely to find new employment? Table 6.4 shows the results of a logit regression for labor force status at the time of the survey for former public sector employees.[12] The dependent variable is a dummy indicating whether or not a redeployee is currently working, and the regression can be interpreted as predicting the probability that a redeployee will have a job at the time of the interview. As discussed above, having a second job while in the civil service is the single most important determinant of current employment, increasing the probability of employment by 20 percent. Most of the other variables in the regression are not significantly different from zero, indicating that they are not highly correlated with the probability of being employed after redeployment. One exception is the work experience variables, which are jointly significant. This indicates that longer work experience increases the probability of finding new work, up to

12 These results are discussed in detail in Alderman, Canagarajah, and Younger (1994), which also reports on more elaborate sector selection models.

Table 6.3. Ghana: average monthly transition probabilities for redeployees

From:	To:				
	Not Working	Under-employed agriculture	One job	One job and underemployed agriculture	Two jobs
Not working	0.951	0.007	0.038	0.000	0.004
Underemployed agriculture	0.002	0.980	0.000	0.018	0.001
One job	0.004	0.000	0.980	0.004	0.011
One job and underemployed agriculture	0.000	0.002	0.001	0.992	0.005
Two jobs	0.000	0.000	0.005	0.000	0.995

Source: Ghana Living Standards Survey and author's calculations.

21 years of experience;[13] after that point the probability begins to decline, perhaps because older redeployees choose to retire or find it difficult to adapt to new work.

The regression also shows that having higher unearned income (mostly pensions, rent, and remittances) lowers the probability of working, a standard result which indicates that leisure is a normal good for redeployees: those who have high unearned income choose to work less. On the other hand, higher severance pay is positively correlated with having a current job. On the basis of a labor/leisure choice, one would expect this coefficient to be negative. One interpretation of this result, consistent with some of our other findings, is that larger amounts of severance pay gave redeployees enough cash to stake a business. While only the profitability of a potential business would matter if redeployees had access to well-functioning credit markets (because creditors would willingly lend to a profitable business), when credit markets do not work well, small operations are limited to self-finance and thus must have significant startup capital in hand. The severance payments may have served to provide that capital.[14]

[13] The experience variable is total years of work, whether in the civil service or not. Similar regressions that include only civil service experience find it to have no correlation with finding a job after redeployment.

[14] Another possible interpretation of this apparent anomaly is that, because higher civil service earnings translated into higher severance pay (based on the standard formula), this variable is capturing an individual effect for "good" workers: people who are more likely to have higher civil service earnings (because they work hard, come to work on time, etc.) and are also more likely to choose to work after redeployment. However, including civil service earnings directly in this logit equation does not alter the coefficient of the severance pay variable or its statistical significance.

Table 6.4. Ghana: logit function for probability of working after redeployment

Variable	Coefficient	T-statistic	Change in probability
Constant	0.6837	−0.7428	
Duration[a]	0.0670	1.5611	0.0076
Duration[b]	−0.1583	−1.7236	−0.0002
Urban resident[a]	−0.3130	−0.3108	−0.0192
Aged 55 or older	−0.4841	−1.2203	−0.0541
Central	−0.3491	−0.8074	−0.0370
Ashanti	−0.6868	−1.9004	−0.0728
Dependency ratio	−0.1574	0.7557	0.0240
Gender	−0.3647	0.2509	0.0089
Dependency ratio × gender	0.8859	1.4961	0.0939
Log (severance pay)	0.1131	2.1416	0.0118
Log (remittances)	−0.1268	−3.4946	−0.0136
Log (unearned income)	−0.1311	−1.9640	−0.0090
Second job holder[a]	2.0491	4.6872	0.2017
Primary[b]	−0.2151	−0.2873	−0.0142
Middle[b]	−0.5425	−1.3491	−0.0549
Secondary or higher[b]	−0.6852	−1.3053	−0.0719
Redeployed in 1987	0.7777	1.2546	0.0716
Redeployed in 1988	0.2431	0.6615	0.0377
Redeployed in 1989	−0.0659	−0.3005	−0.0155
Redeployed in 1990	0.2342	0.4895	0.0254

Dependent variable: Working = 1; Not working = 2
Observations: 506
Log likelihood: −176

Null Hypothesis	Wald-Chi^2	p-value	d.f.
All coefficients = 0	151	0.000	20
All coefficients except constant = 0	59	0.000	19

[a] These variables are calculated as of the time of redeployment. All others are at the time of the interview.

[b] The change in the probability function of these variables is simulated as the mean difference between the function evaluated at 0 (no education) and 1 for every observation.

It is interesting to compare this outcome with the experience in Guinea, where higher amounts of severance were associated with a lower probability of working (Mills and Sahn 1993). While the very different nature of the two labor markets may explain this, another important difference between the programs in Ghana and in Guinea is that in Ghana the government paid severance pay in one lump sum, while in Guinea payments were spread out over time. Again, if redeployees are liquidity constrained and savings opportunities are limited, having the lump sum is much more valuable to those wishing to start a business.

Earnings of redeployees.   In addition to concerns about redeployees' ability to find new work, we are also concerned with what they earn in new jobs compared with their civil service earnings. Overall, average total earnings fell by almost half,[15] indicating a substantial loss in income for redeployees and their households.[16] Yet these losses occur over a heterogeneous group, and dissecting them yields some insight into the determinants of income losses. One approach to this problem, pursued in Alderman, Canagarajah, and Younger (1994), is to estimate earnings functions for working redeployees in the month immediately prior to their redeployment and also in the current month (at the time of the interview). One can then compare coefficients across equations to understand how the returns to different determinants of earnings (human capital variables, worker characteristics, choice of work effort, etc.) affect the losses for different redeployees.

Results from those regressions can be obtained more precisely from a different (but complementary) approach, however. Instead of estimating each earnings function separately, one can subtract the civil service earnings function from the current one and estimate this "differenced" equation whose dependent variable is current earnings less (total) earnings before redeployment.[17] The exact equation is:

$$\ln(y_{cu}) - \ln(y_{cs}) = X\beta + Z_{cu}\gamma_{cu} - Z_{cs}\gamma_{cs} + U\delta + \varepsilon \qquad (1)$$

where y is the redeployee's earnings, X is a vector of time-invariant regressors that affect his or her earnings (e.g. gender, education, year of

---

[15] To some extent, this rather large decline may reflect data problems rather than true reductions in income. Most of the redeployees' current incomes come from farming or self-employment, while most of their earnings while they were civil servants came from wages. It is often the case that farming and self-employed incomes are underreported in surveys, and much more so than wage income, which would generate an exaggerated perception of the income decline in our data. Vijverberg (1988) reports on the general difficulties of using self-employed income data.

[16] Our work concentrates on total earnings from all sources, including second and third jobs. Also, because it is difficult accurately to assess hours worked for the self-employed (a large number of redeployees are currently self-employed), we work with total earnings rather than wage rates.

[17] Glewwe and Hall (1993) discuss the econometric advantages of this approach.

redeployment), Z is a vector of time-varying determinants of earnings (e.g. age, years of experience, number of children), and U is a vector of regressors that are applicable and/or available only for the current period (e.g. the type of current employment). The subscripts indicate time, with cu being the time of the interview and cs being the month just prior to redeployment. The β coefficients are equal to the difference of the coefficients in the current and former earnings functions, $(b_{cu} - b_{cs})$.

Table 6.5 reports results for the estimation of equation (1). Note that, if the two earnings functions were identical, the βs would all be zero and γ_{cs} would equal γ_{cu}. In general, these restrictions are rejected, but an interesting subset is not: we cannot reject the hypothesis that all the γs are equal across equations and that all the βs are zero except for the constant and the location variables (the urban/rural dummy and the region where the redeployee lived before redeployment). Of particular importance is the fact that the slope coefficients on the human capital variables do not differ between equations: only the intercepts do, though the amount that the function shifts down varies with the redeployee's location before redeployment. Thus, for re-deployees, the difference between earnings before and after redeployment is the loss of a premium to civil service employment, manifested in a down-ward shift of their earnings function, rather than different rates of return to their human capital.

The other important feature of equation (1) is the impact of being under-employed. This is captured by including the logit probability for this state (conditional on working) as a regressor in the earnings function. As the probability of underemployment increases, a redeployee's expected change in earnings declines significantly.

Table 6.6 shows the amount that redeployees' expected earnings decline after redeployment, broken down by residence (at the time of redeploy-ment) and the probability of being underemployed (evaluated at 0 and 1). Clearly, the losses are substantial, even for the urban, fully employed group that constitutes the majority of redeployees. For the underemployed, the losses are so large that it probably makes more sense to group them with the unemployed rather than the working.[18]

Welfare status of redeployees' households. The earnings estimates for re-deployees suggest that they have suffered a significant decline in their earnings. For welfare comparisons, it would be preferable to compare the redeployees' *households'* earnings (or, more generally, their consumption) before and after retrenchment, but the survey data do not allow that. We can, however, compare the status of redeployees' households at the time

[18] Repeating the analysis with this assumption yields very similar results. In a more elaborate model, however, Alderman, Canagarajah, and Younger (1994) do find evidence that the few redeployees who have found work in the formal sector (37 workers, or 7 percent of the sample) suffered no decline in earnings.

Table 6.5. Ghana: ordinary least square model of the difference between earnings before and after redeployment

Variable	Estimate	T-statistic	Estimate	T-statistic
Constant	0.132142	0.238803	-0.561247	-2.774823
Civil service duration	-0.013659	-0.303924		
Civil service duration[2]	0.000226	0.200715		
Urban resident	0.408129	2.370343	0.394373	2.325809
Central	-0.429226	-2.581346	-0.374499	-2.475443
Ashanti	-0.048140	-0.283065	-0.003576	-0.023266
Gender	-0.242049	-1.412979		
Primary	0.026843	0.131860		
Middle	-0.165962	-1.035484		
Secondary or university	0.043089	0.189900		
Redeployed in 1987	0.219726	0.873617		
Redeployed in 1988	0.111194	0.483751		
Redeployed in 1989	0.050371	0.238146		
Redeployed in 1990	-0.208318	-1.047503		
Duration[a]	-0.282513	-2.337753	-0.051385	-0.933089
Duration[2a]	0.002198	0.855456	-0.00144945	-1.225967
Aged 55 or older[a]	0.083720	0.294419	0.137403	0.503233
Dependency ratio[a]	-0.322036	-0.958669	-0.187158	-0.776976
Dependency ratio[2a]	0.396403	0.898372	0.151627	0.521753
Duration up To redeployment[b]	0.292371	2.665942		
Duration up To redeployment[2b]	-0.003024	-1.193478		
Aged 55 or older[b]	-0.110071	-0.360591		
Dependency ratio[b]	0.162687	0.614064		
Dependency ratio × gender[b]	-0.075668	-0.219277		
Probability of under-employment	-1.787524	-2.817542	-1.793660	-3.267855
Null Hypothesis	F-statistic	P-value	d.f.	d.f.
Tests between civil service and current earnings				
All comparable betas equal	2.072	0.005	19	404
All betas equal except locations	0.954	0.504	15	404

[a] In the restricted regression, these variables are the *difference* between the value at the time of the survey and the value at redeployment.

[b] These variables are calculated as of the time of redeployment; all others are at the time of the interview.

Table 6.6. Ghana: expected change in earnings after redeployment, by location and job status

	% of civil service earnings	
	Fully employed	Underemployed
Urban		
%	−30	−88
No. of cases	338	32
Rural		
%	−48	−92
No. of cases	44	5
Average (%)	−32	−89

Source: Table 6.5.

they were surveyed (after redeployment) with households from the general population of the GLSS. Median household incomes from the GLSS and for redeployees' households are approximately equal in the two samples—21,110 cedis for the GLSS households vs 20,000 cedis for the redeployees—suggesting that, while redeployees appear to have lost income after redeployment, their households may not be worse off than the general population.[19] Income per capita, however, is 27 percent lower among redeployees' households, but this is probably a result of the fact that household size appears to be underestimated in the GLSS data (Alderman and Higgins 1992). More generally, Table 6.7 indicates the number of redeployee households in each income decile from the GLSS, both currently and at the time of redeployment. As one can see, redeployees' families are underrepresented in the lowest decile, but also in the four highest deciles. Thus, redeployees' households currently are slightly less likely to be extremely poor than Ghanaian households in general, even after suffering the earnings losses associated with redeployment, but they are more likely to fall into the bottom half of the income distribution. Nevertheless, the difference is not overwhelming, and redeployees' households in general appear to be only slightly worse off than the overall population in Ghana. This, combined with the fact that redeployees' income has fallen significantly, suggests that, despite their having come from the lower echelons of the civil service, redeployees' households were better off than the population in

---

19 An important caveat is the apparent underreporting of income in the GLSS survey, which is far below reported expenditures. The Cornell survey does not collect expenditure information, so we have no way of judging whether income underreporting is as severe in our survey as it is in the GLSS. If it were less, however, the implication is that redeployees' households are somewhat worse off than the general population.

Table 6.7. Ghana: distribution of redeployees' per capita household income over GLSS per capita income deciles in three regions

GLSS income decile (three regions)	Redeployee households in each decile	
	Currently	Before redeployment
1	5.5	0.2
2	14.6	3.8
3	12.1	10.9
4	14.0	17.4
5	12.6	14.4
6	10.9	11.9
7	6.9	11.1
8	8.7	9.9
9	7.9	9.7
10	6.7	10.9

Source: Alderman, Canagarajah, and Younger (forthcoming).

general when they worked in the civil service, a fact borne out by the last column of Table 6.7.

Compensation. All redeployees received some form of compensation at the time of redeployment, either severance pay or, for those over 60, pension benefits. Alderman, Canagarajah, and Younger (1993) find that, on average, this compensation offset about one-fourth of the present value of redeployees' lost income stream.

Economic theory suggests that recipients of a one-time windfall payment of this sort will prefer to save it rather than use it for immediate consumption purposes, although a variety of circumstances weigh against doing so in this case. First, redeployees receive their compensation after having lost a job, and may need to spend it while they search for another. Second, financial markets are poorly developed in Ghana, so the opportunities for saving at positive real interest rates are few. Finally, most Ghanaian households are likely to be liquidity constrained, a condition that makes higher consumption out of a windfall more likely. Despite these conditions, however, redeployees did in fact save much of their severance pay: on average, they saved 53 percent of their severance and spent another 8 percent on consumer durables (which are also a means of consumption smoothing). Self-employed redeployees, in particular, allocated a large proportion of their severance pay (41 percent) to the acquisition of business equipment and real estate. This is quite different from the experience in Guinea (Mills and Sahn 1993), where redeployees allocated very little of their severance pay to savings. In addition to the long spells of unemployment experienced in Guinea, the fact that the government paid severance over an extended period of time rather than in a lump sum may also explain Guinean redeployees' low propensity to save or invest in business equipment.

6.4. Conclusions

Our results show clearly that redeployed civil servants in Ghana have suffered significant earnings declines after losing their public sector jobs. There are important caveats to this conclusion, however. Severance payments compensate the earnings loss, but only partially. In addition, one-third of our sample volunteered for redeployment, indicating that they expected to be better off after redeployment even if their earnings were lower (because they wanted to withdraw from the labor force, for example). And there may be a greater bias towards underreporting current income (most of which is from self-employment) than former income (most of which was from wages). Nevertheless, it seems unlikely that these factors could explain completely the loss in earnings that we estimate. Further, while only 15 percent of redeployees' households fell in the lower three deciles of the GLSS income distribution (a standard cut-off for "the poor") prior to redeployment, 32 percent did at the time of our survey. Thus, poverty among redeployees has increased, though it is still roughly equal to poverty in the general population.

Are these consequences unjustifiably severe? That depends on what one believes about the status quo before the redeployment began, especially the fairness of the distribution of public employment and public salaries. If, for example, redeployees had been engaged in socially productive activity while they worked in the civil service, earning salaries commensurate with their skills and actual labor market conditions, then their earnings loss from redeployment is in some sense unfair and deserving of compensation. Unfortunately, that is a poor characterization of the Ghanaian civil service. While some redeployees may have been working in the sense that they showed up at the office for eight hours a day, very few actually did something productive. At the lower echelons, civil service employment in Ghana is usually a thin disguise for transfer payments, a rent for those who are fortunate enough to land a government job. Insofar as most civil servants are not poor and would not be poor in the absence of these transfers, there is no welfare reason to maintain them. Retrenchment of these employees is thus justifiable on social welfare grounds:[20] what the redeployees lose is a rent they should not have had in the first place.

---

[20] There is an argument that some compensation is appropriate because laid-off workers will incur costs while they locate another job. Severance pay is appropriate for this.

The case of the redeployees who are cast into poverty as a result of their redeployment is more complex. Here, there are social welfare reasons for assisting families, though continued public employment may not be the most efficient means of providing such assistance.[21] Indeed, if their productivity is zero in the public sector, there is good reason to suppose that retrenchment will improve efficiency. Nevertheless, retrenchment does cause hardship that is difficult to justify, and some form of compensation seems appropriate. Unfortunately, compensation schemes often are administered poorly and are not well targeted to the households that merit them. In Guinea, for example, recipients of loans for starting new businesses not only failed to repay them, but were also among the wealthiest redeployees rather than the poorest. Kingsbury (1992a, 1992b) and Karp-Toledo (1991) report similar problems in other countries. Perhaps the most effective and administratively efficient approach is to increase severance pay. But to target this at the neediest redeployees requires divergence from traditional severance formulas based on terminal salaries and years of service. In particular, civil servants with lower salaries probably also have less human capital and therefore are most likely to be poor after losing their jobs. Thus, formulas that "flatten" severance pay, favoring the lowest paid workers, are likely to be better targeted to the poor.

Finally, while the results of this research provide important and useful information for policy-makers in Ghana, their generality is very much uncertain. Experiences in Guinea, for example, have been quite different than those in Ghana (see Chapter 7). Much of that difference probably is due to different labor market conditions. Ghana has always had an active informal labor market, and that sector has probably shown healthy growth during the past decade. In Conakry, on the other hand, the Sekou-Touré government worked hard to crush the informal sector, and apparently succeeded. Thus, the most obvious source of readily available employment (because formal enterprises are reducing their own staffing) is in its infancy there. Unfortunately, we know very little about how labor markets function in Africa, meaning that one can only guess about redeployees' labor market experience in any particular country.

---

[21] One must also ask why this relatively small group of poor people merits transfer payments while the poor who are privately employed do not.

References

Alderman, Harold, Sudharshan Canagarajah, and Stephen D. Younger. Forthcoming. "Consequences of Permanent Lay-Off from the Civil Service: Results from a Survey of Retrenched Workers in Ghana." In Rehabilitating Government: Pay and Employment Reform in Developing Economies, D. Lindauer and B. Nunberg, eds.

————— 1993. *Consequences of Permanent Lay-off from the Civil Service: Results from a Survey of Retrenched Workers in Ghana.* Working Paper No. 35. Ithaca, NY: CFNPP.

————— 1994. "A Comparison of Ghanaian Civil Servants' Earnings Before and After Retrenchment." Draft.

—— and Paul Higgins. 1992. *Food and Nutritional Adequacy in Ghana.* Working Paper No. 27. Washington, DC: CFNPP.

de Merode, Louis. 1992. "Implementing Civil Service Pay and Employment Reform in Africa: The Experiences of Ghana, the Gambia, and Guinea." Draft.

Glewwe, Paul, and Gillette Hall. 1993. "Who is Most Vulnerable to Macroeconomic Shocks? Hypothesis Tests Using Panel Data from Peru." Draft.

—— and Kwaku Twum-Baah. 1990. *The Distribution of Welfare in Ghana, 1987–88.* Living Standards Measurement Survey Working Paper No. 75. Washington, DC: World Bank.

Kingsbury, David S. 1992a. "Compensatory Social Programs and Structural Adjustment: A Review of Experience." Bethesda, MD: Development Alternatives, Inc.

—— 1992b. "Programs for Mitigating Adverse Social Impacts During Adjustment: The A.I.D. Experience." Bethesda, MD: Development Alternatives, Inc.

Karp-Toledo, Elaine. 1991. "Les Fonds d'emplo—sont-ils efficaces? Une evaluation socio-economique de la DIRE/FNE au Senegal." Draft.

Mills, Bradford, and David Sahn. 1993. *Is There Life after Public Service: The Fate of Retrenched Workers in Conakry, Guinea.* Working Paper No. 42. Ithaca, NY: CFNPP.

—— et al. 1993. *Public Finance and Public Employment: An Analysis of Public Sector Retrenchment Programs in Ghana and Guinea.* Working Paper No. 52. Ithaca, NY: CFNPP.

Svejnar, Jan, and Katherine Terrell. 1991. *Reducing Labor Redundancy in State-Owned Enterprises.* Working Paper No. 792. Washington, DC: World Bank (Policy Research, and External Affairs Department).

Vijverberg, Wim. 1988. *Profits from Self-Employment: A Case Study of Cote d'Ivoire.* LSMS Working Paper No. 43. Washington, DC: World Bank.

7

Life after Public Sector
Job Loss in Guinea

Bradford Mills and David E. Sahn

7.1. *Introduction*

Donors and policy-makers continue to emphasize reducing the role, and improving the efficiency, of the state as a key component of reform in sub-Saharan Africa economies. Macroeconomic stabilization efforts inevitably focus attention on the size of the wage bill and the attendant strain that is placed on the government's limited budgetary resources. However, public sector wage and employment policies also have important direct impacts on the efficiency of the sector, as well as numerous indirect impacts on the rest of the economy.[1] Thus, the retrenchment of government workers, as well as the rationalization of public sector pay scales and employment policies, have become essential components of structural adjustment programs in sub-Saharan Africa. This paper will focus on the Republic of Guinea's successes and costs of implementing a public sector retrenchment program. Guinea's experience is particularly poignant because of the public sector's initial dominance of economic activity and the presence of severe institutional constraints to effective program implementation.

While there is a general consensus on the need for public sector reform, implementation of programs designed to reduce employment have been hampered by concerns about their political and social costs. Retrenchment programs are often perceived as politically costly because they risk alienating civil servants who form an important political base for most regimes. Further, erosion of civil service support can cripple other reform efforts. Consequently, a number of regimes have lacked the political will to implement retrenchment programs as designed.

The social costs of retrenchment programs have also been an important source of concern and have inhibited implementation efforts. Large layoffs

---

[1] Examples of indirect impacts include: spillovers of public sector wage distortions to private sector labor markets; the deleterious effect of public sector rent seeking on market transaction costs; and the impact of public sector wage flexibility on the effectiveness of nominal exchange rate devaluation.

have the potential of destabilizing private sector labor markets, especially since such programs often occur alongside demand-reducing stabilization policies. Retrenchment programs also raise equity concerns, particularly that women, who are less likely to face job and wage discrimination in the public sector, will be disproportionately hurt. But perhaps of primary concern has been the prospect of retrenched workers being unable to find alternative sources of employment. These issues are explored in the present chapter. The next section presents a brief historical overview of the growth of the public sector in Guinea during the post-independence period, and shows how this precipitated the need for strong reform measures in the mid-1980s. Section 7.3 describes the efforts of the new reform-minded government that took the reigns of power in 1985 to reverse the growth of the public payroll. The transition paths and experiences of departing workers are discussed in Section 7.4. An empirical analysis of the structure of Conakry labor markets and the factors that influence the duration of unemployment experienced by departing public sector workers is presented in Section 7.5. The final section discusses the implications of the results for the design and implementation of public sector retrenchment programs.

7.2. *Historical Context*

In order to understand the acute need for, and challenges of, reducing the size of the civil service and the role of the state in the Guinean economy, one needs to go back to 1958 when independence from France was realized. The new post-independence regime, the First Republic, proceeded to install a state apparatus which was to control all aspects of political and economic life, even at the village level, for the next 26 years. The ruling political party became inseparable from the state apparatus and both were highly centralized under the head of state, Sekou Touré.

As the state endeavored to eliminate all formal private sector activity and became the source of formal sector employment, it grew at a rate of over 7 percent per year throughout the 1970s. The exact number of employees under the First Republic is not known but it is estimated that there were 140,830 government employees in 1979 out of a total population of around 4,400,000 people. The bloated public sector workforce forced the government to allocate a large portion of its resources to support the ballooning public sector. This was especially true during the early 1980s, when the government financed large balance of payments deficits by depleting foreign exchange reserves and accumulating large payment arrears (Arulpragasam and Sahn 1991).

Perhaps most destructively, deteriorating conditions of public sector service throughout the First Republic spawned rent seeking and related corruption which significantly increased the cost of economic transactions.

Nominal wages were frozen between 1965 and 1980 (de Mérode 1991), and remained constant in real terms between 1980 and 1984 (UNDP and World Bank 1992). Further, the wage structure was rigid and compressed, leaving few wage incentives for advancement within the sector. By 1985 the average Guinean civil servant earned 5500 FG per month base pay, about US$18 at the parallel exchange rate. Instead of receiving adequate on-budget wage payment, however, civil servants benefited through their positions from a number of additional allowances and in-kind transfers, especially access to ration shops which sold goods at substantially below parallel market prices. Lack of mechanisms for accountability also encouraged civil servants to put minimum effort into the performance of public sector duties, and to concentrate on using public resources at their disposal for personal gain.

The Second Republic took power in a coup, shortly after the death of Sekou Touré in April 1984. Economic, social, and political disintegration was acute, reserves had been depleted, and the level of debt was untenable. Thus, the new military regime quickly moved to dismantle the state apparatus set up under the First Republic and then implemented liberal economic policies favorable to private enterprise and foreign investment. Economic reform measures were first proposed in the Programme Intérimaire de Redressement Nationale in 1985, which was subsequently elaborated into a structural adjustment program for 1986–1988, Programme de Redressement Economique et Financier (PREF), supported by loans from the World Bank and IMF.

The PREF committed the government to undertake a number of concrete actions to reduce the role of the state in the economy and to liberalize markets. Included in the actions were steps to: drastically devalue the exchange rate to reflect the true value of the currency; eliminate price controls and state marketing agencies to liberalize trade; and shut down state banks and promote commercial banking. But most germane to this paper was the mandate to reduce the number of public sector employees and to privatize or liquidate parastatals.

7.3. The Civil Service Reform Program

7.3.1. Intent and action

As part of the initial economic recovery program outlined in 1985, three targets were set to reduce the number of public sector employees and increase the efficiency of the sector: total public sector employment was to be reduced by 25,000 persons; a new pay and benefits framework was to be introduced; and the skill levels of remaining public sector employees were to be increased. The second phase of PREF, commencing late in 1988, focused on increasing the efficiency of the remaining public sector employees through institutional reform.

The first major step toward realizing the ambitious objectives of the reform program was a census of public sector employees, conducted between December 1985 and April 1986. The census results indicated that 70,989 individuals were employed directly by the civil service; 17,111 more were employed in parastatals, state banks, or attached to mining companies; 12,700 were enrolled in the military; and 2,000 were employed without a specified sector.

The following actions were then initiated to achieve public sector staff reduction targets. First, guaranteed employment for university graduates was terminated. Second, a hiring freeze for civil service positions was imposed. Third, retirement of civil servants over the age of 55 and those with more than 30 years of service was mandated. Fourth, a large number of public sector enterprises and banks were closed and their employees were removed from the public sector payroll. Fifth, employees attached to mining companies were removed from the public sector payroll (although many were re-employed on a contractual basis). Sixth, optional early retirement and voluntary departure packages with substantial benefits packages to civil servants were offered. Finally, mandatory skill testing of all civil service employees was instituted, to be followed by the release of those found to lack required skills.

Concurrently, three programs were developed to lessen the social and political impact of the proposed reductions by enticing employees to leave the public sector voluntarily, and making it less painful for those forced out of their jobs. First, the Administrative Reserve Status program (Disponibilité Spéciale) was instituted in December 1985. The program placed individuals redeployed as part of liquidation or privatization of public sector enterprises on administrative reserve status. This status entitled them to continued payment of base salary for six months after termination of their employment. Under political pressure, salary payments were later extended until December 1988. Subsequently, civil servants who failed the skills test were also placed on Administrative Reserve Status and delays in the confirmation process of test results allowed some of them to remain on reserve status and continue to draw civil service salaries for up to two years after the December 1988 deadline.

Second, as a complement to the forced departures of those from closed enterprises and those who failed skills tests, an attempt was made to provide incentives to induce workers to leave the public sector voluntarily. In particular, the voluntary departure program was created to encourage civil servants to leave the employment of the state. Incentives for departure, of between 500,000 FG and 1,000,000 FG paid over 30 months, were provided. The deadline for enrollment in the voluntary departure program was December 1988, and those who opted to take the civil service skills test, regardless of whether or not the outcome was favorable, forfeited their eligibility for the program.

Third, individuals participating in the Voluntary Departure program were also eligible to receive private enterprise development loans and training from the Bureau d'aide à la reconversion des agents de la fonction publique (BARAF) to facilitate their transition into the private sector.

7.3.2. *Results of the program*

To verify reductions in the size of the public sector, a second census of public sector employees was undertaken at the end of 1989. According to the census results, 32,639 workers had been taken off the public sector payrolls since 1985. Departures of ministry civil service staff accounted for a little over half of all reductions, and redeployments from state banks, parastatals, and mining companies accounted for the remaining departures. Over the same period, the size of the military actually increased from 12,700 to 15,000 persons. Of the 32,639 departures, 10,120 departed under the voluntary departure program; 4700 retired; 6526 retired early; 4245 were removed from Administrative Reserve status; and 5617 were mining sector civil servants removed from the civil service and rehired on a contractual basis. Clearly, in terms of exceeding its target of removing 25,000 persons from the public sector, the census information suggests that the retrenchment program was successful. However, this success was tempered by the questions about the reliability of payroll information and high rates of new hirings.

To boost morale and productivity of remaining workers, wages were increased dramatically during the course of the reform program. In 1986 the civil service salary base was increased by 80 percent and cost of living and transport allowances were added to compensation packages. This followed an even larger pay increase that had occurred in 1985 and resulted in salaries approximately four times higher in 1986 than in 1980. Salary bases were again increased by over 80 percent in 1988, along with additional increases in allowances and premia. Then in April 1989 a new compensation plan was instituted, under which the base salary was determined by an index calculated on the basis of individuals' education and experience levels. Previous allowances for cost of living and transportation were abolished and a comprehensive set of new allowances was defined. These changes resulted in an average increase in real renumeration of 23 percent. More importantly, they represented a first attempt explicitly to link promotions and pay increases to performance.

The trend of yearly salary increases, however, was not altered by the new payroll framework as real compensation was increased again in 1990. Then in 1991, partially as a result of a national strike, the nominal base salary was increased 145 percent, far exceeding the rise in the price level. These latest increases, though politically necessary, had severe budgetary repercussions and were strongly opposed by the international lending community.

In addition to the retrenchment program and efforts to rationalize pay for those who remained, a number of positive steps were taken to improve the institutional structure of the civil service. In late 1988 the Ministry of Reform and Civil Service (MRAFP) was created to institutionalize the civil service reform process. Two departments within the MRAFP and a department within each ministry with links to the MRAFP were created to address institutional organization, skill development, and financial management needs.[2] Despite these accomplishments, there is a common perception that civil service reforms lost momentum and even eroded after 1988. For example, the coverage of the testing program was incomplete and the results often did not translate into appropriate employment decisions.

Transparency and truth in payroll and personnel information has also proved difficult to maintain despite two public sector censuses in four years. A verification exercise in Conakry in 1987 suggested that 5 percent of payroll records were improper, and the second public census in 1989–1990 showed further erosion in the accuracy of payroll information. This inability to maintain payroll information has led to strong suspicions that the actual number of civil servants may be higher than reported. Outside technical assistance has been provided to overhaul and computerize the civil servant roster and payroll system, yet progress in establishing a clear system of accounting for public sector workers continues to move slowly.

The effectiveness of the public sector retrenchment program in reducing the government budget deficit has also been limited by concurrent increases in real wages. Nonetheless, results indicate that, at least initially, efforts to reduce the size of the public sector have had some impact on total government expenditures. A major portion of total government expenditure in the last years of the First Republic was devoted to public sector wages. It is estimated that wage payments comprised 39.9 percent of total government expenditures in 1980 (UNDP and World Bank 1992), but by 1987 wage payments as a share of total expenditures had fallen to only 11.7 percent of total public spending. However, civil service real wages continued to increase, and so between 1987 and 1991 both the real wage bill and wages as a percentage of total public expenditures more than doubled.

While the overall budgetary picture from 1987 to 1991 suggests that the fiscal benefits of the early efforts of public sector reform have been eroded,

---

2 The Office of Administrative Reform Strategies and Programs was set up to provide the rationale and outlines for ministry bureaucratic reorganization and to develop job descriptions and organizational charts within each ministry. The Center for Administrative Improvement was established to improve the efficiency of civil servants. Its specific mandate included: evaluating retraining needs; developing training programs; developing a computerized data base on employees; and developing a standardized system of evaluation and advancement. Finally, a Department of Administrative and Financial Affairs, with links to the MRAFP, was established in every ministry to monitor and administer the ministries' personnel, material, and financial resources.

some positive outcomes remain. Of greatest note is the government's relative success in reallocating overall government expenditure into investment. The portion of total government expenditures going to recurrent expenses decreased between 1987 and 1991. This improvement is partially attributable to large inflows of foreign capital from international donors, where redeployment programs were crucial in obtaining and continuing the flow of this assistance. Thus, from a budgetary standpoint, perhaps the greatest impact of the redeployment programs has been to facilitate the security of foreign assistance by sending a strong signal to the international donor community of the government's commitment to economic reform.

7.4. The Impact of Retrenchment Programs on Redeployed Workers

7.4.1. The data

This section examines the difficulties retrenched public sector employees have faced in transiting into the private sector. The data are based on a self-weighted, representative sample of 1728 households conducted in Conakry in 1990–1991, and a sub-sample of individuals who were redeployed and/or left a public sector job between 1979 and the time the initial survey was conducted.[3] A supplemental "retrenchment" survey then collected additional information on the individuals' labor histories, including: reason for transition, duration of unemployment accompanying the transition, the level of pre- and post-transition wages, and compensation received after departure.

7.4.2. Characteristics of public sector departees

While the formal retrenchment program began in late 1985, efforts to reduce the size of the public sector and accompanying departures began prior to that time and continued after the formal termination of the program in 1988. Overall, during the period 1979–1992, for which we have data, slightly more than half of the departures were motivated by retrenchment.[4] Retirements accounted for 38 percent of departures and finding other work represented roughly 6 percent of departures. It is important to remember,

---

[3] The sub-sample is biased by the lack of representation of individuals who died or migrated from Conakry after transitions from public sector positions, but before implementation of the survey. No specific information is available on the bias introduced by the exclusion of these groups. However, retirees and other cohorts of older retrenched workers are probably under-represented in the sub-sample because of death. On the other hand, urban to rural migration during the period was extremely limited owing to poor economic opportunities in villages, and therefore is probably not a significant source of bias in the sample.

[4] The retrenchment category includes individuals laid off because of government cutbacks, failure of the government skills test, or participation in the voluntary departure program.

however, that these latter categories include those motivated to retire early or find other work, because of the expected reduction in the size of the public service.

An examination of departures by period shows that the frequency of retrenchment is much higher during, but not limited to, the years 1985–1988, when the retrenchment program was most active. However, layoffs from public sector enterprise closings began in the early 1980s prior to the implementation of formal retrenchment programs. Likewise, many individuals placed on the roles of "dispondability special" were released from the public sector after the official termination of retrenchment programs in December 1988.

When one disaggregates departures by reason, a disproportionate number (31 percent) of the retrenched workers were female. While gender bias may be a factor, this finding is due at least partially to the predominate representation of women in the lower age groups, which were more heavily affected by retrenchment. Further, those who were heads of households were less likely to depart because of retrenchment than those who retired or found other employment. As expected, retirees had accumulated the most experience: 26.0 years in their last position and 28.5 years overall. But retrenched workers had also accumulated a significant, albeit smaller, amount of experience before termination of their employment: an average of 12.3 years experience in their last public sector position and 14.9 years' accumulated public sector service. Overall, 42.2 percent of workers leaving the public sector during the retrenchment program had no education.

7.4.3. Transition paths of public sector workers leaving between 1979 and 1992

An examination of individual labor market activities after departing the public sector revealed five paths. First, some left the public sector and did not take other work, at least not through the time that the survey was conducted. Second, some left the public sector, spent a period without work, and then took a private sector position. Third, some left a public sector position and immediately took a private sector position. A fourth type of transition involved leaving a public sector position, spending a period without work, and then entering another public sector position. Finally, several individuals left a public sector position because of retrenchment but immediately took another public sector position.[5]

The current employment status and specific transition paths taken by those who left the civil service between 1980 and 1990 is given in Table 7.1.

---

5 This last type of transition is qualitatively different from the other transitions listed because the individual never actually left the public sector. However, since redeployment was clearly the cause of the transition, they are included with the other types of transition discussed above. In fact, only 1 percent of the transitions are from one public sector job to another without a spell of unemployment. Thus, transition type 5 is not of great importance.

Table 7.1. Guinea: employment status in 1992 of individuals leaving a public sector job between 1978 and 1990 ($N=189$)

	%
Not working:	
since previous public sector position	39.2
with an interim spell in private sector	3.6
All	42.9
Working in private sector with:	
no spell without work from previous public sector position	19.0
a spell without work from previous public sector position	32.9
All	51.9
Working in public sector with:	
no spell without work from previous public sector position	1.1
a spell without work from previous public sector position	4.2
All	5.3
Total	100.0

Source: Mills and Sahn (1995).

The results must be evaluated recognizing that this is a heterogeneous group of workers in terms of the date they left the public service and the reasons for departure. Of those who exited the public sector after 1978, 43 percent were not working at the time of the survey in 1992 (not working includes those who are seeking and those not seeking employment); 52 percent were employed in the private sector, and 5 percent exited a public sector position but were currently employed in another public sector position.

Among those not working at the time of the survey, the overwhelming majority (91 percent) had never re-entered the labor market after leaving the public sector. However, even among individuals employed in the private sector at the time of the survey, 62 percent had experienced a spell without work between leaving the public sector and taking their private sector position. Finally, for the small number of individuals who left a public sector position, 80 percent experienced a spell without work.[6]

For those individuals who left the public sector after 1984 and successfully found other employment, on average, real earnings are over twice their previous levels in the public sector. At the same time, there is a great deal of dispersion in the distribution of earnings changes. This is particularly so

---

[6] It should be emphasized that the 20 percent that had no spell without work after public sector positions clearly indicates that departure from the previous position had been motivated by retrenchment.

among those entering the non-wage sector where 52 percent had lower earnings in their new jobs than at the time of public sector departure, while only 37 percent of the former public sector workers finding wage jobs witnessed a fall in their earnings.

This brief analysis of individual labor histories suggests three things. First, movements out of the public sector to other positions tend to be permanent: 95 percent of transition paths involved leaving the public sector for a private sector position or no work. Second, a relatively high percentage of individuals were either currently without work or had experienced a spell without work upon leaving the public sector.[7]

7.4.4. *Labor market participation*

Table 7.2 examines both the incidence of unemployment and of non-participation in the labor market among those not working during the period that the retrenchment program was formally being implemented, as well as during those years previous and subsequent to the program, when in fact some retrenchment was occurring. In 1992, 36.2 percent of those who were retrenched from the public sector between 1979 and 1990 had not taken another job while 54.4 percent of retirees had not taken another job. However, it would clearly be mistaken to suggest that those who are not working are unemployed, since 35 percent of the retrenched workers and 84 percent of retirees not working are non-participants (no longer searching employment). Further, non-participation is highest in the pre- and post-retrenchment program periods, reflecting an influx onto the job market of former public sector workers who wished to remain active in the labor force, but were forced to retire under the retrenchment program.

From these results, the overall unemployment rate among persons leaving public sector jobs is calculated at 21 percent. This is higher than the overall unemployment rate for Conakry of 12 percent, despite the fact that the majority of redepartees reside in age and gender cohorts with the lowest rates of unemployment (Glick, Sahn and del Ninno 1993). Further, retrenched workers appear to have a higher rate of unemployment overall (20 percent), and during each time period, than for retirees or other departees.

7.4.5. *The welfare of former public sector workers' households*

In order to examine the impact of public sector departure on household welfare we would ideally compare per capita expenditures of households at the time of the survey with their per capita expenditures at the time of departure from the civil service. Unfortunately, data on per capita expenditures at the

---

7 However, it is important to keep in mind that not all individuals without work are structurally unemployed (unable to find suitable job); instead, some are retirees or in other categories of nonparticipants including those not searching because of illness, household duties, perceived poor economic opportunities, and other causes.

Table 7.2. Guinea: labor force and work force participation rates in 1992 by reason for departures from public sector

	Period of departure from public sector			
	1979–90	1979–84	1985–88	1989–90
Retrenched	*N = 94*	*N = 19*	*N = 68*	*N = 7*
% working	63.8	79.0	58.8	71.4
% not working	36.2	21.0	41.2	28.6
of which:				
% participants	64.7	75.0	60.7	100.0
% non-participants	35.3	25.0	39.3	0.0
Retirees	*N = 68*	*N = 25*	*N = 35*	*N = 8*
% working	45.6	36.0	54.3	37.5
% not working	54.4	64.0	45.7	62.5
of which:				
% participants	16.2	0.0	18.7	40.0
% non-participants	83.8	100.0	81.3	60.0
All	*N = 177*	*N = 50*	*N = 108*	*N = 19*
% working	59.9	60.0	59.3	63.2
% not working	40.1	40.0	40.7	36.8
of which:				
% participants	39.4	15.0	45.5	57.1
% non-participants	60.6	85.0	54.5	42.9

Source: Mills and Sahn (1995).

time of departure are not available. However, the data can address the important question of how the welfare of per capita consumption households with public sector departees compares with that of the general population.[8]

The first row of Table 7.3 shows that in 1990, 24 percent of the individuals working in the public sector were from households in the lower 30 percent of the per capita consumption distribution. In contrast, 37 percent of the individuals who transited public sector positions between 1979 and 1990 were in the lower 30 percent of the per capita consumption distribution. Individuals leaving public sector because of redeployment and retirement were particularly vulnerable, with 35 and 44 percent, respectively, falling into the lower 30 percent of the distribution.

However, the subsequent transition path of individuals appears to be far more important than the reason for leaving in determining the probability of

[8] The distribution of household per capita consumption by quintile for the general population is, by definition, 20 percent for each quintile group.

Table 7.3. Guinea: household consumption quintiles in 1990, by reason for leaving the public sector, and 1990 employment status (%)

	Bottom 30%	Quintile					Total	No. of Individuals
		Lowest	2nd	Middle	4th	Highest		
Total in 1990 public sector	23.5	14.7	18.4	17.9	25.8	25.8	100	694
Total leaving public sector between 1979 and 1990	37.1	25.7	23.4	17.7	16.0	17.1	100	175
Reason for leaving:								
Retrenchment	35.1	25.5	23.4	17.0	16.0	18.09	100	94
Not working	38.3	34.0	21.3	14.9	14.9	14.9	100	47
Working	31.9	17.0	25.5	19.2	17.0	21.3	100	47
Retirement	43.9	28.8	25.8	19.7	13.6	12.1	100	66
Not working	50.0	37.5	22.5	20.0	12.5	7.5	100	40
Working	34.6	15.4	30.8	19.2	15.4	19.2	100	26
Found other work	9.1	9.1	9.1	18.2	27.3	36.4	100	11

Source: Mills and Sahn (1995).

the household falling into the lower 30 percent of the per capita household consumption distribution. Among retrenched workers who successfully transited into the private sector before the 1990 survey, 31 percent resided in households in the lower 30 percent compared with 38 percent for redeployees who were not working in 1990. Similarly, among retirees who found other positions in the private sector, 35 percent were from households in the lower 30 percent versus 50 percent of retirees who remained without work.

The above results do not necessarily imply that the households of public sector workers who were laid off and remained unemployed in 1990 were worse off than they were when they were working for the state. It is feasible, given the low education levels we have observed among many of these workers, that they were poor when they were still working for the government. Alternatively, these workers may have been formerly receiving a premium from public sector employment and may now reside in poverty because the socioeconomic profile of their households puts them in a cohort of the general population that has a high poverty risk. The results do imply, however, that individuals who left the public sector and did not undertake alternative employment do face a substantial risk of residing in poor households.

7.4.6. The utilization of compensation programs

There were two primary forms of compensation for workers leaving the public sector: pensions and severance pay. Pension schemes have been in place since before the Second Republic. All public sector workers over 55 years of age or with over 30 years of public service are eligible. As discussed in Section 7.2, severance pay programs were instituted after 1985 as part of the redeployment program and sought to induce the voluntary departure of public sector workers through payments of between 500,000 FG and 1 million FG over 30-month periods. These payments were justified to minimize public sector opposition to reductions and to insure the welfare of transiting public sector workers.

Those leaving the public sector through the voluntary departure program were also, in principle, eligible for loans from BARAF. However, only 3.2 percent of voluntary departees actually secured loans under the program. BARAF also provided technical assistance in starting private enterprises to a number of those securing loans, but provided no training or assistance to the 96.8 percent of voluntary departees who did not secure loans or the larger population of redeployees.

The effectiveness of targeting is clearly shown in Table 7.4, where compensation from last public sector position is examined by reason for leaving the position. Retirees appear to be effectively targeted by pension plans: 87.8 percent received pensions and relatively few, 8.1 percent, received severance benefits. Interestingly, coverage is slightly higher among

Table 7.4. Guinea: compensation for leaving the public sector, by reason of departure, and 1992 employment status (%)

| | Compensation type | | | | | No. of |
	Pension	Severance pay	Pension and severance pay	Nothing	Total	Individuals
All	33.7	33.2	3.7	29.5	100	190
Retirees	82.4	2.7	5.4	9.5	100	74
Not working	79.1	4.7	4.7	11.6	100	43
Working	87.1	0.0	6.5	6.5	100	31
Redeployees	3.0	60.0	3.0	34.0	100	100
Not working	2.6	65.8	5.3	26.3	100	38
Working	3.2	56.5	1.6	38.7	100	62
Found other work	0.0	14.3	0.0	85.7	100	11

Source: Mills and Sahn (1993).

retirees who moved into the private sector than among those who remained without work. By contrast, redeployees' compensation comes primarily from severance pay, 63 percent, with only 6 percent receiving pensions and 34 percent receiving no compensation. The proportion of redeployees receiving compensation was slightly higher among those who did not find another job than among those who found other work. However, as the results of the previous section show, the relationship between severance pay and the duration of unemployment is not statistically significant. Finally, 86 percent of workers leaving a public sector position for another job receive no benefits; but 14 percent who left because they found other work in the private sector received severance payments from the voluntary departure program.

A multinomial logit model is specified to test the relationship between type of compensation received and the personnel characteristics of departees. If compensation has been fairly and equitably disbursed, the probability of receipt should be related solely to the selection criteria for each type of compensation. Specifically, receipt of pensions should be related to age and the duration of public service but not to other personal characteristics such as gender and education level. Similarly, all civil servants should be equally eligible for severance payments, particularly voluntary departure benefits. Thus, the primary factor influencing the receipt of severance payments should be whether the individual left the public sector during the re-deployment program period.

The estimated relationships are given in Table 7.5, using individuals receiving no compensation as the base group.[9] As expected, the dummy variables for persons over 54 years of age, and the variable for years in the public service, increases the probability of receiving retirement benefits. However, the gender parameter is negative and significant. This implies that females, even after controlling for age and duration of service, are less likely to receive retirement benefits. At the same time, the individual's education had no statistically significant impact on the receipt of pensions.

No relationship between the probability of receiving severance pay (compared with the no-compensation base) and personal characteristics is inferred from the data. However, as expected, departure of the public sector during the redeployment period strongly influences the probability of receiving severance pay. Overall, with the exception of gender bias in disbursement of pensions, the results support the assertion that compensation payments have been equitably disbursed.

---

[9] The small group of individuals receiving both pensions and severance pay are included in the severance pay categories.

Table 7.5. Guinea: multinomial logit—a model of type of compensation received for individuals leaving the public sector

Variables	Base: no compensation; $N = 56$			
	Pension only; $N = 64$		Severance pay; $N = 69$	
	Parameter estimate	t-statistic	Parameter estimate	t-statistic
Sex (female = 1)	−2.132	−2.355**	−0.093	−0.183
Age ≥ 55	2.584	1.993**	−2.002	−1.954
Age ≥ 40, < 55	1.114	0.875	−0.524	−0.809
Public service (years)	0.240	4.468**	0.046	1.364
Education level (none = 0)				
Primary	1.184	1.557	0.054	0.092
Secondary	0.314	0.361	−0.505	−0.820
University	−0.489	−0.371	0.319	0.419
Left in redeployment				
period	−0.066	−0.110	2.278	4.952**
Constant	−6.856	−4.556**	−1.514	−2.345**

Model statistics
Log likelihood value: −122.46
Chi-square statistic: 170.98**
No. of observations: $N = 189$

* Significant at the 0.10 level.
** Significant at the 0.05 level.
Source: Mills and Sahn (1995).

7.5. *An Empirical Analysis of Labor Markets and the Factors that Influence the Duration of Unemployment*

This section first establishes evidence of segmentation between wage and non-wage sector labor markets in Conakry and then examines factors that influence the duration of unemployment accompanying job search in the two sectors. The distinction of labor markets by wage and non-wage sectors is particularly relevant for public sector restructuring efforts and their impact on redeployed public sector workers. In addition to the usual transition costs from frictional unemployment, departing public sector workers may experience substantial losses in future earnings when labor markets are segmented, for two reasons. First, if segmentation results from the rationing of wage sector positions, departure from a public sector position can result in the loss of an earnings premium associated with the rationed sector.

Former public sector workers must then choose between entering the non-wage sector or undertaking costly search to find another wage sector position with an accompanying premium. Second, wage sector job loss may attach a stigma to departing public sector workers which lowers the probability of receiving another offer for wage employment. This forces redeployed workers to take non-wage positions or accept lower paying wage sector offers.

7.5.1. *Evidence of a premium for wage sector employment*

In order to establish evidence of an earnings premium, wage and non-wage sector earnings functions are estimated, correcting for endogeneity of sector choice, as part of a switching regression system of equations. Specifically, the system consists of one equation that determines the sector of employment and two equations that determine earnings in the wage and non-wage sectors. (A more detailed presentation of the switching regression system and its statistical properties is found in Mills and Sahn 1993.)

The sector selection equation is specified to be a function of formal measures of human capital, as well as proxies for access to job information networks and household variables which determine the flexibility of labor time. Human capital is expected to be positively related to the probability of obtaining wage sector employment. Thus, older individuals and those with higher educational degrees are expected to be more likely to reside in the wage sector. Further, the education levels of other household members are believed to be important in sector selection because they expand the network of employer contacts and thus increase the probability of finding employment in the wage sector. Residing in the city center is also expected to increase the network of employer contacts and to be positively related to wage sector employment.

Dummy variables for three ethnic groups not indigenous to Conakry—Fula, Malinke, and Forester—are also included in the selectivity equation. These ethnic groups are generally perceived as more likely to be involved in large scale commercial activities with accompanying access to capital. However, it is difficult to postulate if these groups are more or less likely to undertake wage sector employment than the ethnic group indigenous to Conakry, the Suso. It is possible that increased access to capital may make these groups more likely to undertake non-wage employment. On the other hand, they may also have a greater range of wage employer contacts which would increase the probability of finding wage sector employment. Access to employment contacts may also differ by gender. Since wage sector employers and employees are predominantly male, female workers are expected to have less access to information on wage employment opportunities and a lower probability of residing in the wage sector.

Gender, marital status, and number of children are also expected to affect the probability of entering the wage sector through their impact on the individual's flexibility in the allocation of labor time. Since females traditionally have a greater responsibility to household duties, their labor time would be expected to be less flexible and therefore they would be less likely to take wage sector employment. Allocation of labor time is also expected to be less flexible for individuals in households with small children and for married individuals. Finally, a dummy variable for previous departure from a public sector position is included in the sector selection equation to test the hypothesis that public sector job loss has a negative impact on the probability of re-entering the wage sector.

For the earnings equations, the relationships between individual characteristics and earnings are hypothesized to vary between the two sectors. In the wage sector, hourly earnings are expected to be related to formal measures of human capital which serve as signals to potential employers about the employee's ability. Therefore, the returns to schooling levels are expected to be positive and larger at higher degree levels. The returns to age, a proxy for experience, are also expected to be positive, but decreasing, and the returns to duration of employment in the current job are expected to be positive. Further, if wage sector labor markets are rationed, variables such as gender and ethnicity, which are important in the stratification of labor markets in Conakry, influence the probability of finding wage sector employment, but not the determination of wages.

In the non-wage sector, earnings are expected to be strongly related to direct measures of the productivity of the worker. Therefore, functional measures of human capital such as literacy are expected to be positively related to non-wage earnings. The duration of the current enterprise is also expected to yield positive returns to non-wage earnings since individuals accumulate human capital through learning by doing. Similarly, age is expected to have a positive but decreasing return as a proxy for general experience. Returns to physical assets, particularly capital, are also believed to be an important component of non-wage earnings and are expected to show a positive return.

Unlike the wage sector, non-wage sector earnings are expected to be affected by gender and ethnicity through their influence on the opportunity set of enterprise or occupation types available to non-wage workers. Specifically, capital and labor time constraints tend to restrict females to the operation of very small retail enterprises which have lower earnings than other types of enterprise. On the other hand, as discussed, three ethnic groups not indigenous to Conakry—the Fulani, Malinke, and Foresters—are generally perceived to be involved predominantly in large-scale wholesaling and to have extensive commercial linkages with accompanying access to capital. Therefore, the non-wage earnings of these three ethnic groups, after controlling for other factors, are expected to be greater than those of the predominant ethnic group in Conakry, the Suso.

Quarterly dummy variables to control for seasonality in earnings are also included in both the wage and non-wage earnings equations. Since one of the benefits of wage sector employment is a more stable expected stream of earnings over time, these parameters are expected to reveal greater seasonal fluctuations in the non-wage earnings function than in the wage earnings function. Finally, a redeployee dummy variable is added to both the wage and non-wage earnings functions to see if redeployees' earnings tend to be higher or lower than the general population, given the same returns on other earnings characteristics.

Data on 2565 working individuals, from the Cornell Food and Nutrition Policy Program survey of Conakry, Guinea, households, was estimated with the full information maximum likelihood method. The sample is split almost equally between wage and non-wage workers, reflecting the relative size of the two sectors in the Conakry economy. The coefficient estimates for specific groups of variables in the earnings equations, e.g. education variables, are then restricted to be equal in order to perform log-likelihood ratio tests on the significance of the differences in the earnings determinants of the wage and non-wage sectors. The parameter estimates for the sector selection equation are reported in the first two columns of Table 7.6.

The results indicate that age and formal education are positively related to the probability of residing in the wage sector. The education levels of other adult household members also appear to be important in sector selection. University education for other adult male members and secondary education among other adult female members have a positive impact, and primary education among other adult male household members have a negative impact, on the probability of residing in the wage sector.

Perhaps most striking, being female has a very strong negative impact on the probability of participating in wage sector employment, even after controlling for the negative impact of the presence of young children in households. One ethnic group, the Fulani, is also negatively related to wage sector employment. However, residence in the central city area and marriage do not show significant relationships with the probability of working in the wage sector, and neither does being a former public sector employee. Finally, the estimated correlation of the error structures of the sector selection equation and the wage and non-wage earnings equations, $cov(wv)$ and $cov(sv)$, are not significant, suggesting that sector selection does not significantly bias the earnings equations parameter estimates.

The estimated results of the structural sector selection equation are presented in columns (3) and (4) of Table 7.6. The difference between the log of predicted wage and non-wage sector earnings is found to be positively related to the probability of being in the wage sector. This result suggests that perceived sectorial returns do play an important role in sector selection. Further, the magnitude of the other parameter estimates of the structural sector selection equation are very similar to those presented in columns (1) and (2). This is expected, since the estimated correlation between the error

Table 7.6. Guinea: switching regression equation estimates (wage sector = 1)

	System		Structural probit	
	Parameter estimate	t-statistic	Parameter estimate	t-statistic
	(1)	(2)	(3)	(4)
Intercept	−0.2063	(−1.49)	−0.1378	(−0.98)
Age	0.0093	(2.80)**	0.114	(3.52)**
Education				
Primary	0.7663	(10.36)**	0.8125	(11.00)**
Secondary	1.4723	(14.75)**	1.5384	(14.79)**
University	1.8980	(14.58)**	2.0652	(13.39)**
Ethnicity				
Fulani	−0.2342	(−3.11)**	−0.2610	(−3.57)**
Malinke	−0.1310	(−1.58)	−0.0491	(−0.58)
Forester	−0.0682	(−0.56)	0.4166	(0.32)
Sex (female = 1)	−1.1563	(−15.30)**	−1.3173	(−16.11)**
Redeployee	0.0547	(0.37)	0.1699	(1.08)
No. of primary men	−0.0442	(−1.66)**	−0.0472	(−1.76)*
No. of secondary men	0.0563	(1.09)	0.0646	(1.24)
No. of university men	0.2210	(2.29)**	0.2184	(2.34)**
No. of primary women	0.0357	0.87	0.0387	(0.97)
No. of secondary women	0.1584	(2.04)**	0.1571	(2.02)**
No. of university women	0.0797	(0.48)	0.0764	(0.45)
Center city	−0.1369	(−1.48)	−0.1244	(−1.37)
Married	−0.0762	(−0.95)	−0.0466	(−0.57)
No. children < 6	−0.0454	(−1.97)**	−0.0443	(−2.03)**
No. children <1 £, ≥6	−0.0180	(−0.89)	−0.0167	(−0.85)
Premium			0.3387	(3.63)**
$\sigma\omega\omega$	0.5956	(51.86)**		
σss	1.0309	(59.63)**		
ρsv	−0.0678	(−0.24)		
ρsv	−0.0370	(−0.14)		
Log likelihood	−4267.97		−1244.14	
No. of individuals	2565		2565	

* Significant at the 0.10 level.
** Significant at the 0.05 level.

Source: Mills and Sahn (1993).

Table 7.7. Guinea: earnings equations estimates from a switching regression system of equations

	Wage sector		Non-wage sector	
	Parameter estimate	t-statistic	Parameter estimate	t-statistic
Dependent variable: ln (hourly earnings)				
Intercept	4.3808	(16.243)	4.4033	(10.56)**
Age	0.04544	(3.89)**	0.0795	(4.63)**
Age^2	−0.0005	(−3.61)**	−0.0009	(−4.26)**
Education				
Primary	0.1541	(1.57)	0.1333	(0.83)
Secondary	0.2687	(1.84)*	0.1946	(0.59)
University	(0.5817)	(3.56)**	0.8339	(1.75)*
Literate	0.1349	(2.26)**	0.3145	(2.68)**
Duration of last employment	0.0093	(3.96)**	0.0163	(3.85)**
Ethnicity				
Fulani	−0.0163	(−0.36)	−0.0865	(−1.10)
Malinke	−0.0579	(−1/25)	0.1513	(1.77)*
Forester	0.0545	(0.73)	0.3509	(2.79)**
Gender (female = 1)	−0.0854	(−0.74)	−0.4979	(−2.84)
Quarter (1st = 0)				
2nd	0.0651	(1.38)	−0.1109	(−1.44)
3rd	0.1808	(3.99)**	−0.3211	(−3.83)**
4th	0.0338	(0.68)	−0.4739	(−5.50)**
Redeployee	0.1876	(2.23)**	0.4180	(1.69)*
Capital (1,000,000 GF)			0.1600	(11.24)**

* Significant at the 0.10 level.
** Significant at the 0.05 level.

Source: Mills and Sahn (1993).

structure of the earnings equations and the sector selection equation are very small.

Likelihood ratio tests were next applied to the earnings equation estimates, shown in Table 7.7, to examine the overall hypothesis that the returns to individuals' earnings characteristics in the wage and non-wage sectors are significantly different. Examining specific groups of variables, the likelihood ratio tests indicate that the overall structure of returns to education do not differ significantly between sectors. In the wage sector, returns to secondary and university schooling are positive and greater at the later level. Further, the estimated returns to literacy are significantly greater than zero. By contrast, the non-wage sector estimated returns to primary and secondary schooling are lower than wage sector returns and not significantly different from zero, while the estimated returns to university education in the non-wage sector are comparable with those in the wage sector. Most interestingly, the estimated returns to literacy are larger in the non-wage sector, suggesting that functional ability rather than education obtainment may play a greater role in earnings determination in the non-wage sector (Mills and Sahn 1993).

The likelihood ratio tests also reveal that the overall structure of returns to experience are significantly different between sectors. While the estimated returns to age are positive but decreasing in both sectors, estimated initial returns to age are smaller in the wage sector than in the non-wage sector but decrease less rapidly with age. As a result, estimated returns to age peak at 48 years in the wage sector as opposed to 44 years in the non-wage sector. The estimated returns to duration of work at the individual's last job or enterprise are also significant in both sectors and larger in the non-wage sector. In addition, the estimated returns to capital are positive in the non-wage sector.

Ethnicity and gender also have significantly different influences on earnings in the two sectors. As expected, ethnicity has little impact on estimated earnings in the wage sector. However, in the non-wage sector there is an estimated positive relationship between earnings and the Malinke and Foresters ethnic groups versus the baseline ethnic group, Suso. Correspondingly, females have significantly lower earnings in the non-wage sector but show no difference from males in the wage sector. In addition, the data support the assertion that the non-wage sector is more susceptible to seasonal variations in income since the parameter estimates for the seasonal dummy variables are significantly larger in the non-wage earnings equation than in the wage sector earnings equation.

The parameter estimates for the public sector departure dummy variables included in both earnings equations are positive but do not, according to the likelihood ratio tests, differ significantly between the two sectors. This suggests that departing public sector workers who have found other employment in either the wage or the non-wage sector obtain earnings greater than those received by individuals with similar characteristics in the general population who have not been adversely affected by their previous job loss.

7.5.2. *Factors related to the duration of unemployment*

We now estimate the relationship between the duration of unemployment before entrance into the wage or non-wage sector and the characteristics of former public sector workers. The theoretical basis for the empirical model and the expected relationships between worker characteristics and the duration of unemployment are discussed in Mills (1994). The statistical model assumes that the duration of departures follows a Weibull distribution and

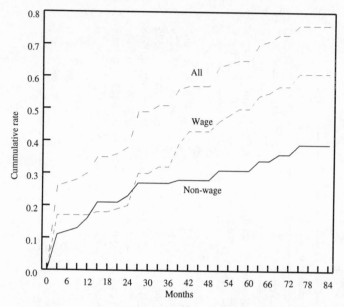

Fig. 7.1. Cumulative rate of exits from unemployment in Guinea, by sector
Source: Mills (1994).

in the two-sector exit model case follows Katz (1986) in assuming that exit times are not correlated across states.

Figure 7.1 presents the non-parametric cumulative rates of exit for all exits and separately for observed wage and non-wage exits. In the calculation of sector-specific exit rates, exits to alternative states are treated as censored at the time of departure. Clearly, the overall average duration of unemployment is quite long, as only half of the observed spells of unemployment end within 27 months. Further, while individuals appear to exit the wage sector at close to a constant rate throughout the seven-year period in the sample, the rate of exits into the non-wage sector declines after 27 months.[10]

The impact of gender, age, education, and severance payments on the duration of unemployment is presented in Table 7.8. For the single exit case, severance payments are estimated to be related to longer durations of unemployment or, correspondingly, a lower probability of exiting unemployment in a given period. However, gender, age, and the number of years of education show no relationship to the duration of unemployment.

When the relationships between the independent variables and the dur-

---

[10] Note that the cumulative rates of exit to the wage and non-wage sectors do not sum to the rate for all exits owing to the presence of censored observations.

Table 7.8. Guinea: duration of unemployment, maximum-likelihood estimates with a weibull parameterizing, single and dual exit state model

| Variable | Single exit state | | Dual exit state | | | |
| | | | Wage sector | | Non-wage sector | |
	Coefficient	Standard error	Coefficient	Standard error	Coefficient	Standard error
Dependent variable = log of unemployment duration						
Intercept	1.2865	1.059	1.3099	1.081	4.4438	1.766**
Gender (female = 1)	−0.2871	0.41	1.0496	0.6075*	−1.9453	0.6429**
Age	−0.0009	0.02	0.0081	0.0212	−0.023742	0.0325
Education (years)	−0.0379	0.032	−0.0388	0.0343	−0.036389	0.05189
Severance pay (received = 1)	0.8995	0.332**	1.213	0.446**	0.36551	0.546
P	0.6693	0.066	0.71309	0.07513**	0.61423	0.10696**
Log-likelihood	−268.1		−188.1		−147.2	
Sample size						
Completed spells	113		69		44	
Censored spells	39		83		108	

* Significant at the 0.10 level.
** Significant at the 0.05 level.
Source: Mills and Sahn (1993).

ation of the unemployment are estimated separately for wage and non-wage exits, a very different story emerges.[11] In line with expectations when labor markets are segmented and wage sector positions rationed, severance payments show a positive relationship to the duration of unemployment in the wage sector. Females also show a positive relationship to the duration of unemployment, suggesting they may face discrimination in the wage sector. By contrast, in the non-wage sector females are estimated to have shorter durations of unemployment. Thus, discrimination in a rationed wage sector may induce females to exit quickly into non-rationed non-wage sector positions.

The Weibull model also estimates whether the hazard rate for exits on unemployment is increasing, $P > 1$, or decreasing, $P < 1$, over time. As expected from the non-parametric estimates, the hazard rate for non-wage exits from unemployment is lower than the wage exit rate.[12] Further, both sectors, as well as the model for all exits, show decreasing hazards over time. This suggests that individuals become less likely to leave unemployment the longer their spell of unemployment lasts.

7.6. Conclusions

The government of Guinea was clearly successful in achieving the specific objective of reducing the number of public sector workers. However, owing to unplanned wage increases and rehirings, the expected macroeconomic benefits from this action have been only partially realized. On the other hand, the retrenchment program has enabled the government to improve the conditions of service and level of education among the public sector workforce, suggesting that some gains have been made in overall public sector efficiency.

The analysis has also shown that, for many of those departing the public sector, the transition from public to private sector work has been extremely costly. Even among those finding other work, a long duration of unemployment usually followed departure from the public sector, and some were earning less than in previous public sector positions. Most alarming, as of 1992, 30 percent of retrenched workers from the peak 1985–1988 period remained unemployed, a rate far higher than the rate of the population at large; while others were no longer searching and had left the labor market.

An examination of the consumption levels of the households of departees also suggests that they are poorer than the general population. This may be

---

[11] Exits to the non-wage sector are treated as observations censored at the time of departure in the wage model, and exits to the wage sector are treated as observations censored at the time of departure in the non-wage model.

[12] However, the two rates are not statistically different.

due, in part, to their low average levels of education and lack of experience in private sector labor markets. In addition, it was found that the current employment status of redeployees is a more important determinant of current household consumption levels than the reason for the transition. On the other hand, the coverage of compensation programs appears to have been widespread and benefits have been equitably distributed.

When the structure of Conakry labor markets were examined, results showed no evidence that former public sector workers are less likely to find wage sector positions. By contrast, human capital and gender were found to have important roles in sector selection. Relative to the general population, former public sector workers also showed higher earnings in the wage and non-wage sectors. However, the two sectors have distinct sets of earnings determinants. In the wage sector, formal measures of human capital, observable to the employer, such as educational degrees, age, and duration at last position, were of primary importance in earnings determination. In the non-wage sector human capital measures were important, but gender and ethnicity, which may reflect differences in the access to capital and flexibility of labor time, also have a significant impact on earnings.

Most interestingly, the predicted premium for employment in the wage sector is negative for the vast majority of individuals. This is particularly true for former public sector workers and suggests that expected earnings alone would not motivate departing public sector workers to remain unemployed while searching for rationed wage sector positions. However, there are several factors that may increase the non-monetary value of wage sector positions. Particularly, seasonal variability of earnings is estimated to be lower in the wage sector. A number of benefits may also arise from access to resources and influence in the wage sector. Unfortunately, these benefits are not quantified.

The results from the single sector and wage/non-wage sector duration of unemployment models highlight the complex nature of job search behavior in a segmented labor market. The results suggest that females face longer durations of unemployment in the wage sector but shorter durations in the non-wage sector. Severance pay was also found to be related to longer durations of unemployment in the single exit state model, but when the durations of unemployment for wage and non-wage exits were estimated separately, the effect was found to be concentrated in the wage sector.

Overall, the results suggest that policy-makers concerned with reducing the social costs of public sector retrenchment should focus on developing assistance mechanisms which increase the rate of workers' re-absorption into the private sector's labor market. The magnitude of the negative premium suggests there may be significant barriers within the non-wage sector to obtaining good employment opportunities. Rationed access to capital and entrepreneurial skills are probably particularly important determinants of the opportunities available in the non-wage sector. Hence, to increase the uptake of retrenched public sector workers, policy-makers may wish to focus assistance from small enterprise training and credit programs on those individuals who are relatively disadvantaged within the non-wage sector, particularly females.

References

Arulpragasam, Jehan, and David E. Sahn. Forthcoming. *Economic Transition in Guinea: Implications for Growth and Poverty*. New York: New York University Press.

———— 1991. *Economic Reform in Guinea: Adjusting for the Past*. Ithaca, NY: CFNPP.

de Mérode, Louis. 1991. *Implementing Civil Service Pay and Employment Reform in Africa: The Experiences of Ghana, The Gambia, and Guinea*. Washington, DC: World Bank.

Glick, Peter, David E. Sahn, and Carlo del Ninno. 1993. "Labor Markets and Time Allocation in Conakry." Ithaca, NY: CFNPP.

Katz, L. 1986. *Layoffs, Recall and the Duration of Unemployment*." Working Paper No. 1825. Cambridge, MA: NBER.

Mills, Bradford. 1994. *The Impact of Gender Discrimination on the Job Search Strategies of Redeployed Public Sector Workers*. Working Paper No. 51. Ithaca, NY: CFNPP.

—— and David Sahn. 1993. "Is There Life After Public Service? The Fate of Retrenched Workers in Conakry Guinea." Cornell Food and Nutrition Policy Program Working Paper 42. Ithaca, NY: CFNPP.

———— 1995. "Reducing the Size of the Public Sector Work Force: Institutional Constraints and Human Consequences in Guinea." *Journal of Development Studies*, 31(4): 505–528.

United Nations Development Programme and World Bank. 1992. *African Development Indicators*. New York and Washington, DC: UNDP and World Bank.

8

Estimating Tax Incidence in Ghana using Household Data

Stephen Younger

8.1. *Introduction*

One of the most common criticisms of structural adjustment policies in Africa is that the burden of fiscal contraction falls disproportionately on the poor (Summers and Pritchett 1993). Most authors have concentrated on the potentially harmful effects of reducing government spending in order to balance budgets,[1] but it is also true that some of the most committed adjusters—Ghana, Uganda, and Tanzania, for example—have addressed their fiscal deficits by increasing tax revenues rather than reducing expenditures. While these increases are often appropriate in a macroeconomic context, policy-makers should be as concerned about the incidence of these new taxes as they are about the incidence of expenditure cuts.

This paper is a first cut at addressing that issue. I use household income and expenditure data from the Ghana Living Standards Survey (GLSS) to examine the question, "Who pays the taxes?" in Ghana. The exercise is admittedly incomplete, but the information it provides should be useful to policy-makers and also should help direct future research efforts on the same theme.

8.2. *Fiscal Policy and Economic Recovery in Ghana*

Ghana is now widely recognized as one of the more interesting and successful cases of adjustment in Africa. Ghana has followed the standard prescription to reduce fiscal deficits with unusual vigor, yet it accomplished this at the same time that expenditures actually rose. As one can see in

---

[1] Sahn (1990) shows that this concern is often unfounded. Overall government expenditures and expenditures on health and education have risen as often as they have fallen in adjusting African economies. In addition, it is not generally true that government expenditures are progressive in Africa; the benefits often go more to the wealthy than to the poor.

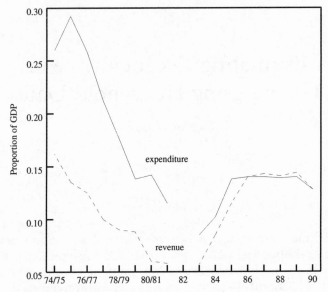

Fig. 8.1. Ghanaian government revenue and expenditures as a proportion of GDP

Figure 8.1,[2] all of the reduction in the fiscal deficit is due to the rapid increase in tax revenues during the adjustment program.[3] Table 8.1 shows that this revenue recovery was broad-based: domestic direct taxes, indirect taxes, and other revenues (mostly grants) have all increased beyond the levels of the late 1970s, while trade taxes have recovered to roughly the same levels. Within these broad groupings, trade taxes have clearly shifted toward import duties[4] and away from taxes on cocoa exports. This partly reflects conscious policy decisions to promote cocoa exports, but the most dramatic declines in cocoa duties have occurred since 1989, when international cocoa prices plummeted and the government protected local farmers by absorbing some of this shock through reduced duties rather than lower producer prices.

Among domestic indirect taxes, excise duties (on alcoholic beverages, tobacco, and soft drinks) recovered quickly after the Economic Recovery Program (ERP) began but have since declined relative to GDP, while

---

2 The data in Figure 8.1 do not include spending that is financed by international project aid flows. Including that spending yields a deficit of between 2 and 3 percent of GDP in recent years (see Younger 1992).

3 The Economic Recovery Program (ERP) began in 1983, and the government continues to work closely with the World Bank and International Monetary Fund, under the rubric of several adjustment credits.

4 These figures include both tariffs and sales taxes on imported goods.

Table 8.1. Ghana: central government revenues by source, 1977/78–1990 (proportions of GDP)

	1977/78	1978/79	1979/80	1980/81	1981/82	1983	1984	1985	1986	1987	1988	1989	1990
Taxes on international transactions	0.050	0.055	0.043	0.013	0.012	0.027	0.030	0.046	0.053	0.060	0.047	0.056	0.044
Import duties	0.015	0.014	0.011	0.008	0.008	0.008	0.009	0.014	0.019	0.017	0.016	0.023	0.018
Sales tax on imported goods	0.000	0.001	0.000	0.000	0.001	0.002	0.003	0.005	0.006	0.006	0.007	0.011	0.013
Purchase tax	0.001	0.001	0.000	0.000	0.000	0.000	0.000	0.001	0.001	0.000	0.000	0.000	0.000
Export duty on cocoa	0.032	0.039	0.032	0.000	0.000	0.015	0.017	0.026	0.027	0.036	0.023	0.022	0.013
Other export duties	0.000	0.000	0.000	0.000	0.000	0.001	0.001	0.001	0.001	0.000	0.000	0.000	0.000
Other taxes on foreign transactions	0.001	0.001	0.000	0.004	0.002	0.001	0.000	0.000	0.000	0.000	0.000	0.000	0.000
Taxes on domestic goods and services	0.021	0.013	0.020	0.025	0.024	0.010	0.021	0.024	0.039	0.036	0.035	0.037	0.036
Cocoa local duty	0.001	0.000	0.004	0.000	0.000	0.000	0.000	0.000	0.000	0.000	0.000	0.000	0.000
Excise duties	0.016	0.010	0.013	0.019	0.019	0.008	0.019	0.019	0.020	0.017	0.014	0.013	0.011
Sales tax on local products	0.003	0.003	0.002	0.003	0.002	0.001	0.002	0.003	0.005	0.011	0.012	0.013	0.011
Other	0.001	0.001	0.001	0.003	0.002	0.000	0.000	0.000	0.000	0.000	0.000	0.000	0.000
Petroleum tax	0.000	0.000	0.000	0.000	0.000	0.000	0.000	0.002	0.013	0.007	0.008	0.011	0.012
Taxes on income and property	0.020	0.014	0.018	0.015	0.017	0.009	0.015	0.022	0.029	0.031	0.038	0.033	0.025
Employees	0.011	0.008	0.007	0.006	0.005	0.003	0.003	0.005	0.006	0.006	0.006	0.005	0.005
Self-employed income tax	0.000	0.000	0.002	0.001	0.004	0.002	0.003	0.005	0.003	0.005	0.005	0.004	0.003
Company tax	0.009	0.006	0.007	0.007	0.008	0.004	0.008	0.013	0.019	0.019	0.026	0.023	0.016
Interest and dividend tax	0.000	0.000	0.000	0.000	0.000	0.000	0.000	0.000	0.000	0.000	0.000	0.000	0.000
Rent income tax	0.000	0.000	0.000	0.000	0.000	0.000	0.000	0.000	0.000	0.000	0.000	0.000	0.000
Other	0.000	0.000	0.001	0.001	0.000	0.000	0.001	0.000	0.000	0.001	0.001	0.001	0.001
Nontax revenue	0.010	0.008	0.006	0.005	0.004	0.010	0.014	0.020	0.016	0.013	0.016	0.010	0.012
Grants	0.000	0.000	0.000	0.001	0.001	0.000	0.003	0.005	0.008	0.008	0.011	0.015	0.014

Source: Republic of Ghana (1992).

revenues from the sales tax and petroleum tax increased more gradually. The latter tax has become particularly important (and controversial) in recent years; the authorities have found it to be a convenient "tax handle" and have raised duties substantially. For the 1993 budget, petroleum taxes were projected to total one-third of all tax revenue, more than 4 percent of GDP (Botchwey 1993). This dramatic increase has fostered a debate over the equity of the petroleum taxes, an issue that I will address in this paper.

Finally, the increase in domestic direct tax revenues has come almost entirely through the company tax (corporate income tax). It is difficult to say much about the incidence of this tax, because the GLSS data are for households, and the links between households and corporate ownership are not clear. Nevertheless, one would suspect that the corporate income tax falls mainly on the wealthy.

8.3. *Incidence of Specific Taxes in Ghana*

8.3.1. *Methodology*

Economists have long recognized the difference between the statutory incidence of a tax and its economic incidence. Those whom the law requires to pay a tax are not necessarily those who suffer the decline in purchasing power associated with the transfer of resources to the government. Rather, households whose demand and supply for products and factors of production are relatively elastic will generally shift the burden of the tax onto those whose demand and supply are inelastic, regardless of who actually must pay the tax. Because economists are interested in the actual welfare changes that result from taxes, we would ideally like to identify the economic rather than statutory incidence of a tax. In practice, however, that is a difficult task, requiring the use of general equilibrium models of the entire economy.[5] Not only is there no such model for Ghana, but even the basic building blocks of such a model—a social accounting matrix and estimates of elasticities—are lacking. Given these limitations, this paper estimates statutory rather than economic tax incidence in an analysis that is comparable with Pechman (1985) for tax policy in the United States, or with Selowsky (1979) and Meerman (1979), who analyze the incidence of government expenditures in a similar fashion. As Pechman points out, the correlation between statutory and economic incidence is high when households' excess demand functions are inelastic, so one way to interpret these

---

5 Shoven and Whalley (1984) discuss the use of computable general equilibrium (CGE) models for analyzing tax policy in the United States. I am not aware of any comparable work for an African economy, although such work might be possible in Cote d'Ivoire and/or Cameroon, the two countries with existing household survey data and CGEs.

results is that they are conditional on the assumption that elasticities are zero.[6]

For consumption-based sales and excise taxes, I have calculated the amount that each household in the GLSS paid in taxes based on its consumption of the taxed commodities and the 1988 tax rates.[7] For direct taxes—mostly taxes on different sources of income—I have used the associated income information and the 1988 income tax schedules.[8] To judge the progressivity of a particular tax or combination of taxes, I order the households by per capita expenditure[9] and then plot their cumulative expenditures and cumulative tax payments against the cumulative proportion of households—so-called Lorenz curves. If expenditures are equal across households, this curve is a straight line from the origin to (1,1). The more convex the curve, the greater the inequality of expenditures (or tax payments). If the Lorenz curve for a tax is more convex than that for expenditures, wealthier households are paying a disproportionately large share of the tax relative to their expenditures: the tax is progressive. Exactly the opposite is true if the Lorenz curve for the tax is less convex.[10] As a summary measure, I calculate a "progressivity coefficient" equal to the area between the two curves. Positive values indicate a progressive tax, and vice-versa for negative values. The measure is bounded by $-(1 + g)$ and $(1 - g)$ where g is the GINI coefficient for expenditures (equal to 0.355 in the case of the GLSS data).

8.3.2. Comparison of GLSS tax calculations with actual tax revenues

Before examining the household level results, it is useful to compare the tax payments that I estimated from the GLSS with the actual tax revenues reported by the government. To do that, Table 8.2 shows government revenues broken down by category along with my estimates scaled up to national levels by multiplying them by the 1988 population of Ghana divided by the population in the GLSS. As one can see, the figures for sales tax revenue and withholding from wages and salaries correspond closely between the two sources, while the others appear to diverge by a large amount. Understanding these differences is important for the discussion of tax incidence that follows. The fact that my self-employment taxes and "other" direct taxes appear larger than the actual tax revenues is probably

---

[6] See Pechman (1985) for a discussion of the realism of this assumption.

[7] The GLSS includes no useful information on import duties, the other important indirect tax in Ghana.

[8] Appendix 8.1 presents these schedules.

[9] Using expenditure rather than income as a measure of welfare is preferable because expenditure data are generally more accurate than income data (Alderman 1992). Expenditure is also more closely related to a household's wealth (or "permanent income") under standard economic theory.

[10] Note that, unlike expenditures, the Lorenz curve for the tax is not bound to be quasi-convex because the households are ordered by expenditure for both curves.

Table 8.2. Ghana: actual government revenue for 1988 compared with estimates from the GLSS

	Actual revenue	Estimate from GLSS	Ratio
Taxes on international transactions[a]	41,926		
Import duties	17,010		
Purchase tax	321		
Export duty on cocoa	24,464	8,809	0.360
Other taxes on foreign transactions	131		
Taxes on domestic goods and services	44,164		
Petroleum tax	8,485	3,142	0.370
Excise duties	15,019	5,284	0.352
Sales tax	20,209	18,356	0.908
Other	451		
Taxes on income and property	39,689		
Employees	6,016	5,696	0.947
Self-employed income tax	5,080	8,264	1.627
Company tax	27,648		
Interest and dividend tax	—		
Rent income tax	29		
Others	916	1,615	1.764
Nontax revenue	16,459		
Grants (mainly from abroad)	11,553		
Total	153,791		

[a] For better comparison with my estimates, I have moved the sales taxes on imported goods from the taxes on international transactions to those on domestic goods and services.

Sources: Republic of Ghana (1992), GLSS, and author's calculations.

just a function of misclassification. I have included household businesses' daily and annual taxes in the self-employment category, but some of these taxes (especially the annual taxes and license fees) probably belong under either the company tax or the non-tax revenues. Similarly, I have compared households' reported tax payments from the expenditure survey with other direct taxes, on the grounds that most of these expenditures are probably for property taxes. But they could also entail payment of other taxes or fees. Altogether, my GLSS calculations for these categories account for only 30 percent of self-employment, company, and other direct taxes combined. This seems low, but is probably not unreasonable given that a household survey like the GLSS will not find a substantial amount of company tax. In addition, households in the GLSS appear to have substantially under-reported their incomes (Alderman and Higgins 1992).

The fact that estimated cocoa revenues are only 36 percent of actual revenues is probably due to farmers' underreporting their sales. Average cocoa yields in Ghana are about 100 kilograms per acre, while the average yield in the GLSS is only 35 kilograms per acre, a shortfall almost exactly equal to the proportion of total cocoa revenues that the GLSS captures.[11] If underreporting increased with production (i.e. if larger farmers report proportionally less of their true harvest), the tax calculations that follow would appear more regressive than the actual situation. This does not appear to be the case, however, yields for cocoa farmers are roughly equal across household expenditure deciles.

The GLSS data capture only 37 percent of the total revenues from the petroleum tax. The most likely explanation of this is that a large proportion of petroleum sales go to firms rather than to final consumers and thus do not show up in a household survey. Virtually all diesel fuel, for example, is consumed by industry (for transport and power generation) rather than by households. The same is probably true of a large proportion of gasoline sales. In the calculations that follow, I will attempt to account for these intermediate sales wherever possible.

The GLSS calculations for excise taxes are also well below actual revenues, a fact that cannot be accounted for by intermediate sales. Rather, it seems likely that households underreport consumption of these goods in the survey. It also seems likely that households with large expenditures on alcohol and tobacco will be more likely to underreport their true consumption. If, in addition, consumption of these items increases more than proportionally with income, wealthier households will have underreported their consumption by proportionally more than poorer ones, so the tax burden will appear more regressive than it actually is.

With these reservations on the quality of the GLSS data in mind, I now turn to my estimates of the progressivity of each of these taxes.

8.3.3. Results on tax incidence

Table 8.3 shows the progessivity coefficient for each of the taxes considered below, the percentage of the tax that households in the lowest 30 percent of the per capita expenditure distribution paid, and the number of households that paid the tax in the GLSS sample. In total, the sample has 3034 households.

Direct Taxes.   Consider first the direct taxes (Figure 8.2). Income taxes are withheld from the wages and salaries of employees in the formal sector. The vast majority of these employees work either in the civil service or in public

---

[11] I have explored a variety of other possibilities for the low levels of cocoa production in the GLSS, including underreporting due to sharecropping, production from corporations (including the Cocoa Marketing Board) rather than households, and an underrepresentation of cocoa farmers in the GLSS sample framework. None of these factors provides a satisfactory explanation of the low production figures.

Table 8.3. Ghana: cocoa yields by household
per capita expenditure deciles

Decile	Yield (kilos/acre)[a]	No. of households
1	32	39
2	22	47
3	32	39
4	36	42
5	41	42
6	53	51
7	23	33
8	32	40
9	33	27
10	47	21

[a] For double-cropped land, yield is calculated
based on half the reported acreage.

Source: GLSS, 1987/88.

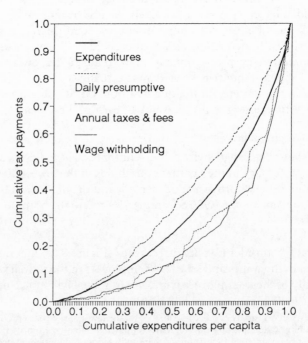

Fig. 8.2. Ghana: Lorenz curves for direct taxes
Source: Ghana Living Standards Survey, 1987/88, and author's calculations.

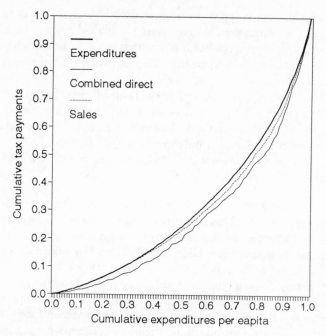

Fig. 8.3. Ghana: Lorenz curve for all direct taxes combined and the sales tax
Source: Ghana Living Standards Survey, 1987/88, and author's calculations.

enterprises, although a few large private enterprises also withhold income tax. The tax is progressive, which is consistent with the findings of Alderman, Canagarajah, and Younger (1993) that public sector employees' households are still somewhat better off than the population in general, despite the much publicized decline in public sector salaries during the early 1980s.

"Daily taxes" are collected mostly from small-scale, self-employed businesses as presumptive income taxes. During the year, 700 households, 23 percent of the sample, paid this type of tax, reflecting the large number of households engaged in self-employed activities and the widespread use of this tax. As one can see in Figure 8.2, the tax is regressive, lending credence to the complaints of small merchants and petty traders about the fairness of this technique.

"Annual taxes and licenses" are income taxes and license fees. These income taxes most likely pertain to larger family-owned enterprises that file an annual income tax return. These firms may or may not be incorporated. The licenses could cover a wide range of government fees, some of which may not be related to income-earning activities (e.g. automobile licenses), but are still included in the household enterprises' costs. Fewer households pay these taxes and fees, and their impact is progressive.

Only 27 households report earning dividends (not shown in the figure), which is not surprising given that most Ghanaian businesses are family-owned or heavily leveraged. But it is true that these 27 households are in the highest expenditure deciles, so that the tax, while unimportant, is highly progressive.

Finally, combining all forms of direct taxation reported in the survey,[12] we find that income and property taxes are progressive as a group, although perhaps not so much as one would expect (Figure 8.3). The main reasons that these direct taxes appear only mildly progressive are, first, the fact that company income taxes are not included here, and second, the regressivity of the presumptive daily income taxes.

Domestic Indirect Taxes.   The impact of the sales tax is essentially proportional (Figure 8.3). This is surprising in an economy where agriculture, which is not affected by the sales tax, accounts for about half of GDP. Nevertheless, Alderman and Higgins (1992) find income elasticities of the demand for food to be very high in Ghana, between 0.9 and 1.0 in all of their estimates. Thus, higher expenditure households include only a slightly smaller proportion of non-taxed food in their consumption than poor households do. Beyond this unusual feature of Ghanaians' expenditures, it is also true that the survey questionnaire often combines items that are likely to be taxed with those that probably are not, which would bias this estimate of progressivity toward zero. For example, wealthier households are probably more likely to buy prescription medicines (which are taxed), while poor households buy traditional medicines (which are not), yet both are included in one expenditure category. Nevertheless, the high income elasticities for food demand imply that a sales tax is unlikely to be very progressive in Ghana.

Figure 8.4 shows the incidence of major non-petroleum excise taxes. The information on these taxes is perhaps the most suspect in this study. It appears that the consumption of alcoholic beverages and tobacco is under-reported in the survey, probably in a way that makes the tax burden appear more regressive than it actually is. In addition, the survey information on alcohol consumption has the same problem of "category confusion" that the sales tax does: all alcohol is lumped together, whether it is beer (which is taxed) or akpteshie, a local gin that effectively avoids taxes because it is produced in the informal sector. These problems make the excise taxes on alcohol and tobacco appear less progressive than one might have thought, with the latter actually looking like a regressive tax. Alcohol taxation, on the other hand, appears to be quite progressive despite these measurement problems.

---

12 This includes the taxes reported in the expenditures section of the survey, which may lead to some double-counting.

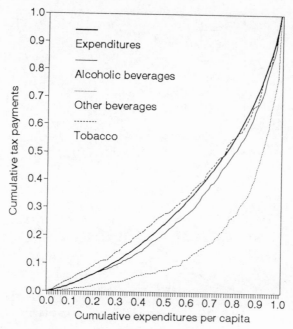

Fig. 8.4. Ghana: Lorenz curve for non-petroleum excise taxes
Source: Ghana Living Standards Survey, 1987/88, and author's calculations.

In addition to direct expenditures on alcohol, alcohol accounts for a large percentage of the expenditures on weddings and funerals, and a proportion of expenditures reported for "meals taken outside the home" are probably for alcoholic beverages. To account for this, I have included 50 percent of the expenditures on weddings and funerals and 20 percent of expenditures for dining out with the direct expenditures on alcohol to produce a "combined" estimate of the excise tax on alcohol. This tax is only slightly progressive, indicating that the burden of expenditures for celebrations can be quite heavy for poorer households.

The last important excise tax is on non-alcoholic beverages (soft drinks). Relatively few households report expenditures on this item and revenues are lower than those from beer and tobacco, but the tax is more progressive than the other excise taxes.

The petroleum tax is currently the most controversial tax in Ghana. It is essentially an excise tax whose importance has grown tremendously in the past few years. Calculating its incidence across the expenditure distribution is not straightforward. To begin, the tax on gasoline and motor oil coming from households' direct consumption of these items is highly progressive, but only 49 households in the GLSS survey reported consuming them. This

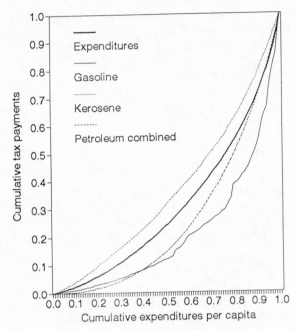

Fig. 8.5. Ghana: Lorenz curves for petroleum excise taxes
Source: Ghana Living Standards Survey, 1987/88, and author's calculations.

is not surprising; automobile ownership is still rare in Ghana.[13] Most of the consumption of petroleum products is by firms rather than households, so understanding the incidence requires (at a minimum) tracing the impact through an input–output table. No such table exists for Ghana, but I have tried at least to capture the impact of the petroleum tax on the public transit sector by assuming that 20 percent of the costs of transport are for fuel. (Input–output tables in Niger, Cameroon, and Madagascar all have coefficients near 0.2 for the value of petroleum inputs to the transport sector.) Consumption of transport services is more balanced across the expenditure distribution than consumption of gasoline, but taxation of transport services (through the tax on gasoline) is still progressive. Combining these two sources of tax revenue from gasoline yields a very progressive tax, as shown in Figure 8.5. Taxes on kerosene, on the other hand, are very regressive. Consumption of kerosene is remarkably flat across households, so that the burden of taxes from this source falls disproportionately on poorer households.

Because gasoline and diesel fuel are often consumed by firms as intermediate inputs rather than by households, it is inappropriate to add up the actual tax payments calculated from the GLSS to estimate the overall

---

13 In addition, civil servants who use government vehicles generally do not pay for gasoline.

impact of the petroleum taxes. Instead, I have calculated a weighted sum of consumption of different petroleum products based on each item's share in the overall consumption of petroleum in the entire economy in 1988. I base each household's proportion of total kerosene and gasoline consumption (direct and through transport) on the actual data reported above, and I assume that diesel consumption is proportional to household expenditures.[14] Figure 8.5 shows that this weighted sum is progressive, but less so than the tax on gasoline alone.

Taxes on international transactions. Tariffs on imports have been and continue to be an important source of tax revenue in Ghana. Unfortunately, the GLSS does not distinguish between imports and domestically produced goods in its questionnaire. What's more, many imports are intermediate goods which would need to be traced through an input–output table. Given this lack of information, one can only guess at the incidence of tariffs, but it is probably not very much different from the roughly proportional incidence of the sales tax (which falls only on formal sector goods).

The one other important tax on international transactions is the tax on cocoa exports. According to the World Bank (1991), this tax amounted to 128,677 cedis per ton in the 1987/88 cropping season.[15] Using this figure and farmers' reported sales (by weight) in the survey yields their tax payments. As Figure 8.6 shows, this tax is regressive and is paid by relatively few households (13 percent of the survey). As I argued in the last section, however, this estimate may be more regressive than true tax payments, if larger farmers underreport their sales by more than small farmers do. Nevertheless, the argument seems less persuasive in this case than it does for the case of excise taxes on tobacco and alcohol. It is easy to understand why heavy consumers of tobacco and alcohol would underreport their consumption more severely, compared with all farmers who have an incentive to underreport that is proportional to their actual output. If cocoa sales represent the bulk of their income, this also implies that the underreporting is evenly spread across the expenditure distribution.

Nevertheless, given the importance of this tax for economic policy, we have investigated the potential underreporting further by checking farmers' yield against the per capita expenditure distribution. As Table 8.3 shows, these are roughly constant, suggesting that underreporting is fairly consis-

[14] Diesel is used primarily for trucks that transport goods rather than people, so its consumption will not show up in a household survey (although some cars and buses also use diesel). Assuming that the impact of a tax on diesel oil is proportional to household expenditure seems reasonable, given that expenditures on items that attract a sales tax are spread evenly across the expenditure distribution.

[15] This is the central government's actual tax revenue. In addition, the Cocoa Board's marketing costs are very high, and one could argue that these are essentially a tax on farmers, combined with a transfer to Cocoa Board employees. I have not included these excessive marketing costs in my calculations here.

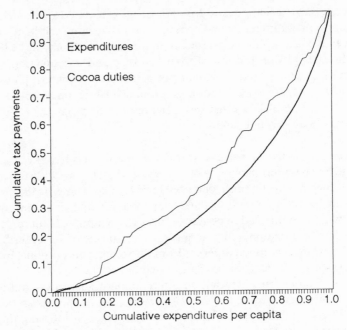

Fig. 8.6. Ghana: Lorenz curves for cocoa duties
Source: Ghana Living Standards Survey, 1987/88, and author's calculations.

tent across the expenditure distribution and, as a result, our measure of fiscal incidence is reliable despite the underreporting.

8.4. *Interpreting the Results: Has Fiscal Stabilization through Increased Tax Revenues Hurt the Poor in Ghana?*

A convincing answer to this question could only come from a much more ambitious study than this one. Nevertheless, the household data from the GLSS combined with the government's revenue data provide interesting information that, if not conclusive, is suggestive of the changes in tax incidence in Ghana during the ERP. Between fiscal 1981/82 and 1987, tax revenues increased from 5 to 12 percent of GDP. Table 8.4 shows that about 70 percent of this increase came from cocoa export duties and non-petroleum excise taxes, both of which are regressive taxes according to the GLSS data. This would make one believe that the tax structure became more regressive in this period. Nevertheless, the data on the cocoa tax are quite misleading when thinking about cocoa farmers' welfare. While it is true that the government's fiscal revenues from cocoa rose substantially in this period, so did farmers' real revenues. Before 1982, the highly over-

Table 8.4. Ghana: sources of revenue as a proportion of total revenue and grants, 1977/78–1990

	1977/78	1978/79	1979/80	1980/81	1981/82	1983	1984	1985	1986	1987	1988	1989	1990
Taxes on international transactions	0.493	0.610	0.499	0.215	0.206	0.483	0.379	0.853	0.693	0.429	0.350	0.413	0.375
Import duties	0.148	0.159	0.122	0.135	0.147	0.137	0.115	0.124	0.137	0.121	0.120	0.168	0.150
Sales tax on imported goods	0.004	0.003	0.003	0.006	0.022	0.043	0.032	0.041	0.042	0.046	0.055	0.083	0.115
Purchase tax	0.011	0.006	0.002	0.002	0.008	0.005	0.004	0.006	0.006	0.002	0.002	0.001	0.001
Export duty on cocoa	0.314	0.429	0.364	0.000	0.000	0.273	0.208	0.229	0.199	0.257	0.172	0.162	0.109
Other export duties	0.005	0.004	0.002	0.001	0.001	0.013	0.017	0.008	0.004	0.000	0.000	0.000	0.000
Other taxes on foreign transactions	0.011	0.009	0.005	0.072	0.027	0.011	0.004	0.000	0.000	0.002	0.001	0.000	0.000
Taxes on domestic goods and services	0.210	0.148	0.232	0.430	0.421	0.172	0.257	0.216	0.285	0.257	0.255	0.273	0.304
Cocoa local duty	0.006	0.000	0.043	0.008	0.000	0.000	0.002	0.000	0.000	0.000	0.000	0.000	0.000
Excise duties	0.157	0.108	0.154	0.316	0.335	0.148	0.233	0.171	0.150	0.122	0.106	0.098	0.096
Sales tax on local products	0.033	0.030	0.028	0.055	0.043	0.019	0.020	0.030	0.037	0.080	0.087	0.093	0.098
Other	0.015	0.010	0.008	0.051	0.043	0.004	0.002	0.000	0.004	0.003	0.003	0.004	0.004
Petroleum tax	0.000	0.000	0.000	0.000	0.000	0.000	0.000	0.016	0.095	0.052	0.060	0.078	0.106
Taxes on income and property	0.202	0.157	0.201	0.260	0.295	0.169	0.185	0.199	0.210	0.223	0.279	0.241	0.216
Employees	0.104	0.085	0.082	0.098	0.085	0.051	0.042	0.048	0.046	0.043	0.042	0.039	0.045
Self-employed income tax	0.000	0.000	0.020	0.019	0.063	0.034	0.036	0.030	0.021	0.034	0.036	0.026	0.025
Company tax	0.092	0.070	0.084	0.117	0.136	0.074	0.098	0.118	0.138	0.137	0.194	0.168	0.137
Interest and dividend tax	0.000	0.000	0.000	0.003	0.006	0.008	0.002	0.002	0.003	0.000	0.000	0.000	0.000
Rent income tax	0.001	0.001	0.002	0.001	0.002	0.001	0.000	0.001	0.001	0.001	0.000	0.000	0.000
Other	0.004	0.001	0.014	0.022	0.001	0.000	0.007	0.000	0.000	0.008	0.006	0.007	0.008
Nontax revenue	0.095	0.084	0.066	0.081	0.068	0.171	0.172	0.170	0.111	0.087	0.116	0.073	0.106
Grants	0.000	0.000	0.002	0.014	0.011	0.006	0.040	0.040	0.053	0.054	0.075	0.099	0.104

Source: Republic of Ghana (1992).

valued exchange rate meant that the cedi value of cocoa sales was very low, leaving very little for the government, the Cocoa Board, and farmers to share between them. Basically, the lions share of cocoa earnings actually went to the importers, who bought the foreign exchange proceeds at a very low exchange rate. The devaluation reduced that implicit subsidy to importers and made it available to both the government and farmers. Thus, both fiscal revenues from cocoa duties and farmers' real producer prices rose after the ERP began.

To account for this phenomenon, I have adjusted the data on cocoa revenues to include an implicit tax from exchange rate overvaluation equal to half the difference between the official and parallel exchange rates times the international price less 15 percent (which is generally considered a reasonable marketing margin for domestic and international transport and processing). Given the severe overvaluation of the currency in the 1970s and early 1980s, this adjustment is a very large number, as much as 15 percent of GDP in some years. Including it makes cocoa taxes the dominant source of tax revenue until the late 1980s (Table 8.5). This also implies that the government's reduced reliance on cocoa taxes has made the overall tax system considerably more progressive.

To be concrete, I have calculated a Lorenz curve for all tax revenues in 1977/78, 1981/82, 1987, and 1990, using weights implied by the government's revenue figures from Table 8.5 (which include the cocoa tax adjustment) for each of those years and proportions of expenditures from the 1987/88 GLSS.[16] Figure 8.7 shows that in both 1977/78 and 1981/82 the overall tax system in Ghana was regressive, and to the same extent in each year. This simply reflects the dominance of cocoa in the tax structure. By 1987, however, the tax system was much less regressive as excise taxes, income taxes, and sales taxes became increasingly important. The data for 1990, the most recent available, show further improvement to a proportional overall tax burden. Thus, the tax policies of the ERP appear to have had a favorable effect on the overall distributional impact of Ghana's tax system.

8.5. Concluding Thoughts on Tax Policy in Ghana

It is important to remember that progressivity is not the only measure of a good tax. Policy makers must also consider the tax's impact on economic efficiency (distortions to the allocation of resources), its administrative

---

16 For the two main taxes on which GLSS provides no useful information, imports and the company tax, I have assumed that the incidence is equal to the sales tax incidence and the annual income tax incidence, respectively. I assume that the small amounts in "other" categories are all distributed proportionally to expenditures.

Table 8.5. Ghana: sources of revenue as a proportion of total revenue, including an adjustment for the implicit tax on cocoa exports arising from exchange rate overvaluation, 1977/78–1990

	1977/78	1978/79	1979/80	1980/81	1981/82	1983	1984	1985	1986	1987	1988	1989	1990
Taxes on international													
transactions	0.838	0.860	0.797	0.643	0.617	0.677	0.606	0.898	0.765	0.468	0.438	0.418	0.391
Import duties	0.047	0.057	0.049	0.062	0.072	0.087	0.073	0.086	0.105	0.113	0.103	0.166	0.146
Sales tax on imported goods	0.001	0.001	0.001	0.003	0.011	0.027	0.020	0.028	0.033	0.043	0.048	0.082	0.112
Purchase tax	0.004	0.002	0.001	0.001	0.004	0.003	0.003	0.004	0.004	0.002	0.002	0.001	0.001
Export duty on cocoa (adjusted)	0.781	0.794	0.743	0.544	0.516	0.545	0.497	0.467	0.386	0.308	0.285	0.169	0.132
Other export duties	0.002	0.001	0.001	0.000	0.001	0.008	0.011	0.006	0.003	0.000	0.000	0.000	0.000
Other taxes on foreign transactions	0.004	0.003	0.002	0.033	0.013	0.007	0.002	0.000	0.000	0.002	0.001	0.000	0.000
Taxes on domestic goods and services	0.067	0.053	0.094	0.199	0.206	0.108	0.163	0.150	0.218	0.239	0.221	0.270	0.296
Cocoa local duty	0.002	0.000	0.017	0.004	0.000	0.000	0.001	0.000	0.000	0.000	0.000	0.000	0.000
Excise duties	0.050	0.039	0.062	0.146	0.164	0.094	0.148	0.118	0.115	0.114	0.091	0.098	0.093
Sales tax on local products	0.010	0.011	0.011	0.025	0.021	0.012	0.013	0.021	0.028	0.074	0.075	0.092	0.095
Other	0.005	0.004	0.003	0.024	0.021	0.003	0.002	0.000	0.003	0.003	0.003	0.004	0.004
Petroleum tax	0.000	0.000	0.000	0.000	0.000	0.000	0.000	0.011	0.073	0.049	0.052	0.077	0.103
Taxes on income and property	0.064	0.057	0.082	0.120	0.144	0.107	0.117	0.138	0.161	0.208	0.241	0.239	0.210
Employees	0.033	0.031	0.033	0.045	0.042	0.033	0.027	0.033	0.035	0.040	0.037	0.039	0.044
Self-employed income tax	0.000	0.000	0.008	0.009	0.031	0.022	0.023	0.021	0.016	0.032	0.031	0.026	0.025
Company tax	0.029	0.025	0.034	0.054	0.067	0.047	0.062	0.082	0.106	0.128	0.168	0.167	0.133
Interest and dividend tax	0.000	0.000	0.000	0.001	0.003	0.005	0.001	0.001	0.002	0.000	0.000	0.000	0.000
Rent income tax	0.000	0.000	0.001	0.001	0.001	0.001	0.000	0.000	0.001	0.001	0.000	0.000	0.000
Other	0.001	0.000	0.006	0.010	0.001	0.000	0.004	0.000	0.000	0.007	0.006	0.007	0.008
Nontax revenue	0.030	0.030	0.027	0.037	0.033	0.108	0.114	0.123	0.090	0.085	0.100	0.072	0.103
Grants	0.000	0.000	0.001	0.006	0.005	0.004	0.027	0.029	0.042	0.054	0.070	0.110	0.113

Source: Republic of Ghana (1992).

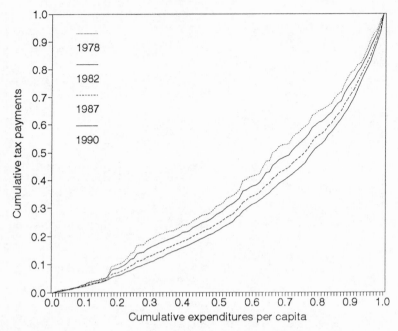

Fig. 8.7. Ghana: Lorenz curves for all taxes, 1977/78, 1981/82, 1987, 1990
Source: Ghana Living Standards Survey, 1987/88, and author's calculations.

efficacy (whether it is a good "tax handle"), and, of course, the utility of the corresponding government expenditures. Nevertheless, progressivity does matter, especially at the political level, where arguments that a tax "hurts the poor" are often more persuasive than considerations of economic or administrative efficiency.

The calculations I have presented here, while rough, can help to inform the debate on tax policy in Ghana in several ways. First, the broad-based taxes are either proportional (in the case of the sales tax) or progressive (the income taxes). Because broad-based taxes are usually less distortionary than particular excise taxes or taxes on trade, it appears that moving toward a greater reliance on broad-based taxes would improve both equity and economic efficiency.[17] To that end, the government's project to establish a value added tax (VAT) is welcome. A VAT's incidence should be similar to the sales tax, but collection is self-enforcing and thus more efficient administratively. On the other hand, the government's continuing attempts to assess reasonable presumptive taxes on self-employed enterprises, the cause of much complaining in Ghana, does in fact appear to be a regressive source of revenue.

Despite the intention to establish better broad-based taxation in 1992 and

[17] The only open question is the administrative costs associated with collecting such taxes.

1993, the government has in fact increasingly turned to two narrow taxes, on petroleum and cocoa. The 1993 budget statement (Botchwey 1993) shows petroleum taxes providing about one-third of all revenues and cocoa duties another 20 percent. As I have shown, the petroleum tax appears to be progressive in Ghana, so complaints that the recent gasoline price increases are falling disproportionately on the poor appear unfounded.[18] In addition, other economic arguments favor taxing petroleum products: there are negative externalities associated with their consumption (pollution); their consumption is correlated with the use of public services (roads); and demand for petroleum products is probably inelastic, so that the efficiency consequences are minor. One should doubt whether these factors have been considered explicitly in setting the current tax rates, but they do favor some level of taxation on petroleum. Within the group of petroleum products, the consumption patterns in the GLSS suggest that taxes on kerosene are regressive, while those on other products are comparably progressive. Thus, a government concerned about the effect of petroleum taxes on the poor might tax gasoline and diesel oil more heavily than kerosene.

There are no similar arguments to defend the cocoa duty. Because of the tradition of cocoa taxation in Ghana and the monopoly on marketing, this tax provides a good tax handle, but it is clearly distortionary and also appears to be regressive. A principal goal of tax policy in Ghana should be to replace this duty with other revenues that are more efficient and equitable. The consumption and production patterns in the GLSS show that the latter criterion is easily met: virtually any tax is more equitable than the cocoa duty. It also seems likely that the cocoa duty is among the most distortionary taxes in Ghana, because it discourages production of a commodity in which the country clearly has a comparative advantage.

Overall, the concern that fiscal stabilization has hurt the poor in Ghana seems unfounded. Reduced reliance on cocoa duties and increased recourse to more progressive direct taxes and the petroleum duty have lessened the poor's share of the overall tax burden. This does not mean that the poor are not paying more in taxes than they used to—virtually everyone in Ghana except cocoa farmers is probably paying more—but the increased burden on the poor has been less relative to their expenditures (and, *a fortiori*, absolutely) than that for wealthier households. It is still possible, of course, that the overall changes in fiscal policy have hurt the poor, but only if the incidence of the benefits of government expenditure is highly regressive. While a careful examination of such incidence would be a difficult project (see Meerman 1979, or Selowsky 1979), Sahn (1990) and Alderman (1990) cast doubt on whether adjustment has shifted expenditures toward the wealthy in Africa and Ghana. Thus, to argue that the ERP's fiscal policy reforms have hurt the poor in Ghana seems implausible.

---

[18] This calculation, however, is subject to a considerable margin of error.

Appendix 8.1. Tables

The following tables show the 1988 personal income tax brackets and weights used in the calculations for Figure 8.2, the expenditure items assumed to pay sales tax, and the importance of outlier corrections for different consumption items.

Table 8A.1. Ghana: 1988 personal income tax schedules[a]

Annual income (cedis)	Rate (%)
First 24,000	Free
Next 30,000	5
Next 30,000	10
Next 225,000	20
Next 225,000	30
Next 225,000	40
Next 225,000	50
Above 984,000	55

[a] Consolidated up to December 1990.

Source: Commissioner of Internal Revenue (1990), *Income Tax Decree of 1975*.

Table 8A.2. Ghana: consumption items covered in the Ghana Living Standard Survey (GLSS)

Item	Sales tax applies?
Lottery tickets	No
Cigarettes, tobacco, cola nuts	Yes
Commercial or home-made soap	Yes
Other personal care and health products	Yes
Home maintenance products	No
Charcoal or wood	No
Matches and candles	Yes
Other fuel for cooking or lighting	No
Gasoline and motor oil	No
Shoes for adults	Yes
Children's shoes	Yes
Domestic or imported cloth	Yes
Material for adult clothing	Yes
Material for children's clothing	Yes
Adult clothing	Yes
Children's clothing	Yes

Table 8A.2. (*cont.*)

Item	Sales tax applies?
Repairs and other expenses for vehicles	No
Public transport, taxis, etc.	No
Home repairs, painting, insurance, etc.	No
Books, notebooks, newspapers, stationery, etc.	No
Table top stoves and coal pots	Yes
Medicines	Yes
Medical services and expenses	No
Kitchen equipment	Yes
Lanterns and lamps	Yes
Furniture	No
Linen	Yes
Envelopes, writing paper, stamps, and telephones	No
Hairdressing, haircuts, etc.	No
Domestic servants	Yes
Jewelry, watches	No
Entertainment	No
Taxes	No
Reimbursement of loans and interest	No
Susu	No
Weddings and dowries	No
Funerals	No
Gifts	Yes
Bread or wheat flour	Yes
Macaroni and spaghetti	Yes
Biscuits and cakes	Yes
Refined oil	Yes
Butter or margarine	Yes
Alcoholic beverages	Yes
Non-alcoholic beverages	Yes
Maggi$_{TM}$ cubes	Yes
Milk or milk powder	Yes
Milk products (except butter)	Yes
Other foods eaten away from home	No
All other food items	No

Note: For the following items, I assume that sales tax is applied to the use value only: sewing machines, gas or other full-sized stoves, refrigerators or freezers, air conditioners, fans, radios, radio/cassette players, phonographs, stereo equipment, video equipment, washing machines, black-and-white TV sets, color TV sets, bicycles, motorbikes, cars, other vehicles, and cameras.

Table 8A.3. Ghana: information on outlier corrections in the sample

Proportion of expenditure allocated to:	No. of households	Mean	Standard deviation	Alternate cutoff	No. of outliers
Alcoholic beverages	1199	0.0016	0.0019	0.10	0
Weddings and funerals	2332	0.0119	0.0277	0.10	18
Non-alcoholic beverages	413	0.0008	0.0009	0.05	0
Gasoline	47	0.0869	0.0849	0.10	1
Kerosene	2650	0.0233	0.0218	0.10	18
All items with sales tax	3019	0.1664	0.0984	0.70	19
Tobacco	915	0.0589	0.0667	0.10	7
Public transport	2714	0.0040	0.0048	0.10	2
Reported tax payments	2181	0.0027	0.0071	0.45	0
Cocoa[a]	376	35.5	51.9	—	4
Daily income tax	695	0.0287	0.0478	0.45	1
Annual income tax	349	0.0181	0.0372	0.45	1
Taxes on dividend income	27	0.0192	0.0277	0.30	2
Wage/salary withholding	878	0.0231	0.0624	0.45	3

[a] Cocoa data are for yield (in kilos/acre).

References

Alderman, Harold. 1990. *Downturn and Economic Recovery in Ghana: Impacts on the Poor.* Monograph No. 10. Ithaca, NY: CFNPP.

——1992. *Incomes and Food Security in Ghana.* Working Paper No. 26. Ithaca, NY: CFNPP.

——Sudharshan Canagarajah, and Stephen D. Younger. 1993. *Consequences of Permanent Lay-off from Civil Service: Results from a Survey of Retrenched Workers in Ghana.* Working Paper No. 35. Ithaca, NY: CFNPP.

——and Paul Higgins. 1992. *Food and Nutritional Adequacy in Ghana.* Working Paper No. 27. Ithaca, NY: CFNPP.

Botchwey, K. 1993. Budget speech (unpublished).

Johnson, Martin, Andrew McKay, and Jeffrey Round. 1989. "Household Income and Expenditure Sub-aggregates from the Ghana Living Standards Survey 1988." Coventry: University of Warwick Development Research Centre, Department of Economics.

Meerman, Jacob. 1979. *Public Expenditure in Malaysia: Who Benefits and Why.* New York: Oxford University Press.

Pechman, Joseph. 1985. *Who Paid the Taxes, 1966–85.* Washington, DC: Brookings Institution.

Republic of Ghana. 1992. *Quarterly Digest of Statistics* (March).

Sahn, David. 1990. *Fiscal and Exchange Rate Reforms in Africa: Considering the Impact on the Poor.* Monograph No. 4. Ithaca, NY: CFNPP.

Selowsky, Marcelo. 1979. *Who Benefits from Government Expenditure: A Case Study of Colombia.* New York: Oxford University Press.

Shoven, John, and John Whalley. 1984. "Applied General Equilibrium Models of Taxation and International Trade." *Journal of Economic Literature,* 22.

Summers, Lawrence, and Lant Pritchett. 1993. "The Structural Adjustment Debate." *American Economic Review,* 83(2).

World Bank. 1989. "Ghana Living Standards Survey, First Year Report." Unpublished.

——1991. "Ghana: Progress on Adjustment." Report No. 9475-GH. Washington, DC: World Bank.

Younger, Stephen D. 1992. "Aid and the Dutch Disease: Macroeconomic Management When Everybody Loves You." *World Development,* 20(11).

9

Growth Linkages in Madagascar: Implications for Development Strategies

Paul Dorosh and Steven Haggblade

9.1. *Introduction*

In the late 1970s, Madagascar launched an ambitious investment program as part of its *investir à outrance* (invest to the limit) development strategy to spur economic growth. For a few short years during the investment boom, the economy surged forward, fueled by massive capital inflows and short-term commercial bank loans at market interest rates. When scheduled payments of interest and principal on the loans coincided with a decline in terms of trade in the early 1980s, however, a balance-of-payments crisis ensued. As part of the stabilization and structural adjustment efforts supported by the IMF and the World Bank, the investment program was scaled back, government spending was slashed, and government controls on markets were gradually reduced.

Although the role of the public sector has diminished in Madagascar, government investment, as embodied in the public investment program, remains an important part of the country's development efforts. With investment resources limited, strategic allocation of national investment is a crucial element of the transition from structural adjustment to long-run economic growth. The *investir à outrance* development push placed a major emphasis on industry to the relative neglect of agriculture. The investments in agriculture that were made during the 1970s and 1980s focused on large-scale irrigated rice perimeters, such as Lac Alaotra,[1] as well as on increased production of export crops, particularly coffee. Overall, the results of most of these investments have been disappointing. After a decade of stabilization and structural adjustment, as the country had hopes of achieving sustained economic growth, it was important that the earlier mistakes were not repeated, but that scarce resources were used efficiently and equitably.

---

[1] See Barghouti and Lenoigne (1990) for an analysis of economic returns to large scale irrigation projects in Madagascar.

In setting priorities, the microeconomic profitability of the investment, for example the costs and benefits directly resulting from the investment project, plays a major role. But initial project selection is also guided by overall development strategy, incorporating a blend of objectives including economic growth, income distribution, and regional or spatial criteria. Here, linkages between the project outcome at a microeconomic level and its impact on the rest of the economy also become important (Bell, Hazell, and Slade 1982). A thorough understanding of the tradeoffs involved in alternative growth paths, including potential multiplier effects and impacts on income distribution, provides a fundamentally important input into public decision-making.

This chapter examines the implication of alternative growth strategies on the level and distribution of income in Madagascar. We focus on growth linkages emanating from the three key sectors of the Malagasy economy—paddy (the major food crop), coffee (the major export crop), and the formal manufacturing sector.

After a brief discussion of the roles of agriculture and industry in the Malagasy economy, we present a semi-input–output (SIO) model for projecting the income and employment consequences of these three alternative growth strategies. The model uses a social accounting matrix (SAM) as a framework for tracing the interrelationships among productive sectors, households, and other institutions in the economy. The results focus on the tradeoffs between investments in rice, export crops, and manufacturing. The final section offers policy conclusions.

9.2. *Agriculture and Industry in the Malagasy Economy*

The choices between investment in agriculture versus industry—and, within agriculture, between food crops and export crops—are especially important given the large size of the agricultural sector and the limited resources available in Madagascar. Agriculture provides the primary source of income for three-quarters of Madagascar's population and is second only to services in generating value added (Table 9.1). The formal industrial sector, dominated by food processing and textiles, remains small, accounting for only 8.6 percent of GDP and 3 percent of employment.

By value, farm output is concentrated in rice (paddy), export crops (coffee, vanilla and cloves), root crops, and livestock. Paddy, the major staple, is grown throughout Madagascar, mostly by small farmers on irrigated land. In the central highlands (Hauts-Plateaux), paddy cultivation forms the base of the rural economy. Coffee, vanilla, and cloves are grown on the east and north coasts.

Apart from the short-lived investment boom, Madagascar's economy

Table 9.1. Madagascar: listing of SAM accounts

SAM row accounts	1984 gross output (m FMG)	% of value added
Activities		
Paddy, irrigated low-input	59,973	2.4
Paddy, irrigated high-input	87,315	2.7
Paddy, rainfed	20,918	1.1
Coffee, low-input	21,534	1.3
Coffee, high-input	7,201	0.4
Vanilla and cloves	14,569	0.9
Nontraditional export crops	—	—
Industrial crops (cotton, groundnuts, sugarcane)	14,176	0.5
Other agriculture (livestock, tubers, perishables)	487,485	26.1
Mining, energy, and water	85,298	2.0
Rice milling	169,988	0.2
Formal manufacturing	84,885	2.3
Informal industries	403,829	6.8
Private services (commerce, construction, services)	1,001,088	45.0
Public services	203,799	8.2
Commodities		
Paddy		
Coffee		
Vanilla and cloves		
Nontraditional export crops		
Industrial crops		
Other agriculture (livestock, tubers, perishables)		
Mining, energy and water		
Rice		
Formal manufacturing		
Informal industries		
Private services (commerce, construction, services)		
Public services		
Households		
Large urban areas		
Secondary urban centers		
Large farms		
Small farms		
Rural nonfarm poor		
Rural nonfarm rich		
Institutions (corporations, financial, nonprofits)		
Government		
Rest of world		
Capital		

Source: Dorosh and Haggblade (1992).

Table 9.2. Madagascar: sectoral growth and investment, 1973–1990

	1973–77	1978–80	1981–82	1983–87	1988–90
Real GDP					
(bn 1987 FMG)					
Agricultural	760.8	740.7	756.7	824.7	922.1
Industry	347.5	380.8	316.0	299.6	335.5
Services	1224.5	1311.9	1273.9	1200.8	1307.3
Real GDP	2332.9	2433.4	2346.6	2325.1	2564.9
Real GDP per capita					
('000 1987 FMG)	306.5	286.7	262.6	232.6	226.7
Real GDP growth					
rates (%)					
Agriculture	0.86	1.03	0.67	2.51	3.16
Industry	−0.31	4.76	−13.17	4.99	0.67
Real GDP	−0.06	2.49	−3.59	1.38	3.37
Real GDP per capita	−2.57	−0.27	−6.13	−1.50	0.16
Investment per capita					
('000 1987 FMG)	35.2	39.0	31.9	23.4	37.0
Investment/GDP (%)	11.4	13.5	12.0	10.1	16.3
Rice production					
('000 metric tons)	1931.2	2025.3	2030.3	2192.6	2329.0
Per capita rice					
production[a] (kg)	168.8	159.1	151.4	146.2	137.2

[a] Rice equivalent equal to 0.67 kg of milled rice per kg of paddy.

Sources: World Bank (1993); Bernier and Dorosh (1993).

stagnated from the early 1970s to the late 1980s.[2] Nationalization of industries and increasing government intervention in markets resulted in a disappointing 0.06 percent average annual decline in real GDP from 1973 to 1977 (Table 9.2). The *investir à outrance* strategy in the late 1970s was designed to take advantage of high world coffee prices and readily available credit on world markets to jump-start the economy with massive investments in industry and infrastructure. Investment as a share of GDP rose to 13.5 percent in the 1978–1980 period, up from an average of 11.4 percent of GDP from 1973 to 1977. During these boom years, industrial output grew by an average of 4.76 percent per year, though the growth rate of agriculture was only 1.03 percent per year.

Unfortunately, declining world coffee prices, increased debt servicing obligations and tighter world credit markets in the early 1980s brought about a balance of payments crisis before many of the investment projects

[2] Further details on the Malagasy economy and economic policies are found in Dorosh, Bernier, and Sarris (1990), Dorosh (1994), and in Chapter 2 above.

were completed. With foreign exchange shortages limiting imports of intermediate and capital goods, value added in industry fell by an average of 13.17 percent per year in 1981 and 1982, to a level 9.1 percent below the average output of 1973–1977. The industrial sector recovered somewhat thereafter, as price controls were gradually eliminated and official lending helped ease foreign exchange constraints from 1983 to 1987. Industrial growth was a mere 0.67 percent per year from 1988 to 1990, however, despite an overall gain in real GDP averaging 3.16 percent per year in this period.

In contrast to industry, the agriculture sector fared better under structural adjustment. Since liberalization of agricultural markets, beginning in 1983, value added in agriculture increased by an average of 2.51 percent per year from 1982 to 1987 and by 3.16 percent per year from 1987 to 1990. However, rice output per capita declined by 20.6 percent between 1975 and 1988 before increasing slightly in 1989 and 1990, and rice imports averaged 8.2 percent of total rice availability over the second half of the 1980s (Bernier and Dorosh 1993). Production of traditional export crops also declined in value after the late 1970s.

Political turmoil in the early 1990s reversed the growth in GDP following the major trade liberalization of 1987 and 1988. Several key reforms undertaken under structural adjustment were reversed and more stringent government controls were reimposed on foreign exchange and trade. Whether economic growth is restored will depend in part on the policies of the new Malagasy government with regard to the extent of liberalization of key markets and other policies affecting economic incentives and private investment. A key aspect of the government's own investment strategy, having major implications for both growth and equity, will be the sectoral allocation of public investment.

Discouraged by the disappointing record of past investments in large-scale irrigated rice perimeters and in manufactured goods, many now argue that a heavier emphasis on export crops will yield the greatest prospects for long-run growth. A thorough understanding of the tradeoffs involved in alternative growth paths, including potential multiplier effects and impacts on income distribution, provides a fundamentally important input in public decision-making.

9.3. *Modeling Linkages in the Malagasy Economy*

9.3.1. *Overview of the model*

Investment, like new technology, directly increases output in the target sector. In the process, this increased output stimulates demand for production inputs and for consumer goods required by the households earning income in the new production units. Because of these twin sources of demand, increased output generates not only direct income growth within a sector but also indirect increases in demand for other goods and services in the economy. Where excess capacity exists, the increased demand translates into higher output and consequently higher incomes. Thus, the total income gain generated by growth in a given sector includes the direct sectoral income plus the indirect earnings generated in other sectors.

The measurement of these indirect effects requires a model that relates sectoral output, household income, consumer demand, and inter-industry input linkages. Since supply responsiveness across sectors determines how effectively growing demand will translate into increased domestic output and income, any model must make clear assumptions about supply elasticities in all sectors of the economy.

One option, the input–output model, embodies the classic approach to this question. It sets total supply in each sector (Z) equal to the two sources of demand, inter-industry input demand (AZ) and final consumption demand (F). Final demand includes consumption by households (βY) and exogenous sources of demand such as exports (E). The value added share (v) in gross commodity output (Z) determines income (Y).

$$Z = AZ + F$$
$$= AZ + \beta Y + E$$
$$= AZ + \beta v Z + E \qquad (1)$$

Presuming supply to be perfectly elastic in all sectors, total output and incomes become determined by the level of exogenous demand (E) and the matrix of multipliers $(I-M)^{-1}$, where M offers shorthand notation for the parameters $(A + \beta)$.

$$Z = (I - M)^{-1} E \qquad (2)$$

Because they assume perfectly elastic supply in all sectors, input–output models overestimate output responses following from any intervention. Yet in reality, some sectors in most developing countries face supply constraints. This is especially true for agriculture, where land, labor, rainfall, and technology frequently limit output. Industrial output is also often constrained by lack of capital. By ignoring supply constraints altogether, input–output models typically exaggerate the size of the inter-sectoral linkages. In the case of crop-based agriculture, input–output models overstate growth multipliers by a factor of 2 to 5 (Haggblade, Hammer, and Hazell 1991).

A more realistic approach, and the one adopted here, is to use a semi-input–output (SIO) model. While retaining many of the basic assumptions of the IO approach, the SIO model differs in that it introduces supply rigidities in some sectors. The following two equations, contrasted with (1) and (2) above, capture the SIO model's essential distinction. By classifying all economic sectors as either supply-constrained (Z_1) or perfectly elastic in supply (Z_2), the SIO model permits output responses only in some sectors (Z_2). In supply-constrained sectors (Z_1), increases in domestic demand merely reduce net exports (E_1), which then become endogenous to the system.[3]

$$Z_1 = A_1 Z + \beta_1 v_1 Z + E_1$$
$$Z_2 = A_2 Z + \beta_2 v_2 Z + E_2 \qquad (3)$$

$$\begin{bmatrix} E_1 \\ Z_2 \end{bmatrix} = (1 - M^\star)^{-1} \begin{bmatrix} Z_1 \\ E_2 \end{bmatrix} \qquad (4)$$

The model used here is built around a condensed SAM that includes 12 commodity accounts, 15 activities, 6 household groups, 1 other non-government institution, the government, the rest of the world, and 1 capital account (Table 9.1).[4]

The semi-input–output (SIO) model is described graphically in Figure 9.1. For simplicity of exposition, the model collapses the 12 SAM commodity accounts still further, into the following three categories: (Z_1), paddy; (Z_2), other supply-constrained commodities (tradables such as coffee, industrial crops, minerals, and formal manufacturing); and (Z_3), commodities highly elastic in supply (non-tradables such as services, informal industries, perishable agriculture, plus the tradables, vanilla and cloves).

Following along in Figure 9.1, consider the consequences of public or private investments in paddy production. Regardless of the technology chosen, be it rehabilitation of small irrigated perimeters or investment in large-scale irrigated rice schemes, the immediate impact of this investment is to increase paddy supply. In round 1, this directly raises farm income by 0.49 Madagascar franc (FMG) for every 1 FMG of increased paddy supply. This direct injection triggers a series of responses that increase income even more.

In round 2, the economy registers increased demand for the inputs used in paddy production plus increased farm household spending on consumer goods. These twin channels increase domestic demand for paddy, other supply-constrained tradables, and the highly elastic supply of non-tradable domestic services, informal manufactures and perishable agricultural commodities. For paddy and other supply-constrained tradables, this increase in demand does not stimulate further domestic production: it merely decreases

---

[3] A formal exposition of the SIO model is found in Appendix 2 of Dorosh, Haggblade, et al. (1991).

[4] The SAM used in this study is a condensed version of the SAM described in Dorosh et al. (1991). Details of the modifications for the purpose of the modeling here are found in Dorosh, Haggblade et al. (1991).

net exports. In contrast, because of the elastic supply of non-tradables, increased demand leads to higher output and higher domestic incomes in these other sectors, most of them outside of agriculture.

The increased production of commodities with elastic supply (Z_3) once again raises demand for production inputs and consumer goods. In round 3, this increases demand in all three sectors. As before, production of paddy and other supply-constrained commodities does not increase. Instead, net exports decrease still more. For this reason, as equation (4) indicates, exports in these supply-constrained sectors become endogenous to the model. Yet once again, output and incomes rise in the activities with highly elastic supply. This induces further rounds of successively dampening demand increases.

In total, the indirect effects of the irrigation investment, from round 2 on, stimulate another 1.31 FMG in national income for every 1 FMG of increased paddy supply. Thus, the total increase resulting from paddy investments equals $0.49 + 1.31 = 1.80$.

Investments in coffee production or formal manufacturing will generate the same sequence of events. They differ only in that the shock, the initial supply increase, will occur in sector Z_2. Since coffee and formal manufacturing generate different input demands than paddy and a different distribution of income, the second-round demand shifts will differ from the paddy results in both composition and magnitude. Ultimately, the total income gain will also be different.

9.3.2. Underlying premises

The semi-input–output (SIO) model falls into the general family of linear, fixed-price models. For the SIO model to generate sensible predictions, each of these characteristics must offer reasonable approximations of reality.

Linearity. As with many kinds of economic models, the SIO requires that all relationships be expressed as linear functions. For intermediate inputs, this standard assumption suggests that increases in output require additional inputs in fixed proportions. For household consumption, it requires that consumption expenditures rise in tandem with income. Although marginal expenditures or input demands may differ from the average, the increments must be expressed as linear functions of output and income.

In general, this simplification does not pose great problems. Non-linear systems can be approximated by linear functions in the short run. And they offer considerable conveniences in computing model solutions.

Fixed prices. Fixed prices likewise vastly simplify computational requirements by side-stepping cumbersome issues of substitution in production and consumption. Input–output coefficients and marginal budget shares, which remain fixed in a fixed-price world, become endogenous variables in

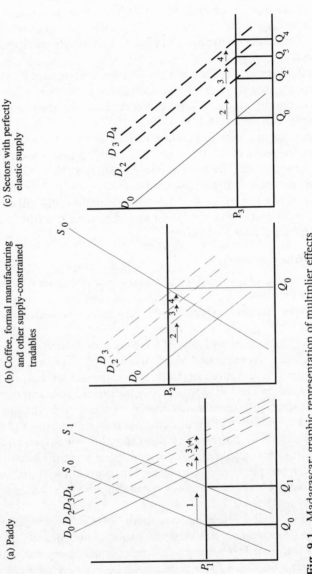

Fig. 9.1. Madagascar: graphic representation of multiplier effects

(a) Paddy
(b) Coffee, formal manufacturing, and other supply-constrained tradables
(c) Sectors with perfectly elastic supply

	Paddy (Inelastic supply, imported good)	Coffee (Inelastic supply, exported good)	Non-traded (Perfectly elastic supply)
Round 1	Invest in paddy Increase in supply Increase in farmer income		
Round 2	Increased demand (final and intermediate goods); supply fixed at Q_1 Exports decrease Domestic output and income unchanged	Increased demand (final and intermediate goods); supply fixed at Q_0 Exports decrease Domestic output and income unchanged	Increased demand (final and intermediate goods) Increased output Increased income
Rounds 3 and 4	Increased demand (final and intermediate goods); supply fixed at Q_1 Exports decrease Domestic output and income unchanged	Increased demand (final and intermediate goods); supply fixed at Q_0 Exports decrease Domestic output and income unchanged	Increased demand (final and intermediate goods) Increased output Increased income

a world where relative prices vary. While computational convenience is not a strong rationale for imposing fixed prices, it does offer a strong incentive to investigate the plausibility of such an assumption.

For tradable goods, most analysts agree that the fixed-price assumption is appropriate in small countries. World markets will determine their price level. Madagascar, a small country, takes world prices as given in all markets except vanilla and cloves, where they account for over half of world trade. We will return to the fixed-price characteristic of vanilla and cloves in a moment.

For non-traded goods, such as services, informal manufactured goods, and many perishable agricultural commodities, fixed prices depend on firms' ability to increase output at constant cost. Formally, this requires a perfectly elastic output supply. Because of the considerable unemployment and excess capacity present in Madagascar, especially in the 1984 base year for which the SAM was constructed, the constant cost assumption appears to be a reasonable approximation of reality.

Vanilla and cloves, too, even though they are tradable commodities, are highly elastic in supply. The output of wild gathered crops requiring primarily harvesting labor can be increased at constant cost so long as wage rates do not rise. Given current underemployment, it appears that vanilla and cloves supply can be considered highly elastic, at least in the short run.

At some point, as expansion and liberalization proceed, supply constraints may develop in some of Madagascar's non-tradable sectors. When this day arrives, the SIO model will overstate income multipliers emanating from sectoral growth. Consequently, some sort of adjustment will be required to capture the income-dampening effects of the inflation that will follow. Recent experiments suggest that, in the face of upward-sloping non-tradable supply, SIO models overstate true income multipliers by 10–25 percent (Haggblade, Hammer, and Hazell 1991). So the simplest accommodation would involve rule-of-thumb discounting based on these results. A much more complicated alternative is to use a computable general equilibrium model.[5]

9.4. Model simulations

The following results explore the three most commonly considered alternative investment strategies for Madagascar: food crops (rice), export crops (coffee), and manufacturing. In agriculture, we model what observers consider the most likely sources of agricultural growth, those focused on improved small farmer technology. High-input technology, and, in the case of rice, rehabilitation of small-scale irrigation perimeters rather than large-

---

5 See Dorosh (1994) for a description of a CGE model for Madagascar.

scale perimeters or rainfed cultivation, seem the most viable avenues for future investment. For manufacturing, we focus on the formal sector,[6] where, after decades of neglect, supply-side investment seriously constrains growth.

The model simulation assumes that consumers spend additional income the same way they have in the past, that is, that average budget shares equal marginals, and that savings are not translated into investment expenditure in the short run. Thus, investment is taken as exogenous.

9.4.1. *Impact on growth*

Income. Under these assumptions, a 1 FMG increase in agricultural output will generate roughly 2 FMG in national income, 1.802 FMG for paddy and 1.974 FMG for coffee (Table 9.3). In contrast, manufactured goods produce only half as much income, 0.963 FMG for every 1 FMG in increased output. This difference arises primarily because of smaller value added generated by the direct increase in manufacturing output. Material inputs used in formal manufacturing account for 70 percent of the value of production. Consequently, value added per unit of output stands at only 30 percent. Yet in the agricultural sectors, the value added in total output is much higher—49 percent in paddy and 63 percent for coffee.

If direct increase in paddy production generates only 0.49 FMG in income per unit of output, where does the remaining 1.310 FMG (1.802–0.492) come from? It comes from the second- and third-round linkages, the input demand and consumption growth emanating from the injection of agricultural growth. Clearly the linkages are important. They account for over two-thirds of total income created in all three sectors (Table 9.3).

All three sectors generate large linkages. But in agricultural they are larger, primarily because of larger initial income (value added) and consequently a larger second round of consumer spending on local goods and services.

Investment requirements. Ultimately, the efficiency of alternative investment strategies depends on how much investment is required to initiate output growth in the first place. Once output grows by 1 FMG, the income consequences are broadly similar in the two agricultural sectors, though only half as large in manufacturing.

---

[6] Small-scale and informal manufacturing is not appropriate for comparison in these simulations. Because capital requirements are so very small in informal and small-scale manufacturing activities, most observers consider them to be constrained by discriminatory policies, working capital, or demand, but not by investment capital (Kilby, Liedholm, and Meyer 1984; Haggblade, Liedholm, and Mead 1986; Liedholm and Mead 1987; Page and Steel 1984). While public intervention in support of these small enterprises is appropriate, that intervention will primarily involve removal of discriminatory policies, provision of infrastructure, including a well-functioning credit system, and a method of fostering a pattern of general economic growth that generates buoyant demand to which these small enterprises can respond.

Table 9.3. Madagascar: multiplier decomposition under improved small farmer technology[a]

	Effect of a 1 FMG increase		
	Paddy output	Coffee output	Formal manufacturing output
Change in national income			
Initial direct increase	0.492	0.632	0.303
Multiplier effects	1.310	1.343	0.660
Total income increase	1.802	1.974	0.963
Investment multiplier, high returns scenario			
Investment required	0.387	0.641	1.000
National income generated per unit of investment	4.651	3.079	0.964
Investment multiplier, low returns scenario			
Investment required	0.644	1.282	3.000
National income generated per unit of investment	2.797	1.540	0.321

[a] These simulations model high-input technologies for paddy and coffee, and average budget shares for households.

Source: Model simulations.

The investment necessary to increase output of paddy, coffee, and formal sector manufactured goods by 1 FMG differs substantially from one another. Given that investment data in all sectors suffer from considerable uncertainty, Table 9.3 offers both optimistic and pessimistic projections for each of the three sectors under review. For paddy and coffee, the analysis presents two investment scenarios, based on traditional cost–benefit analysis.[7] The paddy scenarios show the costs and benefits for rehabilitation of small irrigated perimeters in the high plateaus using traditional and input-intensive technologies (AIRD 1991). These yield pessimistic and optimistic projections, respectively. The coffee scenarios are based on FAO (1989) under high and low world coffee price assumptions. For the formal manufacturing sector, it is clear that some industries, such as textiles and food processing, require lower fixed investments than others, such as chemicals, metal products, and pharmaceuticals. Synthesizing from a variety of sources, Table 9.3 contrasts two alternative incremental capital–output

7 See Appendix Table 9A.1 for details of the calculations.

ratios (ICORs) for manufacturing, 1 for the low-investment industries and 3 for the more capital-intensive ones (World Bank 1978; Liedholm and Mead 1987; World Bank 1991).

Although these investment costs vary considerably across locations (rural vs urban) and over time (short-run investments in paddy vs longer-run investments in coffee and manufacturing), it appears that, under best- and worst-case settings for each investment opportunity, policy-makers can increase paddy output at significantly lower investment cost than for coffee or manufactured goods. Investment requirements for producing one unit of paddy range from 0.4 to 0.6; this compares with 0.6 to 1.3 in coffee and 1.0 to 3.0 in manufacturing. Under the most optimistic scenario for each activity, paddy requires investments 30–60 percent lower than for coffee and manufacturing.

Income/investment multipliers. Given low investment costs and high income per unit of output, paddy generates the largest income multipliers of the three. In the worst-case setting, assuming high-input technology but low marginal increase in output, 1 FMG invested in paddy rehabilitation will generate 2.8 FMG in national income (GDP). The same 1 FMG invested in coffee, under current low world prices, would yield only 1.5 FMG in national income, while the gain from a similar investment in manufactured goods is still smaller, only 0.3 FMG in value added.

Even with more optimistic assumptions on efficiency of investment in manufacturing, the pessimistic, low-yield scenario for paddy still results in a much larger gain in GDP—2.8 FMG from paddy vs 0.964 FMG for manufacturing (Table 9.3). Similarly, returns to investment in paddy under the low yield scenario are larger than returns to investment in coffee under the high world coffee price scenario. Thus, on efficiency grounds it appears that investments in agriculture—especially paddy—yield much higher returns than investments in manufacturing.[8]

9.4.2. Employment and income distribution

Investment in agriculture also generates more employment, particularly for unskilled labor, than does investment in manufacturing (Table 9.4). For each 1 million FMG increase in output of paddy and coffee, employment increases by 2.9 and 2.6 jobs, respectively; the same 1 million FMG increase in manufacturing output increases employment by only 1.1 jobs. Moreover, more than 90 percent of the employment generated with increased paddy and coffee output is for unskilled labor, compared with 82 percent from an increase in manufacturing investment.

---

[8] These scenarios differ slightly from those in Dorosh and Haggblade (1993). For rice, the pessimistic scenario now models a high input technology but with only a small marginal increase in output of 1.5 metric tons/ha. For coffee, only the value of incremental coffee output is used in the multiplier calculations here.

Table 9.4. Madagascar: employment consequences of alternative growth strategies[a]

	Effect of a 1m FMG increase		
	Paddy output	Coffee output	Formal manufacturing output
Employment generated ('000s of jobs)			
Skilled jobs	0.024	0.046	0.036
Semi-skilled jobs	0.148	0.202	0.170
Unskilled jobs	2.757	2.392	0.941
Total jobs	2.929	2.640	1.147
Employment generated (%)			
Skilled jobs	0.8	1.7	3.1
Semi-skilled jobs	5.1	7.7	14.8
Unskilled jobs	94.1	90.6	82.0
Total jobs	100.0	100.0	100.0

[a] These simulations model high-input technologies for paddy and coffee, and average budget shares for households.

Source: Model simulations.

Because the greater employment generated by paddy and coffee is concentrated among unskilled workers, these investments result in a more equitable distribution of income as well (Table 9.5). The rural poor, who constitute 88 percent of Madagascar's poor (Dorosh, Bernier, and Sarris 1990), enjoy a much larger gain in incomes when agricultural output is increased. With increased paddy output, the rural poor earn 54 percent of all income created, while they receive only 34 percent from coffee and 25 percent from manufactured goods.

Surprisingly, the change in urban household income is approximately the same for all three sectors, i.e. 0.20–0.30 FMG per unit of output increased. How is it possible that agriculture-led growth generates at least as much urban income as that focused on urban manufacturing? The answer lies in spatial linkages.

9.4.3. *Spatial linkages*

Not surprisingly, rural incomes rise most with increases in paddy and coffee, the two agricultural outputs (Table 9.6). In absolute terms, rural incomes rise by 1.38 FMG for each 1 FMG increase in output of paddy, nearly three times as much as that resulting from increased manufacturing output. Three-quarters of the gain in incomes generated from increased paddy output accrue to rural households. For both coffee and manufactured goods, the income share earned by rural households is about 50 percent.

Table 9.5. Madagascar: income distribution consequences of alternative growth strategies[a]

	Result of a 1 FMG increase in output		
	Paddy supply	Coffee supply	Formal manufacturing supply
Income distribution (FMG)			
Government income	0.067	0.436	0.175
Institutions	0.142	0.164	0.116
Households			
Urban	0.213	0.323	0.219
Rural rich	0.408	0.389	0.214
Rural poor	0.972	0.663	0.238
Total income	1.802	1.975	0.962
Income distribution (%)			
Government income	3.7	22.1	18.2
Institutions	7.9	8.3	12.1
Households			
Urban	11.8	16.4	22.8
Rural rich	22.6	19.7	22.2
Rural poor	53.9	33.6	24.7
Total income	100.0	100.0	100.0

[a] These simulations model high-input technologies for paddy and coffee, and average budget shares for households.

Source: Model simulations.

The large urban centers attract 20–50 percent of all income gains under each of the three growth scenarios. Although the percentages vary, absolute income increments are roughly comparable for paddy and manufacturing. For coffee, however, urban income generation is roughly double that of the other two sectors. The large urban linkages for coffee arise mainly because 45 percent of crop value accrues to the government and traders as commodity taxes and commercial margins.

Secondary cities, so important in many decentralized schemes of development, appear unaffected by any of these strategies. Yet a growing contingent of geographers, regional planners, anthropologists, and public finance economists have become increasingly concerned about the importance of these small towns in fostering an equitable and decentralized pattern of economic growth (Bendavid-Val 1989; Karaska and Belsky 1987; Rondinelli 1983; Evans 1989).

Decomposing the total income gain reveals that direct income accrues, as expected, primarily in rural areas for paddy and in urban areas for

Table 9.6. Madagascar: spatial implications of alternative growth strategies[a]

	Result of a 1 FMG increase in output		
	Paddy	Coffee	Formal manufacturing
Total income, by location (FMG)			
Large urban centers			
Households	0.177	0.272	0.185
Institutions	0.142	0.164	0.116
Government	0.067	0.436	0.175
Total	0.386	0.872	0.476
Secondary cities			
Households	0.036	0.051	0.034
Rural areas households	1.380	1.052	0.452
Total income	1.802	1.975	0.962
% share of total income			
Large urban centers			
Households	9.8	13.8	19.2
Institutions	7.9	8.3	12.1
Government	3.7	22.1	18.2
Total	21.4	44.2	49.5
Secondary cities			
Households	2.0	2.6	3.5
Rural areas households	76.6	53.3	47.0
Total income	100.0	100.0	100.0

[a] These simulations model high-input technologies for paddy and coffee, and average budget shares for households.

Source: Model simulations.

manufacturing (Table 9.7). Coffee, however, generates large direct income in urban areas, primarily through heavy taxation.

Yet indirect linkages run strongly in both directions (Table 9.8). Agricultural growth generates urban income through increases in demand for private services and informal manufactures. Conversely, manufacturing generates rural income through increases in demand for non-tradable agricultural products such as milk, meat, and vegetables. The share of indirect income accruing to rural households is roughly the same for all three types of investment, 42–50 percent.

In fact, in absolute magnitude, indirect linkages from agriculture to large cities are double those from manufacturing (Table 9.8). This result arises because of the high use of imported inputs in formal manufacturing as well as the higher import content of urban consumption.

Table 9.7. Madagascar: direct impact on spatial distribution of income[a]

| | Result of a 1 FMG increase in output | | |
	Paddy	Coffee	Formal manufacturing
Initial direct income, by location			
Large urban centers			
Households	0.000	0.000	0.074
Institutions	0.006	0.041	0.055
Government	0.000	0.376	0.145
Total	0.006	0.417	0.274
Secondary cities			
Households	0.000	0.000	0.013
Rural areas households	0.485	0.215	0.016
Total direct income	0.491	0.632	0.303
% share of direct income increment			
Large urban centers			
Households	0.0	0.0	24.4
Institutions	1.2	6.5	18.2
Government	0.0	59.5	47.9
Total	1.2	66.0	90.4
Secondary cities			
Households	0.0	0.0	4.3
Rural areas households	98.8	34.0	5.3
Total direct income	100.0	100.0	100.0

[a] These simulations model high-input technologies for paddy and coffee, and average budget shares for households.

Source: Model simulations.

9.5. *Conclusions*

9.5.1. *Sectoral priorities*

Structural adjustment in Madagascar succeeded in generating only a few short years of per capita economic growth after 1988 before political turmoil and a subsequent reversal of liberalization measures led to economic declines again in the early 1990s. Restoring and sustaining this growth will require market reforms, sound government policies, and appropriate public sector investments as part of a coherent overall development strategy.

The simulation results presented in this chapter strongly suggest that an agriculturally based investment strategy—particularly one focused on

Table 9.8. Madagascar: indirect impact on spatial distribution of income[a]

| | Result of a 1 FMG increase in output | | |
	Paddy	Coffee	Formal manufacturing
Indirect income multipliers, by location			
Large urban centers			
Households	0.177	0.272	0.111
Institutions	0.136	0.123	0.061
Government	0.067	0.060	0.030
Total	0.380	0.455	0.202
Secondary cities			
Households	0.036	0.051	0.021
Rural areas households	0.895	0.837	0.436
Total indirect income	1.311	1.343	0.659
% share of total income			
Large urban centers			
Households	13.5	20.3	16.8
Institutions	10.4	9.2	9.3
Government	5.1	4.5	4.6
Total	29.0	33.9	30.7
Secondary cities			
Households	2.7	3.8	3.2
Rural areas households	68.3	62.3	66.2
Total indirect income	100.0	100.0	100.0

[a] These simulations model high-input technologies for paddy and coffee, and average budget shares for households.

Source: Model simulations.

rehabilitation of small irrigated paddy perimeters—will generate the most rapid income growth, the most jobs, the most equitable income distribution, and the most rapid urban economic growth. Even under the most optimistic assumptions about manufacturing and the most pessimistic returns in agriculture, paddy investments outperform those in manufacturing by a factor of 3. And over half of the agricultural income accrues to the rural poor, compared with only 25 percent for manufacturing. On both equity and efficiency grounds, investments in paddy emerge as the priority option.

As an additional bonus, the urban spinoffs projected from agricultural growth appear surprisingly strong. Both paddy and coffee generate substantial income and employment in large urban centers.

Yet, like manufacturing, they make little impact on secondary urban centers. This is surprising, and disappointing, given the considerable emerging interest in decentralized urbanization. In a modeling exercise such as this, parameters built on present locational patterns may not faithfully forecast the future growth of small towns. Given the large volume of evidence from elsewhere on the importance of rural towns, it would be premature to discount the rural town linkages based on this one empirical exercise (Anderson and Leiserson 1980; Haggblade, Hazell, and Brown 1989; Bendavid-Val 1989; Karaska and Belsky 1987; Evans 1989). Clearly, more field work is warranted. Perhaps, too, the secondary cities of Madagascar have simply not benefited from the basic infrastructural investments that elsewhere facilitate agricultural processing and marketing linkages.

9.5.2. *Sustaining the growth linkages*

Growth linkages across urban–rural boundaries have been shown to be significant for both urban and rural investments. Nearly one-quarter of the income generated from increased paddy production accrues to urban households and institutions (including the government). Similarly, rural households earn almost one-half the total income generated from investments in formal sector manufacturing. Government policies can help assure that these growth linkages achieve their full potential.

First, attention to rural infrastructure—roads, electricity, water, and communications—is especially important since it will both affect the ability of non-farm sectors to respond to the increased demand of farm households, and facilitate the response of farm sectors to increased demand of non-farm households. To ensure that spinoffs achieve their full potential, ongoing decisions about the sighting, construction, maintenance, and finance of rural infrastructure will be required. In all these phases, local decision-making and the ability to mobilize local resources will be key. This makes local governments important actors in agriculture-led growth strategies. To play their role effectively, the local authorities must enjoy the necessary political and financial authority as well as the management skills necessary to mobilize local resources and coordinate decision-making.

Second, direct intervention on behalf of non-farm and secondary farm activities can effectively accelerate their growth. To enjoy the full benefit of the agriculturally induced demand stimulus, evidence suggests that supporting supply-side interventions can be cost-effective (Haggblade, Hazell, and Brown 1989). While working capital credit programs have proven most popular, policy reform and technical assistance can also be viable if judiciously targeted.

The experience of the late 1970s with the failed investment push in Madagascar illustrates the importance of project design, funding, and policy environment for sustainable growth. In addition to these factors, maximizing the efficiency of scarce government resources for public investment will require an appropriate sectoral focus as part of the overall development strategy. The growth linkage analysis here provides evidence that an agriculturally focused growth strategy, with collateral incentives and support for rural infrastructure and non-farm enterprises, will likely yield the most rapid and equitable pattern of growth for Madagascar.

Appendix 9.1. Investment Data

Table 9A.1 presents calculations of the marginal returns to investment in paddy and robusta coffee.

Table 9A.1. Madagascar: returns to investment in agriculture

(a) Paddy: rehabilitation of small irrigated perimeters

	Pessimistic (traditional technology)	Optimistic (high-input technology)
Investment cost (FMG/ha)	241,564	242,133
Marginal increase in output (MT/ha)	1.5	2.5
Investment cost per MT increase in production (FMG/MT)	161,043	96,853
Price of paddy (FMG/MT)	250,000	250,000
Value of output per FMG invested (FMG)	1.552	2.581
Incremental capital output ratio	0.644	0.387

(b) Robusta coffee project: mixed replanting and pruning, high-input technology[a]

	Pesimistic (low world price)	Optimistic (high world price)
Investment cost (m FMG)	4,896	4,896
Additional output of coffee (m FMG)	3,820	7,639
FMG value of coffee output per FMG invested	0.780	1.560
Incremental capital output ratio	1.282	0.641

[a] Benefits and costs for the Coffee project are amortized annual values calculated at a discount rate of 10 %.

Sources: AIRD (1991); FAO (1989); and authors' calculations.

References

Anderson, Dennis, and Mark Leiserson. 1980. "Rural Non-farm Employment in Developing Countries." *Economic Development and Cultural Change*, 28 (2): 227–248.

Associates for International Resources and Development. 1984. "Etude du Secteur Rizicole: Rapport Finale." Somerville, MA: AIRD. Draft.

—— 1991. "Madagascar: Irrigated Sub-Sector Review: An Economic and Financial Analysis." Somerville, MA: AIRD. Draft.

Barghouti, Shawki, and Guy Lemoigne. 1990. *Irrigation in Sub-Saharan Africa: The Development of Public and Private Systems*. Technical Paper No. 123. Washington, DC: World Bank.

Bell, C.P., P. Hazell, and R. Slade. 1982. *Project Evaluation in Regional Perspective: A Study of an Irrigation Project in Northwest India*. Baltimore, MD: Johns Hopkins University Press.

Bendavid-Val, Avrom. 1989. "Rural–Urban Linkages: Farming and Farm House-holds in Regional and Town Economies." *Review of Urban and Regional Development*, 2: 89–97.

Bernier, René, and Paul Dorosh. 1993. *Constraints on Rice Production in Madagascar: The Farmer's Perspective*. Working Paper No. 34. Ithaca, NY: CFNPP.

Dorosh, Paul. 1994. *Structural Adjustment, Growth and Poverty in Madagascar: A CGE Analysis*. Monograph No. 17. Ithaca, NY: CFNPP.

—— and Steve Haggblade. 1993. "Agriculture-led Growth: Foodgrains versus Export Crops in Madagascar." *Agricultural Economics*, 9: 165–180.

—— —— et al. 1992. *Agricultural Growth Linkages in Madagascar*. Working Paper No. 22. Ithaca, NY: CFNPP.

—— René E. Bernier, and Alexander H. Sarris. 1990. *Macroeconomic Adjustment and the Poor: The Case of Madagascar*. Monograph No. 9. Ithaca, NY: CFNPP.

—— —— Armand Roger Randrianarivony, and Christian Rasolomanana. 1991. *A Social Accounting Matrix for Madagascar: Methodology and Results*. Working Paper No. 6. Ithaca, NY: CFNPP.

Evans, Hugh Emrys. 1989. "Rural–Urban Linkages: Draft Final Report." Washington, DC: Urban Development Division, World Bank. Unpublished.

Food and Agriculture Organization (FAO). 1989. "Madagascar: Projet de Finance-ment du Sous Secteur Café—rapport de préparation." Rapport du Programme de Coopération FAO/Banque Mondiale Centre d'Investissement 18/89 CP-MAG27. Rome: FAO.

Haggblade, S., J. Hammer, and P. Hazell. 1991. "Modeling Agricultural Growth Multipliers." *American Journal of Agricultural Economics*, 73(2): 361–374.

—— P. Hazell, and J. Brown. 1989. "Farm–NonFarm Linkages in Rural Sub-Saharan Africa." *World Development*, 17(8): 1173–1201.

—— Carl Liedholm, and Donald C. Mead. 1986. "The Effect of Policy and Policy Reforms on Non-Agricultural Enterprises and Employment in Developing Countries: A Review of Past Experiences." EEPA Discussion Paper No. 1. Cambridge, MA: Harvard Institute for International Development.

Karaska, Gerald J., and Eric S. Belsky. 1987. "Rural/Urban Dynamics in Regional Planning: Examples from Underdeveloped Regions." In Patterns of Change in Developing Regions., R. Bar-El et al., eds. Boulder, CO: Westview Press.

Kilby, Peter, Carl Liedholm, and Richard L. Meyer. 1984. "Working Capital and Nonfarm Rural Enterprises." In Undermining Rural Development with Cheap Credit., D. Adams, D. Graham, and J.D. Von Pischke, eds. Boulder, CO: Westview Press.

Liedholm, Carl, and Mead, Donald. 1987. "Small Scale Industries in Developing Countries: Empirical Evidence and Policy Implications." MSU International Development Papers No. 9. East Lansing, MI: Department of Agricultural Economics, Michigan State University.

Page, John, and Steel, William F. 1984. *Small Enterprise Development: Economic Issues from African Experience."* Technical Paper No. 26. Washington, DC: World Bank.

Rondinelli, Dennis. 1983. *Secondary Cities in Developing Countries: Policies for Diffusing Urbanization.* Beverly Hills, CA: Sage Publications.

World Bank. 1978. *Employment and Development of Small Enterprises.* Sector Policy Paper. Washington, DC: World Bank.

—— 1991a. *World Development Report.* New York: Oxford University Press.

—— 1991b. "Madagascar-Beyond Stabilization to Sustainable Growth." Report No. 9101-MAG. Washington, DC: World Bank.

—— 1993. *World Tables.* Washington, DC: World Bank.

10

Sectoral Investment Priorities for Renewed Growth in Zaire

Solomane Koné and Erik Thorbecke

10.1. *Introduction*

Zaire is characterized by chronic and escalating inflation and a disintegrated economy with widespread poverty. This is despite not only its rich natural endowment in minerals and abundant fertile soils, but also several IMF and World Bank stabilization and structural adjustment programs (SSAPs) starting as early as 1967.[1] The two major and recent programs were in 1983 and 1986–1987. Zaire's historically poor economic management and very partial implementation of policy reforms largely explain this poor performance.

Rising government current expenditures, mainly on goods and services, have caused unsustainable levels of budget deficits. Financing through money supply has largely contributed to chronic inflation (Tshishimbi, Glick, and Thorbecke 1991). Therefore, a major part of a viable stabilization program should consist of a substantial cut, or at least a freeze, in current expenditures in addition to a tight monetary policy. At the same time, major structural impediments to output growth, particularly in traditional agriculture, need to be removed, or at least relaxed, through institutional changes and an investment strategy in transport and agricultural infrastructure. The real need for these reforms raises the fundamental question of their short- and long-run impact on growth and the standard of living of the poor.

This study deals with the direct and indirect effects of structural reforms and macroeconomic policies on growth and poverty in Zaire. In particular, the focus is on: (1) the effects of the major structural obstacles in traditional agriculture on household income distribution and output growth; (2) the link between growth and poverty alleviation and the types of structural change that might contribute to both; and (3) the expected effects on growth and on the standard of living of the poor of not only a cut or a freeze of public expenditures with or without an increase in investment in traditional

---

[1] See e.g. Tabatabai (1993) and Noble (1993).

agriculture and transport sectors, but also improved targeting of current implicit subsidies for government services.

The study goes beyond previous poverty related studies on Zaire by adopting a social accounting matrix (SAM) framework to capture the main features and the initial conditions of the Zairian socioeconomic system in the base year (1987), and to diagnose the underlying structural causes of poverty. This SAM is the first fully integrated one for Zaire. It links together the different SAM modules estimated by Maton (1992a), and incorporates additional features. Because the SAM framework is comprehensive and also imposes consistency by reconciling data from different sources, the well-known problems of data availability and reliability in Zaire are somewhat lessened but certainly not resolved.

The chapter is organized in the following manner. Section 10.2 provides an overview of the different IMF and World Bank adjustment programs in Zaire and the structural impediments to growth. Section 10.3 describes the Zaire SAM and identifies the status and behavior of poor households within the SAM. In Section 10.4, the SAM framework is used to primarily analyze the policy issues, mentioned previously, through a multiplier-cum-structural path analysis and multiplier-based policy experiments. In addition to the conventional unconstrained fixed-price multipliers, constrained multipliers, assuming inelastic supply in traditional agriculture, are derived to capture the direct and indirect effects of the structural bottlenecks.

The latter impose severe constraints on output growth not only in traditional agriculture but also in other sectors. The comparison of both types of multiplier provides rough estimates of the extent to which these obstacles affect household incomes and output growth. The policy experiments attempt to simulate the impact of some policy measures that were included in the 1986–1987 SSAP. Finally, Section 10.5 draws the main conclusions and policy implications of the study.

10.2. Overview of Adjustment Experiences, Macroeconomic Performance, and Structural Impediments to Growth in Zaire Post-Civil War Period

The post-civil war economic history of Zaire can be divided into three main periods: (1) the 1967 stabilization program and the growth and expansionary policies, 1967–1974; (2) the crisis and multiple stabilization policies, 1975–1982; and (3) the major stabilization and structural reforms, 1983–1990, subdivided into the IMF major stabilization program, 1983–1986, and the IMF and World Bank structural reforms of the economy, 1987–1990. The 1983–1990 period is considered as the main reform phase because of the broad scope and the longer term perspective of the measures employed (World Bank 1989). The 1983 program aimed at restoring macroeconomic stability and improving efficiency, while that of 1986–1987 aimed at promoting growth through improvements in macroeconomic management, removing structural barriers through reforms of the agricultural, manufacturing, transport, and public sectors, providing incentives to the private sector, and restoring external balance through the non-traditional tradable sector.

These programs have been reviewed and discussed in great detail by Tshishimbi and Glick (1990), Tshishimbi, Glick, and Thorbecke (1991), and to some extent the World Bank (1989). In sum, after a growth period from 1968 to 1974 marked by expansionary policies subsequent to favorable terms of trade, the overall macroeconomic performance of Zaire has been very disappointing despite the several aborted attempts at SSAPs, particularly since the mid-1970s after the sharp drop in copper prices.

Besides external shocks, two main internal factors have not only limited the effectiveness of the various programs but also led to the continued need for reforms in Zaire. First, the financial drain of parastatals and expansionary fiscal and monetary policies was aggravated by government noncompliance with the targets of the programs on the spending side. Government expenditure targets were often exceeded, particularly in the category of goods and services; conversely, spending in crucial sectors such as health, education, and transport were less than targeted. Overall, the budget deficit reached unsustainable levels by the end of the 1980s. The financing of the deficits through money creation has in turn been a primary source of chronic and escalating inflation.[2] By 1990, the IMF and the World Bank had suspended their assistance to Zaire owing to non-compliance.

Second, a number of structural impediments affecting primarily traditional agriculture have limited the effects of some reform policies in agriculture, such as price and marketing liberalization, in addition to constraining overall economic growth. The main obstacles are marketing; transport-related problems caused by the high fuel cost, lack of spare parts and agricultural support services to provide fertilizer and high quality seeds to farmers; and, chiefly, a very inadequate road system.[3] As a result, the output response, wherever positive, was both very marginal and largely attributable to an increase in cultivated area since Zaire is not constrained by land availability (Tshishimbi and Glick 1990).

Another consequence of these problems in the agricultural sector has been a drastic rise in food imports that supply urban markets, mainly

[2] In January 1993, President Mobutu attempted to introduce 5 million zaire bank notes (about US$2) as a way to counteract a more than 7000 percent annual inflation rate (Makau 1993), which was about 85 percent from 1986 to 1988.

[3] Transport costs take up about 90 percent of the wholesale margin, which is more than 40 percent of the retail value of a number of food items produced in Bandundu and sold in Kinshasa (see Jabara 1990).

Kinshasa. This strategy initially kept urban food prices from rising significantly, but hurt farmers where the poor are concentrated. Yet there is evidence that Zairian farmers do respond to price incentives in an environment favorable to trade (World Bank 1989).

10.3. *A Social Accounting Matrix (SAM) for Zaire*

The SAM for Zaire,[4] based on the path-breaking preliminary SAM by Maton (1992a), has a base year of 1987. This represents not only the year when the first set of consistent macroeconomic data (including the informal sector) was made available through a joint Zairian Institut National de Statistique (INS)/World Bank effort, but also the most recent year of relatively stable economic and financial indicators (given Zaire current economic chaos). In addition, the impact of some of the 1986/87 adjustment measures can be examined using a SAM for this period. The SAM transaction table can be found in Koné and Thorbecke (1994). It is a 35 × 35 consisting of 8 factors of production, 9 socioeconomic groups, 14 production activities, government, public, and private companies, combined capital, and the rest of the world accounts.

10.3.1. *Production activities*

There are 2 agricultural and 12 non-agricultural activities, shown in rows and columns 19–32 of the SAM. Agriculture includes farming, livestock, fishing, and forestry. It is divided into traditional and modern types.[5] Traditional agriculture is mainly of a subsistence type, from which an estimated 5 million smallholder households (representing a total population of 26 million) derive their livelihood. It is characterized by rudimentary techniques of production. The main factors of production are family labor, self-produced seeds and cuttings, and land, which is generally in abundant supply in Zaire. The use of unskilled salaried labor, improved seeds, and fertilizer is very limited.

In contrast, modern agriculture employs only about 120,000 farmers organized in modern skill categories (managerial, technical, skilled, and unskilled), and uses modern and diversified factors such as buildings, machinery, fertilizer, pesticides, and high quality seeds and plants. The sector largely consists of enterprises exploiting plantations and agro-industries of palm-oil, coffee, tea, tobacco, and timber.

Among non-agricultural activities, the sector "Imputed Rent" is a dummy

---

4 See Koné and Thorbecke (1994) for more details about this SAM.
5 See Ben-Senia (1992) for a detailed description of both types of agriculture in Bandundu, which is a major producing region.

activity used to impute the production of banking services. Mining is the primary source of foreign exchange, government revenues, and modern sector employment. It is dominated by the parastatal Générale des Carrières et des Mines (Gécamines), the second largest modern sector employer (about 40,000 employees) next to the government and provider of a large share of tax revenues (about 25 percent in 1984–1989). The main mining products are copper, diamond, cobalt, crude oil, and gold.

The other non-agricultural activities consist of three manufacturing activities (food industries, textiles, and other manufacturing) producing almost entirely for the domestic market, utilities, construction, transport and communications, commerce, banking and insurance, private services, and government services. Private services include activities such as real estate, hotels and restaurants, and repairs. Government services are expenditures of the central and local administration on personnel, goods and services, and investment to provide those services, a marginal part of which consists of domestic services to households. Unfortunately, no data were available to distinguish government services by type such as health and education.

Table 10.1 shows the total output and value added of production activities in 1987 million zaires, estimated at 1,134,097 million and 852,035 million zaires, respectively. Total agricultural output amounted to 285,399 million zaires, and traditional agriculture alone accounted for 269,141 million zaires (94 percent of the total). In fact, traditional agriculture had the greatest share of total output (23.31 percent), followed by commerce (21.21 percent) and mining (11.88 percent). The same ranking holds for value added: traditional agriculture (28.67 percent), commerce (23.25 percent), and mining (12.41 percent). Utilities had the lowest share of output and value added (1.09 and 1.03 percent), preceded by banking and insurance (1.14 and 1.15 percent). The very high sectoral ratios of value added to total output (ranging from about 47 percent for food and beverages to about 92 percent for agriculture) suggest very low shares of intermediate inputs.

Table 10.1 also shows the relative importance of informal activities in terms of value added. Overall, they account for more than 62 percent of total value added. Owing to declining formal real incomes, informal activities have rapidly grown in recent years.[6] They predominate in traditional agriculture (100 percent), commerce (73.91 percent), private services (71.24 percent), and construction (61.84 percent). They are non-negligible in food industries, textiles, and other manufacturing, and to a lesser extent in transport and in mining. On the other hand, modern agriculture, utilities, banking and insurance, and government services are dominated by parastatals.

---

[6] World Bank (1989). A large number of illegal and unreported trade activities such as smuggling, bribery, and illegal taxation are not included in this SAM; see e.g. MacGaffey (1988).

Table 10.1. Zaire: total output and formal/informal value added of production activities, 1987 (m zaires)[a]

Production Activities	(1) Total output	(2) % total ouput	(3) Total value added	(4) % total added	(5) Value added/ total output	(6) Formal value added	(7) Informal value added	(8) % sector formal	(9) % sector informal	(10) % total formal	(11) % total informal
Traditional agriculture	264,351	23.31	244,237	28.67	92.39	0	244,237	0.00	100.00	0.00	45.87
Modern agriculture	14,210	1.25	11,342	1.33	79.82	11,342	0	100.00	0.00	3.55	0.00
Mining	134,681	11.88	105,759	12.41	78.53	79,690	26,069	75.35	24.65	24.94	4.90
Food, beverages, tobacco	78,162	6.89	36,990	4.34	47.32	23,203	13,787	62.73	37.27	7.26	2.59
Textiles	27,337	2.41	16,275	1.91	59.53	10,260	6,015	63.04	36.96	3.21	1.13
Other manufacturing	56,715	5.00	27,568	3.24	48.61	18,889	8,679	68.52	31.48	5.91	1.63
Utilities	12,402	1.09	8,815	1.03	71.08	8,815	0	100.00	0.00	2.76	0.00
Construction	71,890	6.34	42,059	4.94	58.50	16,051	26,008	38.16	61.84	5.02	4.88
Commerce	240,595	21.21	198,109	23.25	82.34	51,681	146,428	26.09	73.91	16.17	27.50
Transportation and communications	62,751	5.53	31,833	3.74	50.73	23,965	7,868	75.28	24.72	7.50	1.48
Private services	78,408	6.91	66,484	7.80	84.79	19,119	47,365	28.76	71.24	5.98	8.90
Banking and insurance	12,973	1.14	9,785	1.15	75.43	9,785	0	100.00	0.00	3.06	0.00
Government services	79,622	7.02	52,779	6.19	66.29	46,779	6,000	88.63	11.37	14.64	1.13
Total	1,134,097	100	852,035	100	75.13	319,579	532,456	37.51	62.49	100	100

[a] Column (5) = column (3) / column (1); (8) = (5) / (3); (9) = (7) / (3)

Source: Computed from the Zaire SAM.

10.3.2. *The factors of production*

Labor and capital are the two major categories of factors. Labor is further divided into two informal types (unpaid and paid labor) and four formal types (unskilled, low-, medium-, and high-skilled labor).[7] Capital, derived as a residual, was simply divided into formal and informal. The latter refers to the remuneration of capital in traditional agriculture and urban informal activities, while the former is that of the modern sector. In total, there are eight specific factors of production.

Unpaid labor consists of the imputed value of labor of the household head (or the independent) and that of active family members who work in family-owned farms or in urban informal businesses. In the latter, there are also apprentices who may not be family members. Many relatively well-educated workers have turned to urban informal activities where returns are generally higher than in the formal sector (World Bank 1989).

Table 10.2 shows the value added accruing to the various factors of production and their relative importance in each activity. Overall, labor accounts for 68 percent of total value added (50 percent informal labor, and 18 percent formal labor), and capital, 32 percent (20 percent formal capital, and 12 percent informal capital). Unpaid labor has the largest share in value added (40 percent) followed by formal capital (20 percent), informal capital (12 percent), paid labor (11 percent), and the remainder 17 percent by formal labor types. Unpaid labor predominates particularly in traditional agriculture (82 percent) and commerce (42 percent).

10.3.3. *External trade*

Receipts of the rest of the world (RoW) consist of imports of final goods, intermediate goods, capital goods, and payments of the government to the RoW. Expenditures are comprised of exports of production activities, where mining accounts for the largest share (76 percent); export taxes and other foreign payments to the government of Zaire, and net capital operations obtained as a residual.

10.3.4. *Government revenues and expenditures*

Government revenues consist of income taxes on formal sector households and urban independents, taxes on goods and services, duties on imported final goods and services, profit taxes and transfers from domestic companies, duties on imported intermediate goods, taxes on capital goods, and export taxes and income from abroad. Expenditures consist of imputed subsidies to households of 2071 million zaires, government services of 83,384 million zaires, and payments abroad of 22,441 million zaires. Expenditures on

---

[7] The average number of years of formal education in these skill categories in Kinshasa was, respectively, 4.09, 6.32, 7.09, and 14.26 (Lewis 1991).

Table 10.2. Zaire: value added of production activities according to factors of production, 1987 (m zaire)

	Unpaid labor	Paid labor	Unskilled labor	Low skill labor	Medium skill labor	High skill labor	Informal capital	Formal capital	Total value added	Informal labor	Formal labor	Total labor	Total capital
Traditional agriculture	201,495	6,106	0	0	0	0	36,636	0	244,237	207,601	0	207,601	36,636
Modern agriculture	0	0	4,036	1,369	555	557	0	4,825	11,342	0	6,517	6,517	4,825
Mining	17,957	1,690	12,796	4,443	4,484	4,749	6,422	53,218	105,759	19,647	26,472	46,119	59,640
Food, beverages, and tobacco	7,076	4,741	4,228	1,676	2,692	1,528	1,970	13,079	36,990	11,817	10,124	21,941	15,049
Textiles	3,502	1,437	1,301	516	828	471	1,076	7,144	16,275	4,939	3,116	8,055	8,220
Other manufacturing	4,823	2,148	2,477	982	1,579	895	1,708	12,956	27,568	6,971	5,933	12,904	14,664
Utilities	0	0	171	380	987	622	0	6,655	815	0	2,160	2,160	6,655
Construction	8,174	15,071	3,989	2,594	3,179	2,079	2,763	4,210	42,059	23,245	11,841	35,086	6,973
Commerce	82,780	50,286	3,500	2,501	9,119	7,472	13,362	29,089	198,109	133,066	22,592	155,658	42,451
Transportation and communications	599	2,052	1,493	1,006	2,850	1,148	5,217	17,468	31,833	2,651	6,497	9,148	22,685
Private services	4,486	9,678	2,720	497	737	394	33,201	14,771	66,484	14,164	4,348	18,512	47,972
Banking and insurance	0	0	959	685	2,495	2,046	0	3,600	9,785	0	6,185	6,185	3,600
Government services	5,817	0	0	10,470	20,532	9,736	183	6,041	52,779	5,817	40,738	46,555	6,224
Total	336,709	93,209	37,670	27,119	50,037	31,697	102,538	173,056	852,035	429,918	146,523	576,441	275,594

Source: Computed from the Zaire SAM.

personnel, goods and services, and investment operate mainly through the activity "government services."

10.3.5. Companies: income, expenditures, and savings

Companies represent all formal private and public enterprises. Their sole income source is formal capital, which consists of the total operating surplus or gross profits of 173,056 million zaires. This income is expended on transfers to households (54,580 million zaires), imputed rent (6189 million zaires), and direct taxes and transfers to the government (23,627 million zaires). The remainder 88,655 million zaires, going to the combined capital account, represents the undistributed profits after taxes (or savings), which together with savings of households of 13,335 million zaires and from abroad of 17,550 million zaires (obtained as a residual), constitute total savings and total investment in Zaire of 119,540 million zaires in 1987.

10.3.6. Households: incomes, expenditures, and savings

Nine groups of households are defined according to the socioeconomic category of the head: two agricultural (traditional and modern farmers) and seven non-agricultural (informal urban salaried workers, urban independents, unskilled workers, skilled workers, foremen, cadres, and civil servants). They received incomes based primarily on their respective ownership of the various assets (types of labor skills and capital). Other incomes are received from private (or non-government) transfers, and imputed subsidies. The latter assumed a subsidy of about 20 percent of the actual cost of government services consumed by the various households. Private transfers are different payments of companies to non-agricultural households.[8]

Also shown in the SAM are household expenditures on, respectively, food and non-food items produced by production activities, expenditures on taxes and imported goods, and savings.[9]

10.3.7. The poor and the Zairian socioeconomic structure (or the SAM)

Of the various budget-based poverty studies on Zaire, only those by Tabatabai (1993) for Kinshasa and Bandundu, Ben-Senia (1992) for rural Bandundu, and to some extent the World Bank (1989) attempted explicitly to identify the poor by estimating poverty lines and to analyze poverty in relation to a number of household characteristics.[10] Using a SAM, this study goes beyond the latter studies by taking into account the relationship between poverty and the underlying Zairian socioeconomic structure.

---

[8] See Maton (1992a). These transfers somewhat compensate for the non-inclusion of undeclared earnings (or income from side activities), which are an important additional source of urban household income.

[9] Saving rates by household groups were assumed since no saving data were available; see Koné and Thorbecke (1994).

[10] These studies and a number of others such as Houyoux (1973, 1986, 1987) are briefly reviewed in Koné and Thorbecke (1994).

Table 10.3. Zaire: household incomes by source, and household characteristics, 1987

Income source	Traditional farmers	Modern farmers	Unskilled workers	Civil servants
Socioeconomic groups[a]				
(m zaires)				
Unpaid labor	201,495	0	0	0
Paid labor	6,106	0	0	0
Unskilled labor	0	4,036	33,634	0
Low-skill labor	0	1,369	0	10,470
Medium-skill labor	0	555	0	20,532
High-skill labor	0	557	0	9,736
Informal capital	36,636	0	0	0
Private transfers	0	0	0	818
Imputed subsidies	339	13	174	178
Total	244,576	6,530	33,808	41,734
(percentages)				
Unpaid labor	82.39	0.00	0.00	0.00
Paid labor	2.50	0.00	0.00	0.00
Unskilled labor	0.00	61.81	99.49	0.00
Low-skill labor	0.00	20.96	0.00	25.09
Medium-skill labor	0.00	8.50	0.00	49.20
High-skill labor	0.00	8.53	0.00	23.33
Informal capital	14.98	0.00	0.00	0.00
Private transfers	0.00	0.00	0.00	1.96
Imputed subsidies	0.14	0.20	0.51	0.43
Total	100.00	100.00	100.00	100.00
Household size[b] (no. of persons)	5.26	3.9	4.8	4.4
No. of households[c]	5,106,521	119,419	366,520	299,200
% of total	66.01	1.54	4.74	3.87
Total population	26,860,300	465,734	1,759,296	1,316,480
% of total	70.06	1.21	4.59	3.43
Per household income (zaires)	47,895	54,681	92,241	139,485
Per capita income (zaires)	9,105	14,021	19,217	31,701

[a] The socioeconomic household groups are ranked by increasing order of average household incomes.
[b] Guestimated by the authors based on estimates of household sizes in Kinshasa and Bandundu; see Lewis (1991).
[c] Based on estimates by Shapiro (1992).
Source: Computed from the Zaire SAM unless otherwise indicated.

Informal urban workers	Skilled workers	Independent urban	Foremen	Cadres	Total
0	0	135,214	0	0	336,709
87,103	0	0	0	0	93,209
0	0	0	0	0	37,670
0	15,280	0	0	0	27,119
0	14,076	0	14,874	0	50,037
0	0	0	0	21,404	31,697
0	0	65,902	0	0	102,538
8,629	600	39,306	750	4,482	54,585
400	114	753	63	37	2,071
96,132	30,070	241,175	15,687	25,923	735,635
0.00	0.00	56.06	0.00	0.00	45.77
90.61	0.00	0.00	0.00	0.00	12.67
0.00	0.00	0.00	0.00	0.00	5.12
0.00	50.81	0.00	0.00	0.00	3.69
0.00	46.81	0.00	94.82	0.00	6.80
0.00	0.00	0.00	0.00	82.57	4.31
0.00	0.00	27.33	0.00	0.00	13.94
8.98	2.00	16.30	4.78	17.29	7.42
0.42	0.38	0.31	0.40	0.14	0.28
100.00	100.00	100.00	100.00	100.00	100.00
4.5	4.6	4.1	4.9	5.8	4.96
541,661	168,887	1,066,838	44,864	21,914	7,735,824
7.00	2.18	13.79	0.58	0.28	100.00
2,437,475	776,880	4,374,036	219,834	127,101	38,337,136
6.36	2.03	11.41	0.57	0.33	100.00
177,476	178,048	226,065	349,657	1,182,942	95,095
39,439	38,706	55,138	71,359	203,956	19,189

The first and crucial step is to identify the poor within the SAM. In Table 10.3 households are ranked by increasing order of their average income. The best-off are those headed by cadres, while the worst-off are headed by traditional farmers, followed by modern farmers and unskilled workers. The latter three had incomes below the 1987 national average household income of 95,095 zaires (about US$723).

Three categories of vulnerable household are considered: traditional and modern farmers; the urban poor, consisting of the unskilled and the urban informal salaried workers; and civil servants and, some skilled workers[11] who are losers from adjustments. To distinguish this latter group, they will be referred to as the "new poor" in the remainder of the paper. However, the groups of modern farmers and civil servants are not homogeneous because of large within-group differences in skill levels, and thus in incomes.

Since food constitutes a central share of household expenditures in Zaire (44 percent), it should be noted that, except for traditional farmers, all household groups are net buyers of food items supplied mainly through imports because of transport and marketing problems already discussed.

10.4. *SAM-Based Multiplier Analysis*

We derive unconstrained and constrained (or mixed) fixed-price multipliers. The former, which have conventionally dominated the literature, assume excess capacity throughout the economy; i.e., supply is perfectly elastic in all sectors, and an exogenous increase in demand is sufficient to stimulate output and income growth with prices remaining constant. It has been argued that this assumption is very unrealistic in the short run regarding the agricultural sector in most developing countries, where supply response can be very low for a number of structural reasons such as land, labor, or technology constraints (Thorbecke 1993). To circumvent this shortcoming and allow for limited or no supply response in agriculture, SAM-based constrained or mixed multipliers have recently been derived by Subramanian and Sadoulet (1990) using an Indian village SAM, by Lewis and Thorbecke (1992) using a small region SAM in Kenya, and by Parikh and Thorbecke (1993) using two Indian village SAMs. While the former two studies assumed completely inelastic supply in agriculture, Parikh and Thorbecke allowed for a limited degree of supply response. They argued that the "true" multipliers lie somewhere in between the unconstrained fixed-price and mixed multipliers.[12] Therefore, the former multiplier holds up to an exogenously specified full capacity level. The mixed multiplier is

---

11 The World Bank (1989) and Tabatabai (1993) considered only two types of poor: the "long-term" poor who remain poor because of lack of participation in the growth process, and the "new" or "short-term" poor who bear the short-term burden of adjustment.

12 This point was also made by Lewis and Thorbecke (1992).

then used for the remaining demand such that the final multiplier is the sum of the two types of multiplier.

In this study, mixed multipliers assuming complete inelastic supply in traditional agriculture are derived for Zaire in order to account for the full effect of the major structural impediments. The unconstrained multipliers are also derived. The comparison of both multipliers can provide rough estimates of the extent to which these supply-side obstacles impede output and income growth.

10.4.1. *The unconstrained fixed-price multipliers framework*

Two preliminary assumptions are necessary to transform a SAM transaction table to a multiplier model. First, as conventionally assumed, the government, the rest of the world, and the capital accounts are exogenous, while all other accounts (i.e. factors of production, production activities, household groups, and companies) are endogenously determined. Second, the different behavioral and technical relations in the SAM are approximated by fixed linear transformations, which will warrant excess capacity throughout the economy allowing prices to remain constant.

The SAM transaction table (T) is then converted into a matrix of average expenditure propensities (A) by dividing each element in the SAM accounts by its corresponding column total (y_n). The matrix A consists of two sub-matrices, A_n and A_l, respectively, the average expenditure propensities for the endogenous accounts and the average leakages (l_s) from the system (aggregate savings, imports, and taxes).

From the definition of A_n, each endogenous total income (y_n) in the transaction matrix can be expressed as follows (Pyatt and Round 1979):

$$y = A_n y_n + x \qquad (1)$$

where x is the sum of exogenous accounts. Equation (1) is rewritten as

$$Y_n = (I - A_n)^{-1} x \qquad (2a)$$

$$Y_n = M_a x. \qquad (2b)$$

In a similar fashion, the leakages can be expressed as follows:

$$I = A_l Y_n \qquad (3)$$

$$Y_n = A_l M_a x. \qquad (4)$$

Equation (2b) shows that a given exogenous change in x will operate through the multiplier matrix M_a (called accounting multipliers) to determine the effect on endogenous incomes y_n. Since M_a depends on A_n, it assumes unitary expenditure elasticities. While this assumption may be acceptable for all other elements of A_n, it is certainly unrealistic for A_{32}. Clearly, households do respond differently at the margins.

Therefore, one can specify a matrix of marginal expenditure propensities (C_n) based on the observed different household expenditure elasticities (ε_{hi}). Formally,

$$\varepsilon_{hi} = MEP_{hi} \,/\, AEP_{hi} \tag{5a}$$

$$MEP_{hi} = \varepsilon_{hi} \bullet AEP_{hi} \tag{5b}$$

$$\sum MEP_{hi} = 1 \tag{5c}$$

where MEP_{hi} and AEP_{hi} are, respectively, the marginal and average expenditure propensities of household group h for activity i. Equation (5b) was used to derive the C_n matrix for Zaire (Koné and Thorbecke 1994). In this case, C_n formally differs from A_n in the following way: $C_{13}=A_{13}$, $C_{33}=A_{33}$, $C_{21}=A_{21}$, $C_{22}=A_{22}$, but $C_{32}\neq A_{32}$.

Given that C_n is non-singular, M_c, the fixed-price multiplier matrix, can be derived by rewriting (2a) and (2b) in the following way:[13]

$$dy_n = (I - C_n)^{-1}dx \tag{6a}$$

$$dy_n = M_c dx \tag{6b}$$

10.4.2. *Constrained or mixed multipliers framework*

Two sets of sectors are distinguished: supply-constrained (or exogenous) sectors in which supply is inelastic, and non-supply-constrained (or endogenous) sectors in which excess capacity is assumed. Then, mixed multipliers are derived as in (7a) below (Lewis and Thorbecke 1992). The vectors y and x and the matrix C are defined as previously, except the subscripts nc and c refer to non-supply and supply-constrained sectors respectively; R is a matrix of marginal expenditure propensities of factors, institutions, and activities of the nc sectors on output of the c sectors, while Q is those of the c sectors on the nc sector output; and I and 0 are the identity and null matrices, respectively.

$$d\begin{bmatrix} y_{nc} \\ x_c \end{bmatrix} = \begin{bmatrix} (I-C_{nc}) & 0 \\ -R & -I \end{bmatrix}^{-1} \begin{bmatrix} I & Q \\ 0 & -(I-C_c) \end{bmatrix} d\begin{bmatrix} x_{nc} \\ y_c \end{bmatrix} \tag{7a}$$

The multiplication of the first two terms on the right-hand side of (7a) yields the constrained or mixed multiplier matrix, M_m:

$$d\begin{bmatrix} y_{nc} \\ x_c \end{bmatrix} = M_m d\begin{bmatrix} x_{nc} \\ y_c \end{bmatrix} \tag{7b}$$

---

13 Similarly, the leakages are expressed as: $d_l = C_l M_c dx$.

Total incomes and output of the nc sectors (dy_{nc}) can be stimulated either by an exogenous increase in demand for their output (dx_{nc}) or by an increase in exogenous output (supply-driven) of the c sectors (dy_c). In the former case, for example, an increase in government expenditures will stimulate output and incomes in those sectors (dy_{nc}) through the multiplier effects, which will in turn lead to a change in final demand for the c sectors (dx_c), e.g., an adjustment in net exports. On the other hand, an increase in demand for the c sectors will stimulate output and incomes through increases in output of the nc sectors and an increase in imports of goods produced by the c sectors, i.e. a decrease in net exports. This will be reflected in the matrix M_m by negative multiplier values along the row of the constrained (or c) sector (say, traditional agriculture).

10.4.3. *Effects of structural obstacles and growth on poverty alleviation*

The derived unconstrained and constrained multipliers[14] are used to analyze the effects of the major structural obstacles to the supply of traditional agricultural products on household incomes and output growth, and the relationship between economic growth and poverty alleviation.[15]

Value added and output multipliers help determine the activities and the household expenditure patterns that best promote economic growth. Tables 10.4 and 10.5 show, respectively, the value added and output unconstrained and mixed multipliers (columns (1) and (2)), where activities are ranked by decreasing size of their unconstrained multipliers. In column (3) the ratios of the mixed to the fixed-price multipliers reveal the extent to which the multipliers decline as a result of inelastic supply in traditional agriculture. Finally, column (4) shows the ranking of activities by decreasing size of their mixed multipliers.[16] The reduction in the size of the output multipliers is larger than that of value added owing to the nature of intersectoral linkages in the economy. Overall, the mixed multipliers represent 58 percent of their unconstrained fixed-price levels for total value added, and 54 percent for total output.

The activities that best promote value added growth, respectively, are

---

[14] The multipliers' matrices M_c and M_m as well as their detailed description are provided in Koné and Thorbecke (1994).

[15] The mixed multipliers assume inelastic supply in traditional agriculture to capture implicitly the disincentives to output growth largely attributed to the ill-functioning transport and marketing system. Modern agriculture is not supply-constrained, given its better endowment and smaller size. Furthermore, supply in the manufacturing sector could have also been considered as constrained owing to a lack of foreign exchange to import raw materials. However, this problem is ignored here since, in principle, it was to be resolved through the 1987 industrial structural adjustment credit (ISAC). The transport sector could have also been supply-constrained. However, being a non-tradable, its negative multiplier values cannot represent an increase in imports, though they may reflect the associated cost to the economy of having no or limited capacity in transport, most of which is captured by the inelastic supply in traditional agriculture.

[16] See Lewis and Thorbecke (1992).

Table 10.4. Zaire: value added fixed-price and mixed multipliers for production activities, 1987

Production Activities	(1) Fixed-price multipliers (FPM)	(2) Mixed multipliers (MM)	(3) MM/FPM	(4) Mixed multipliers ranking
Traditional agriculture	2.893	1.605	0.555	1
Commerce	2.434	1.441	0.592	2
Private services	2.314	1.414	0.611	3
Construction	2.134	1.255	0.588	4
Textiles	2.039	0.951	0.466	11
Modern agriculture	1.974	1.213	0.614	5
Government services	1.958	1.196	0.611	6
Agro-food industries	1.942	0.798	0.411	13
Banking and insurance	1.917	1.194	0.623	7
Transport and communications	1.708	1.086	0.636	10
Mining	1.704	1.096	0.643	8
Other manufacturing	1.612	0.933	0.579	12
Utilities	1.577	1.096	0.695	8
Mean multipliers	2.02	1.18	0.58	

Source: Extracted from the multiplier matrices, M_c and M_m.

traditional agriculture, commerce, private services, and construction under both the unconstrained and constrained cases. The informal sector is predominant in these activities. They also best stimulate output growth, but only under excess capacity in all sectors, and the ranking is slightly different. With inelastic supply in traditional agriculture, construction best stimulates output growth, followed by transport and communications, government services, and commerce. These sectors are not as heavily dependent (directly or indirectly) on traditional agriculture, unlike sectors such as food industries and textiles.

Activities with formal sector predominance such as utilities, other manufacturing, mining, transport and communications, and banking and insurance tend to have little effect on value added and output growth under excess capacity in all sectors. Mining, despite its importance as the main source of foreign exchange and government revenue, is typically an enclave with limited intersectoral linkages. Therefore, Zaire's continued reliance on mining exports will only lead to limited growth and increased poverty since it excludes the majority of the population, mostly engaged in traditional agriculture and urban informal activities.

In order to clarify the structural and behavioral mechanisms underlying

Table 10.5. Zaire: output fixed-price and mixed multipliers for production activities, 1987

Production Activities	(1)	(2)	(3)	(4)
	Fixed-price multipliers (FPM)	Mixed multipliers (MM)	MM/FPM	Mixed multipliers ranking
Traditional agriculture	3.934	1.737	0.44	7
Construction	3.510	2.012	0.57	1
Commerce	3.509	1.815	0.52	4
Private services	3.306	1.771	0.54	5
Agro-food industries	3.288	1.336	0.41	13
Textiles	3.241	1.385	0.43	12
Government services	3.155	1.855	0.59	3
Transport and communications	2.965	1.904	0.64	2
Modern agriculture	2.932	1.635	0.56	10
Banking and insurance	2.923	1.690	0.58	9
Other manufacturing	2.917	1.759	0.60	6
Mining	2.658	1.620	0.61	11
Utilities	2.512	1.691	0.67	8
Mean multipliers	3.142	1.708	0.54	

Source: Extracted from the multiplier matrices, M_c and M_m.

the global effects (direct and indirect) provided by the multipliers, structural path analysis (SPA) can be used to identify the whole network of paths along which a given influence is transmitted from one sector of origin (activities, factors, or households) to its ultimate destination.[17] For the purpose of illustration, the most important paths from an exogenous injection into traditional agriculture, commerce, private services, construction, and mining are shown in Table 10.6.

10.4.4. *Household income multipliers*

Per capita rather than total household income multipliers are used to determine the activities that best promote the alleviation of poverty through increased incomes accruing to the poor (Tables 10.7a and b). An exogenous injection into, respectively, traditional agriculture, commerce, private services, and construction will have the greatest impact on overall household per capita income, in addition to their positive output effects discussed above, under both excess capacity and inelastic supply in traditional agriculture. On the other hand, utilities, other manufacturing, mining, and

[17] See Defourny and Thorbecke (1984). The complete and exhaustive set of SPA for any given pole of origin and any given pole of destination is available on request from the authors.

Table 10.6. Zaire: most important paths of the impact on household incomes of an exogenous injection into traditional agriculture, commerce, private services, contruction, or mining, 1987 (using unconstrained fixed-price multipliers M_c)

(1) Exogenous injection into production activities[a]	(2) Factor type income[a]	(3) Household type income	(4) Global influence on household income[b]	(5) Global influence on food consumption[c]	(6) % of global influence along path(s) shown
1. Traditional agriculture	0.765 → Unpaid labor	0.598 → Traditional farmers	1.183	0.655	85
		0.402 → Urban independents	1.03	0.216	70
2. Commerce	0.32 → Unpaid labor	0.598 → Traditional farmers	0.766	0.424	61
		0.402 → Urban independents	0.71	0.149	47
	0.195 → Paid labor	0.934 → Informal salaried workers	0.378	0.133	82
3. Private services	0.385 → Informal capital	0.643 → Urban independents	0.791	0.166	55
		0.357 → Traditional farmers	0.679	0.376	44
	0.112 → Paid labor	0.934 → Infromal salaried workers	0.294	0.103	52
4. Construction	0.185 → Paid labor	0.934 → Informal salaried workers	0.371	0.131	59
5. Mining	0.1 → Unpaid labor	0.598 → Traditional farmers	0.598	0.331	21
	0.104 → Unpaid labor	0.598 → Traditional farmers	0.423	0.234	31
	0.074 → Unskilled labor	0.893 → Unskilled workers	0.098	0.047	72

[a] The arrows indicate the direct influence (impact) of a given exogenous injection. The values are taken from the C-matrix, the matrix of marginal expenditure propensities (see Koné and Thorbecke 1994).

[b] The global influence measures the total (direct and indirect) effects induced by a given exogenous injection. The values are given by M_c, the matrix of unconstrained fixed-price multipliers.

[c] Column (5) equals column (4) multiplied by the marginal expenditure propensity on food of the corresponding household group (in Koné and Thorbecke 1994).

Table 10.7(a). Zaire: household per capita income multipliers for production activities, 1987 (× 10m): unconstrained fixed-price multipliers (FPM)

Production activities	Traditional farmer	Rank	Modern farmer	Rank	Unskilled worker	Rank	Civil servant	Rank	Informal paid worker	Rank
Traditional agriculture	0.441	1	0.214	12	0.315	11	0.45	13	0.917	4
Modern agriculture	0.154	11	0.83	14	1.471	1	0.77	4	0.649	12
Mining	0.157	10	0.342	5	0.558	2	0.516	9	0.628	13
Agro-food	0.227	5	0.287	6	0.447	6	0.515	10	0.873	5
Textiles	0.229	4	0.283	7	0.442	7	0.511	11	0.865	6
Other manufacturing	0.166	8	0.241	10	0.37	9	0.454	12	0.773	8
Utilities	0.107	14	0.205	13	0.222	14	0.688	5	0.558	14
Construction	0.223	6	0.357	4	0.528	5	0.683	6	1.521	2
Commerce	0.285	2	0.252	9	0.347	10	0.619	7	1.549	1
Transport	0.162	9	0.222	11	0.315	11	0.517	8	0.859	7
Private services	0.253	3	0.257	8	0.415	8	0.434	14	1.204	3
Banking	0.152	12	0.431	1	0.532	3	1.292	2	0.658	10
Government services	0.181	7	0.366	3	0.233	13	1.566	1	0.72	9
Imputed rent	0.152	12	0.431	1	0.532	3	1.292	2	0.658	10
Mean FPM	0.206		0.337		0.48		0.736		0.888	

Table 10.7(a). (*Cont.*)

Production activities	Skilled worker	Rank	Independent	Rank	Foreman	Rank	Cadre	Rank	Total	Rank
Traditional agriculture	0.519	13	2.356	1	1.056	13	3.255	14	0.696	1
Modern agriculture	1.121	14	1.064	10	1.293	8	4.778	5	0.42	8
Mining	0.617	8	1.077	9	1.082	11	4.164	8	0.353	12
Agro-food	0.617	8	1.331	5	1.194	9	3.56	11	0.439	7
Textiles	0.612	10	1.397	4	1.192	10	3.71	9	0.447	6
Other manufacturing	0.537	12	1.051	11	1.067	12	3.312	12	0.349	13
Utilities	0.776	6	0.896	14	1.684	4	5.302	4	0.292	14
Construction	0.841	5	1.296	6	1.493	5	4.419	7	0.493	4
Commerce	0.673	7	1.624	3	1.464	6	4.724	6	0.561	2
Transport	0.601	11	1.134	7	1.294	7	3.626	10	0.364	11
Private services	0.509	14	1.808	2	1.028	14	3.302	13	0.524	3
Banking	1.303	2	1.021	12	3.035	2	10	1	0.416	9
Government services	1.954	1	1.082	8	3.711	1	8.043	3	0.452	5
Imputed rent	1.303	2	1.021	12	3.035	2	10	1	0.416	9
Mean FPM	0.856		1.297		1.688		5.157		0.445	

Source: Computed from the unconstrained and constrained fixed-price multipliers matrices (M_c and M_m, respectively).

Table 10.7(b). Zaire: household per capita income multipliers for production activities, 1987 (× 10m): mixed multipliers (MM); traditional agriculture is supply-constrained

Production Activities	Traditional farmer	Rank	Modern farmer	Rank	Unskilled worker	Rank	Civil servant	Rank	Informal paid worker	Rank
Traditional agriculture	0.244	1	0.119	14	0.175	12	0.25	14	0.509	8
Modern agriculture	0.038	13	0.774	1	1.388	1	0.652	4	0.408	13
Mining	0.065	6	0.297	5	0.492	2	0.421	8	0.435	10
Agro-food	0.052	10	0.202	8	0.322	7	0.337	12	0.51	7
Textiles	0.063	8	0.203	7	0.323	6	0.342	11	0.52	6
Other manufacturing	0.063	8	0.19	10	0.296	9	0.349	10	0.558	5
Utilities	0.033	14	0.169	13	0.169	13	0.613	5	0.405	14
Construction	0.089	4	0.292	6	0.433	5	0.546	6	1.242	1
Commerce	0.134	2	0.178	11	0.239	11	0.465	7	1.234	2
Transport	0.068	5	0.176	12	0.248	10	0.42	9	0.661	4
Private services	0.116	3	0.19	9	0.317	8	0.294	13	0.919	3
Banking	0.042	11	0.377	2	0.453	2	1.179	1	0.429	11
Government services	0.064	7	0.31	4	0.15	14	1.447	3	0.478	9
Imputed rent	0.042	11	0.377	2	0.453	2	1.179	3	0.429	11
Mean MM	0.08		0.275		0.39		0.607		0.624	
Mean MM/Mean FPM	0.386		0.817		0.811		0.824		0.703	

Table 10.7(b). (*Cont.*)

Production activities	Skilled worker	Rank	Independent	Rank	Foreman	Rank	Cadre	Rank	Total	Rank
Traditional agriculture	0.288	14	1.307	1	0.586	14	1.806	14	0.386	1
Modern agriculture	0.984	4	0.445	11	1.015	8	3.923	5	0.238	8
Mining	0.508	7	0.581	5	0.86	9	3.479	7	0.207	10
Agro-food	0.412	12	0.399	14	0.776	12	2.273	13	0.164	14
Textiles	0.417	10	0.511	7	0.785	11	2.485	11	0.186	11
Other manufacturing	0.415	11	0.498	9	0.819	10	2.547	10	0.176	11
Utilities	0.689	5	0.504	8	1.508	4	4.761	4	0.282	13
Construction	0.683	6	0.581	5	1.173	5	3.431	8	0.282	4
Commerce	0.495	8	0.815	3	1.101	6	3.606	6	0.323	2
Transport	0.49	9	0.628	4	1.067	7	2.926	9	0.215	9
Private services	0.348	13	1.076	2	0.699	13	2.29	12	0.308	3
Banking	1.173	2	0.432	12	2.771	2	9.192	1	0.242	6
Government services	1.818	1	0.461	10	3.432	1	7.185	3	0.269	5
Imputed rent	1.173	2	0.432	12	2.771	2	9.192	1	0.242	6
Mean MM	0.707		0.619		1.384		4.221		0.244	
Mean MM/Mean FPM	0.826		0.478		0.82		0.818		0.55	

Source: Computed from the unconstrained and constrained fixed-price multipliers matrices (M_c and M_m, respectively).

transport will have the least impact under excess capacity, with food industries, utilities, textiles, and other manufacturing benefiting the most under supply constraints in traditional agriculture. Traditional farmers will benefit the most from an injection into traditional agriculture, commerce, private services, and textiles under both scenarios. However, modern farmers benefit from modern agriculture only under supply constraints in traditional agriculture, in which case they rely more on their own production. Otherwise, they benefit the most from banking, government services, construction, and mining.

Under both excess capacity and supply constraints, the unskilled benefit most from modern agriculture, mining, banking, and construction; the informal salaried workers are most positively affected by commerce, construction, and private services. Finally, the civil servants gain the most from government services, banking, modern agriculture, and utilities.

10.4.5. *Policy experiments*

Through policy experiments, this section analyzes the impact of a number of the adjustment policies on output, value added, and household incomes using 1987 as the base year. The methodology adopted here is similar to that in Keuning and Thorbecke (1992), which can formally be expressed as follows:

$$M_c X_i = Y_i \qquad (8a)$$
$$M_m X_i = Y_i \qquad (8b)$$

where, the subscript i refers to a given experiment; M_c and M_m are defined as previously; Y_i is a 32×3 matrix of endogenous incomes generated directly and indirectly by each of the three sources of exogenous injections (government expenditures, exports, and investment) represented by the 32×3 X_i matrix. The resulting total endogenous incomes y_i are obtained by summing along the rows of Y_i.[18] In essence, the methodology amounts to postulating different sets of X_i and determining their impact on the y_i through the multiplier process. The different y_i are then compared with the set of base year incomes y_0, in a comparative static sense. The dynamic process involved in the determination of the new y_i is not made explicit in this framework.

Experiment 1 considers a 20 percent decrease in mining exports while all other exogenous variables are fixed at their 1987 level in order to simulate the independent effect of the drop in actual export volume of *Gécamines* resulting from its rehabilitation plan. Experiment 2 compares an equivalent 20 percent decrease in total agricultural exports while other exogenous variables (including mining exports) remain fixed as in 1.

---

[18] Formally, $Y_i e = y_i$; where e is a 3×1 vector of units and y_i is a 32×3 vector of the total incomes of each of the 32 endogenous variables.

Experiment 3 simulates the impact of the agricultural and transport sector reforms to address major structural bottlenecks. Specifically, as stipulated in the three-year Public Investment Program (PIP) under the 1986/87 SSAP, the government current expenditures are cut by 12 percent (10,100 million zaires) and reallocated to investment both in traditional agriculture (9700 million zaires) and an emergency rural roads program (400 million zaires). Another 5635 million zaires is invested in transport infrastructures, of which 300 million zaires was anticipated from a rural road tax and 5335 million was assumed to be provided by the structural adjustment loan. Finally, exports and all other exogenous variables are kept at their 1987 level.

Experiment 4 postulates the same investment spending as in experiment 3, but financed entirely by a substantial cut in current expenditures. Thus, instead of current expenditures being cut by 12 percent, as in experiment 3, they are reduced by 18 percent, since no new foreign capital inflows are provided through the adjustment loan.

In experiment 5, the government eliminates subsidies for services to the rich in order to provide free services to the poor. Thus, user fees are eliminated for the poor, a move financed by savings from both the subsidy cut at the upper level (skilled workers, urban independents, foremen, and the cadres) and a streamlining of current expenditures. Total government spending and other exogenous variables remain at their 1987 level. Experiment 6 simply combines experiments 3 and 5 into one experiment.

10.4.6. *Results of the policy experiments*

The results are shown in Table 10.8. They are expressed as percentage changes relative to the base SAM. The comparison of experiments 1 and 2 suggests that a 20 percent decrease in mining exports leads to a greater decline in output, value added, and household incomes than a corresponding 20 percent decrease in agricultural exports in the short run. It is noteworthy, however, that the multiplier analysis in Section 10.4 showed that, of all the activities, traditional agricultural best promotes output and value added growth, and mining ranks among the activities that least promote output and value added growth. These results are, in fact, not contradictory. The most important reason is that mining accounts for the largest share of exports in absolute terms (with the value of exports estimated at 172,385 million zaires compared with 15,217 million zaires for agriculture). Therefore, a 20 percent decrease in mining exports is naturally not only much larger in absolute terms but also has more of an impact than the corresponding percentage decrease in agricultural exports. It should also be noted that, while almost 100 percent of mining products are exported, the domestic demand for agricultural products represents 94 percent of total production. Owing to chronic transport and marketing problems, about 40 percent of total production is consumed by the farmers themselves, while urban markets are increasingly supplied by imports. Clearly, there is great

Table 10.8. Zaire: results of policy experiments with supply constraints in traditional agriculture, 1987 (Base = 100)[a] (% change)

	Experiment 1: 20% decrease mining exports	Experiment 2: 20% decrease agricultural total exports	Experiment 3: Invest in trad. ag. and transport through SAL and 12% cut current expend.	Experiment 4: Invest in trad. ag. and transport through 18% cut current expend.	Experiment 5: 100% subsidies to poor households and zero to upper income groups	Experiment 6: Experiments 3 and 5 combined
Production						
Traditional agriculture[b]	2.69	-0.39	2.54	3.09	-0.31	2.23
Modern agriculture	-1.99	-5.22	0.81	0.43	0.28	1.08
Mining	-20.00	0.00	0.00	0.00	0.00	0.00
Food industries	-3.28	-0.53	1.26	0.59	0.33	1.59
Textiles	-4.93	-0.66	1.17	0.03	0.10	1.27
Other manufacturing	-4.13	-0.40	0.32	-0.67	-0.53	-0.21
Utilities	-8.07	-0.45	0.20	-0.96	-0.66	-0.46
Construction	-0.49	-0.04	0.27	0.17	-0.04	0.22
Commerce	-3.80	-0.46	0.96	0.08	-0.17	0.79
Transport and communications	-3.93	-0.48	7.03	5.91	-0.56	6.46
Private services	-3.90	-0.49	1.53	0.72	-0.23	1.30
Banking and insurance	-7.08	-0.48	0.77	-0.12	-0.23	0.40
Government services	-0.53	-0.07	-10.26	-16.15	-5.80	-16.06
Imputed Rent	-8.82	-0.45	0.87	0.08	-0.34	0.52
Sub-total	-4.27	-0.40	0.67	-0.13	-0.60	0.07
Payments to factors						
Unpaid labor	-2.26	-0.66	2.35	1.97	-0.15	2.20
Paid labor	-0.33	-0.04	0.10	0.03	-0.01	0.09
Unskilled labor	-8.87	-0.78	0.81	0.37	-0.04	0.78
Low-skill labor	-4.93	-0.44	-3.38	-5.96	-2.29	-5.67
Medium-skill labor	-3.94	-0.29	-3.44	-6.26	-2.48	-5.92
High-skill labor	-5.27	-0.33	-2.48	-4.72	-1.88	-4.36
Informal capital	-3.41	-0.57	2.32	1.83	-0.14	2.18
Formal capital	-8.82	-0.44	0.86	0.08	-0.35	0.52
Sub-total	-2.23	-0.27	0.57	0.17	-0.23	0.34

Table 10.8. (cont.)

	Experiment 1: 20% decrease mining exports	Experiment 2: 20% decrease agricultural total exports	Experiment 3: Invest in trad. ag. and transport through SAL and 12% cut current expend.	Experiment 4: Invest in trad. ag. and transport through 18% cut current expend.	Experiment 5: 100% subsidies to poor households and zero to upper income groups	Experiment 6: Experiments 3 and 5 combined
Incomes of companies	−8.82	−0.44	0.86	0.08	−0.35	0.52
Household incomes						
Traditional farmers	−2.46	−0.64	2.30	1.91	0.55	2.86
Modern farmers	−7.30	−0.63	−0.72	−1.95	0.12	−0.60
Unskilled workers	−8.83	−0.78	0.81	0.37	2.55	3.36
Civil servants	−4.58	−0.34	−3.11	−5.68	−0.09	−3.19
Informal paid workers	−3.80	−0.37	0.97	0.28	1.94	2.91
Skilled workers	−4.52	−0.37	−3.32	−5.96	−2.71	−6.02
Urban independents	−3.64	−0.60	2.09	1.62	−0.49	1.60
Foremen	−4.16	−0.30	−3.23	−5.94	−2.77	−5.99
Cadres	−5.88	−0.35	−1.90	−3.88	−1.76	−3.65
Sub-total	−3.72	−0.55	1.16	0.37	0.16	1.32

[a] Figures are calculated as $[(Xsim - X87 \text{ base}) / X87 \text{ base}] \times 100$; i.e. $[(\text{absolute change in } X \text{ vis à vis } 1987 \text{ base}) / XSAM - 1] \times 100$.

[b] Figure indicates change in net exports as a % of total supply. (Domestic production is considered fixed at its base level.)

Source: Authors' calculations.

potential for increased production in agriculture through exports and further increases in domestic demand once the major obstacles, both on the production and the distribution side, are removed. In combination, the experiments and multiplier analysis suggest that, although mining is much less effective in promoting economic growth and incomes than the agricultural sector, a decline in mining exports will have harsher consequences for the poor than a comparable percentage fall in agriculture. The main reasons are that, not only is supply constrained in traditional agriculture in the short run, but also agricultural exports play a minor role in the Zairian economy.

In the medium run, economic growth and poverty alleviation can be promoted by the type of short-run structural reforms approximated by experiments 3, 4, and 6, though their overall short-term output, value added, and household income gains will be limited. Of particular interest is that the foreign financing associated with experiment 3, which allows government to limit the reduction in current expenditures relative to experiment 4, confers little benefit on the poor, primarily benefiting skilled workers. The difference in overall value added between experiments 3 and 4 is also quite small.

Experiment 5 does not incorporate any structural adjustment measures with medium- to long-run benefits. It simply attempts to target subsidies in the form of government services to the poor. The outcome is inferior to the simulations that involve investments in traditional agriculture. Nevertheless, experiment 4 provides an interesting example of an outcome where the incomes of the poor increase, despite falling total production. Experiment 6 can be preferred, since it most improves the incomes accruing to vulnerable households—traditional farmers, the unskilled, and informal workers—while hurting particularly civil servants, skilled workers, and to a marginal extent modern farmers. However, it is also the most challenging set of policy changes to implement, especially from a political economy perspective.

10.5. Conclusions and Policy Implications

Based on a SAM framework, this chapter deals with the direct and indirect effects of macroeconomic policies and structural reforms on growth and poverty alleviation in Zaire. Three types of poor socioeconomic groups were identified: the farmers (traditional and modern); the urban poor (the unskilled and the urban informal salaried workers); and the "new poor" (the majority of civil servants who have recently seen a dramatic and steady decline in their formal real incomes, and the skilled workers to some extent). Constrained and unconstrained multipliers as well as multiplier-based policy experiments were used to analyze a number of issues.

First, the most important finding from the multiplier analysis is that economic growth and poverty alleviation are in fact interrelated. Medium-to long-term growth and incomes accruing to the poor will best be promoted by stimulating activities mainly in traditional agriculture, commerce, private services, and construction. The resulting increase in incomes accruing to the poor and the nature of their pattern of expenditures will in turn sustain growth. This finding makes a more convincing argument than that presented by the World Bank (1989), that sustained economic growth combined with policies to foster the participation of the poor will reduce poverty in the medium to long term.

Second, development of small enterprises to address urban unemployment and promote entrepreneurship, along with high labor intensity public work programs to ease the adjustment period for the urban poor and unemployed, were major policy objectives in Zaire (World Bank 1989). For these types of project, decision-makers should focus mostly on commerce, private services, and construction. Informal activities are currently predominant in these sectors. Investment in construction can particularly focus on rural and transport infrastructures.

Third, a government commitment to simultaneously restoring macroeconomic stability and removing most of the major structural impediments largely in traditional agriculture will strongly support the growth and poverty alleviation mechanisms discussed above. A substantial cut in current expenditures, mainly on goods and services, should be a major component of the fiscal side of a stabilization program. This is because any attempt at increasing tax revenues (other than those from mining exports) is unlikely to materialize or be successful in the short run, and simulating a substantial cut in current expenditures had favorable distributional outcomes, especially when accompanied by a shift toward investing in traditional agriculture.

While not modeled, the financial assistance through the SAL could be allocated in the short run to crucial social sectors such as education and health instead of investment in roads and rural infrastructure, emphasized in the analysis. But in any case, other measures involving institutional change will be required, such as improved systems of marketing and the distribution of fertilizer and quality seeds. Overall growth and poverty alleviation will be promoted in the medium run only to the extent that the major structural impediments to supply response in traditional agriculture are removed, or at least relaxed (a situation approximated by experiment 7). Activities such as agro-food industries and textiles will particularly benefit because of their stronger linkages with agriculture.

Fourth, the analysis showed that formal sector activities in general, and mining in particular, have weak linkages with the rest of the economy in terms of stimulating growth and household incomes, whereas the effects of increasing agricultural exports will be substantially greater. However, since output in traditional agriculture is constrained as long as the major supply obstacles prevail, rising mining exports can serve as a short-term cushion but not as a solution to growth and poverty alleviation.

Fifth, policy experiments that involve increasing free government services to the poor, through both an elimination of current levels of subsidies to the rich and a reallocation of expenditures, led to only marginal improvements in the standard of living of the poor because of the low historical levels of such subsidies in Zaire. However, greater availability of "free" government services to the poor is likely to raise significantly the effective demand for them and, accordingly, to require investment in expanding capacity which the government may not be able to sustain in the short run in addition to the needed investment in agriculture and transport. A lack of disaggregated data did not permit distinguishing these services by functional type such as health and education.

Finally, although the policies analyzed in this study are crucial structural ones, the effects of other macroeconomic policies, such as changes in the tax and tariff structures, or a devaluation, could not be directly simulated owing to the limitations of the static fixed-price multipliers framework. However, the short-term impact of a devaluation on output growth and farmers' incomes, through its impact on the supply of tradables, is likely to be very marginal because of supply constraints in traditional agriculture and weak linkages of mining. Besides upper-income groups, a devaluation may hurt some of the urban poor in the short run because of their relative higher expenditure intensity on traded goods, some of which could have been supplied domestically in the short run (e.g. food). The medium-run positive effects will depend largely on the speed at which the structural obstacles are removed, and the response of non-agricultural incomes to a more robust economy.

References

Ben-Senia, Mohamed. 1992. "Rural Bandundu: Agricultural Production, and Household Consumption and Poverty." Final Report Prepared for CFNPP. Ithaca, NY: CFNPP.

Defourny, Jacques, and Erik Thorbecke. 1984. "Structural Path Analysis and Multiplier Decomposition within a Social Accounting Matrix Framework." *Economic Journal*, 94: 111 136.

Houyoux, Joseph. 1973. *Budgets Ménagers, Nutrition et Mode de Vie à Kinshasa.* Kinshasa: Presses Universitaires du Zaire.

—— 1986. *Consommation des Produits Vivriers à Kinshasa et dans les Grandes Villes du Zaire, 1986.* Kinshasa: BEAU.

—— 1987. *Budgets des Menages, Kinshasa, 1986.* Kinshasa: Bureau d'Etudes d'Amenagement et d'Urbanisme (BEAU).

Institut National de la Statistique-Zaire (INS). 1990. "Synthèse de révision des comptes nationaux et résultats du Programme de Révision des Comptes Nationaux au Zaire." Kinshasa. Photocopy.

Jabara, Cathy L. 1990. "Zaire: Transport and Marketing Costs for Bandundu Subsector Model." Draft Report. Ithaca, NY: CFNPP.

Keuning, Steven, and Erik Thorbecke. 1992. "The Social Accounting Matrix and Adjustment Policies: The Impact of Budget Retrenchment on Income Distribution." In *Adjustment and Equity in Indonesia*, Erik Thorbecke et al., eds. Paris: OECD.

Koné, Solomane, and Erik Thorbecke. 1994. "Macroeconomic Policies and Poverty Alleviation in Zaire: A Social Accounting Matrix Approach." Unpublished photocopy.

Lewis, Blane D. 1991. "Household Expenditure Behavior in Kinshasa and Bandundu Town." Final Report. Ithaca, NY: CFNPP.

—— and Erik Thorbecke. 1992. "District-Level Economic Linkages in Kenya: Evidence Based on a Small Regional Social Accounting Matrix." *World Development*, 20: 881 897.

MacGaffey, Janet. 1988. *Entrepreneurs and Parasites: The Struggle for Indigenous Capitalism in Zaire.* Cambridge: Cambridge University Press.

Makau, wa Mutua. 1993. "Zaire: Permanent Anarchy?" *Africa Report*, 38(3): 52.

Maton, Jeff. 1992a. "Measuring the Sensitivity of the Income of the Poor to Changes in Sectoral Outputs and Changes in Income Distribution: Simulations by Means of a Simplified SAM for Zaire (1987)," Final Report; and "Methodological Procedures Applied in Constructing the SAM of Zaire." Ithaca, NY: CFNPP.

—— 1992b. "How Do The Poor in Kinshasa Survive: Miracle, Enigma or Black Box?" Ithaca, NY: CFNPP.

Noble, Kenneth B. 1993. "In Zaire, Starvation is Growing in a Wealthy Land." *New York Times*, May 16.

Parikh, Alka, and Erik Thorbecke. 1993. "Impact of Rural Industrialization on Village Life and Economy: A SAM Approach." Ithaca, NY: CFNPP.

Pyatt, Graham, and Jeffrey I. Round. 1979. "Accounting and Fixed Price Multipliers in a Social Accounting Matrix Framework." *Economic Journal,* 89: 850 873.

Shapiro, David. 1992. "Final Report on Employment and Labor Cost." Washington, DC: CFNPP, June 17; and "Final Report on Labor Markets in Kinshasa and Bandundu." Ithaca, NY: CFNPP.

Subramanian, Shankar, and Elizabeth Sadoulet. 1990. "The Transmission of Production Fluctuations and Technical Change in a Village Economy: A Social Accounting Matrix Approach." *Economic Development and Cultural Change,* 39: 131 173.

Tabatabai, Hamid. 1993. "Poverty and Food Consumption in Urban Zaire." Revised Report. Ithaca, NY: CFNPP.

Thorbecke, Erik. 1993. "Intersectoral Linkages and their Impact on Rural Poverty Alleviation: A Social Accounting Matrix Approach." Paper prepared for and under the auspices of UNIDO. May.

Tshishimbi, wa Bilenga, and P. Glick. 1990. "Stabilization and Structural Adjustment in Zaire Since 1983." Ithaca, NY: CFNPP. Photocopy.

——— and Erik Thorbecke. 1991. "Missed Opportunity for Adjustment in a Rent-Seeking Society: The Case of Zaire." Ithaca, NY: CFNPP. Photocopy.

World Bank. 1989. "Country Assessment and Policy Issues. Volume I: A Poverty Profile; Volume II: Annexes." Confidential Report No. 7812-ZR. Washington, DC: World Bank.

PART IV

Agriculture, Food Policy Reforms, and Welfare Outcomes

11

Perpetuating Poverty for Malawi's Smallholders: External Shocks and Policy Distortions

Yves Van Frausum and David E. Sahn

11.1. *Introduction*

Although Malawi was regarded as one of sub-Saharan Africa's best economic performers during the post-independence years, and was lauded for adopting an agriculture-based, export-promotion development strategy (Acharya and Johnston 1978), more recent literature has painted a rather bleak picture of the country's achievements, especially during the 1980s (Sahn, Arulpragasam, and Merid 1990). This pessimistic characterization is a consequence of a number of factors. First was the slow rate of growth during the 1980s, averaging –1.0 percent per capita per annum, in contrast to 2.9 percent in the period 1960–1979. Second was the increasing recognition that Malawi's agriculture-based, export-oriented strategy was achieved by the imposition of a strict duality in the agricultural sector whereby the estate enclave fared well, largely as a result of the exploitation of the peasant subsector (Kydd and Christiansen 1982). And third, and perhaps most important, was the emerging evidence of high levels of malnutrition and infant mortality, indicators of the extraordinary depth and breadth of poverty in Malawi (Centre for Social Research 1988; World Bank 1989).

Malawi's faltering struggle to grow at a rate in excess of population growth is partially attributable to the series of shocks that buffeted the economy during the late 1970s and 1980s. In particular, after increasing 0.7 percent per year between 1970 and 1977, the terms of trade declined at an average annual rate of 15.5 percent between 1977 and 1980. After a slight reversal in the early 1980s, the terms-of-trade decline continued in earnest from 1984 onward. Indeed, the oil shocks, declining prices for agricultural exports, and the sharp increase in transport costs because of the war in Mozambique did serious harm to the economy. This harm was compounded by a variety of other factors, such as the decline in remittances coming from Malawian workers in South Africa, the repatriation of wages and profits earned by foreign capital and labor in Malawi, and drought that hurt agriculture, the backbone of Malawi's economy.

In response to the economic crisis that gripped Malawi as it entered the 1980s, the International Monetary Fund (IMF), World Bank, and bilateral donors lined up behind the government. Balance-of-payment support and policy advice were generously provided, with the two often intertwined in the form of conditions for the disbursement of financing.

The main focus of donor-financed adjustment efforts during the 1980s was on reforming agriculture. Particular conditions revolved around reducing taxation of smallholders, removing the subsidy on fertilizer, and privatizing and liberalizing marketing arrangements, including rationalizing the activities of agricultural parastatals. The basic structural features of the rural sector—in particular the policy-induced divisions between the smallholder and estate subsectors—remained intact, however (Sahn and Arulpragasam 1991a). At the macro level, a variety of objectives were agreed upon during the years under adjustment, including increasing and diversifying revenue sources, reducing and reorienting government spending, limiting new credits and their diversion to the private sector, and rationalizing interest rates (World Bank 1981, 1983, 1985).

As intimated above, despite the efforts of the donor community and the government during the 1980s, policy and balance-of-payment support failed in the short term to bring about observable and sustained improvements in the economy. Neither was there any evidence to suggest success in the corollary of development—the alleviation of poverty. In order to gain some insight on the effect of exogenous factors and policy on economic performance during the past decade, the remainder of this paper will be devoted to presenting an econometric model and carrying out policy simulations with the model to explore the relative contributions of shocks and decision-making on macroeconomic performance, sectoral value added, and the corresponding functional income distribution by major household groups.

The next section of the paper is devoted to describing the prototype model and its limitations. This is followed in Section 11.3 by running counterfactuals, using the model to determine the effects of alternative scenarios concerning policies and shocks. In particular, outcomes of interest include both macroeconomic performance—including gross domestic product (GDP) growth, balance of payments, inflation, and debt—and sectoral outcomes, such as growth of smallholder agriculture, estate agriculture, and non-agriculture. In addition, in order to gain some insights into the distributional implications of alternative policies, the results from the model runs that distribute value added by sector according to major functional groups, including smallholders and estate workers, are presented. The final section summarizes the most salient lessons learned from the exercise.

11.2. *Description of the Model*

The formal modeling of economies under adjustment, especially when distributional outcomes are important, is extremely challenging. First, it is necessary to trace macro policy changes to the level of economic activity by sector, and thereafter, factor income must be distributed to household types or groups. The weak data base and the fact that, unlike the case of a SAM-based CGE, this model does not start with an empirically consistent description of the economy imply a considerable degree of aggregation. Furthermore, the prototype model presented in this paper is primarily of use for identifying relationships in the economy and determining how alternative policies would have affected the direction of change in key indicators during the 1980s. In addition, owing to the weaknesses of the data base and the fact that the functioning of markets has been impeded by the extensive government intervention in administration of prices, a number of variables that one would ideally endogenize are in fact exogenous in this model. Of particular importance is that prices of agricultural products, nominal wages, and interest rates are exogenous, along with the nominal exchange rate. (The complete list of equations and exogenous variables is found in the appendices.)

The prototype model is composed basically of five blocks (plus a few miscellaneous equations): the production block, balance-of-payment block, government finance block, prices block, and monetary sector block. Within each block there is a series of stochastic equations and/or identities. Altogether, the model, briefly described below, is composed of 60 equations.[1]

11.2.1. *Production block*

The production block of the model consists of a number of equations that predict output in agriculture and industry as well as construction value added. These, in addition to the level of government expenditures (on wages, goods, and grants), are used to predict, in a reduced-form equation, GDP at factor cost. Nearly two-thirds of the tertiary sector—or 30 percent of GDP at factor cost—is therefore not explicitly modeled; we are in fact assuming that services are a markup over production in the other sectors.

Agriculture, counting for 36 percent of GDP and nearly all export revenue, is disaggregated into maize and cash crops produced by smallholders and export crops produced by the estates.[2] The dualistic nature of Malawi's agriculture involves clear, government-delineated legal and institutional rules regarding crop production, marketing arrangements, pricing, and land

---

[1] For a detailed discussion of the model, see Van Frausum and Sahn (1993).
[2] The share of agricultural value added in the 1980s was roughly 29 percent for smallholders and 8 percent for estates.

tenure.[3] In spite of this, the estate and smallholder subsectors compete for factors of production and agricultural inputs.

Maize, most of which is local varieties, is produced primarily by smallholders and is mostly for subsistence.[4] The surplus is marketed through the Agricultural Development and Marketing Corporation (ADMARC), the parastatal marketing agency, and in recent years, since the liberalization of marketing regulations, through private traders as well. The second component of smallholder output is smallholder cash crops, proxied by the weighted sum of dark-fired, sun-and air-cured, and oriental tobacco (marketed through ADMARC), groundnuts, and cotton production. Excluded were rice and pulses, which have been exported in significant volume in only one or two years. Coffee also was excluded since it has accounted for 1.4–5.0 percent of export revenues in the last half of the 1980s. Estate sector production, consisting of barley, flue-cured tobacco, tea, and sugar, is marketed at close to world market prices.

Modeling agricultural production proved to be difficult. Ideally we would estimate production functions for each crop separately, but information on allocation of inputs by crops was not available. The absence of reliable time-series data on labor input and land under cultivation by subsector, coupled with the unreliable nature of time-series data on the use of fertilizer by smallholders and estates, was indeed a problem. The data limitations commended essentially employing a supply response function to determine how output is related to relative prices, weather, and any secular changes captured by a time trend. In such a model, the variable we are explaining is planned output, which is not actually observed. We use realized output as a proxy. This is reasonable, given that stagnant yields and the virtual absence of technological change in both smallholder and estate agriculture indicate that changes in output have been largely determined by acreage in cultivation.[5]

In addition, the maize model includes a relative price variable of maize to fertilizer. Owing to the fact that smallholder fertilizer is subsidized and rationed, and given the excess demand, the price that clears the market is expected to be the unsubsidized price as determined by imports for use by estates (Sahn and Arulpragasam 1991b). In the cash-crop equation, the price of cash crops relative to the minimum wage rate is also included, as it is expected that a higher supply price of hired labor will reduce labor demand and subsequently cash-crop production.

---

[3] For further discussion, see Sahn and Arulpragasam (1991a).

[4] According to the annual surveys of agriculture (1983/84–1988/89), 92.5 percent of the maize (hectarage) was local varieties, 1.7 percent was composite, and only 5.8 percent hybrid. Most of the hybrid maize was produced by the 25 percent of smallholders whose landholding exceeded 1.5 hectares (Sahn, Arulpragasam, and Merid 1990).

[5] For a discussion of the failure of agricultural research to spur technological change in Malawi, see Kydd (1989).

As far as the estate sector equation is concerned, there is a strong effect on production from the price of estate crops relative to the minimum wage. The increase in the price of labor will discourage hiring by estate producers, which leads to a consequent decline in output. Higher fertilizer prices, also as expected, reduce estate production.

The industrial production index is explained as a supply function of imports of intermediate goods, capital stock of equipment (a measure derived from deflated imports of equipment), capital stock of infrastructure (a measure derived from deflated, fixed capital formation by the government), and an interaction term capturing the specific environment during the 1980s. Value added in the construction sector is regressed upon gross fixed capital formation (*GFCF*) of government and of the private sector. This is not a genuine production equation but relates the value-added component of construction output to investment activity. Subsectoral production in agriculture, and value added from construction, industrial production, and government expenditure on wages–goods–grants feed somewhat less conventionally into two equations that predict GDP at factor cost in constant prices, one including and the other one excluding the subsistence sector.

11.2.2. *Balance-of-payment block*

The balance-of-payment (BOP) block gives a detailed picture of the current account; it shows how the current account balance is ultimately transformed into external debt. The central equation is exports at constant prices (f.o.b.). Exports of tobacco, tea, sugar, groundnuts, cotton, coffee, pulses, rice, and maize are simply regressed on agricultural production indices (smallholder cash crops and estate crops). Other exports, counting for no more than 10 percent of export revenues, are regressed on a time trend and a proxy for price competitiveness (a real exchange rate indicator). Exports of nonfactor services are regressed on the time trend, a price competitiveness indicator, and number of departing visitors.

On the import side, we first determine foreign exchange availability (excluding foreign borrowing) after subtracting debt servicing and other factor payments from export revenues and exogenous official transfers. In the extreme case where no foreign savings inflows occur, the foreign exchange availability variable will put a cap on imports of goods and nonfactor services.[6] We then use a stochastic foreign-exchange-constrained imports function, where right-hand-side variables include foreign exchange availability (the sum of the value of total exports plus long-term borrowings

---

[6] Of course, net capital inflows do occur, allowing imports to be somewhat more demand-driven. Thus, in reality, we may have two regimes of imports determination (foreign-exchange-constrained or demand-constrained) calling for a disequilibrium econometrics approach; that, unfortunately, did not give satisfactory results and had to be abandoned. Instead, we use a function where supply of foreign exchange constrains imports.

minus factor payments) and an interaction of foreign exchange availability and creditworthiness.[7]

Imports of capital goods, intermediate inputs, fertilizer, and so forth are derived from the total import function, assuming exogenous shares. Total external debt is modeled as a simple identity: one-year lagged debt (revalued at the current exchange rate) plus the balance of the current account. A deficit adds to debt, and a surplus reduces debt. Provision can be made for partial debt cancellation. Non-government external debt is computed as a residual, as we have accounted for government external borrowing and principal repayment elsewhere in the model (the government finance block). The debt service ratio is determined in an identity: interest payments plus principal repayments divided by exports of goods and services.

11.2.3. Government finance block

The government finance block is made up entirely of nonstochastic equations. Current revenue is determined by imports (c.i.f.) and GDP at factor cost (actually less the subsistence sector, since the latter's income is not explicitly taxed). Official transfers (a BOP item) are exogenous. Government external debt service and interest payments on domestic debt are endogenized as a function of external and domestic debt outstanding, although with a one-year lag. The sum of government expenditure on wages, goods, grants, and fixed capital formation is derived as an identity: total government revenue plus domestic and foreign borrowing less debt service, loans to sectors, and change in cash position (treated as an exogenous variable). A share parameter, which is the actual distribution of government expenditure observed for each year, is used next to determine separately current and capital expenditures. In effect, expenditures are determined by the financing constraint—i.e., revenues including borrowing.[8] Government-fixed capital formation adds to the stock of infrastructure. The government stock of external debt is written as an identity: one-year lagged debt plus new borrowing less repayments; all are expressed in foreign currency.

11.2.4. Price block

The price block includes essentially the retail price index (RPI), the GDP deflator, the real wage rate in the private sector, and an equation for the free (black) market exchange rate. Also endogenized are the deflators for gross fixed capital formation and government expenditure on wages–goods–grants. The RPI and GDP deflator are estimated in percentage changes, and the set

---

[7] The purpose of the interaction term is to capture the supply of some of the shorter-term credits to recipients such as private sector agents and parastatals.

[8] Of course, it may be the case that in certain years the government had set an expenditure target, then determined borrowing requirements as the residual—i.e. the expenditure and borrowing variables switch roles in the equation. This option, however, is not followed in our simulations.

of explicative variables is virtually identical in both equations: import prices adjusted for import duties, ADMARC producer prices, and indirect tax rates. Finally, a variable defined as "advances to government and parastatals divided by real GDP" appears in the RPI equation and translates the effect of nominal money supply on price inflation.

The real wage rate in the private sector is positively correlated with the terms of trade (TOT), labor productivity, government-administered real minimum wage rate, number of registered work seekers, and number of Malawian workers abroad (e.g. in South Africa). However, the latter two variables contribute little in explaining the real wage rate, and were subsequently dropped from the equation. Population (proxy for labor supply) and nominal exchange rate exert a negative effect on the real wage rate.[9]

11.2.5. *The monetary block*

The dimensions of the monetary sector block are kept to the bare minimum. Instead of describing in detail the assets and liabilities structure of the central bank and the commercial banking system, we have simply modeled total advances from commercial banks as a function of foreign exchange availability (which feeds into the monetary base) and the real interest rate. Advances from commercial banks to the private sector are then derived by subtracting commercial bank advances to government and parastatals from total advances (thus taking into account the crowding-out effect). The latter variable is a policy instrument: the government can indeed borrow domestically either directly from the central bank (high-powered money) or from the commercial banking sector.[10]

11.3. *Household Functional Groups*

One consequence of the lack of household survey data in Malawi was that the model described above is limited to the analysis of sectoral output. Given our interest in income distribution, we have added a functional income distribution module as a partial remedy for the model's shortcoming. The prototype model's production block endogenizes smallholder maize and cash-crops' production, estate production, industrial production, and value added of construction in constant prices. Government expenditure on wages (government finance block) is a good proxy for value added in the

---

[9] Considerable collinearity exists between terms of trade and population: a regression of *TOT* on population yields a determination coefficient of 0.93, which explains why bringing *TOT* and population together in a single specification requires our having recourse to Ridge regression technique.

[10] Crowding out has an effect on capital formation (indirectly through imports of capital goods); and (excess) money supply, proxied by total advances, fuels inflation.

government services sector, whereas value added of the "other services" sector is computed basically as a markup over value added of the sectors, which are explicitly treated in the model.

The first step is to convert our constant-prices production measures generated by the model (there are six in all) into current-prices value added. For this conversion, we have used, in addition to the production measures, the price indices available in the prototype model. We have also tried to adjust for the impact of changing prices and volumes of intermediate inputs, but with little success—a fact that reflects the deficiencies of the Malawian national accounts methodologies.

In a second step, the derived sectoral value added is distributed by sector over labor remuneration and capital remuneration (i.e. gross profit), which includes depreciation. Factor shares are computed initially from the Annual Economic Survey 1980–1983 (National Statistical Office 1989). On estates two-thirds of the value added accrues to labor, while in industry the figure is only 40 percent. In contrast, almost all government value added is payments to labor, while other services roughly split between labor and capital. Since ownership and labor are not distinct in smallholder agriculture, value added in that sector is attributed almost entirely to labor remuneration, with the exception of a small share for depreciation. Nonetheless, a key decision in terms of defining the functional groups to be included in the model was the delineation between large (i.e. better-off) and small (poor) smallholder households. We obviously did not wish to treat smallholders as a homogeneous group, owing to the variability in landholding size and the assertion that the size of landholding is a primary determinant of incomes. However, distinctions among smallholder households are best based on an empirical question: how does the size of holding influence incomes? To make this determination, we employed the same regional household survey (to be discussed in greater detail below) to examine the relationship between landholding size and income. The results, found in Table 11.1, suggest that over the bottom four landholding quintiles there is no trend in per capita expenditures, although household expenditures increase noticeably over the first three deciles, reflecting the smaller household size for those households in the bottom landholding quintiles. In contrast, for the largest landholding households, with an average farm size of 2.7 hectares, the expenditure figures jump noticeably. On the basis of these descriptive data, coupled with a simple, double log-quadratic function wherein landholdings are used to predict expenditures, we chose 1.5 hectares as a cutoff point to distinguish functional groups of poor and better-off smallholders to be incorporated in the model.

A more serious problem is that the reported factor shares vary over time. Once again, in spite of the intrinsic weakness of Malawian labor market statistics (e.g. incomplete coverage), we attempt to endogenize labor income shares. The methodology followed was first to fit a model to predict sectoral

Table 11.1. Malawi: expenditures by household landholding quintile

Quintile	Hectares cultivated	Per capita hectares cultivated	Monthly household expenditures	Monthly per capita expenditures
All	1.5	0.23	56.5	9.0
1	0.6	0.13	38.6	8.1
2	1.0	0.19	46.7	8.3
3	1.3	0.22	54.9	9.0
4	1.7	0.26	52.5	7.9
5	2.7	0.36	91.0	11.9

Source: Sahn, Arulpragasam, and Merid (1990).

wage rates and employment.[11] We can then compute an implicit sectoral labor income and labor income share (since sectoral value added is known). Then we calibrate this implicit labor income share to match the period average shares from government statistics.

11.4. *Policy Simulations*

We now turn to the policy simulations using the model. Counterfactuals are run to test the six scenarios, each of which represented either key policy decisions relating to the adjustment program or external shocks to which Malawi was trying to adjust. The context of each policy/shock is first discussed briefly, and then the model results are presented.

The results of the alternative scenarios outlined below are compared with a base case, which in essence is the systematic behavior of the model. That is, the base case is a dynamic simulation, assuming that all the policies and the external environment were as observed. It separates systematic model behavior from random factors not explained by the prototype model. Obviously, the better the tracking capability of the econometric model, the more confidence we will have in the results of the counterfactuals. To summarize the tracking capability of the model, Theil and Mean Absolute Percentage Error (MAPE) indexes are reported for key variables (see Table 11.2). The threshold for Theil is one, meaning that a no-change prediction is at least as good as the model's prediction, thus casting doubt on the

---

[11] Three real wage rate equations were estimated: one for private sector workers, which included industry and other workers, one for estate workers, and one for construction workers. Four employment equations are estimated: for estate workers, construction workers, workers in industry, and workers in other productive services. Since virtually all of the smallholder and government shares of value added accrue to labor, estimating functions for these groups was not necessary as depreciation is assumed to stay constant.

Table 11.2. Malawi: coefficient of Theil and MAPE (dynamic simulation) (%)

Variable	Theil	MAPE
Maize	0.56	4.0
Cash	0.21	6.4
Estate	0.52	3.6
Value added, construction sector	0.89	10.7
Constant prices exports	0.37	5.2
Total factor payments (BOP)	0.23	3.5
External debt (kwacha)	0.19	3.0
Creditworthiness	0.47	5.4
Imports at current prices (goods and services)	0.51	8.9
Government expenditure on goods, services, wages, and capital formation (current prices)	0.32	3.9
Retail price index	0.18	2.2
Deflator, GDP	0.14	1.5
Real wage rate	0.31	2.7
Index of industrial production	0.77	3.5
Government expenditure on goods, services, wages (constant prices)	0.55	3.9
GDP at factor cost, constant prices	0.99	2.6
GDP at market prices, current prices	0.47	5.3
Debt service ratio	0.39	6.5

Source: Malawi model simulations.

model's reliability. Overall the model appears to behave well in the dynamic simulation. Our major concern is the high Theil coefficient for GDP at factor cost, although the MAPE is still reasonably low at 2.6 percent.

Since there are a large number of endogenous variables in the model, for the sake of keeping the presentation within manageable bounds, we concentrate our discussion on an examination of a few equations that we feel are most interesting: maize production; smallholder cash-crop production; estate crop production; construction value added; industrial production; exports at constant prices; GDP deflator; GDP at factor costs; real minimum wage rate; government current expenditures; and debt service ratio.

11.5. Transport Costs

Owing to the civil war in neighboring Mozambique, Malawi witnessed a dramatic increase in the costs of importing, while at the same time the prices received for exports were depressed. In particular, as trade was diverted from the ports in Mozambique, primarily to Durban, South Africa, shipping costs per metric ton increased dramatically, reflecting the fivefold increase in the average length of routes to ocean ports—from 800 to 3500 kilometers. Calculating the shipment factor, defined as the ratio of the difference between f.o.b. and c.i.f. prices divided by f.o.b. prices, shows that between 1980 and 1984 shipment costs increased by approximately two and one half times. Because the Nacala rail line is being rehabilitated in Mozambique, and the Northern Corridor route through Tanzania is being developed, these transport costs are expected to moderate in the early 1990s, although the pace of the decline will be conditioned by the regional security situation. In the transport scenario, we basically assume that the transport bottleneck did not occur, so that the shipment factor is lower during the 1980s (pegged to the level observed in 1979).

It is clearly the case that, in the absence of the transport shock, other exogenous variables would have behaved differently, and many of the other policy decisions that followed from the increased transport costs would also have been altered. Although a limitation of the model is that it does not endogenize government decision-making—for example, with regard to the nominal exchange rate or administered prices—we feel that it is worthwhile expanding the transport shock simulation to incorporate other assumptions. In particular, these include: (1) that in the absence of the war, which caused the transport bottleneck, there would have been no refugees from Mozambique; (2) that the nominal devaluation would not have been deemed necessary, and the exchange rate would have remained at the 1979 level of 0.8169 kwacha per US dollar, rather than being devalued at an average annual rate of 12 percent per year; (3) that nominal interest rates on both deposits and lending would have been lower, the former pegged to the inflation rate and the latter to inflation plus 4 percent; and (4) that the need for government net borrowing from central and commercial banks would have been reduced, at least in nominal terms. In addition, we assume that relative prices (of agricultural products) would have followed the pattern actually observed, but the rate of change of both the numerator and denominator of these ratios has been modified to coincide with the simulated rather than actual inflation figures.[12]

Among the exogenous variables that are not modified, compared with the base-case scenario, are implicit tax rates, factor receipts (in the BOP), official transfers, and government external borrowing. These assumptions may not seem realistic, but without an indication as to how these variables might have behaved counterfactually we preferred not to modify them in order to avoid the model's being driven by too many exogenous variables other than the shipment factor.

---

[12] The GDP deflator and imported inflation values of 3.8 and 4.3 percent per annum, respectively, observed in the counterfactual contrast with the 15.3 and 20.4 percent, respectively, observed in actuality.

The simulation results confirm that the transportation shock did dramati-cally affect the economic performance of Malawi in the 1980s (Table 11.3). In addition, the absence of the higher transport margin would have resulted in a slightly smaller share of the income distribution going to the poor smallholders (Table 11.4). Gross profits initially gain in the absence of the transportation bottleneck, their share of value added being over 2 percent higher compared with the average base-case share of 32 percent over the 1980s. Also, losing out initially, in the years 1980–1984, are other labor in the private sector and government workers, while estate labor gains. Small-holder labor gains in the second half of the 1980s because the counterfactual exchange rate is kept constant; this avoids the inevitable losses to labor that follow from a devaluation. On balance, however, the poor would have fared much better in the absence of the transport shock as real GDP at factor cost would have been up by an average 17.5 percent in the period 1985–1989, compared with the observed level of GDP. This translates into a GDP growth of 3.7 percent per year against 2.3 percent per year observed. Per capita GDP would thus have grown by 0.4 percent per year against a drop of 1.1 percent in reality. Maize production would be higher by an average 6.1 percent as a result of lower fertilizer prices. Smallholder cash-crop production is very price-sensitive, and the large fluctuations of the deviations from the base-case scenario are not a reflection of the instability of the model, but of relative prices. The model captures this very well.[13] Therefore it is not surprising that during the 1980s the counterfactual also varies markedly from year to year. The average gain is around 14 percent, owing to lower fertilizer prices. Estate production is, on average, 15.1 percent higher, although in 1988 and 1989 this moderates to around 13 percent. Real exports are thus 15.0 percent higher than in the base case.

Higher exports and lower import costs would, in a first instance, have contributed to a lowering of Malawi's external debt if import demand had been somewhat demand-driven. However, the import function retained in our model is driven by foreign exchange availability and creditworthiness or debt service, and since exports, creditworthiness, and debt service improve significantly in the early and mid-1980s the model allows imports to run higher at the expense of external debt. The creditworthiness variable plays the role of a stabilizer in the model so that, although external debt (in US dollars) is 22 percent higher counterfactually in 1989, the country's credit-worthiness still shows an improvement of 14 percent in 1989, whereas the resulting counterfactual debt service ends up being lower than the observed debt service ratio. Industrial production, spurred by higher investment and greater availability of imported intermediate inputs, would be, on average,

13 An illustration of the observed fluctuations in cash-crop output is that its constant prices value fell 35 percent in 1982, only to jump back up to 82 percent in 1984. The model easily explains the lower output levels in 1982 and 1983 as a result of lower cash-crop prices relative to the wage rate in 1982 and lower cash-crop prices relative to the maize price in 1983.

Table 11.3. Malawi: counterfactual simulations

Scenario/period	Maize	Cash	Estate	VAConstr	Industry	Exports	GDPdef	WageReal	GovCurr	GDP	DebtServ
Transport shock											
1980–84	1.004	1.138	1.131	1.197	1.123	1.132	0.774	1.010	1.218	1.125	0.841
1985–89	1.061	1.140	1.151	1.168	1.257	1.150	0.414	1.200	1.212	1.175	0.884
Exchange rate devaluation											
1980–84	0.988	1.297	1.180	1.154	1.069	1.202	1.241	0.775	1.322	1.142	0.813
1985–89	0.977	1.266	1.214	1.196	1.113	1.238	1.191	0.883	1.328	1.158	0.876
Current account deficit											
1980–84	1.000	1.000	1.000	0.934	0.937	1.000	1.001	1.000	0.878	0.945	0.776
1985–89	1.000	1.000	1.000	0.963	0.957	1.000	0.999	1.000	0.905	0.960	0.727
Agriculture pricing policy											
1980–84	0.936	1.945	1.000	1.053	1.040	1.174	1.002	0.998	1.058	1.057	0.890
1985–89	0.966	1.371	1.000	1.015	1.030	1.091	1.001	1.000	1.011	1.030	1.001
Agriculture pricing policy and minimum wage											
1980–84	0.935	1.715	0.940	1.008	1.014	1.087	1.017	1.048	0.962	1.009	0.936
1985–89	0.966	1.327	0.937	0.978	0.995	1.029	1.016	1.050	0.909	0.980	1.014

Source: Sahn and Van Frausum (1995).

Table 11.4. Malawi: functional distribution of income with respect to base case

Scenario	Smallholders		Estate labor	Government labor	Other labor	Profits	Total
	<1.5ha	>1.5ha					
Base Case	0.1297	0.1204	0.0434	0.1248	0.2616	0.3200	1
Transport scenario							
1980–84	0.1252	0.1155	0.0452	0.1142	0.2581	0.3418	1
1985–89	0.1277	0.1199	0.0433	0.1123	0.2714	0.3256	1
Exchange rate scenario	0.1157	0.1096	0.0360	0.1464	0.2086	0.3838	1
Current account scenario	0.1367	0.1286	0.0452	0.1148	0.2611	0.3136	1
Agricultural pricing scenario	0.1418	0.1555	0.0388	0.1187	0.2407	0.3045	1

Source: Sahn and Van Frausum (1995).

25.7 percent higher than actual. Government real expenditure is seesawing quite a lot in the counterfactual simulation, but the average level is up by 21.7 percent between 1985 and 1989, largely as a result of increased tax revenues, translating into higher expenditures.

11.6. *Exchange Rate*

During the 1970s, Malawi's exchange rate was initially pegged to the British pound, then to a weighted average of the US dollar and pound, and then in 1975, to the standard drawing rights (SDR). Beginning in 1984, the Malawi Kwacha was pegged to a weighted basket of currencies of major trading partners. There was a series of nominal devaluations during the 1980s (on average, of 12.7 percent per year). Domestic inflation actually resulted in little sustained real exchange rate devaluation: the IMF measure of the real effective exchange rate stood at 98 in the period 1978–1979, against an average of 101 in 1980–1984 and 91.1 in 1985–1989.

Malawi's exchange rate policies have not been the primary focus of adjustment. This is partially a reflection of the fact that shadow exchange rates indicate a general pattern of overvaluation on the order of 25–50 percent both before and since adjustment. This is small relative to the gross distortions in other countries, such as Ghana, Somalia, Guinea, Tanzania, and Nigeria, where nominal devaluations tenfold or more were the centerpiece of reforms. Despite the absence of gross distortions, there remains an important question as to how Malawi would have fared if it had aligned its exchange rate before the shocks of the 1980s and maintained it at the equilibrium level thereafter. To test the impact of adopting a more competitive exchange rate, we have plugged into an exchange rate scenario the shadow exchange rate. This would have meant a devaluation of almost 41 percent, from 0.8169 to 1.15 kwacha per US dollar, in 1980 followed by annual devaluations of 16 percent on average, slightly more than those actually observed (Sahn, Arulpragasam, and Merid 1990).

In addition to the modified exchange rate scenario, we have also made the following assumptions: (1) government net borrowing from the central and commercial banks is adjusted to account for the now different domestic inflation rate; (2) deposit interest rate equals inflation rate; (3) lending interest rate equals inflation rate plus 4 percent; and (4) domestic prices, which remain exogenous in the model, follow approximately the general inflation trend (i.e., 16.4 percent per annum). The movement in relative maize-to-cash-crop prices observed during the 1980s is replicated.

A 41 percent devaluation in 1980 would raise the deflator of GDP by an extra 24 percent compared with the base cost during the period 1980–1984, and would boost nominal government revenue, owing largely to the increase

in estate and smallholder cash-crop production (Table 11.3).[14] This increase in exports in turn would have contributed to a much greater level of
nominal government expenditure than in the base case, which translates
also into a large increase in real terms since the deflator of government
expenditure (which, among other things, is a function of lagged minimum
wages) increases at a rate slower than the general price level. GDP at factor
costs would not also have been up by 15.0 percent during the period
1983–1989 if the government had decided to add the windfall revenue to its
cash reserves; GDP growth would have been significantly lower.

Maize production is down slightly, partly as a result of the substitution to
export crops and of the higher fertilizer prices (in kwacha terms). Cash-crop
production would be up by nearly 30 percent in the 1980–1984 period,
despite the higher price of fertilizer. This increase is due to a higher relative
price of cash crops to the wage rate. Estate production is also benefiting
considerably from the devaluation, the average increase being 1902 percent
between 1980 and 1989. Industrial production is 9.1 percent higher than in
the base case over the decade. This is explained entirely by higher investment and imports of intermediate inputs. A modified specification of the
industrial production equation, allowing for an import substitution response
to a permanently lower real exchange rate, yields even higher industrial
output. (However, in our scenario, domestic inflation is allowed to erode
the real devaluation.) Real exports also shoot up by 14.1 percent above the
base case, and debt service is down by 15.5 percent over the decade. Our
conclusion is that, although Malawi might have staved off a severe recession
with a competitive devaluation policy, stagflation during the second half of
the decade was almost unavoidable.

Concerning the distribution of value added in the exchange rate scenario,
gross profits' share in GDP advances by an average 6.4 percent, from the
period average of 32 percent to the counterfactual 38.4 percent, mostly at
the expense of private sector labor remuneration (down 5.3 percent) and
labor remuneration in the estate sector (down 0.7 percent), and in the
smallholder sector (down 1.2 percent). The model predicts that labor in the
government sector would increase its income share by an average of 2.2
percent because of increased hiring resulting from higher tax revenues, and
not because of increased real wages.

---

14 The precipitous decline in cash-crop production that occurred in 1982 is avoided under
the counterfactual, since under the simulation minimum wages would not have displayed the
same increase relative to the price of cash crops that in the base case and actual case contributed to a decline in cash-crop production.

11.7. *Balance-of-Payment Support for the Current Account*

Credits from multilateral and bilateral sources have contributed significantly to financing Malawi's current account deficit—and therefore imports—during the past decade. Structural adjustment loans from the World Bank and other forms of development assistance, including bilateral loans and grants, have indeed been important in Malawi, as in the rest of Africa. At the same time, IMF-and World Bank-inspired stabilization policies sought to reduce imbalances in the external accounts (through a reduction of imports) and in the domestic budget by cutting down on expenditures and reducing credit supply, and thus reducing the budget deficit. Stabilization policies are by nature deflationary. Malawi's performance in reducing external imbalances followed a distinctive pattern of "two steps forward, one step backward. Improvements secured over a number of years by determined government action were followed by disturbances that upset macro-balances and set back the effort to stabilize. The economy had insufficient reserves or flexibility to cope with the series of shocks to which it remained exposed" (Gulhati 1989: 38).

In order to determine the growth contribution of external financing, we have, counterfactually, halved the period-average current account deficit to 3.3 percent of GDP at current market prices in the years 1980–1989. The reduction in foreign savings inflows is shared about equally by government and non-government (including parastatals) foreign borrowing. The immediate impact of the exogenously imposed BOP constraint is a reduction in imports.[15] Construction activity, industrial production, and real government expenditure all fall (Table 11.3). This largely contributes to the gain in the share of value added accruing to the poor (Table 11.4). Nevertheless, there is a resulting loss in GDP at factor cost of 5.5 percent from 1980 to 1984, resulting in an overall decline in income for the poor. Not shown in the table, although equally interesting, is the fact that during the period 1982–1988 half the initial loss is recouped. This can be explained by a virtuous external debt mechanism: lower initial current account deficit leads to lower external debt (down 22 percent by 1988), lower debt servicing (down 26.1 percent), and thus more foreign exchange available to finance imports. Our conclusion, therefore, is that balance-of-payment support during a "bad" year will cushion the recession, but that in the long run GDP growth is not raised unless the country undergoes structural changes. Of course, our findings are determined by the fact that the prototype

---

[15] The prototype model does not indicate that smallholder and estate production are affected by lower fertilizer imports: fertilizer use does not appear as an explicative variable in the agricultural supply functions, although a severe foreign exchange constraint may in reality depress agricultural production through lower fertilizer inputs. Furthermore, lower fertilizer inputs also mean lower quality of tobacco and thus lower export prices fetched.

econometric model does not endogenize technical change, and the model does not assume that technical change is intrinsically enhanced by structural adjustment lending.

11.8. *Smallholder Cash-Crop Export Parity Pricing*

Malawi's dualistic agriculture is delineated by legal and institutional rules regarding crops to be produced, marketing arrangements, pricing, and land tenure. Smallholder agriculture is concentrated on maize, cassava, and other subsistence crops, in addition to cash crops such as oriental, sun-and air-cured tobacco, groundnuts, and cotton. Up until recently, smallholders have had little recourse but to rely on ADMARC to purchase their crops, although recent liberalization efforts have encouraged privatization of the marketing function, especially for food crops. Given the role of ADMARC in setting prices, particularly for export crops, it is instructive to note that, in contrast to estate producers, smallholders have been heavily taxed. Some have argued that, in fact, this is part of a strategy to keep the reservation wage rate low, thereby enabling estates to have access to cheap labor.

A review of nominal protection coefficients for export crops paints a clear picture of significant taxation (Table 11.5). Although the levels of taxation have fallen somewhat in comparison with the 1970s and early 1980s in accordance with the conditions of Malawi's structural adjustment program, this was generally due to declining world prices during the second half of the 1980s, rather than to increased producer prices. In contrast, maize prices have remained slightly above export parity for most years. While it could be argued that the correct border price for comparison is the import parity price, it would seem that Malawi's switching from importer to exporter justifies a price anywhere in a wide band between the two (Sahn and Arulpragasam 1991b).

We therefore next consider a scenario wherein export parity pricing for smallholder cash crops is adopted. Smallholder cash-crop prices are increased by the amount of negative protection. The only other modification to exogenous variables in the scenario is that the implied fertilizer subsidy is next subtracted from government expenditure through a reduction in domestic borrowing by the government. Since, as discussed earlier, the relevant marginal price is that of the estate sector, the effects of adopting border prices for inputs are not felt through changing relative prices.

Results indicate that the level of maize production over the decade would be on average 4.9 percent below the base case (Table 11.3). Smallholder cash-crop production would gain 65.8 percent, while estate production remains unaffected as long as the wage rate is not adjusted upward. The average annual gain in value added in the construction sector and in government expenditure would rise by 3.4 and 3.5 percent, respectively.

Table 11.5. Malawi: nominal protection coefficients (NPCs) for tobacco and groundnuts, 1980–1989[a]

	Tobacco	Groundnuts
1980	0.46	0.56
1981	0.31	0.37
1982	0.17	0.88
1983	0.34	0.92
1984	0.39	0.92
1985	0.89	1.42
1986	0.49	0.84
1987	0.35	1.05
1988	0.26	1.02
1989	0.24	1.00

[a] NPCs for tobacco are for a composite of varieties of smallholder tobacco.

Source: Sahn and Van Frausum (1995).

The increase in government expenditure despite the removal of the fertilizer subsidy is explained by an increase in explicit tax revenue brought about by higher imports, financed out of higher export revenue (up by 11.6 percent on average) in response to a reduction of cash-crop taxation and higher overall activity levels. External debt would end 6.8 percent higher by 1989 compared with the base case, because imports are increasing at a more rapid pace than exports—a result of the fact that the level of imports is determined by foreign exchange availability as well as creditworthiness, both of which have improved concurrent with the parity pricing regime. This, however, does not endanger the debt service ratio, which is on parity in 1989, although 5.4 percent lower than the base case when viewed over the entire 1980s. Industrial production would exceed the base case by an average of 3.5 percent, all of which results in an average annual increase in GDP at factor cost of 4.4 percent in the 1980s.

Finally, a sensitivity analysis was carried out on the above export parity pricing scenario when 20 percent is added to the minimum wage rate in every year compared with the observed pattern. This is to reflect the possibility that the reservation wage rate increases in response to higher smallholder incomes from cash-crop production, which would encourage government to alter the administered wage as well. The results indicate a few significant changes (see Table 11.3). Cash-crop production would fall below the levels reached in the previous scenario. We do not know exactly how realistic our assumption might be regarding the reservation wage rate, but a 20 percent increase would lead to a significantly lower level of estate production (–6.3 percent). Real exports would nevertheless be up by an average of 6.4 percent. The increase in the minimum wage rate almost wipes out earlier gains in industrial production and, more significantly, lowers real government expenditure (–6.4 percent). Overall, GDP at factor cost would remain at parity with the base case. The real wage rate would be up by 5 percent, leaving the general price level 1.7 percent higher by 1989.

As expected, smallholders would gain from export parity pricing for cash crops: smaller farmers (< 1.5 hectares) see their income share increase by nearly 3 percent. Farmers with over 1.5 hectares of land, who account for a much larger share of cash-crop production, gain by over 5 percent. Income shares drop for all other income categories.

11.10. *Conclusions*

This paper has presented a prototype econometric model of Malawi, showing the implications of alternative policies and external conditions on economic performance and poverty during the 1980s. Outcomes, which in most cases are reliable in terms of the direction and broad magnitude of change, were largely limited to the levels of sectoral outputs, government finance, balance of payments, and prices. A further attempt was made to examine functional income distribution at a high level of aggregation.

Some interesting findings emerge from the exercise. First, Malawi was indeed hurt badly by the transport shock that buffeted the economy. In particular, the bottleneck cost Malawi, on the average, 1.5 percent in annual GDP growth over the 1980s. These costs were due to lower export revenue and reduced imports of intermediate and capital goods. But while these external conditions hurt, the response of the donor community greatly mitigated the negative effects of external shocks. In particular, the provision of concessional financing was of great help in cushioning the blow of the transport shock on the incomes of poor and non-poor alike. However, while there is much to be said for donors holding interest rates for loans to Malawi below market rates, the current account scenario suggests some less promising effects of external borrowing in general. Specifically, the short-term effects of restricting imports to meet a lower current deficit target will be adverse on levels of output, although medium-term results indicate that the relative gap between the actual and counterfactual GDP levels stabilizes rapidly. This implies that the long-term growth rates of the economy in general, and the welfare of the poor in particular, are not appreciably affected because, among other things, debt servicing will be lower in the future, and thus more foreign exchange will be available for financing imports. Eventually one can imagine that counterfactual, long-term growth rates will exceed actual growth rates in the current regime, with generous current account deficit financing. What would invalidate our conclusion is some "proof" that BOP support leads the economy to adjust structurally by speeding up technical change, management decision-making capability, and so forth.

Regarding the role of the setting of the nominal price for agricultural products, there is little question that the taxation of smallholder crops reduced export earnings. This in turn filtered through the economy to reduce value added in the construction sector, industrial output (through dampening imports), and GDP. But perhaps of greater interest is that, not only would GDP have been up 4.4 percent, on average, during the course of the 1980s if parity pricing cum removal of fertilizer subsidies had been adopted, but the smallholders' income share, net of depreciation, would have been substantially higher. Thus, the failure to adopt basic agricultural pricing reforms had deleterious effects upon the poor.

Perhaps of greater importance than the specific results of the counterfactual, however, is the fact that the model does indicate a high level of price responsiveness in agriculture, in terms of substitution between cash crops and maize, the importance of the fertilizer-to-crop price, and the relation of minimum wage to crop price. Regarding the latter, there is little question that higher nominal wages would result in lower output in the estate and smallholder export crop sectors. The deleterious effect of higher wages on output, furthermore, filters through the economy to reduce government revenues, savings, and expenditures. This, of course, points to the fact that it is important that any increases in the administered real minimum wage be a reflection of productivity gains to avoid any medium- and long-term negative effects on output.

Appendix 11.1. Exogenous Variables in Dynamic Simulation (Base Case)

Rainfall
Time
ADMARC producer price of maize
ADMARC producer price of cash crops
ADMARC producer price index (weighted average of maize, other food crops and cash crop prices)
Import price of fertilizer (c.i.f.) in US dollars
Smallholder fertilizer price in kwacha
Weighted price index of trading partners (consumption prices or wholesale prices) for 10 regions or countries
Shipment factor
Exchange rate (official)

Lending interest rate

Deposit interest rate

Import price index (= unit value index) in US dollars and filtered from shipment factor

Export price index (= unit value index) in US dollars and filtered from shipment factor

Implicit import tax rate

Implicit other indirect taxes rate

Implicit direct taxes rate

Export revenue: factor revenue in US dollars

Official transfers in US dollars

Population

Minimum wage rate

Productivity growth in industry

Government domestic borrowing from central and commercial banks

Government foreign borrowing expressed in US dollars

Government expenditure: loans (e.g. to parastatals)

Net increase or decrease in government cash position

Government: principal repayment rate on external debt

Government: implicit interest rate on domestic debt

Government: implicit interest rate on external debt

Implicit interest rate/dividend rate on non-government external liabilities

Share of intermediate inputs imports (excluding fertilizer and fuels) in total c.i.f. imports

Number of refugees

Number of departing visitors (tourists)

Velocity of money

Share of fertilizer imports in total c.i.f. imports

Share of fertilizer sales to smallholders in total fertilizer imports

Stock of foreign direct investment

Appendix 11.2. A prototype Econometric Model for Malawi

Production block

(1) maize production (ton)	=	$f1$ (rainfall, time, (maize price/fertilizer price), (maize price/cash crops price))
(2) maize availability per capita (kg)	=	(production – exports + imports)/population
(3) cash-crop production smallholder (constant prices)	=	$f3$ (time, (cash crops price/minimum wage rate), (cash crops price/maize price), (cash crops price/fertilizer price))

(4) estate crop production   =   *f*4 (rainfall, time, (price estate crops/price
   (constant prices)   fertilizer), (price estate crops/wage rate))
(5) value added construction   =   *f*5 (gross fixed capital formation government,
   sector (constant prices)   gross fixed capital formation private sector)
(6) index industrial   =   *f*6 (constant prices imports of intermediate
   production   goods, capital stock GOV – GFCF, capital
                                      stock equipment, time, (import
                                      deflator/wage rate))
(7) GDP factor cost   =   *f*7 (index industrial production, VA
   (constant prices)   construction, constant prices GOV
                                      expenditure on wages + goods + grants,
                                      maize production, cash crops production,
                                      estate crop production)
(8) GDP factor cost   =   *GDPfc*—*f*8 (maize production, cash crops
   (–subsistence sector)   production)
   (constant prices)
(9) GDP factor cost   =   *GDPfc* (constant prices) • GDPdef
   (–subsistence sector)
   (current prices)

Balance-of-payments block

(10) exports80 (f.o.b.)   =   *f*10.1 (cash crop production smallholders,
   (constant prices)   estate crop production) + *f*10.2 (wage rate
                                      shipment factor)/(exchange rate • $price
                                      index of competitors, time)
(11) exports (f.o.b.) (current =   exports (FOB) • export deflator
   prices)
(12) exports non-factor   =   *f*12 (time, *GDPdef*/($price index of
   services   competitors • exchange rate), number of
                                      visitors)
(13) export revenue: net   =   *f*13 (time, number of refugees)
   private transfers
(14) export revenue: factor   =   exports factor receipts (US$) • exchange rate
   receipts (*K*)
(15) GOV: interest payments   =   implicit interest rate • stock external debt
   (foreign debt)   (GOV,*t* – 1)
(16) other factor payments   =   implicit interest and dividends rate • stock
                                      other external liabilities (non-GOV,*t* – 1)
(17) total factor payments   =   GOV interest payments on foreign debt +
                                      other factor payments
(18) official transfers   =   official transfers (US$) • exchange rate
(19) foreign exchange   =   exports goods + exports non-factor services +
   availability   export revenue net private transfers +
                                      export revenue factor receipts + official
                                      transfers – total factor payments

(20) imports (goods + non-factor services) (current prices) = $f20$ ((foreign exchange availability + government external borrowing – government foreign debt repayment), creditworthiness)

(21) current account (+ surplus, – deficit) = foreign exchange availability – Imports (goods + non-factor services)

(22) imports goods (c.i.f.) = $f22$ (imports goods + non-factor services)

(23) external debt (t) = [external debt $(t-1)$/exchange rate $(t-1)$] · [exchange rate (t) – current account (t)]

(24) non-government external liabilities (kwacha) = external debt – GOV stock external debt

(25) creditworthiness = external debt/exports of goods

(26) imports capital goods/imports (c.i.f.) (current prices) = $f26$ (advances to government/advances to private sector)

(27) imports capital goods (constant prices) = imports capital goods (curr. pr.)/($price index competitors · shipment factor · exchange rate)

(28) imports intermedt. goods / imports (c.i.f.) (current prices) exclud. fertilizer, petroleum products, construction prod. = exogenous

(29) imports intermediate goods (constant prices) = imports intermediate goods (current prices)/import price index

(30) imports fertilizer (smallholders) (ton) = imports (c.i.f.) · share total fertilizer imports in imports (c.i.f.) · share smallholder fertilizer in total fertilizer imports/import price fertilizer

(31) imports fertilizer (estates) (ton) = total fertilizer imports – imports fertilizer (smallholders)

(32) debt service ratio = [GOV interest payments foreign debt + GOV debt repayment + (implicit interest rate non-GOV debt + implicit principal repayment rate non-GOV debt) · non-GOV debt]/(exports goods + exports non-factor services + exports factor services)

Government finance block

(33) GOV: import taxation revenue = implicit import tax rate · imports (c.i.f.)

(34) GOV: other indirect tax revenue = implicit tax rate (ind) · $GDPfc$ – subsistence sector

(35) GOV: other domestic revenue = implicit tax rate (oth.) · $GDPfc$ – subsistence sector

(36) GOV: interest payments, domestic debt = implicit interest rate · stock domestic debt $(t-1)$

(37) GOV: total interest payments = GOV interest payments on foreign debt + GOV interest payments on domestic debt

(38) GOV: foreign debt repayment = implicit repayment rate • stock external GOV debt $(t-1)$

(39) GOV: expenditure excl. debt service = import taxation revenue + other indirect tax revenue + other domestic revenue + official transfers + net domestic borrowing + foreign (current prices) borrowing – loans to sectors – total interest payments – foreign debt repayment – change in cash position and other financing

(40) GOV: expenditure, wages + goods + grants (current prices) = GOV expenditure • distribution parameter

(41) GOV: expenditure, wages + goods + grants (constant prices) = GOV expenditure $(w + g + g)$/deflator $(w + g + g)$

(42) GOV: expenditure, gross fixed cap form (current prices) = GOV expenditure • (1 – distribution parameter)

(43) GOV: expenditure, GFCF (constant prices) = GFCF (curr. pr.)/deflator GFCF

(44) Capital stock of GOV – GFCF = capital stock GOV – GFCF $(t-1)$ + GOV – GFCF (t)

(45) GOV: stock domestic debt (t) = stock domestic GOV – debt$(t-1)$ + net domestic borrowing (t)

(46) GOV: stock foreign debt (t) (in US$) = stock of foreign debt $(t-1)$ + foreign borrowing (t) – foreign debt repayment (t)

(47) GOV: stock foreign debt(t) (in kwacha) = stock foreign debt (t) in US$ • exchange rate

Prices block

(48) retail price index = $f48$ (import deflator, import tax rate, money supply proxy, ADMARC – price index, per capita maize availability, other indirect taxes rate)

(49) GDP – deflator = $f49$ (import deflator, import tax rate, ADMARC price index, per capita maize availability, nominal minimum wage rate, other indirect taxes rate)

(50) real wage rate private sector = $f50$ (population, terms of trade, real minimum wage rate, productivity index private sector, nominal exchange rate)

(51) deflator GFCF = $f51$ (*GDPdef*, wage rate private sector, import deflator)

(52) deflator GOV – expenditure $(w + g + g)$ = $f52$ (*GDPdef*)

(53) free market exchange rate   = $f53$ (*GDPdef*, \$price of competitors,
       K/US\$ creditworthiness)

Monetary sector

(54) advances from   = $f54$ (foreign exchange availability, real interest
       commercial banks   rate on savings deposits)

(55) advances to GOV +   =   exogenous
       parastatals by RBM and
       commercial banks

(56) advances to GOV +   =   advances to GOV + parastatals by Reserve
       parastatals by   Bank of Malawi and commercial banks
       commercials banks

(57) advances to private sector   =   advances from commercial banks – advances
       by commercial banks   to GOV + parastatals from commercial
                                        banks

Miscellaneous equations

(58) gross fixed capital
       formation by private   = $f58$ (imports capital goods, real price of
       sector (constant prices)   GFCF $\cdot$ (1 + lending interest rate)

(59) capital stock equipment   = $0.9 \cdot$ capital stock equipment $(t-1)$ +
       (t) (constant prices)   imports capital goods (t)

(60) productivity index private   =   index industrial production/employment
       sector

References

Acharya, N., and B. Johnston. 1978. *Two Studies of Development in Sub-Saharan Africa.* World Bank Staff Papers. Washington, DC: World Bank.

Bourguignon, Francois, William Branson, and Jaime de Melo. 1989. *Macroeconomic Adjustment and Income Distribution: A Macro-Micro Simulation Model.* Technical Paper. Paris: OECD.

Centre for Social Research. 1988. *The Characteristics of Nutritionally Vulnerable Sub-Groups within the Smallholder Sector of Malawi: A Report from the 1980/81 NSSA.* Zomba: Center for Social Research, University of Malawi.

de Janvry, A., and E. Sadoulet. 1987. "Agricultural Price Policy in General Equilibrium Models: Results and Comparisons." *American Journal of Agricultural Economics.* 69(2): 230-246.

Gulhati, R. 1989. *Malawi: Promising Reforms, Bad Luck.* Washington, DC: World Bank, Economic Development Institute.

International Fertilizer Development Center. 1989. *Malawi Smallholder Fertilizer Marketing Survey.* Prepared for Ministry of Agriculture, Government of Malawi. Muscle Shoals, AL: IFDC.

International Monetary Fund. 1990a. *Direction of Trade Yearbook.* Washington, DC: IMF.

—— 1990b. *International Financial Statistics.* Washington, DC: IMF.

Kydd, J. 1989. "Maize Research in Malawi: Lessons from Failure." *Journal of International Development,* 1(1): 112–144.

—— and R. Christiansen. 1982. "Structural Change in Malawi since Independence: Consequences of a Development Strategy based on Large-Scale Agriculture." *World Development,* 10(5): 355–375.

Ministry of Agriculture. 1980. *Annual Survey of Agriculture.* Malawi: MOA.

National Statistical Office. 1989. *Annual Economic Survey, 1980–1983.* Malawi: NSO.

Robert R. Nathan Associates. 1987. *The Impact of the Fertilizer Subsidy Removal Program on Smallholder Agriculture in Malawi: Annexes.* Presented to Ministry of Agriculture, Malawi Government and U.S. Agency for International Development, Contract No. PDC-0000-I-04-6135-00, Work Order No. 004.

Sahn, David E., and Jehan Arulpragasam. 1991a. "Land Tenure, Dualism, and Poverty in Malawi." In *Including the Poor,* Michael Lipton, ed. Baltimore, MD: Johns Hopkins University Press (forthcoming).

—— —— 1991b. "The Stagnation of Smallholder Agriculture in Malawi: A Decade of Structural Adjustment." *Food Policy* (forthcoming).

—— —— and Lemma Merid. 1990. *Policy Reform and Poverty in Malawi: A Review of a Decade of Experience.* Monograph No. 7. Ithaca, NY: CFNPP.

—— and Yves Van Frausum. 1995. "Economic Growth, Equity and Agricultural Policy in Malawi." *Journal of African Economies,* 3(3).

Sarris, Alexander. 1990. *A Macro–Micro Framework for Analysis of the Impact of Structural Adjustment on the Poor in Sub-Saharan Africa.* Monograph No. 5. Ithaca, NY: CFNPP.

Scobie, Grant M. 1989. *Macroeconomic Adjustment and the Poor: Toward a Research Strategy*. Monograph No. 1. Ithaca, NY: CFNPP.

Thorbecke, Erik 1990. *Adjustment, Growth, and Income Distribution in Indonesia*. Paris: OECD Development Centre.

Van Frausum, Yves, and David E. Sahn. 1993. "An Econometric Model for Malawi: Measuring the Effects of External Shocks and Policies." *Journal of Policy Modeling*, 15(3).

——— 1991. *An Econometric Model for Malawi: Measuring the Effects of External Shocks and Policies*. Working Paper No. 13. Ithaca, NY: CFNPP.

World Bank. 1981. *Report and Recommendation of the President of the International Bank for Reconstruction and Development to the Executive Directors on a Structural Adjustment Loan to the Republic of Malawi* (June 4). Washington DC: World Bank.

——— 1983. *Report and Recommendation of the President of the International Bank for Reconstruction and Development to the President of the International Development Association on a Proposed Credit of SDR 51.9 Million to the Republic of Malawi for a Second Structural Adjustment Project* (November 29). Washington DC: World Bank.

——— 1985. *Report and Recommendation of the President of the International Bank for Reconstruction and Development to the Executive Directors on a Proposed Credit of SDR 28 Million and a Proposed African Facility Credit of SDR 37.4 Million to the Government of Malawi for a Third Structural Adjustment Operation* (November 25). Washington DC: World Bank.

——— 1989. *Malawi Country Economic Memorandum: Growth through Poverty Reduction*. Washington, DC: World Bank.

12

Market Liberalization and the Role of Food Aid in Mozambique

Paul Dorosh, Carlo del Ninno, and David E. Sahn

12.1. *Introduction*

Momentous changes swept Mozambique from 1987 to 1993. Major economic reforms were enacted, liberalizing markets after more than a decade of pervasive state controls. A severe drought struck in 1991 and 1992, decimating harvests and threatening widespread famine. Most important, a settlement of the long civil war was finally reached in late 1992, bringing hope of peace and improved welfare to the country's large rural population.

Foreign aid has played an extremely important role in this tumultuous period. Foreign capital inflows in support of structural adjustment in Mozambique averaged US$673.6 million (47.9 percent of GDP) between 1987 and 1991, financing imports of goods and services, mainly to urban areas. Massive inflows of food aid, in particular, were instrumental in providing food to millions of people during the drought. Food aid was a crucial element of urban food supplies even before the drought, as the civil war disrupted domestic food production and flows of grain to urban centers.

This chapter examines the impact of foreign aid on food markets and poverty in Mozambique. As the civil war ends and rural recovery takes place, foreign aid will likely be reduced. Given the liberalization of markets as part of structural adjustment, reductions in capital inflows and food aid imports will directly affect market prices. How will the poor be affected? What role, if any, remains for food aid? To analyze these issues, we develop a multi-market model of supply and demand for major food commodities and present a series of simulations covering various scenarios and policy options.

Section 12.2 reviews the recent macroeconomic history of Mozambique, with a focus on aid flows and the real exchange rate. We present a range of estimates of the extent of real exchange rate appreciation arising from foreign capital inflows using a variation of the standard "elasticities approach" to an analysis of exchange rate devaluations.

Section 12.3 outlines a simple multi-market model covering the major food commodities in Mozambique, urban households in the capital city,

Maputo, and rural households in the southernmost three provinces of the country. The core of the model consists of data on levels of expenditures by urban households in Maputo from a household survey conducted in 1991– 1992 and econometric estimates of demand parameters. Disaggregation of household expenditures in the model permits an analysis of the impacts of trade and agricultural pricing policies on supply and demand for yellow and white maize, rice, wheat and bread, export crops, and other food.

Model simulations of several policy alternatives and the impact of restored agricultural production on prices, incomes, and commodity supply and demand follow in Section 12.4. First, we present simulations of the effects of likely reductions in foreign aid and the implications of a postwar recovery of the rural economy. The focus of the analysis then shifts to more micro issues, in particular the role of food aid in the transition period. Using the multi-market model, we examine the consequences of changes in the level of yellow maize food aid on market prices and real incomes. Then, we extend the multi-market analysis to estimate effects of market liberalization and changes in food aid inflows on the extent and depth of poverty, on the basis of data on individual households from the Maputo survey.

The concluding section highlights the major lessons of the simulations and implications for food policy in Mozambique.

12.2. *Aid Flows, Macro Policy, and the Real Exchange Rate*

After independence in 1975, Mozambique's government opted for central planning of the economy with heavy state controls of markets. Government parastatals became increasingly involved in all facets of the economy, including agriculture, industry, and trade, and official prices were set for most products, including food and export crops. Civil war, drought, and poor economic policy led to a dismal economic performance during most of the 1980s and eventually led to the adoption of significant economic reforms in the mid-1980s. Central to the reform effort was tighter fiscal policy, exchange rate devaluations and agricultural price liberalization.

12.2.1. *Exchange rate policy*

During the first half of the 1980s, the Mozambique government made only small adjustments in the nominal metical–US dollar exchange rate, despite rapid domestic inflation. Between 1980 and 1986, the total depreciation of the nominal exchange rate was only 24.7 percent, while domestic prices (as measured by the official consumer price index) rose by 221.9 percent. As a result, the real exchange rate[1] appreciated by 61.2 percent.

The above measure of the real exchange rate does not accurately reflect relative prices for many transactions, however, because of widespread

---

[1] Measured using the nominal exchange rate deflated by the official consumer price index.

parallel markets in foreign exchange coupled with quotas on imports.[2] With demand for foreign exchange at the official price far exceeding supply of foreign exchange available for imports (or capital flight), parallel market exchange rates were 186 percent higher than the official exchange rate in the early 1980s (1980–1983 average), testifying to the huge rents associated with the import licensing system.

Exchange rate devaluation was a major part of the macroeconomic reform program. After initial devaluations in 1987 totaling over 600 percent, from 40.4 to 289.4 meticais to the US dollar, the nominal exchange rate depreciated by another 870 percent to 2526 meticais to the US dollar. Although domestic inflation in this period was also high (the CPI rose by 433 percent), the real exchange rate depreciated by 63.8 percent between 1987 and 1992.

12.2.2. *The role of foreign aid*

With structural adjustment measures came a large influx of foreign aid from Western donors. Aid inflows grew from 17.1 percent of GDP in the 1980–1986 period to an average of 47.9 percent between 1987 and 1991.

After liberalization of imports and foreign exchange in 1992, the nominal exchange rate was determined essentially by supply and demand for foreign exchange. (A small premium nonetheless remained on the parallel market, reflecting some remaining restrictions on foreign exchange transactions.) But there is an important sense in which the exchange rate was still not in equilibrium. Despite the massive devaluations of the metical, Mozambique's trade deficit remained large, financed by capital inflows. It is likely that in the future, as the economy recovers, foreign aid and net capital inflows will decrease. Should this happen, a depreciation of the real exchange rate will be required to equilibrate supply and demand for foreign exchange.

The simplest method for estimating the size of the real exchange rate depreciation required to re-equilibrate the foreign exchange market with lower foreign aid inflows is the elasticities approach, by which the depreciation of the nominal exchange rate required to attain a given balance of trade surplus or deficit is calculated using base level exports and imports and estimates of elasticities of import demand and export supply.

The supply of exports and demand for imports are assumed to depend only on nominal prices, and cross-price effects do not exist. The approach is straightforward: a change in the (nominal) exchange rate raises the price of exports and imports, inducing a decline in import demand and an increase in export supply according to the relevant elasticities.

Defining the trade balance (in foreign currency terms), B as

$$B = PX^w \bullet X - PM^w \bullet M \tag{1}$$

---

[2] Until the trade liberalization of 1992, foreign exchange for imports was allocated through the system of import licensing.

and assuming that world prices of importables and exportables are fixed (PX^w is price of exports; X is exports, PM^w is price of imports, and M is imports), the change in the trade balance dB arising from a devaluation is:

$$dB / dE = (1 / E) \bullet PX^w \bullet X \bullet \varepsilon_x - PM^w \bullet M \bullet \varepsilon_{m'} \qquad (2)$$

where ε_x is the elasticity of supply of exports and ε_m is the (compensated) price elasticity of demand for imports.[3]

Non-traded goods are left in the background in the elasticities approach. Implicitly, some nominal variable is held fixed, so that changes in the nominal exchange rate and nominal prices of importables and exportables translate into changes in relative prices. (If all nominal prices and incomes in an economy increase by the same percentage, there would be no change in relative prices and in theory, no change in any real variables.)

Dornbusch (1975) presents an explicit formulation for non-traded goods and the real exchange rate for the elasticities approach.[4] Assuming that the price of non-traded goods is held constant (or is used as the numeraire) and that exportables are not consumed domestically, the effect on the trade balance, given fixed world prices as above, is:

$$dB / dE = (1 / E) \bullet [PX^w \bullet X \bullet \varepsilon_x - PM^w \bullet M \bullet (\varepsilon_{m'}^* + \eta_m)] / (1 - a\eta_m), \qquad (3)$$

where ε_m^* is the compensated price elasticity of demand for imports, η_m is the income elasticity of demand for imports, and a is the budget share of imports in total demand: $a = M/Y$. The term $a\eta_m$ is thus equal to the marginal propensity to consume imports, $\partial M/\partial Y$ or m:

$$a \bullet \eta m = M / Y (\partial M / \partial Y)(Y / M) = \partial M / \partial Y = m. \qquad (4)$$

Thus, the total effect of the exchange rate change is determined by the total price elasticity of demand for imports, $\varepsilon_m = \varepsilon_m^* + \partial_m$, and the marginal propensity to consume importables out of total income. Equation (3) reduces to (2) when m equals zero and the total price elasticity of demand is used in the denominator.

The above adjustment for income effects is especially important for the case of Mozambique, since foreign aid funds a large share of national expenditures and because the marginal propensity to consume imports out of foreign aid is high.[5] In other words, foreign-aid-financed imports do not simply substitute for imports that would otherwise be imported commercially.

Aid-financed imports can have another effect: they may supply intermediate and capital goods which can increase current and future domestic

[3] A derivation of the formula is found in Dorosh and Bernier (1994).
[4] See Dorosh and Bernier (1994: Appendix 2) for a formal presentation of the effects of a change in foreign capital inflows on the real exchange rate.
[5] The degree of substitutability of foreign-aid-financed imports for commercial imports is also a key parameter in the analysis of the effects of counterpart funds on the money supply and inflation (see Roemer 1989).

production and real incomes. The level of foreign capital inflows may be especially critical for firms accustomed to preferential access to foreign exchange in the transition from a controlled economy to a liberalized market economy. To model these effects fully, however, we would need a more complete specification of domestic production, including intermediate input use.

12.2.3. *Empirical estimates*

Table 12.1 presents estimates of the effects of a reduction in foreign capital inflows on the equilibrium real exchange rate using the simple elasticities approach. The base levels for the calculations are the 1991 levels of imports and exports; the real exchange rate depreciations shown correspond to a reduction in foreign capital inflows by 61 percent, from 51 to 20 percent of 1992 GDP. Ideally, the import demand and export supply elasticities would be estimated econometrically, but detailed data on trade flows, tariffs, and domestic prices (with which to estimate implicit tariffs) are not available. As an alternative, sensitivity analysis is performed using a range of parameter values reported for econometric estimates for developing countries (Khan and Reinhart 1990). Price elasticities of import demand are varied from 0.1 to 0.5 and a conservative range of export supply elasticities (0–1.0) is chosen.[6]

The table illustrates two major points. First, the effects of changes in the export supply elasticity are smaller than the effects of changes in the price elasticity of import demand. This is because the level of imports, equal to 78.1 percent of GDP in 1991, is much larger than the level of exports (27 percent of GDP in 1992). Second, with income effects of a reduction in capital inflow not fully accounted for, the required depreciation of the real exchange rate is very large. Using the mid-range value for the price elasticity of import demand of 0.3 and a conservative estimate of the export supply elasticity of 0.7, reductions in foreign capital inflows from 51 to 20 percent of GDP would result in a real depreciation of 74 percent, holding trade policy and other factors constant.

Table 12.2 shows the changes in the real exchange rate when income effects of a decline in capital inflows are more fully taken into account. Compensated price elasticities of import demand vary from 0.1 to 0.3 and export supply elasticities range from 0.7 to 1.3. Marginal propensities to import (out of additional income) also vary, from 0.4 to 0.6.[7] Again, no change in trade policy (implicit tariff rates or export taxes), is modeled.[8]

---

[6] Khan and Reinhart (1990) report a range of 0.7–1.3 for econometrically estimated export supply elasticities.

[7] Khan and Reinhart (1990) report ranges of compensated price elasticities of import demand of 0.1–0.5, and 0.7–1.3 for export elasticities of demand. Reported income elasticities of import demand range from 0.7 to 1.3.

[8] The implied import demand elasticities for the various combinations of compensated price and income elasticities are given in Dorosh and Bernier (1994: Appendix Table 1).

Table 12.1. Mozambique: real exchange rate depreciation resulting from reduced capital inflows

	Import Demand Elasticity (% depreciation)		
	0.1	0.3	0.5
Export supply elasticity			
0.0	398	133	80
0.3	196	99	66
0.7	117	74	54
1.0	89	62	47
Memorandum items			
Target trade deficit/GDP	0.2		
1992 exports (bn metacais)	721		
1992 imports (bn metacais)	2086		
1992 GDP (bn metacais)	2670		
Trade deficit/GDP	0.511		

Source: IMF (1992), and authors' calculations.

The values in the first row of Table 12.2 (with the marginal propensity to import equal to zero) replicate results using the simple elasticities approach. As before, the depreciation resulting from the reduction in capital inflows with price elasticities of export supply and import demand equal to 1.0 and 0.3, respectively (the elasticity case), is 62 percent.[9] At the other extreme, if the marginal propensity to import out of foreign capital inflows is unity, then a cutback of foreign aid inflows will require no real exchange rate depreciation, since imports will drop the same amount as capital inflows with no price adjustment necessary. This is the case where the imports financed by foreign aid are totally non-substitutable for other commercial imports. Marginal propensities to import are typically 0.2–0.3, but, given the large share of imports in total expenditures in Mozambique (52 percent in 1992), the marginal import propensity is likely to be larger, on the order of 0.4–0.6.[10]

Given the above range for marginal import propensities, the real exchange rate depreciation required to restore equilibrium with a reduction in capital

[9] Note that the compensated and uncompensated price elasticities of import demand are equal in this case, since the marginal propensity to import (and therefore the income elasticity of demand) are zero.

[10] The marginal propensity to import $\partial M/\partial Y = (\partial M/\partial Y)(Y/M)(M/Y) = \eta \cdot a$, where M is imports, Y is income or expenditures, η is the income (expenditure) elasticity of import demand $(\partial M/\partial Y) * (Y/M)$, and a is the average budget share (M/Y). Given $a = M/Y = 0.5$, and η between 0.9 and 1.3, m is 0.45–0.65.

Table 12.2. Mozambique: real exchange rate depreciation resulting from reduced capital inflows (including income effects)

	Elasticites (% depreciation)		
	Low	Medium	High
Marginal propensity to import ($\partial M / \partial Y$)			
0.0	196	90	62
0.4	117	54	37
0.5	98	45	31
0.6	78	36	25

Memorandum items
Target trade deficit/GDP = 0.2
Low elasticities: Export supply elasticity (ε_s) = 0.3;
    import price elasticity (compensated) $\eta_m^* = 0.1$
Medium elasticities: (ε_s) = 0.7, $\eta_m^* = 0.2$
High elasticities: (ε_s) = 0.1, $\eta_m^* = 0.3$

Sources: IMF (1992), and authors' calculations.

inflows to only 20 percent of 1992 GDP ranges from 25 percent with relatively elastic export supply and import demand to 117 percent under assumptions of highly inelastic price responsiveness. Using the mid-range guesstimates for price elasticities and a marginal propensity to import of 0.5, the required depreciation is 45 percent.[11]

Of course, a cutback in foreign aid inflows of this magnitude (as well as the large real exchange rate depreciation) imply massive changes in the economy which are by no means captured in a simple model based on trade elasticities. The parameter estimates chosen are borrowed from other developing countries and in general are estimated from considerably smaller changes in prices, imports and exports than those assumed here. A recovery in domestic production after peace is established would itself bring about significant changes in the economy. Nonetheless, the point of this exercise is to understand the direction and broad magnitudes of changes in real exchange rates under various scenarios. Despite the uncertainties regarding parameters and supply effects, it is clear that a cutback in foreign aid inflows without other changes in policy or external conditions would lead to substantial real exchange rate depreciation, perhaps on the order of 30 percent or more.

[11] Note that the implied price elasticity of import demand is high (0.7, on the upper end of the reported range of 0.4–0.7), despite a conservative estimate of 0.2 for the compensated price elasticity of import demand because of the large marginal propensity to import (0.5).

12.3. *The Multi-Market Model*

Changes in the real exchange rate affect prices, supply, and demand of commodities throughout the economy. In addition, agricultural policies, trade restrictions, and other government policies, as well as non-economic factors such as weather, all impact on markets, in particular on agricultural and food markets. To analyze the effects of policy changes and external shocks on supply and demand for agricultural commodities, household food consumption, and real incomes, we develop a multi-market model, designed to capture the major interactions across commodity markets.[12]

12.3.1. *The data and descriptive statistics*

The base data for the model consist of estimated levels of consumption expenditures by households, production, trade, and prices for the eight commodities included. Household expenditure estimates (e.g. volumes and quantities) in urban areas are derived from the 1991–1992 Food Security Department/Cornell Food and Nutrition Policy Program integrated survey of 1816 households in Maputo. Data on expenditures and incomes for rural households are considerably less certain, and are derived from sectoral level data on production and producer prices, as well as the data on expenditure patterns of the urban poor. Results are given in Table 12A.1.

The integrated household survey was conducted over a seven month period, October 1991–April 1992. The multi-purpose survey was designed to collect detailed information on household structure, consumption, prices, incomes, labor market activities, morbidity, child nutrition and feeding practices, and housing characteristics. The sample was a self-weighted random sample of households in greater Maputo (including Maputo City, Matola, and Inhaca).

12.3.2. *Model structure*

Eight commodities are included in the model: yellow maize, white maize, rice, wheat, export crops and vegetables (including fruits, roots and tubers, and pulses), meat (including fish and other food not listed above), and non-agriculture. All are produced domestically except yellow maize and wheat, and all are traded internationally, although trade in vegetables and meat is very small and is fixed exogenously in the model. Households are divided into three groups: Maputo non-poor, Maputo poor, and "rural" (the rest of the population of the three southern provinces of Maputo, Inhambane, and Gaza).

---

12 See Braverman and Hammer (1986) for a formal presentation of a multi-market model in another African context. Further details concerning the model construction are also found in Dorosh and Bernier (1994).

The model determines the level of domestic production of agricultural commodities given rural prices; non-agricultural production is fixed exogenously. Rural prices are linked to urban consumer prices by a fixed marketing margin.[13]

Consumption of both urban and rural households is a function of household income and consumer prices. (For rural households, the consumer price is equal to the producer price.) Non-agricultural output is fixed and non-agricultural income varies with the price of non-agricultural goods in the model.[14] Agricultural incomes are determined by quantities produced and their prices.

The method by which prices are obtained varies according to whether the commodity is traded or non-traded. For traded goods, the domestic price level is determined by world prices and the exchange rate. Net imports adjust so that total supply equals demand.[15] For non-traded goods (vegetables and meat), net imports are set to the base level of imports, and the model solves for the consumer price that clears the market, equating supply and demand.

For traded goods, consumer prices are linked to border prices by the exchange rate, tariffs, marketing costs, and, in cases where the official consumer price is fixed, rents. For commodities where the level of net imports is not fixed, rents are zero and the consumer price is determined by the border price. The level of net imports adjusts to equate supply and demand. For yellow maize, which is imported in fixed amounts under foreign aid agreements, the quantity of net imports is fixed, the consumer price adjusts to equate supply and demand, and rents are earned by those able to buy at the official border price and sell at the market clearing price.

The numeraire of the model is the price index of non-traded goods, which is computed from the price of non-traded agriculture (vegetables and meat) and non-traded non-agricultural goods. The exchange rate adjusts so that exogenous foreign capital inflows equal the excess of import demand over export supply. Given the fixed price index of non-traded goods, the nominal exchange rate is equivalent to the real exchange rate.

[13] The marketing margin is fixed as a constant percentage markup between rural and Maputo prices.

[14] An alternate assumption would be to fix non-agricultural income in real terms, with the overall price level used as the deflator.

[15] World prices are themselves endogenous, depending on the choice of elasticity of export supply parameter. An export supply function from the rest of the world is included, with Mozambique's import price positively related to the level of its imports reflecting higher marketing costs associated with smuggling larger quantities of goods across borders:

$$M_i = M0_i \cdot [1 + \varepsilon_i^m \cdot (PW_i/PW0_i - 1)].$$

For goods that are traded freely on international markets, such as export goods and rice, the elasticity of export supply ε_i^m is made very large, so that the world price is essentially fixed. For goods such as white maize, which is traded across land borders, this elasticity may be less than infinity, but still greater than zero. In all the simulations presented in Section 12.3, ε_i^m is made very large and world prices are exogenous.

12.3.3. Model parameters

The major sets of parameters that influence the behavior of the model are supply elasticities and demand parameters. The former derive mainly from estimates from other countries and theoretical restrictions on the matrix of parameters (symmetry of cross-price elasticities of supply and zero homogeneity). Own-price elasticities of supply range from 0.1 to 0.4. The demand parameters derive from econometric estimates using the urban survey data. The methodology, discussed in Dorosh, del Ninno, and Sahn (1994), involved estimating a system of equations in an Almost Ideal Demand System (AIDS) framework (Deaton and Muellbauer 1990).

Perhaps the most important findings implied for the demand parameters is that for the poor, yellow maize is an inferior good, with an income elasticity of −0.571 (Appendix Table 12A.2), and that the cross price effects between yellow and white maize grain are small.[16] In fact, it was found that an increase in yellow maize price results in a small decline in white maize consumption. This is explained by the dominance of the income effect. More specifically, while the positive compensated elasticities (not shown) indicate that the two commodities are indeed net substitutes, the income effect dominates in the Slutsky decomposition to result in the uncompensated effect being negative.

12.3.4. Poverty line

In addition to the behavioral parameters discussed above, another key model parameter is the level of income that distinguishes the urban poor and non-poor. The poverty line for Maputo, discussed in detail elsewhere (del Ninno and Sahn 1994), is derived using the system of demand discussed above to identify the income level below which a household can be expected not to achieve an adequate level of food energy intake based on normative standards.[17,18]

In the simulations, we employ the demand model to estimate the equivalent income for different vectors of prices which are also endogenized in the model. In other words, we estimate a new level of income that will

16 Different budget shares for the poor and non-poor were used to calculate the different elasticities used in the model, although, in recognition of space limitations, only the results for the poor are shown.

17 See Osmani (1982) and Foster, Greer, and Thorbecke (1984) for a more complete discussion of the methodology employed. While shortcomings with this method are acknowledged, for the most part they revolve around the difficulty in making comparisons of poverty levels across space and time where there are shifts in activity levels, household characteristics, tastes, and wealth. These problems are not germane to this exercise. For a more complete discussion of the merits and limits of the approach used to set the poverty line, see Ravallion (1993).

18 The level of consumption that we chose for our normative standard is 2500 calories per adult equivalent. In addition, we also defined an ultra-poverty line, which will be used in the next section, based on an intake of 2000 calories per adult equivalent.

enable the household to achieve the same level of money metric utility prior to policy change that generates a new vector of prices. Furthermore, recognizing that income is a function of prices in the model, the model also adjusts the vector of nominal household incomes in conjunction with arriving at new levels of equivalent incomes that correspond to the policy changes modeled.

12.4. *Policy Simulations*

In this section, a number of simulations using the multi-market model are presented. The first set of simulations examines the effects of economy-wide changes in policy or economic conditions. Changes in the level of foreign aid inflows leading to a real exchange rate depreciation, rural recovery, and a combination of the two scenarios are modeled. Next, we analyze the effects of increased yellow maize imports, a policy designed to increase food consumption and incomes of the poor in Maputo. For this simulation, sensitivity analysis of key assumptions in the model structure and parameters are performed to test the robustness of the policy implications. Finally, we extend the multi-market analysis to address the question: how would the calorie consumption and budget shares of each household below the poverty line change if the prices and incomes changed according to the model simulations? We further determine how the head count and depth of poverty measures change in the population as a result of the price shifts and aggregate income changes derived from the model.

12.4.1. *Real exchange rate depreciation*

Simulation 1 models the effect of a reduction in net foreign exchange inflows of 20 percent which lead to a real depreciation of 25.1 percent (Table 12.3). As a result, real prices of tradable goods rise by the same percentage in general. Higher prices for these goods reduce demand and spur increased production so that net imports of these goods fall. Imports of white maize fall by 33.0 percent. Imports of rice and wheat fall by 5.5 and 11.4 percent, respectively, while exports of agricultural products rise by 3.4 percent.

Production of tradable goods rises significantly. White maize production increases by 2.6 percent, rice production increases by 1.4 percent, and export crop production increases by 3.4 percent. Agricultural incomes rise in real terms, but non-agricultural incomes fall in terms of overall purchasing power as prices of tradable goods rise. Real incomes of the urban poor and non-poor fall by 0.9 and 2.5 percent, respectively. Rural incomes are essentially unchanged, rising by 0.2 percent, as the decline in real non-agricultural income offsets the gains in agricultural income.

These simulation results imply that a cutback in foreign aid with the ensuing real exchange rate depreciation is likely to increase real agricultural

Table 12.3. Mozambique: real exchange rate depreciation, rural recovery, and food aid simulations

	Simulation 1: Real exchange rate depreciation	Simulation 2: Rural recovery	Simulation 3: Simulations 1 and 2 combined	Simulation 4: Increased food aid by 15%
Production				
White maize	2.59	21.75	24.91	0.10
Rice	1.43	21.75	23.49	0.12
Export crops	3.41	23.53	27.74	0.23
Vegetables	1.40	14.89	16.50	-0.45
Meat	-0.06	19.50	19.44	0.37
Consumption				
Yellow maize total	0.00	0.00	0.00	8.98
Urban non-poor	1.69	-15.97	-14.51	0.82
Urban poor	-1.63	15.44	14.03	28.71
Rural	0.00	0.00	0.00	0.00
White maize total	-9.03	1.37	-7.70	-0.21
Urban non-poor	-9.49	1.59	-8.04	1.46
Urban poor	-9.65	0.81	-8.94	-0.92
Rural	-8.79	1.36	-7.42	-0.73
Rice	-4.48	10.63	5.66	-1.77
Wheat	-11.41	10.13	-2.40	2.51

Real incomes			
Urban non-poor	-0.92	8.95	0.20
Urban poor	-2.53	13.63	3.63
Rural	0.22	11.54	-0.07
Yellow maize price	14.35	-25.73	-37.07
Non-agricultural goods price	8.89	6.15	0.43
Exchange rate	25.10	0.00	-0.36
White maize price	25.10	0.00	-0.36
White maize imports	-33.04	-40.73	-0.86

Source: Mozambique model simulations.

incomes and thus benefit or at least not severely harm the rural population. Urban groups are likely to suffer more.

It should be noted that the model simulation is only a partial equilibrium result. Non-agricultural output is held fixed in the model and thus private non-agricultural incomes are likewise fixed in terms of the price of non-agriculture. Moreover, the government sector is not modeled and there is no direct linkage between inflows of foreign capital and changes in aggregate demand. Thus, the negative effects on real incomes may well be overstated.

12.4.2. *Rural rehabilitation*

With the end to the civil war and the re-establishment of rural security in Mozambique, it is hoped that many *deslocados* will be able to return to rural areas and begin farming again. Some of the effects of such an occurrence are modeled in simulation 2. Agricultural production is exogenously increased by 20 percent, leading to shifts in prices and incomes. The final increase in agricultural production is determined endogenously by the model.

The large increase in agricultural production leads to reduced net imports for traded crops and lower prices for non-traded crops. Exports of agricultural products rise by 23.5 percent in this simulation and imports of rice increase by 8.7 percent as the direct impact of increased domestic supply is offset by the gains in demand arising from increased real incomes.[19] White maize production increases by 21.8 percent, resulting in a 40.7 percent drop in white maize imports.

Real incomes of the urban poor and non-poor rise by 13.6 and 9.0 percent, respectively, as a result of lower prices for non-traded agriculture, with only a 6.2 percent increase in the price of non-agricultural consumer goods. Rural real incomes rise by 11.5 percent, less than the 20 percent increase in agricultural output because the price of non-tradable goods falls and because the gain in non-agricultural real incomes is small.

This simulation does not capture many other likely impacts of rural rehabilitation including likely increases in non-agricultural rural production and changes in the real exchange rate arising from massive shifts in production. The major thrust of the results is clear, however: that is, urban households also benefit from rural rehabilitation as food prices of non-tradable goods fall. These benefits for Maputo households materialize only if marketing linkages between rural producers and the Maputo markets function well so that the additional local production can reach the city. Moreover, the importance of markets runs both ways. Azam and Faucher (1988) provide evidence that the availability of consumer goods in rural areas is an important factor promoting agricultural marketed surpluses.

---

[19] Note also that local production of rice accounts for only 43.8 percent of total rice consumption in the 1991 base data, the rest being supplied by imports. Thus, a 20 percent increase in local production represents only an 8.8 percent increase in total supply (if imports are unchanged).

12.4.3. *Real exchange rate depreciation and rural recovery combined*

In simulation 3, the combined effects of a real exchange rate depreciation and rural recovery are combined. The result is large increases in real incomes for all households. Rural households gain most (11.9 percent), as the benefits of the real exchange rate depreciation add to the gains from the rural recovery. The total gain in export crop production is 27.7 percent, compared with only 16.5 percent for non-tradable agriculture (vegetables, roots and pulses). The gain for the urban poor is again larger than for the urban non-poor as a 15 percent decline in the yellow maize price, arising from demand shifts toward meat and rice, has a larger positive effect on their real incomes.

12.4.4. *Market liberalization and food aid imports:* *sectoral level outcomes*

In addition to the issues of exchange rates and rural recovery discussed above, another concern that arises in the context of reform is the implications, particularly for the urban poor, of market liberalization and the reduction in the level of food aid. In the mid-1980s, the government instituted a system of food rationing in Maputo and Beira, the Novo Sistema de Abestecimento (NSA). This was designed as a way of ensuring food security, which relied on the food aid provided by donors. More specifically, a system was set up where consumers could purchase subsidized yellow maize grain, yellow maize flour, rice, and sugar. The food aid was consigned to state-run enterprises at far below world market prices. These enterprises were supposed to distribute the commodities to licensed shops, which in turn were supposed to sell it to cardholders at administered prices. (See Alderman, Sahn and Arulpragasam 1991 for a more complete discussion of the NSA.)

In practice, by the early 1990s the system of food rationing was not meeting its intended food security objectives. In the first place, only two-thirds of the households in Maputo actually had ration cards. Lower-income households, as well as households headed by migrants and heads with less education had a lower probability of having a card. But even more troubling is the fact that, despite official prices being one-half to one-third lower than parallel market prices, in practice this was not of great benefit to either the poor or the non-poor, neither of whom had access to the rationed products at official prices. This finding is illustrated by the fact that only 20 percent of the cardholder households relied exclusively on the ration system for yellow maize grain, with an additional 8 percent consuming from the subsidy scheme in combination with other market and non-market sources (Table 12.4). For yellow maize flour, the comparable figures were 6 percent relying exclusively on the ration system, and 5 percent relying on the ration system in combination with other markets. For rice and sugar, only 25 and

Table 12.4. Mozambique: share of cardholder and all households consuming commodities distributed through the NSA and the source of products consumed (%)

Commodity	Share of all households consuming product	Share of consuming households by source of product					
		Parallel market only	Off-ration, retail shops only	Ration system only	Ration system and other sources[a]	Other sources[b]	Total
Yellow maize grain							
Cardholders	37.1	39.5	21.4	19.8	8.1	8.8	100.0
All	34.3	47.2	20.1	13.8	5.6	13.3	100.0
Yellow maize flour							
Cardholders	45.7	70.7	9.0	6.2	5.4	8.7	100.0
All	44.1	73.3	9.5	4.1	3.6	9.5	100.0
Rice							
Cardholders	92.7	47.6	14.9	5.6	19.4	12.5	100.0
All	90.5	54.9	15.3	3.7	12.9	13.3	100.0
Sugar							
Cardholders	96.6	56.6	13.6	5.7	13.4	10.7	100.0
All	95.0	61.9	14.7	3.8	8.8	10.9	100.0

[a] These include ration shops in combination with one or more of the following: parallel market, off-ration from retail shops, gifts, and own-production.

[b] These include any combination of two or more of the following: dumbanengue, loja, gifts, and own-production.

Source: Sahn and Desai (1994).

20 percent, respectively, of households who had cards made any purchases at the ration shops. Putting together the information on the frequency of participation in the ration system, and the mean quantity of off-take, we found that for yellow maize grain only 7.6 percent of the food aid that was supposed to be sold by the ration shops was actually purchased through the ration system. The comparable figure for yellow maize flour, also supplied in the form of food aid supposedly destined for official markets, was only 3.0 percent. The vast majority of product for all rationed commodities, instead of being sold through the ration system, was diverted to the *dumbanengue*, the open air, unlicensed parallel market, where prices are determined by supply and demand, and thus are significantly in excess of administered prices. In addition, off-ration purchases from retail shops were also important sources of product. For maize, retail shop prices were just slightly higher than the administered prices, while for rice and sugar they were nearly the same as parallel market (i.e. *dumbanengue*) prices (Sahn and Desai 1994).

The diversion of food aid from official to open markets, where prices rather than quantities clear markets, suggests that the social costs of abandoning the food subsidy system will be minimal for some, and imperceptible for most households, since they are already primarily reliant on the parallel markets. Furthermore, by eliminating the rationing scheme, the enormous rents that accrued to traders receiving products at the official price and marketing them on the open market at high prices could instead accrue to the Treasury. This would greatly enhance the budgetary position of the government, without a commensurate loss of consumer welfare.

The compelling arguments for eliminating the ration shops have been coupled with arguments that food aid is increasingly inappropriate in a liberalized system of food marketing, even in urban Maputo, especially in light of the possible disincentive effects on agriculture. The counter-argument is that, even though food aid is diverted from official to parallel markets where it is sold at a price determined by supply and demand, it has proven instrumental in feeding poor and rich alike. Thus, food aid to the cities should be continued, or even increased, since it represents a important means of combating what remains a serious poverty problem. This call to maintain or increase the use of large donations of food aid has become particularly contentious, however, as the prospects for peace raise concerns over the possible disincentive effects of food aid on rural producers.

In order to gain some insight into the appropriateness of continued food aid as a means of alleviating poverty in an environment where prices will be determined by supply and demand, and where liberalized markets transmit price signals to consumers and producers alike, we ran simulation 4, where yellow maize imports destined for the Maputo market are increased by 15 percent over the base 1991 level. It is assumed that these imports are funded through additional foreign aid inflows, and that there is no rationing of product through official channels.

The results indicate that the price of yellow maize falls sharply as the 15 percent increase in yellow maize supply is sold on the Maputo market. The demand parameters indicate that, in contrast to the urban poor, the urban non-poor households are not very responsive to price changes, (i.e., their demand is price inelastic), so the increased supply of yellow maize must be consumed almost entirely by the urban poor. The yellow maize market clears with a 37.1 percent decrease in the yellow maize price and a 28.7 percent increase in yellow maize consumption by the urban poor.

Changes in the yellow maize price affect markets for other commodities as well, by increasing the demand for wheat, meat, and non-agricultural goods and lowering demand for substitutes for yellow maize: white maize, rice, and vegetables, roots, and pulses. Prices of non-tradable vegetables, roots, and pulses tend to fall because of reduced demand, thus shifting production incentives away from these goods, and towards tradable agricultural commodities and non-agricultural production. Production of white maize, rice, and export crops rises slightly (by 0.1–0.2 percent), while production of vegetables, roots, and pulses falls by 0.5 percent.

This gain in production takes place in spite of a small appreciation of the real exchange rate (a reduction in the price of tradables relative to non-tradables). Because the cost of the incremental yellow maize imports is small on a macroeconomic scale, $2.1 million,[20] the real exchange rate appreciates by only 0.4 percent. (Although the price of vegetables, roots, and pulses falls, this is outweighed by an increase in the prices of other non-tradable goods such as non-agricultural goods and meat.)

The increase in yellow maize imports thus has little effect on the white maize market. The 37.1 percent decrease in the yellow maize price, in itself, leads to only a 0.9 percent decrease in demand for white maize by the urban poor (and a 1.5 percent increase in demand by the urban non-poor).[21] The small real exchange rate appreciation only slightly lowers white maize prices relative to prices of non-tradable goods in general. But the decline in the price of vegetables, roots, and pulses as demand shifts towards yellow maize outweighs the effects of the real exchange rate appreciation and actually leads to a slight increase in incentives for production of white maize. White maize imports fall by 0.9 percent.

The net effect of the changes in prices and agricultural production is to increase aggregate real incomes of the urban poor by 3.6 percent, mainly because of lower food prices. Aggregate real incomes of the urban non-poor increase only slightly since these households consume relatively little yellow

[20] The 15 percent increase in yellow maize imports is equal to 11,500 tons of yellow maize, valued at $182.6 per ton c.i.f.

[21] Unlike the poor, for the urban non-poor yellow maize is not a net substitute for white maize. The low magnitude of the positive compensated elasticity is offset by the income effect, so the uncompensated cross-price elasticity of white maize demand with respect to the price of yellow maize is slightly negative.

maize. Because the terms of trade shift against rural households as the prices of vegetables, roots, and pulses, and grains fall, real incomes of rural households fall very slightly (−0.1 percent).

Sensitivity analysis was performed to ensure that key parameters, even those empirically estimated, would not alter the conclusions reached. More specifically, we experimented with the following: changing the own-price elasticity of demand for yellow maize by urban non-poor from 0.0 to −0.2; changing the cross-price elasticity of demand for white maize with respect to a change in the yellow maize price from −0.046 to 0.150 for the poor and from 0.004 to 0.200 for the urban non-poor; making the non-poor more price-responsive; assuming that white maize imports are fixed in the short run (owing to problems in information flows or other market imperfections), which would mean that any decline in white maize demand would affect domestic demand, and thus prices, not the level of imports; and changing the original assumption that yellow maize sold in Maputo is consumed only by urban households, so that the maize finds its way into rural markets throughout the southern region of the country, implying that the same price holds for all consumers. This last assumption provides an upper bound for the magnitude of the effects of leakages outside the Maputo market, not only because it assumes outflows of aid from Maputo to the countryside, but also because the yellow maize marketed is sold in rural areas at the same price as in Maputo. In reality, even if there were market flows to the countryside, prices in rural markets would be higher than in Maputo because of the large transport and other marketing costs. In addition, we experimented with various combinations of the above.

Results indicated that, under a wide range of assumptions on model parameters and structure, a policy of open market sales of increased yellow maize imports is an effective self-targeting mechanism for increasing real incomes of the Maputo poor, without having any significant deleterious effects on rural producers. Several key parameters drive this result. First, there are the own-price elasticities of demand for yellow maize, which are larger in magnitude for the poor than for the non-poor. Second, Maputo comprises a relatively small share of regional consumption of white maize. Third, cross-price effects on the white maize market are small, even with a change from the econometrically estimated parameters and fixed white maize imports. Fourth, white maize is a traded commodity, whose price is set internationally. And fifth, a large share of Maputo's white maize consumption is from commercial imports, which will bear the brunt of any decrease in demand for white maize (Dorosh, del Ninno, and Sahn 1994).

12.4.5. *Market liberalization and the effect of food aid on poverty*

Given the price and nominal income changes derived above, we next examined the implication for levels of poverty. Only results for the simulation 4 where changes in prices dominate the results, are analyzed here. No

Table 12.5. Mozambique: poverty level and depth for alternative policy simulations

	Poverty line (meticais per capita/month)	Poverty Indexes		
		Head count	Poverty gap	FGTP$_2^a$
At current prices				
Poverty line	32,400	33.96	9.70	3.99
Ultra poverty line	21,380	12.99	2.90	1.08
15% increase in yellow maize imports				
Poverty line	26,944	22.82	5.87	2.29
Ultra poverty line	16,610	5.46	1.22	0.45

[a] FGTP$_2$ is described in Foster, Greer, and Thorbecke (1984).
Source: Model simulations.

results for the effects of a real exchange rate depreciation and rural recovery (simulations 1–3) are presented, since for these scenarios large changes in non-agricultural incomes among urban households (not captured in the multi-market model) are likely to have significant effects on income distribution within the poor and non-poor household groups.

As a result of an increase in the supply of yellow maize imports of 15 percent, calorie intake of the poor will increase by 12.4 percent. As with the earlier simulations, this increase is due primarily to a rise in the consumption of yellow maize, the least expensive source of calories. The substitution effects increase the calorie shares for yellow maize from 44.1 percent in the base case to 50.4 percent, under the import scenario found in simulation 4.

How do the above exogenous price and supply changes of yellow maize affect the actual head count of poor and the depth of poverty?[22]

Prior to intervention (the base case), 34.0 percent of the households are below the poverty line, and 13.0 percent are classified as ultra-poor (Table 12.5). The average depth of poverty is 9.7 percent. We find that a 15 percent increase in yellow maize imports will reduce the number of poor from 34.0 to 22.8 percent of the population, reflecting a 16.8 percent decline in the level of income required to be classified as poor. This drop in the share and depth of poverty, once again, is attributable to a decline in the prices, which reduces the corresponding level of income required to achieve the normative calorie consumption levels. But even more dramatic is the decline in the share of ultra-poor, falling from 13.0 to 5.5 percent of the population while the ultra-poverty gap falls to just 1.2 from 5.9 percent. This reflects a 22.3 percent fall in the ultra-poverty line.

[22] For a discussion of the poverty measures employed, see Foster, Greer, and Thorbecke (1984).

12.5. *Conclusions*

With the restoration of peace and the end of the drought, reductions in foreign aid inflows from their levels of the early 1990s are likely. In this chapter we have shown that the real exchange rate depreciation resulting from a decline in aid inflows will tend to improve agricultural price incentives and spur production. If, in addition, non-price factors such as the return of refugees to their farms, rebuilding of marketing infrastructure, and adequate rainfall prevail, a substantial increase in agricultural production may occur, with substantial benefits for rural households in terms of higher incomes and for urban households in terms of lower food prices.

Before an anticipated recovery of the agricultural sector occurs, however, there remains a need for targeted poverty alleviation programs in urban areas, particularly in Maputo. In this context we have explored the effectiveness of the food subsidy program designed to provide a minimum food ration to the poor. We found that access to ration cards is slightly greater for lower income households and for households where the head has more education and has resided in Maputo, and in his or her current domicile, for a longer period of time. Given that the NSA ration prices for yellow maize grain and flour, and usually rice, were substantially lower than on the open market, one would expect that, even if serving only two-thirds of the households, any move to liberate markets and eliminate price controls would have deleterious effects on the food security of the poor. In practice, however, this was not the case. The level of off-takes from the rationing system was low, as consumers, rich and poor alike, were dependent primarily upon the non-rationed market sources. Practically speaking, the parallel markets have become the main source for the food aid products, supposedly destined for the NSA ration scheme, which are instead being diverted to open markets.

The compelling arguments for the elimination of the NSA, however, should not be viewed as arguments for the elimination of food aid which was the source of the product supposedly destined for the official markets. In particular, it is clear that the food aid, although not reaching the intended beneficiaries through the NSA, is nonetheless feeding them through the parallel market channels. The implication of the paramount importance of the *dumbanengue*, supplied largely through the illegal diversion of food aid, is that the continuation of the provision of food aid remains essential, given the supply shortfalls that are a consequence of the internal conflict and shortage of foreign exchange earnings for commercial imports. In fact, the multi-market simulations, using parameter estimates derived from the 1991/92 Maputo household survey, show that, since yellow maize is a self-targeting commodity, an effective short- to medium-run poverty alleviation strategy would be to increase the quantity of food aid imports sold in the Maputo market above the levels of 1991/92 as a means of raising calorie intake.

These results therefore suggest that the provision of food aid in the future should also be tied to a rationalization of the system through which the commodities are marketed, with specific attention being given to eliminating the rents that accrue to those procuring the food aid at low official prices and selling them at the parallel market price instead of the official price. This suggests adopting a strategy such as auctioning the food aid, or a similar mechanism that will facilitate a unification of the market where prices do the clearing.

Of perhaps equal importance to the effectiveness of a commercial food aid program in Maputo is the evidence that marginal changes in the level of yellow maize sales in Maputo *vis à vis* the levels of 1991/92 are unlikely to have major effects on rural price incentives. This is because in normal years a large share of white maize consumed in Maputo is likely to be imported from Swaziland and the Republic of South Africa, especially in the form of flour. Even if the cross-price effects of lowering yellow maize imports depressed demand for white maize, the most immediate impact would be to reduce white maize imports, before reducing the domestic price of white maize.

However, even if increased domestic production replaced imported white maize, the simulations show that the decline in the price of white maize is likely to be small. The urban poor's budget shares to white maize products is trivial relative to aggregate domestic supply, so there is little sector-wide impact of a decline in their demand for white maize. Conversely, the urban non-poor who consume white maize not only are small consumers of yellow maize, but also are not nearly as price-responsive. Thus, their demand for white maize also changes little. Third, it is also the case that the areas proximate to Maputo are not major maize producing regions. As long as the yellow maize food aid is initially sold in Maputo, the potential for substantial amounts of yellow maize to be transported and marketed in producing areas is not in the realm of financial feasibility.

Finally, the above benefits of supplying yellow maize food aid to Maputo do not necessarily apply to other urban centers in Mozambique and almost certainly do not apply to rural areas in postwar Mozambique in years of normal harvest. Demand characteristics of non-Maputo households are not necessarily the same as those in Maputo. In isolated markets, impacts of substitution effects on prices may be larger as flows of white maize and other commodities from outside the region are limited. Addressing these issues fully would require data on rural household incomes and expenditure patterns, as well as information on market flows of commodities, a high priority for further data collection efforts.

Structural adjustment in Mozambique has brought about much-needed market liberalization, particularly for agricultural commodities. As the country recovers from drought and civil war, prospects of increased agricultural food production and stable food supplies are good. Yet, there remains a role for government intervention in alleviating poverty in Maputo through open market sales of yellow maize food aid, at least during the transition period before real incomes and food security improve significantly. Because yellow maize is self-targeting and the disincentive effects on production are likely to be small, continued food aid sales in Maputo have relatively low costs. This limited intervention, working through the market for the delivery of food aid to its intended consumers, does much to alleviate the costs of adjustment to the urban poor.

Appendix 12.1. Equations of the Mozambique Multi-market Model

Supply, demand, and incomes

(1) $\quad X_i = X0_i \bullet \prod_j (PP_j / PP0_j)^{\varepsilon^t_{i,j}}$

(2) $\quad UC_{i,h} = UC0_{i,h} \bullet \prod_j (PC_j / PC0_j)^{\varepsilon^D_{i,j,h}} \bullet (Y_h / Y_h 0)^{\eta_{i,h}}$

(3) $\quad RC_i = RC0_i \bullet \prod_j (PP_j / PC0_j)^{\varepsilon^D_{i,j,h}} \bullet (Y_h / Y_h 0)^{\eta_{i,h}}$

(4) $\quad CD_i = \sum_h UC_{i,h} + RC_i$

(5) $\quad YNAG_h = YNAG0_h \bullet (PC_{NA} / PC0_{NA})$

Prices

(6) $\quad YAG_h = \sum_i PP_i \bullet X_i \bullet w_{ih}$

(7) $\quad PM_i = PW_i \bullet ER \bullet (1 + tm_i)$

(8) $\quad M_{it} = M0_{it} \bullet [1 + \varepsilon^M_{i,t} \bullet (PW_{it} / PW0_{it} - 1)]$

(9) $\quad PC_{it} = PM_{it} \bullet (1 + trmarg_i)$

(10) $\quad PC_i = PP_i \bullet (1 + marg_i)$

Model closure

(11) $\quad X_i = C_i - M_i$

(12) $\quad PC_{NA} = PNT_{NA}\alpha^{NA} \bullet [ER \bullet (1 + TM_{NA}) \bullet PWM_{NA}]^{(1 - \alpha^{NA})}$

(13) $PNT = PNT_{NA}^{\beta_1^{NT}} \bullet PC_{vegs}^{\beta_2^{NT}} \bullet PC_{meat}^{(1-\beta_1^{NT}-\beta_2^{NT})}$

(14) $ER = ER0 \bullet CHFSAV \bullet (1-\beta)/[X \bullet (1+\varepsilon_x) - P_m M \bullet (1+\eta^m)]$

Variables of the model

CD_i	Total consumption of good i
$CHFSAV$	Change in foreign savings (dollars)
ER	Exchange rate (meticais/dollar)
M_{it}	Net imports of tradable good it
PC_i	Consumer price of good i
PM_{it}	Border price of tradable good it (meticais)
PNT	Nontraded good price index for non-traded goods
PP_i	Producer price of commodity i
PW_{it}	World price of tradable good it (dollars)
RC_i	Rural consumption of good i
$UC_{i,h}$	Urban consumption of good i by household h
Xi	Output of sector i
Y_h	Income of household h
YAG_h	Agricultural income of household h
$YNAG_h$	Non-agricultural income of household h

Source: Dorosh, Del Ninno, and Sahn (1994)

Appendix 12.2.
Base data and model parameters

Base data on supply and demand of the commodities in the Mozambique multi-market model are given in Table 12A.1. Table 12A.2 presents the demand elasticities estimated for urban poor households in Maputo. These same elasticities are also used for rural poor households.

Table 12A.1. Mozambique: base data on supply and demand, 1991

	Domestic production	Imports	Marketing	Total supply	Maputo non-poor	Maputo poor	Maputo total	Rural South consumption	Total demand
Value (bn metacais)									
Yellow maize	0.0	491.2	39.4	530.6	156.2	161.5	317.7	212.9	530.6
White maize	150.7	169.7	76.7	397.0	182.9	63.5	246.4	150.7	397.0
Rice	37.2	423.1	262.2	722.5	548.0	145.4	693.4	29.1	722.5
Wheat	0.0	439.0	439.0	877.9	633.5	154.7	788.2	89.7	877.9
Vegetables	1,505.2	798.0	913.2	3,216.4	2,073.8	588.6	2,662.4	554.0	3,216.4
Meat	916.1	266.7	716.4	1,899.2	1,513.2	199.0	1,712.2	187.0	1,899.2
Export crops	48.0	−100.8	52.8	0.0	—	—	—	—	—
Non-food	465.0	10,767.0	—	11,232.0	2,777.0	326.0	3,103.0	387.0	11,232.0[c]
Total	3,122.2	13,253.8	2,499.6	18,875.6	7,884.5	1,638.8	9,523.3	1,610.4	18,875.6[c]
Quantity ('000 metacais)									
Yellow maize	0.0	128.1	—	128.1	37.7	39.0	76.7	51.4	128.1
White maize	79.3	38.4	—	117.7	28.5	9.9	38.4	79.3	117.7
Rice	10.1	57.4	—	67.5	47.1	12.5	59.6	7.9	67.5
Wheat	0.0	106.7	—	106.7	77.0	18.8	95.8	10.9	106.7

[a] Rural South production only.
[b] Includes marketing margins.
[c] Includes non-household demand.

Sources: FSC/CFNPP household survey; Mozambique unpublished national accounts table; IMF (1992); and authors' calculations.

Table 12A.2. Mozambique: urban poor and rural demand elasticities

Quantity	Price							Income
	Yellow maize	White maize	Rice	Wheat	Vegetables	Meat	Non-agriculture	
Yellow maize	-0.552	0.013	0.080	0.014	0.213	0.034	0.026	0.172
White maize	0.004	-0.856	0.016	0.051	0.232	-0.102	0.145	0.510
Rice	0.019	-0.012	-0.668	0.143	-0.237	-0.276	-0.020	1.052
Wheat	-0.065	0.009	0.152	-1.077	-0.047	-0.097	0.228	0.897
Vegetables	0.054	0.031	-0.034	0.013	-0.617	-0.043	0.045	0.551
Meat	-0.166	-0.095	-0.321	-0.176	-0.491	-0.219	-0.514	1.980
Non-agriculture	-0.138	-0.018	-0.033	0.010	-0.189	-0.078	-0.977	1.423

Source: Mozambique multi-market model.

References

Alderman, Harold, David E. Sahn, and Jehan Arulpragasam. 1991. "Food Subsidies in an Environment of Distorted Exchange Rates: Evidence from Mozambique." *Food Policy*, 16(8): 395–404.

Azam, J.P., and J.J. Faucher. 1988. "The Case of Mozambique." In *The Supply of Manufactured Goods and Agriculture Development*, J.C. Berthelemy, J.P. Azam, and J.J. Faucher, eds. Development Centre Papers. Paris: Organization for Economic Cooperation and Development.

Braverman, Avishay, and Jeffrey S. Hammer. 1986. "Multimarket Analysis of Agricultural Pricing Policies in Senegal." In *Agricultural Household Models: Extensions, Applications, and Policy*, Inderjit Singh, Lyn Squire, and John Strauss, eds. Baltimore, MD.: Johns Hopkins University Press.

Deaton, Angus, and John Muellbauer. 1990. "An Almost Ideal Demand System." *American Economic Review*, 70: 312–326.

del Ninno, Carlo, and David E. Sahn. 1994. *The Determinants of Poverty and Income Distribution in Mozambique*. Working Paper No. 56. Ithaca, NY: CFNPP.

Dornbusch, Rudigier. 1975. "Exchange Rates and Fiscal Policy in a Popular Model of International Trade." *American Economic Review*, 65: 859–871.

Dorosh, Paul, and René Bernier. 1994. *Agricultural and Food Policy Issues in Mozambique: A Multi-Market Analysis*. Working Paper No. 63. Ithaca, NY: CFNPP.

—— Carlo del Ninno, and David E. Sahn. 1994. *Food Aid and Poverty Alleviation in Mozambique: The Potential for Self-Targeting with Yellow Maize*. Working Paper No. 50. Ithaca, NY: CFNPP.

Foster, J., Joel Greer, and Erik Thorbecke. 1984. "A Class of Decomposable Poverty Measures." *Econometrica*, 52: 761–766.

International Monetary Fund. 1992. *Republic of Mozambique: Statistical Annex.* Washington, DC: IMF.

Khan, Mohsin S., and C.M. Reinhart. 1990. "Relative Price Responsiveness of Foreign Trade in Developing Countries." Washington, DC: International Monetary Fund. Unpublished.

Osmani, S. 1982. *Economic Inequality and Group Welfare*. New York: Oxford University Press.

Ravallion, Martin. 1993. "Poverty Comparisons." Washington, DC: World Bank. Draft.

Roemer, Michael. 1989. "The Economics of Counterpart Funds Revisited." *World Development*, 17: 795–808.

Sahn, David E., and Jaikishan Desai. 1994. *The Emergence of Parallel Markets in a Transition Economy: The Case of Mozambique*. Working Paper No. 53. Ithaca, NY: CFNPP.

13

Do Cheap Imports Harm the Poor?
Rural–Urban Tradeoffs in Guinea

Jehan Arulpragasam and Carlo del Ninno

13.1. *Introduction*

The markets for food commodities have been profoundly affected by structural adjustment in Guinea. Trade, exchange, and price reform have jointly altered both the quantities of food items available on domestic markets and the prices at which they are sold. The reform of Guinea's exchange regime, together with concurrent liberalization of trade, have led to a massive influx of food imports into the country. Between 1983 and 1992 the volume of rice imports increased by 227 percent, the volume of wheat flour increased by 81 percent, sugar by 472 percent, and cooking oil by 517 percent. In the five years between 1987 and 1992 alone, the volume of rice imports increased by 109 percent, the volume of wheat flour by 18 percent, sugar by 18 percent, and cooking oil by 125 percent. Data on foreign exchange sales show that the value of total food imports increased by 16 percent between 1989 and 1992. Food import purchases accounted for approximately 50 percent of total private sector foreign exchange demand during this period.

The escalating level of food imports in the context of Guinea's open economy has raised several concerns related to the consequences of liberalized exchange and trade policies on the welfare of urban and rural households alike. First, the exchange rate devaluations integral to adjustment and stabilization focus on raising the prices of tradable commodities relative to non-tradables. Such devaluations are expected to be especially detrimental to urban households which tend to consume larger shares of imported goods than do rural households. The vulnerability of urban households to exchange rate devaluation, furthermore, is likely to have increased with liberalization in Guinea owing to the increase in levels of imported foods consumed nationally.

Second, whereas exchange and trade reforms are generally expected to benefit rural households in the context of adjustment programs, in the short term these reforms may be acting at cross-purposes in Guinea. Whereas the relative increase in the price of tradable commodities resulting from devaluation is expected to be beneficial for rural producers by increasing rural revenues from tradable crops, most rural smallholder households in Guinea (with the exception of coffee-producing smallholders in the forest) have yet to engage in significant production for the export market.[1] The mean percentage of household revenue from export crops nationally is 3.3 percent. For example, only 0.1 percent of rural households in Guinée Maritime cultivate coffee and only 1.9 percent cultivate pineapple, the two export crops for which data are reported (GOG 1991a). Rather, in Guinea (internationally) nontraded crops continue to be the primary source of agricultural revenue. The relative price movement from devaluation, by lowering the relative price of non-tradable commodities, is expected to increase the demand for these commodities and thus to stimulate domestic production of nontraded domestic crops and possibly the rural agricultural incomes derived therein. In Guinea, however, the primary crop is locally produced rice. The large-scale increase in the volume of food imports in general and rice imports in particular as a result of reform has led to increasing concerns that any benefit to rural households from devaluation is being negated by a fall in the demand for locally produced rice and for other staples as a result of import liberalization.

This chapter will examine the consumption consequences on the poor of altered relative prices of traded and nontraded food items. In particular, the chapter will concentrate on how policies that change the relative price of imported versus domestically produced crops consequently affect sectoral outcomes and household incomes, as well as consumption, food-energy intake, and poverty among urban households specifically. The chapter concentrates particularly on the debate over rice, which is the primary domestically produced crop, the single largest import commodity, and the most important food consumed in Guinea.

13.2. Policy Reform and Food Imports

13.2.1. Exchange rate and tariff liberalization and food imports

The severance from a fixed exchange rate regime has probably been the most dramatic and important reform undertaken by Guinea, owing to the magnitude of the initial devaluation as well as to the subsequent move to a more flexible exchange rate regime. The nominal exchange rate experienced a 17-fold devaluation between the last quarter of 1985 and the first quarter of 1986, bringing the official rate roughly in line with the parallel rate.

---

[1] The lagging production for the export market is due in part to reasons associated with infrastructural constraints to the export market and to weak international markets (Arulpragasam and Sahn 1994).

Over the course of the reform period, the Guinea franc has been gradually devalued in nominal terms on the basis of a managed peg. Since 1986, the nominal exchange rate devaluations averaged 16.6 percent a year. The central bank, the Banque Central de la République de Guinée (BCRG), effectively sets the nominal rate after assessing net private sector foreign exchange demand each week (through a misleading process named a foreign exchange "auction") and with an eye on net public sector supply of foreign exchange.[2]

Reform of the exchange rate regime was also accompanied in 1986 by swift changes in Guinea's trade and tariff regime. Whereas under the First Republic all official trade was the purview of parastatal import and export entities, since 1984 the state monopoly on trade was terminated. The private sector has since been permitted to import all commodities. Import licensing was abolished in 1986. Importers, moreover, are now permitted to purchase foreign exchange from the BCRG.[3] The tariff structure was also initially dramatically simplified in 1986. The basic tariff rate was set at 10 percent (with certain food items facing a tariff as low as 2 percent) as opposed to the dispersed and generally higher tariffs that had been in place prior to reform. The tariff on rice was initially eliminated altogether.

As mentioned above, the reform of exchange and trade policies of 1986 has resulted in a rapid increase in the volume of food commodity imports. In particular, the availability of rice, the primary crop produced and the main staple in Guinea, has increased markedly with reform primarily as a result of the increase in rice imports following liberalization. In the five years from 1984 to 1989, rice imports (commercial and food aid) doubled, increasing by close to 100,000 metric tons. Aggregate estimates show that between 1977 and 1979 (during the era of state-controlled import) imported rice accounted for only about 20 percent of rice available domestically; between 1989 and 1992 (after liberalization) it accounted for close to 40 percent of total domestic rice supplies. Whereas per capita rice availability nationally averaged close to 50 kilograms per year between 1980 and 1982, it had risen to an average of about 70 kilograms per capita per year between 1989 and 1990.

The increased availability of imported rice has certainly meant increased consumption of imported rice in rural areas. Of the approximately 87 percent of Guinée Maritime farm households that purchase rice, 68 percent

---

2 An effort is also made to maintain a degree of stability within the foreign exchange markets and to keep the official rate within a few points of the parallel rate. More recently the central bank has also aimed at meeting target annual devaluation rates agreed upon with the World Bank and the IMF.

3 Permission to access the auction initially required prior approval by the BCRG of the type, quantity, and value of goods to be imported. In 1989, however, the advanced verification of import declarations was abolished. Moreover, since 1992, exporters have been allowed to retain up to 25 percent of their foreign exchange denominated export receipts on deposit for use on authorized transactions.

purchased imported rice and 36 percent consumed only imported rice by the late 1980s (GOG undated (a)). This percentage has risen recently, with imported rice now constituting an estimated 8 percent of total household budgets in the coastal region (Appendix Table 13A.1).[4]

Imported staples, including imported rice and bread made from imported wheat flour, are even more important in urban areas relative to the rest of the country. Descriptive statistics from a recent household survey in urban Conakry (CFNPP/ENCOMEC 1990–1992) provide important data on consumption and expenditure patterns. Imported rice dominates the diet in Conakry. On average, imported rice constituted 60.1 percent of the quantity of all starchy staples consumed per capita and 83.8 percent of all rice consumed (Table 13.1). These percentages were even higher among the poor. The poor consume as much as 68.4 percent of their starchy staples in the form of imported rice. Expenditure shares on imported rice also reveal the greater importance of imported rice in the food consumption pattern among poorer households. The expenditure share to imported rice increases from 2.4 percent among the richest quintile to 6.8 among the middle quintile and to 12.3 percent among the poorest quintile. The consumption of imported rice, moreover, is widespread in Conakry. Among all households, 79.4 percent consume some imported rice; among poor households, 87.7 percent consume some imported rice (Arulpragasam 1994b).

Besides imported rice, bread made from imported wheat flour is the next most important staple consumed in Conakry. Bread represents 4.1 percent of total expenditures among all households, and in quantity terms it constitutes 17.3 percent of all starchy staples consumed. As is the case with imported rice, bread too constitutes a higher expenditure share the poorer the quintile. The consumption of bread is widespread in Conakry, where, like elsewhere in urban Africa, taste as well as preparation time dictate the choice of bread over other staples. Indeed, 88.2 percent of all households consume bread, with no marked difference in the percentage of households consuming bread among poor and nonpoor households (Arulpragasam 1994b).

Imported staples, in the form of imported rice and bread combined, thus constitute as much as 77.4 percent of the total quantity of starchy staples consumed in the capital and 84.5 percent of the total quantity of starchy staples consumed by the poor (Table 13.1). In contrast, locally produced staples account for only 22.6 percent of the total quantity of starchy staples consumed in the city. Local rice, the most important crop cultivated locally in terms of land allocation and production levels, constitutes only 1.5 percent of total expenditures among the average population in Conakry and

---

[4] Indeed, the price of imported rice is often lower than that of local rice throughout Guinea, although the discount for imported rice is lower in producing regions and in areas further from Conakry, lending credit to the argument that there is a quality premium paid for local rice (Arulpragasam and Sahn 1994).

Table 13.1. Guinea: consumption per capita of staple grains in Conakry, 1990/91

	Poor			Nonpoor			All		
	Metric tons	Kilograms per capita	% of total starchy staples	Metric tons	Kilograms per capita	% of total starchy staples	Metric tons	Kilograms per capita	% of total starchy staples
Imported rice	33.247	71.33	68.41	39.344	81.30	54.49	72.591	76.41	60.09
Local rice	4.291	9.21	8.83	9.721	20.09	13.46	14.012	14.75	11.60
Other grains, roots, tubers	3.222	6.91	6.63	10.084	20.84	13.97	13.306	14.01	11.02
Bread	7.838	16.82	16.13	13.051	26.97	18.08	20.889	21.99	17.29
Total staple grains	48.598	104.27	100.00	72.200	149.20	100.00	120.798	127.16	100.00
Population	466,070			483,930			950,000		

Sources: CFNPP/ENCOMEC survey; PNAFR (1993a); Ministere du Plan et des Finances/PADSE (GOG 1991a); Ministere de l'Agriculture et des Ressources Animales (GOG 1992b).

accounts for only 11.6 percent of the total consumption of starchy staples. Whereas the expenditure share to local rice is marginally higher among the poor relative to the nonpoor, in quantity terms local rice accounts for only 8.8 percent of total starchy staples consumed by the poor and 11.6 percent of staples consumed by the average population. In fact, only about 30 percent of Conakry's population consumes any local rice at all, choosing instead to consume most of their rice in the form of imported varieties. A similar story is evident in the case of other locally produced grains, roots, and tubers (such as sorghum, maize, millet, fonio, yam, and cassava). Whereas on average this commodity group accounts for 2.0 percent of total expenditures, their share of total starchy staples consumed ranges from 14.0 percent among the nonpoor to 6.6 percent among the poor.

While expenditure shares provide important insight into consumption patterns, data on food energy intake provide a more direct indication of welfare from the nutritional perspective. Table 13.2 presents daily per capita caloric intake and share of calories by commodity group across expenditure groups. Across the entire sample, the mean daily per capita caloric intake is 2348. The mean caloric intake in Conakry thus lies above the generally accepted minimum adult equivalent caloric requirement of 2200, or the per capita caloric requirement of 2000. However, while the nonpoor exceed these benchmark levels with a mean daily per capita caloric intake of 2796, the poor fall below this level with an estimated food-energy intake of 1721, pointing to the potential of serious undernutrition among the poor.

The source of households' caloric intake by commodity reflects the calorie prices of each commodity. Among the starchy staples, imported rice is in fact the cheapest source of calories. Rice commercially imported from Vietnam, Taiwan, Pakistan, and Thailand (riz Asiatique) is generally not parboiled, is of low quality (usually 35 percent broken), and is one-third cheaper on the Conakry retail market than locally produced rice (riz locale). The average caloric price of imported rice is also 280 percent cheaper than other cereals, roots, and tubers. While bread is more expensive a source of calories than local rice, it too is 53 percent cheaper a calorie source than the category of other local staples. Imported rice accounts for 31.8 percent of caloric intake among all households and 42.3 percent of caloric intake among the poor; bread accounts for 9.3 percent of caloric intake among all households and 9.1 percent among the poor (Table 13.2).

Households with higher expenditure levels generally derive an increased share of calories from non-rice sources owing to the diversification of the diet away from rice. Oil, fish, and vegetables are the other important sources of calories in the diet.

13.2.2. Policy concerns

The high level of national cereal imports and the high share of food imports in household consumption have raised policy-makers' concerns on

Table 13.2. Guinea: daily per capita caloric intake by commodity group in Conakry, by quintile (%)

| | Poverty classification | | Per capita expenditure quintile | | | | | All |
	Poor	Nonpoor	1	2	3	4	5	
Local rice	5.85	6.81	6.31	5.53	8.08	6.94	6.55	6.74
Imported rice	42.27	28.27	44.51	39.82	34.01	30.30	21.15	31.81
Other grains, roots, tubers	3.68	5.38	3.37	4.45	5.45	5.49	5.54	5.05
Bread	9.12	9.66	8.67	9.28	8.86	8.96	10.09	9.28
Meat	2.17	4.59	1.73	2.52	3.59	4.22	5.77	3.94
Fish	9.60	8.02	9.84	9.23	9.16	8.79	7.01	8.56
Milk and dairy	0.31	0.96	0.24	0.39	0.79	0.77	1.24	0.78
Vegetables	6.87	6.51	6.68	7.06	7.42	6.53	5.87	6.62
Fruit	2.38	4.78	2.34	2.79	3.48	4.52	6.06	4.19
Butter and oil	10.92	10.61	10.89	11.35	11.03	12.22	10.39	11.16
Spices	0.88	0.95	0.84	0.89	0.94	1.08	1.07	0.99
Sugar	3.40	3.56	3.17	3.55	3.52	3.16	3.91	3.51
Beverages	0.04	0.18	0.02	0.06	0.07	0.13	0.36	0.16
Food away from home	2.51	9.72	1.38	3.09	3.60	6.89	15.00	7.22
Caloric shares	100.00	100.00	100.00	100.00	100.00	100.00	100.00	100.00
Calories	1720.72	2796.30	1500.36	1930.07	2292.69	2687.94	3330.57	2348.32
N	636	1089	345	345	345	345	345	1725

Source: CFNPP/ENCOMEC survey data.

two separate counts. First, it has been argued that the increased levels of imported cereals are acting as a disincentive to the production of all local staples and particularly of local rice. The availability of cheaper imported rice on rural retail markets has raised the controversial argument that the adjustment policy of rice import liberalization constitutes a food security threat to the nation by transmitting a production disincentive to domestic rice farmers (Hirsch 1986; Filippi-Wilhelm 1987; and Thenevin 1988). Indeed the price of imported rice is often lower than that of local rice throughout Guinea, with any discount for imported rice being lower in producing regions and in areas further from Conakry (Arulpragasam and Sahn 1994). Imported rice, it is argued, may thus be substituting for domestic rice at the cost of real incomes among rural producers. Reflecting similar concerns raised elsewhere in West Africa, this argument makes a case for raising tariffs on imported rice and other food commodities in Guinea. In its most extreme form, the argument is made that a tariff on imports can increase production, raise rural real income, and, by increasing the supply of domestic foods, result in little if no loss in consumption and calorie intake among urban consumers. Additionally tariffs on imports would contemporaneously be one of the easiest ways in which to address problems related to weak levels of government revenue generation.

It was in response to these concerns that the Government of Guinea (GOG) has taken measures aimed specifically at reducing rice imports and their sale in the interior. Alarm at the sudden increase in the volume of imported rice, together with the imperatives of generating increased government revenue, have resulted in the gradual escalation of tariff levels in Guinea since initial trade liberalization in 1986. While rice imports were initially free of tariff charges upon import liberalization in 1986, an import tariff of 10 percent was in place on rice by 1990. Import tariffs on most other food items meanwhile were raised from 2 percent in 1986 to 10 percent in 1988, and to 20 percent in 1990.

Several non-tariff restrictions on the exchange market contributed further to increasing the real price of imports. Indeed, even after liberalizing internal trade in 1986, the GOG continued to require approval (*autorisations de transit*) prior to moving imported rice into areas of the interior. In 1989 a restriction was instituted prohibiting the use of credit for the purchase of foreign exchange. In 1990 a further requirement was imposed that importers make an advance deposit of 20 percent of the value of consumer imports ordered in order to access foreign exchange from the central bank. This policy was focused specifically at restricting the increase in rice imports, and it severely restricted demand, given the working capital constraints of smaller importers. While the latter requirement was eliminated in 1992, the tariff on rice was increased from 10 to 20 percent, and tariffs on all other food imports were increased from 20 to 30 percent. More recently there have been additional proposals for further tariff increases on rice for the purposes of both tariff revenue generation and for the protection of local production of rice (Caputo 1991).

13.3. A Multi-Market Model

The dramatic increase in the level of food imports arising from trade liberalization in Guinea, together with concurrent devaluations and fluctuations in the real exchange rate arising from exchange and trade policy changes, have thus increasingly exposed the welfare of Guinean consumers and producers to external sector policies and prices. In the context of Guinea's new, open economy, changes in world prices, the exchange rate and tariffs can be expected to have important effects on the price of food, on the demand for local produce, and thus on the real incomes of urban and rural households as well as on their food consumption levels. Increased levels of food imports resulting from liberalization may be harming domestic agriculture; rice imports may be acting as a disincentive to local rice production. Alternatively, tariff policies to protect domestic agriculture may harm both urban and rural consumers. Indeed, among poor households, even marginal changes in food prices could severely compromise welfare as measured by food consumption and food energy intake. It is specifically to address and analyze these issues, introduced above, that a multi-market model is developed in this section. The modeling draws upon the multi-market techniques outlined in Dorosh, del Ninno, and Sahn (1994); Braverman, Hammer, and Ahn (1987); and Braverman and Hammer (1986).

13.3.1. Model structure

The model is regional in focus in that it is calibrated on data from Guinée Maritime.[5] The model consists of 13 commodity groups. Among these, six commodities are traded internationally, namely imported rice, bread (wheat), sugar, beverages, oil, and nonfoods. There is some domestic production of the latter two commodities; the other four internationally traded goods are imported but are not produced domestically.[6] The model also includes seven domestically produced commodities: local rice, other domestic staples, meat and dairy, fish, vegetables, spices, and fruits. Included as "other domestic staples" are roots, tubers, and cereals such as maize, fonio, sorghum, millet, manioc, yam, and taro. These commodities are treated as

---

[5] In addition to the fact that data for this region are most reliable (including, for example, estimations of regional imports, the level of rural consumption of imported food, and price data), it is in this region that the pervasiveness of imported food is greatest and that the issue of imported rice competing with local rice most relevant.

[6] Although there is clearly some production of beverages domestically, reliable aggregate production data are unavailable. Moreover, in Conakry and Guinée Maritime, imported beverages form a substantial part of the market in value terms.

nontraded goods that are produced domestically and are not traded inter-nationally.[7,8]

The model determines equilibrium prices, production quantities, and im-port levels in the market for each good. (The model equations are outlined in Appendix 13.1.) In the case of traded food commodities, imports adjust to meet demand and clear the market at the fixed international price multiplied by the exchange rate and a fixed trading margin.[9] In the case of nontraded domestic food commodities, domestic prices adjust to clear the market. In the case of the nonfood commodity, price is computed as a weighted average of its traded and nontraded components. The price of nontraded goods is the model's numeraire and is composed of a weighted share of nontraded agricultural and non-agricultural price indices. With the nontraded price index being fixed, the nominal exchange rate is in effect the real exchange rate. The nominal exchange rate can adjust to equate foreign capital inflows to the trade deficit.

The model determines production levels. While non-agricultural produc-tion is fixed exogenously, supply of each of the domestically produced food commodities is determined endogenously at equilibrium rural prices. Rural producers inherently select a production pattern that optimizes agricultural profits based on prices. Rural prices are related to urban prices by the factor of a fixed transformation and marketing margin.

Consumption levels, a primary focus of this model, are based on house-hold income levels and household response to consumer prices. Households are divided into three groups: urban (Conakry) poor households, urban (Conakry) nonpoor households, and rural (Guinée Maritime) households. Urban (Conakry) household incomes are derived in their entirety from non-agricultural sources. Non-agricultural (nonfood) output and incomes vary with the price of the non-agricultural commodity in the model, the level of nonfood output being fixed. In addition to non-agricultural incomes, rural households derive an important share of their incomes from agricultural production. The agricultural incomes of rural households are determined by the quantities of agricultural goods they produce and each good's respective rural producer price.[10,11]

Demand and supply parameters are essential to determining the model

---

7 There are some net "domestic imports" into Guinée Maritime of three of the domestically produced goods. In particular, meat and dairy, vegetables, and spices are imported domes-tically from Haute and Moyenne Guinée. These domestic import levels are fixed exogenously.

8 The percentage of frozen imported meat and fish consumed in Guinea is not considered important enough to treat separately.

9 In the case of cooking oil, which is imported and produced domestically, imports adjust to meet the excess demand over domestic supply. As a simplifying assumption, domestic and imported cooking oil are treated as a homogeneous product.

10 Rural consumer and producer prices are assumed to be the same, and both are a fixed margin of urban consumer prices.

11 For a more detailed discussion of the theoretical and operational structure of the model, see Arulpragasam (forthcoming).

outcomes. The demand elasticity matrices utilized in the model for the populations of the urban poor, the urban nonpoor, and rural households are based on parameters estimated from the CFNPP/ENCOMEC dataset. The Almost Ideal Demand System (AIDS) was estimated using a three-stage least square econometric model in which per capita expenditure was treated as an endogenous variable and instrumented accordingly. Symmetry and homogeneity restrictions, as dictated by demand theory, were imposed on the system. A sample of 1557 households was used for the demand estimation.[12] Since some of these households did not consume certain commodities, the selectivity bias among the sample of consumers, inherent in the decision to consume or not to consume a given commodity, was corrected for using the estimated inverse Mills ratio as an instrument (Heien and Wessells 1990).

Supply parameters utilized in the model are derived from estimates from other countries, discussions with policy-makers, and theoretical restrictions on the matrix of parameters, namely symmetry of cross-price elasticities of supply and homogeneity of degree zero in prices.[13]

The multi-market model also requires base data for household consumption levels by household group, production levels by commodity, trade, and prices for each of the model's 13 commodity groups. These base sectoral data are derived from a variety of sources including available government sectoral statistics and studies, import statistics, and agricultural survey data.

13.3.2. *The poverty line and poverty measures*

Both the definition of urban household groups as poor and nonpoor and subsequent discussion on the effect of policy and exogenous changes on poverty dictate the determination of a poverty line. Here the poverty line is first normatively designated in terms of a threshold level of food energy intake.[14] The poverty line is then translated into money-metric terms by projecting, with the estimated demand parameters and for a given price vector, that level of per capita expenditures that would be associated with per capita consumption of the calorie-denominated poverty line. Utilization of a full demand system to determine the expenditure-level-designated poverty line has several advantages. The poverty line assigned in this manner reflects actual behavioral choices and thus indicates the utility level associated with a consumer's cost minimization at given prices. By the same token, this specification will permit an examination of the effect of price changes on the poverty line.

---

12 For greater detail on the sample and sample selection, see Arulpragasam (1994b), Arulpragasam and del Ninno (1993), and del Ninno and Sahn (1990).

13 For a more detailed description of the model and model parameters, see Arulpragasam (1994a).

14 A level of 2000 calories per capita is chosen as the food-energy-level-denominated poverty line.

Table 13.3. Guinea: AIDS estimated income and own-price elasticities of food commodities in Conakry

	Income elasticities			Own-price elasticities		
	Poor	Nonpoor	All	Poor	Nonpoor	All
Local rice	0.644	0.594	0.652	−1.893	−2.020	−1.874
Imported rice	0.338	−0.531	0.069	−0.592	−0.151	−0.455
Other coarse grains	1.069	1.068	1.062	−0.857	−0.859	−0.872
Bread	0.510	0.265	0.397	−0.673	−0.523	−0.604
Meat	1.317	1.230	1.239	−0.930	−0.955	−0.952
Fish	0.408	0.098	0.314	−0.727	−0.610	−0.692
Vegetables	0.515	0.308	0.460	−0.644	−0.510	−0.608
Fruit	1.152	1.102	1.114	−0.968	−0.980	−0.977
Butter and oil	0.467	0.227	0.396	−0.823	−0.751	−0.801
Spices	0.325	−0.092	0.193	−0.697	−0.522	−0.642
Sugar	0.381	0.070	0.248	−0.543	−0.319	−0.447
Beverages	1.584	1.323	1.420	−1.304	−1.171	−1.221
Nonfoods	1.473	1.374	1.437	−1.207	−1.066	−1.041

Source: Arulpragasam (1994a), from CFNPP/ENCOMEC dataset.

The welfare effect of a change in a set of prices can thus be measured as the amount of income by which consumers must be compensated so as to be as well off after the change as before. Thus, in the simulations to follow, a new poverty line can be computed for a new equilibrium vector of prices and real incomes generated by the multi-market model for any given simulated policy change.

With the estimation of a new poverty line, moreover, the effect of policy-induced price and income changes on poverty can also be examined. Three alternative poverty measures will be utilized to assess the effect of policy on poverty: the headcount index, the poverty gap index, and the Foster–Greer–Thorbecke (FGT) sensitivity index.

13.3.3. *Demand elasticities*

Imported rice has the lowest income elasticity[15] among staples and has the greatest variation across expenditure groups (Table 13.3); in fact, it is an inferior good among the nonpoor. The other commodities for which there

[15] Elasticities are computed using the formulas utilized by Blanciforti and Green (1983) and Laraki (1990) for the linear approximation of the AIDS model:

$$\varepsilon_{ik} = \delta_{ik} / w_i - \beta_i w_k / w_i \qquad \forall i \neq k$$
$$\varepsilon_{ik} = -1 + \delta_{ik} - \beta_i \qquad \forall i = k$$
$$a_i = 1 + \beta_i / w_i$$

is a notably higher income elasticity among the poor are bread, sugar, fish, and condiments (spices), other foods that constitute the "basic" diet among the poor in Conakry. The income elasticities for all other staples, furthermore, are much higher than those for imported rice.

The three commodities with the lowest (absolute value) own-price elasticities are three imported commodities. Imported rice, sugar, and bread have own-price elasticities of −0.455, −0.447, −0.604 respectively (Table 13.3). The relatively inelastic demand for these commodities reflects the fact that they are basic to the diet and are thus least responsive to price changes.

Most of the cross-price effects estimated by the model are relatively small.[16] Several cross-price elasticities, however, are quite important. Of greatest policy significance are the cross-price effects between local and imported rice. Not only are the two goods clearly substitutes, with positive compensated and uncompensated cross-price elasticities, but the effect of the price of imported rice on the demand for local rice is large. A 10 percent increase in the price of imported rice results in a 9.7 percent increase in the demand for local rice.[17] Increasing the price of imported rice through trade or exchange policies would thus be expected to result in a large shift in demand for local rice.

The large share of imported rice in the consumer budget results in large income effects associated with price changes of imported rice. The inverse relationship between the price of imported rice and the consumption of other grains, of roots and tubers, of meat and dairy products, and of nonfood items is due to the income effect dominating the substitution effects. In fact, the compensated (Hicksian) cross-price elasticities between these goods and imported rice are positive, indicating that they are pure substitutes of imported rice. However, increases in the price of imported rice do not result in net increases in consumption of these commodities because real income declines as a result of the higher price of imported rice. The same large income effects are also true of the cross-price relationships between bread and meat and dairy products as well as between bread and nonfood goods. Trade and exchange policies that increase the price of imported foods may therefore have net *negative* effects on the demand for many local non-tradables owing to income effects that are larger than substitution effects.[18]

---

16 For the complete matrix, see Arulpragasam and del Ninno (1993).

17 Conversely, a 10 percent increase in the price of local rice results in a 2.12 percent increase in the demand for imported rice.

18 The other strong cross-price effects to highlight are those associated with price changes of the nonagricultural (or nonfood) good. In particular, an increase in the price of the composite nonfood good decreases consumption of local rice, imported rice, other grains, roots, and tubers, fruits, and beverages. Once again, this inverse relationship is due to large negative income effects overriding positive substitution effects.

13.4. *Policy Simulations*

The multi-market model, in conjunction with estimated demand system parameters, permits a study of the consequences of tariff and exchange policies on consumers and producers. The sectoral outcomes of the multi-market model, moreover, can then be extended to analyze outcomes at the household level. Estimated demand parameters are utilized to examine the effect of policy-induced price and real income changes (derived from the multi-market model) on consumption and food-energy uptake among households. The focus is particularly on examining how expenditure and calorie shares and levels would be affected among the poor as a result of a given policy change. Moreover, utilizing the notion of compensated income variation discussed above, the analysis is extended to examining the effect of a given policy change on urban poverty.

Three sets of simulation results are presented in this section. The first set of simulations examines the effects of tariffs on markets, household welfare, and urban poverty. In particular, the focus will be on assessing the arguments for the imposition of a tariff on imported rice. The second set of simulations examines the sectoral and household level effects of exchange rate devaluation. Changes in the exchange rate and factors that affect the exchange rate alter household consumption patterns, food energy intake, and poverty. In this context the welfare effects of a reduction in capital inflow will also be examined. The final set of simulations examines the multi-market effects of two likely non-price sources of welfare improvement in Guinea. These are an increase in non-agricultural incomes and a reduction in domestic marketing margins for agricultural produce.

13.4.1. *Changing tariffs*

The argument for increased tariff levels on food commodities has centered both on the need to increase government revenues and on the need to protect domestic agriculture. The multimarket model can be used to examine how effective tariff policy can be in fulfilling these objectives.

Sectoral level outcomes. Simulation 1 in Table 13.4 demonstrates the sectoral effects of a 10 percentage point tariff increase on all imported commodities. In effect, this represents the actual increase in tariffs undertaken by the Government of Guinea over the period 1990–1993. The tariff on imported rice was increased from 10 to 20 percent, and tariffs on other food imports were increased from 20 to 30 percent.

The prices of all imported commodities increase as a consequence of the tariff increase. Households reduce their consumption of imported rice, wheat, cooking oil, and sugar. Urban poor households experience the sharpest reduction in their levels of consumption, reducing imported rice

Table 13.4. Guinea: simulated sectoral effects of tariff increase (% changes)

	Simulation 1: Increase all food tariffs by 10%			Simulation 2: Increase tariff on rice by 30%		
	Urban poor	Urban nonpoor	Rural	Urban poor	Urban nonpoor	Rural
Consumption						
Local rice	9.57	11.13	−0.24	13.27	15.47	0.39
Imported rice	−4.87	−0.30	−4.23	−15.04	−0.93	−14.58
Cereals, roots, tubers	−1.97	−1.88	0.06	−2.30	−2.15	0.20
Bread	−5.95	−5.26	−4.89	−1.00	−2.55	−0.41
Meat and dairy	−1.15	−0.19	0.09	−1.99	−0.44	0.20
Fish	0.04	−0.13	0.66	0.17	−0.66	1.04
Vegetables	−0.15	−0.62	0.41	−0.17	−0.92	0.80
Fruit	−0.39	−0.40	0.68	−0.26	−0.64	1.44
Butter, oil	−4.46	−3.27	−3.89	3.06	3.27	3.97
Spices	−0.07	0.57	0.23	−0.03	0.58	0.47
Sugar	−5.52	−4.79	−5.33	−2.11	−4.59	−1.21
Beverages	−14.32	−11.48	−12.98	−5.59	−2.79	−2.67
Nonfood	−2.26	−1.43	−0.98	−4.41	−2.74	−2.00
Production						
Local rice		1.12			2.19	
Cereals, roots, tubers		−0.31			−0.25	
Meat and dairy		−0.39			−0.56	
Fish		0.23			0.21	
Vegetables		0.04			0.18	
Fruit		0.12			0.39	
Butter, oil		1.89			−0.41	
Spices		0.47			0.73	
Consumer prices						
Local rice		3.86			7.36	
Imported rice		9.09			27.27	
Cereals, roots, tubers		−0.09			0.65	
Bread		8.33			0.00	
Meat and dairy		−1.96			−2.78	
Fish		0.91			0.84	
Vegetables		0.20			0.74	
Fruit		0.40			1.31	
Butter, oil		8.33			0.00	
Spices		2.40			3.68	
Sugar		8.33			0.00	
Beverages		8.33			0.00	
Nonfood		−0.34			−0.78	
Imports						
Imported rice		−2.30			−7.54	
Wheat		−3.11			−0.82	
Butter, oil		−4.89			4.32	
Sugar		−1.73			−0.85	
Beverages		−12.24			−3.13	
Nonfood		−1.86			−3.61	
Real incomes						
Urban poor		−2.18			−3.45	
Urban nonpoor		−1.18			−1.55	
Rural		−1.19			−1.55	
Food tariff revenue		57.46			72.44	

Source: Model simulations.

Simulation 3: Increase tariff on rice by 30% with increased rice production			Simulation 4: Decrease tariffs on rice by 10%			Simulation 5: Decrease marketing margins by 30%		
Urban poor	Urban nonpoor	Rural	Urban poor	Urban nonpoor	Rural	Urban poor	Urban nonpoor	Rural
44.02	48.18	23.45	−4.45	−5.18	−0.13	18.48	19.92	−2.14
−17.13	−6.57	23.31	5.02	0.31	4.87	−1.91	−4.80	6.10
−1.49	−1.36	1.33	0.76	0.71	−0.06	13.47	13.50	−1.72
−1.26	−3.28	−1.63	0.34	0.86	0.15	−0.16	−0.38	5.16
−2.18	−1.08	1.94	0.66	0.14	−0.05	3.80	3.59	−2.51
0.60	−0.01	0.53	−0.06	0.22	−0.34	−0.65	−0.96	1.40
0.21	−0.31	0.90	0.06	0.31	−0.26	4.06	2.84	−0.47
0.02	−0.77	2.59	0.08	0.21	−0.47	5.63	5.68	−2.57
−0.19	−1.70	0.19	−1.02	−1.09	−1.31	0.26	0.29	0.48
0.42	1.01	0.20	0.01	−0.19	−0.15	4.73	3.33	−1.75
−4.98	−9.19	−4.24	0.71	1.54	0.42	−1.91	−2.97	6.15
−6.15	−2.76	−0.91	1.88	0.94	0.93	−1.59	−0.71	15.00
−3.87	−2.39	0.83	1.47	0.91	0.69	−1.50	1.12	4.82
	−2.79			−0.73			0.56	
	0.82			0.09			1.12	
	−0.04			0.19			1.74	
	0.34			−0.07			0.06	
	0.49			−0.06			1.22	
	0.92			−0.13			1.73	
	0.35			0.13			−0.47	
	0.75			−0.24			0.81	
	−9.12			−2.44			−8.32	
	27.27			−9.09			0.00	
	1.91			−0.20			−15.91	
	0.00			0.00			0.00	
	−0.18			0.94			−2.71	
	1.38			−0.27			0.25	
	1.52			−0.24			−6.71	
	3.08			−0.42			−5.32	
	0.00			0.00			0.00	
	3.79			−1.22			−6.79	
	0.00			0.00			0.00	
	0.00			0.00			0.00	
	0.13			0.27			0.52	
	−11.89			2.52			0.30	
	−1.29			0.28			1.03	
	−0.73			−1.43			0.53	
	−2.02			0.29			0.48	
	−2.73			1.06			3.24	
	−2.14			1.21			3.00	
	−3.03			1.19			1.83	
	−1.35			0.52			1.61	
	−1.24			0.55			2.27	
	66.73			−26.85			0.87	

consumption by 4.9 percent, bread by 6.0 percent, cooking oil by 4.5 percent, and sugar by 5.5 percent.

As a consequence of the tariff increase, there is indeed a switch in demand to certain domestic crops, resulting in increased prices and production. Most important, the demand for local rice increases significantly in urban areas, by 9.6 percent among the urban poor and 11.1 percent among the urban nonpoor. The net increase in total demand for local rice stimulates an increase in the producer (and consumer) price for local rice by 3.9 percent, and instigates a 1.1 percent increase in local rice production.

Despite production gains, however, real incomes decline among all household groups as a result of the tariff increases. Although net nominal rural incomes increase marginally with the increase in domestic production and producer prices as a consequence of the enhanced tariff structure, the general increase in the level of consumer prices negates any real income increases even among rural households.

Simulation 2 in Table 13.4 examines, specifically, the effect of proposed increases in the tariff on imported rice by 30 percentage points.[19] Net consumption of imported rice falls by 10.3 percent. The higher price for imported rice, however, is indeed successful in increasing the consumption and production of local rice. Local rice consumption and production rise by a net 2.2 percent. In fact there is a marginal net increase in the consumption demand of all locally produced goods except for meat, other cereals, roots and tubers, and non-agricultural goods, all of which are luxury goods. However, the increase in demand for domestic crops following the tariff on imported rice drives up the consumer prices for all domestic crops. Together with the large tariff-induced increase in the price of imported rice, these price increases result in a substantial increase in houshold-specific consumer price indices.

Urban households experience marked declines in food consumption as a result of tariff-induced income and price changes. Rural households do not face the same fall in consumption as do urban households as a result of the tariff. The nominal incomes of rural households actually increase with tariff imposition as a consequence of increased agricultural incomes from increased demand, production, and producer prices of most domestic crops, and especially that of local rice. In addition to increased production of local rice, rural households increase their production of fish, vegetables, and spices.[20] Increased nominal incomes of 1.2 percent and higher import prices

[19] The simulation increases the tariff rate on imported rice from its 1990 base rate of 10 percent to 40 percent, a 27.27 percent increase. The consumer price of all other imported foods remain at their world prices.

[20] Meat and other cereals, roots, and tubers face a decline in production resulting from the decline in demand and prices for these luxury goods. Moreover, local rice production increases at a cost to the production of local palm oil as producers switch into rice and out of oil, the demand for which is satisfied by increased imported oil at the fixed world price.

result in marginal consumption increases of many domestic foods by rural households. The inflationary effects of a tariff on rice, however, are harmful to the real income of all consumers, including rural households. As a result of the tariff, urban poor households experience a 3.5 percent loss in real income. Moreover, inflation also completely erodes the marginal nominal income gain by rural households.

Only the government would experience any clear increase in real income as a result of the tariff. Despite a reduction in rice imports, the higher tariff level for imported rice would result in government food tariff revenues augmenting by 72.4 percent.

The effect of a tariff on imported rice on rural real income clearly is a consequence of already high levels of rural consumption of imported rather than local rice. What would be the prospect of a tariff on imported rice given higher initial levels of production and consumption of local rice? Simulation 3 in Table 13.4 demonstrates the effect of a 30 percent tariff on imported rice *after* a 30 percent increase in domestic production.[21] Even if domestic rice production were to reach higher levels to begin with, the imposition of a protective tariff on rice would still not improve household welfare of either rural or urban households as measured by real incomes.

Simulation 4 in Table 13.4 conversely examines the real income effects of a 10 percent *tariff reduction* on imported rice. The decrease in the price of imported rice increases consumption of imported rice among all households, and especially by the urban poor whose consumption of the commodity increases by 5.0 percent. Moreover, the reduction in the price of imported rice allows households marginally to increase their demand for some other imports such as bread and sugar as well as some domestic crops such as meat, dairy, and oil. Consumption of local rice decreases among all household groups, falling by 4.5 percent among the urban poor, but by only 0.13 percent among rural households. The fall in demand results in a 2.4 percent reduction in the price of local rice. Total production however declines by less than 1 percent.

Increased demand for non-agricultural goods drives up the price of non-agricultural goods and thus urban nominal incomes. Furthermore, the decline in the price of imported rice and the resulting decline in the consumer prices of many domestic crops results in additional gains to real incomes; real incomes of urban poor households rise by 1.2 percent as a result of the 10 percent tariff reduction. Moreover, despite nominal income losses to rural households, consumer price deflation results in real income gains even among rural households.

---

[21] Under optimistic scenarios, and given recent estimated growth rates in rice production, it may be argued that such an increase in production over the next few years is not so unrealistic. Also, some of the higher estimates of current rice production for Guinea are larger than the generally accepted base estimates by factors of 1.3 and above.

Table 13.5. Guinea: simulations of welfare effects on the urban poor

Poverty measures	Base run	Simulations				
		1	2	3	4	5
P_0	35.59	38.84	40.58	40.29	32.99	33.97
P_1	9.94	11.28	12.31	12.09	9.01	9.50
P_2	3.91	4.55	5.07	4.96	3.47	3.76

Effect on poverty and household consumption among the poor. While the above analysis examined sectoral level outcomes and consumption changes among aggregate household groups, the focus of this section is to examine the effect of the devaluation-induced price and income changes among the poor at the household level as well as the effect of these policy-induced changes on poverty. Table 13.5 examines how the sectoral effects of the various tariff policies discussed above translate into household level outcomes in terms of expenditure and food-energy consumption patterns among the poor, and how they affect the level and extent of poverty.

The concurrent increase in all imported food commodity tariffs by 10 percentage points reduces average per capita expenditure by 2.2 percent, but decreases daily per capita calorie consumption among the reference group of poor households by 4.2 percent, from 1720 to 1647. The higher prices of imported foods increase the expenditure shares but reduce the calorie shares that the poor derive from their cheaper staples, in particular from imported rice and bread. Instead, calorie shares are reallocated toward domestic foods that are more expensive sources of calories (such as local rice, fish, and vegetables) but whose relative price has declined as a consequence of the tariff increases. As a result of the decline in food-energy intake resulting from the tariffs, the poverty line (as measured by the expenditure level associated with the threshold calorie level given consumption behavior) increases, putting an additional 3.3 percent of all households below the poverty line as measured by P_0. The average poverty gap (or income shortfall from the poverty line), P_1, increases from 9.9 to 11.3; the P_2 Foster–Greer–Thorbecke sensitivity index increases by 16.5 percent, from 3.9 to 4.6.

The effect of increasing the tariff on rice alone by 30 percentage points is even more detrimental to food-energy consumption among the reference poor population. The tariff decreases the calorie intake share from imported rice from 46.9 to 43.3 while also causing the 3.5 percent fall in real incomes discussed earlier. The combined effects of decreased real income and substitution away from what used to be the cheapest source of calories signifies a 7.4 percent decrease in total daily per capita caloric intake among the reference group, to 1593. The lower real expenditure level, combined with higher prices, results in the expenditure-denominated poverty line increasing by 9.1 percent over the base poverty line. A 30 percent increase in the tariff on imported rice thus increases the number households under the poverty line from 35.6 to 40.6 percent of the total population. The average poverty gap, the P_1 index, increases from 9.9 to 12.3 (Table 13.5).

A *reduction* in the tariff on imported rice, on the other hand, would clearly contribute to poverty reduction. As a result of a 10 percent decrease in the tariff on imported rice, the number of households in poverty would decline from 35.6 percent of the total population in the base case to 33.0 percent after the 10 percent reduction in the rice tariff (Table 13.5, simulation 4).

Lowering the tariff on imported rice would thus be a simple and effective policy by which the government could increase real incomes in both urban and rural areas and also alleviate poverty. Moreover, even if increased tariffs were targeted to be a source of increased government revenue, rice should not be the commodity to target for tariff increases. There are other commodities that could shoulder a higher tariff rate so that tariff revenue would increase with less of an increase in poverty. Table 13.6 demonstrates the summary results of the effect of a 10 percent tariff increase on each of the imported commodities in the model on average real per capita expenditure and calorie levels, on poverty measures, and on government revenue. A tariff on rice, although increasing nonmining tariff revenues by 2.5 percent, has the biggest detrimental effect on average real per capita expenditure and calorie levels as well as on all poverty measures. The P_0 measure increases by 4.9 percent to 37.3 from a base measure of 35.6. A 10 percent increase in the tariff on oil would have the next largest effect on urban poverty, resulting in a 2.4 percent increase in P_0, and moreover it would increase nonmining tax revenues by only 0.9 percent. Placing a tariff on wheat flour would result in tariff revenue increases that approach the magnitude of increase from the rice tariff, but this policy would have a similar effect on urban poverty as would the tariff on oil.[22] A 10 percent tariff on sugar, in contrast, would result in tariff revenues that almost equal the magnitude of revenues from an equivalent rice tariff. Moreover, the poverty implications of a tariff on sugar are much less serious. A 10 percent tariff on sugar hardly affects the headcount index. If the government sees no option but to increase tariffs so as to increase revenues, an increase in the tariff on sugar, for example, would be as effective as a tariff on rice in raising revenues and would have less of a detrimental effect on poverty than would a tariff on rice. Decreasing the tariff on rice while elevating the tariff on sugar, for example, would in fact assist in poverty reduction at little cost to government revenue.

---

[22] It should be noted, however, that, since there is a domestic processing industry that transforms flour to bread, the income effects of a tariff on flour would be greater than estimated here.

Table 13.6. Guinea: summary effects of a 10% tariff on alternative food commodities: Conakry

	Base run	Tariff increase of 10%			
		On rice	On oil	On wheat	On sugar
Total per capita monthly expenditure (real GNF)	14,799	14,626	14,724	14,667	14,754
Total per capita daily calories	1,720	1,674	1,700	1,699	1,713
Poverty line (real GNF)	20,250	20,925	20,575	20,525	20,325
Poverty measures					
P_0	35.594	37.333	36.464	36.464	35.942
P_1	9.938	10.795	10.352	10.288	10.033
P_2	3.906	4.317	4.102	4.072	3.951
Government tariff revenue (% chase)					
Food tariff revenue	0.00	25.50	9.45	20.45	24.09
Nonmining tax revenue	0.00	2.54	0.94	2.04	2.40
Total revenue and grants	0.00	0.73	0.27	0.58	0.69

Source: Model simulations.

13.4.2. *Decreased marketing margins*

Marketing and transformation costs are high in Guinea. The high cost of domestic transportation, for example, resulted in the cost of transporting one kilogram of rice from Boke to Conakry in 1987 being three times as expensive as that of transporting a kilogram of rice from Bangkok to Conakry (Arulpragasam and Sahn 1994). These costs can act as impediments to domestic commerce and production. Policies that lower these rural–urban marketing wedges, such as the numerous road projects undertaken in Guinea as well as policies that facilitate internal commerce by eliminating red tape and road checks, can be expected to affect the levels of domestic production, imports, consumption, and real urban and rural incomes.

Simulation 5 in Table 13.4 presents the results of a simulated 30 percent reduction in marketing (and transformation) margins. The reduction in margins lowers the urban consumer price of domestically produced commodities as well as the rural consumer price of imported goods. It is the urban consumer prices that are presented in simulation 5.[23] Among the urban poor in Conakry, this price movement results in increased consumption of local rice (by 18.5 percent), of other cereals, roots, and tubers (by 19.9 percent), and in decreased consumption of imported rice (by 1.9 percent) and bread (by 0.2 percent) for which the relative prices have increased. The increased urban demand for domestic agricultural products is met in part by increased production in all commodities (with the exception of oil). Increased urban demand for domestic products is also met by the decreased consumption of these products by rural households which switch toward the consumption of more imported foods for which rural consumer prices have declined because of the reduced marketing margins.

The net effect of the reduction in marketing margins is an increase in the real incomes of each of the three household groups. Among urban households, nominal incomes increase by 0.5 percent as a result of an increase in the price of the nontraded component of non-agricultural goods. Real urban incomes increase by more than that owing to the general fall in the urban consumer price indices for each household group. Consequently real incomes increase by 1.8 percent among the urban poor and by 1.6 percent among the urban nonpoor. For rural households, nominal incomes increase by 3.6 as a result of increased demand for domestic agricultural produce, higher producer prices, and the consequent increase in production. Nevertheless, with the reduction in marketing margins, rural real incomes still increase by a net 2.3 percent. Decreasing marketing margins by 30 percent can therefore benefit the incomes of the urban poor by even more than can a 10 percent reduction in the rice tariff. Moreover, the reduction in

[23] The large reduction in the consumer price of other cereals, roots, and tubers is due to a 30 percent reduction in a large observed transformation margin in addition to the marketing margin.

marketing margins benefits rural consumers almost as much as the 2.7 percent increase in their real incomes from a simulated 30 percent increase in the production of local rice. The reduction in marketing margins is notable in that it results in all three household groups experiencing real income gains of between 1.5 and 2.5 percent. The reduction in marketing margins also results in the number of urban households in poverty dropping from 35.6 to 34.0 percent as a consequence of the reduction in marketing margins.

13.5. *Conclusions*

The liberalization of the exchange regime and of imports in Guinea in 1986 has likely had a positive effect on food consumption and food energy uptake among consumers compared with the pre-reform period. The volume of all food imports has increased dramatically since reform. Rice imports increased by over three times, wheat imports close to doubled, and imports of cooking oil increased by over six times between 1983 and 1992. Increased levels of production (as a result of increased consumer prices) and of imports (as a result of private sector participation in imports, access of foreign exchange to the private sector, and a realigned exchange rate) resulted in increased per capita rice availability in Guinea. Moreover, the availability of more imported rice, despite being of poor quality, has therefore given consumers access to rice which has been on average approximately 30 percent cheaper than that of local rice since 1986.

Trade and exchange liberalization in Guinea, by permitting increased food imports, has in particular affected the market for local rice, the primary agricultural crop produced in Guinea. Multi-market simulation results examined the effect that the availability of imported rice at decreased prices currently has on local rice production upon accounting for substitution effects in demand, rural supply response, and the corresponding equilibrium adjustments in the markets for other foods. It was found that the ready availability of imported rice at lower real prices increases the volume of rice imported and undoubtedly leads to a reduction in the domestic production of rice. Indeed, model simulation results showed that a 9.1 percent decrease in the price of imported rice (presented in the form of a tariff reduction) results in a 2.5 percent increase in rice imports and a 0.7 percent decrease in rice production.

The multi-market analysis, however, also reveals that the benefits to urban and rural welfare of cheaper imported rice in Guinea surpass the real income costs of a production decrease. Simply put, imported rice is by far the cheapest priced calorie source in the diet and commands such a large food expenditure share that movements in its real price are the single most important element in dictating the level of total food-energy uptake among consumers. The share of imported rice is so large, especially in the budget of poor urban consumers, that the income effects associated with changes in its price are extremely important in determining the level of consumption of all food and hence in determining ultimate welfare outcomes. In particular, for urban households, a decrease in the price of imported rice results in increased demand and consumption not only of imported rice but also of most other imported commodities, of non-agricultural goods, and of most local produce other than local rice and oil. As a result, both nominal and real incomes in urban areas increase with a fall in the price of imported rice.

Reductions in the price of imported rice, surprisingly, also raise rural real incomes despite lowering both rice production and rural nominal incomes. Even among rural consumers in coastal Guinea, the expenditure share to imported rice is due largely to its current pervasiveness on rural markets and its discounted price relative to local rice. Many of these rural households are net consumers of rice, and even among those that are not, purchased rice plays an important food security role during the *soudure* (dry season). A decrease in the price of imported rice, while decreasing the price and the production of local rice and marginally reducing the production of food such as fruits, vegetables, and fish, will increase price, production, and rural revenue from oil, other staples, and meat. Most importantly, although nominal rural incomes will decline, in rural areas real incomes increase with a reduction in the price of imported rice owing to the corresponding decrease in the rural consumer price index.

Any attempt to curtail rice imports, therefore, whether it be through the imposition of tariff or non-tariff barriers, will increase the price of imported rice to the detriment of both urban and rural households. In particular, the multi-market model was used to analyze the effects of proposed tariff increases on rice. Simulation results reveal that, although a 30 percent increase in the tariff on rice would increase the production of local rice by 2.2 percent, the consumption of imported rice would decrease sharply among the urban poor and among rural households. Real incomes of all three household groups would decline. The percentage of urban households in poverty would also increase. Indeed, the tariff increases on all food commodities actually instituted in Guinea between 1990 and 1993, while contributing to agricultural production increases, are estimated to have decreased urban real incomes by 2.2 percent and rural real incomes by 1.2 percent, thereby increasing poverty.

The gradual reimposition of tariffs since liberalization is hence harmful to both urban and rural welfare. It is debatable, moreover, whether the gains in government revenue from tariffs, which are marginal, are worth the welfare costs. While it is clear that Guinea urgently needs to search for alternative sources of government revenues, a 10 percent tariff on rice increases tariff revenues by only 2.5 percent, while increasing the number of urban households in poverty by close to 5.0 percent. Furthermore, even if

revenue generation from tariffs on agricultural commodities were impera-
tive, simulation results revealed that it would be possible to raise that revenue from an increased tariff on a commodity other than rice, such as sugar,
at a lesser cost both to poverty and also to calorie intake among the poor.

Foreign assistance and government policies that focus on lowering marketing and transformation costs of agricultural produce can enhance the
welfare of both urban and rural households. Multi-market simulation results
show, for example, that the reduction of high urban–rural marketing
margins in Guinea will increase domestic production, lower prices, and
increase nominal and real incomes. Thus, projects that lower the cost of
transportation to traders, such as rural road projects, as well as projects that
lower the cost of transformation, such as projects to reduce the high cost of
milling cereals, will contribute to production improvements and real welfare
gains. Similarly, efforts to improve local private enterprise and thus incomes
from non-agricultural sources, although inflationary, will nevertheless also
increase demand for agricultural produce, increase production, and improve
real incomes of both urban and rural households. It is policies such as these,
which foster local demand for agricultural commodities without resorting to
increased protectionism, that also hold the most promise for Guinean
consumers to experience future welfare improvements.

Appendix 13.1. Guinea
Multi-market Model Equations

Supply, demand, and incomes

(1) $S_i = S0_i \bullet \left[1 + \sum \varepsilon_{i,j}^s \bullet (PP_j / PP0_j - 1) \right]$

(2) $D_i^u = D0_i^u \bullet \left[1 + \sum \eta_{i,j,h}^u \bullet (PC_j / PC0_j - 1) + \gamma_{i,h}^u \bullet (Y_h^u / Y0_h^u - 1) \right]$

(3) $D_i^r = D0_i^r \bullet \left[1 + \sum \eta_{i,j,h}^r \bullet (PP_j / PP0_j - 1) + \gamma_{i,h}^r \bullet (Y_h^r / Y0_h^r - 1) \right]$

(4) $D_i = \sum D_i^u + D_i^r$

(5) $YNAG_h = YNAG0_h \bullet PC_{NA} / PC0_{NA'}$

(6) $YAG_h = \sum PP_i \bullet S_i \bullet \theta_{ih}$

Prices

(7) $\quad PM_i = PW_i \bullet ER \bullet (1 + t_i)$

(8) $\quad PC_i = PM_i \bullet (1 + mt_i)$

(9) $\quad PC_i = PP_i \bullet (1 + m_i)$

Model closure

(10) $\quad S_i = D_i - (M_i + DM_i)$

(11) $\quad PC_{NA} = PNT_{NA}^{\alpha^{NA}} \bullet [ER \bullet (1 + TM_{NA}) \bullet PWM_{NA})^{(1-\alpha^{NA})}$

(12) $\quad PNT = PNT_{NA}^{\beta^{NT}} \bullet PNT_{AG}^{(1-\beta^{NT})}$

(13) $\quad PNT_{AG} = \prod \left(\dfrac{PC_k}{PC0_k} \right)^{\phi_k} + \prod \left(\dfrac{PP_k}{PP0_k} \right)^{\xi_k}$

(14) $\quad ER = ER0 \bullet [1 - CHFSAV \bullet (1-\beta) / (P_x X \bullet \varepsilon_x - P_m M \bullet \eta_m)]$

Variable/key parameter

D_i	Total consumption (demand) of good i
D_i^u	Urban consumption (demand) of good i
D_i^r	Rural consumption (demand) of good i
S_i	Domestic production of good i
M_i	Net international imports of good i
DM_i	Net interregional domestic trade of good i
Y_h	Total income of household h
$YNAG_h$	Non-agricultural income of household h
YAG_h	Agricultural income of household h
ER	Real exchange rate
PP_i	Producer price of good i
PC_i	Consumer price of good i
PW_i	World price (in dollars) of traded good i
PM_i	Border price of imported good i (in guinea francs)
PNT	Price index of non-tradable goods
$CHFSAV$	Change in foreign savings
t_i	Tariff on good i
m_i	Rural–urban marketing margin of good i
mt_i	Import marketing margin of good i
$\eta_{i,h}$	Price elasticity of demand for good i
$\gamma_{i,h}$	Income elasticity of demand for good i
$\varepsilon_{i,h}^s$	Elasticity of supply of good i

Source: Arulpragasam (1994a).

Appendix 13.2. Baseline supply and demand in Guinea

Table 13A.1 presents the multi-market baseline supply and demand for 1990/91.

Table 13.A1. Guinea: multi-market baseline supply and demand, 1990/91

	Demand (metric tons)					Supply (metric tons)			
	Conakry poor	Conakry nonpoor	Conakry total	Rural (Guinée Maritime) total	Total demand	Rural (Guinée Maritime) production	Domestic trade	Imports	Total supply
Imported rice	33,247	39,344	72,591	49,542	122,133	0	(44,867)	167,000	122,133
Local rice	4,291	9,721	14,012	98,450	112,462	112,462	0	0	112,462
Other grains, roots, tubers	3,222	10,084	13,305	58,081	71,386	71,386	0	0	71,386
Bread[a]	7,838	13,051	20,889	12,469	33,358	0	(23,050)	56,408	33,358
Meat and dairy	4,032	15,246	19,278	12,610	31,888	22,087	9,800	0	31,888
Fish	8,391	14,519	22,910	15,569	38,479	38,479	0	0	38,479
Vegetables	13,579	25,570	39,149	51,610	90,760	84,617	6,143	0	90,760
Fruits	6,865	26,660	33,525	30,686	64,211	64,211	0	0	64,211
Oils	2,879	5,248	8,128	6,671	14,798	2,422	0	12,376	14,798
Condiments	3,279	5,414	8,693	13,325	22,018	12,690	9,328	0	22,018
Sugar	2,062	3,417	5,480	4,634	10,113	0	(20,201)	30,314	10,113
Beverages	157	717	874	305	1,179	0	0	1,179	1,179
Nonfoods	1.78	6.64	8.42	7.30	1.57	5.69	0.00	0.00	1.57

[a] A 0.8 transformation factor is applied to imported wheat in producing bread.

Source: CFNPP/ENCOMEC survey; Projet National d'Appui a la Filière Riz; Ministere du Plan et des Finances/PADSE (GOG 1991a), "Enquete sur les Informations Prioritaires, Rapport final et Annexes Statistiques;" Ministere de l'Agriculture et des Ressources Animales (GOG 1991b).

References

AGRER/GOG. 1991. "Etude de Securité Alimentaire." Draft version. Conakry: Ministère du Plan et de la Cooperation Internationale.

—— 1992. "Macro-économie et dimensions sociales de l'ajustement—Rapport Définitif." Conakry: AGRER/GOG.

Arulpragasam, Jehan. 1994a. "The Effects on Food Markets, Household Food Consumption, and Urban Poverty of Price, Trade and Exchange Policies in Guinea: A Multimarket Analysis." Ph.D. dissertation, University of North Carolina, Chapel Hill, NC.

—— 1994b. "The Effects of Trade and Exchange Policies on Food Markets, Household Food Consumption, and Urban Poverty in Guinea: A Multimarket Analysis." Cornell University Food and Nutrition Policy Program Working Paper, March 1994. Ithaca, NY: Cornell University Food and Nutrition Policy Program.

—— and Carlo del Ninno. 1993. "Price Changes and their Effects on Consumption in Conakry." *ENCOMEC Findings Bulletin No. 12*. Washington, DC: CFNPP.

—— and David E. Sahn. Forthcoming. *Economic Transition in Guinea: Implications for Growth and Poverty*. New York: New York University Press.

—— —— 1994. "Policy Failure and the Limits of Rapid Reform: Lessons from Guinea." In *Adjusting to Policy Failure in African Economies*, David E. Sahn, ed. Ithaca, NY: Cornell University Press.

Associates for International Resources and Development (AIRD). 1989. "Agricultural Sector Assessment, Republic of Guinea." Somerville, MA: AIRD.

Banque Central de la République de Guinée (BCRG). 1989. "Rapport Annuel D'Activites au 31 Decembre 1989." Conakry: BCRG.

—— 1993. "Rapport Préliminaire d'Activities 1992." Draft. March 1993. Conakry: BCRG.

—— Various years. "Bulletin Trimestriel d'Etudes et de Statistiques," Nos. 4, 5, 7, 8, 9 and 15. Conakry: BCRG.

Benz, Hélène. 1992. "Quelques Élements sur les Importations et le Commerce du Riz en Guinée." Montpellier: CIRAD.

Blanciforti, L. and R. Green. 1983. "An Almost Ideal Demand System: A Comparison and Application to Food Groups." *Agricultural Economic Research*, 35: 1–10.

Braverman, Avishay and Jeffrey S. Hammer. 1986. "Multimarket Analysis of Agricultural Pricing Policies in Senegal." In *Agricultural Household Models: Extensions, Applications, and Policy*, Inderjit Singh, Lyn Squire, and John Strauss, eds. Baltimore, MD: Johns Hopkins University Press.

—— —— and Choong Yong Ahn. 1987. "Multimarket Analysis of Agricultural Pricing Policies in Korea." In *The Theory of Taxation for Developing Countries*, David Newbery and Nicholas Stern, eds. New York: Oxford University Press.

—— —— and Anne Gron. 1987. "Multimarket Analysis of Agricultural Price Policies in an Operational Context: The Case of Cyprus." *World Bank Economic Review*, 1(2): 337–356.

Caputo, E. 1991. "Rapport d'Evolution d'un Programme National D'Appui à la Filière Riz en Guinée." Conakry: CCCE.

Chalfant, James A. 1987. "A Globally Flexible, Almost Ideal Demand System." *Journal of Business and Economic Statistics*, 5: 233–242.

Deaton, Angus, and John Muellbauer. 1980. "An Almost Ideal Demand System." *American Economic Review*, 70: 312–326.

del Ninno, Carlo and David E. Sahn. 1990. "Survey Methodology and Preliminary Results of Household Welfare in Conakry: A Progress Report." Ithaca, NY: Cornell University Food and Nutrition Policy Program. Draft.

Dorosh, Paul, Carlo del Ninno and David E. Sahn. 1994. "Food Aid and Poverty Alleviation in Mozambique: The Potential for Self-Targeting with Yellow Maize." Cornell Food and Nutrition Policy Program Working Paper 50. Ithaca, NY: Cornell University.

Filippi-Wilhelm. 1987. "Circuits de Commercialisation et de Distribution en Guinée." Vol. 1. Conakry: UNCTAD/UNDP.

—— 1988. "Circuits de Commercialisation et de Distribution en Guinée." Vol. 2. Conakry: UNCTAD/UNDP.

Forbeau, Francis, and Yannick Meneux. 1989. "Riz Local ou Riz Importé en Guinée?" Montpellier: Institute de Recherches Agronomique Tropicales (IRAT).

Foster, James, Joel Greer, and Erik Thorbecke. 1984. "A Class of Decomposable Poverty Measures." *Econometrica*, 52(3): 761–766.

Guinea, Government of (GOG). 1986. "Enquête Légère sur la Consommation des Ménages de la Ville de Conakry, 30/09/84–3/11/84." Conakry: Ministère du Plan et de la Coopération International. Photocopy.

—— 1989a. "Loi de Finances pour l'année 1989." Conakry: Ministère de l'Economie et des Finances.

—— 1989b. "Rapport Annuel 1988: Situation et Perspectives Economiques 1988–91." Conakry: Ministère du Plan et del'Coopération Internationale.

—— 1989c. "Recensement General de la Population et de l'Habitat, 1983, Analyse des Resultats Definitifs." Conakry: Ministère du Plan et de la Coopèration Internationale and Direction Nationale de la Statistique et del'Informatique.

—— 1990a. "Loi de Finances pour 1990." Conakry: Ministère de l'Economie et des Finances.

—— 1990b. "Rapport Economique et Social 1989." Conakry: Ministère du Plan et de la Coopération Internationale.

—— 1990c. "Resultats du Recensement National de l'Agriculture." Conakry: Ministère du Plan et de la Coopération Internationale and Direction Nationale de la Statistique et del'Informatique.

—— 1991a. "Dimensions Sociales de l'Ajustement Structurel (DSA) Enquête sur les Informations Prioritaires (ESIP)—Rapport Final." Conakry: Ministère du Plan et des finances.

—— 1991b. "Rapport Economique et Social 1990." Conakry: Ministère du Plan et de la Cooperation Internationale.

—— 1992a. "Rapport Économique et Social 1991." Conakry: Ministère du Plan et des finances.

—— 1992b. "Rapport Générale de l'Enquête Agricole Permanente Campagne 1991–1992." Vols. 1 and 2. Conakry: Ministère de l'Agriculture et des Ressources Animales (MARA).

—— 1993a. "Cadrage Macro-économique Annuel 1993." Draft, May. Conakry: Ministère du Plan et des finances.

Guinea, Government of (GOG). 1993b. "Synthese des Conclusions de la Mission du Fonds sur l'Execution du Programme 1992."

——Various Issues. "Evolution de l'Indice des Prix à la Consommation des Ménages de Conakry." Conakry: Ministère du Plan et de la Coopération International.

——Undated (a). "Etude sur la Filière-Riz en Guinée Maritime." Conakry: Ministère du Plan et de la Coopération Internationale and Ministère du Développement Rural. Photocopy.

——Undated (b). "Enquête Filière-Riz Haute Guinée 1986–87." Conakry: Ministère de l'Agriculture et Ressources Animales.

——Undated (c). "Enquête sur les Dépenses des Ménages de la Ville de Conakry, December 1986–January 1987." Conakry: Ministère du Plan et de la Coopération International.

——Undated (d). "Rapport sur les Conditions de Vie des Menages de Conakry de 1986–88." Conakry: Ministère du Plan et de la Coopération Internationale. Photocopy.

Hanrahan, Charles E. and Steven Block. 1988. "Food Aid and Policy Reform in Guinea." Prepared for USAID/Conakry. Cambridge, MA: ABT Associates.

Heien, Dale, and Cathy Wessells. 1990. "Demand System Estimation with Microdata: A Censored Regression Approach." *Journal of Business and Economic Statistics*, 8: 365–371.

Hirsch, Robert. 1986. "Rapport d'un Mission Préliminaire sur le Secteur Rizicole Guinéen." Paris: Caisse Centrale de Coopèration Economique.

International Monetary Fund (IMF). 1986. "Guinea—Recent Economic Developments." Washington, DC: IMF.

——1987. "Guinea—Recent Economic Developments." Washington, DC: IMF.

——Various years. *International Financial Statistics*. Washington, DC: IMF.

Laraki, Karim. 1990. "Ending Food Subsidies: Nutritional, Welfare, and Budgetary Effects." *World Bank Economic Review*, 3: 395–408.

Lowdermilk, Melanie. 1989. "Food Needs Assessment 1989–90." Washington, DC: E/DI.

Nellum, A. L., and Associates. 1980. "Guinea Agricultural Sector Report."

PICK. Various years. *Work Currency Yearbook*.

Porte Autonome de Conakry (PAC). 1993. "Statistiques Comparées—Janvier à Décembre 1991 et 1992." Conakry: Ministère du Commerce, des Transports et du Tourisme.

Projet National d'Appuis à la Filière Riz (PNAFR). 1992. "Note de Conjoncture 1992 Section Commercialisation." Conakry: MARA/PNAFR.

——1993a. "Note de Conjoncture des Importations de Riz." Conakry: MARA/PNAFR.

——1993b. "Note de Conjoncture Suivi des Prix et des Marchées de Riz." Conakry: MARA/PNAFR.

Pujo, Laurence. 1993. "La Filière riz en Guinée Forestière." Montpellier: CIRAD.

Reveco. 1988. "Les Cicuits d'Approvisionnement de Conakry Riz Importé—Riz Local." Conakry: UNDP/UNCTAD.

Thenevin, Pierre. 1988. "Politique de Relance de la Filière Rizicole et Approvisionnement en Riz Local de la Guiné:; Identification et Feasibility de Quelques Actions." Photocopy.

United States Agency for International Development. 1987a. "An Evaluation of United States Food Aid in Guinea." Conakry: USAID. Photocopy.

—— 1987b. "Guinea Foreign Exchange System." Conakry: USAID. Photocopy.

—— 1989. "Guinea Grant Food Assistance Programs Second Mid-Term Evaluation." Conakry: USAID.

—— 1990. "Guinea Foreign Exchange System Report for CY 1989." Draft. Conakry: USAID. Photocopy.

World Bank. 1981. "Revolutionary People's Republic of Guinea—Country Economic Memorandum." Washington, DC: World Bank.

—— 1984a. "Guinea: Agricultural Sector Review." Washington, DC: World Bank.

—— 1984b. "Guinea: The Conditions for Economic Growth, A Country Economic Memorandum." Washington, DC: World Bank.

—— 1990. "Republic of Guinea—Country Economic Memorandum." Vols. 1 and 2. Washington, DC: World Bank.

14

More than just Peanuts (Groundnuts): Aid Flows and Policy Reform in The Gambia

Paul A. Dorosh and Mattias K.A. Lundberg

14.1. *Introduction*

In many ways, The Gambia's experience in the early 1980s paralleled that of many other countries in sub-Saharan Africa. World prices of groundnuts, The Gambia's major export good, fell along with the prices of other major agricultural export commodities in Africa. The drought that struck much of West Africa reduced yields in Gambian agriculture as well. And as world credit markets tightened, foreign borrowing became increasingly difficult for nearly all developing countries. Finally, inappropriate domestic economic policies contributed to the economic decline. More specifically, fiscal deficits, pricing policies, and large levels of foreign borrowing in previous years helped precipitate a balance-of-payments crisis. Yet, structural characteristics of the Gambian economy, particularly the country's small size, which enabled foreign aid to play an extremely important role in the economy, and The Gambia's open borders with neighboring Senegal, differentiate The Gambia's economic experience from that of other countries of sub-Saharan Africa.

The Gambia undertook initial policy reforms in the early 1980s, apart from the financial support of the World Bank and IMF, but most major reforms began only with the Economic Recovery Program (ERP), launched in 1985. The ERP brought about substantial changes in economic incentives through liberalization of agricultural marketing, changes in tariffs, and a devaluation of the exchange rate. These policy reforms, together with substantial assistance from international donor agencies and governments, and the fortunate coincidences of increased export (groundnut) prices in world markets, the end of the drought, and lower import (rice) prices, enabled the ERP to achieve its goals to a large extent. By the end of the 1980s, the current account was in surplus, budgetary deficits were small, and national income had increased.

In this chapter, we focus on how the major components of the ERP and external shocks affected income distribution, in particular the welfare of the poor, in The Gambia. Changes in world groundnut prices and domestic groundnut policies are highlighted, given the importance of groundnuts as a source of rural incomes and in foreign trade. We also place major emphasis on the role of foreign aid in the economic recovery. The analysis is based on a set of policy simulations using a computable general equilibrium (CGE) model with a disaggregated structure of households.

In the next section we present a brief description of the structure of the Gambian economy, followed by a discussion of The Gambia's experiences during the past decade of policy reform and structural adjustment. Section 14.3 outlines the Gambia CGE model. Model simulations of external shocks and policy measures undertaken as part of the ERP are presented in Section 14.4. The concluding section highlights the major lessons illustrated by the policy simulations.

14.2. *Economic Crisis and Reform*

The Gambia is one of Africa's smallest, poorest, and most densely populated countries. Geographically, the country consists of a narrow band of land on both sides of the Gambia River, bordered on three sides by neighboring Senegal. In 1989/90 the total population was estimated at 862,000, or roughly 76 people per square kilometer, with an annual per capita GDP of about US$260. More than two-thirds of the population live in rural areas, and the vast majority of the population is engaged in rainfed agriculture. Groundnuts, the most important crop, are produced primarily for export, and other crops (cereals, fruits, and vegetables) are produced primarily for domestic consumption.[1]

The Gambia's small size and its open borders with Senegal have important implications. Lacking a significant industrial base, The Gambia imports most manufactured goods, almost all processed foods, and nearly 20 percent of primary food crops. One-third of all imports, with a value equal to more than 10 percent of GDP, are re-exported to Senegal through cross-border trade. The open borders also make Senegal's agricultural price policy, in particular the producer price of groundnuts, an important factor in determining farmer incomes and The Gambia's own exports of processed groundnut products.

Up until the mid-1970s, The Gambia experienced positive real growth in GDP per capita as a result of modest policies and a favorable external environment. However, policies instituted during the 1970s overwhelmed the public sector and left the economy vulnerable to shocks, which came as the

---

[1] See Jabara (1990, 1994) for more detailed discussions of The Gambia's economy and economic policies.

twin apocalyptic horsemen of many African economic crises: drought and a decline in the international terms of trade. The economic collapse in The Gambia was severe in its magnitude but also in its swiftness. From 1975 to 1980, the current account plummeted from equilibrium to a deficit worth more than 30 percent of GDP.

14.2.1. *The origins of the crisis*

The First Development Plan of 1976–1981 boosted investment in basic social and economic infrastructure. This investment program was funded primarily by highly concessional foreign loans, but also by government budget surpluses on the current account and domestic borrowing. An estimated 40 percent of total development expenditure was channeled to the creation of new state-owned enterprises, and the number of parastatals doubled during that period.

In addition to the spending on the development program, the Government of The Gambia (GOTG) increased recurrent expenditure and imports. The number of established posts in the government doubled and by 1981 the budget deficit equalled 10.9 percent of GDP (Table 14.1). More troubling, imports financed by foreign borrowing worsened the trade deficit, which averaged 21.6 percent of GDP from 1976 to 1981. The Gambia's foreign debt increased sevenfold in real terms during that period, from 13 to 176 percent of GDP.

Terms-of-trade shocks, the macroeconomic turmoil, and inappropriate pricing policy adversely affected the groundnut sector as well. Throughout the 1970s, the Gambia Produce Marketing Board (GPMB) implicitly taxed groundnut producers by placing a large but stable wedge between the prices paid to farmers and the export price, resulting in significant operating surpluses. This fund was used to support food subsidies, and for a variety of non-agricultural activities, such as the provision of low-interest loans to civil servants (McPherson and Posner 1991). As the public sector deficit increased, the withdrawal of funds from the GPMB's reserves intensified.

When the world price of groundnuts fell more than a third between 1975/76 and 1984/85, the value and volume of groundnut exports declined and the GPMB suffered financial losses. With their reserves gone (having been used to subsidize the expansionary policies of the late 1970s and early 1980s), the GPMB was unable to intervene to raise producer prices to stimulate production, and groundnut production began to decline.

The Sahelian drought made things even worse, reducing the volume and increasing the variability of rainfall. Between 1974 and 1987, average rainfall declined by 36 percent in western Gambia and 24 percent in eastern Gambia, and variability increased to 50 percent in the middle of the cropping season (McPherson and Posner 1991). Farmers responded to the drought and the drop in prices by shifting out of cash crops and into food crops. Between 1974/75 and 1984/85, the area planted to groundnuts de-

Table 14.1. The Gambia: macroeconomic summary, 1975–1990

	1975	1976–81	1982–85	1986–90
Real GDP (m 1987 dalasis, market prices)				
End of period	1103.2	1375.3	1581.8	1845.2
Real GDP/capita ('000 1987 dalasis/person)				
End of period	2.070	2.096	2.115	2.109
Annual change in GDP (%)	−2.14	4.17	3.76	3.15
Annual change in GDP deflator (%)				
Average	15.63	9.26	21.19	16.59
End of period	15.63	2.29	54.92	12.94
Budget deficit/GDP (%)				
Average	−2.99	−7.37	−4.74	−3.00
End of period	−2.99	−10.86	−0.35	−0.41
Trade deficit (G&NFS)/GDP (%)				
Average	3.03	−21.64	−11.39	−10.11
End of period	3.03	−20.37	−7.44	−10.70
Exchange rate (dalasis/$)				
Average	1.98	2.00	3.25	7.37
End of period	1.98	2.10	3.46	7.50
Total external debt ($m)				
Average	13.4	82.87	223.45	322.24
End of period	13.4	176.00	245.00	352.10

Sources: IMF (1993); World Bank (1993).

clined by nearly one-third, while the area planted to coarse grains (maize, millet, and sorghum) increased by nearly two-thirds (FAO 1991, data tapes).

14.2.2. *The depths of the crisis*

Although export earnings and real GDP continued to fall in the early 1980s, increased foreign aid and foreign borrowing postponed the total collapse of the economy. Ironically, the increase in foreign financing may have been partly responsible for the severity of the crisis, since it allowed the government of The Gambia to maintain its ambitious investment program and high levels of consumption.[2]

Initial efforts at stabilization took place as part of two stand-by agreements signed with the IMF in 1982 and 1984. The Gambian government

[2] In July 1981, the GOTG survived a violent revolt and attempted coup d'état, which reduced foreign exchange earnings from tourism. A desire to preclude further unrest may have influenced the government's decision to maintain high levels of recurrent expenditure (see McPherson and Radelet 1991).

attempted to increase government receipts and reduce consumer subsidies, partly by eliminating explicit price ceilings for urban consumers and also by increasing producer prices.[3] At the same time, foreign assistance declined to historical levels of the mid-1970s, requiring the Gambian government to cut expenditure even more sharply. Higher debt service payments and an expanded wage bill reduced the government's room for maneuver, forcing a reduction in the provision of services and the consumption of imports. By early 1986, the total external debt increased to nearly twice the value of GDP, and payments arrears were more than twice official export earnings.

14.2.3. *Economic recovery*

Real structural changes were necessary to boost foreign exchange receipts, to compensate for declining world groundnut prices, discourage capital flight, and encourage growth and diversification in the private domestic productive base. Therefore, in 1985/86 the Gambian government introduced the Economic Recovery Program (ERP). The ERP had three basic components: price and exchange rate liberalization, public sector rationalization, and demand management. Because The Gambia was in arrears to the IMF, the ERP was introduced without support from either an IMF stand-by agreement or additional assistance from bilateral donors (Radelet 1992).

In the first year of the ERP, most retail prices were decontrolled, import duties were raised, export duties were reduced or eliminated, and the dalasi was allowed to float freely. Prices for public and parastatal monopoly services were raised and subsidies were reduced on other services. In January 1986 interbank foreign exchange auctions were inaugurated, resulting in a nominal depreciation of 49 percent in the first month and the virtual elimination of the premium on foreign exchange on the parallel market.

Many urban households suffered directly from the ERP as the Gambian government reduced the size of the public sector by reducing expenditure, laying off workers, freezing wages, and selling off parastatal enterprises. Over the two year-period 1985–1987, nearly a quarter of the government labor force was eliminated. Fortunately, a decline in world rice prices beginning in mid-1986 helped offset the adverse effects of the devaluation on urban households.[4]

For rural households, changes in groundnut pricing and marketing had major impacts on real incomes. The groundnut producer price was increased from 620 to 1260 dalasis per ton in a series of price adjustments in 1985/86,

---

[3] As a condition of the stand-by arrangement, the GPMB increased the producer prices for groundnuts for the 1982/83 season. Higher producer prices combined with good weather to achieve a record harvest, but that year the world groundnut price collapsed, plunging the GPMB into debt. The GPMB was forced to borrow to pay for groundnut purchases, since their reserves had been used by the GOTG to finance the earlier public investment program. As a result, domestic credit grew 45 percent in 12 months.

[4] The importance of the decline in rice prices at this crucial juncture for the political acceptability of the ERP is emphasized by Radelet (1992).

Table 14.2. The Gambia: domestic and world prices for groundnuts, 1984–1990

	1984	1985	1986	1987	1988	1989	1990
(1) Gambia producer price (D/ton)	450	620	1260	1800	1500	1100	1650
(2) Senegal producer price (CFA/ton)	70	80	90	90	90	70	70
(3) Senegal producer price (D/ton)	731	1026	2186	1742	2639	1754	2088
(4) Price ratio ((3)/(1))	1.63	1.65	1.73	0.97	1.76	1.59	1.27
(5) Domestic price Banjul (D/ton)	933	1229	2337	3235	2883	2373	3257
(6) f.o.b. Banjul ($/ton)	588.0	467.4	241.6	219.5	249.4	302.0	331.0
(7) f.o.b. Banjul (D/ton)	2105	1804	1677	1552	1674	2292	2608
(8) Implicit export tax (%)	125.7	46.9	−28.2	−52.0	−42.0	−3.4	−19.9

Notes: Producer prices are for unshelled groundnuts. Calculated using parallel exchange rate. Domestic price Banjul is unshelled groundnuts adjusted for transformation and marketing costs. Calculated using official exchange rate. The implicit export tax is defined as $[(7)/(5)-1] \times 100$.

Sources: Jabara (1990); IMF (1987, 1988); *Banque Centrale des Etats de l'Afrique de l'Ouest* (various issues); Cowitt (1989); and authors' calculations.

but the depreciation of the exchange rate kept domestic groundnut prices below those in Senegal and on the world market (Table 14.2). A further increase to 1800 dalasis per ton in 1986/87 raised the domestic producer price above the export price (Banjul) and the producer price in Senegal, leading to losses for the GPMB. Given lower world prices, the producer price for groundnuts was again reduced by nearly 20 percent in 1987/88 and the groundnut export tax was eliminated. In addition, as part of the general trend towards privatization, groundnut marketing and exporting were liberalized, enabling private traders to buy directly from farmers and to export groundnuts.

The Gambian government began the second phase of the ERP during 1988/89, again with the support of donor agencies, and after reaching a debt rescheduling agreement with the London Club of creditors in January. The primary objective of this phase was to improve the performance of the government and parastatal agencies, to make the parastatals attractive for sale, or simply to eliminate them and transfer their functions to the private sector.

Despite a deterioration in the weather with a consequent decline in agricultural production, real GDP grew by 5.2 percent in 1989/90 and was 19.4 percent higher than in 1984/85, before the onset of the ERP. During the reform period, exports of groundnut products had likewise increased, by 49 percent in special drawing line terms. The current account deficit including official transfers was only 2.7 percent of GDP, down from 6.4 percent in 1983/84. Including grants, the government budget now showed a surplus equal to 2 percent of GDP, compared with a deficit of 9 percent of GDP in 1984/85 (IMF 1992a). Only the large increase in foreign debt, from US$176.0 million in 1981 to $352.1 million in 1990, diminished the luster of the economic recovery (Table 14.1).

14.3. The CGE Model[5]

In order to trace the effects of the complex set of external shocks and policy changes on household incomes, we use a CGE model of the Gambian economy and conduct a series a counterfactual simulations. The "neoclassical structuralist" model presented here follows the work of Dervis, de Melo, and Robinson (1982); Benjamin and Devarajan (1985); and Condon, Dahl, and Devarajan (1987), among others. Unlike an earlier CGE model of The Gambia (Radelet 1990), the CGE model used for the simulations in this chapter includes a disaggregated structure enabling an analysis of changes in income distribution across a broad classification of households.

A social accounting matrix (SAM) for 1989/90 forms the data base for the model (Jabara, Lundberg, and Sireh Jallow 1992).[6] Macroeconomic and sectoral aggregates are taken from the national accounts (Central Bureau of Statistics 1991); household information is derived from a 1989/90 survey of rural and urban households (Jabara et al. 1991) and national accounts aggregates for the same year.

The model describes production of 16 activities, each producing a single commodity (Table 14.3). A seventeenth commodity, non-competitive imports, for which there is no domestic production, is also included. Production of groundnuts and groundnut products (cake and oil) are treated as separate activities. The large re-export trade is also specified as an activity, using non-competitive imports as the major input.

Despite the small size of The Gambia geographically, the rural labor market is separated from the urban market. Four types of labor (skilled and unskilled in both urban and rural areas) are modeled, each assumed to be fixed in supply. Capital is also fixed in the short run (one year). A single aggregate capital stock enters the production functions; returns to capital are allocated to seven types of capital: corporate capital, urban housing, urban informal capital, rural informal capital, rural housing, and agricultural capital/land owned by the poor and non-poor rural households, respectively.

Four household types are modeled: urban non-poor, urban poor, rural

[5] A listing of the equations and variables of the model is found in Appendix 14.1. See Dorosh and Lundberg (1993) for a more detailed description of the CGE model.

[6] A number of minor modifications to the SAM found in Jabara, Lundberg, and Sireh Jallow (1992) are described in Dorosh and Lundberg (1993: Appendix 1).

Table 14.3. The Gambia: value added and exports by sector, 1989/90

Activity	Value added		Exports	
	Dalasis	%	Dalasis	%
Agriculture	543.4	29.8	131.3	10.9
Groundnuts	158.5	8.7	71.0	5.9
Rice	43.1	2.4	0.0	0.0
Coarse grains	101.7	5.6	0.0	0.0
Fruit/vegetables/roots	90.3	5.0	35.9	3.0
Livestock/fishing/forestry	149.8	8.2	24.4	2.0
Industry	111.3	6.1	102.9	8.5
Groundnut processing	22.9	1.3	86.0	7.1
Manufacture and industry	88.5	4.9	17.0	1.4
Services	1167.6	64.1	973.6	80.6
Construction	74.2	4.1	0.0	0.0
Transport, communications, and utilities	158.6	8.7	43.2	3.6
Domestic informal trade	61.0	3.3	0.0	0.0
Domestic formal trade	196.9	10.8	0.0	0.0
Reexport trade	200.0	11.0	723.2	59.9
Private services	139.0	7.6	207.3	17.2
Public services	153.8	8.4	0.0	0.0
Urban housing	95.0	5.2	0.0	0.0
Rural housing	89.2	4.9	0.0	0.0
Total	1822.3	100.0	1207.8	100.0

Source: Gambia SAM adapted from Jabara, Lundberg, and Sireh Jallow (1992).

non-poor, and rural poor. Here the poor are defined as households in the lower 70 percent of total household expenditures within each region. On average, per capita incomes in urban areas in The Gambia are 2.9 times those in rural areas (Table 14.4). Per capita incomes of the urban non-poor are 6.7 times those of the rural poor. Three other institutions are also included in the model: formal enterprises, government, and the rest of the world. In the model, all transfers between institutions (including households) have been netted out. Value added generated by each production activity j is specified as a constant elasticity of substitution (CES) production function, with quantities of intermediate inputs modeled as fixed shares of the quantity of output produced. Elasticities of substitution between capital and labor are chosen so as to give elasticities of supply equal to 0.8 for groundnuts, rice, livestock and forestry, manufacturing, construction, and transport and communications, and 1.5 for all other non-government sectors.[7]

[7] The elasticity of substitution for the government sector (whose output in the model is essentially determined by exogenous demand for government services) is equal to 0.8.

Table 14.4. The Gambia: income shares, 1989/90

	Urban poor	Urban nonpoor	Urban total	Rural poor	Rural nonpoor	Rural total	Gambia total
Labor income							
Skilled	41.6	40.8	41.2	2.5	5.7	4.0	24.0
Unskilled	42.1	24.5	32.7	66.6	44.3	56.2	43.6
Entrepreneurial income	5.5	24.4	15.6	3.7	4.8	4.2	10.3
Housing	7.2	6.7	6.9	12.1	9.5	10.9	8.8
Land rents	0.9	0.2	0.5	6.7	15.1	10.6	5.2
Interest received	0.5	0.6	0.5	0.4	0.1	0.2	0.4
Transfers	2.2	2.9	2.6	8.0	20.5	13.8	7.8
Total	100.0	100.0	100.0	100.0	100.0	100.0	100.0
Population ('000)	172.9	74.1	247.0	430.5	184.5	615.0	862.0
Per capita income ('000 dalasis/person)	2.55	6.80	3.83	1.01	2.06	1.33	2.04

Sources: Gambia SAM adapted from Jabara, Lundberg, and Sireh Jallow (1992).

Internationally traded goods are treated as imperfect substitutes for goods domestically produced and consumed, following Armington (1969). In an analogous manner, export goods and goods produced for the local market are modeled as imperfect substitutes. Elasticities of substitution between local and traded goods, levels of trade, and levels of domestic production for each commodity are given in Appendix Table 14A.1. World prices are assumed to be fixed.

Household incomes are determined by returns to factors of production controlled by the households (Table 14.4). Including the value of imputed wages, the urban poor receive 83.7 percent of their income from labor, compared with 69.1 percent for the rural poor. Entrepreneurs are found in all urban income classes: returns to informal sector capital account for 5.5 percent of incomes of the urban non-poor and 22.4 percent of incomes for the urban poor. Returns to agricultural land are significant only for rural households, contributing 15.1 and 6.7 percent of incomes of rural non-poor and poor, respectively.

The value of household consumption of each commodity is specified as a fixed share function of nominal expenditures (Appendix Table 14A.2). Savings are a linear function of income. Both recurrent and investment expenditures of the government are fixed in real terms.

In the model, the total level of private investment is determined by net savings (total savings less the value of government investment). Value of investment by sector of destination j is assumed to be a fixed share of total fixed investment. The composition of capital by activity is also fixed.

Markets for commodities clear as prices adjust to equate supply and demand. In the labor market, wages adjust to bring labor demand in line with fixed labor supply. The nominal exchange rate and foreign savings are fixed exogenously, leaving changes in the aggregate price index to bring about movements in the real exchange rate and equilibrium in the rest of the world accounts.

For each year of the dynamic simulations, capital stock is updated according to the previous period's net investment by sector. The base level labor supplies of both skilled and unskilled labor are also increased exogenously by a constant population growth rate.

14.4. Policy Simulations

The Gambian economy underwent a marked transformation in the mid-1980s as changes in terms of trade, foreign aid, and government policies affected incentives for production, consumption, and investment. In order to shed light on the impacts of the various external and policy shocks on household incomes, the CGE model outlined in the preceding section is used to simulate the Gambian economy during the major period of the Economic Recovery Program, 1985–1990.

The simulations presented here compare the effects of the various shocks with a base run that models the path of the economy with no changes in world prices, foreign capital inflows, or government spending in real terms (Appendix Table 14A.3). A number of shocks are simulated, including changes in government spending, movements in world prices of groundnuts and rice, and changes in taxes on these commodities. The roles of foreign aid inflows and the drought are highlighted with separate runs.

14.4.1. *Simulation 1: No adjustment (cutbacks in foreign aid)*

In the mid-1980s, The Gambia borrowed substantial amounts of funds from international donors—loans that provided the resources for government investments to spur economic development. In the absence of the Economic Recovery Program, donor funding would likely have diminished to a level sufficient to cover only interest payments due on past loans, a decline in foreign aid of about $18 million (Radelet 1990). Simulation 1 models the economy without the ERP by reducing foreign savings by $18 million relative to the base run in each year of the simulation. Government investment spending is reduced by the same dalasi value as the reduction in foreign aid inflow.

Reductions in foreign aid result in sharp declines in real incomes and investment in simulation 1 (Table 14.5). Smaller inflows of foreign aid (foreign savings) reduce the total pool of savings in the economy available for investment. Since government investment is exogenously reduced by the same value, there is no direct impact on the supply of savings available for private investment. However, the decline in investment spending reduces aggregate demand, and in particular demand for construction services and other investment goods. Government investment by 66.5 percent and total investment falls by 51.3 percent in year 1 (1986) relative to the base run.

The construction sector, heavily dependent on investment demand, experiences a collapse in output of similar magnitude (51.8 percent).

Lower aggregate demand also leads to lower prices of non-traded goods (including construction), while prices of traded goods tend to remain unchanged since they are tied to world prices. Thus, the real exchange rate, the relative price of traded to non-traded goods, approximated here by the nominal exchange rate divided by the GDP deflator, rises (depreciates) by 3.6 percent in year 1 (5.1 percent in year 5). This shift in relative prices leads to increased production of traded agricultural goods (groundnuts, rice, vegetables). Overall agricultural production increases by 0.2 percent, while industry (including construction) falls by 11.5 percent. Exports of groundnuts (to Senegal) and groundnut products through Banjul rise by 4.5 and 7.5 percent, respectively, in year 1. Overall exports increase by 7.8 percent in year 1, while imports, discouraged by the higher prices, fall by 5.6 percent.

Table 14.5. The Gambia: simulations 1 and 2—no adjustment (reduced foreign aid) and reduced government spending (%)

	No adjustment (reduced foreign aid)		Reduced government spending	
	Year 1	Year 5	Year 1	Year 5
GDP	-2.5	-5.4	-0.9	0.6
Consumption	-2.0	-7.0	-0.9	0.5
Total investment	-51.3	-40.8	13.5	9.1
Private investment	-20.7	-8.1	115.8	63.5
Public investment	-66.5	-66.5	-37.3	-33.6
Government consumption	0.0	0.0	-16.3	-9.9
Government revenues	-1.4	-3.5	1.1	2.5
Real exchange rate	3.6	5.0	0.0	0.4
Exports	7.8	4.1	0.6	2.2
Imports	-5.6	-8.1	0.6	2.2
Foreign savings	-128.6	-128.6	0.0	0.0
Sectoral production				
Agriculture	0.1	-3.1	0.0	-1.1
Industry	-11.5	-14.9	2.7	2.1
Services	4.8	2.6	0.2	3.5
Public administration	-4.7	-4.8	-17.4	-11.3
Total production	-0.7	-3.3	-0.7	1.1
Household incomes				
Urban poor	-2.3	-7.6	-2.0	1.9
Urban non-poor	-1.4	-7.3	-1.6	1.5
Rural poor	-1.1	-7.4	0.1	-1.3
Rural non-poor	-1.9	-3.3	0.4	0.4
Total	-1.7	-6.6	-0.8	0.7

Source: The Gambia model simulations.

All household groups suffer a loss of real income when foreign capital inflows decline.[8] Initially, the urban population suffers most from the decline in foreign saving and investment spending in urban areas. Real incomes of the urban poor fall by 2.4 percent in year 1. The decline in real incomes of the urban non-poor is slightly less (1.5 percent) because returns to urban entrepreneurial capital actually rise by 3.7 percent in real terms. Rural households suffer only small declines in real income initially as the real exchange rate depreciation leads to increased production of tradable

[8] The population of each household group grows at an exogenous growth rate in each dynamic simulation. Reported percentage changes in household real incomes compared with the base run thus reflect percentage changes in both total incomes and per capita incomes.

agricultural goods. Over time, however, the effects of reduced government investment in agriculture lead to reduced real wages for unskilled rural labor while returns to land increase. As a result, by year 5 real incomes of the rural poor have fallen by 7.4 percent relative to the base run, similar to the declines in real incomes of urban households (who are adversely affected by the lower urban capital stock). Rural large landowners (the rural non-poor) gain relative to other groups in the economy because of the increase in returns to land, although their income is still 3.3 percent lower than in the base run in year 5.

14.4.2. *Simulation 2: Reduced government expenditures*

In simulation 2, the historical pattern of government real expenditures is modeled. Real recurrent expenditures are reduced by 16.3 percent in 1985 of simulation 2; real government investment is 37.4 percent lower than the base run in 1985 (Table 14.5).

The decline in government spending frees up total savings for private investment which more than doubles.[9] Total investment increases by 13.6 percent. Although real GDP is slightly lower than the base case in the first three years of the simulation, the additional capital stock created from higher levels of investment result in a gain in real GDP of 0.7 percent relative to the base run by year 5.

The shift in composition of spending from the public to private sector has little impact on the real exchange rate in this simulation. Agricultural production suffers over time from the decline in government investment; year 5 agricultural output is 1.2 percent less than in the base run. Output of the industrial and service sectors, which benefit from increased private investment, are 2.2 and 3.6 percent higher than the base run in year 5.

Changes in real income are small in this scenario. Initially, incomes fall by 2.0 percent for the urban poor and 1.6 percent for the urban non-poor as expenditures by the government on urban wages and goods fall. Rural incomes rise slightly because private investment expenditures spur the construction and carpentry sectors—sectors that have stronger rural linkages. By year 5, however, the increased levels of private investment, mainly in urban activities, lead to gains in urban real incomes. With lower public investment in rural activities, real incomes of the rural poor fall by 1.4 percent while real incomes of the rural non-poor stagnate.

14.4.3. *Simulations 3–6: Groundnut prices and policy*

Changes in world prices of groundnuts (f.o.b. Banjul), Senegal's producer price, and producer prices in The Gambia were all important factors behind the large fluctuations in protection/taxation of the groundnut sector in The

---

[9] Implicitly, net borrowing by the government from the banking sector is reduced, making available more funds for private investment.

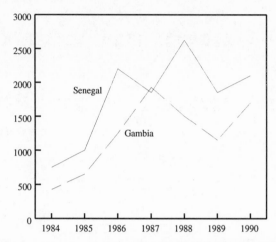

Fig. 14.1. Groundnut producer prices, The Gambia and Senegal, 1984–1990
Source: Table 14.2.

Gambia. In the early 1980s, producer prices were kept low relative to border prices, resulting in a large implicit export tax of over 50 percent in 1985 (See Table 14.2). Unfortunately, the substantial increase in producer prices in 1986 and 1987 coincided with a sharp decline in world prices of groundnut products, so that domestic prices rose to almost twice the border price in 1987. Sharp reductions in producer prices combined with rising world prices eliminated the export subsidy by 1989. Throughout the period, Senegal's producer price converted to dalasis using the parallel exchange rate was greater than The Gambia's producer price except for 1987.

Simulations 3–6 shed light on some of the effects of these movements in world prices and producer prices. The effects of movements in Senegal's producer prices and world export prices are shown in simulations 3 and 4. Simulation 5 models changes in implicit export taxes/subsidies. The combined effects of all three factors (Senegal's producer price, world export prices, and implicit export taxes) are given in simulation 6.

In dollar terms, Senegal's producer price of groundnuts rose significantly after 1985 (Figure 14.1). Simulation 3 shows the effects of the 45.8 percent increase in 1986 and the high Senegal prices in subsequent years. Higher prices for exports to Senegal result in an increase in groundnut production of 9.9 percent. Cross-border groundnut exports increase by 71.0 percent, while exports of groundnut products through Banjul decrease by 18.8 percent. The increased income from groundnut exports leads to increased spending on non-traded goods and an appreciation of the real exchange rate by 1.6 percent. Reduced exports of groundnut products reduce export tax revenues and government net savings, leading to a drop in private

Table 14.6. The Gambia: simulations 3–6—effects of changes in groundnut prices and policy (%)

	Increased groundnut prices in Senegal, simulation 3		Lower world price, simulation 4		Lower world price with change in export tax, simulation 5		Combined effects of changes in groundnut prices and policy, simulation 6	
	Year 1	Year 5	Year 1	Year 5	Year 1	Year 5	Year 1	Year 5
GDP	0.6	0.4	-3.1	-3.2	-3.2	-3.7	-2.0	-2.8
Consumption	1.1	0.7	-1.6	-2.4	-0.5	-0.9	0.6	0.0
Total investment	-0.6	-0.4	-12.0	-8.8	-17.4	-17.2	-14.6	-15.4
Private investment	-1.7	-0.9	-36.2	-20.1	-52.5	-39.1	-44.1	-35.1
Public investment	0.0	0.0	0.0	0.0	0.0	0.0	0.0	0.0
Government consumption	0.0	0.0	0.0	0.0	0.0	0.0	0.0	0.0
Government revenues	-2.9	-2.1	-5.9	-5.5	-15.7	-21.3	-15.3	-20.5
Real exchange rate	-1.6	-1.1	3.9	3.2	1.1	-1.3	-0.7	-2.1
Exports	1.1	0.7	-1.7	-2.2	-2.1	-3.5	-0.5	-2.4
Imports	1.1	0.7	-1.7	-2.2	-2.0	-3.5	-0.5	-2.3
Foreign savings	0.0	0.0	0.0	0.0	0.0	0.0	0.0	0.0
Sectoral production								
Agriculture	0.5	0.4	-0.8	-0.5	0.1	0.6	0.5	0.7
Industry	-1.7	-1.3	-8.5	-7.1	-2.9	-0.3	-4.1	-1.1
Services	-0.0	-0.0	3.2	1.3	1.3	-3.3	1.1	-2.9
Public administration	0.1	0.0	-0.0	-0.0	0.0	0.1	0.1	0.1
Total production	-0.3	-0.2	-0.6	-1.2	0.0	-1.5	-0.3	-1.5
Household incomes								
Urban poor	-1.8	-1.5	0.2	-1.7	-0.9	-5.2	-2.5	-5.6
Urban non-poor	-1.4	-1.1	0.6	-1.1	-0.7	-4.9	-2.0	-5.2
Rural poor	4.1	3.0	-4.0	-3.3	0.2	3.6	4.2	5.7
Rural non-poor	3.9	2.8	-3.5	-3.1	-0.2	3.1	3.7	5.4
Total	0.8	0.5	-1.3	-2.2	-0.4	-1.3	0.4	-0.5

Source: The Gambia model simulations.

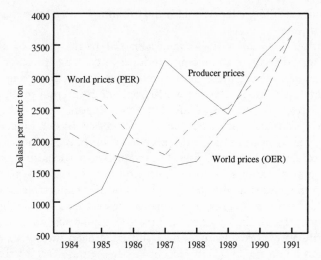

Fig. 14.2. The Gambia: groundnut border prices, 1984–1990

Notes: Producer price is farmgate price plus marketing costs to f.o.b. Banjul; world price (PER) is calculated at the parallel exchange rate; world price (OER) is calculated at the official exchange rate.

Source: Table 14.2.

investment as the total pool of savings in the economy diminishes. Urban household incomes fall as groundnut processing declines by 13.5 percent and the construction sector slumps slightly. Real incomes of the rural poor and rural non-poor rise by 4.2 and 3.9 percent respectively, although total agricultural output at constant prices increases by only 0.5 percent (Table 14.6).

In simulation 4, the decline in world prices of groundnut products, f.o.b. Banjul, is modeled, holding Senegal's price constant (Figure 14.2). Groundnut production falls 11.2 percent as world prices of groundnut product exports decline by 48.3 percent in year 1. Cross-border trade becomes relatively more remunerative and groundnut exports to Senegal increase by 30.0 percent. Real GDP declines by 3.1 percent as the terms-of-trade shock reduces real incomes for farmers and export tax revenues for the government (Table 14.6). Total investment falls by 12.0 percent and output of the construction sector declines by 12.6 percent. Lower overall export earnings lead to a depreciation of the real exchange rate of 3.9 percent. Re-export trade increases by 6.7 percent however, largely because of the real exchange rate depreciation resulting from falling world groundnut prices. Not surprisingly, rural incomes fall most with the decline in groundnut prices, by 4.0 percent for the rural poor and 3.6 percent for the rural non-poor. Urban incomes change little in the first year of the simulation, but the sharp declines in investment reduce capital stock over time, so that by year 5 urban incomes fall by 1.8 percent for the urban poor and 1.1 percent for the urban non-poor.

Simulation 4 assumes that changes in the world price of groundnut products lead directly to changes in producer prices since the export tax rate (implicit in official producer prices paid by the GPMB) is held fixed. In simulation 5, this rate is varied as world prices of groundnut products (f.o.b. Banjul) change. In the first year of the simulation, the border price of groundnut products (before tax) actually increases by 5.8 percent despite the 48 percent decline in the world price of groundnut products as the 46.9 percent export tax becomes a 28.2 percent export subsidy.[10] In contrast to simulation 4, exports of groundnut products increase by 12.4 percent relative to the base run and unofficial cross-border exports decrease by 3.5 percent. Government net revenues decline even further, despite the increase in exports of groundnut products, since the export tax on groundnuts is replaced by an export subsidy. The result is an even further drop in total savings and investment to 17.5 percent below the base case level. With the change in export tax policy, the burden of the decline in world groundnut prices falls mainly on the urban population as lower investment spending reduces urban incomes by 0.9 and 0.7 percent for the poor and non-poor groups, respectively. Rural producers see little change in real incomes thanks to the offsetting domestic tax policy.

Over the five years of the simulation, the export tax and domestic producer prices vary sharply according to the historical pattern. In year 5, the combination of a recovery in world groundnut prices (relative to year 1) and low export taxes increases groundnut producer prices by 18.6 percent in real terms compared with the base run. Rural household incomes are 3.7 percent higher than the base run for the rural poor and 3.2 percent higher for the rural non-poor. Urban household incomes are 5.0–5.2 percent lower than in the base run since urban capital stocks decline (the result of several years of lower investment).

The total effects of movements in world prices and changes in implicit export taxes/subsidies on groundnuts are shown in simulation 6 (Table 14.6). Overall, the rural population enjoys significant gains in real incomes as producer prices for groundnuts increase. Real producer prices are on average 25.3 percent higher than in the base run for the five-year simulation as a whole, and groundnut production increases by an average of 12.0 percent. There is a sharp contrast in the change in incomes of urban and rural households. By year 5 of the simulation, real incomes of the rural poor are 5.7 percent higher than in the base run; real incomes of the urban poor (who are less poor and less numerous than their rural counterparts) are 5.7 percent lower.

---

[10] Both the export tax and the export subsidy are measured as a percentage of the f.o.b. price (see Table 14.2).

14.4.4. *Simulations 7 and 8: Rice prices and policy*

Prior to the liberalization of rice marketing in mid-1985 as part of the ERP, wholesale distribution of imported rice was a monopoly of the Gambia Produce Marketing Board (GPMB); retail prices of imported rice were also fixed. Although rice imports were taxed at 23 percent, this tariff was not completely passed on to domestic rice consumers. Subsidies to the GPMB covering its losses on distribution of imported rice reduced the net taxation.[11]

World rice prices fell in 1986 shortly after the liberalization of the dalasi in January of the year. This happy coincidence helped reduce the retail price of rice in Banjul, after the initial doubling of prices that accompanied the devaluation. World prices fell by nearly 41 percent from 1984 to 1986,[12] then rose to a level approximately 30 percent higher than the 1985 level by 1988 before stabilizing somewhat. As world prices rose, the rice import tariff was reduced, cushioning the impact of higher world prices on domestic consumers.

Simulation 7 shows the effects of changes in the world price of rice on the Gambian economy (Table 14.7). Overall production, savings, and investment change very little in any year since the rice production sector is small in terms of value added generated and since rice accounts for only a small share of total imports. Changes in consumer prices, rather than changes in macro variables, dominate the results.

In year 1, the world rice price drops 27.3 percent, leading to a 20.2 percent decline in the average real price of rice for consumers. Rice imports increase by 44.7 percent, with overall imports increasing by only 0.2 percent. Although lower rice prices discourage production, which drops by 6.6 percent, lower consumer prices contribute to a real exchange rate depreciation of 2.5 percent and a gain in real incomes averaging 2.3 percent. As world prices rise in the latter years of the simulation, real incomes fall below the base period.

In simulation 8, changes in both world prices and import tariffs are modeled. Since there were only minimal changes in rice import tariff rates until 1989 (year 4 of the simulation), only year 5 results are shown in Table 14.7. Lowering the import tariff on rice from 30 to 10 percent (comparing simulations 7 and 8) helps offset the decline in real incomes associated with higher import prices of rice for all household groups. Real incomes decline by an average of 1.4 percent in simulation 8 relative to the base run, a 1 percent improvement compared with simulation 7. Lower tariffs reduce government revenues and total investment, however. Total investment falls

11 The subsidies were less than 23 percent of the c.i.f. value of rice imports, so that domestic prices were still somewhat higher than border prices (see Jabara 1990: 98–100).

12 The f.o.b. Bangkok price for 100 percent brokens fell from $214/ton in 1984 to $126/ton in 1984 (Johm 1988).

Table 14.7. The Gambia: simulations 7 and 8—changes in world rice prices and import tariffs (%)

	New rice price, simulation 7		New rice price with lower import tariff simulation 8
	Year 1	Year 5	Year 5
GDP	2.25	−1.51	−1.43
Consumption	3.24	−2.16	−1.41
Total investment	0.24	−0.20	−2.55
Private investment	0.73	−0.46	−5.79
Public investment	0.00	0.00	0.00
Government consumption	0.00	0.00	0.00
Government revenues	2.99	−2.93	−3.90
Real exchange rate	2.51	−1.74	−0.61
Exports	0.25	−0.25	0.28
Imports	0.25	−0.25	0.28
Foreign savings	0.00	0.00	0.00
Sectoral production			
Agriculture	−0.01	−0.01	0.01
Industry	0.14	−0.13	−0.67
Services	0.02	−0.02	0.20
Public administration	−0.01	0.01	0.01
Total production	0.04	−0.04	-0.06
Household incomes			
Urban poor	2.84	−2.80	−1.70
Urban non-poor	1.24	−1.25	−0.86
Rural poor	3.09	−3.09	−1.65
Rural non-poor	2.40	−2.39	−1.39
Total	2.33	−2.33	−1.38

Source: The Gambia model simulations.

by 2.6 percent in year 6 of simulation 8 compared with the drop of only 0.2 percent in year 6 of simulation 7.

14.4.5. *Simulation 9: Combined effects of changes in policy and terms of trade*

Simulation 9 (Table 14.8) shows the combined effects of changes in policy (reduced government expenditures and changes in trade taxes on groundnuts and rice) and terms of trade (world prices of groundnuts and rice). There is a pronounced difference in the total effects on urban and rural household groups. For urban groups, the negative effects of reduced government expenditures in year 1 and lower world prices for groundnuts

Table 14.8. The Gambia: simulations 9–12 (%)

	Combined effects of changes in policy and terms of trade, simulation 9		End of the drought, simulation 10		Increased capital inflows, simulation 11		Total policy package and external shocks, simulation 12	
	Year 1	Year 5	Year 1	Year 5	Year 1	Year 5	Year 1	Year 5
GDP	-0.6	-3.4	2.0	2.2	0.5	3.1	2.0	1.9
Consumption	2.9	-0.7	2.4	2.7	0.9	4.9	6.5	6.6
Total investment	-0.4	-8.4	2.1	2.0	15.5	32.3	16.4	27.5
Private investment	73.6	23.4	6.3	4.6	46.8	73.4	124.4	105.2
Public investment	-37.3	-33.6	0.0	0.0	0.0	0.0	-37.3	-33.6
Government consumption	-16.3	-9.9	0.0	0.0	0.0	0.0	-16.3	-9.9
Government revenues	-12.0	-21.2	1.3	1.5	0.4	2.9	-11.3	-16.7
Real exchange rate	2.2	-2.2	-0.4	-0.5	-1.8	-4.9	-0.0	-7.0
Exports	0.4	0.3	0.3	0.5	-2.9	-4.4	-2.1	-3.2
Imports	0.4	0.3	0.3	0.4	1.9	6.7	2.7	7.9
Foreign savings	0.0	0.0	0.0	0.0	46.1	117.2	46.1	117.2
Sectoral production								
Agriculture	0.4	-0.4	6.7	6.9	-0.0	-0.3	7.3	6.3
Industry	-1.0	0.2	2.0	2.1	3.3	8.8	3.8	12.0
Services	1.5	1.1	-1.1	-0.9	-1.9	-0.9	-1.3	-0.6
Public administration	-17.3	-11.2	0.0	0.0	-0.0	-0.0	-17.3	-11.2
Total production	-0.8	-0.3	1.1	1.3	-0.1	1.6	0.1	2.9
Household incomes								
Urban poor	-1.8	-4.8	1.0	1.3	0.8	6.8	-0.2	2.9
Urban non-poor	-2.4	-4.0	0.5	0.7	0.6	5.7	-1.4	2.2
Rural poor	7.5	2.4	4.6	4.8	0.5	1.9	13.3	9.1
Rural non-poor	6.6	4.2	3.4	3.6	1.0	3.3	11.6	10.8
Total	1.8	-1.0	2.2	2.4	0.7	4.6	4.9	5.8

Source: The Gambia model simulations.

(f.o.b. Banjul) outweigh the benefits of lower prices for imported rice. Real incomes decline by 1.86 percent for the urban poor and 2.47 percent for the urban non-poor. Rural households enjoy income gains of 7.58 and 6.67 percent for the poor and non-poor, respectively, as the effects of higher groundnut prices in Senegal and lower world rice prices dominate. In the dynamic simulation, real income gains are less for rural households and real income losses larger for urban households, mainly owing to the effects of the increase in world rice prices over time modeled.

14.4.6. *Simulation 10: Effects of the drought*

In Simulation 10, productivity of crop production (groundnuts, rice, coarse grains, and vegetables and roots) is exogenously increased by 10 percent over the base run productivity to simulate the effects of an end to the drought.[13] Simulated production of these crops increases by 9.3–12.3 percent in year 1 while overall agricultural production (including livestock and forestry) rises by 6.7 percent (Table 14.8). Cross-border exports of groundnuts increase by 18.4 percent, and exports of groundnut products increase by 11.9 percent. In spite of a small decline in real prices of crops, real incomes in the rural sector rise by 4.7 percent for the rural poor and 3.5 percent for the rural non-poor. Urban households also benefit somewhat, particularly the urban poor, for whom the decline in food prices is more important given the larger share of food in total expenditures (44.7 percent for the urban poor versus 32.8 percent for the urban non-poor).[14]

Overall, real GDP is 2.0–2.3 percent higher in each year of the simulation as a result of the end of the drought. Real investment is only 2.1 percent greater in the base run since much of the increase in real incomes accrues to rural households with low savings rates (2.6 percent for rural poor households compared with a national average of 7.5 percent).

14.4.7. *Simulation 11: Increased capital inflows*

Simulation 11 (Table 14.8) parallels simulation 1 (reduced capital flows). Historically, capital inflows after the introduction of the ERP in 1985 were not only maintained at the pre-ERP level, but were considerably higher. The balance-of-trade deficit was on average $11.5 million higher from 1986 to 1990 ($23.6 million) than in the 1985 level ($12.1 million) (IMF 1992b).

As foreign savings increase in simulation 11, total savings and investment rise substantially (by 15.6 percent in year 1 and 32.3 percent in year 5) and the real exchange rate appreciates by 1.8 percent in year 1 and 4.9 percent in year 5. Because of the additional investment, real GDP is 3.1 percent higher than the base run in year 5, compared with only 0.6 percent higher than the base run in year 1.

---

[13] The 10 percent figure follows that used by Radelet (1990).
[14] The budget shares for food given above do not include expenditures on non-competitive imports.

The rural poor gain little from the inflow of foreign capital in this scenario. With government investment held fixed in real terms, increased foreign capital only enables additional private investment that is concentrated in urban activities. Moreover, the real exchange rate depreciation tends to depress rural incomes. Incomes of the rural poor increase by only 1.9 percent over the base run level in year 5; incomes of the urban poor are 6.8 percent higher.

14.4.8. *Simulation 12: Total package*

Simulation 12 models the combined effects of the policy changes and external shocks discussed in simulations 2–11. Real GDP is 2.0 percent higher than the base run in both year 1 and year 5 (Table 14.8). Rural households benefit substantially: real incomes of rural households rise by 13.3 and 11.6 percent for the rural poor and non-poor, respectively, in year 1. Real incomes of the urban households fall slightly in year 1, but the increase in urban capital stocks resulting from the large increase in private investment lead to more than a 2 percent gain in urban real incomes in year 5.

The relative importance of the various policy changes and external shocks on real incomes is indicated in Table 14.9. For the rural population, drought, the increase in Senegal's groundnut prices, and the decline in world rice prices in year 1 are the major factors behind the large gains in real incomes. Changes in the government's policies—reducing government expenditures, lower export taxes on groundnuts—have relatively small, but positive, effects of rural incomes. The real income gains for year 5 are smaller than for year 1 because world rice prices are higher than the base run in the latter years of the simulation.

For urban households, government policies had a more significant, but generally negative, effect on real incomes. Cuts in government expenditures lowered urban wage incomes, and reductions in export taxes on groundnuts led to diminished construction activity by reducing total savings and investment in the economy. Increased foreign savings inflows helped offset this latter effect, however. Changes in terms of trade had much smaller effects. By year 5 of the simulation, the crucial role of foreign capital inflows on urban income stands out. Only the reduction in government expenditures (which permits increased private investment), the end of the drought, the reduction in import tariffs on rice, and the increase in foreign savings had positive effects on urban incomes, with the effects of the former three factors being relatively small. Apart from the effects of the increase in foreign capital inflows, which added 6.8 and 5.8 percent to real incomes of the urban poor and non-poor, respectively, real incomes would decline by more than 3 percent in year 5.

Table 14.9. The Gambia: summary of simulation results

Simulations	Household incomes					
	Real GDP	Urban poor	Urban non-poor	Rural poor	Rural non-poor	All Gambia
Year 1						
No adjustment	-2.5	-2.3	-1.4	-1.1	-1.9	-1.7
Reduced government expenditures	-0.9	-2.0	-1.6	0.1	0.4	-0.8
Higher groundnut prices in Senegal	0.6	-1.8	-1.4	4.1	3.9	0.8
Lower groundnut export prices (Banjul)	-3.1	0.2	0.6	-4.0	-3.5	-1.3
Lower export tax on groundnuts	-3.2	-0.9	-0.7	0.2	-0.2	-0.4
Total groundnut package	-2.0	-2.5	-2.0	4.2	3.7	0.4
World rice price changes	2.2	2.8	1.2	3.0	2.4	2.3
Lower rice import tariff	-0.6	-1.8	-2.4	7.5	6.6	1.8
Simulations 2–8 combined						
End of the drought	2.0	1.0	0.5	4.6	3.4	2.2
Increase capital inflows	0.5	0.8	0.6	0.5	1.0	0.7
Total package	2.0	-0.2	-1.4	13.3	11.6	4.9

Year 5

No adjustment	-5.4	-7.6	-7.3	-7.4	-3.3	-6.6
Reduced government expenditures	0.6	1.9	1.5	-1.3	0.4	0.7
Higher groundnut prices in Senegal	0.4	-1.5	-1.1	3.0	2.8	0.5
Lower groundnut export prices (Banjul)	-3.2	-1.7	-1.1	-3.3	-3.1	-2.2
Lower export tax on groundnuts	-3.7	-5.2	-4.9	3.6	3.1	-1.3
Total groundnut package	-2.8	-5.6	-5.2	5.7	5.4	-0.5
World rice price changes	-1.5	-2.8	-1.2	-3.0	-2.3	-2.3
Lower rice import tariff	0.1	1.1	0.4	1.5	1.0	1.0
Simulations 2–8 combined	-3.4	-4.8	-4.0	2.4	4.2	-1.0
End of the drought	2.2	1.3	0.7	4.8	3.6	2.4
Increase capital inflows	3.1	6.8	5.7	1.9	3.3	4.6
Total package	1.9	2.9	2.2	9.1	10.8	5.8

Source: The Gambia model simulations.

14.5. *Summary and Conclusions*

The Gambia has often been cited as an example of successful structural adjustment. Following the implementation of the Economic Recovery Program, real GDP increased by 14.7 percent between 1986 and 1990. The model simulations presented here suggest that there were significant improvements in equity as well. However, a large part of these imports in income levels and distribution was the result of changes in exogenous factors and increased capital inflows, and not the direct results of policy change.

Radelet (1992) emphasizes the importance of a decline in world rice prices that happily coincided with The Gambia's exchange rate devaluation in 1985 in the political economy of acceptance of the reforms. The simulations suggest that lower rice prices contributed to a short-run gain in real incomes of 2.8 percent for the urban poor and 2.3 percent for the population as a whole. Even with the benefit of lower rice prices, real incomes of urban households fell by 0.2 and 1.4 percent for the poor and non-poor, respectively, in the model simulations, showing the total effects of all policy changes and external shocks.

In the longer run, however, foreign capital inflows played a more important role in the economic recovery. Without an adjustment program and lower capital inflows, average household incomes in The Gambia decline by 1.7 percent in the static simulation. Because the capital inflows provide funds for investment, the long-term loss in real incomes with reduced capital inflows is even larger (6.6 percent). The increase in foreign capital inflows that accompanied the ERP was especially important for urban households in the longer run. Although all households benefited from the increase in economic activity associated with the increased capital inflows, the urban population gained most in the simulations since much of the new investment was concentrated on urban activities. These increased capital flows in themselves resulted in real income gains of 6.8 and 5.7 percent for the urban poor and non-poor, respectively. Without the capital inflows, urban real incomes would have declined by more than 3 percent.

The biggest gains in real incomes were enjoyed by the rural population, though.[15] The end of the drought accounted for more than half of the 9.1 percent gain in real incomes of the rural poor in year 5 of the simulations (and about one-third of the real income gain of the rural non-poor). Terms of trade changes, particularly the increase in Senegal's producer prices (expressed in dalasis), more than offset the effects of the decline in world prices of groundnut products. Since the average rural household is a net consumer of rice, the decline in world rice prices also added to rural incomes. In contrast to the urban households, though, short-run capital inflows did not

---

[15] The effects of the removal of fertilizer subsidies are not modeled here, however.

benefit the rural population much since the adverse effects of the accompanying real exchange rate appreciation tended to offset the gains from increased expenditures in the domestic economy.

The model simulations should of course be interpreted with caution, given the numerous assumptions made in constructing the SAM and the model. In particular, the shares of value added of a particular type (e.g. skilled labor or informal sector capital) paid to each type of household are fixed over time and for each policy simulation. Changes in this distribution of factor returns to households would affect the resulting income distributions. The shares of investment by sector of destination are also fixed, so that medium-run effects of policy changes that alter investment incentives may be understated. The role and level of cross-border trade also deserves further analysis.

In spite of these caveats, several general policy lessons emerge from the analysis. First, foreign aid inflows can provide a significant cushion to mitigate the negative effects of adjustment on the urban poor. To the extent that these funds are channeled into rural activities and commodities, there are potential benefits for rural households as well. The Gambia's small size enabled a level of funding in per capita terms that may not be feasible with other countries, however. In absolute terms, The Gambia's levels of foreign aid and borrowing are small when compared with other sub-Saharan countries. In per capita terms, and in comparison with the size of the economy, external support for the adjustment process has been enormous: aid inflows per capita to The Gambia were 3.8 times higher than the average for sub-Saharan Africa in 1987–1989 (Table 14.10).

Second, reduced government expenditures do not necessarily benefit the rural population in the long run if private investment in rural areas is not forthcoming. There remain short-run gains from the depreciation of the real exchange rate associated with lower government spending, but these can be outweighed by declines in government investment in rural areas. Maintaining these government investments in agriculture and rural infrastructure plays a very important role in raising the incomes of the rural poor.

Third, groundnut pricing policies have large effects on income distribution in The Gambia, with very clear tradeoffs between urban and rural incomes. The implicit tax revenues earned from keeping groundnut prices low generate funds for investments that are largely concentrated in urban areas. Rural incomes are especially sensitive to changes in producer prices of groundnuts. The complicating factor is cross-border trade, since an increase in parallel exports limits both the potential gains to urban groups through taxation of groundnuts and the potential losses of producer revenues through sales at low official prices. Similarly, an increase in Senegal's producer price leads to higher rural incomes at the expense of urban incomes as groundnut processing and official exports decline.

The openness of The Gambia's economy has made it very susceptible to world price shocks and also has limited the effectiveness of agricultural

Table 14.10. The Gambia:comparison of debts and development assistance[a]

	The Gambia	Sub-Saharan Africa average
Net ODA (current US$)		
1975–77	14.0	71.8
1978–80	41.7	130.3
1981–83	52.7	160.3
1984–86	68.0	194.2
1987–89	91.7	284.0
Net ODA per capita (current US$)		
1975–77	25.1	10.1
1978–80	67.7	17.4
1981–83	78.1	19.7
1984–86	90.3	21.7
1987–89	111.6	29.0
Net ODA/GDP (%)		
1975–77	10.3	1.7
1978–80	19.3	2.9
1981–83	25.1	3.8
1984–86	43.2	5.2
1987–89	44.8	8.8
Total external debt (current US$)		
1975–77	22.3	398.1
1978–80	89.2	964.8
1981–83	198.3	1557.5
1984–86	248.5	2128.1
1987–89	330.0	3096.3
Total external debt per capita (current US$)		
1975–77	40.0	57.4
1978–80	144.2	128.7
1981–83	291.9	191.3
1984–86	331.8	238.2
1987–89	401.4	316.2
Total external debt/GDP (%)		
1975–77	16.2	9.6
1978–80	40.3	21.4
1981–83	94.7	36.6
1984–86	155.1	56.4
1987–89	160.5	96.1

[a] Figures are three-year moving averages.
Sources: World Bank (1992, 1991, 1981).

price policy. Moreover, its dependance on agriculture keeps it vulnerable to changes in climatic conditions. Favorable changes in terms of trade and weather played a major role in The Gambia's economic recovery in the 1980s. Policy reforms were less important, with the exception of limiting the taxation of agriculture, which had very positive overall income distribution effects. Continued large foreign aid inflows were perhaps the sole indispensable part of the reform process and are likely to continue to be crucial for sustained and rapid economic growth.

Appendix 14.1.
Equations of the Gambia Model

Prices:

(1) $PM_i = \overline{PWM_i} \bullet (1 + \overline{TM_i}) \bullet \overline{ER}$

(2) $PE_i \bullet (1 + \overline{TE_i}) = \overline{PWE_i} \bullet \overline{ER}$

(3) $PPT_i \bullet XPT_i = PPD_i \bullet XPD_i + \dfrac{PE_i}{(1 + margx_i)} \bullet E_i$

(4) $PVA_j = PPT_j(1 - tprod_j) - \displaystyle\sum_i PC_i a_{ij}$

(5) $PC_i \bullet XT_i = PPD_i(1 + margd_i + dtax_i) \bullet XPD_i + PM_i(1 + margm_i + itax_i) \bullet M_i$

(6) $PK_j = \displaystyle\sum_i PC_i \bullet imat_{ij}$

(7) $PPTACT_j = \displaystyle\sum_i PPT_i \bullet outmat_{ji}$

(8) $PINDEX = \displaystyle\sum_i \theta_i \bullet PC_i$

Production

(9) $XPTACT_j = CES(L_{1j}, L_{2j}, K_j)$

(10) $XPT_i = \displaystyle\sum_j XPTACT_j \bullet outmat_{ji}$

Trade

(11) $\quad XPT_i = AT_i[\gamma_i E_i^{\psi_i} + (1-\gamma_i)XPD_i^{\psi_i}]^{1/\psi_i}, \qquad$ for i = exported goods

(12) $\quad \dfrac{E_i}{XPD_i} = \left(\dfrac{PE_i^*}{PPD_i} \bullet \dfrac{(1-\gamma_i)}{\gamma_i}\right)^{\phi_i}, \qquad PE_i^* = \dfrac{PE_i}{1+margx_i}$

$\quad\quad \phi_i = \dfrac{1}{\varphi_i - 1}, \qquad$ for i = exported goods

(13) $\quad XT_i = AC_i[\delta_i M_i^{-\rho_i} + (1-\delta_i)XPD_i^{-\rho_i}]^{-1/\rho_i}, \qquad$ for i = imported goods

(14) $\quad \dfrac{M_i}{XPD_i} = \left(\dfrac{PPD_i^*}{PM_i^*} \bullet \dfrac{\delta_i}{1-\delta_i}\right)^{\sigma_i}, \qquad \sigma_i = \dfrac{1}{1+\rho_i}, \qquad$ for i = imported goods

$\quad\quad PPD_i^* = PPD_i(1+margd_i+dtax_i),$ and $PM_i^* = PM_i(1+margm_i+itax_i)$

(15) $\quad XT_i = XPD_i, \qquad$ for i = non-imported goods

(16) $\quad XPT_i = XPD_i, \qquad$ for i = non-exported goods

Factor markets

(17) $\quad W_{lc,j}/r_j = \dfrac{\alpha_{lc,j}}{1-\displaystyle\sum_{lc}\alpha_{lc,j}} \bullet \dfrac{K_j^{1+\rho_j}}{K_{lc,j}^{1+\rho_j}}$

(18) $\quad \displaystyle\sum_j L_{lc,j} = \overline{LS}_{lc}$

(19) $\quad r_j = \left(1-\displaystyle\sum_{lc}\alpha_{lc,j}\right) \bullet AD_j^{-\rho} \bullet K_j^{-\rho-1} \bullet PVA_j \bullet Q_j^{1+\rho}$

Household income, savings

(20) $\quad LCSAL_{lc} = \displaystyle\sum_j wdist_{j,lc} \bullet W_j \bullet LC_{lc,j}$

(21) $\quad RETK_{kc} = \displaystyle\sum_j (PVA_j \bullet XPTACT_j - ACTSAL_j) \bullet shrkc_{kc,j}$

(22) $\quad ACTSAL_j = \displaystyle\sum_{lc} WA_{lc} \bullet wdist_{j,lc} \bullet L_{j,lc}$

(23) $\quad RENT_i = \overline{PWM}_i \bullet (TM_i - tmr_i) \bullet \overline{M}_i, \qquad$ for i = imq

(24) $\quad Y_h = \displaystyle\sum_{lc}(shr_{lc,h} \bullet LCSAL_{lc}) + \sum_{kc}(shr_{kc,h} \bullet RETK_{kc}) + \sum_{imq}(rentshr_{imq,h} \bullet RENT_{imq})$

(25) $\quad SAVHH_h = sO_h \bullet \left(\dfrac{PINDEX}{PINDEX0}\right) + mps_h \bullet Y_h$

(26) $\quad RURHHSAV = \sum_{rh} SAVHH_{rh}$

(27) $\quad YD_h = Y_h - SAVHH_h - tdir_h \bullet Y_h$

Intermediate demand

(28) $\quad INT_i = \sum_j a_{ij} XPTACT_j$

(29) $\quad INT_{10} = \sum_j a_{ij} XPTACT_j$

$\qquad +(MARGXIT + MARGMIT + MARGDIT) / PC_{10}$

(30) $\quad MARGXIT = \sum_i PE_i \bullet margx_i / (1 + margx_i) \bullet E_i$

(31) $\quad MARGMIT = \sum_i PM_i \bullet margm_i \bullet M_i$

(32) $\quad MARGDIT = \sum_i PPD_i \bullet margd_i \bullet XPD_i$

Household consumption

(33) $\quad PC_i \bullet CD_{ih} = cles_{ih} \bullet YD_h$

(34) $\quad CD_i = \sum_h CDHH_{i,h}$

Government

(35) $\quad GD_i = \beta_i^G \bullet \overline{GDTOT}$

(36) $\quad GR = TARIFF + DUTY + PRODTX + DSALETX + ISALETX + DIRTX$

(37) $\quad TARIFF = \sum_i \overline{TM}_i \bullet \overline{PWM}_i \bullet M_i \bullet ER$

(38) $\quad DUTY = \sum_i \overline{TE}_i \bullet PE_i \bullet E_i$

(39) $\quad PRODTX = \sum_j tprod_j \bullet PPTACT_j \bullet XPTACT_j$

(40) $\quad DSALETX = \sum_i dtax_i \bullet PPD_i \bullet XPD_i$

(41) $\quad ISALETX = \sum_i itax_i \bullet PM_i \bullet M_i$

(42) $\quad DIRTX = \sum_h tdir_h \bullet Y_h$

(43) $GOVSAV = GR - \sum_i PC_i \bullet GD_i$

Investment

(44) $ID_i = \sum_j imat_{ij} \bullet DK_j$

(45) $GID_i = gio_i \bullet \overline{GOVIVT}$

(46) $VGOVIVT = \sum_i PC_i \bullet GID_i$

(47) $PK_j \bullet DK_j = KIO_j \bullet (SAVINGS - RURHHSAV - TOTDSTK - VGOVIVT$
$+ RKIO_j \bullet RURHHSAV)$

(48) $TOTDSTK = \sum_i PC_i \bullet DSTK_i$

(49) $SAVINGS = TOTHHSAV + GOVSAV + ENTFSAV + \overline{FSAV} \bullet ER$

(50) $TOTHHSAV = \sum_h SAVHH_h$

(51) $YENTF = \sum_{KC} shr_{kc,corps} \bullet YENTF$

(52) $ENTFSAV = YENTF - tdir_{corps} \bullet YENTF$

(53) $DEPRECIA = \sum_j DEPR_j \bullet PK_j \bullet K_j$

(54) $DKTOT = \sum_j DK_j$

National income

(55) $YGDP = \sum_j PVA_j \bullet XPTACT_j + PRODTX + TARIFF + DUTY$
$+ DSALETX + ISALETX - DEPRECIA$

Model closure

(56) $\sum_i PWM_i \bullet M_i = \sum_i PWE_i \bullet E_i + \overline{FSAV}$

(57) $XT_i = INT_i + CD_i + GD_i + ID_i + GID_i + DST_i$

Dynamic equations

(58) $\overline{LS}_{lc,t+1} = \overline{LS}_{lc,t} \bullet (1 + lsgr_{lc})$

(59) $\overline{K}_{i,t+1} = \overline{K}_{i,t} \bullet (1 - depr_i) + DK_i + gkio_i \bullet \overline{GOVIVT}$

(60) $GDK_j = GKIO_j \bullet GOVIVT$

Endogenous variables

ACTSAL	Wage bill by activity j
CD	Total consumer demand of good i
CDHH	Consumer demand for good i by household h
DEPRECIA	Total value of depreciation
DIRTX	Direct tax
DK	Real investment by activity j
DKTOT	Total real investment
DSALETX	Sales tax on domestic goods
DST	Change in stocks of good i
DUTY	Export duties
ENTFSAV	Formal enterprise savings
GD	Government consumption of good i
GDK	Government investment by sector
GID	Government investment demand for good i
GOVSAV	Government savings
GR	Government revenue
ID	Private investment demand for good i
INT	Intermediate use of good i
ISALETX	Sales tax on imported goods
L	Labor use (demand) in activity j
LCSAL	Total wage bill for labor of type lc
M	Imports
MARGDIT	Total marketing margin on domestic goods
MARGMIT	Total marketing margin on imports
MARGXIT	Total marketing margin on exports
PC	User price of good i
PE	Domestic price of exported goods
PINDEX	National consumer price index
PK	Price of capital goods in activity j
PM	Domestic price of imported goods
PPD	Price of domestically produced goods
PPT	Price of output of good i
PPTACT	Price output of activity j
PRODTX	Revenue from producer taxes
PVA	Price of value added of activity j
PWE	World export price in dollars
RENT	Rent from import quotas on good i
RETK	Total returns to capital of type kc
RURHHSAV	Rural household savings
SAVHH	Savings by household h
SAVINGS	Total value of savings

TARIFF	Tariff revenue
TOTDSTK	Total change in stocks
TOTHHSAV	Total household savings
VGOVIVT	Nominal value of government investment
WA	Average wage rate
XPD	Domestic sales of production of commodity i
XPT	Domestic output of commodity i
XPTACT	Output of activity j
XT	Supply of commodity i
Y	Household income
YENTF	Formal enterprise income
YGDP	Definition of GDP

Exogenous variables

ER	Exchange rate (dalasis/dollar)
FSAV	Foreign savings
DSTK	Change in stocks
E	Exports
GDTOT	Total government consumption
GOVIVT	Total government investment
K	Capital stock in activity j
LS	Labor supply
PWM	World import price in dollars
TE	Export tariff rate
TM	Import tariff rate

Activities (16)

Groundnuts, rice, coarse grains, fruits/vegetables/roots, livestock/forestry, groundnut processing, manufacturing, construction, transport/communications/utilities, domestic informal trade, domestic formal trade, re-export trade, private services, public services, urban housing, rural housing

Labor types

Skilled, unskilled

Household types

Urban non-poor
Urban poor (lower 70 percent of total expenditures per household)
Rural non-poor
Rural poor (lower 70 percent of total expenditures per household)

Capital

Rural informal

Agricultural land—non-poor
Agricultural land—poor
Rural housing
Urban informal
Corporate capital surplus
Urban housing

Appendix 14.2.
Base Data and Model Parameters

Tables 14A.1 and 14A.2 present trade levels and parameters, and household budget shares. Base simulation results are given in Table 14A.3.

Table 14A.1. The Gambia: trade levels and parameters, 1989/90 (m dalasis)

	Production	Imports	Exports	Elasticity of Substitution
Groundnuts	199.4	0.0	67.5	2.0
Rice	48.3	91.3	0.0	2.0
Coarse grains	114.1	30.8	0.0	2.0
Fruits, vegetables	103.3	25.8	32.7	2.0
Livestock, forestry	201.6	15.6	22.2	0.9
Groundnut products	117.0	0.0	77.1	2.0
Manufacturing	231.0	14.1	16.5	0.9
Construction	183.9	0.0	0.0	0.9
Transport, communications	292.0	0.0	43.2	0.9
Informal trade	71.5	0.0	0.0	0.4
Formal trade	253.7	0.0	0.0	0.4
Re-exports	723.1	0.0	723.1	2.0
Private services	390.8	0.0	207.3	0.7
Public services	231.8	0.0	0.0	0.4
Urban housing	95.0	0.0	0.0	0.4
Rural housing	89.2	0.0	0.0	0.4
Non-competitive imports	0.0	1191.0	0.0	2.0
Total	3345.9	1368.5	1189.4	—

Sources: Gambia CGE model, Dorosh and Lundberg (1993).

Table 14A.2. The Gambia: household budget shares, 1989/90 (%)

	Urban poor	Urban non-poor	Rural poor	Rural non-poor
Groundnuts	1.0	1.1	3.0	1.9
Rice	11.6	4.7	16.3	12.6
Coarse grains	8.0	6.6	11.9	9.7
Fruits, vegetables	7.1	6.8	6.0	5.5
Livestock, forestry	12.9	11.3	12.4	11.6
Groundnut products	3.9	2.3	3.1	2.4
Manufacturing	9.4	11.3	9.1	8.5
Construction	0.0	0.0	0.0	0.0
Transport, communications	6.2	8.4	2.6	2.3
Informal trade	0.0	0.0	0.0	0.0
Formal trade	0.0	0.0	0.0	0.0
Re-exports	0.0	0.0	0.0	0.0
Private services	11.0	14.1	8.2	8.1
Public services	0.5	0.4	0.5	0.7
Urban housing	12.3	13.4	0.0	0.0
Rural housing	0.0	0.0	10.9	12.4
Non-competitive imports	16.1	19.6	16.0	24.2
Total expenditures	100.0	100.0	100.0	100.0
(m dalasis)	364.2	374.8	424.6	348.3
Marginal propensity to save (%)	7.4	11.1	2.6	8.4

Sources: Gambia CGE model, Dorosh and Lundberg (1993).

Table 14A.3. The Gambia: base simulation results

	% change versus 1985 values				
	1986	1987	1988	1989	1990
GDP	2.45	4.94	7.47	10.08	12.76
Consumption	2.46	4.93	7.45	10.04	12.71
Total investment	4.71	9.54	14.51	19.62	24.88
Private investment	15.64	31.69	48.18	65.13	82.60
Government investment	−37.60	−17.21	−10.64	−38.48	−39.17
Government consumption	−16.34	−31.83	−20.52	−13.13	−9.93
Government revenues	2.49	5.03	7.65	10.35	13.16
Real exchange rate	−0.11	−0.20	−0.29	−0.39	−0.48
Exports	2.43	4.88	7.38	9.95	12.62
Imports	2.40	4.82	7.30	9.84	12.48
Foreign savings	6.45	26.40	11.80	15.39	14.87
Sectoral production					
Agriculture	3.20	6.44	9.72	13.04	16.42
Industry	3.42	6.83	10.26	13.72	17.25
Services	1.87	3.81	5.83	7.98	10.25
Public administration	0.08	0.15	0.23	0.31	0.39
Total production	2.32	4.68	7.09	9.58	12.16
Household incomes					
Urban poor	1.76	3.54	5.39	7.34	9.43
Urban non-poor	2.16	4.32	6.53	8.83	11.24
Rural poor	3.03	6.00	8.95	11.89	14.83
Rural non-poor	2.41	4.85	7.34	9.88	12.49
Total	2.30	4.61	6.95	9.35	11.84

Source: The Gambia model simulations.

References

Armington, P. 1969. *A Theory of Demand for Products Distinguished by Place of Production*. IMF Staff Papers 16. Washington, DC: IMF.

Banque Centrale des Etats de l'Afrique de l'Ouest. Various issues. *La Commercialisation de l'Arachide au Senegal*. Dakar: BCEAO.

Benjamin, Nancy, and Shantayanan Devarajan. 1985. *Oil Revenues and Economic Policy in Cameroon: Results from a Computable General Equilibrium Model*. World Bank Staff Working Paper. Washington, DC: World Bank.

Central Bureau of Statistics. 1991. *National Accounts of the Gambia*. Banjul: Ministry of Finance and Economic Affairs.

Condon, Timothy, Henrik Dahl, and Shantayanan Devarajan. 1987. *Implementing a Computable General Equilibrium Model*. Report No. 290. Washington, DC: World Bank.

Cowitt, Philip. 1989. *World Currency Yearbook, 1988–89*. New York: International Currency Analysis, Inc.

Dervis, Kemal, Jaime de Melo, and Sherman Robinson. 1982. *General Equilibrium Models and Development Policy*. Washington, DC: World Bank.

Dorosh, Paul A., and Mattias K. Lundberg. 1993. *Aid Flows and Policy Reforms: A General Equilibrium Analysis of Adjustment and the Poor in The Gambia*. Working Paper 46. Ithaca, NY: CFNPP.

Food and Agriculture Organization (FAO). 1991. Data tapes. *Production Series*. Rome: FAO.

International Monetary Fund. 1987. *The Gambia: Recent Economic Developments*. Washington, DC: IMF.

—— 1988. *The Gambia: Recent Economic Developments*. Washington, DC: IMF.

—— 1992a. "Background Paper and Statistical Appendix." Unpublished. Washington, DC: IMF.

—— 1992b. *International Financial Statistics Yearbook*. Washington, DC: IMF.

—— 1993. *International Financial Statistics Yearbook*. Washington, DC: IMF.

Jabara, Cathy L. 1990. *Economic Reform and Poverty in the Gambia: A Survey of Pre- and Post-ERP Experience*. Monograph No. 8. Ithaca, NY: CFNPP.

—— 1994. "Structural Adjustment in a Small Open Economy: The Case of The Gambia." In *Adjusting to Policy Failure in African Economies*, David E. Sahn, ed. Ithaca, NY: Cornell University Press.

—— Mattias Lundberg, and Abdoulie Sireh Jallow. 1992. *A Social Accounting Matrix for The Gambia*. Working Paper No. 20. Ithaca, NY: CFNPP.

—— Mattias Lundberg, Marjatta Tolvanen, and Rohey Wadda. 1991. *Incomes, Nutrition and Poverty in the Gambia: Results from the CFNPP Household Survey*. Ithaca, NY: CFNPP.

Johm, Ken. 1988. "Production and Consumption Trends and their Implications." In *Policy Issues for Rice Development in the Gambia*, Sambou Kinteh and Joachim von Braun, eds. Washington, DC: International Food Policy Research Institute.

McPherson, Malcolm F., and Joshua Posner. 1991. *Structural Adjustment and Agriculture in sub-Saharan Africa: Lessons from The Gambia*. Development Discussion

Paper No. 410. Cambridge, MA.: Harvard Institute for International Development.

—— and Steven C. Radelet. 1991. "Economic Reform in The Gambia: Policies, Politics, Foreign Aid, and Luck." In *Reforming Economic Systems in Developing Countries*, Dwight H. Perkins and Michael Roemer, eds. Cambridge, MA: Harvard Institute for International Development.

Radelet, Steven C. 1990. "Economic Recovery in The Gambia: The Anatomy of an Economic Reform Program." Ph.D. dissertation, Harvard University.

—— 1992. "Reform without Revolt: The Political Economy of Economic Reform in The Gambia." *World Development*, 20(8).

World Bank. 1981. *Accelerated Development in sub-Saharan Africa*. Washington, DC: World Bank.

—— 1991. *World Tables*. Washington, DC: World Bank.

—— 1992. *African Development Indicators*. Washington, DC: World Bank/UNDP.

—— 1993. *World Tables*. Washington, DC: World Bank.

15

Price Movements and Economic Reform in Ghana: Implications for Food Security

Harold Alderman and Gerald Shively

15.1. *Introduction*

The decade following Ghana's economic reforms of 1983 was the longest sustained period of economic growth in Ghana's history. These reforms followed several decades of relative neglect of Ghana's agricultural sector (Tabatabai 1986), widespread deterioration of national infrastructure, and rapid spread of parallel markets, especially for agricultural inputs (Jebuni and Seini 1992). Since the implementation of Ghana's Economic Recovery Programme (ERP), progress has been steady both in terms of growth of income per capita and in the provision of social services.

In part, because of the severity of the decline, the adjustment experience in Ghana differs considerably from elsewhere in sub-Saharan Africa: by 1983, few government services and subsidies remained to be cut, and few imports actually reached the country. Nevertheless, concerns regarding the effects of structural adjustment on individual welfare have been raised by a number of authors.[1] Among these are concerns over prices and food security. In this chapter we take food security as one measure of welfare, while recognizing that this is but one component from a list that includes freedom from disease, access to safe water, adequate shelter, and education, and security of fundamental political and human rights as well as the standard measurement of welfare in terms of income. Nevertheless, the nutritional fate of the poor during adjustment has been a common focus of concern, and so food security seems a fitting indicator for us to adopt.

Agricultural prices are our point of departure. Price changes can have a rapid impact on food security and hence nutritional levels. Such changes can also contribute to long-run structural changes in an economy. The

---

1 See e.g. the UNICEF volumes edited by Cornia, Jolly, and Stewart (1987).

performance of agricultural markets, however, is our central focus. In a developing country, the commodity marketing system is arguably the most important infrastructure. The impact of economic reforms on its performance is therefore of critical importance for both short- and medium-term national food security. Moreover, if markets transmit information successfully, then the price impacts of liberalization will pervade an economy. To the extent that these price impacts are positive, large portions of the population will benefit. If, on the other hand, such impacts are negative, or if markets are segmented, sluggish, or overresponsive, then liberalization may have deleterious results, prices may not reflect relative values in the economy, and a variety of efficiency losses may result. In these important cases, market interventions may be justified to enhance household welfare.[2]

With reference to Ghana, therefore, we will focus attention on three questions: (1) Did the economic reforms of the 1980s have a significant impact on the household and market level food prices? (2) Were these prices effectively transmitted across regions and commodities? (3) Have internal patterns of agricultural trade contributed to increased price volatility? Each of these issues will be addressed in turn, with particular reference to the pre- and post-adjustment periods in Ghana, and with a view to whether there is a need to undertake market level—as opposed to household level—interventions to improve food security. Before addressing these questions, however, we examine the nature of structural adjustment in Ghana, its linkages to agricultural markets, and the importance of these linkages for welfare outcomes.

15.2. Adjustment and Welfare Linkages

Since its independence, Ghana has taken a lead for the African continent in testing the possibilities—and, often, the limitations—of development theories. It retains this role in regard to structural adjustment, having one of the earliest and most comprehensive adjustment programs in sub-Saharan Africa (Alderman 1991). In some respects, however, Ghana's program is atypical of reform packages, or at least it represents one end of a spectrum. Indeed, Ghana's adjustment experience has differed considerably from elsewhere in sub-Saharan Africa.[3] For example, economic contraction was not part of Ghana's recovery program: the economy had fully contracted prior to the adoption of reforms. Similarly, the country had neither the creditworthiness to be sensitive to an interest rate shock nor the foreign

---

2 As is well known, Ghana has accompanied its economic reforms with a Programme to Mitigate the Social Costs of Adjustment (PAMSCAD). The majority of the programs, however, were not designed to mitigate impacts of adjustment so much as to ensure that significant groups were not bypassed by economic growth (Alderman 1991).

3 For some comparisons, see Harvey (1991).

reserves to maintain a trade deficit. Thus, Ghana's massive devaluation was followed by an increase rather than a decrease in the volume of imports.[4]

Moreover, while the government reduced its deficit, it did so by raising revenues and by shifting investments to aid and loan packages which, although not large by African standards, exceeded the level of foreign resource flows prior to the reform program. Government spending in the aggregate rose appreciably after the adjustment program began. Furthermore, there is little indication that reform programs lowered incomes—and thereby increased food insecurity—for large numbers of Ghanaian households (Alderman 1994). Unfortunately, neither is there strong evidence that income growth by itself has had time to enhance household welfare or reduce household level food insecurity.

In addition to its impact on total income, fiscal reforms can influence household welfare by means of line item budget adjustments, in particular through reallocation of funds available for health and other human services. Although this broader perspective on household welfare goes beyond our current focus, it is worth noting that some evidence suggests that, in general, health (and education) expenditures in Africa did not suffer disproportional cuts when fiscal austerity was imposed (Sahn 1992). Indeed, in Ghana expenditures on health and education rose dramatically during the first phase of adjustment (Alderman 1991).

Although Ghana had neither a contraction of the general economy nor a contraction of services as part of its economic restructuring, there is yet another pathway that can plausibly affect food security, that of changes in relative prices. In principle, price changes in agricultural markets can be traced back to adjustment policies through changes in domestic and international trade as well as through fiscal policies. The former includes changes in exchange rates as well as the dismantling of barriers to internal or foreign trade. In Ghana, the most important agricultural commodity thus affected was rice.

Changes in fiscal policies may affect prices by reductions in subsidies or increases in taxes on food items. Second round effects on food prices may also be observed if subsidies on fertilizer or fuel are reduced or if economy-wide credit constraints affect producers or input suppliers. For example, Jebuni and Seini (1992) examine the role of subsidy removal and privatization on the trade in agricultural inputs and conclude that the response of private agents to the removal of subsidies, especially on fertilizer, has been poor, mainly as a result of credit shortages and uncertainty regarding the continuation of Ministry of Agriculture privatization efforts. While most official distribution channels have shut down, few private traders have taken their place, and the price of fertilizer has steadily increased. Jebuni and Seini

---

[4] Devaluation did, however, serve an important economic function, as it shifted economic rents and allowed price signals to allocate resources more efficiently.

conclude that adjustment related impacts on fertilizer policy will be borne by rice, millet, and maize farmers—who are predominantly poor.[5] Such second round effects stemming from lags in private markets replacing official channels may have appreciable impact on an entire economy (von Braun and Puetz 1987).

Given the rather weak state of Ghana's transportation infrastructure prior to the adjustment period, and the critical role that transportation plays in market performance, changes in transport costs might be another avenue where adjustment may affect consumers. Jebuni and Seini report that while the nominal cost for tractor hire went up considerably as a result of adjustment efforts, in real terms farmers paid 70 percent less for plowing and 30 percent less for carting in 1990 than they did in 1980. One possible explanation is that the negative impacts of fuel price increases up to that date were mitigated by increased flows of spare parts.

Despite the fact that the impact of such indirect effects is hard to determine a priori, adjustment policies are typically viewed as directly increasing food prices and thus placing vulnerable individuals at increased risk of malnutrition. However, price rises need not always be the rule.[6] Fiscal reforms may have little effect on the prices faced by the poorest households, as these households often are not the main recipients of subsidies prior to adjustment. Similarly, devaluations often have little effect on the price of foods consumed by the poor. In part, this is because—with the exception of rice and maize in some, but not all, African countries—many of the staple foods consumed by the most vulnerable households are not traded on the international market. Additionally, in some cases devaluations have been accompanied by liberalized trade which reduces rents (particularly to parallel market traders) and achieves economies of scale. Thus, reforms can lead to lower domestic prices for imports even when border prices for a reference commodity (evaluated at the official exchange rate) appear to rise.[7] Similarly, improvements in domestic trade may result in higher producer prices yet lower consumer prices.

Even with well-functioning domestic markets, changes in international economic forces can affect agriculture through price volatility. For example, Krueger, Schiff, and Valdés (1988) show that international price volatility typically exceeds domestic price volatility under protection. In general, protection may shift price volatility from consumers to either producers or the fiscal deficit. Increased openness may therefore result in increased price uncertainty for producers and consumers of *traded* goods. This emphasis is important: while increased variability can have detrimental impacts on

---

[5] In contrast, the impact of a similar chain of events pertaining to pesticides is estimated to be borne primarily by upper quintile farmers, principally those growing cocoa.

[6] A number of examples of declining prices are presented in Sahn (1993).

[7] An illustration for Maputo, Mozambique, is presented in Alderman, Sahn, and Arulpragasam (1991).

both consumption and production of agricultural commodities (Sahn and Delgado 1989; Binswanger and Rosenzweig 1986), price volatility generally *decreases* when formerly autarkic markets are opened.

Commodity traders play a role as well. In general, traders move commodities from areas of low demand to areas of relatively higher demand, at higher prices. As pointed out by Drèze and Sen (1989), this is simply the way that traders make profits. As a result, if a region is characterized by well-functioning markets, disparities in prices beyond differences in transport costs will tend to dissipate. But when market traders respond slowly or overcompensate to price changes, price variability may be exacerbated. Indeed, the impact of adjustment on price volatility, as on price levels, depends in part on the behavior of market intermediaries. Therefore, if prices are indeed related to welfare, well-functioning markets are a necessary condition for improvements in welfare for at least some groups.[8] But this raises an important question: namely, how strong is the link between prices and household welfare?

Lavy et al. (1992) indicate that both nutritional status and mortality in Ghana are sensitive to food prices.[9] While hardly unprecedented—similar results have been documented for Cote d'Ivoire (Thomas, Lavy, and Strauss 1992)—a strong relationship between individual food prices and nutritional outcome is not automatic. Given the diversity of diet in all regions of the country, there is extensive substitution between food items which mitigate the impact of any single food price movement. The findings of Lavy et al. are, however, in keeping with observed impacts of prices on overall nutrient intakes in the country. Despite extensive substitution between commodities, calorie availability at the household level responds to grain prices and, to a lesser degree, cassava prices (Alderman and Higgins 1992).

Despite the methodological soundness of the study by Lavy et al., the relationship indicated cannot be interpreted as evidence that economic reforms have had a negative impact on nutrition. The evidence that an increase in maize prices will increase mortality rates is also evidence that a decrease will reduce them. Similarly, although rural consumers do reduce their total calorie consumption by 6 percent if maize prices increase 10 percent, they will also increase consumption commensurate with a decrease in prices (Alderman and Higgins 1992). The critical direction of price changes is an empirical not a theoretical issue.

To summarize, empirical evidence suggests what may appear obvious, namely that nutrition in Ghana is responsive to changes in food prices in general, and to grain prices in particular. Furthermore, price levels as well

---

[8] Of course, well functioning markets may not be sufficient. This is the primary point raised by Drèze and Sen (1989: 90) with regard to the alleviation of famines.

[9] This is indicated using cross-sectional price variation. However, there is also a strong univariate correlation when prices and malnutrition rates are plotted over time (United Nations 1989).

as price variability may depend critically on the performance of agricultural markets. Prices may be affected by adjustment policies in a variety of ways. First, adjustment may have a direct impact on prices through fiscal restraint and reductions in direct or indirect subsidies. Second, adjustment may affect prices directly through devaluations that lead to increases in the prices of imported commodities. Third, adjustment may have an indirect impact on prices. These indirect effects arise because adjustment policies may influence the ways in which commodities are marketed, as well as the costs of commodity marketing. Fourth, liberalized trade may achieve economies of scale or reduce parallel market trade, potentially reducing consumer prices. At the same time, liberalization may increase price volatility for tradable commodities and reduce price volatility in formerly autarkic markets. In each case, the market mechanism is important for transmitting food price movements across regions and sectors.

15.3. *Food Price Levels in the 1980s*

This section depicts the trends and patterns of price levels during the pre- and post-adjustment period. Drawing upon, and updating, results reported by Alderman and Shively (1991), we consider eight food commodities, but focus on maize, an important item in the diet of most poor individuals. In addition to examining trends in prices, we examine how these price levels have been affected by exchange rate movements. Finally, we place the food price movements in a relative welfare context by examining the ratio of the maize price to the minimum wage throughout the period.

15.3.1. *Trends and patterns in prices*

Conceptually, it should be a simple matter to indicate any trends in prices, even in the context of appreciable interyear variability. Data availability and quality, however, often leave such investigations open to question. For example, Tabatabai (1988) found two series from the same government ministry that indicate either increases or decreases in wholesale prices in the 1970s. Many price series that are available are discontinuous. Most are unweighted averages over regions and seasons or both. Others make little distinction between official prices and those at which goods are available to most consumers.[10]

Alderman and Shively (1991), however, analyzed monthly food prices obtained from Ministry of Agriculture regional offices. These data correspond to prices in a number of rural and urban markets (rather than regional or

---

[10] For example, one price series reported by the Statistical Service shows an apparent *decline* in the real retail price of maize in Accra during both 1982 and 1983 relative to 1980 and 1981. This is hardly consistent with the famine that most of the population experienced in 1983.

national averages) for the period January 1970–July 1990. Depending upon the commodity in question, up to 36 rural and urban markets were included in the analysis.[11] Regressing the logarithm of real prices, deflated by urban and rural CPI indices, on time (in months) and other variables, they find strong statistical evidence that both wholesale and retail real prices of all commodities have declined since 1984. Contrary to conventional wisdom, this food price decline began in the 1970s, in keeping with overall world price movements. For most commodities except rice and yams, however, the rate of decline accelerated after 1984. For example, the trend coefficients for maize reported in Table 15.1 imply that the average *monthly* real decline in the wholesale price of maize was 0.06 percent a month (0.7 percent a year) in the pre-recovery period and 0.13 percent a month (1.6 percent a year) after the initiation of the recovery. In the earlier period, the downward trend was particularly pronounced for rice (nearly 4 percent a year).

One plausible explanation for this acceleration is a period of consistently favorable weather and yield increases for some crops such as maize. A further explanation may be found in falling marketing costs; although fuel prices have increased since 1984, trucks and spare parts have been more readily available and more funds have been available for road construction and repairs. Note that these factors are not mutually exclusive. They may all play some role in explaining the consistent pattern. For example, the pattern observed in millet prices provides some indication of the role of transport. A regression covering 2038 market observations nationwide indicates that the savannah region and the rest of the country had virtually identical trends during the pre-adjustment period. In the post-adjustment period, however, the downward movement in millet prices in the nationwide sample is twice that of the Northern and Upper Regions. This trend is consistent with improvements in transportation from the geographically restricted producing regions to other markets that have been made in the second half of the decade.

To a large degree, the exception of rice in the overall pattern reinforces, rather than contradicts, the general results. Rice is the only commodity studied that is consistently imported or exported. One would expect, therefore, that the changes in policies regarding the exchange rate determination since 1983 would affect this commodity in a different manner from that of other food crops.[12] The price of rice continued to decline throughout the

---

[11] Data for most markets and commodities reflect prices through July 1990. For five markets—Bolgatanga, Cape Coast, Makola (greater Accra), Sunyani, and Techiman—maize prices have been extended through July 1993.

[12] While maize is also potentially a tradable good, government restrictions, as well as the distinction between yellow and white maize on the world market, have effectively segmented the local market from the world market. Wheat is also imported as a government monopoly. However, it is not a major component of diets in general, and particularly not of the poor.

Table 15.1. Ghana: regressions indicating price trends of food prices, 1970–1993

Independent variable	Wholesale Price of:					Retail Price of:			
	Maize[a]	Sorghum	Millet[a]	Cassava	Gari[b]	Yam	Rice	Maize[a]	Gari
Constant	3.148 (112.078)	3.910 (84.590)	3.724 (72.619)	2.065 (18.155)	3.548 (56.361)	4.132 (85.035)	4.382 (114.524)	3.237 (42.872)	3.042 (38.797)
Time trend prior to 1983	-5.967^{-04} (−3.100)	-5.505^{-04} (−1.834)	-1.582^{-03} (−4.220)	7.283^{-04} (0.955)	-1.034^{-03} (−2.498)	-7.542^{-04} (−2.549)	-3.260^{-03} (−13.356)	-9.717^{-04} (−2.468)	1.922^{-04} (0.413)
Time trend after 1984	-1.330^{-03} (−13.293)[c]	-1.710^{-03} (−9.665)[c]	-2.099^{-03} (−9.918)[c]	-2.647^{-05} (−0.053)[c]	-1.659^{-03} (−7.644)[c]	-8.656^{-04} (−4.820)	-1.445^{-03} (−10.585)[d]	-1.908^{-03} (−9.261)[c]	-1.193^{-03} (−4.325)
Urban	0.009 (0.775)	0.019 (1.292)	5.811^{-03} (0.321)	0.089 (2.900)	−0.052 (−1.792)	0.181 (9.988)	6.589^{-03} (0.448)	−0.023 (−0.476)	0.166 (5.057)
Upper region	−0.014 (−1.061)	−0.165 (−9.671)	—	0.569 (7.055)	−0.224 (−1.965)	0.071 (3.396)	−0.101 (−6.077)	0.045 (1.452)	0.369 (10.233)
Northern region	−0.185 (−8.536)	−0.279 (−12.473)	−0.043 (−2.033)	0.769 (9.937)	—	−0.303 (−10.990)	−0.057 (−2.251)	−0.151 (−3.474)	—[b]
January	0.250 (8.957)	−0.212 (−6.050)	−0.059 (−1.442)	0.061 (0.857)	0.145 (2.191)	0.133 (3.185)	−0.126 (−3.654)	0.225 (3.919)	0.117 (1.799)
February	0.262 (9.413)	−0.150 (−4.279)	-8.794^{-03} (−0.214)	0.045 (0.638)	0.097 (1.494)	0.121 (2.861)	−0.086 (−2.462)	0.247 (4.310)	0.084 (1.297)
March	0.356 (12.698)	−0.149 (−4.223)	0.020 (0.490)	-2.122^{-03} (−0.030)	0.122 (1.847)	0.134 (3.182)	−0.081 (−2.275)	0.334 (5.782)	0.064 (0.987)
April	0.437 (15.471)	−0.116 (−3.294)	0.076 (1.823)	0.057 (0.800)	0.132 (1.952)	0.216 (5.120)	−0.062 (−1.743)	0.435 (7.531)	0.083 (1.267)
May	0.494 (17.576)	−0.058 (−1.652)	0.126 (3.003)	0.144 (2.038)	0.130 (1.940)	0.317 (7.308)	−0.051 (−1.415)	0.495 (8.773)	0.154 (2.363)

Table 15.1. (cont.)

Independent variable	Wholesale Price of:				Retail Price of:				
	Maize[a]	Sorghum	Millet[a]	Cassava	Gari[b]	Yam	Rice	Maize[a]	Gari
June	0.500	−0.036	0.146	0.079	0.140	0.337	−0.053	0.497	0.142
	(17.828)	(−1.027)	(3.446)	(1.124)	(2.127)	(7.594)	(−1.482)	(8.709)	(2.178)
July	0.374	−0.025	0.121	0.034	0.075	0.287	−0.027	0.409	0.071
	(13.226)	(−0.714)	(2.796)	(0.489)	(1.142)	(6.392)	(−0.740)	(7.138)	(1.092)
August	0.133	0.010	0.086	0.074	0.015	0.132	5.887^{-03}	0.159	0.078
	(4.678)	(0.287)	(2.000)	(1.061)	(0.226)	(3.038)	(0.164)	(2.745)	(1.182)
October	0.027	−0.045	−0.047	−0.026	−0.014	−0.044	−0.055	8.806^{-03}	0.018
	(0.946)	(−1.241)	(−1.075)	(−0.365)	(−0.205)	(−1.039)	(−1.552)	(0.152)	(0.279)
November	0.098	−0.123	−0.091	−0.052	−0.047	0.055	−0.105	0.110	−0.061
	(3.412)	(−3.440)	(−2.077)	(−0.738)	(−0.706)	(1.303)	(−2.899)	(1.884)	(−0.930)
December	0.115	−0.283	−0.190	−0.040	−0.016	0.064	−0.165	0.096	−0.089
	(3.998)	(−7.842)	(−4.452)	(−0.558)	(−0.230)	(1.508)	(−4.573)	(1.630)	(−1.307)
Imported (before 1983)	—	—	—	—	—	—	−0.118		
							(−2.806)		
Imported (after 1983)	—	—	—	—	—	—	0.280[d]		
							(5.829)		
R^2	0.297	0.251	0.267[e]	0.131	0.189	0.242	0.134	0.364	0.323
N	3,386	2,085	1,232[e]	1,341	664	1,782	2,244	850	770

Note: T-statistics are in parentheses. The maize series includes data through July 1993 for selected markets; all other commodity series include data through April 1990 only.

[a] Savannah regions only.

[b] No observations available for Tamale.

[c] Indicates that the coefficient is significantly less than the corresponding coefficient for the earlier period (p, 0.01 two-tailed test).

[d] Indicates that the coefficient is significantly greater than the corresponding coefficient for the earlier period (p, 0.01 two-tailed test).

[e] Millet results reported are for Upper and Northern Regions only. Similar trends and significance are observed for the prices from the full sample, although the sales are clearly concentrated in the savannah regions.

1980s, but at a significantly slower pace than in the earlier period. More-over, the relatively few markets that distinguish imported from domestic rice provide evidence regarding the change of trade regimes since the initiation of the economic recovery period. Imported rice was apparently 10 percent cheaper than domestic rice before 1983 and over 25 percent more expensive at the wholesale level after 1984. Such a pattern is consistent with the devaluations of the cedi associated with the adjustment policies during this period.[13]

As Tabatabai (1988) correctly observes, however, declining food prices during contraction could reflect falling real incomes for nonproducers and hence reduced demand. Although there are few direct indicators of the dis-tribution of income growth between 1984 and 1990, average per capita income increased by over 15 percent in that period. The continuing price decline, then, indicates either increased production in the latter period or lower marketing costs, or both.

If one graphs prices, one notes that much of the price movement fol-lowing adjustment occurred early in the adjustment period. This is vexing, because if the price movement was dominated by the immediate post-drought period it would be difficult to distinguish drought recovery from one-time gains from liberalization. Taking different end points for the maize price trend, the downward trend for maize price between 1986 and July 1993 appears similar to that prior to 1983. While this is half of the 1984–1986 monthly decline, it confirms that the reforms in Ghana have not only not raised prices, but have not slowed long term secular trends.

15.3.2. The exchange rate–price link

A major policy prescription of nearly every orthodox stabilization package is exchange rate reform: relatively weak exchange rates are viewed as necessary for improvements in capital inflows as well as trade improvements, although they are also believed to have detrimental impacts on the poor in the short term through increases in the price of food and fuel. Younger (1992) investigates the movement of food prices and the exchange rate using an autoregressive moving average procedure (Box and Tiao 1975). Using a two-step method, the relationship between a driving variable (in this case the nominal exchange rate) and a dependent variable (the food component of the consumer price index) may be studied. In the first step, the dependent variable is generated as the error term from a regression of the change in the national CPI for food (in logarithmic form) on seasonal dummies and a dummy variable for the drought period (1983 and 1984). This procedure effectively removes the seasonal trend in the price series.

---

13 This increase, however, was relatively small compared with the nominal change in the official exchange rate, which moved from 2.75 cedis per dollar in the first quarter of 1983 to 30.30 cedis per dollar in the first quarter of 1984.

In the second step, this dependent variable (denoted here as CPI) is regressed on its lagged value and log differences in the exchange rate are lagged one and two periods. Younger reports the following equation (standard errors in parentheses):

$$CPI_t = -0.46\ CPI_{t-1} + 0.05\ EXCHANGE\ RATE_{t-1} + 0.06\ EXCHANGE\ RATE_{t-2}$$

$$(0.15) \qquad\qquad (0.012) \qquad\qquad\qquad (0.014) \qquad (1)$$

Integrating the resulting function allows one to indicate the magnitude and speed of the response of food prices to changes in the exchange rate. Younger notes that, while a large nominal devaluation in Ghana raised prices, the cumulative elasticity of prices to exchange rate changes was only on the order of 5–10 percent. As is illustrated in Figure 15.1, the impact of a 100 percent devaluation is only an 8 percent increase in food prices, all of which comes after the first two months. This is clearly a small (but statistically significant) response. The comparatively small magnitude of this relationship may have two explanations. First, it is quite possible that scarcity costs (shadow prices of foreign exchange) rather than official prices determined the market prices of those foods that were imported. This issue, however, may pertain more to an earlier period in Ghana characterized by import quotas and a distorted currency. For example, in a study of overall price movements (not merely food price movements), Chibber and Shafik (1991) conclude that official devaluations had no affect on inflation. In part, the exchange rate–price linkage may be weak as a result of the parallel market premium prior to the devaluation. Second, one should note that few food commodities consumed in Ghana were actually traded on inter-

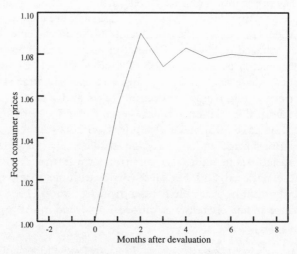

Fig. 15.1. Response to 100 percent devaluation in Ghana
Source: Younger (1992).

national markets during the adjustment period. This point remains valid even in the 1990s. In addition, Younger finds no evidence to suggest that devaluation affects the parallel market rate, concluding that the primary effect of an official devaluation would be on the relative importance of black market trade. Thus, any welfare impacts of adjustment, as they occurred through food price adjustments to devaluation, must be considered moderate.[14]

15.3.3. *Minimum wage–food price ratios*

Even if inflation is not directly caused by devaluation, it was—and is—a feature of the economy. An important issue therefore is whether wage changes keep pace with changes in the cost of living. While wage indices provide a reasonable indicator of trends in earning power, there are only a few countries for which price and wage series reflect the position of low-income households. Alternatively, from the perspective of food security, one can use the amount of food an unskilled worker can purchase with a day's wage as an indicator of real income. While no single food commodity is a precise deflator of wages, the number of kilos of grain obtained for each day of employment provides a tangible indicator of purchasing power. This statistic has the additional advantage of allowing some accessible inter-country comparisons. For our calculations, we use the daily minimum wage as a indicator of wages for unskilled workers.

In Ghana, unlike many countries, the majority of workers earn more than the minimum wage; less than 10 percent of all individuals who reported a wage in the 1987–1988 Ghana Living Standards Survey (GLSS) indicated that their wage was below the legal minimum. The rate is only slightly higher—at 15 percent—for the small subset of those individuals who reported receiving a wage for agricultural labor. A survey conducted by Cornell and Fudtech Consultants in Brong-Ahafo and Upper East in 1990 found the percentage of individuals earning below minimum wages essentially the same as in the GLSS.

Although labor markets in Ghana suffer from a range of imperfections, there is little evidence of increased unemployment throughout the study period (Alderman 1991; Beaudry and Sowa 1989). In addition, the differential between urban wages and returns to agricultural activity in Ghana is rather small, and somewhat less than in neighboring countries (Appleton and Collier 1991). Thus, the legal minimum serves as a reasonable indicator of minimum earning capacity of workers throughout the period.

Table 15.2 indicates the ratio of the minimum wage to the price of maize—often, but not always, the cheapest source of calories in Ghana

---

[14] The case of rice, as we shall discuss in Section 15.4.4 below, is noteworthy. In particular, while the rice market is the one most affected by liberalization, it is also one of the least integrated markets in the country.

Table 15.2. Ghana: minimum wages in terms of kilograms of maize that could be purchased with a day's wages in four regions

	Accra	Bolgatanga	Kumasi	Techiman
1975				
June	—	7.77	—	—
December	—	6.67	—	—
1980				
June	0.75	0.69	0.64	0.71
December	0.87	2.50	1.03	—
1981				
June	1.22	1.32	1.14	2.00
December	1.60	1.92	2.06	2.40
1982				
June	1.10	1.16	1.20	1.71
December	—	1.99	1.11	1.50
1983				
June	0.51	0.33	0.28	0.58
December	—	0.82	0.74	0.98
1984				
June	0.98	1.06	0.97	1.08
December	2.90	2.15	4.05	5.09
1985				
June	3.12	2.99	2.98	3.94
December	2.67	3.84	3.21	3.85
1986				
June	1.71	2.62	1.88	2.12
December	2.17	3.54	2.36	2.81
1987				
June	1.03	1.65	1.10	1.37
December	1.37	1.53	1.41	1.73
1988				
June	1.05	1.25	1.11	1.31
December	1.90	2.08	2.22	2.71
1989				
June	2.47	3.09	3.62	4.55
December	2.91	3.32	3.82	4.02
1990				
May	1.83	3.45	—	2.57

Sources: Maize prices from PPMED regional price data; minimum wages from Alderman (1991).

(Alderman and Shively 1991). The June and December prices are reported for four markets, although the major source of variation is over time and not regions. The minimum wage was revised in eight of the ten years covered. It nevertheless could neither adapt to the June seasonal price rise, nor always keep pace with inflation. In particular, it clearly was an insufficient basis for individual subsistence during the drought of 1983. Moreover, given that a kilogram of maize provides roughly 1.5 times the calorie requirement of an adult, in many years of the decade the wage rate was insufficient for an individual adequately to support dependents. While the situation improved in 1985, the minimum wage then eroded until 1989. Even at its peak during the decade, the wage fell well below the level in the middle of the 1970s. For example, in 1975 the minimum wage would purchase between 6.0 and 7.5 kilograms of maize depending on the market and month, while in 1987 the agricultural wage (which was 50 percent above the minimum wage) would purchase only 4–6 kilograms of maize per day of wage employment depending on the season.[15]

It should be noted that the minimum wage in a number of African countries is often as variable, and occasionally as low, as that in Ghana (Alderman 1992). For example, in Mozambique it has ranged between 2.75 and 10.6 kilos of maize meal (at the official, controlled price) in the short period between January 1987 and the end of 1990. The trend during this period of structural adjustment was clearly downward. Similarly, the maize equivalent of the minimum wage in Malawi ranged between 2.4 and 6.0 kilograms a day in the three-year span between January 1986 and February 1989. While the post-drought figures for Ghana are not famine levels,[16] they imply comparatively little leeway (in either a cross-country or a temporal perspective) for high dependency ratios, or little cushion for spells of either seasonal or structural unemployment.

15.4. Market Performance

Adequate performance of agricultural markets is critical to the transmittal of prices through private marketing mechanisms: it is through these signals that scarcity values in the economy are reported. When markets transmit information successfully and completely, the impacts of liberalization are reflected in market prices. In a well functioning market, these impacts manifest themselves across regions and commodities relatively rapidly. To

15 The median wage reported in the 1987–1988 GLSS was 300 cedis, or 75 percent more than the minimum wage. If the value of allowances and in-kind support is included, the median wage was 363, or twice the minimum.

16 This is indicated, for example, in Table 15.2 with the low wages in June 1983. This level is lower than that in the nadir of the disastrous Bengal Famine of 1943, when a day's work, if available, would purchase 0.6 kilogram of rice (Sen 1981).

the extent that liberalization confers positive impacts in terms of the levels
or variability of prices, the transmission of these benefits may depend on
the integration and speed of response of market mechanisms. Addressing
the question of how adjustment programs impact the poor must therefore
examine how well markets perform the task of transmitting price information. In this section, we investigate the degree to which agricultural
markets in Ghana perform this task. We use three primary measures of
performance: market integration, speed of adjustment, and the index of
market connectedness.

15.4.1. *Framework*

A number of studies of market linkages in Ghana use bivariate correlations
to assess efficiency (Asante, Asuming-Brempong, and Bruce 1989). The
limitations of this method in providing market information, however, are
widely recognized (Harriss 1979). Thus, to study markets in Ghana, we use
a dynamic model introduced by Ravallion (1986):[17]

$$P_{1t} = \sum_{j=1}^{m} \alpha_{1j}P_{1t-j} + \sum_{k=2}^{n}\sum_{j=0}^{m} \beta_{1j}^{k}P_{kt-j} + \gamma_1 X_{1t} + \theta_{1t} \tag{2}$$

$$P_{it} = \sum_{j=1}^{m} \alpha_{ij}P_{it-j} + \sum_{j=0}^{m} \beta_{ij}P_{1t-j} + \gamma_i X_{it} + \theta_{it} \qquad (i = 2,\ldots,n) \tag{3}$$

for $n \neq m$, where k indicates markets and j indicates lags; prices in a reference
market are denoted as P_1 while other markets are indicated generically; X
indicates any other seasonal or temporal factor, such as a drought, that may
influence the speed or degree of price transmittal across markets.

If $\beta_{ij} = 0$ for all values of j in equation (2), then the ith market is
segmented from the central market (denoted by subscript 1). On the other
hand, if $\beta_{io} = 1$, then prices are immediately transmitted. Moreover, if
markets are integrated in the long run, then $\Sigma\alpha_{ij} + \Sigma\beta_{ij} = 1$. In addition, this
model can also test the possibilities of short-run integration, which are less
immediate than instantaneous price transmittal.

Timmer (1987) and Heytens (1986) make two modifications of this
model. First, they work in the logarithm of prices. This implies ad valorem
marketing costs rather than a fee per quantity handled. Second, they
simplify estimation and interpretation by assuming a single lag structure for
price formation rather than the six lags that Ravallion uses. Thus, one can
reformulate Ravallion's model as

$$(P_{it} - P_{it-1}) = (\alpha_j - 1)(P_{it-1} - P_{1t-1}) + \beta_{i0}(P_{1it} - P_{1it-1})$$

$$+ (\alpha_i + \beta_{i0} + \beta_{i1} - 1)P_{1t-1} + \gamma X + \mu_{it} \tag{4}$$

This expresses the temporal change in a peripheral market as a function of

---

17 See also Alderman (1993).

the spatial price spread in the last period, the temporal change in the central, or reference, market, and the price level in the reference market in the last period. Seasonal and policy variables can be included. Equation (4) can be further manipulated to derive

$$P_{it} = (1 + b_1)P_{it-1} + b_2(P_{1t} - P_{1t-1}) + (b_3 - b_1)P_{t-1} + \gamma X + \mu_{it} \qquad (5)$$

where

$$b_1 = \alpha_i - 1, \qquad b_2 = \beta_{i0}, \qquad b_3 = \alpha_i + B_{i0} + \beta_{i1} - 1 \qquad (6)$$

In long-run equilibrium conditions, $(P_{1t} - P_{1t} - 1) = 0$. If one assumes also that $\gamma = 0$, then $(1 + b_1)$ and $(b_3 - b_1)$ are, respectively, the contribution of local and central market price history to current prices. In a well-integrated market, the latter will have a comparatively strong influence on the local price level. Timmer suggests that the ratio indicates the relative magnitude of the two influences. He defines this ratio as the index of market connectedness (IMC) with values less than 1 indicating short-run market integration:[18]

$$IMC = \frac{1 + b_1}{b_3 - b_1} \qquad (7)$$

Clearly, although it is only approximate, this index is useful for comparative purposes not only because of the above-mentioned truncation of the lag structure, but also because the vector of parameters denoted by γ may not be insignificant. Timmer (1987) also argues that b_2 is a measure of the degree to which changes in prices in the reference market are transmitted to other markets. This parameter is expected to be close to 1, although even if markets are perfectly integrated some difference from 1 could reflect a mixture of absolute and proportional marketing costs.

15.4.2. *Market integration*

As mentioned, each of these approaches has features that are useful for our study of Ghana. The key is to adapt the models to the specific context under investigation. One particular focus is the Upper East Region, which is relatively poor and is considered an area of food insecurity. It is the main millet-consuming region in the country, with sorghum being a secondary grain. Maize is only occasionally grown. The region is linked to the rest of the country by a single trunk road through Tamale and further to the maize-exporting areas of Brong-Ahafo and Ashanti.[19] Because of the linear nature of the trade link and because the Upper East imports maize, we can investigate the potential relation of other grain prices in the Upper East to maize prices using a recursive structure.

---

18 The choice of the cutoff is somewhat arbitrary although indicative.

19 A map of Ghana indicating the major markets and transport routes is provided in Alderman and Shively (1991).

We can take equation (2) as explaining the formation of maize prices in the principal maize market, Techiman. This price will be influenced by a number of markets. It is not, however, determined by the price in the Upper East, which, under an analogy with standard models in international trade, can be assumed to be a "small country" price-taker. P_1 (the maize price in Techiman), therefore, need not be considered as simultaneously determined in estimations of P_n (the maize price in the main market in the Upper East, Bolgatanga).

The purpose here is to study not market integration *per se*, but rather the implications for adjustment policies and any interventions to stabilize prices. The question is, what effect does government action in one commodity market have beyond the specific intervention?[20] The relation of other grain prices to maize prices is an important policy issue inasmuch as the government may intervene in the maize market, but is unlikely to do so in millet or sorghum markets.

Thus, we extend the Ravallion single commodity model with the inclusion of the lagged local prices of millet (and/or sorghum). The justification again goes back to the standard trade model for an importer. Under competitive assumptions, the local price for an imported commodity (maize) is the c.i.f. price; changes in local demand should not influence this price although they will influence the quantity traded. In fact, as reported in Table 15.3 (tests 5 and 6), we cannot reject the hypothesis that the millet or sorghum prices in the preceding four periods had no influence on maize prices—that is, that the four coefficients for lagged millet prices (or for sorghum prices) were individually and jointly not significant. Although this observation is important, and is discussed further below, it is not a strict test of the hypothesis that the Bolgatanga maize price is determined by the price in Brong-Ahafo alone, and hence is not a strict test of fully integrated markets.

A test of whether contemporaneous millet or sorghum prices influence maize prices is also needed. Adding current millet and sorghum prices to models 3 and 4, respectively, indicated that contemporaneous millet and sorghum prices do influence local maize prices even after prices in Techiman are included; current millet and sorghum prices were statistically significant when added to the two models, with t-statistics of 12.0 and 7.7, respectively.

The test indicates that either Bolgatanga is not a price-taker in regards to maize or, more likely, that current market events in Techiman are too slowly or incompletely transmitted to the Upper East; in the model with maize prices as the dependent variable, the current Techiman price was incompletely transmitted. While prices appear integrated, they are not instantaneously so.

[20] Ideally, this effort should be augmented with a study that traces the long-run impact of a supply shift of one commodity on all prices. However, not only does this require a set of price and cross-price elasticities, which are unavailable, but it would not trace out the time path.

Table 15.3. Ghana: test statistics for dynamic model of grain markets in Bolgatanga

Model	Test	F-statistic
Base: Maize prices as a function of Techiman maize prices and period dummy variables	Significance of model: $$P^{BOMZ} = f(P^{TEMZ})$$	$F(4,110) = 71.23$
1. Inclusion of 1-period lagged maize prices	$\alpha_{t-1}^{BOMZ} = 0$, $\beta_{t-1}^{TEMZ} = 0$ (Joint significance relative to base model)	$F(2,108) = 49.97$
2. Inclusion of 2-period lagged maize prices	$\alpha_{t-2}^{BOMZ} = 0$, $\beta_{t-2}^{TEMZ} = 0$ (Joint significance relative to model 1)	$F(2,106) = 1.74$
3. Inclusion of 4-period lagged maize prices	$\alpha_{t-2}^{BOMZ} = 0$, $\alpha_{t-3}^{BOMZ} = 0$, $\alpha_{t-4}^{BOMZ} = 0$, $\beta_{t-2}^{TEMZ} = 0$, $\beta_{t-3}^{TEMZ} = 0$, $\beta_{t-4}^{TEMZ} = 0$ (Joint significance relative to model 1)	$F(6,102) = 3.39$
4. Inclusion of 5-period lagged maize prices	$\alpha_{t-5}^{BOMZ} = 0$, $\beta_{t-5}^{TEMZ} = 0$ (Joint significance relative to model 3)	$F(2,100) = 0.32$
5. Inclusion of 4-period lagged maize prices and 4-period lagged local millet prices	$\alpha_{t-1}^{BOMI} = 0$, $\alpha_{t-2}^{BOMI} = 0$, $\alpha_{t-3}^{BOMI} = 0$, $\alpha_{t-4}^{BOMI} = 0$ (Joint significance relative to model 3)	$F(4,98) = 1.23$
6. Inclusion of 4-period lagged maize prices and 4-period lagged local sorghum prices	$\alpha_{t-1}^{BOGC} = 0$, $\alpha_{t-2}^{BOGC} = 0$, $\alpha_{t-3}^{BOGC} = 0$, $\alpha_{t-4}^{BOGC} = 0$ (Joint significance relative to model 3)	$F(4,94) = 1.70$
7. Inclusion of 4-period lagged maize prices (same as model 3)	Rejection of hypothesis that $$\beta_t^{TEMZ} + \beta_{t-1}^{TEMZ} + \beta_{t-2}^{TEMZ} + \beta_{t-3}^{TEMZ}$$ $$+ \beta_{t-4}^{TEMZ} + \alpha_{t-1}^{BOMZ}$$ $$+ \alpha_{t-2}^{BOMZ} + \alpha_{t-3}^{BOMZ} + \alpha_{t-4}^{BOMZ} = 1$$	$F(1,102) = 0.38$
8. Millet prices as a function of Techiman maize prices, lagged local millet prices, and period dummy variables. Corresponds to model 3 with millet prices as dependent variable.	Significance of model	$F(12,103) = 32.08$
9. (Same as model 8)	Rejection of hypothesis that $$\beta_t^{TEMZ} + \beta_{t-1}^{TEMZ} + \beta_{t-2}^{TEMZ} + \beta_{t-3}^{TEMZ}$$ $$+ \beta_{t-4}^{TEMZ} + \alpha_{t-1}^{BOMI}$$ $$+ \alpha_{t-2}^{BOMI} + \alpha_{t-3}^{BOMI} + \alpha_{t-4}^{BOMI} = 1$$	$F(1,103) = 0.15$
10. Sorghum prices as a function of Techiman maize prices, lagged local sorghum prices, and period dummy variables. Corresponds to model 3 with sorghum prices as dependent variable.	Significance of model	$F(12,98) = 41.56$
11. (Same as model 10)	Rejection of hypothesis that $$\beta_t^{TEMZ} + \beta_{t-1}^{TEMZ} + \beta_{t-2}^{TEMZ} + \beta_{t-3}^{TEMZ}$$ $$+ \beta_{t-4}^{TEMZ} + \alpha_{t-1}^{BOGC}$$ $$+ \alpha_{t-2}^{BOGC} + \alpha_{t-3}^{BOGC} + \alpha_{t-4}^{BOGC} = 1$$	$F(1,98) = 0.002$

Note: Superscripts denote the market and real commodity price as follows: BOMZ = Bolgatanga wholesale maize; TEMZ = Techiman wholesale maize; BOMI = Bolgatanga wholesale millet; BOGC = Bolgatanga wholesale sorghum.

Using the millet price as a dependent variable indicates that movement in maize prices in the reference market largely explains movement in millet prices. More surprisingly, movement in local maize prices adds no additional explanation to the model; that is, when Bolgatanga millet prices are regressed on current and lagged *maize* prices in Techiman, as well as lagged Bolgatanga *millet* prices, the lagged Bolgatanga maize prices do not improve the fit of the model. Thus, local maize prices may not contain information that is not conveyed by Techiman maize prices and lagged millet prices. Similarly, when Techiman and lagged Bolgatanga *maize* prices are included in the model, millet prices add no additional information.

This is an important observation since, in a smoothly functioning market, prices would incorporate all available information. If each commodity price contains all information, two sets of prices *from the same market* would contain the same information. This hypothesis cannot be rejected with the data on millet or maize prices in Bolgatanga.

This condition, however, does not apply to sorghum prices in Bolgatanga. Instead, lagged local sorghum and lagged local maize prices both contain information beyond that contained in the other set of prices when the current price of sorghum is the dependent variable. This is indicated by the joint significance of the respective block of prices when added to a model that includes current and lagged maize prices in Techiman as well as the alternative set of lagged prices from Bolgatanga. This may be explained by the use of sorghum in beer-making in the Upper East. Brewers, most of whom operate on a small scale, likely trade and store only that commodity. Sorghum may then constitute a conceptually separate (although physically contiguous) market.

Complete market segmentation implies that none of the Techiman prices significantly influence Bolgatanga prices. This implication can be rejected for maize, millet, and sorghum in Bolgatanga. On the other hand, short-run integration—indicated by the coefficient of *current* Techiman prices being 1—is also rejected in all models. Tests of the restrictions necessary for long-run integration are also reported in Table 15.3 (tests 7, 9, and 11). These restrictions are not rejected at plausible levels of significance.

In summary, it appears that most grain markets in Ghana are integrated with each other. Such interconnected markets weaken the rationale for separate regional stabilization policies. In addition, price shocks (and stabilization) are apparently transmitted across commodities; that is, a rise or decline in maize prices strongly influences subsequent movements in sorghum and millet prices. This cross-commodity integration implies that either trade or storage of maize will also influence commodities that are only locally traded. Furthermore, these findings suggest that commodity-specific impacts of adjustment will filter into other commodities, albeit with some delay. However, these results raise the important question, how long is the necessary delay? The length of delay in transmitting information is impor-

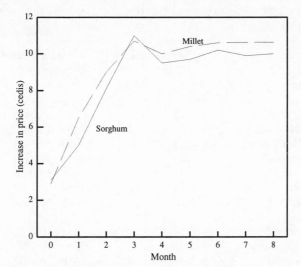

Fig. 15.2. Ghana: Impact on millet and sorghum prices of a 10-cedi increase in the price of maize

Note: Calculations are based on equations found in Alderman and Shively (1991).

tant because it determines the lag with which beneficial changes reach outlying areas, or, conversely, the degree to which the rural poor may be insulated from price volatility.

15.4.3. *Speed of adjustment*

Figure 15.2 indicates the speed and magnitude that price movements in the Techiman maize market transmit to millet and sorghum prices in Bolgatanga. These simulations show that a sustained increase of 10 cedis in the price of maize (1985 prices) leads to roughly a similar increase in the prices for the two other grains in the outlying market.[21] This change occurs rapidly and, as indicated in the test of the sums of parameters above, is stable in the long run. A more transitory movement in the price of maize—say, a fluctuation that lasts only one period—will, of course, have a much smaller impact on the other market.

If markets reach an equilibrium in the long run, as is implied by the test of restrictions above, the model can be reformulated in first differences (Ravallion 1986). We will, therefore, turn to the model of Timmer (1987) and Heytens (1986). Although this model is based on a single period lag—

---

[21] Mean prices for maize, millet, and sorghum in Bolgatanga in the period covered were 29.6, 36.3, and 35.1, respectively.

Table 15.4. Ghana: indices of market connectedness and price transmittal

Market	Index of market connectedness	Parameter of price transmittal[a,d]
Maize[a]		
Sunyani[a]	0.23	0.92 (0.048)
Bolgatanga[a]	1.01	0.33 (0.083)
Cape Coast[a]	0.83	1.23 (0.173)
Kumasi[a]	0.82	0.48 (0.122)
Makola (Accra)[b]	0.51	0.65 (0.093)
Millet[a]	1.76	0.42 (0.106)
Sorghum[a]	1.62	0.37 (0.100)
Rice		
Tamale[a]	2.19	0.19 (0.064)
Bolgatanga[a]	2.71	0.39 (0.120)
Kumasi[a]	4.39	0.18 (0.131)
Makola[a]	11.75	0.20 (0.079)
Bolgatanga[c]	0.87	0.54 (0.134)
Cassava		
Kumasi[a]	0.64	0.051 (0.184)

[a] Reference market is Techiman.
[b] Reference market is Kumasi.
[c] Reference market is Tamale.
[d] Standard errors in parentheses.
Source: Our calculations from PPMED data.

which is rejected with these data—it provides a useful simplification for discussion. Table 15.4 presents the indices of market connectedness (IMC) and parameter of price transmittal discussed above for a series of maize markets, using Techiman as the reference market. The maize markets appear relatively connected, using Timmer's benchmark of 1 as an indicator. Indeed, the connectedness indicator (low when the reference market rather than local conditions influences the local price) is lower for maize than those reported by Timmer for Indonesian maize or by Heytens for yams and gari in Nigeria.

Table 15.4 also indicates the degree of market connectedness for millet and sorghum. The underlying models link the change in millet and sorghum prices with the change in *maize* prices in Techiman. Although less connected to Techiman maize prices than are maize prices, the index nevertheless shows that millet and sorghum prices have a fair amount of response to maize prices. That an appreciable amount of price transmittal occurs between maize prices in Techiman and millet and sorghum prices in Bolgatanga reinforces the conclusion that any success the government has in moderating maize prices and their fluctuations will have an impact on consumers of other grains.[22]

The models in first differences, as well as the more complete models with multiple lags, do not reveal any consistent seasonal patterns or a significant difference in the drought period of January 1983–June 1984. Similarly, no time trend in market integration is observed. This, of course, does not imply that there are no seasonal price patterns in Ghana; it only suggests that the links between markets do not appear to vary over seasons. This contrasts with a less complete version where current prices in one market are regressed on current prices in the reference market. Such models show significant seasonal and drought effects. Such patterns seem to be short-run effects only, which may affect the speed of price transmittal, but not the degree.

15.4.4. *The special case of rice*

Table 15.4 also indicates the IMC and price transmittal parameter for a number of rice market links. If changes in the reference market are fully transmitted to the local market, the parameter of price transmittal will be 1. Mink (1989) argues that rice markets in Ghana are not as efficient as those for maize, millet, and sorghum. The results here support his contention. Price transmittal among rice markets is virtually nonexistent; local market conditions dominate the reference market. Similarly, in a four-period lag model similar to the maize models discussed above linking Kumasi and Makola (Accra), the coefficients of the price variables sum to 0.71. This indicates that the markets are not integrated in the long run. The sum is only 0.53 in a model with a single lag.

However, Tamale rice prices appear well-integrated with Bolgatanga. Similarly, there is a fair amount of price transmittal, although the coefficient is significantly different from 1. One would expect, of course, that the Savannah markets would be insulated from imports to a degree, and hence more closely linked to each other.

Rice, it seems, is an exception to the market integration story in Ghana; rice markets do not function as well as maize and coarse grain markets. Transmittal of price movements between Accra (where rice is largely imported) and the forest and savannah zones is relatively poor. This variation reflects differences in quality. In addition, transportation costs are likely to segregate effectively the savannah market from the coast. Imported rice, apparently, has only a localized impact, and domestic price fluctuations do not transmit to Accra, nor even across other internal markets. Given this, as well as the low share that rice has in either consumers' budgets or their

---

[22] Alderman (1993) tested the hypotheses of market integration using two additional related econometric techniques. The results confirm that price formation within a given market often (but not always) utilizes information efficiently.

diets, the government probably cannot use rice imports or storage to stabilize overall food budgets. The intention here is not to suggest that food aid consisting of rice might not help stabilize demands for foreign exchange, but it does reinforce the notion that rice imports will have only a small direct impact on household welfare outside of, perhaps, the major metropolitan centers. Furthermore, to the extent that devaluations impacted imported rice, these price increases would not have been transmitted to other regions, nor to other commodities. Any welfare impact of adjustment on non-urban consumers through this channel, therefore, has been moderate if not entirely absent.

15.4.5. *The pre- and post-adjustment experiences*

Is there any evidence that market integration has changed in response to new economic policies? Dummy variables for post-1983 or for drought periods as well as for seasons included in the models of integration for maize prices do not indicate any trends or seasonal patterns.[23] In contrast to the maize models, the rice models indicate a seasonal pattern as well as a difference between pre-1983 and post-1983 periods. As Mink (1989) has argued, this seasonal pattern, with larger price spreads in the third quarter, may reflect patterns of food aid and imports, which disrupt the southward flow of locally produced rice. The trend that indicates larger price differentials over time may reflect the changes in the availability and price of imports since 1984.

In summary, given the geographical barriers to market performance in Ghana, the results presented here are somewhat reassuring. With the exception of rice markets, price transmittal is relatively efficient and rapid. This suggests that agricultural markets in Ghana are providing both the physical transformation of commodities through time and space, and the economic transmission of cost information, both of which are essential market functions (Timmer 1987). There is no strong evidence to suggest that these functions have been compromised in any way during the post-adjustment period.

15.5. *Food Price Variability and Internal Trade*

Much of the preceding discussion has focused on the impact of adjustment on welfare as it occurs through food price levels. In this section we examine price volatility. We look first to the empirical evidence on the variability of maize prices in the pre- and post-adjustment periods. This leads into a discussion of the role of grain trade, in particular seasonal storage, and

---

[23] However, the International Fund for Agricultural Development (IFAD) presents data that show poor market integration in 1977–1978.

marketing margins, in generating variability in food prices. In fact, much of the concern over the welfare effects of structural adjustment is a concern over policies that create, as well as redistribute, economic advantage. If market intermediaries are in a position to exploit rapid movements in prices, such concerns may not be unfounded. Indeed, such issues go beyond mere academic interest. For example in Ghana, at various times, populist reaction to profiteering has led to attempts to fix prices and to regulate traders extensively (Kraus 1988). Frustration at the ineffectiveness of such regulation has led, on the one hand, to such acts as the razing of the Makola market in Accra and, on the other hand, to recent market liberalization. Unfortunately, relatively few data on actual market activities in Ghana are available.

Nevertheless, the magnitude and variability of price margins in Ghana are indisputable. It is less clear what implications such variability has for income distribution, household welfare, and policy. For example, if the main consequence of price variability for rural households is an uncertain value for their marketed output, then policy might be oriented toward stabilizing farm-gate prices or providing better price forecasts during the planting season. In contrast, if the main impact falls on consuming households, policy might be oriented toward employment or income enhancements during critical periods. Further, if prices reflect production shocks that in turn influence rural incomes, policies to increase food availability need to be augmented with policies to stabilize overall farm incomes (Alderman 1992; Sarris 1992). Similarly, the impacts of market interventions by the government, if any, revolve in part on how government policies change the marketing decisions of thousands of private agents (farmers and merchants).[24] Hence, this section focuses on the role of private trade in seasonal storage, its contribution to price formation through marketing margins, and the relationship of these factors to adjustment programs.[25]

15.5.1. Empirical evidence on price variability

We examine the issue of price variability on two levels. On a purely descriptive level, we examine price variability during the study period, as well as typical seasonal peaks. We then investigate the evidence for changes in price variability between the pre- and post-1983 period using wholesale maize prices from Bolgatanga and more formal econometric methods.

The coefficients of variation for food prices in three markets are reported in Table 15.5. The three markets represent, albeit imperfectly, the three main agro-ecological zones: savannah, forest, and coastal. The prices of

24 This is illustrated in Sarris (1992).
25 Greater emphasis is placed on grains, although perishable and bulky roots, tubers, and plantains have as large a share of urban budgets as do grains—an indication of extensive marketing channels (Alderman and Higgins 1992)—since those markets are more likely to be affected by trade policy.

Table 15.5. Ghana: measurements of real price variability

(a) Coefficients of variation in real prices

Market	Wholesale maize	Retail maize	Wholesale millet	Wholesale sorghum	Wholesale cassava	Wholesale gari	Retail gari	Wholesale yams	Wholesale plantains	Wholesale cocoyams	Wholesale rice
Excluding 1983											
Bolgatanga	35	35	37	38	30	—	39	45	45	41	34
Cape Coast	31	35	—	—	33	32	32	32	36	29	32[a]
Techiman	41	40	41	45	61	—	42	39	63	52	32
Including 1983											
Bolgatanga	43	42	39	40	30	—	48	45	45	41	39
Cape Coast	63	68	—	—	33	64	60	32	36	29	32[a]
Techiman	50	41	46	51	63	—	64	59	67	69	36

(b) Comparison of pre- and post-1983 coefficients of variation in real prices, all markets

Commodity	Pre-1983 coefficient of variation	Post-1983 coefficient of variation
Cassava	57.8	55.7
Maize (wholesale)	37.7	37.4
Maize (retail)	39.5	37.0
Millet	31.7	36.2
Rice	39.2	29.3
Yams	43.6	41.6

[a] Because a large number of data points in the Cape Coast wholesale rice series were missing, the complete price series for wholesale rice in Makola has been substituted.

Notes: — indicates not available. *N* varies; the minimum number of cases for any food item is 197 for the series including 1983, and 187 for the series excluding 1983.

plantain and root crops appear to be as variable as those of grains, even though these crops are available throughout the year. In general, Techiman prices are, in non-drought years, more variable than the prices in Bolgatanga and Cape Coast. This finding is unexpected, since Techiman is more centrally located and, therefore, better placed to be able to stabilize prices through internal trade.When 1983 is included in the calculation of price variation, the coefficients of variation increase, often markedly, particularly for Cape Coast maize and gari. Gari prices appear more variable than grain prices when 1983 is included and less variable when 1983 is excluded.

The lower portion of Table 15.5 reports simple price variances for five commodities (cassava, maize, millet, rice, and yams) over the pre- and post-1983 periods. These data suggest that price variances have been relatively stable, or even somewhat lower, during the adjustment period. However, the coefficient of variation is a somewhat imprecise measure. To examine the nature of price volatility in our sample further, we focus on Bolgatanga, the main market of the Upper East region. Wholesale maize prices for each month between January 1978 and July 1993 are used. Data for 1983—for previously argued reasons—have been dropped from the analysis. This places 60 observations in the pre-1983 period and 115 observations in the post-1983 period.

We adopt an autoregressive conditionally heteroskedastic (ARCH) model as developed by Engle (1982). The model posits an error structure in which the unconditional variance is homoskedastic, but in which errors at any time t, conditional on errors during previous periods, are not. Thus, the possibility of a specific time varying pattern in conditional variances is possible, as is a variance conditional on some exogenous factors. The model also provides a testable hypothesis regarding a time varying error process. The main structure of our model is given by equations (8) and (9).

$$\ln price_t = \beta_0 + \beta_1 time + \beta_2 D_{post83} + \varepsilon_t \tag{8}$$

$$\varepsilon_t^2 = \alpha_0 + \alpha_1 \varepsilon_{t-1}^2 + \sum_{j=2}^{J} \gamma_j D_{season_j} + \delta D_{post83} \tag{9}$$

Equation (8) describes price movements over time and (9) describes the deseasonalized variance at time t conditional on lagged-variance and a post-adjustment indicator. Here D_{post83} is a dummy variable equal to 1 in the period 1984–1993 and 0 otherwise, and the three seasonal dummy variables correspond to the periods October–December (season 2), January–March (season 3), and April–June (season 4). Equations (8) and (9) were estimated jointly using maximum likelihood under the assumption that the unconditional errors are normally distributed. Alternative assumptions and estimation procedures are sometimes used; interested readers should consult Greene (1990). Here we adopt a single-period seasonally adjusted lag structure which proves sufficient to ensure that the error process in these

Table 15.6. Ghana: results of autoregressive conditional heteroskedasticity (ARCH) model

Independent variable	Parameter estimate	Standard error
(a) Equation (1). Dependent variable: log of real wholesale maize price		
Constant	3.200	0.035
Time trend	0.0016	$0.36e^{-03}$
Post-1983 dummy	−0.234	0.052
(b) Equation (2). Dependent variable: price variance		
Constant	0.071	0.021
Variance$_{t-1}$	0.720	0.147
Post-1983 dummy	−0.039	0.018
Season 2	−0.005	0.019
Season 3	−0.028	0.013
Season 4	−0.025	0.013
$N = 175$		

Source: Our calculations from PPMED data.

data is stationary.[26] The regression results reported in Table 15.6 reveal a lower level of wholesale maize prices in the post-1983 period. This is in keeping with the results of the regressions reported in Table 15.1. In addition, the results of the variance regression present some interesting evidence. In particular, with $a_1 = 0.72$, current and previous period residuals appear strongly correlated at standard significance levels. Most importantly for our current focus, the coefficient on the post-1983 dummy variable is −0.039, which suggests that a small downward trend in maize price variance occurs in the post reform period. The null hypothesis that this coefficient is equal to zero could be rejected at the 95 percent confidence level, although the overall estimation appears rather weak.[27]

Our limited sample, of course, precludes one from making any strong generalizations beyond the Bolgatanga maize market. However, to the extent that the Bolgatanga market is one of the more geographically isolated markets in Ghana, one might speculate that price spreads in other maize markets may have moderated as well. As for the welfare implications, we note that, while the moderation in price variance has been slight, it never-

[26] Generalizations to longer lag structures are straightforward. For the model presented here, including up to four lags in the variance structure does not substantially change our results.

[27] The log-likelihood ratio is −5.5 and the test statistic $W = 11.0$. The statistic is distributed chi-square (10). This value falls below the 95 percent confidence interval value of 25.19. A second maximum likelihood estimation which eschewed seasonal adjustment gave similar results overall, but a somewhat larger log-likelihood ratio and a test statistic of 20.5 compared with a 95 percent confidence interval cutoff of 18.55.

theless bodes well for net purchasers of grain. The extent to which risk premia have been reduced for producers, and whether such a reduction has been able to offset declining producer prices, are more difficult issues to assess. However, the possibility for gains in producer welfare, at least in theory, does exist.

15.5.2. Seasonal price movements

The total price variability in Table 15.5 combines both seasonal price movement and interannual variability. The ARCH model attempts to control for the former in order to shed light on the latter. In this subsection, we concentrate on seasonal food price patterns. In Ghana, detrended seasonal price movements (the monthly dummy variables in Table 15.1) show that maize prices usually peak in June, and reach a low a few months later in September. Similarly, the price of millet also peaks in June, although the trough does not occur until December, the same month as the lowest price for sorghum. Cassava prices show virtually no seasonal pattern, while prices of yams have a seasonality nearly as pronounced as that of maize.

There is, however, considerable variation around the expected seasonal pattern. For example, June was the most common peak month for maize prices in all markets studied; but June was the peak month in only 5 of the 16 years in Bolgatanga. Similarly, in a 21-year period in Cape Coast, June was the peak month for maize prices in only 7 years. Peak and trough months for millet and sorghum appear as dispersed as for maize, while the peaks for yam and cassava prices are yet more diverse.

The magnitudes of annual price rises vary greatly by crop; maize price increases are substantially greater than millet or sorghum increases, despite the fact that maize is harvested in two periods. Seasonal price changes for rice are generally lower than for other grains, although this difference, to a degree, depends on whether the northern markets are aggregated with the coastal import-dominated markets. Although seasonal price rises for cassava (which has no pronounced seasonal production pattern) are not as marked as for other crops, the proportional increase is large relative to price movements for grains in non-African developing countries.

This seasonal price spread can be explained by storage losses, transport costs, interest charges, post-harvest distress sales, and trader collusion. Each point may be partially valid; nevertheless, their empirical foundations are limited. Furthermore, adjustment-related policy reforms can be expected to impact directly only two of these, namely transport and credit. Entrenched views that adjustment affects marketing margins may therefore be more a matter of vague generalization than of fact. Moreover, although the rank ordering of the proportional price increases is consistent with differences in storage losses of the various crops, seasonal increases are large relative to estimates of the physical and financial costs of storage.

Sarris (1992) explores this point by regressing $(P_2 - P_1)/P_1$ on the deviation from trend production where the subscripts 1 and 2 denote the harvest and post-harvest season, respectively. He shows that when a harvest exceeds trend the decrease in lean season prices is significantly less than the decrease in the harvest season price.

If the seasonal pattern were a cost markup only and losses and interest rates were independent of yields, then the level of the harvest would not affect the components of cost and thus should not affect the price. Similarly, if the driving force behind seasonal price movements were the inability of households to store grain—because of either a lack of physical capacity or a pressing need for cash—one might see more grain sold in the early season, hence a *greater* decline in the early season price during bountiful years relative to normal years. With this particular motive for sales, storage would not increase. This pattern would result in a positive coefficient on the deviation from trend variable. In fact, the coefficient of the deviation from trend was negative for all three crop aggregations that Sarris explored. Sarris argues that this pattern reflects a shift in stocks normally sold in the early season to being sold in the later season. This shift would be proportionally greater relative to overall supplies in the post-harvest period and would, therefore, lead to a larger decrease in prices in that season when the deviation from trend was positive. Thus, seasonal patterns are behavioral as well as mechanical.

Replicating Sarris's approach with five principal maize markets between 1978 and 1993 supports Sarris's observations on the importance of the size of the harvest. However, our analysis also shows that the seasonal price spread has been increasing since 1984 as indicated by the following post-1983 trend:[28]

$$+ \frac{0.026}{(0.007)} \textit{Time post-1983} - \frac{0.0012}{(0.0003)} \textit{production} \tag{10}$$

The pre-1983 variable shows that a similar pattern was not observed for the years prior to adjustment. If the variable for production is removed, the time trend coefficient drops in half to 0.011 (0.006). Statistically, this is because production has also trended upward; practically, it implies that production increases are mitigating a contemporaneous trend; the net impact is indicated by the trend coefficient when production is not included in the regression. The regression looks at the price spread in percentage terms. Given a decline in overall prices, and hence in the denominator, the net decline of 0.011 implies a nearly constant real absolute seasonal price rise.

15.5.3. *Seasonal storage, purchases, and sales*

Urban consumers, understandably, purchase food regularly throughout the year, and rely little on home storage. This raises a key question: who stores the grain that is sold in the later months of the cropping year? Although the

---

[28] The variable is named such in order to tie it to the recovery program. However, given the drought dummy variable, it actually covers post-1984.

Ghana Food Distribution Corporation (GFDC) and the Ghana Warehousing Corporation (GWC) serve some institutional and military storage requirements, they have not yet been able to provide storage to meet private demand.

To some extent it appears that farmers may hold grain for both speculation and to smooth income.[29] Studies by Alderman (1992) and Southworth, Jones, and Pearson (1979) indicate that a large portion of the maize sold by farm households is sold in the pre-harvest months between March and June, a finding that parallels findings in neighboring countries.[30] Although these studies agree that farm households in West Africa do not concentrate their commodity sales in the immediate post-harvest months, there is less agreement on whether households with larger surpluses are more or less likely to delay their sales. For example, Asante, Asuming-Brempong, and Bruce (1989) found that less than 12 percent of households with over six acres of planted maize held part of their 1988 harvest for six months or more, while half the households that produced less than six acres of maize in their sample did so. They hypothesize that this was because larger farmers were able to sell to the government, but only in the immediate post-harvest period.

Asante et al. also provide evidence that on-farm losses in Ghana are unlikely to be in the neighborhood of 20–30 percent despite the common assumption. These results were duplicated in the 1987–1988 GLSS survey as well as a subsequent survey of 600 households randomly drawn from the population of the Upper East and Brong-Ahafo (Alderman 1992). Although these data neglect losses in transit and degradation of the nutrient value, farmers report that damaged grain is fed to animals and therefore retains significant economic value. Nevertheless, high estimates of on-farm losses persist. Greeley (1987) documents the policy errors that can be made using such an erroneous assumption.

The prevailing evidence from African markets also implies that traders do not generally hold an appreciable share of interseasonal storage (Jones 1972). Results from a survey of rural traders in Ghana reinforces this perspective. In particular, based on a survey of 102 traders in Brong-Ahafo, a grain-exporting region, and the Upper East, one of the most food-insecure regions in the country,[31] it appears that these traders store mainly for pipeline

---

29 Surveys that obtain farmers' reasons for the timing of sales (Asante, Asuming-Brempong, and Bruce 1989; Southworth, Jones, and Pearson 1979) generally indicate that farmers recognize potential profit, although holding reserves for unexpected cash needs is also reported as a reason for delayed sales.

30 See Alderman (1992), Sahn and Delgado (1989), Ellsworth and Shapiro (1989). Also note that the Food and Agriculture Organization (FAO 1989) states (somewhat inaccurately) that no data on the timing of arrivals are available. Nevertheless, the absence of such data did not prevent a claim that "there is a rush to sell in September and October."

31 These data were collected by a Cornell–Fudtech team between March and June 1990. These data may be better considered a case study than a sample survey; in the absence of a

supplies, and see their interest in rapid turnover rather than in storage and speculation.[32] Indeed, the opportunity cost for traders of storing is high: on average, traders in the sample could turn over their stock 3.7 times in a month and earn 5.3 percent on the average sale.[33]

Using these turnover and markup figures, one can estimate that traders might expect to earn about 15–20 percent a month on their capital.[34] This implies that traders have little incentive to tie up capital in speculative storage. One implication of adjustment policies is therefore apparent. If the costs of borrowing are higher because of credit shortages, the costs of working capital will be higher and the incentives for quick turnover will be even greater. This may reduce the size of working stock and diminish buffers against transitory food shortages. One might expect that, to the extent that the economic reforms constricted credit for traders, a potential welfare risk might exist for consumers under transitory grain shortages.

Besides high costs of storage and movement, it is commonly held that traders manipulate prices either by monopsony buying at harvest time and/or through cartels led by market queens. The former market structure would hurt producers (without affecting consumer prices), while the latter would affect the consumer price. Both would increase merchants' profits.

In the first instance, one means by which traders could extract monopsony profits from farmers might be through a creditor–debtor relationship. However, Southworth, Jones, and Pearson (1979) indicate that the overwhelming majority of loans given by traders in Brong-Ahafo were without explicit interest charges. Similar results were reported in the Cornell–Fudtech survey. Thus, the prudent assumption would be that traders do not have many opportunities to earn interest from credit transactions. Nevertheless, traders may still use tied transactions to keep farmers at a bargaining disadvantage. Such a concern recurs regularly in the literature. Again, Southworth, Jones, and Pearson (1979) provide one of the few empirical estimates of how widespread such practices have been: a quarter of the farmers in their sample sold to the trader who provided loans. Far fewer loans to farmers—never mind fewer tied loans—were found in the Cornell–Fudtech survey. Since long-distance traders serving the main urban

complete listing of traders analogous to census tracts used in sampling, it is difficult to conduct a random draw of traders.

[32] At the time of interview, 70 percent of the traders in the survey reported that they intended their current stocks to last one week or less, and over half the traders reported that their current supplies were obtained in the previous week; only 20 percent claimed to have held supplies over one month.

[33] The estimated markup over costs for all reported transactions was 8.2, slightly higher than for maize trade alone, a result consistent with margins observed for groundnut and cassava by Austin Associates (1990).

[34] Note, however, that this is not strictly analogous to an interest rate or similar measures of the opportunity of capital because the figure also includes the return for the traders' labor and management.

centers predominated in the Southworth study, the scale of transactions may have encouraged credit provision to ensure supply. If so, such credit would be a cost of operation paid by the trader rather than a means of exploiting farmers. To a large degree this is plausible. Neither the farmers in the Southworth study nor those in the more recent Asante survey reported that they had difficulty finding buyers. Nor did either study find that farmers relied on traders to tell them what prices prevailed. When farmers have information on market prices and a choice of traders to whom to sell (as well as the option of waiting to sell), monopsony purchasing cannot be the norm.

As for the second concern, although market queens influence local conditions, there are no studies that quantify the extent of this influence. Indeed, because prices in Ghanaian markets are not posted and are generally determined by private negotiation between purchasers and traders, no mechanism by which price collusion can be directly enforced has been proposed in the literature. A market queen may, however, restrict entry. If she is able to monitor only the number of traders and not their volume, restrictions of entry may fail to affect market-clearing conditions. Note that under such circumstances the market queen still has an incentive to restrict entry because reducing the number of traders admitted raises the share of total profits for any included agent, a portion of which may be extracted as rent or fee for inclusion. The fact that market queens have local influence, then, is insufficient to indicate the welfare effects of such a position.[35]

15.5.4. *Summary*

In this section we have provided evidence suggesting that no appreciable increase in overall price volatility has accompanied Ghana's downward trend in commodity prices. This is not to say that prices are not volatile: they are. But available data do not indicate an increase in the variability of prices overall. There may be several reasons for this. First, evidence indicates that spatial markups are predominately real costs of transport and handling. Given that transport costs may have fallen—and themselves stabilized—in the post-adjustment period, this may lead to moderation in price variances. Second, survey evidence indicates that monopsony purchases and tied transactions are not widespread and that market traders are not contributing to price volatility.

Third, we have found that farmers smooth stocks and that on-farm losses are moderate. Since we also argue that traders generally work on turnover and that principal agents for storage, at least outside the main urban centers, are farm households, decreased volatility may reflect conditions—such as continued favorable weather—at the farm level. As indicated in this and

---

[35] At any rate, some evidence suggests that, while traders have lower per capita incomes than food farmers (although the distribution is somewhat more upwardly skewed), they do not appear to be as vulnerable to negative terms-of-trade shocks as their counterparts in neighboring Cote d'Ivoire (Appleton and Collier 1991).

other studies (Alderman 1992, Sarris 1992), the government could replace a portion of this household-level storage—and perhaps reduce price variance further—but at considerable cost and with little gain to consumers. Since stocks are a fair proportion of a farm household's capital portfolio, and since the ability to bear risks may correlate with income, the poor and middle-income farmers who are hypothesized to hold collectively the bulk of grain stocks in Ghana are likely to be particularly sensitive to price fluctuations. The variability of production, then, would discourage storage and hence contribute to interseasonal price increases. Methods of reducing risk, therefore, may be possible entry points for both enhancing household welfare and reducing price volatility.

Moreover, while traders in some markets may erroneously overreact to new information (Ravallion 1985), thereby exacerbating price rises, we find no evidence of systematic uncompetitive behavior on the part of market traders. Indeed, this section has pointed more to information flows and to the riskiness of markets than to technical features or collusion as the cause of seasonal price patterns. Nevertheless, given sharp movements in prices in Ghana that are not easily explained by changes in supply or by accurate changes in supply forecasts—for example, the pronounced increase in maize prices in May and June of 1990—hyper-responsiveness in price expectations in Ghana may well be the case. Adjustment, *per se*, is not at issue here. Nevertheless, evidence does suggest that credit shortages could have welfare impacts through reduced trader stocks. Technical solutions—where they are identified and are cost-effective—will help reduce risk and therefore will affect the behavioral aspects of seasonal price increases. But failure to understand the role of risk-averse and credit-constrained households in price formation will result in an oversell of the ease of commodity price stabilization policies.

15.5. *Conclusions*

The results presented in this chapter confirm that real wholesale and retail prices of food in Ghana have been declining since the 1970s. Price trends in the 1980s have been characterized by a sharp rachet downward at the beginning of the recovery period and a continuing trend subsequently. Although this trend would not reduce the concern for transitory high food prices that all governments share, it does indicate that the markets have improved and that the production potential has increased. The other side of the food security equation—household purchasing power—is not directly addressed in this paper; but if prices continue moderating and markets remain functioning, income and employment policies deserve consideration as a possible entry point for government efforts to enhance household welfare.

Our results also show that, with the exception of rice, markets in Ghana appear to function reasonably well. Although price signals in the major markets do not transmit instantly to each other, markets do appear to be integrated in the long term. Moreover, prices are transmitted across commodities fairly well; price movements for maize influence price movements for sorghum and millet. Both these observations indicate that price stability in any one market will contribute to the same stability in others. This is not, by itself, justification for price stabilization policies either through trade or storage, but it does argue for simplification in any proposed price stabilization program. Concerning rice, the market channel appears to break between the savannah producers and the coastal markets. Food imports, therefore, including food aid, will probably not assist in stabilizing the northern markets. Moreover, studies that estimate the impact of such imports on local producers should disaggregate the coastal market channels from other regions. But again, such breaks in the physical market for rice appear to pre-date adjustment and may be part of the natural landscape in Ghana.

In addition, we find some limited evidence that price volatility has declined through the study period. Although the reduction in price variance has been slight, it may bode well for producers. While lower prices in isolation hurt producers, both reductions in price volatility and overall increases in yields are more favorable. The overall welfare impacts on producers, therefore, are indeterminant.

Finally, we find no appreciable evidence of widespread on-farm losses in storage. Yet the assumption that such losses are high persists. Not only could erroneous estimates of these losses lead to misleading estimates of domestic food availability, but they may lead to inaccurate policy prescriptions as well. In particular, one justification for the level of storage under the GFDC that is offered is that there is a need for more efficient storage. This may be, but a benefit–cost analysis of this particular role for government involvement in grain storage (there are other objectives as well) must be based on an accurate assessment of alternatives. In the face of accumulating household-level data, anecdotes or outdated generalizations need not be the basis for the underlying assumptions.

In summary, this analysis of price and market data from Ghana does not make a compelling case for increased government involvement in commodity markets to mitigate the effects of structural adjustment. To be sure, prices are variable over seasons and between years, and sometimes markedly so. However, no market failures can be found among the main markets, with the exception of rice, which is a minor component of consumers' budgets and diets. Our analysis of intermarket price transmittal suggests that a well functioning commodity market exists in Ghana. The trend in prices is downward, even during the post-adjustment period, and markets appear sufficiently competitive as to prevent traders from enjoying excess margins. Furthermore, the severe devaluations associated with Ghana's economic recovery programme appear to have had little impact on the overall price level for food, and their impact, if any, on the cross-border trade of maize has been favorable. In short, it appears that Ghana's impressive (and largely atypical) post-adjustment period was facilitated by well functioning markets, and that adjustment policies have had little detrimental impact on the market mechanism itself. Nevertheless, efficient markets are not necessarily equitable markets. The problems of fairly distributing economic opportunity in Ghana persist.

References

Alderman, Harold. 1991. *Downturn and Economic Recovery in Ghana: Impacts on the Poor.* Monograph No. 10. Ithaca, NY: CFNPP.

—— 1992. *Incomes and Food Security in Ghana.* Working Paper No. 26. Ithaca, NY: CFNPP.

—— 1993. "Intercommodity Price Transmittal: Analysis of Markets in Ghana." *Oxford Bulletin of Economics and Statistics,* 55(1): 43–64.

—— 1994. "Ghana: Adjustment's Star Pupil?" In *Adjusting to Policy Failure in African Economies,* David E. Sahn, ed. Ithaca, NY: Cornell University Press.

—— and Paul Higgins. 1992. *Food and Nutritional Adequacy in Ghana.* Working Paper No. 27. Ithaca, NY: CFNPP.

—— David Sahn, and Jehan Arulpragasam. 1991. "Food Subsidies in an Environment of Distorted Exchange Rates: Evidence from Mozambique." *Food Policy,* 16(5):395–404.

—— and Gerald Shively. 1991. *Prices and Markets in Ghana.* Working Paper No. 10. Ithaca, NY: CFNPP.

Appleton, Simon, and Paul Collier. 1991. *Agriculture and the Macroeconomy: Consequences of Negative External Shocks in Ghana and the Cote d'Ivoire: 1979–1987.* World Development Programme Research Working Paper. Geneva: International Labour Office.

Asante, Edward, S. Asuming-Brempong, and P. A. Bruce. 1989. *Ghana: Grain Marketing Study.* Accra: Ghana Institute of Management and Public Administration, and Washington, DC: World Bank.

Austin Associates, Inc. 1990. "Agricultural Marketing in Ghana: Status and Recommendations for Improvement." Report to USAID. Photocopy.

Beaudry, P., and N. Sowa. 1989. "Labour Markets in an Era of Adjustment: A Case Study of Ghana." Montreal: University of Montreal. Photocopy.

Binswanger, Hans P., and Mark Rosenzweig. 1986. "Behavioral and Material Determinants of Production Relations in Agriculture." *Journal of Development Studies,* 22(3): 503–539.

Box, G., and G. Tiao. 1975. "Intervention Analysis with Applications to Economic and Environmental Problems." *Journal of the American Statistical Association,* 70(March): 70–79.

Chibber, Ajay, and Nemat Shafik. 1991. "The Inflationary Consequences of Devaluation with Parallel Markets: The Case of Ghana." In *Economic Reform in sub-Saharan Africa,* A. Chibber and S. Fischer, eds. Washington, DC: World Bank.

Cornia, Giovanni Andrea, Richard Jolly, and Frances Stewart. 1987. *Adjustment with a Human Face.* Oxford: Clarendon Press for UNICEF.

Drèze, Jean, and Amartya Sen. 1989. *Hunger and Public Action.* Oxford: Clarendon Press.

Ellsworth, Lynn, and Kenneth Shapiro. 1989. "Seasonality in Burkina Faso Grain Marketing: Farmer Strategies and Government Policy." In *Seasonal Variability in Third World Agriculture: The Consequences for Food Security,* David Sahn, ed. Baltimore, MD: Johns Hopkins University Press.

Engle, Robert. 1982. "Autoregressive Conditional Heteroskedasticity with Estimates of the Variance of United Kingdom Inflations." *Econometrica*, 50(4): 987–1008.

Food and Agriculture Organization (FAO). 1989. "Marketing and Storage of Stable Food Crops Strategy Study." Rome: FAO. Photocopy.

Greeley, Martin. 1987. *Postharvest Losses, Technology, and Employment: The Case of Rice in Bangladesh.* Boulder, CO: Westview Press.

Greene, William H. 1990. *Econometric Analysis.* New York: Macmillan.

Harriss, Barbara. 1979. "There is Method in my Madness: Or Is It Vice Versa? Measuring Agricultural Market Performance." *Food Research Institute Studies*, 17(2): 197–218.

Harvey, Charles. 1991. "Recovery from Macro-economic Disaster in sub-Saharan Africa." In *States or Markets? Neo-liberalism and the Development Policy Debate*, Christopher Colclough and James Manor, eds. Oxford: Clarendon Press.

Heytens, Paul J. 1986. "Testing Market Integration." *Food Research Institute Studies*, 20(1): 25–41.

Jebuni, Charles D., and Wayo Seini. 1992. *Agricultural Input Policies under Structural Adjustment: Their Distributional Implications.* Working Paper No. 31. Ithaca, NY: CFNPP.

Jones, William. 1972. *Marketing Staple Food Crops in Tropical Africa.* Ithaca, NY: Cornell University Press.

Kraus, Jon. 1988. "The Political Economy of Food in Ghana." In *Coping with Africa's Food Crises*, Naomi Chazan and Timothy Shaw, eds. Boulder, CO: Lynne Reinner.

Krueger, Anne O., Maurice Schiff, and Alberto Valdés. 1988. "Agricultural Incentives in Developing Countries: Measuring the Effects of Sectoral and Economy-Wide Policies." *World Bank Economic Review*, 2(3): 255–271.

Lavy, Victor, John Strauss, Duncan Thomas, and Phillippe de Vreyer. 1992. "Quality of Health Care, Survival and Health Outcomes in Ghana." Washington, DC: World Bank. Photocopy.

Mink, Stephen. 1989. "Ghana: Policy and Performance in the Agricultural Sector During the Economic Recovery Program." Draft working paper. Washington, DC: World Bank.

Ravallion, Martin. 1985. *Markets and Famines.* Oxford: Oxford University Press.

—— 1986. "Testing Market Integration." *American Journal of Agricultural Economics*, 68(1): 102–109.

Sahn, David. 1992. "Public Expenditures in sub-Saharan Africa during a Period of Economic Reforms." *World Development*, 20(5): 673–693.

—— 1993. "The Impact of Macroeconomic Adjustment on Incomes, Health and Nutrition in Africa." Ithaca, NY: CFNPP. Photocopy.

—— and Christopher Delgado. 1989. "The Nature and Implications for Market Interventions of Seasonal Food Price Variability." In *Seasonal Variability in Third World Agriculture: The Consequences for Food Security*, David Sahn, ed. Baltimore, MD: Johns Hopkins University Press.

Sarris, Alexander H. 1992. *Options for Public Intervention to Enhance Food Security in Ghana.* Monograph No. 14. Ithaca, NY: CFNPP.

Sen, Amartya. 1981. *Poverty and Famines: An Essay on Entitlement and Deprivation.* Oxford: Oxford University Press.

Southworth, V. Roy, William O. Jones, and Scott R. Pearson. 1979. "Food Crop Marketing in Atebubu District, Ghana." *Food Research Institute Studies*, 17(2): 157–195.

Tabatabai, H. 1986. *Economic Decline, Access to Food and Structural Adjustment in Ghana.* World Employment Programme Research Working Paper. Geneva: International Labour Office.

—— 1988. "Agricultural Decline and Access to Food in Ghana." *International Labour Review*, 127(6): 703–734.

Thomas, Duncan, Victor Lavy, and John Strauss. 1992. *Public Policy and Anthropometric Outcomes in Cote d'Ivoire.* Living Standards Measurement Study Working Paper No. 89. Washington, DC: World Bank.

Timmer, C. Peter. 1987. "Corn Marketing." In *The Corn Economy of Indonesia*, C. Peter Timmer, ed. Ithaca, NY: Cornell University Press.

von Braun, Joachim, and Detlev Puetz. 1987. "An African Fertilizer Crisis: Origin and Economic Effects in The Gambia." *Food Policy*, 12(4): 337–348.

Younger, Stephen D. 1992. "Testing the Link between Devaluation and Inflation: Time Series Evidence from Ghana." *Journal of African Economics*, 1(3): 369–394.

United Nations, Subcommittee on Nutrition. 1989. *SCN News*, 1989(4): 3.

INDEX